THE UNITED STATES
EXECUTIVE BRANCH

THE UNITED STATES EXECUTIVE BRANCH

*A Biographical Directory of
Heads of State and Cabinet Officials
M–Z*

Edited by Robert Sobel and David B. Sicilia

GREENWOOD PRESS
Westport, Connecticut • London

Library of Congress Cataloging-in-Publication Data

The United States Executive Branch : a biographical directory of heads of state and cabinet officials / edited by Robert Sobel and David B. Sicilia.
    p. cm.
  Rev. ed. of: Biographical directory of the United States executive branch, 1774–1989. 1990.
  Includes bibliographical references.
  ISBN 0–313–31134–X (set : alk. paper)—ISBN 0–313–32593–6 (v. 1 : alk. paper)—
ISBN 0–313–32594–4 (v. 2 : alk. paper)
  1. Statesmen—United States—Biography—Dictionaries. 2. United States—Officials and
employees—Biography—Dictionaries. 3. Cabinet officers—United
States—Biography—Dictionaries. 4. Presidents—United States—Biography—Dictionaries.
5. Vice-Presidents—United States—Biography—Dictionaries. I. Sobel, Robert, 1931 Feb. 19–
II. Sicilia, David B. III. Sobel, Robert, 1931 Feb. 19–   Biographical directory of the
United States executive branch, 1774–1989.
E176.U575   2003
351.73′092′2—dc21   2002028434
[B]

British Library Cataloguing in Publication Data is available.

Library of Congress Catalog Card Number: 2002028434
ISBN: 0–313–31134–X (set)
     0–313–32593–6 (v. 1)
     0–313–32594–4 (v. 2)

First published in 2003

Greenwood Press, 88 Post Road West, Westport, CT 06881
An imprint of Greenwood Publishing Group, Inc.
www.greenwood.com

Printed in the United States of America

The paper used in this book complies with the
Permanent Paper Standard issued by the National
Information Standards Organization (Z39.48–1984).

10 9 8 7 6 5 4 3 2 1

Contents

APPENDIXES

Preface

More than 600 men and women have served in the cabinets of American presidents. Researchers in American political history who have an adequate library at their disposal may discover basic information about most of them without too much difficulty. But it can be challenging to track down essential information about many former members of the executive branch. When investigating the most prominent and famous cabinet members, the researcher may have to wade through voluminous writings before finding a sought-after date, event, award, or other biographical detail. Finding information on those who served in minor posts for short and uneventful periods of time is even more of a challenge. For those who wish to study a particular department or administration, the effort may be tedious and time-consuming. These volumes have been written and compiled for individuals such as these as well as for the general student of political history.

The United States Executive Branch contains career biographies of all cabinet heads, as well as of presidents, vice-presidents, and presidents of the Continental Congress. Only individuals confirmed in office by the Senate have been included; acting cabinet officials—of whom there were many, especially in the nineteenth century—are not included here because nearly all served for very short periods of time. Each biography includes the most significant dates in the subject's life and information about family, religious affiliation, career prior to and after cabinet duty, organizational affiliations, awards and honors, major publications, and date and place of death. In addition, each entry concludes with one or more bibliographic references to important primary and secondary works to be consulted for additional information. Following the preface are two sections—the first covering presidential administrations and the second listing heads of state and cabinet officials. The individual biographies are followed by a series of appendixes in which six categories of key information are compiled.

The United States Executive Branch: A Biographical Directory of Heads of States and Cabinet Officials includes fifty entirely new entries covering George H.W. Bush's administration (since 1989, when the previous edition appeared), both of Bill Clinton's terms and the initial round of cabinet officers in President George W. Bush's administration. The book also updates the older entries where appropriate. Through this volume, especially the appendixes, one can see key patterns in our nation's political life. A brief review of the "Place of Birth" appendix, for example, reveals that the Middle Atlantic states have contributed a disproportionately high percentage of cabinet officers for their populations. The cabinet members new to this edition are, as a group, more racially and ethnically diverse and more engaged in a variety of prominent (noncabinet) public activities than their predecessors.

The individual biographies were written by teams of historical researchers. The pre-1971 entries were undertaken by Karen Bragg, Tapper Bragg, Janice Daar, Aaron Hause, Arthur Kurzweil, Richard Mark, Karen Mitura, Connie Panzarino, Mark Rosenblatt, Joseph Sconzo, and Dennis Steigerwald. The writers for the period from 1971 through 1977 were Kenny Franks, Margaret Karafian, Michael Kass, Stephan Manzi, William Maynard, Patricia Page, Steven Rosman, Barbara Simpson, Roy Sudlow, Helene Vecchione, Harry Weber, and Carolynn Weinstock. The 1977–1989 biographies were written by Golda Blum, Miriam Delphin, Jay Goodale, Denise Holton, Angela Malacari, Andrew Myers, Jocelyn Nuttall, Lynn Poppe, and David Sarnoff. The new entries for this edition, covering the years 1989 through 2001, were written by Phil Bagley, Rachel Ban, Jeremy Brett, Herbert Brewer, Robert T. Chase, Jeffrey Coster, William J. Lombardo, Stephanie Muravchik, Johnathan O'Neill, Brian C. Phelan, Jonathan Setliff, Matthew Wasniewski, Scott W. Webster, and Edmund Wehrle. Jennifer Lesar helped locate some particularly obscure information. My wife Leila helped with a number of administrative matters. Cynthia Harris at Greenwood has been a sage and supportive editor throughout the project.

I am especially grateful to Jeff Coster, who began by writing a few entries, then was drawn into the maelstrom to become, in effect, managing editor of the project. He ultimately contributed 16 original entries to this volume, updated some 200 others, and worked meticulously and relentlessly to update the appendixes. His work on this new edition was simply indispensable.

At the early stages of work on this volume, my dear friend, former mentor, and colleague Robert Sobel—who brought me into this project—died in his home on Long Island, New York. A professor and prolific author for more than four decades, Bob touched the lives of thousands of students and countless readers. For me, completing this volume without him was a labor both of love and of sorrow.

David B. Sicilia
College Park, Maryland

Presidential Administrations

FIRST ADMINISTRATION OF GEORGE WASHINGTON (1789–1793)

Office	Name
Office	**Name**
Pres.	Washington, George
Vice-Pres.	Adams, John
Secy. State *ad int.*, 1789	Jay, John
Secy. State, 1789–93	Jefferson, Thomas
Secy. Treas.	Hamilton, Alexander
Secy. War	Knox, Henry
Atty. Gen.	Randolph, Edmund J.
Postm. Gen., 1789–91	Osgood, Samuel
Postm. Gen., 1791–93	Pickering, Timothy

SECOND ADMINISTRATION OF GEORGE WASHINGTON (1793–1797)

Office	Name
Office	**Name**
Pres.	Washington, George
Vice-Pres.	Adams, John
Secy. State, 1793–94	Jefferson, Thomas
Secy. State, 1794	Randolph, Edmund J.
Secy. State *ad int.*, 1795; Secy. State, 1795–97	Pickering, Timothy

Secy. Treas., 1793–95	Hamilton, Alexander
Secy. Treas., 1795–97	Wolcott, Oliver, Jr.
Secy. War, 1793–95	Knox, Henry
Secy. War *ad int.*, 1795–96	Pickering, Timothy
Secy. War, 1796–97	McHenry, James
Atty. Gen., 1793–94	Randolph, Edmund J.
Atty. Gen., 1794–95	Bradford, William
Atty. Gen., 1795–97	Lee, Charles
Postm. Gen., 1793–95	Pickering, Timothy
Postm. Gen., 1795–97	Habersham, Joseph

ADMINISTRATION OF JOHN ADAMS (1797–1801)

Office	Name
Pres.	Adams, John
Vice-Pres.	Jefferson, Thomas
Secy. State, 1797–1800	Pickering, Timothy
Secy. State *ad int.*, 1800	Lee, Charles
Secy. State, 1800; *ad int.*,* 1800–01	Marshall, John
Secy. Treas., 1797–1801	Wolcott, Oliver, Jr.
Secy. Treas. *ad int.*, 1801	Dexter, Samuel
Secy. War, 1797–1800	McHenry, James
Secy. War *ad int.*, 1800	Stoddert, Benjamin
Secy. War, 1800–01	Dexter, Samuel
Atty. Gen.	Lee, Charles
Postm. Gen.	Habersham, Joseph
Secy. War, 1798–1801	Stoddert, Benjamin

FIRST ADMINISTRATION OF THOMAS JEFFERSON (1801–1805)

Office	Name
Pres.	Jefferson, Thomas
Vice-Pres.	Burr, Aaron

---

*While Chief Justice.

Secy. State *ad int.*, 1801	Lincoln, Levi
Secy. State, 1801–05	Madison, James
Secy. Treas., 1801	Dexter, Samuel
Secy. Treas., 1801–05	Gallatin, Albert
Secy. War	Dearborn, Henry
Atty. Gen.	Lincoln, Levi
Postm. Gen., 1801	Habersham, Joseph
Postm. Gen., 1801–05	Granger, Gideon
Secy. Navy, 1801	Stoddert, Benjamin
Secy. Navy *ad int.*, 1801	Dearborn, Henry
Secy. Navy, 1801–05	Smith, Robert

SECOND ADMINISTRATION OF THOMAS JEFFERSON (1805–1809)

Office	Name
Pres.	Jefferson, Thomas
Vice-Pres.	Clinton, George
Secy. State	Madison, James
Secy. Treas.	Gallatin, Albert
Secy. War, 1805–09	Dearborn, Henry
Atty. Gen., 1805–06	Breckinridge, John
Atty. Gen., 1807–09	Rodney, Caesar A.
Postm. Gen.	Granger, Gideon
Secy. Navy	Smith, Robert

FIRST ADMINISTRATION OF JAMES MADISON (1809–1813)

Office	Name
Pres.	Madison, James
Vice-Pres.	Clinton, George
Secy. State, 1809–11	Smith, Robert
Secy. State, 1811–13	Monroe, James
Secy. Treas.	Gallatin, Albert
Secy. War, 1809–12	Eustis, William
Secy. War *ad int.*, 1813	Monroe, James
Secy. War, 1813	Armstrong, John

Atty. Gen., 1809–11	Rodney, Caesar A.
Atty. Gen., 1812–13	Pinkney, William
Postm. Gen.	Granger, Gideon
Secy. Navy, 1809	Smith, Robert
Secy. Navy, 1809–12	Hamilton, Paul
Secy. Navy, 1813	Jones, William

SECOND ADMINISTRATION OF JAMES MADISON (1813–1817)

Office	Name
Pres.	Madison, James
Vice-Pres., 1813–14	Gerry, Elbridge
Secy. State, 1813–14; *ad int.*, 1814–15; Secy. State, 1815–17	Monroe, James
Secy. Treas., 1813–14	Gallatin, Albert
Secy. Treas. *ad int.*, 1814	Jones, William
Secy. Treas., 1814	Campbell, George W.
Secy. Treas., 1814–16	Dallas, Alexander J.
Secy. Treas., 1816–17	Crawford, William M.
Secy. War, 1813–14	Armstrong, John
Secy. War *ad int.*, 1814–15	Monroe, James
Secy. War *ad int.*, 1815	Dallas, Alexander J.
Secy. War, 1815–16	Crawford, William H.
Secy. War *ad int.*, 1816–17	Graham, George
Atty. Gen., 1813–14	Pinkney, William
Atty. Gen., 1814–17	Rush, Richard
Postm. Gen., 1813–14	Granger, Gideon
Postm. Gen., 1814–17	Meigs, Return J., Jr.
Secy. Navy, 1813–14	Jones, William
Secy. Navy, 1815–17	Crowninshield, Benjamin W.

FIRST ADMINISTRATION OF JAMES MONROE (1817–1821)

Office	Name
Pres.	Monroe, James
Vice-Pres.	Tompkins, Daniel D.

Secy. State *ad int.*, 1817	Rush, Richard
Secy. State, 1817–21	Adams, John Q.
Secy. Treas.	Crawford, William H.
Secy. War, 1817–21	Calhoun, John C.
Atty. Gen., 1817	Rush, Richard
Atty. Gen., 1817–21	Wirt, William
Postm. Gen.	Meigs, Return J., Jr.
Secy. Navy, 1817–18	Crowninshield, Benjamin W.
Secy. Navy *ad int.*, 1818–19	Calhoun, John C.
Secy. Navy, 1819–21	Thompson, Smith

SECOND ADMINISTRATION OF JAMES MONROE (1821–1825)

Office	Name
Pres.	Monroe, James
Vice-Pres.	Tompkins, Daniel D.
Secy. State	Adams, John Q.
Secy. Treas.	Crawford, William H.
Secy. War	Calhoun, John C.
Atty. Gen.	Wirt, William
Postm. Gen., 1821–23	Meigs, Return J., Jr.
Postm. Gen., 1823–25	McLane, John
Secy. Navy, 1821–23	Thompson, Smith
Secy. Navy, 1823–25	Southard, Samuel L.

ADMINISTRATION OF JOHN QUINCY ADAMS (1825–1829)

Office	Name
Pres.	Adams, John Q.
Vice-Pres.	Calhoun, John C.
Secy. State	Clay, Henry
Secy. Treas.	Rush, Richard
Secy. War, 1825–28	Barbour, James
Secy. War *ad int.*, 1828	Southard, Samuel L.
Secy. War, 1828–29	Porter, Peter B.
Atty. Gen.	Wirt, William

Postm. Gen.	McLean, John
Secy. Navy	Southard, Samuel L.

FIRST ADMINISTRATION OF ANDREW JACKSON (1829–1833)

Office	Name
Pres.	Jackson, Andrew
Vice-Pres., 1829–32	Calhoun, John C.
Secy. State, 1829–31	Van Buren, Martin
Secy. State, 1831–33	Livingston, Edward
Secy. Treas., 1829–31	Ingham, Samuel D.
Secy. Treas., 1831–33	McLane, Louis
Secy. War, 1829–31	Eaton, John H.
Secy. War *ad int.*, 1831	Taney, Roger B.
Secy. War, 1831–33	Cass, Lewis
Atty. Gen., 1829–31	Berrien, John M.
Atty. Gen., 1831–33	Taney, Roger B.
Postm. Gen.	Barry, William T.
Secy. Navy, 1829–31	Branch, John
Secy. Navy, 1831–33	Woodbury, Levi

SECOND ADMINISTRATION OF ANDREW JACKSON (1833–1837)

Office	Name
Pres.	Jackson, Andrew
Vice-Pres.	Van Buren, Martin
Secy. State, 1833	Livingston, Edward
Secy. State, 1833–34	McLane, Louis
Secy. State, 1834–37	Forsyth, John
Secy. Treas., 1833	McLane, Louis
Secy. Treas., 1833	Duane, William J.
Secy. Treas., 1833–34	Taney, Roger B.
Secy. Treas., 1834–37	Woodbury, Levi
Secy. War, 1833–36	Cass, Lewis
Secy. War *ad int.*, 1836–37	Butler, Benjamin F.

Atty. Gen., 1833	Taney, Roger B.
Atty. Gen., 1833–37	Butler, Benjamin F.
Postm. Gen., 1833–35	Barry, William T.
Postm. Gen., 1835–37	Kendall, Amos
Secy. Navy, 1833–34	Woodbury, Levi
Secy. Navy, 1834–37	Dickerson, Mahlon

ADMINISTRATION OF MARTIN VAN BUREN (1837–1841)

Office	Name
Pres.	Van Buren, Martin
Vice-Pres.	Johnson, Richard M.
Secy. State	Forsyth, John
Secy. Treas.	Woodbury, Levi
Secy. War	Poinsett, Joel R.
Atty. Gen., 1837–38	Butler, Benjamin F.
Atty. Gen., 1838–39	Grundy, Felix
Atty. Gen., 1840–41	Gilpin, Henry D.
Postm. Gen., 1837–40	Kendall, Amos
Postm. Gen., 1840–41	Niles, John M.
Secy. Navy, 1837–38	Dickerson, Mahlon
Secy. Navy, 1838–41	Paulding, James K.

ADMINISTRATION OF WILLIAM HENRY HARRISON (1841)

Office	Name
Pres.	Harrison, William H.
Vice-Pres.	Tyler, John
Secy. State	Webster, Daniel
Secy. Treas.	Ewing, Thomas
Secy. War	Bell, John
Atty. Gen.	Crittenden, John J.
Postm. Gen.	Granger, Francis
Secy. Navy	Badger, George E.

ADMINISTRATION OF
JOHN TYLER (1841–1845)

Office	Name
Pres.	Tyler, John
Secy. State, 1841–43	Webster, Daniel
Secy. State *ad int.*, 1843	Legaré, Hugh S.
Secy. State *ad int.*, 1843; Secy. State, 1843–44	Upshur, Abel P.
Secy. State *ad int.*, 1844	Nelson, John
Secy. State, 1844–45	Calhoun, John C.
Secy. Treas., 1841	Ewing, Thomas
Secy. Treas., 1841–43	Forward, Walter
Secy. Treas., 1843–44	Spencer, John C.
Secy. Treas., 1844–45	Bibb, George M.
Secy. War, 1841	Bell, John
Secy. War, 1841–43	Spencer, John C.
Secy. War, 1843–44	Porter, James M.
Secy. War, 1844–45	Wilkins, William
Atty. Gen., 1841	Crittenden, John J.
Atty. Gen., 1841–43	Legaré, Hugh S.
Atty. Gen., 1843–45	Nelson, John
Postm. Gen., 1841	Granger, Francis
Postm. Gen., 1841–45	Wickliffe, Charles A.
Secy. Navy, 1841	Badger, George E.
Secy. Navy, 1841–43	Upshur, Abel P.
Secy. Navy, 1843–44	Henshaw, David
Secy. Navy, 1844	Gilmer, Thomas W.
Secy. Navy, 1844–45	Mason, John Y.

ADMINISTRATION OF
JAMES K. POLK (1845–1849)

Office	Name
Pres.	Polk, James K.
Vice-Pres.	Dallas, George M.
Secy. State	Buchanan, James
Secy. Treas.	Walker, Robert J.

Secy. War	Marcy, William L.
Atty. Gen., 1845–46	Mason, John Y.
Atty. Gen., 1846–48	Clifford, Nathan
Atty. Gen., 1848–49	Toucey, Isaac
Postm. Gen.	Johnson, Cave
Secy. Navy, 1845–46	Bancroft, George
Secy. Navy, 1846–49	Mason, John Y.

ADMINISTRATION OF
ZACHARY TAYLOR (1849–1850)

Office	Name
Pres.	Taylor, Zachary
Vice-Pres.	Fillmore, Millard
Secy. State	Clayton, John M.
Secy. Treas.	Meredith, William M.
Secy. War *ad int.*, 1849	Johnson, Reverdy
Secy. War, 1849–50	Crawford, George W.
Atty. Gen.	Johnson, Reverdy
Postm. Gen., 1849–50	Collamer, Jacob
Secy. Navy	Preston, William B.
Secy. Interior	Ewing, Thomas

ADMINISTRATION OF
MILLARD FILLMORE (1850–1853)

Office	Name
Pres.	Fillmore, Millard
Secy. State, 1850	Clayton, John M.
Secy. State, 1850–52	Webster, Daniel
Secy. State *ad int.*, 1852	Conrad, Charles M.
Secy. State, 1852–53	Everett, Edward
Secy. Treas., 1850	Meredith, William M.
Secy. Treas., 1850–53	Corwin, Thomas
Secy. War, 1850	Crawford, George W.
Secy. War, 1850–53	Conrad, Charles M.
Atty. Gen., 1850	Johnson, Reverdy

Atty. Gen., 1850–53	Crittenden, John J.
Postm. Gen., 1850	Collamer, Jacob
Postm. Gen., 1850–52	Hall, Nathan K.
Postm. Gen., 1852–53	Hubbard, Samuel D.
Secy. Navy, 1850	Preston, William B.
Secy. Navy, 1850–52	Graham, William A.
Secy. Navy, 1852–53	Kennedy, John P.
Secy. Interior, 1850	Ewing, Thomas
Secy. Interior, 1850	McKennan, Thomas M.T.
Secy. Interior, 1850–53	Stuart, Alexander H.H.

ADMINISTRATION OF FRANKLIN PIERCE (1853–1857)

Office	Name
Pres.	Pierce, Franklin
Vice-Pres.	King, William R.
Secy. State	Marcy, William L.
Secy. Treas.	Guthrie, James
Secy. War	Davis, Jefferson
Atty. Gen.	Cushing, Caleb
Postm. Gen.	Campbell, James
Secy. Navy	Dobbin, James C.
Secy. Interior	McClelland, Robert

ADMINISTRATION OF JAMES BUCHANAN (1857–1861)

Office	Name
Pres.	Buchanan, James
Vice-Pres.	Breckinridge, John C.
Secy. State, 1857–60	Cass, Lewis
Secy. State, 1860–61	Black, Jeremiah S.
Secy. Treas., 1857–60	Cobb, Howell
Secy. Treas. *ad int.*, 1860	Toucey, Isaac
Secy. Treas., 1860–61	Thomas, Philip F.
Secy. Treas., 1861	Dix, John A.

Secy. War, 1857–61	Floyd, John B.
Secy. War *ad int.*, 1861; Secy. War, 1861	Holt, Joseph
Atty. Gen., 1857–60	Black, Jeremiah S.
Atty. Gen., 1860–61	Stanton, Edwin M.
Postm. Gen., 1857–59	Brown, Aaron V.
Postm. Gen., 1859–61	Holt, Joseph
Postm. Gen., 1861	King, Horatio
Secy. Navy, 1857–61	Toucey, Isaac
Secy. Interior, 1857–61	Thompson, Jacob

FIRST ADMINISTRATION OF ABRAHAM LINCOLN (1861–1865)

Office	**Name**
Pres.	Lincoln, Abraham
Vice-Pres.	Hamlin, Hannibal
Secy. State	Seward, William H.
Secy. Treas., 1861–64	Chase, Salmon P.
Secy. Treas., 1864–65	Fessenden, William P.
Secy. War, 1861–62	Cameron, Simon
Secy. War, 1862–65	Stanton, Edwin M.
Atty. Gen., 1861–64	Bates, Edward
Atty. Gen., 1864–65	Speed, James
Postm. Gen., 1861–64	Blair, Montgomery
Postm. Gen., 1864–65	Dennison, William
Secy. Navy	Welles, Gideon
Secy. Interior, 1861–63	Smith, Caleb B.
Secy. Interior *ad int.*, 1863; Secy. Interior, 1863–65	Usher, John P.

SECOND ADMINISTRATION OF ABRAHAM LINCOLN (1865)

Office	**Name**
Pres.	Lincoln, Abraham
Vice-Pres.	Johnson, Andrew

Office	Name
Secy. State	Seward, William H.
Secy. Treas.	McCulloch, Hugh
Secy. War	Stanton, Edwin M.
Atty. Gen.	Speed, James
Postm. Gen.	Dennison, William
Secy. Navy	Welles, Gideon
Secy. Interior	Usher, John P.

ADMINISTRATION OF ANDREW JOHNSON (1865–1869)

Office	Name
Pres.	Johnson, Andrew
Secy. State	Seward, William H.
Secy. Treas.	McCulloch, Hugh
Secy. War, 1865–(68)*	Stanton, Edwin M.
Secy. War *ad int.*, 1867–68	Grant, Ulysses S.
Secy. War, 1868–69	Schofield, John M.
Atty. Gen., 1865–66	Speed, James
Atty. Gen., 1866–68	Stanbery, Henry
Atty. Gen. *ad int.*, 1868	Browning, Orville H.
Atty. Gen., 1868–69	Evarts, William M.
Postm. Gen., 1865–66	Dennison, William
Postm. Gen. *ad int.*, 1866; Postm. Gen., 1866–69	Randall, Alexander W.
Secy. Navy	Welles, Gideon
Secy. Interior, 1865	Usher, John P.
Secy. Interior, 1865–66	Harlan, James
Secy. Interior, 1866–69	Browning, Orville H.

FIRST ADMINISTRATION OF ULYSSES S. GRANT (1869–1873)

Office	Name
Pres.	Grant, Ulysses S.
Vice-Pres.	Colfax, Schuyler

---

*See biography for details.

Secy. State, 1869	Washburne, Elihu B.
Secy. State, 1869–73	Fish, Hamilton
Secy. Treas., 1869–73	Boutwell, George S.
Secy. War, 1869	Rawlins, John A.
Secy. War, 1869	Sherman, William T.
Secy. War, 1869–73	Belknap, William W.
Atty. Gen., 1869–70	Hoar, Ebenezer R.
Atty. Gen., 1870–71	Akerman, Amos T.
Atty. Gen., 1872–73	Williams, George H.
Postm. Gen.	Creswell, John A.J.
Secy. Navy, 1869	Borie, Adolph E.
Secy. Navy, 1869–73	Robeson, George M.
Secy. Interior, 1869–70	Cox, Jacob D.
Secy. Interior, 1870–73	Delano, Columbus

SECOND ADMINISTRATION OF ULYSSES S. GRANT (1873–1877)

Office	Name
Pres.	Grant, Ulysses S.
Vice-Pres., 1873–75	Wilson, Henry
Secy. State	Fish, Hamilton
Secy. Treas., 1873–74	Richardson, William A.
Secy. Treas., 1874–76	Bristow, Benjamin H.
Secy. Treas., 1876–77	Morrill, Lot M.
Secy. War, 1873–76	Belknap, William W.
Secy. War, 1876	Robeson, George M.
Secy. War, 1876	Taft, Alphonso
Secy. War, 1876–77	Cameron, James D.
Atty. Gen., 1873–75	Williams, George H.
Atty. Gen., 1875–76	Pierrepont, Edwards
Atty. Gen., 1876–77	Taft, Alphonso
Postm. Gen., 1873–74	Creswell, John A.J.
Postm. Gen., 1874	Marshall, James W.
Postm. Gen., 1874–76	Jewell, Marshall
Postm. Gen., 1876–77	Tyner, James N.
Secy. Navy, 1873–77	Robeson, George M.
Secy. Interior, 1873–75	Delano, Columbus
Secy. Interior, 1875–77	Chandler, Zachariah

ADMINISTRATION OF
RUTHERFORD B. HAYES (1877–1881)

Office	Name
Pres.	Hayes, Rutherford B.
Vice-Pres.	Wheeler, William A.
Secy. State	Evarts, William M.
Secy. Treas.	Sherman, John
Secy. War, 1877–79	McCrary, George W.
Secy. War, 1879–81	Ramsey, Alexander
Atty. Gen.	Devens, Charles
Postm. Gen., 1877–1880	Key, David M.
Postm. Gen., 1880–81	Maynard, Horace
Secy. Navy, 1877–80	Thompson, Richard W.
Secy. Navy *ad int.*, 1880–81	Ramsey, Alexander
Secy. Navy, 1881	Goff, Nathan, Jr.
Secy. Interior	Schurz, Carl

ADMINISTRATION OF
JAMES A. GARFIELD (1881)

Office	Name
Pres.	Garfield, James A.
Vice-Pres.	Arthur, Chester A.
Secy. State	Blaine, James G.
Secy. Treas.	Windom, William
Secy. War	Lincoln, Robert T.
Atty. Gen.	MacVeagh, Wayne
Postm. Gen.	James, Thomas L.
Secy. Navy	Hunt, William H.
Secy. Interior	Kirkwood, Samuel J.

ADMINISTRATION OF
CHESTER A. ARTHUR (1881–1885)

Office	Name
Pres.	Arthur, Chester A.
Secy. State, 1881	Blaine, James G.

Secy. State, 1881–85	Frelinghuysen, Frederick T.
Secy. Treas., 1881	Windom, William
Secy. Treas., 1881–84	Folger, Charles J.
Secy. Treas., 1884	Gresham, Walter Q.
Secy. Treas., 1884–85	McCulloch, Hugh
Secy. War	Lincoln, Robert T.
Atty. Gen., 1881	MacVeagh, Wayne
Atty. Gen., 1882–85	Brewster, Benjamin H.
Postm. Gen., 1881–82	James, Thomas L.
Postm. Gen., 1882–83	Howe, Timothy O.
Postm. Gen., 1883–84	Gresham, Walter Q.
Postm. Gen. *ad int.*, 1883; *ad int.*, 1884; Postm. Gen., 1884–85	Hatton, Frank
Secy. Navy, 1881–82	Hunt, William H.
Secy. Navy, 1882–85	Chandler, William E.
Secy. Interior, 1881–82	Kirkwood, Samuel J.
Secy. Interior, 1882–85	Teller, Henry M.

FIRST ADMINISTRATION OF GROVER CLEVELAND (1885–1889)

Office	Name
Pres.	Cleveland, Grover
Vice-Pres.	Hendricks, Thomas A.
Secy. State	Bayard, Thomas F.
Secy. Treas., 1885–87	Manning, Daniel
Secy. Treas., 1887–89	Fairchild, Charles S.
Secy. War	Endicott, William C.
Atty. Gen.	Garland, Augustus H.
Postm. Gen., 1885–88	Vilas, William F.
Postm. Gen., 1888–89	Dickinson, Donald M.
Secy. Navy	Whitney, William C.
Secy. Interior, 1885–88	Lamar, Lucius Q.C.
Secy. Interior, 1888–89	Vilas, William F.
Secy. Agricult., 1889	Colman, Norman J.

ADMINISTRATION OF
BENJAMIN HARRISON (1889–1893)

Office	Name
Pres.	Harrison, Benjamin
Vice-Pres.	Morton, Levi P.
Secy. State, 1889–92	Blaine, James G.
Secy. State, 1892–93	Foster, John W.
Secy. Treas., 1889–91	Windom, William
Secy. Treas., 1891–93	Foster, Charles
Secy. War, 1889–91	Proctor, Redfield
Secy. War, 1891–93	Elkins, Stephen B.
Atty. Gen.	Miller, William H.H.
Postm. Gen.	Wanamaker, John
Secy. Navy	Tracy, Benjamin F.
Secy. Interior	Noble, John W.
Secy. Agricult.	Rusk, Jeremiah M.

SECOND ADMINISTRATION OF
GROVER CLEVELAND (1893–1897)

Office	Name
Pres.	Cleveland, Grover
Vice-Pres.	Stevenson, Adlai E.
Secy. State, 1893–95	Gresham, Walter Q.
Secy. State, 1895–97	Olney, Richard
Secy. Treas.	Carlisle, John G.
Secy. War	Lamont, Daniel S.
Atty. Gen., 1893–95	Olney, Richard
Atty. Gen., 1895–97	Harmon, Judson
Postm. Gen., 1893–95	Bissell, Wilson S.
Postm. Gen., 1895–97	Wilson, William L.
Secy. Navy	Herbert, Hilary A.
Secy. Interior, 1893–96	Smith, Hoke
Secy. Interior, 1896–97	Francis, David R.
Secy. Agricult.	Morton, Julius S.

FIRST ADMINISTRATION OF WILLIAM McKINLEY (1897–1901)

Office	Name
Pres.	McKinley, William
Vice-Pres.	Hobart, Garret A.
Secy. State, 1897–98	Sherman, John
Secy. State, 1898	Day, William R.
Secy. State, 1898–1901	Hay, John
Secy. Treas.	Gage, Lyman J.
Secy. War, 1897–99	Alger, Russell A.
Secy. War, 1899–1901	Root, Elihu
Atty. Gen., 1897–98	McKenna, Joseph
Atty. Gen., 1898–1901	Griggs, John W.
Postm. Gen., 1897–98	Gary, James A.
Postm. Gen., 1898–1901	Smith, Charles E.
Secy. Navy	Long, John D.
Secy. Interior, 1897–99	Bliss, Cornelius N.
Secy. Interior, 1899–1901	Hitchcock, Ethan A.
Secy. Agricult.	Wilson, James

SECOND ADMINISTRATION OF WILLIAM McKINLEY (1901)

Office	Name
Pres.	McKinley, William
Vice-Pres.	Roosevelt, Theodore
Secy. State	Hay, John
Secy. Treas.	Gage, Lyman J.
Secy. War	Root, Elihu
Atty. Gen. (Jan.–Mar.)	Griggs, John W.
Atty. Gen. (Apr.–Sept.)	Knox, Philander C.
Postm. Gen.	Smith, Charles E.
Secy. Navy	Long, John D.
Secy. Interior	Hitchcock, Ethan A.
Secy. Agricult.	Wilson, James

FIRST ADMINISTRATION OF THEODORE ROOSEVELT (1901–1905)

Office	Name
Pres.	Roosevelt, Theodore
Secy. State	Hay, John
Secy. Treas., 1901–02	Gage, Lyman J.
Secy. Treas., 1902–05	Shaw, Leslie M.
Secy. War, 1901–04	Root, Elihu
Secy. War, 1904–05	Taft, William H.
Atty. Gen., 1901–04	Knox, Philander C.
Atty. Gen., 1904–05	Moody, William H.
Postm. Gen., 1901–02	Smith, Charles E.
Postm. Gen., 1902–04	Payne, Henry C.
Postm. Gen., 1904–05	Wynne, Robert J.
Secy. Navy, 1901–02	Long, John D.
Secy. Navy, 1902–04	Moody, William H.
Secy. Navy, 1904–05	Morton, Paul
Secy. Interior	Hitchcock, Ethan A.
Secy. Agricult.	Wilson, James
Secy. Comm. and Labor, 1903–04	Cortelyou, George B.
Secy. Comm. and Labor, 1904–05	Metcalf, Victor H.

SECOND ADMINISTRATION OF THEODORE ROOSEVELT (1905–1909)

Office	Name
Pres.	Roosevelt, Theodore
Vice-Pres.	Fairbanks, Charles W.
Secy. State, 1905	Hay, John
Secy. State, 1905–09	Root, Elihu
Secy. State, 1909	Bacon, Robert
Secy. Treas., 1905–07	Shaw, Leslie M.
Secy. Treas., 1907–09	Cortelyou, George B.
Secy. War, 1905–08	Taft, William H.
Secy. War, 1908–09	Wright, Luke E.
Atty. Gen., 1905–06	Moody, William H.

Atty. Gen., 1906–09	Bonaparte, Charles J.
Postm. Gen., 1905–07	Cortelyou, George B.
Postm. Gen., 1907–09	Meyer, George von L.
Secy. Navy, 1905	Morton, Paul
Secy. Navy, 1905–06	Bonaparte, Charles J.
Secy. Navy, 1906–08	Metcalf, Victor H.
Secy. Navy, 1908–09	Newberry, Truman H.
Secy. Interior, 1905–07	Hitchcock, Ethan A.
Secy. Interior, 1907–09	Garfield, James R.
Secy. Agricult.	Wilson, James
Secy. Comm. and Labor, 1905–06	Metcalf, Victor H.
Secy. Comm. and Labor, 1906–09	Straus, Oscar S.

ADMINISTRATION OF WILLIAM H. TAFT (1909–1913)

Office	Name
Pres.	Taft, William H.
Vice-Pres.	Sherman, James S.
Secy. State	Knox, Philander C.
Secy. Treas.	MacVeagh, Franklin
Secy. War, 1909–11	Dickinson, Jacob M.
Secy. War, 1911–13	Stimson, Henry L.
Atty. Gen.	Wickersham, George W.
Postm. Gen.	Hitchcock, Frank H.
Secy. Navy	Meyer, George von L.
Secy. Interior, 1909–11	Ballinger, Richard A.
Secy. Interior, 1911–13	Fisher, Walter L.
Secy. Agricult.	Wilson, James
Secy. Comm. and Labor	Nagel, Charles

FIRST ADMINISTRATION OF WOODROW WILSON (1913–1917)

Office	Name
Pres.	Wilson, Woodrow
Vice-Pres.	Marshall, Thomas R.

Secy. State, 1913–15	Bryan, William J.
Secy. State *ad int.*, 1915; Secy. State, 1915–17	Lansing, Robert
Secy. Treas.	McAdoo, William G.
Secy. War, 1913–16	Garrison, Lindley M.
Secy. War, 1916–17	Baker, Newton D.
Atty. Gen., 1913–14	McReynolds, James C.
Atty. Gen., 1914–17	Gregory, Thomas W.
Postm. Gen.	Burleson, Albert S.
Secy. Navy	Daniels, Josephus
Secy. Interior	Lane, Franklin K.
Secy. Agricult.	Houston, David F.
Secy. Comm.	Redfield, William C.
Secy. Labor	Wilson, William B.

SECOND ADMINISTRATION OF WOODROW WILSON (1917–1921)

Office	Name
Pres.	Wilson, Woodrow
Vice-Pres.	Marshall, Thomas R.
Secy. State, 1917–20	Lansing, Robert
Secy. State, 1920–21	Colby, Bainbridge
Secy. Treas., 1917–18	McAdoo, William G.
Secy. Treas., 1918–20	Glass, Carter
Secy. Treas., 1920–21	Houston, David F.
Secy. War	Baker, Newton D.
Atty. Gen., 1917–19	Gregory, Thomas W.
Atty. Gen., 1919–21	Palmer, A. Mitchell
Postm. Gen.	Burleson, Albert S.
Secy. Navy	Daniels, Josephus
Secy. Interior, 1917–20	Lane, Franklin K.
Secy. Interior, 1920–21	Payne, John B.
Secy. Agricult., 1917–20	Houston, David F.
Secy. Agricult., 1920–21	Meredith, Edwin T.
Secy. Comm., 1917–19	Redfield, William C.
Secy. Comm., 1919–21	Alexander, Joshua W.
Secy. Labor	Wilson, William B.

ADMINISTRATION OF
WARREN G. HARDING (1921–1923)

Office	Name
Pres.	Harding, Warren G.
Vice-Pres.	Coolidge, Calvin
Secy. State	Hughes, Charles E.
Secy. Treas.	Mellon, Andrew W.
Secy. War	Weeks, John W.
Atty. Gen.	Daugherty, Harry M.
Postm. Gen., 1921–22	Hays, Will H.
Postm. Gen., 1922–23	Work, Hubert
Postm. Gen., 1923	New, Harry S.
Secy. Navy	Denby, Edwin
Secy. Interior, 1921–23	Fall, Albert B.
Secy. Interior, 1923	Work, Hubert
Secy. Agricult.	Wallace, Henry C.
Secy. Comm.	Hoover, Herbert C.
Secy. Labor	Davis, James J.

FIRST ADMINISTRATION OF
CALVIN COOLIDGE (1923–1925)

Office	Name
Pres.	Coolidge, Calvin
Secy. State	Hughes, Charles E.
Secy. Treas.	Mellon, Andrew W.
Secy. War	Weeks, John W.
Atty. Gen., 1923–24	Daugherty, Harry M.
Atty. Gen., 1924–25	Stone, Harlan F.
Postm. Gen.	New, Harry S.
Secy. Navy, 1923–24	Denby, Edwin
Secy. Navy, 1924–25	Wilbur, Curtis D.
Secy. Interior	Work, Hubert
Secy. Agricult., 1923–24	Wallace, Henry C.
Secy. Agricult. *ad int.*, 1924; Secy. Agricult., 1924–25	Gore, Howard M.
Secy. Comm.	Hoover, Herbert C.
Secy. Labor	Davis, James J.

SECOND ADMINISTRATION OF
CALVIN COOLIDGE (1925–1929)

Office	Name
Office	**Name**
Pres.	Coolidge, Calvin
Vice-Pres.	Dawes, Charles G.
Secy. State	Kellogg, Frank B.
Secy. Treas.	Mellon, Andrew W.
Secy. War, 1925	Weeks, John W.
Secy. War, 1925–29	Davis, Dwight F.
Atty. Gen.	Sargent, John G.
Postm. Gen.	New, Harry S.
Secy. Navy	Wilbur, Curtis D.
Secy. Interior, 1925–28	Work, Hubert
Secy. Interior *ad int.*, 1928–29; Secy. Interior, 1929	West, Roy O.
Secy. Agricult.	Jardine, William M.
Secy. Comm., 1925–28	Hoover, Herbert C.
Secy. Comm. *ad int.*, 1928; Secy. Comm., 1928–29	Whiting, William F.
Secy. Labor	Davis, James J.

ADMINISTRATION OF
HERBERT C. HOOVER (1929–1933)

Office	Name
Office	**Name**
Pres.	Hoover, Herbert C.
Vice-Pres.	Curtis, Charles
Secy. State	Stimson, Henry L.
Secy. Treas., 1929–32	Mellon, Andrew W.
Secy. Treas., 1932–33	Mills, Ogden L.
Secy. War, 1929	Good, James W.
Secy. War, 1929–33	Hurley, Patrick J.
Atty. Gen.	Mitchell, James D.
Postm. Gen.	Brown, Walter F.
Secy. Navy	Adams, Charles F.
Secy. Interior	Wilbur, Ray L.
Secy. Agricult.	Hyde, Arthur M.
Secy. Comm., 1929–32	Lamont, Robert P.

Secy. Comm. *ad int.*, 1932; Secy. Comm., 1932–33	Chapin, Roy D.
Secy. Labor, 1929–30	Davis, James J.
Secy. Labor, 1930–33	Doak, William N.

FIRST ADMINISTRATION OF FRANKLIN DELANO ROOSEVELT (1933–1937)

Office	Name
Pres.	Roosevelt, Franklin D.
Vice-Pres.	Garner, John N.
Secy. State	Hull, Cordell
Secy. Treas., 1933–34	Woodin, William H.
Secy. Treas. *ad int.*, 1934; Secy. Treas., 1934–37	Morgenthau, Henry, Jr.
Secy. War, 1933–36	Dern, George H.
Secy. War *ad int.*, 1936–37	Woodring, Henry H.
Atty. Gen.	Cummings, Homer S.
Postm. Gen.	Farley, James A.
Secy. Navy	Swanson, Claude A.
Secy. Interior	Ickes, Harold L.
Secy. Agricult.	Wallace, Henry A.
Secy. Comm.	Roper, Daniel C.
Secy. Labor	Perkins, Frances

SECOND ADMINISTRATION OF FRANKLIN DELANO ROOSEVELT (1937–1941)

Office	Name
Pres.	Roosevelt, Franklin D.
Vice-Pres.	Garner, John N.
Secy. State	Hull, Cordell
Secy. Treas.	Morgenthau, Henry, Jr.
Secy. War, 1937–40	Woodring, Henry H.
Secy. War, 1940–41	Stimson, Henry L.
Atty. Gen., 1937–39	Cummings, Homer S.

Office	Name
Atty. Gen. *ad int.*, 1939; Atty. Gen., 1939–40	Murphy, Frank
Atty. Gen., 1940–41	Jackson, Robert H.
Postm. Gen., 1937–40	Farley, James A.
Postm. Gen., 1940–41	Walker, Frank C.
Secy. Navy, 1937–39	Swanson, Claude A.
Secy. Navy, 1939 (acting); *ad int.*, 1939–40; Secy. Navy, 1940	Edison, Charles
Secy. Navy, 1940–41	Knox, Frank
Secy. Interior	Ickes, Harold L.
Secy. Agricult., 1937–40	Wallace, Henry A.
Secy. Agricult., 1940–41	Wickard, Claude R.
Secy. Comm., 1937–38	Roper, Daniel C.
Secy. Comm. *ad int.*, 1938–39; Secy. Comm., 1939–40	Hopkins, Harry L.
Secy. Comm., 1940–41	Jones, Jesse H.
Secy. Labor	Perkins, Frances

THIRD ADMINISTRATION OF FRANKLIN DELANO ROOSEVELT (1941–1945)

Office	Name
Pres.	Roosevelt, Franklin D.
Vice-Pres.	Wallace, Henry A.
Secy. State, 1941–44	Hull, Cordell
Secy. State, 1944–45	Stettinius, Edward R.
Secy. Treas.	Morgenthau, Henry, Jr.
Secy. War	Stimson, Henry L.
Atty. Gen., 1941	Jackson, Robert H.
Atty. Gen., 1941–45	Biddle, Francis
Postm. Gen.	Walker, Frank C.
Secy. Navy, 1941–44	Knox, Frank
Secy. Navy, 1944–45	Forrestal, James V.
Secy. Interior	Ickes, Harold L.
Secy. Agricult.	Wickard, Claude R.
Secy. Comm.	Jones, Jesse H.
Secy. Labor	Perkins, Frances

FOURTH ADMINISTRATION OF
FRANKLIN DELANO ROOSEVELT (January–April 1945)

Office	Name
Pres.	Roosevelt, Franklin D.
Vice-Pres.	Truman, Harry S
Secy. State	Stettinius, Edward R.
Secy. Treas.	Morgenthau, Henry, Jr.
Secy. War	Stimson, Henry L.
Atty. Gen.	Biddle, Francis
Postm. Gen.	Walker, Frank C.
Secy. Navy	Forrestal, James V.
Secy. Interior	Ickes, Harold L.
Secy. Agricult.	Wickard, Claude R.
Secy. Comm., Jan.–Mar.	Jones, Jesse H.
Secy. Comm., Mar.–Apr.	Wallace, Henry A.
Secy. Labor	Perkins, Frances

FIRST ADMINISTRATION OF
HARRY S TRUMAN (1945–1949)

Office	Name
Pres.	Truman, Harry S
Secy. State, 1945	Stettinius, Edward R.
Secy. State, 1945–47	Byrnes, James F.
Secy. State, 1947–49	Marshall, George C.
Secy. Treas., 1945	Morgenthau, Henry, Jr.
Secy. Treas., 1945–46	Vinson, Fred M.
Secy. Treas., 1946–49	Snyder, John W.
Secy. War, 1945	Stimson, Henry L.
Secy. War, 1945–47	Patterson, Robert P.
Secy. War, 1947	Royall, Kenneth C.
Secy. Defense, 1947–49	Forrestal, James
Atty. Gen., 1945	Biddle, Francis
Atty. Gen., 1945–49	Clark, Tom C.
Postm. Gen., 1945	Walker, Frank C.
Postm. Gen., 1945–47	Hannegan, Robert E.

Postm. Gen., 1947–49	Donaldson, Jesse M.
Secy. Navy, 1945–47	Forrestal, James
Secy. Interior, 1945–46	Ickes, Harold L.
Secy. Interior, 1946–49	Krug, Julius A.
Secy. Agricult., 1945	Wickard, Claude R.
Secy. Agricult., 1945–48	Anderson, Clinton P.
Secy. Agricult., 1948–49	Brannan, Charles F.
Secy. Comm., 1945–46	Wallace, Henry A.
Secy. Comm. *ad int.*, 1946–47; Secy. Comm., 1947–48	Harriman, W. Averill
Secy. Comm., 1948–49	Sawyer, Charles
Secy. Labor, 1945	Perkins, Frances
Secy. Labor, 1945–48	Schwellenbach, Lewis B.
Secy. Labor *ad int.*, 1948–49	Tobin, Maurice J.

SECOND ADMINISTRATION OF HARRY S TRUMAN (1949–1953)

Office	**Name**
Pres.	Truman, Harry S
Vice-Pres.	Barkley, Alben W.
Secy. State	Acheson, Dean G.
Secy. Treas.	Snyder, John W.
Secy. Defense, 1949	Forrestal, James
Secy. Defense, 1949–50	Johnson, Louis A.
Secy. Defense, 1950–51	Marshall, George C.
Secy. Defense, 1951–53	Lovett, Robert A.
Atty. Gen., 1949	Clark, Tom C.
Atty. Gen., 1949–52	McGrath, J. Howard
Atty. Gen., 1952–53	McGranery, James P.
Postm. Gen.	Donaldson, Jesse M.
Secy. Interior, 1949	Krug, Julius A.
Secy. Interior *ad int.*, 1949–50; Secy. Interior, 1950–53	Chapman, Oscar L.
Secy. Agricult.	Brannan, Charles F.
Secy. Comm.	Sawyer, Charles
Secy. Labor	Tobin, Maurice J.

FIRST ADMINISTRATION OF
DWIGHT DAVID EISENHOWER (1953–1957)

Office	Name
Pres.	Eisenhower, Dwight D.
Vice-Pres.	Nixon, Richard M.
Secy. State	Dulles, John F.
Secy. Treas.	Humphrey, George M.
Secy. Defense	Wilson, Charles E.
Atty. Gen.	Brownell, Herbert, Jr.
Postm. Gen.	Summerfield, Arthur E.
Secy. Interior, 1953–56	McKay, Douglas
Secy. Interior, 1956–57	Seaton, Frederick A.
Secy. Agricult.	Benson, Ezra T.
Secy. Comm.	Weeks, Sinclair
Secy. Labor, 1953	Durkin, Martin P.
Secy. Labor *ad int.*, 1953–54; Secy. Labor, 1954–57	Mitchell, James P.
Secy. Health, Education and Welfare, 1953–55	Hobby, Oveta Culp
Secy. HEW, 1955–57	Folsom, Marion B.

SECOND ADMINISTRATION OF
DWIGHT DAVID EISENHOWER (1957–1961)

Office	Name
Pres.	Eisenhower, Dwight D.
Vice-Pres.	Nixon, Richard M.
Secy. State, 1957–59	Dulles, John F.
Secy. State, 1959–61	Herter, Christian A.
Secy. Treas., 1957	Humphrey, George M.
Secy. Treas., 1957–61	Anderson, Robert B.
Secy. Defense, 1957	Wilson, Charles E.
Secy. Defense, 1957–59	McElroy, Neil H.
Secy. Defense *ad int.*, 1959–60, Secy. Defense, 1960–61	Gates, Thomas S., Jr.
Atty. Gen., 1957	Brownell, Herbert, Jr.
Atty. Gen. *ad int.*, 1957–58; Atty. Gen., 1958–61	Rogers, William P.

Postm. Gen.	Summerfield, Arthur E.
Secy. Interior	Seaton, Frederick A.
Secy. Agricult.	Benson, Ezra T.
Secy. Comm., 1957–58	Weeks, Sinclair
Secy. Comm. *ad int.*, 1958–59	Strauss, Lewis L.
Secy. Comm. *ad int.*, 1959; Secy. Comm., 1959–61	Mueller, Frederick H.
Secy. Labor	Mitchell, James P.
Secy. HEW, 1957–58	Folsom, Marion B.
Secy. HEW, 1958–61	Flemming, Arthur S.

ADMINISTRATION OF
JOHN F. KENNEDY (1961–1963)

Office	Name
Pres.	Kennedy, John F.
Vice-Pres.	Johnson, Lyndon B.
Secy. State	Rusk, D. Dean
Secy. Treas.	Dillon, C. Douglas
Secy. Defense	McNamara, Robert S.
Atty. Gen.	Kennedy, Robert F.
Postm. Gen., 1961–63	Day, J. Edward
Postm. Gen., 1963	Gronouski, John A.
Secy. Interior	Udall, Stewart L.
Secy. Agricult.	Freeman, Orville L.
Secy. Comm.	Hodges, Luther H.
Secy. Labor, 1961–62	Goldberg, Arthur J.
Secy. Labor, 1962–63	Wirtz, W. Willard
Secy. HEW, 1961–62	Ribicoff, Abraham A.
Secy. HEW, 1962–63	Celebrezze, Anthony J.

FIRST ADMINISTRATION OF
LYNDON B. JOHNSON (1963–1965)

Office	Name
Pres.	Johnson, Lyndon B.
Secy. State	Rusk, D. Dean

Secy. Treas.	Dillon, C. Douglas
Secy. Defense	McNamara, Robert S.
Atty. Gen.	Kennedy, Robert F.
Postm. Gen.	Gronouski, John A.
Secy. Interior	Udall, Stewart L.
Secy. Agricult.	Freeman, Orville L.
Secy. Comm., 1963–65	Hodges, Luther A.
Secy. Comm., 1965	Connor, John T.
Secy. Labor	Wirtz, W. Willard
Secy. HEW	Celebrezze, Anthony J.

SECOND ADMINISTRATION OF LYNDON B. JOHNSON (1965–1969)

Office	Name
Pres.	Johnson, Lyndon B.
Vice-Pres.	Humphrey, Hubert H.
Secy. State	Rusk, D. Dean
Secy. Treas., 1965	Dillon, C. Douglas
Secy. Treas., 1965–69	Fowler, Henry H.
Secy. Defense, 1965–68	McNamara, Robert S.
Secy. Defense, 1968–69	Clifford, Clark M.
Atty. Gen., 1965–67	Katzenbach, Nicholas de B.
Atty. Gen., 1967–69	Clark, Ramsey
Postm. Gen., 1965	Gronouski, John A.
Postm. Gen., 1965–68	O'Brien, Lawrence F.
Postm. Gen., 1968–69	Watson, William M.
Secy. Interior	Udall, Stewart L.
Secy. Agricult.	Freeman, Orville L.
Secy. Comm., 1965–67	Connor, John T.
Secy. Comm., 1967–68	Trowbridge, Alexander G.
Secy. Comm., 1968–69	Smith, Cyrus R.
Secy. Labor	Wirtz, W. Willard
Secy. HEW, 1965	Celebrezze, Anthony J.
Secy. HEW, 1965–68	Gardner, John W.
Secy. HEW, 1968–69	Cohen, Wilbur J.
Secy. Housing and Urban Development, 1966–69	Weaver, Robert C.

Secy. HUD, 1969	Wood, Robert C.
Secy. Transport., 1966–69	Boyd, Alan S.

FIRST ADMINISTRATION OF RICHARD M. NIXON (1969–1973)

Office	Name
Pres.	Nixon, Richard M.
Vice-Pres.	Agnew, Spiro T.
Secy. State, 1969–73	Rogers, William P.
Secy. State, 1973	Kissinger, Henry A.
Secy. Treas., 1969–70	Kennedy, David M.
Secy. Treas., 1970–72	Connally, John B.
Secy. Treas., 1972–73	Shultz, George P.
Secy. Defense, 1969–73	Laird, Melvin R.
Atty. Gen., 1969–72	Mitchell, John N.
Atty. Gen., 1972–73	Kleindienst, Richard G.
Postm. Gen.	Blount, Winton
Secy. Interior, 1969–71	Hickel, Walter J.
Secy. Interior, 1971–73	Morton, Rogers C.B.
Secy. Agricult., 1969–71	Hardin, Clifford M.
Secy. Agricult., 1971–73	Butz, Earl L.
Secy. Comm., 1969–72	Stans, Maurice H.
Secy. Comm., 1972–73	Peterson, Peter G.
Secy. Labor, 1969–70	Shultz, George P.
Secy. Labor, 1970–73	Hodgson, James D.
Secy. HEW, 1969–70	Finch, Robert H.
Secy. HEW, 1970–73	Richardson, Elliot L.
Secy. HUD, 1969–73	Romney, George W.
Secy. Transport., 1969–73	Volpe, James A.

SECOND ADMINISTRATION OF RICHARD M. NIXON (1973–1974)

Office	Name
Pres.	Nixon, Richard M.
Vice-Pres., 1973	Agnew, Spiro T.

Vice-Pres., 1973–74	Ford, Gerald R.
Secy. State	Kissinger, Henry A.
Secy. Treas., 1973–74	Shultz, George P.
Secy. Treas., 1974	Simon, William E.
Secy. Defense, 1973	Richardson, Elliot L.
Secy. Defense, 1973–74	Schlesinger, James R.
Atty. Gen., 1973–74	Richardson, Elliot L.
Atty. Gen., 1974	Saxbe, William B.
Secy. Interior	Morton, Rogers C. B.
Secy. Agricult.	Butz, Earl L.
Secy. Comm.	Dent, Frederick B.
Secy. Labor	Brennan, Peter J.
Secy. HEW	Weinberger, Caspar W.
Secy. HUD	Lynn, James T.
Secy. Transport.	Brinegar, Claude S.

ADMINISTRATION OF GERALD R. FORD (1974–1977)

Office	Name
Pres.	Ford, Gerald R.
Vice-Pres.	Rockefeller, Nelson A.
Secy. State	Kissinger, Henry A.
Secy. Treas.	Simon, William E.
Secy. Defense, 1974–76	Schlesinger, James R.
Secy. Defense, 1976–77	Rumsfeld, Donald
Atty. Gen., 1974–75	Saxbe, William B.
Atty. Gen., 1975–77	Levi, Edward H.
Secy. Interior, 1974–75	Morton, Rogers C.B.
Secy. Interior, 1975	Hathaway, Stanley K.
Secy. Interior, 1975–77	Kleppe, Thomas
Secy. Agricult., 1974–76	Butz, Earl L.
Secy. Agricult., 1976–77	Knebel, John
Secy. Comm., 1974–75	Dent, Frederick B.
Secy. Comm., 1975–76	Morton, Rogers C.B.
Secy. Comm., 1976–77	Richardson, Elliot L.
Secy. Labor, 1974–75	Brennan, Peter J.
Secy. Labor, 1975–76	Dunlop, John T.

Secy. Labor, 1976–77	Usery, Willie J., Jr.
Secy. HEW, 1974–75	Weinberger, Caspar W.
Secy. HEW, 1975–77	Matthews, Forrest D.
Secy. HUD, 1974–75	Lynn, James T.
Secy. HUD, 1975–77	Hills, Carla
Secy. Transport., 1974–75	Brinegar, Claude S.
Secy. Transport., 1975–77	Coleman, William

ADMINISTRATION OF JIMMY CARTER (1977–1981)

Office	Name
Pres.	Carter, Jimmy
Vice-Pres.	Mondale, Walter F.
Secy. State, 1977–80	Vance, Cyrus R.
Secy. State, 1980–81	Muskie, Edmund S.
Secy. Treas., 1977–79	Blumenthal, W. Michael
Secy. Treas., 1979–81	Miller, G. William
Secy. Defense	Brown, Harold
Atty. Gen., 1977–79	Bell, Griffin B.
Atty. Gen., 1979–81	Civiletti, Benjamin R.
Secy. Interior	Andrus, Cecil D.
Secy. Agricult.	Bergland, Bob S.
Secy. Comm., 1977–79	Kreps, Juanita M.
Secy. Comm., 1979–81	Klutznick, Philip M.
Secy. Labor	Marshall, Freddie R.
Secy. HEW, 1977–79	Califano, Joseph A., Jr.
Secy. HEW, 1979–81	Harris, Patricia R.
Secy. HUD, 1977–79	Harris, Patricia R.
Secy. HUD, 1979–81	Landrieu, Moon E.
Secy. Transport., 1977–79	Adams, Brockman
Secy. Transport., 1979–81	Goldschmidt, Neil E.
Secy. Energy, 1977–79	Schlesinger, James R.
Secy. Energy, 1979–81	Duncan, Charles W., Jr.
Secy. Health and Human Svcs.	Harris, Patricia R.
Secy. Education	Hufstedler, Shirley M.

FIRST ADMINISTRATION OF RONALD REAGAN (1981–1985)

Office	Name
Pres.	Reagan, Ronald W.
Vice-Pres.	Bush, George H.W.
Secy. State, 1981–82	Haig, Alexander M., Jr.
Secy. State, 1982–85	Shultz, George P.
Secy. Treas., 1981–85	Regan, Donald T.
Secy. Treas., 1985	Baker, James A., III
Secy. Defense	Weinberger, Caspar W.
Atty. Gen.	Smith, William French
Secy. Interior, 1981–83	Watt, James G.
Secy. Interior, 1983–85	Clark, William P.
Secy. Agricult.	Block, John R.
Secy. Commerce	Baldridge, Malcolm
Secy. Labor	Donovan, Raymond J.
Secy. HUD	Pierce, Samuel R., Jr.
Secy. Transport., 1981–83	Lewis, Andrew
Secy. Transport., 1983–85	Dole, Elizabeth H.
Secy. Energy, 1981–82	Edwards, James
Secy. Energy, 1982–85	Hodel, Donald P.
Secy. Health and Human Svcs., 1981–83	Schweiker, Richard
Secy. Health and Human Svcs., 1983–85	Heckler, Margaret M.
Secy. Education	Bell, Terrel H.

SECOND ADMINISTRATION OF RONALD REAGAN (1985–1989)

Office	Name
Pres.	Reagan, Ronald W.
Vice-Pres.	Bush, George H.W.
Secy. State, 1982–85	Shultz, George P.
Secy. Treas., 1985	Regan, Donald T.
Secy. Treas., 1985–88	Baker, James A., III
Secy. Treas., 1988–89	Brady, Nicholas F.

Secy. Defense, 1985–87	Weinberger, Caspar W.
Secy. Defense, 1987–89	Carlucci, Frank C., III
Atty. Gen., 1985	Smith, William French
Atty. Gen., 1985–88	Meese, Edwin, III
Atty. Gen., 1988–89	Thornburgh, Richard L.
Secy. Interior, 1985	Clark, William P.
Secy. Interior, 1985–89	Hodel, Donald P.
Secy. Agricult., 1985–86	Block, John R.
Secy. Agricult., 1986–89	Lyng, Richard E.
Secy. Commerce, 1985–87	Baldridge, Malcolm
Secy. Commerce, 1987–89	Verity, C. William, Jr.
Secy. Labor, 1985	Brock, William E., III
Secy. Labor, 1985–89	McLaughlin, Ann D.
Secy. HUD	Pierce, Samuel R., Jr.
Secy. Transport., 1985–87	Dole, Elizabeth H.
Secy. Transport., 1987–89	Burnley, James H., IV
Secy. Energy, 1985	Hodel, Donald P.
Secy. Energy, 1985–89	Herrington, John
Secy. Health and Human Svcs., 1985	Heckler, Margaret M.
Secy. Health and Human Svcs., 1985–89	Bowen, Otis R.
Secy. Education, 1985	Bell, Terrel H.
Secy. Education, 1985–88	Bennett, William John
Secy. Education, 1988–89	Cavazos, Lauro F.

ADMINISTRATION OF GEORGE H.W. BUSH (1989–1993)

Office	Name
Pres.	Bush, George H.W.
Vice-Pres.	Quayle, James Danforth, III
Secy. State, 1989–92	Baker, James A., III
Secy. State, 1992–93	Eagleburger, Lawrence S.
Secy. Treas.	Brady, Nicholas F.
Secy. Defense	Cheney, Richard B.
Atty. Gen., 1989–91	Thornburgh, Richard L.
Atty. Gen., 1991–93	Barr, William P.

Secy. Interior	Lujan, Manuel, Jr.
Secy. Agricult., 1989–91	Yeutter, Clayton K.
Secy. Agricult., 1991–93	Madigan, Edward R.
Secy. Commerce, 1989–92	Mosbacher, Robert A.
Secy. Commerce, 1992–93	Franklin, Barbara H.
Secy. Labor, 1989–90	Dole, Elizabeth H.
Secy. Labor, 1990–93	Martin, Lynn M.
Secy. HUD	Kemp, Jack F.
Secy. Transport., 1989–91	Skinner, Samuel K.
Secy. Transport., 1992–93	Card, Andrew H., Jr.
Secy. Energy	Watkins, James D.
Secy. Health and Human Svcs.	Sullivan, Louis W.
Secy. Education, 1989–90	Cavazos, Lauro F.
Secy. Education, 1990–93	Alexander, Lamar
Secy. Veterans Affairs	Derwinski, Edward J.

ADMINISTRATION OF WILLIAM J. CLINTON (1993–2001)

Office	**Name**
Pres.	Clinton, William J.
Vice-Pres.	Gore, Albert, Jr.
Secy. State, 1993–97	Christopher, Warren M.
Secy. State, 1997–2001	Albright, Madeleine K.
Secy. Treas., 1993–94	Bentsen, Lloyd
Secy. Treas., 1994–99	Rubin, Robert E.
Secy. Treas., 1999–2001	Summers, Lawrence H.
Secy. Defense, 1993–94	Aspin, Les
Secy. Defense, 1994–97	Perry, William J.
Secy. Defense, 1997–2001	Cohen, William S.
Atty. Gen.	Reno, Janet
Secy. Interior	Babbitt, Bruce
Secy. Agricult., 1993–94	Espy, Mike
Secy. Agricult., 1995–2001	Glickman, Dan
Secy. Commerce, 1993–96	Brown, Ronald H.
Secy. Commerce, 1996–97	Kantor, Michael
Secy. Commerce, 1997–2000	Daley, William M.
Secy. Commerce, 2000–2001	Mineta, Norman Y.

Secy. Labor, 1993–97	Reich, Robert B.
Secy. Labor, 1997–2001	Herman, Alexis M.
Secy. HUD, 1993–97	Cisneros, Henry G
Secy. HUD, 1997–2001	Cuomo, Andrew M.
Secy. Transport., 1993–97	Peña, Federico
Secy. Transport., 1997–2001	Slater, Rodney E.
Secy. Energy, 1993–97	O'Leary, Hazel R.
Secy. Energy, 1997–98	Peña, Federico
Secy. Energy, 1998–2001	Richardson, William
Secy. Health and Human Svcs.	Shalala, Donna E.
Secy. Education	Riley, Richard W.
Secy. Veterans Affairs, 1993–97	Brown, Jesse
Secy. Veterans Affairs, 1998–2001	West, Togo D., Jr.

ADMINISTRATION OF GEORGE W. BUSH (2001–)

Office	Name
Pres.	Bush, George W.
Vice-Pres.	Cheney, Richard B.
Secy. State	Powell, Colin
Secy. Treas.	O'Neill, Paul H.
Secy. Defense	Rumsfeld, Donald H.
Atty. Gen.	Ashcroft, John
Secy. Interior	Norton, Gale A.
Secy. Agricult.	Veneman, Ann M.
Secy. Commerce	Evans, Donald
Secy. Labor	Chao, Elaine
Secy. HUD	Martinez, Melquiades
Secy. Transport.	Mineta, Norman Y.
Secy. Energy	Abraham, Spencer
Secy. Health and Human Svcs.	Thompson, Tommy
Secy. Education	Paige, Rod
Secy. Veterans Affairs	Principi, Anthony

Heads of
State and Cabinet Officials

PRESIDENTS OF THE CONTINENTAL CONGRESS (1774–1789)

Name	Date Elected
Elias Boudinot	Nov. 4, 1782
Nathaniel Gorham	June 6, 1786
Cyrus Griffin	Jan. 22, 1788
John Hancock	May 24, 1775
John Hancock	Nov. 23, 1785
John Hanson	Nov. 5, 1781
Samuel Huntington	Sept. 28, 1779
John Jay	Dec. 10, 1778
Henry Laurens	Nov. 1, 1777
Richard Henry Lee	Nov. 30, 1784
Thomas McKean	July 10, 1781
Henry Middleton	Oct. 22, 1774
Thomas Mifflin	Nov. 3, 1783
Peyton Randolph	Sept. 5, 1774
Peyton Randolph	May 10, 1775
Arthur St. Clair	Feb. 2, 1787

PRESIDENTS

Name	Dates
Adams, John	1797–1801
Adams, John Q.	1825–29
Arthur, Chester A.	1881–85
Buchanan, James	1857–61
Bush, George H.W.	1989–93
Bush, George W.	2001–
Carter, Jimmy	1977–1981
Cleveland, Grover	1885–89; 1893–97
Clinton, William J.	1993–2001
Coolidge, Calvin	1923–29
Eisenhower, Dwight D.	1953–61
Fillmore, Millard	1850–53
Ford, Gerald R.	1974–77
Garfield, James A.	1881–85
Grant, Ulysses S.	1869–77
Harding, Warren G.	1921–23
Harrison, Benjamin	1889–93
Harrison, William H.	1841
Hayes, Rutherford B.	1877–81
Hoover, Herbert C.	1929–33
Jackson, Andrew	1829–37
Jefferson, Thomas	1801–09
Johnson, Andrew	1865–69
Johnson, Lyndon B.	1963–69
Kennedy, John F.	1961–63
Lincoln, Abraham	1861–65
Madison, James	1809–17
McKinley, William, Jr.	1897–1901
Monroe, James	1817–25
Nixon, Richard M.	1969–74
Pierce, Franklin	1853–57
Polk, James K.	1845–49
Reagan, Ronald W.	1981–89
Roosevelt, Franklin D.	1933–45
Roosevelt, Theodore	1901–09
Taft, William H.	1909–13

Taylor, Zachary	1849–50
Truman, Harry S	1945–53
Taylor, John	1841–45
Van Buren, Martin	1837–41
Washington, George	1789–97
Wilson, Woodrow	1913–21

VICE-PRESIDENTS

Name	Dates	President
Adams, John	1789–97	Washington
Agnew, Spiro T.	1969–74	Nixon
Arthur, Chester A.	1881	Garfield
Barkley, Alben W.	1949–53	Truman
Breckinridge, John C.	1857–61	Buchanan
Burr, Aaron	1801–05	Jefferson
Bush, George H.W.	1981–89	Reagan
Calhoun, John C.	1825–29	J.Q. Adams
Calhoun, John C.	1929–32	Jackson
Cheney Richard B.	2001–	G.W. Bush
Clinton, George	1805–09	Jefferson
Clinton, George	1809–13	Madison
Colfax, Schuyler	1869–73	Grant
Coolidge, Calvin	1921–23	Harding
Curtis, Charles	1929–33	Hoover
Dallas, George M.	1845–49	Polk
Dawes, Charles G.	1924–29	Coolidge
Fairbanks, Charles W.	1905–09	T. Roosevelt
Fillmore, Millard	1849–50	Taylor
Ford, Gerald R.	1973–74	Nixon
Garner, John N.	1933–41	F.D. Roosevelt
Gerry, Elbridge	1813–14	Madison
Gore, Albert	1993–2001	Cinton
Hamlin, Hannibal	1861–65	Lincoln
Hendricks, Thomas A.	1885	Cleveland
Hobart, Garret A.	1897–99	McKinley
Humphrey, Hubert H., Jr.	1964–69	L.B. Johnson
Jefferson, Thomas	1797–1801	Adams

Johnson, Andrew	1865	Lincoln
Johnson, Lyndon B.	1961–63	Kennedy
Johnson, Richard M.	1837–41	Van Buren
King, William R. deV.	1853	Pierce
Marshall, Thomas R.	1913–21	Wilson
Mondale, Walter	1977–81	Carter
Morton, Levi P.	1889–93	B. Harrison
Nixon, Richard M.	1953–61	Eisenhower
Quayle, Danforth	1989–93	G.H.W. Bush
Rockefeller, Nelson A.	1974–77	Ford
Roosevelt, Theodore	1901	McKinley
Sherman, James S.	1908–12	Taft
Stevenson, Adlai E.	1893–97	Cleveland
Tompkins, Daniel D.	1817–25	Monroe
Truman, Harry S	1945	F.D. Roosevelt
Tyler, John	1841	W.H. Harrison
Van Buren, Martin	1833–37	Jackson
Wallace, Henry A.	1941–45	F.D. Roosevelt
Wheeler, William A.	1877–81	Hayes
Wilson, Henry	1873–75	Grant

SECRETARIES OF STATE

Name	Dates	President
Acheson, Dean G.	1949–53	Truman
Adams, John Q.	1817–25	Monroe
Albright, Madeleine	1997–2001	Clinton
Bacon, Robert	1909	T. Roosevelt
Baker, James A., III	1989–92	G.H.W. Bush
Bayard, Thomas F.	1885–89	Cleveland
Black, Jeremiah	1860–61	Buchanan
Blaine, James G.	1881	Garfield
Blaine, James G.	1889–92	B. Harrison
Bryan, William J.	1913–15	Wilson
Buchanan, James	1845–49	Polk
Byrnes, James F.	1945–47	Truman
Calhoun, John C.	1844–45	Tyler
Cass, Lewis	1857–60	Buchanan

Christopher, Warren	1993–97	Clinton
Clay, Henry	1825–29	J.Q. Adams
Clayton, John M.	1849–50	Taylor
Colby, Bainbridge	1920–21	Wilson
Conrad, Charles M.	*ad int.*, 1852	Fillmore
Day, William R.	1898	McKinley
Dulles, John F.	1953–59	Eisenhower
Eagleburger, Lawrence S.	1992–93	G.H.W. Bush
Evarts, William M.	1877–81	Hayes
Everett, Edward	1852–53	Fillmore
Fish, Hamilton	1869–77	Grant
Forsyth, John	1834–37	Jackson
Forsyth, John	1837–41	Van Buren
Foster, John W.	1892–93	B. Harrison
Frelinghuysen, Frederick T.	1881–85	Arthur
Gresham, Walter Q.	1893–95	Cleveland
Haig, Alexander M., Jr.	1981–82	Reagan
Hay, John M.	1898–1905	McKinley
Herter, Christian A.	1959–61	Eisenhower
Hughes, Charles E.	1921–25	Harding
Hull, Cordell	1933–44	F.D. Roosevelt
Jay, John	1789–90	Washington
Jefferson, Thomas	1790–94	Washington
Kellogg, Frank B.	1925–29	Coolidge
Kissinger, Henry A.	1973–74	Nixon
Kissinger, Henry A.	1974–77	Ford
Knox, Philander C.	1909–13	Taft
Lansing, Robert	1915–20	Wilson
Lee, Charles	*ad int.*, 1800	J. Adams
Legaré, Hugh S.	*ad int.*, 1843	Tyler
Levi, Lincoln	*ad int.*, 1801	Jefferson
Livingston, Edward	1831–33	Jackson
Madison, James	1801–09	Jefferson
Marcy, William L.	1853–57	Pierce
Marshall, George C.	1947–49	Truman
Marshall, John	*ad int.*, 1800	J. Adams
Marshall, John	1800–01	
McLane, Louis	1833–34	Jackson
Monroe, James	1811–17	Madison

Muskie, Edmund S.	1980–81	Carter
Olney, Richard	1895–97	Cleveland
Pickering, Timothy	1795–97	Washington
Pickering, Timothy	1797–1800	J. Adams
Powell, Colin	2001–	G.W. Bush
Randolph, Edmund J.	1794	Washington
Rogers, William P.	1969–73	Nixon
Root, Elihu	1905–09	T. Roosevelt
Rush, Richard	*ad int.*, 1817	Monroe
Rusk, D. Dean	1961–63	Kennedy
Rusk, D. Dean	1963–69	L.B. Johnson
Seward, William H.	1861–65	Lincoln
Seward, William H.	1865–69	A. Johnson
Sherman, John	1897–1900	McKinley
Shultz, George P.	1982–89	Reagan
Smith, Robert	1809–11	Madison
Stettinius, Edward R., Jr.	1944–45	F.D. Roosevelt
Stimson, Henry L.	1929–33	Hoover
Upshur, Abel P.	1843–44	Tyler
Van Buren, Martin	1829–31	Jackson
Vance, Cyrus	1977–80	Carter
Washburne, Elihu B.	1869	Grant
Webster, Daniel	1841–43	W.H. Harrison
Webster, Daniel	1850–52	Fillmore

SECRETARIES OF THE TREASURY

Name	Dates	President
Anderson, Robert B.	1957–61	Eisenhower
Baker, James A., III	1985–89	Reagan
Bentsen, Lloyd	1993–94	Clinton
Bibb, George H.	1844–45	Tyler
Blumenthal, Michael W.	1977–79	Carter
Boutwell, George S.	1869–73	Grant
Brady, Nicholas F.	1989–93	G.H.W. Bush
Bristow, Benjamin H.	1874–76	Grant
Campbell, George W.	1814	Madison
Carlisle, John G.	1893–97	Cleveland

Chase, Salmon P.	1861–64	Lincoln
Cobb, Howell	1857–60	Buchanan
Connally, John B.	1970–72	Nixon
Cortelyou, George B.	1907–09	T. Roosevelt
Corwin, Thomas	1850–53	Fillmore
Crawford, William H.	1816–17	Madison
Crawford, William H.	1817–25	Monroe
Dallas, Alexander	1814–16	Madison
Dexter, Samuel	*ad int.*, 1801	Adams
Dillon, C. Douglas	1961–63	Kennedy
Dillon, C. Douglas	1963–65	L.B. Johnson
Dix, John A.	1861	Buchanan
Duane, William J.	1833	Jackson
Ewing, Thomas	1841	W.H. Harrison
Fairchild, Charles S.	1887–89	Cleveland
Fessenden, William P.	1864–65	Lincoln
Folger, Charles J.	1881–84	Arthur
Forward, Walter	1841–43	Tyler
Foster, Charles	1891–93	B. Harrison
Fowler, Henry H.	1965–69	L.B. Johnson
Gage, Lyman J.	1901–02	McKinley
Gallatin, Albert	1801–09	Jefferson
Gallatin, Albert	1809–14	Madison
Glass, Carter	1918–20	Wilson
Gresham, Walter Q.	1884	Arthur
Guthrie, James	1853–57	Pierce
Hamilton, Alexander	1789–95	Washington
Houston, David F.	1920–21	Wilson
Humphrey, George M.	1953–57	Eisenhower
Ingham, Samuel D.	1829–31	Jackson
Jones, William	*ad int.*, 1814	Madison
Kennedy, David M.	1969–70	Nixon
MacVeagh, Franklin	1909–13	Taft
Manning, Daniel	1885–87	Cleveland
McAdoo, William G.	1913–18	Wilson
McCulloch, Hugh	1865	Lincoln
McCulloch, Hugh	1865–69	A. Johnson
McCulloch, Hugh	1884–85	Arthur
McLane, Louis	1831–33	Jackson

Mellon, Andrew W.	1921–23	Harding
Mellon, Andrew W.	1923–29	Coolidge
Meredith, William M.	1849–50	Taylor
Miller, G. William	1977–79	Carter
Mills, Ogden L.	1932–33	Hoover
Morgenthau, Henry, Jr.	1934–45	F.D. Roosevelt
Morrill, Lot M.	1876–77	Grant
O'Neill, Paul H.	2001–	G.W. Bush
Regan, Donald T.	1981–85	Reagan
Richardson, William A.	1873–74	Grant
Rubin, Robert	1995–99	Clinton
Rush, Richard	1825–29	J.Q. Adams
Shaw, Leslie M.	1902–07	T. Roosevelt
Sherman, John	1877–81	Hayes
Shultz, George P.	1972–74	Nixon
Simon, William E.	1974	Nixon
Simon, William E.	1974–77	Ford
Snyder, John W.	1946–53	Truman
Spencer, John C.	1825	Tyler
Summers, Lawrence H.	1999–2001	Clinton
Taney, Roger B.	1833–34	Jackson
Thomas, Philip F.	1860–61	Buchanan
Vinson, Frederick M.	1945–46	Truman
Walker, Robert J.	1845–49	Polk
Windom, William	1881	Garfield
Windom, William	1889–91	B. Harrison
Wolcott, Oliver, Jr.	1795–1800	Washington
Woodbury, Levi	1834–37	Jackson
Woodbury, Levi	1837–41	Van Buren
Woodin, William H.	1933–34	F.D. Roosevelt

SECRETARIES OF WAR*

Name	Dates	President
Alger, Russell A.	1897–99	McKinley
Armstrong, John	1813–14	Madison

*Position merged with that of Secretary of the Navy into the National Military Establishment under Department of Defense by the National Security Act of 1947.

Baker, Newton D.	1916–21	Wilson
Bancroft, George	(acting) 1845	Polk
Barbour, James	1825–28	J.Q. Adams
Belknap, William W.	1869–76	Grant
Bell, John	1841	W.H. Harrison
Butler, Benjamin F.	*ad int.*, 1836–37	Jackson
Calhoun, John C.	1817–25	Monroe
Cameron, James D.	1876–77	Grant
Cameron, Simon	1861–62	Lincoln
Cass, Lewis	1831–36	Jackson
Conrad, Charles M.	1850–53	Fillmore
Crawford, George W.	1849–50	Taylor
Crawford, William H.	1815–16	Madison
Dallas, Alexander	*ad int.*, 1815	Madison
Davis, Dwight F.	1925–29	Coolidge
Davis, Jefferson	1853–57	Pierce
Dearborn, Henry	1801–09	Jefferson
Dern, George H.	1933–36	F.D. Roosevelt
Dexter, Samuel	1800–01	Adams
Dickinson, Jacob M.	1909–11	Taft
Eaton, John H.	1829–31	Jackson
Elkins, Stephen B.	1891–95	B. Harrison
Endicott, William C.	1885–89	Cleveland
Eustis, William	1809–12	Madison
Floyd, John B.	1857–61	Buchanan
Garrison, Lindley M.	1913–16	Wilson
Good, James W.	1929	Hoover
Grant, Ulysses S.	*ad int.*, 1867–68	A. Johnson
Holt, Joseph	*ad int.*, 1861	Buchanan
Hurley, Patrick J.	1929–33	Hoover
Johnson, Reverdy	*ad int.*, 1849	Taylor
Knox, Henry	1785–94	Washington
Lamont, Daniel S.	1893–97	Cleveland
Lincoln, Robert T.	1881	Garfield
Lincoln, Robert T.	1881–85	Arthur
Marcy, William L.	1845–49	Polk
McCrary, George W.	1877–79	Hayes
McHenry, James	1796–1800	Washington
Monroe, James	*ad int.*, 1813–14	Madison

Monroe, James	1814–15	
Patterson, Robert P.	1945–47	Truman
Pickering, Timothy	*ad int.*, 1795–96	Washington
Poinsett, Joel R.	1837–41	Van Buren
Porter, James M.	1843–44	Tyler
Porter, Peter B.	1828–29	J.Q. Adams
Proctor, Redfield	1889–91	B. Harrison
Ramsey, Alexander	1879–81	Hayes
Rawlins, John A.	1869	Grant
Root, Elihu	1899–1904	McKinley
Royall, Kenneth C.	1947	Truman
Schofield, John M.	1868–69	A. Johnson
Sherman, William T.	1869	Grant
Southard, Samuel L.	*ad int.*, 1828	J.Q. Adams
Spencer, John C.	1841–43	Tyler
Stanton, Edwin M.	1862–65	Lincoln
Stanton, Edwin M.	1865–67; 1868	A. Johnson
Stimson, Henry L.	1940–45	F.D. Roosevelt
Stimson, Henry L.	1945	Truman
Stoddert, Benjamin	*ad int.*, 1800	J. Adams
Taft, Alphonso	1876	Grant
Taft, William H.	1904–08	T. Roosevelt
Taney, Roger B.	*ad int.*, 1831	Jackson
Weeks, John W.	1921–23	Harding
Weeks, John W.	1923–25	Coolidge
Wilkins, William	1844–45	Tyler
Woodring, Henry H.	1936–40	F.D. Roosevelt
Wright, Luke E.	1908–09	T. Roosevelt

SECRETARIES OF THE NAVY*

Name	Dates	President
Adams, Charles F.	1929–33	Hoover
Badger, George E.	1841	W.H. Harrison
Bancroft, George	1845–46	Polk
Bonaparte, Charles J.	1905–06	T. Roosevelt

---

*Positions merged with that of Secretary of War into the National Military Establishment under Department of Defense by the National Security Act of 1947.

Borie, Adolph	1869	Grant
Branch, John	1829–31	Jackson
Calhoun, John C.	*ad int.*, 1818–19	Monroe
Chandler, William E.	1882–85	Arthur
Crowninshield, Benjamin W.	1815–17	Madison
Crowninshield, Benjamin W.	1817–18	Monroe
Daniels, Josephus	1913–21	Wilson
Dearborn, Henry	*ad int.*, 1801	Jefferson
Denby, Edwin	1921–24	Harding
Dickerson, Mahlon	1834–38	Jackson
Dobbin, James C.	1853–57	Pierce
Edison, Charles	1939–40	F.D. Roosevelt
Forrestal, James V.	1944–47	F.D. Roosevelt
Gilmer, Thomas W.	1844	Tyler
Goff, Nathan, Jr.	1881	Hayes
Graham, William A.	1850–52	Fillmore
Hamilton, Paul	1809–12	Madison
Henshaw, David	1843–44	Tyler
Herbert, Hilary A.	1893–97	Cleveland
Hunt, William H.	1881–82	Garfield
Jones, William	1813–14	Madison
Kennedy, John P.	1852–53	Fillmore
Knox, W. Frank	1940–44	F.D. Roosevelt
Long, John D.	1897–1902	McKinley
Mason, John Y.	1844–45	Tyler
Mason, John Y.	1846–49	Polk
Metcalf, Victor H.	1906–08	T. Roosevelt
Meyer, George Von L.	1909–13	Taft
Moody, William H.	1902–04	T. Roosevelt
Morton, Paul	1904–05	T. Roosevelt
Newberry, Truman H.	1908–09	T. Roosevelt
Paulding, James K.	1838–41	Van Buren
Preston, William B.	1849–50	Taylor
Ramsey, Alexander	*ad int.*, 1880–81	Hayes
Robeson, George M.	1869–77	Grant
Smith, Robert	1801–09	Jefferson
Southard, Samuel L.	1823–25	Monroe
Southard, Samuel L.	1825–29	J.Q. Adams
Stoddert, Benjamin	1798–1801	J. Adams

Swanson, Claude	1933–39	F.D. Roosevelt
Thompson, Richard W.	1877–80	Hayes
Thompson, Smith	1819–23	Monroe
Toucey, Isaac	1857–61	Buchanan
Tracy, Benjamin F.	1889–93	B. Harrison
Upshur, Abel P.	1841–43	Tyler
Welles, Gideon	1861–65	Lincoln
Welles, Gideon	1865–69	A. Johnson
Whitney, William C.	1885–89	Cleveland
Wilbur, Curtis D.	1924–29	Coolidge
Woodbury, Levi	1831–34	Jackson

SECRETARIES OF DEFENSE*

Name	Dates	President
Aspin, Les	1993–94	Clinton
Brown, Harold	1977–81	Carter
Carlucci, Frank C., III	1987–89	Reagan
Cheney, Richard B.	1989–93	G.H.W. Bush
Clifford, Clark M.	1968–69	L.B. Johnson
Cohen, William	1997–2001	Clinton
Forrestal, James V.	1947–49	Truman
Gates, Thomas S., Jr.	1959–61	Eisenhower
Johnson, Louis M.	1949–50	Truman
Laird, Melvin R.	1969–73	Nixon
Lovett, Robert A.	1951–53	Truman
McElroy, Neil H.	1957–59	Eisenhower
McNamara, Robert S.	1961–63	Kennedy
McNamara, Robert S.	1963–68	L.B. Johnson
Marshall, George C.	1950–51	Truman
Perry, William	1994–97	Clinton
Richardson, Elliot L.	1973–74	Nixon
Rumsfeld, Donald	1975–77	Ford
Rumsfeld, Donald	2001–	G.W. Bush
Schlesinger, James R.	1973	Nixon

*Position created by the National Security Act of 1947, merging Departments of War and Navy into the National Military Establishment under Department of Defense.

Schlesinger, James R.	1973–75	Ford
Weinberger, Caspar W.	1981–87	Reagan
Wilson, Charles E.	1953–57	Eisenhower

ATTORNEYS GENERAL

Name	Dates	President
Akerman, Amos J.	1870–71	Grant
Ashcroft, John	2001–	G.W. Bush
Barr, William P.	1991–93	G.H.W. Bush
Bates, Edward	1861–64	Lincoln
Bell, Griffin B.	1977–79	Carter
Berrien, John M.	1829–31	Jackson
Biddle, Francis B.	1941–45	F.D. Roosevelt
Black, Jeremiah	1857–60	Buchanan
Bonaparte, Charles J.	1906–09	T. Roosevelt
Bradford, William	1794–95	Washington
Breckinridge, John	1805–06	Jefferson
Brewster, Benjamin H.	1882–85	Arthur
Brownell, Herbert, Jr.	1953–58	Eisenhower
Browning, Orville H.	*ad int.*, 1868	A. Johnson
Butler, Benjamin	1833–37	Jackson
Civiletti, Benjamin R.	1979–81	Carter
Clark, Tom C.	1945–49	Truman
Clark, W. Ramsey	1967–69	L.B. Johnson
Clifford, Nathan	1846–48	Polk
Crittenden, John J.	1841	W.H. Harrison
Crittenden, John J.	1850–53	Fillmore
Cummings, Homer S.	1933–39	F.D. Roosevelt
Cushing, Caleb	1853–57	Pierce
Daugherty, Harry M.	1921–24	Harding
Devens, Charles	1877–81	Hayes
Evarts, William M.	1868–69	A. Johnson
Garland, Augustus H.	1885–89	Cleveland
Gilpin, Henry D.	1840–41	Van Buren
Gregory, Thomas W.	1914–19	Wilson
Griggs, John W.	1898–1901	McKinley
Grundy, Felix	1838–39	Van Buren

Harmon, Judson	1895–97	Cleveland
Hoar, Ebenezer R.	1869–70	Grant
Jackson, Robert H.	1940–41	F.D. Roosevelt
Johnson, Reverdy	1849–50	Taylor
Katzenbach, Nicholas De B.	1965–67	L.B. Johnson
Kennedy, Robert F.	1961–63	Kennedy
Kennedy, Robert F.	1963–65	L.B. Johnson
Kleindienst, Richard G.	1972–73	Nixon
Knox, Philander C.	1901–04	McKinley
Lee, Charles	1795–97	Washington
Lee, Charles	1797–1801	J. Adams
Legaré, Hugh S.	1841–43	Tyler
Levi, Edward H.	1975–77	Ford
Lincoln, Levi	1801–04	Jefferson
MacVeagh, Wayne	1881	Garfield
MacVeagh, Wayne	1881	Arthur
Mason, John Y.	1845–46	Polk
McGranery, James P.	1952–53	Truman
McGrath, James H.	1949–52	Truman
McKenna, Joseph	1897–98	McKinley
McReynolds, James C.	1913–14	Wilson
Meese, Edwin, III	1985–88	Reagan
Miller, William H.	1889–93	B. Harrison
Mitchell, John N.	1969–72	Nixon
Mitchell, William D.	1929–33	Hoover
Moody, William H.	1904–06	T. Roosevelt
Murphy, Frank	1939–40	F.D. Roosevelt
Nelson, John	1843–45	Tyler
Olney, Richard	1893–95	Cleveland
Palmer, Alexander M.	1919–21	Wilson
Pierrepont, Edwards	1875–76	Grant
Pinkney, William	1811–14	Madison
Randolph, Edmund J.	1789–94	Washington
Reno, Janet	1993–2001	Clinton
Richardson, Elliot L.	1973–74	Nixon
Rodney, Caesar A.	1807–11	Jefferson
Rogers, William P.	1958–61	Eisenhower
Rush, Richard	1814–17	Madison
Rush, Richard	*ad int.*, 1817	Monroe

Sargent, John G.	1925–29	Coolidge
Saxbe, William B.	1974	Nixon
Saxbe, William B.	1974–75	Ford
Smith, William French	1981–85	Reagan
Speed, James	1864–66	Lincoln
Stanbery, Henry	1866–68	A. Johnson
Stanton, Edwin M.	1860–61	Buchanan
Stone, Harlan F.	1924–25	Coolidge
Taft, Alphonso	1876–77	Grant
Taney, Roger B.	1831–33	Jackson
Thornburgh, Richard L.	1988–89	Reagan
Thornburgh, Richard L.	1989–91	G.H.W. Bush
Toucey, Isaac	1848–49	Polk
Wickersham, George W.	1909–13	Taft
Williams, George H.	1872–75	Grant
Wirt, William	1817–25	Monroe
Wirt, William	1825–29	J.Q. Adams

POSTMASTERS GENERAL

Name	Dates	President
Barry, William T.	1829–35	Jackson
Bissell, Wilson S.	1893–95	Cleveland
Blair, Montgomery	1861–64	Lincoln
Blount, Winton M.	1969–73	Nixon
Brown, Aaron V.	1857–59	Buchanan
Brown, Walter F.	1929–33	Hoover
Burleson, Albert S.	1913–21	Wilson
Campbell, James	1853–57	Pierce
Collamer, Jacob	1849–50	Taylor
Cortelyou, George B.	1905–07	T. Roosevelt
Creswell, John A.J.	1869–70	Grant
Day, J. Edward	1960–63	Kennedy
Dennison, William	1864–66	Lincoln
Dickinson, Donald M.	1887–89	Cleveland
Donaldson, Jesse M.	1947–53	Truman
Farley, James A.	1933–40	F.D. Roosevelt
Gary, James A.	1897–98	McKinley

Granger, Francis	1841	W.H. Harrison
Granger, Gideon	1801–14	Jefferson, Madison
Gresham, Walter Q.	1883–84	Arthur
Gronouski, John A.	1963	Kennedy
Gronouski, John A.	1963–65	L.B. Johnson
Habersham, Joseph	1795–97	Washington
Habersham, Joseph	1797–1801	J. Adams
Hall, Nathan K.	1850–52	Fillmore
Hannegan, Robert E.	1945–47	Truman
Hatton, Frank	1884–85	Arthur
Hays, William H.	1921–22	Harding
Hitchcock, Frank H.	1909–13	Taft
Holt, Joseph	1859–61	Buchanan
Howe, Timothy O.	1882–83	Arthur
Hubbard, Samuel D.	1852–53	Fillmore
James, Thomas L.	1881–82	Garfield
Jewell, Marshall	1874–76	Grant
Johnson, Cave	1845–51	Polk
Kendall, Amos	1835–37	Jackson
Kendall, Amos	1837–40	Van Buren
Key, David M.	1877–80	Hayes
King, Horatio	1861	Buchanan
Marshall, James W.	1874	Grant
Maynard, Horace	1880–81	Hayes
McLean, John	1823–25	Monroe
McLean, John	1825–29	J.Q. Adams
Meigs, Return J., Jr.	1814–17	Madison
Meigs, Return J., Jr.	1817–23	Monroe
Meyer, George von L.	1907–09	T. Roosevelt
New, Harry S.	1923	Harding
New, Harry S.	1923–29	Coolidge
Niles, John M.	1840–41	Van Buren
O'Brien, Lawrence F.	1965–69	L.B. Johnson
Osgood, Samuel	1789–91	Washington
Payne, Henry C.	1902–04	T. Roosevelt
Pickering, Timothy	1791–95	Washington
Randall, Alexander W.	1866–69	A. Johnson
Smith, Charles E.	1898–1902	McKinley
Summerfield, Arthur E.	1953–61	Eisenhower

Tyner, James N.	1876–77	Grant
Vilas, William F.	1885–88	Cleveland
Walker, Frank C.	1940–45	F.D. Roosevelt
Wanamaker, John	1889–93	B. Harrison
Watson, William M.	1968–69	L.B. Johnson
Wickliffe, Charles A.	1841–45	Tyler
Wilson, William L.	1895–97	Cleveland
Work, Hubert	1922–23	Harding
Wynne, Robert J.	1904–05	T. Roosevelt

SECRETARIES OF THE INTERIOR

Name	Dates	President
Andress, Cecil	1977–1981	Carter
Babbitt, Bruce	2001	Clinton
Bollinger, Richard A.	1909–11	Taft
Bliss, Cornelius N.	1897–99	McKinley
Browning, Orville H.	1866–69	A. Johnson
Chandler, Zachariah	1875–77	Grant
Chapman, Oscar L.	1950–53	Truman
Clark, William P.	1983–85	Reagan
Cox, Jacob D., Jr.	1869–70	Grant
Delano, Columbus	1870–75	Grant
Ewing, Thomas	1849–50	Taylor
Fall, Albert B.	1921–23	Harding
Fisher, Walter L.	1911–13	Taft
Francis, David R.	1896–97	Cleveland
Garfield, James R.	1907–09	T. Roosevelt
Harlan, James	1865–66	A. Johnson
Hathaway, Stanley K.	1975	Ford
Hickel, Walter J.	1969–71	Nixon
Hitchcock, Ethan A.	1898–1907	McKinley
Hodel, Donald P.	1985–89	Reagan
Ickes, Harold L.	1933–46	F.D. Roosevelt
Kirkwood, Samuel J.	1881–82	Garfield
Kleppe, Thomas	1975–77	Ford
Krug, Julius A.	1946–49	Truman
Lamar, Lucius Q.C.	1885–88	Cleveland

Lane, Franklin K.	1913–20	Wilson
Lujan, Manuel, Jr.	1989–93	G.H.W. Bush
McClelland, Robert	1853–57	Pierce
McKay, Douglas J.	1953–56	Eisenhower
McKennan, Thomas M.T.	1850	Fillmore
Morton, Rogers C.B.	1971–73	Nixon
Morton, Rogers C.B.	1974–75	Ford
Noble, John W.	1889–93	B. Harrison
Norton, Gale	2001–	G.W. Bush
Payne, John B.	1920–21	Wilson
Schurz, Carl	1877–81	Hayes
Seaton, Frederick A.	1956–61	Eisenhower
Smith, Caleb	1861–63	Lincoln
Smith, Hoke	1893–96	Cleveland
Stuart, Alexander H. H.	1850–53	Fillmore
Teller, Henry M.	1882–85	Arthur
Thompson, Jacob	1857–61	Buchanan
Udall, Stewart L.	1961–63	Kennedy
Udall, Stewart L.	1963–69	L.B. Johnson
Usher, John P.	1863–65	Lincoln
Vilas, William F.	1888–89	Cleveland
Watt, James G.	1981–83	Reagan
West, Roy O.	1928–29	Coolidge
Wilbur, Ray L.	1929–33	Hoover
Work, Hubert	1923–28	Coolidge

SECRETARIES OF AGRICULTURE

Name	Dates	President
Anderson, Clinton B.	1945–48	Truman
Benson, Ezra T.	1953–61	Eisenhower
Bergland, Robert S.	1977–81	Carter
Block, John R.	1981–86	Reagan
Brannan, Charles F.	1948–53	Truman
Butz, Earl L.	1971–74	Nixon
Butz, Earl L.	1974–76	Ford
Colman, Norman J.	1889	Cleveland
Espy, Mike	1993–94	Clinton
Freeman, Orville L.	1961–63	Kennedy

Freeman, Orville L.	1963–69	L.B. Johnson
Glickman, Dan	1995–2001	Clinton
Gore, Howard M.	1924–25	Coolidge
Hardin, Clifford M.	1969–71	Nixon
Houston, David F.	1913–20	Wilson
Hyde, Arthur M.	1929–31	Hoover
Jardine, William M.	1928–29	Coolidge
Knebel, John	1976–77	Ford
Lyng, Richard E.	1986–89	Reagan
Madigon, Edward	1991–93	G.H.W. Bush
Meredith, Edwin T.	1920–21	Wilson
Morton, Julius S.	1893–97	Cleveland
Rusk, Jeremiah M.	1889–93	B. Harrison
Veneman, Ann	2001–	G.W. Bush
Wallace, Henry A.	1933–40	F.D. Roosevelt
Wallace, Henry C.	1921–23	Harding
Wallace, Henry C.	1923–24	Coolidge
Wickard, Claude R.	1940–45	F.D. Roosevelt
Wilson, James	1897–1901	McKinley
Wilson, James	1901–09	T. Roosevelt
Wilson, James	1909–13	Taft
Yeutter, Clayton K.	1989–91	G.H.W. Bush

SECRETARIES OF COMMERCE AND LABOR*

Name	Dates	President
Cortelyou, George B.	1903–04	T. Roosevelt
Metcalf, Victor H.	1904–05	T. Roosevelt
Nagel, Charles	1909–13	Taft
Strauss, Oscar S.	1906–09	T. Roosevelt

SECRETARIES OF COMMERCE**

Name	Dates	President
Alexander, Joshua W.	1919–21	Wilson
Baldrige, Malcolm	1981–87	Reagan

*Department established by Congress, February 1903; split into Department of Commerce and Department of Labor, March 1913.
**Established following dissolution of Department of Commerce and Labor, March 1913.

Brown, Ronald H.	1993–96	Clinton
Chapin, Roy D.	1932–33	Hoover
Connor, John T.	1965–67	L.B. Johnson
Daley, William	1997–2000	Clinton
Dent, Frederick B.	1973–74	Nixon
Dent, Frederick B.	1974–75	Ford
Evans, Donald	2001–	G.W. Bush
Franklin, Barbara H.	1992–93	G.H.W. Bush
Harriman, W. Averill	1947–48	Truman
Hodges, Luther H.	1961–63	Kennedy
Hodges, Luther H.	1963–65	L.B. Johnson
Hoover, Herbert C.	1921–23	Harding
Hoover, Herbert C.	1923–28	Coolidge
Hopkins, Harry L.	1938–40	F.D. Roosevelt
Jones, Jesse H.	1940–45	F.D. Roosevelt
Kuntor, Mickey	1996–97	Clinton
Klutznick, Philip M.	1979–81	Carter
Kreps, Juanita	1977–79	Carter
Lamont, Robert P.	1929–32	Hoover
Mineta, Norman	2000–01	Clinton
Morton, Rogers C.B.	1975–76	Ford
Mosbacher, Robert A.	1989–92	G.H.W. Bush
Mueller, Frederick H.	1959–61	Eisenhower
Peterson, Peter G.	1972–73	Nixon
Redfield, William C.	1913–19	Wilson
Richardson, Elliot L.	1976–77	Ford
Roper, Daniel C.	1933–38	F.D. Roosevelt
Sawyer, Charles	1948–53	Truman
Smith, Cyrus R.	1968–69	L.B. Johnson
Stans, Maurice H.	1969–72	Nixon
Strauss, Oscar S.	*ad int.*, 1958	Eisenhower
Trowbridge, Alexander B.	1967–68	L.B. Johnson
Verity, C. William, Jr.	1987–89	Reagan
Wallace, Henry A.	1945–48	Truman
Weeks, Sinclair	1953–58	Eisenhower
Whiting, William F.	1928–29	Hoover

SECRETARIES OF LABOR*

Name	Dates	President
Brennan, Peter J.	1973–74	Nixon
Brennan, Peter J.	1974–75	Ford
Brock, William E., III	1985–87	Reagan
Chao, Eluine	2001–	G.H.W. Bush
Davis, James J.	1921–23	Harding
Davis, James J.	1923–29	Coolidge
Davis, James J.	1929–30	Hoover
Doak, William N.	1930–33	Hoover
Dole, Elizabeth H.	1989–90	G.H.W. Bush
Donovan, Raymond J.	1981–85	Reagan
Dunlop, John T.	1975–76	Ford
Durkin, Martin P.	1953	Eisenhower
Goldberg, Arthur J.	1961–62	Kennedy
Hermary, Alexis	1997–2001	Clinton
Hodgson, James D.	1970–73	Nixon
Marshall, F. Ray	1977–81	Carter
Martin, Lynn	1991–93	G.H.W. Bush
McLaughlin, Ann D.	1987–89	Reagan
Mitchell, James P.	1954–61	Eisenhower
Perkins, Frances	1933–45	F.D. Roosevelt
Reich, Robert	1993–97	Clinton
Schwellenbach, Lewis B.	1945–48	Truman
Shultz, George P.	1969–70	Nixon
Tobin, Maurice J.	1948–53	Truman
Usery, Willie J., Jr.	1976–77	Ford
Wilson, William B.	1913–21	Wilson
Wirtz, William W.	1962–63	Kennedy
Wirtz, William W.	1963–69	L.B. Johnson

*Established following dissolution of Department of Commerce and Labor, March 1913.

SECRETARIES OF HEALTH, EDUCATION, AND WELFARE*

Name	Dates	President
Califano, Joseph	1977–79	Carter
Celebrezze, Anthony J.	1962–63	Kennedy
Celebrezze, Anthony J.	1963–65	L.B. Johnson
Cohen, Wilbur J.	1968–69	L.B. Johnson
Finch, Robert H.	1969–70	Nixon
Flemming, Arthur S.	1958–61	Eisenhower
Folsom, Marion B.	1955–58	Eisenhower
Gardner, John W.	1965–69	L.B. Johnson
Harris, Patricia R.	1979–80	Carter
Hobby, Oveta C.	1953–55	Eisenhower
Matthews, Forrest D.	1975–77	Ford
Ribicoff, Abraham A.	1961–62	Kennedy
Richardson, Elliot L.	1970–73	Nixon
Weinberger, Caspar W.	1973–74	Nixon
Weinberger, Caspar W.	1974–75	Ford

SECRETARIES OF HOUSING AND URBAN DEVELOPMENT

Name	Dates	President
Ciseros, Henry	1993–97	Clinton
Cuomo, Andrew	1997–2001	Clinton
Harris, Patricia R.	1977–79	Carter
Hills, Carla	1975–77	Ford
Kemp, Jack	1989–93	G.H.W. Bush
Landrieu, Moon E.	1979–81	Carter
Lynn, James T.	1973–74	Nixon
Lynn, James T.	1974–75	Ford
Martinez, Mel	2001–	G.W. Bush
Pierce, Samuel R., Jr.	1981–89	Reagan
Romney, George W.	1969–73	Nixon
Weaver, Robert C.	1966–69	L.B. Johnson
Wood, Robert C.	1969	L.B. Johnson

*Department established 1953; split into Department of Health and Human Services and Department of Education, 1979.

SECRETARIES OF TRANSPORTATION

Name	Dates	President
Adams, Brockman	1977–79	Carter
Boyd, Alan S.	1967–69	L.B. Johnson
Brinegar, Claude S.	1973–74	Nixon
Brinegar, Claude S.	1974–75	Ford
Burnley, James H., IV	1987–89	Reagan
Card, Andrew H., Jr.	1992–93	G.H.W. Bush
Coleman, William	1975–77	Ford
Dole, Elizabeth H.	1983–87	Reagan
Goldschmidt, Neil E.	1979–81	Carter
Lewis, Andrew	1981–83	Reagan
Mineta, Norman	2001–	G.W. Bush
Peña, Federico	1993–97	Clinton
Skinner, Samuel K.	1989–91	G.H.W. Bush
Slater, Rodney	1997–2001	Clinton
Volpe, John A.	1969–73	Nixon

SECRETARIES OF EDUCATION*

Name	Dates	President
Alexander, Lamar	1991–93	G.H.W. Bush
Bell, Terrel H.	1981–84	Reagan
Cavazos, Lauro F.	1988–89	Reagan
Cavazos, Lauro F.	1989–90	G.H.W. Bush
Bennett, William J.	1985–88	Reagan
Hufstedler, Shirley M.	1979–81	Carter
Paige, Rod	2001–	G.W. Bush
Riley, Richard	1993–2001	Clinton

SECRETARIES OF HEALTH AND HUMAN SERVICES*

Name	Dates	President
Bowen, Otis R.	1985–89	Reagan
Harris, Patricia R	1980–81	Carter

*Established following dissolution of Department of Health, Education, and Welfare, 1979.

Heckler, Margaret	1983–85	Reagan
Schweiker, Richard	1981–83	Reagan
Shalala, Donna	1993–2001	Clinton
Sullivan, Louis W.	1989–93	G.H.W. Bush
Thompson, Tommy	2001–	G.W. Bush

SECRETARIES OF ENERGY

Name	Dates	President
Abraham, Spencer	2001–	G.W. Bush
Duncan, Charles W., Jr.	1979–81	Carter
Edwards, James	1981–82	Reagan
Watkins, James D.	1989–93	G.H.W. Bush
Hodel, Donald P.	1982–85	Reagan
Herrington, John	1985–89	Reagan
O'Leary, Hazel	1993–97	Clinton
Peña, Federico	1997–98	Clinton
Richardson, William B.	1998–2001	Clinton
Schlesinger, James	1977–79	Carter

SECRETARIES OF VETERANS AFFAIRS

Name	Dates	President
Brown, Jesse	1993–97	Clinton
Derwinski, Edward J.	1989–92	G.H.W. Bush
Principi, Anthony	2001–	G.W. Bush
West, Togo D., Jr.	1998–2001	Clinton

M

MacVEAGH, Franklin

Born on a farm near Phoenixville, Pa., November 22, 1837; son of Major John and Margaret (Lincoln) MacVeagh; brother of Wayne MacVeagh, attorney general under Garfield; Methodist; married Emily Eames in 1868; father of five children; educated partly by private tutors and partly at Freeland Seminary (now Ursinus College), at Collegeville, Pa.; graduated from Yale in 1862; entered Columbia Law School in New York City, graduating in 1864; admitted to the bar in 1864, he practiced law in Philadelphia; moved to Chicago where he became affiliated with a wholesale grocery chain; organized Franklin MacVeagh & Co., wholesale grocers, in 1871; director of the Commercial National Bank for 28 years; leader in the formation of the Citizens Committee against Graft, becoming its first president in 1874; although nominally a Republican, he supported Cleveland's candidacy; became Democratic candidate for U.S. senator in 1894 but was defeated; split with the Democratic Party over the free silver issue and returned to the Republican Party; appointed SECRETARY OF THE TREASURY by President Taft on March 8, 1909, serving until March 4, 1913; founder of the Municipal Art League of Chicago; died July 6, 1934. **References:** Herbert Smith Duffy, *William Howard Taft* (1939); Norman M. Wilensky, *Conservatives in the Progressive Era: The Taft Republicans of 1912* (1965).

MacVEAGH, Wayne

Born in Phoenixville, Pa., April 19, 1833; son of Major John and Margaret (Lincoln) MacVeagh; brother of Franklin MacVeagh, secretary of the treasury under Taft; Methodist; married Letty Minor Lewis in 1856; married Virginia Rolette Cameron in 1866; attended school at Pottstown; graduated Yale in 1853; studied law in office of James L. Lewis in West Chester, Pa.; admitted to bar in 1856 and began practice of law; district attorney for Chester County, 1859–1864; became captain of emergency infantry in 1862; made major of Union cavalry regiment, 1863; chairman of Republican state central committee of Pennsylvania, 1863; appointed U.S. minister to Turkey on June 4, 1870, and served until 1872; opposed Grant; delegate to state constitutional convention, 1872–1873; moved to Philadelphia in 1876; counsel for Pennsylvania Railroad Company; appointed ATTORNEY GENERAL in the cabinet of President Garfield on March 5, 1881, continued under Arthur, and served from March 7, 1881, to November 13, 1881; most important contribution was securing indictment of Guiteau; active in Civil Service Reform Association and Indian Rights Association; returned to practice in Philadelphia; chosen ambassador to Italy on December 20, 1893; joined Washington law firm of McKenny and Flannery, counsel for D.C. and Pennsylvania Railroads, 1897; chief counsel for United States in Venezuela arbitration of 1903; died on January 11, 1917. **References:** W.R. Thayer, *The Life and Letters of John Hay*, 2 vols. (1915); Theodore C. Smith, *Life and Letters of James Abram Garfield*, 2 vols. (1st ed., 1925; 2d ed., 1968).

MADIGAN, Edward Rell

Born in Lincoln, Ill., January 13, 1936, son of Earl T., town alderman and owner of a taxi company, and Theresa (Loobey) Madigan; married Evelyn Marie George in 1955; father of Kimberly, Kellie Madigan Clapper, and Mary Elizabeth Madigan Gyori; A.A. in business administration, Lincoln College, 1955; manager of the family business, Yellow & Lincoln Cab Company, 1955–1958, and manager/owner, 1958–1973; Republican member, Illinois General Assembly, 1967–1972; chairman, Illinois House Committee on Reapportionment, 1971–1972; Republican member from Illinois, U.S. House of Representatives, 1973–1991, representing the state's 21st district, 1973–1981, and following reapportionment, 15th district, 1981–1991; a congressional authority on farm issues; ranking minority member, House Agriculture Committee; member, House Committee on Energy and Commerce, and Subcommittees on Conservation and Credit, Health and the Environment, Commerce, Transportation and Tourism, and Telecommunications; helped pass 1981 Clean Air Act revision and 1985 Farm Bill; chairman, Republican Research Committee, 1981–1982; Republican chief deputy whip, 1987–1989, but lost bid for House minority whip to Georgia Congressman and future Speaker of the House Newt Gingrich, 1989; appointed by President George H.W. Bush as SECRETARY OF AGRICULTURE and served from March 8, 1991, until the end of Bush's term on January 20, 1993; head of a 1991 inspection team to determine how to avert starvation in the former Soviet Union; criticized by consumer activists for not addressing hunger problems in the United States; lobbied for protections of American agricultural interests in the Uruguay Round of the General Agreement on Tariffs and Trade talks, 1991; delegate, Illinois State Republican Convention, 1966, and Republican National

Convention, 1980; member, Board of Zoning Appeals, Lincoln, 1967–1973; member, board of directors, Olympic Federal Savings and Loan Association, Berwyn, Ill., 1983–1990, a failed S&L whose bailout cost millions in taxpayer dollars, though Madigan donated all of his fees to charity; recipient, Outstanding Legislator award, Illinois Association of School Superintendents, 1968, Outstanding Public Service award, Lincoln College Alumni Association, 1974, and honorary degrees from Lincoln College, 1975, James Milliken University, 1977, and Illinois Wesleyan University, 1979; former member, Illinois Jaycees (former vice-president), Lincoln Chamber of Commerce, Elks, Kiwanis, Eagles, Union League Club of Chicago; died of complications from lung cancer on December 7, 1994, in Springfield, Ill. **References:** *New York Times* (March 22, 1989; January 26, 1991; December 9, 1994); *The Economist* (November 16, 1991); *Who's Who in American Politics, 1991–1992; Current Biography Yearbook 1992.*

—Rachel Ban

MADISON, James

Born at Port Conway, Va., March 16, 1751; son of James, justice of the peace and plantation owner, and Eleanor ("Nellie") Rose (Conway) Madison; Episcopalian; married Dorothea ("Dolley") Payne Todd (1768–1849) on September 15, 1794; stepfather of a child from Mrs. Madison's first marriage; B.A., College of New Jersey (now Princeton University), 1771, where he studied law and theology, 1771–1772; admitted to the bar in Virginia, 1774; member, committee of safety, Orange County, Va., 1774–1775; delegate, Virginia Provincial Convention, Williamsburg, 1776, which called for independence and set up a state government; member, Virginia House of Delegates, 1776, 1784–1787, and 1800–1801; helped pass the state's Statute of Religious Freedom, 1785; member, Virginia Privy Council, 1777–1779; delegate from Virginia, Continental Congress, 1779–1783 and

James Madison (Library of Congress)

1786–1788; delegate from Virginia, Annapolis Convention, 1786, and Constitutional Convention, Philadelphia, 1787, where he was instrumental in creating the federal government structure and drafting the final version of the U.S. Constitution; coauthor, along with Alexander Hamilton and John Jay, under the pseudonym "Publius," of the series of editorials known as "The Federalist," arguing for the ratification of the Constitution, 1787–1788; delegate, Virginia ratifying convention, 1787–1788; member from Virginia, U.S. House of Representatives, 1789–1797 (1795–1797 as a Democratic-Republican); helped draft and push passage of federal Bill of Rights, 1791, and became leader of the congressional opposition to Secretary of the Treasury Hamilton's economic policies that became the Democratic-Republican Party; drafted Virginia Resolutions condemning the Alien and Sedition Acts and asserting the right of states to judge the constitutionality of acts of Congress, 1798; appointed by President Jefferson as SECRETARY OF STATE and served from May 2, 1801, until the end of Jefferson's second term, resigning on March 3, 1809; supported the purchase of the Louisiana Territory from France, 1803, the U.S. Navy's suppression of Barbary pirates, 1803-1805, and after protesting French and British violations of American neutrality in the Atlantic, the American trade embargo, 1807–1809; nominated for president by the Democratic-Republic Party in 1808, he won 122 electoral votes and defeated Federalist challenger Charles E. Pinckney to become the fourth PRESIDENT OF THE UNITED STATES; inaugurated on March 4, 1809; won 128 electoral votes in 1812 to be reelected over challenger DeWitt Clinton and served for two full terms until March 4, 1817; after trying as secretary of state to avoid war, was pressured by "War Hawks" in Congress into requesting a declaration of war against Britain in June 1812, triggering the War of 1812; despite the British occupation and burning of Washington, D.C., August, 1814, the war ended on favorable terms for the United States with the Treaty of Ghent, 1814, and stimulated a renewed sense of popular nationalism; after the war, recommended strengthening U.S. manufacturing, finance, trade, and transportation infrastructure; rector, UVA, 1826–1836; delegate and cochairman, Virginia State Constitutional Convention, 1829; member, and later president, American Colonization Society, an organization advocating manumission and the resettlement of former slaves in Africa; died on June 28, 1836, at his estate, Montpelier, Orange County, Va., where he is interred. **References:** J.C.A. Stagg, *Mr. Madison's War* (1983); Robert Allen Rutland, *James Madison: The Founding Father* (1987) and *The Presidency of James Madison* (1990); Donald R. Hickey, *The War of 1812: The Forgotten Conflict* (1989); Drew R. McCoy, *The Last of the Fathers: James Madison and the Republican Legacy* (1989); Jack N. Rakove, *James Madison and the Creation of the American Republic* (1990) and *Original Meanings: Politics and Ideas in the Making of the Constitution* (1996); Lance Banning, *The Sacred Fire of Liberty: James Madison and the Founding of the Federal Republic* (1995); Richard Matthews, *If Men Were Angels: James Madison and the Heartless Empire of Reason* (1995); Guy Padula, *Madison v. Marshall: Popular Sovereignty, Natural Law, and the United States Constitution* (2001).

—Jeffrey Coster

MANNING, Daniel

Born in Albany, N.Y., August 16, 1831; son of John and Eleanor (Oley) Manning; married Mary Little on October 11, 1853; father of James Hilton, Frederick Clinton, Anastasia, and Mary Elizabeth; married Mary Margaret Fryer on November 19, 1884; attended common schools; became page for state assembly in 1841; was paper boy for Albany *Atlas* (later *Argus*); *Argus* reporter for state senate, 1858–1871; made Associated Press reporter for State Assembly in 1863; associate editor of *Argus*, 1865; chosen legislative correspondent for *Brooklyn Eagle*; became director of National Commercial Bank of Albany in 1873; made president of *Argus* in 1873; took part in Democratic state convention in Syracuse, 1874; headed New York delegation to Democratic National Convention in St. Louis, 1876 and 1880; secretary of Democratic state committee in 1879; chosen vice-president of National Bank of Albany in 1881, and president, 1882; chairman of Democratic State Committee, 1881, 1882, and 1883; supported Cleveland, 1884; appointed SECRETARY OF THE TREASURY in the cabinet of President Cleveland on March 6, 1885, and served from March 8, 1885, to May 31, 1887; most important contributions were desire for stoppage of silver coinage and government purchase of silver, and condemnation of reduction of Treasury surplus; became director of Albany Electric Illuminating Company; died in Albany, N.Y., on December 24, 1887. **References:** Robert McElroy, *Grover Cleveland: The Man and the Statesman* (1923); Robert I. Vexler, ed., *Grover Cleveland, 1837–1908: Chronology, Documents, Bibliographical Aids* (1968).

MARCY, William Learned

Born in Sturbridge (now Southbridge), Mass., December 12, 1786; son of Jedediah and Ruth (Learned) Marcy; married Dolly Newell on September 27, 1812, and after her death married Cornelia Knower in 1825; father of six children; educated at the academy at Leicester and at Woodstock Academy, Union, Conn.; attended Brown University, graduating in 1808; taught school at Newport, R.I.; moved to Troy, N.Y.; studied law and was admitted to the bar in 1811, commencing his practice at Troy; volunteered and served in the War of 1812; recorder of Troy, 1816–1818; adjutant general of New York State Militia in 1821; editor of the *Troy Budget*, which became an organ of the Democratic Party; comptroller of New York state in 1823; moved to Albany, N.Y.; associate justice of the New York Supreme Court, 1829–1831; elected to the U.S. Senate as a Democrat on December 5, 1831, serving as chairman of the Judiciary Committee; resigned his Senate seat when he won the governorship of New York in 1832; three-term governor, 1833–1839; appointed commissioner of Mexican claims by President Van Buren, 1839–1842; appointed to the cabinet of President Polk as SECRETARY OF WAR on March 6, 1845, entering upon his duties March 8, 1845, and serving until March 8, 1849; advocated the Tariff of 1846; appointed SECRETARY OF STATE by President Pierce on March 7, 1853, serving until March 4, 1857; negotiated 24 treaties, including the significant Gadsden Purchase with Mexico and the Reciprocity Treaty with Great Britain; coined the phrase "To the victor belong the spoils"; died at Ballston Spa, N.Y., July 4, 1857; interment in Rural Cemetery, Albany, N.Y. **References:** Charles Allan McCoy, *Polk and the Presidency* (1957); Roy Franklin Nichols, *Franklin Pierce: Young Hickory of the Granite Hills* (1969).

MARSHALL, (Freddie) Ray

Born in Oak Grove, La., August 22, 1928; raised in a Baptist orphanage; at age 15, ran away, overstated his age, and enlisted in the U.S. Navy, serving during World War II; A.B. in economics, Millsaps College, Jackson, Miss., 1949; M.A. in economics, Louisiana State University, 1950; Ph.D. in economics, University of California, Berkeley, 1954; Fulbright Scholar in Finland, 1955–1956; instructor in economics, San Francisco State College, 1952; associate professor, University of Mississippi, 1953–1954; professor, Louisiana State University, 1957–1962, University of Texas, Austin, 1962–1967, University of Kentucky, Lexington, 1967–1969; director, Center for the Study of Human Resources, University of Texas, 1970–1977; appointed by President Carter as SECRETARY OF LABOR, serving from January 27, 1977, until the end of Carter's term on January 20, 1981; contributions included raising safety standards to reduce workers' exposure to various cancer-causing chemicals; worked to make the Occupational Safety and Health Administration (OSHA) a more efficient organization; involved in negotiations that settled the United Coal Miners' strike, 1977–1978; Audre and Bernard Rapoport Professor of Economics and Public Affairs, Lyndon B. Johnson School of Public Affairs, University of Texas, Austin, 1981–1998, professor emeritus, 1998– ; chairman, advisory committee, Center for the Study of Human Resources; former chairman, Federal Committee on Apprenticeships, and Committee on Political Discrimination, American Economics Association; former member, National Council on Employment Policy; former president, National Rural Center and Industrial Relations Research Association; former member, National Skills Standard Board, Advisory Commission on Labor Diplomacy; former cochairman, Commission on the Skills of the American Workforce; member, board of directors, Economic Policy Institute; member, Commission on State and Local Public Service; chairman, National Center on Education and the Economy; president, International Labor Rights Fund; author of more than 30 books, including *The Negro in Organized Labor* (1965), *The Negro Worker* (1967), *Rural Workers in Rural Labor Markets* (1974), *Human Resources and Labor Markets* (1975), *Labor Economics: Wages, Employment and Trade Unionism* (rev. 1976), *The Role of Unions in the American Economy* (1976), *An Economic Strategy for the 1980's* (1981), *Work and Women in the Eighties* (1983), and *Unheard Voices: Labor and Economic Policy in a Competitive World* (1987); honored in 1999 as the namesake of the Ray Marshall Center for the Study of Human Resources. **References:** *Time* (December 27, 1976; January 3, 1977); *U.S. News & World Report* (January 10, 1977); *International Who's Who, 1988–1989*; Burton I. Kaufman, *The Presidency of James Earl Carter, Jr.* (1993); Gary M. Fink and Hugh Davis Graham, eds., *The Carter Presidency: Policy Choices in the Post-New Deal Era* (1998).

MARSHALL, George Catlett, Jr.

Born in Uniontown, Pa., December 31, 1880; son of George Catlett, a coke and coal merchant, and Laura (Bradford) Marshall; Episcopalian; married Elizabeth ("Lily") Carter Coles (1874–1927) on February 11, 1902; married Katherine Boyce (Tupper) Brown (1882–1978) on October 15, 1930; stepfather of Molly, Clifton Stevenson, and Allen Tupper Brown, who was killed in action in Italy, 1944; graduated as senior first captain of the corps of cadets, with a degree in civil engineering, from Virginia Military Institute (VMI), 1901; commissioned second lieutenant of infantry, U.S. Army, 1902, and promoted to first lieutenant, 1907, captain, 1916, major, 1920, lieutenant colonel, 1923, colonel, 1933, brigadier general, 1936, major general, 1939, and general of the army, temporarily in 1944, permanently in 1946; commandant, Danville (Va.) Military Institute, 1901; stationed in the Philippines, 1902–1903, and Oklahoma and Texas, 1903–1906; assigned to Army Service Schools, Fort Leavenworth, Kans., 1906–1910, graduating from Infantry-Cavalry School, 1907, and Army Staff College, 1908, and serving as instructor, Department of Military Engineering, 1908–1910; inspector-instructor, Massachusetts National Guard, Boston, 1911–1912; stationed with Fourth Infantry in Arkansas, Minnesota, and Texas, 1912–1913; aide-de-camp to Major General Hunter Liggett, the Philippines, 1913–1916, and to Major General J. Franklin Bell, San Francisco and Governors Island, N.Y., 1916–1917; served with the American Expeditionary Force in France during World War I, 1917–1919, as assistant chief of staff, First Division, 1917–1918, staff officer, General Headquarters, 1918 and 1919, assistant chief of staff, First Army, 1918, and chief of staff, Eighth Corps, 1918–1919; aide-de-camp to General John J. Pershing, France and Washington, 1919–1924; executive officer, Fifteenth Infantry Regiment, Tientsin, China, 1924–1927; instructor, Army War College, Washington, 1927; assistant commandant in charge of instruction, U.S. Army Infantry School, Fort Benning, Ga., 1927–1932; commander of National Guard and Civilian Conservation Corps (CCC) units in Georgia and South Carolina, 1932–1933; senior instructor, Illinois National Guard, Chicago, 1933–1936; commander, Fifth Infantry Brigade, Third Division, Vancouver Barracks, Wash., and CCC District, 1936–1938; assistant chief of staff, War Plans Division, War Department, Washington, 1938; deputy U.S. Army chief of staff, 1938–1939, acting chief of staff, 1939, and chief of staff, 1939–1945; during World War II, he administered a U.S. Army and Army Air Force of over 8 million soldiers, reorganized the War Department, was President Franklin Roosevelt's chief military adviser, and was critical to the development of Allied forces strategy; special representative, with the rank of ambassador, of

President Harry Truman to mediate the civil war in China, 1945–1947; appointed by Truman as SECRETARY OF STATE and served from January 1, 1947, until the end of Truman's first term in office on January 20, 1949; his most important contribution was the creation of the European Recovery Program ("Marshall Plan") of U.S. aid to rebuild war-torn Europe, announced at Harvard University, June 5, 1947, and enacted 1948; also helped lay the diplomatic groundwork for the creation of the North Atlantic Treaty Organization; president, American Red Cross, 1949–1950; after the outbreak of the Korean War, he reentered government when Truman appointed him SECRETARY OF DEFENSE, where he served from September 21, 1950, until September 12, 1951, and helped rebuild the army, supported Truman's decision to remove General Douglas MacArthur from command of UN forces in Korea in 1951, unsuccessfully promoted universal military training, and weathered vicious smears on his patriotism by Senator Joseph McCarthy; appointed by President Dwight Eisenhower as head of U.S. delegation to the coronation of Queen Elizabeth II of the United Kingdom, 1953; named "Man of the Year" by *Time* magazine, 1944; decorated Distinguished Service Medal with First Oak Leaf Cluster, Silver Star, Congressional Gold Medal; recipient of many other military and civilian honors, awards from 16 foreign countries, including the French Legion of Honor and British Knight Grand Cross, 16 honorary degrees from colleges and universities, and the Nobel Peace Prize, 1953, the first career soldier to win that award; chairman, American Battle Monuments Commission, 1949–1959; member, board of visitors, VMI, 1946–1954; author of *Memoirs of My Service in the World War, 1917–1918* (1976); died on October 16, 1959, in Washington, D.C.; interment in Arlington National Cemetery. **References:** Forrest C. Pogue, *George C. Marshall*, 4 vols. (1963–1987); Robert H. Ferrell, *George C. Marshall* (1966); Larry Bland, ed., *The Papers of George Catlett Marshall*, 6 vols. (1983–); Donald R. McCoy, *The Presidency of Harry S. Truman* (1984); Thomas Parrish, *Roosevelt and Marshall: Partners in Politics and War* (1989); Mark A. Stoler, *George C. Marshall: Soldier–Statesman of the American Century* (1989); Ed Cray, *General of the Army: George C. Marshall, Soldier and Statesman* (1990); *Smithsonian* (August 1997); James Barber, *George C. Marshall: Soldier of Peace* (1997); Michael Hogan, *A Cross of Iron: Harry S. Truman and the Origins of the National Security State, 1945–54* (1998).

—Jeffrey Coster

MARSHALL, James William

Born in Clarke County, Va., August 14, 1822; never married; spent early years in Mount Sterling, Ky.; attended local schools of Clarke County; graduated Dickinson College, Carlisle, Pa., in 1848; became professor at Dickinson College, 1848–1850, and was made full professor of foreign languages, 1850–1861; appointed U.S. consul at Leeds, England, in 1861, and served until

1865; chosen first assistant postmaster general in 1869; appointed POSTMASTER GENERAL in the cabinet of President Grant on July 3, 1874, and served from July 7, 1874, to August 23, 1874; again made first assistant postmaster general and served as such until the end of Grant's administration; became general superintendent of railway mail service; died in Washington, D.C., on February 5, 1910. **References:** Philip R. Moran, *Ulysses S. Grant, 1822–1885: Chronology, Documents, Bibliographical Aids* (1968); Ulysses S. Grant III, *Ulysses S. Grant, Warrior and Statesman* (1969).

MARSHALL, John

Born near Germantown (now Midland), Va., September 24, 1755; son of Thomas, farmer and Revolutionary War soldier, and Mary Randolph (Keith) Marshall: Episcopalian; married Mary Willis ("Polly") Ambler on January 3, 1783; father of ten children; attended school in Westmoreland County, Va., 1769–1770, and lectures on law by George Wythe at the College of William and Mary, 1779–1780; read law and was admitted to the bar in Virginia, 1780; joined Virginia militia as first lieutenant in a regiment of "Minutemen" in 1775 and later joined General George Washington's Continental Army, was promoted to captain in 1777, and served until 1781; practiced law in Fauquier County, Va., 1781–1783, and Richmond, 1783–1797; elected to Virginia House of Delegates, 1782–1784, 1787–1791, and 1795–1797, first from Fauquier, then from Henrico County; member, Committee on the Courts of Justice, and Governor's Council, 1782–1795; delegate to Virginia's constitutional convention, 1788, as a supporter of the federal Constitution; declined offers from President Washington to serve as attorney general or U.S. ambassador; appointed by President John Adams as one of three U.S. commissioners to France in what became known as the "XYZ Affair," 1797–1798; member from Virginia, U.S. House of Representatives, 1799–1801, winning elections in 1798 and 1800; appointed by President John Adams as SECRETARY OF STATE and served from June 6, 1800, until the end of Adams's term in office on March 4, 1801; maintained U.S. neutrality in the Anglo-French conflict and negotiated settlements to commercial and territorial disputes with Britain and Spain; appointed by President Adams as chief justice of the U.S. Supreme Court in 1801, where he served until his death in 1835, establishing important precedents in Court powers and constitutional law, including judicial review, federal government supremacy over states, and the sanctity of contracts and property rights, in such cases as *Marbury v. Madison* (1803), *Fletcher v. Peck* (1810), *McCulloch v. Maryland* (1819), *Dartmouth College v. Woodward* (1819), and *Gibbons v. Ogden* (1824); delegate, Virginia state constitutional convention, 1829–1830; author of *The Life of George Washington* (5 vols., 1804–1807) and *A History of the Colonies Planted by the English on the Continent of North America* (1824); died on July 6, 1835, in Philadelphia, Pa.; interment in Richmond. **References:** Albert J. Beveridge, *The Life of John Marshall*, 4 vols. (1916–1919); Robert Faulkner, *The Jurispru-*

dence of John Marshall (1968); Ralph A. Brown, *The Presidency of John Adams* (1975); Charles F. Hobson, *The Great Chief Justice: John Marshall and the Rule of Law* (1996); Jean Edward Smith, *John Marshall: Definer of a Nation* (1996); Herbert Alan Johnson, *The Chief Justiceship of John Marshall, 1801–1835* (1997); David Scott Robarge, *A Chief Justice's Progress: John Marshall from Revolutionary Virginia to the Supreme Court* (2000); R. Kent Newmyer, *John Marshall and the Heroic Age of the Supreme Court* (2001); Guy Padula, *Madison v. Marshall: Popular Sovereignty, Natural Law, and the United States Constitution* (2001); James F. Simon, *What Kind of Nation: Thomas Jefferson, John Marshall and the Epic Struggle to Create a United States* (2002).

—Jeffrey Coster

MARSHALL, Thomas Riley

Born at North Manchester, Ind., March 14, 1854; son of Dr. Daniel M. and Martha (Patterson) Marshall; Presbyterian; married Lois Irene Kimsey on October 2, 1895; no children; moved with his family to Illinois, Kansas, and Missouri, finally returning to Indiana; after attending the public schools, he entered Wabash College, Crawfordsville, Ind., graduating in 1873; studied law at Fort Wayne, Ind., and was admitted to the bar in 1875, commencing the practice of his profession in Columbia City, Ind.; taught Sunday school at the Presbyterian Church; served on the local school board; nominated and elected governor of Indiana in 1908, serving until 1913; Indiana's favorite son for president of the United States at the 1912 Democratic National Convention; when the nomination went to Woodrow Wilson, he accepted the vice-presidential nomination; elected VICE-PRESIDENT on the Democratic ticket in November 1912, serving two full terms, from March 4, 1913, until March 3, 1921, having been reelected with President Wilson in November 1916; acted as ceremonial head of the United States when the president was out of the country promoting the League of Nations; coined the phrase: "What this country needs is a really good five-cent cigar"; member of the Federal Coal Commission in 1922 and 1923; trustee of Wabash College; upon retiring from political office, he returned to Indiana, making his home in Indianapolis; died in Washington, D.C., on June 1, 1925; buried in Indianapolis. **References:** John Morton Blum, *Woodrow Wilson and the Politics of Morality* (1956); Norman Gordon Levin, *Woodrow Wilson and World Politics* (1968).

MARTIN, (Judith) Lynn Morley

Born in Evanston, Ill., December 26, 1939; daughter of Lawrence William, an accountant, and Helen Catherine (Hall) Morley; married John Martin, an engineer and business owner, in 1960 (divorced 1978); mother of Julia Catherine and Caroline; married Harry D. Leinenweber, a U.S. district court judge, in January 1987; stepmother of Jane, John, Stephen, Justin, and Thomas Leinenweber; attended Catholic and public schools in Chicago area; graduated from William Howard Taft High School, 1957; B.A. cum laude in English, University of Illinois, Champaign-Urbana, 1960; taught high school English, government, and economics, Du Page County and Rockford, Ill., 1961–1969; member, Winnebago County Board, 1972–1976, and member, finance and public works committees; Republican member, Illinois House of Representatives, 1977–1979, and Illinois Senate, 1979–1981, sitting on the appropriations committee in each house; Republican member from Illinois's 16th district, U.S. House of Representatives, 1981–1991; member of House Budget, Armed Services, Administration, and Rules Committees; vice-chair of the House Republican Conference, the first woman elected to a congressional leadership post, 1985; cochair, House Ethics Task Force, 1989; appointed by President George H.W. Bush as SECRETARY OF LABOR and served from February 22, 1991, until January 20, 1993; major contributions include creating a model workplace program in the department, campaigning against "glass ceilings" for women and minorities, and improving coal-mining safety; fellow, John F. Kennedy School of Government, Harvard University, 1993; A.B. Davee Clinical Professor of Public Management, J.J. Kellogg Graduate School of Management, Northwestern University, 1993– ; cochair, Bush-Quayle presidential campaign committee, 1988; unsuccessful Republican candidate for U.S. Senate, 1990; chair, Deloitte & Touche's Council of the Advancement of Women; headed independent company-wide investigation of sexual harassment charges at Mitsubishi Motors Manufacturing of America, 1996–1997; member, board of directors, Ameritech, Harcount General, Dreyfus Funds, TRW Inc., Ryder Systems, and Chicago's Lincoln Park Zoo; named one of Outstanding Young Women in America, U.S. Jaycees, one of "Ten Rising Stars of American Politics," *U.S. News & World Report*, 1987, Republican Woman of the Year, 1989, a Mother of the Year, National Mother's Day Committee, 1992; member, American Association of University Women, Junior League, Council on Foreign Relations, Phi Beta Kappa. **References:** *Current Biography Yearbook 1989;* Charles Kolb, *White House Daze: The Unmaking of Domestic Policy in the Bush Years* (1994); *Who's Who, 2001.*

—Edmund Wehrle

MARTINEZ, Melquiades Rafael

Born in Sagua La Grande, Cuba, October 23, 1946; son of Melquiades C., a veterinarian, and Gladys V. (Ruiz) Martinez; Roman Catholic; married Kathryn ("Kitty") Tindal on June 13, 1970; father of Lauren Elizabeth, John Melquiades, and Andrew Tindal; came to United States in 1962 as part of Operation Pedro Pan, an airlift of 14,000 children out of communist-controlled Cuba; lived with foster families in Orlando, Fla., until joined by his parents and sister in 1966; naturalized, 1971; received B.A. in 1969 and J.D. in 1973 from Florida State University; admitted to the bar for the state of Florida and for the middle district of Florida,

U.S. District Court, 1973, for the U.S. Supreme Court, 1979, and for the southern district of Florida, 1986; certified National Board Trial Advocacy; private practice in Orlando as personal injury lawyer, 1973–1998, as partner, Martinez, Dalton, Dellecker and Wilson, 1973–1985, then as attorney, Martinez, Dalton, Dellecker, Wilson and King, 1985–1998; active in public service in Orlando, including as member, board of directors, Catholic Social Services, 1978–1986, founder and chairman, Mayor's Hispanic Advisory Committee, 1981–1982, chairman, board of commissioners, Orlando Housing Authority, 1983–1986, member, Orlando Utilities Commission, 1992–1997 (president, 1995–1997), and as chairman, Orange County, 1998–2001; won praise for promoting quality-of-life issues, including reducing overcrowded schools and overrapid development in the Orlando area and cutting property taxes; defeated for Republican nomination for Florida governor, 1994; appointed by Governor Jeb Bush to chair Florida's Growth Management Study Commission, 1999; cochair of Florida's Bush for President campaign and Republican elector for Florida, 2000; appointed SECRETARY OF HOUSING AND URBAN DEVELOPMENT by President George W. Bush, taking office on January 24, 2001, the first Cuban American ever to hold a U.S. cabinet post, and charged with pushing through a proposal to increase tax credits to allow for the construction and purchases of over 100,000 new homes; member, Florida Bar Association (member, board of governors, young lawyers section, 1981–1982), Academy of Florida Trial Lawyers (director, 1981–1985, treasurer, 1986–1987, president, 1988–1989), and Ninth Judicial Circuit (judicial nomination commission, 1986); former member of board, Catholic Charities, Orlando (including as vice-president), Greater Orlando Aviation Authority, and Orlando/Orange County Expressway Authority; he and his wife have taken Cuban and Vietnamese refugees into their home. **References:** *Washington Post* (December 26, 2000); *Who's Who in America, 2000.*

—Jeffrey Coster

MASON, John Young

Born near Hicksford (now Emporia), Va., April 18, 1799; son of Edmunds and Frances Ann (Young) Mason; married Mary Anne Port on August 9, 1821; father of eight children; after completing his preparatory education at the local schools, he attended the University of North Carolina at Chapel Hill, graduating in 1816; studied law at the Litchfield Law School, Litchfield, Conn., and was admitted to the bar in 1819, commencing the practice of law in Hicksford, Va.; elected a member of the Virginia General Assembly from 1823 to 1831; represented a Tidewater district at the constitutional convention in 1830; elected as a Democrat to the U.S. House of Representatives, serving from March 4, 1831, to November 11, 1837; a Jacksonian Democrat, he broke with President Jackson by his refusal to vote for the rechartering of the National Bank; chairman of the House committee on foreign affairs; resigned from Congress on November 11, 1837, having been appointed U.S. district judge for the eastern district of Virginia; president of the James River and Kanawha Company in 1849; delegate to the state constitutional convention of 1850; invited to join the cabinet of President Tyler as SECRETARY OF THE NAVY on March 14, 1844, serving until March 10, 1845; appointed ATTORNEY GENERAL by President Polk on March 6, 1845, entering his duties on March 11, 1845, and terminating the office on September 9, 1846; reappointed SECRETARY OF THE NAVY by President Polk from September 9, 1846, until March 8, 1849; resumed the practice of law in Richmond, Va., from 1849 to 1854; appointed U.S. minister plenipotentiary to France on January 22, 1854, serving until his death; died in Paris, France, on October 31, 1859; interred in Hollywood Cemetery, Richmond, Va. **References:** Robert J. Morgan, *A Whig Embattled: The Presidency under John Tyler* (1954); Charles Allan McCoy, *Polk and the Presidency* (1960).

MATHEWS, (Forrest) David

Born at Grove Hill, Ala., December 6, 1935; son of Forrest Lee and Doris M. (Pearson) Matthews; married Mary Chapman on January 24, 1960; father of Lee Ann and Lucy Macleod; A.B. in history and classical Greek, University of Alabama, 1958, M.A., 1959; Ph.D. in the history of American education, Columbia University, 1965; served in the U.S. Army, 1958–1959; with the University of Alabama as lecturer, dean of men, executive assistant to the president, executive vice-president, 1960–1968, and president, 1969–1980; appointed by President Gerald Ford as SECRETARY OF HEALTH, EDUCATION, AND WELFARE and served from August 8, 1975, until the end of Ford's term on January 20, 1977; more conservative in his views than his predecessor, Caspar Weinberger, which was reflected in his questioning the "effectiveness" of busing as a way to achieve racial balances in public schools; during administration apparent widespread fraud was uncovered in the federal Medicaid program; trustee, president, and chief executive officer, Kettering Foundation, 1981– ; member, board of directors, Alabama Community and Technical Services Agency, 1968, Academy for Education Development, National Civic League, Miles College; member, Southern Regional Educational Board, National Programming Council for Public Television, Internal Program Advisory Committee, American Council on Education, executive committee, Public Agenda; chairman, Council on Public Policy Education, Committee on Educational Opportunities for Minority Groups, National Association State Universities and Land-Grant Colleges, 1971–1972; trustee, Gerald R. Ford Foundation; recipient, Outstanding Young Man award, Alabama Jaycees, 1968, one of the ten Outstanding Young Men in the Nation award, 1969, Nicholas Murray Butler medal, Columbia University, 1976, Alabama Administrator of the Year award, Alabama Conference of Black Mayors, 1976, Brotherhood award, National Conference of Christians and Jews, 1979, and 14 honorary degrees; member, Phi Beta Kappa, Phi Alpha Theta, Phi Delta Kappa, Omicron Delta Kappa. **References:** *Current Biography Yearbook 1976*; National Journal, *Ford's Presidency* (1976).

MAYNARD, Horace

Born in Westboro, Mass., August 30, 1814; son of Ephraim and Diana (Cogswell) Maynard; Presbyterian; married Laura Ann Washburn on August 30, 1840; father of Edward Maynard, U.S. consul to Turks Island in 1866, and six other children; attended common schools of Westboro; prepared at Milbury Academy; graduated Amherst College in 1838; moved to Knoxville, Tenn.; became tutor at East Tennessee College (now University of Tennessee) and made professor of mathematics, 1842–1843; studied law, was admitted to the bar in 1844, and began practice in Knoxville; candidate for district elector in 1852; was presidential elector on Whig ticket of Scott and Graham; was state elector on Fillmore ticket, 1856; elected to 35th, 36th, and 37th Congresses and served from March 4, 1857, to March 3, 1863; received LL.D. from Amherst College in 1860; campaigned for Bell and Everett in 1860; fought withdrawal of Tennessee from Union; made attorney general of Tennessee, 1863–1865; was presidential elector on Republican ticket of Lincoln and Andrew Johnson in 1864; became trustee of East Tennessee University in 1865; chosen delegate to South Loyalist convention at Philadelphia in 1866; elected to 39th through 43d Congresses and served from July 24, 1866, to March 3, 1875; was unsuccessful candidate for governor of Tennessee in 1874; minister to Turkey, March 9, 1875, to May 1880; appointed POSTMASTER GENERAL in the cabinet of President Hayes on June 2, 1880, and served from August 25, 1880, to March 4, 1881; retired to private life; died in Knoxville, Tenn., on May 3, 1882; interment in Old Gray Cemetery. **References:** James Park, *Life and Services of Horace Maynard* (1903); Arthur Bishop, *Rutherford B. Hayes, 1822–1893: Chronology, Documents, Bibliographical Aids* (1969).

McADOO, William Gibbs

Born near Marietta, Ga., October 31, 1863; son of Judge William Gibbs McAdoo, officer in the Mexican War; Episcopalian; married Sarah Houston Fleming on November 18, 1885; father of Harriet, Francis, Nona, William, and Sally; after death of first wife married Eleanor Randolph Wilson, daughter of President Wilson, in a White House ceremony on May 7, 1914; father by second marriage of Ellen and Mary; divorced in 1934; married Doris I. Cross on September 14, 1935; briefly attended University of Tennessee; appointed deputy clerk of 6th U.S. Circuit Court of Appeals in Tennessee in May 1882; admitted to the bar in 1885; practiced at Chattanooga, Tenn., until 1892, when he moved to New York City and entered into law partnership with William McAdoo (no relation), formerly assistant secretary of the navy; in 1902 became president and director of two companies later consolidated as the Hudson and Manhattan Railroad Company, which, on March 8, 1904, completed the first tunnel under the Hudson River; vice-chairman of the Democratic National Committee in 1912 and acting chairman for the greater part of the campaign; appointed SECRETARY

OF THE TREASURY in the cabinet of President Wilson on March 6, 1913; most important contributions were conducting four successful Liberty Bond drives, establishing war risk insurance law that later was extended to include life insurance for the armed forces, and serving as chairman of the Federal Reserve Board, which he helped institute in 1913; resigned from office on December 16, 1918; served as director general of U.S. railroads during the period of government operation from 1917 to his resignation on January 10, 1919; resumed law practice first in New York and later in Los Angeles, Calif.; was a prominent candidate for the Democratic presidential nomination in the conventions of 1920 and 1924 but failed to secure nomination; chairman of the California delegation to the Democratic National Conventions of 1932 and 1936; elected U.S. senator from California in 1933 and served until his resignation in 1939; retired from political life and became chairman of the board of directors of the American President Steamship Lines; supported the League of Nations, Prohibition, and women's suffrage; author of *The Challenge—Liquor and Lawlessness vs. Constitutional Government* (1928); died in Washington, D.C., on February 1, 1941. **References:** William Gibbs McAdoo, *Crowded Years* (1931); *Who Was Who in America*, vol. 1 (1943); *Encyclopedia Americana*, vol. 18 (1968).

Secretary of the Treasury William G. McAdoo and his son William, Jr., who was in the aviation branch of the Navy. (National Archives)

McCLELLAND, Robert

Born in Greencastle, Pa., August 1, 1807; son of John and Eleanor Bell (McCulloh) McClelland; Methodist; married Sarah E. Sabine in 1837; graduated Dickinson College in 1829; taught; studied law; admitted to Chambersburg bar in 1831; moved to Pittsburgh and began practice; moved to Monroe, Mich., in 1833; organized new state government and Democratic Party; active in state constitutional convention of 1835; declined offer of first bank commissioner of state; declined attorney generalship of Michigan; was member of board of regents of University of Michigan in 1837 and 1850; elected to 28th, 29th, and 30th Congresses and served from March 4, 1843, to March 3, 1849; made Cass's chief Michigan lieutenant and aided him in presidential campaign of 1848; member of state constitutional convention, 1850; elected governor of

Michigan in 1850 and 1852; appointed SECRETARY OF THE INTERIOR in the cabinet of President Pierce and served from March 7, 1853, to March 5, 1857; most important contributions were reduction of corruption in land, Indian and pension bureaus, efficient operations of bureaus, placing Indians on reservations, settlement of annuities in goods, opposition to homestead legislation, and making pensions available to only the indigent; returned to Michigan and practiced law, 1857; member of Michigan constitutional convention in 1867; toured Europe in 1870; died in Detroit, Mich., on August 30, 1880; interment in Elwood Cemetery. **References:** Alfred Nevin, *Men of Mark of Cumberland Valley, Pennsylvania* (1876); Irving J. Sloan, ed., *Franklin Pierce, 1804–1869: Chronology, Documents, Bibliographical Aids* (1968).

McCRARY, George Washington

Born near Evansville, Ind., August 29, 1835; son of James McCrary, farmer, and Matilda (Forest) McCrary; Unitarian; married Helen Galett in 1857; family moved to Van Buren County, Iowa; studied for brief intervals at school and academy; taught country school at 18; studied law in Keokuk with John W. Rankin and Samuel F. Miller; admitted to bar in 1856; began practice; elected state representative, 1857; became state senator on committee of Indian affairs and judiciary, 1861–1865; entered partnership with Rankin when Miller became justice of Supreme Court, 1862; was representative to Congress from March 4, 1869, to March 3, 1877; published *A Treatise on the American Law of Elections*; appointed SECRETARY OF WAR in the cabinet of President Hayes on March 12, 1877, and served until his resignation on December 11, 1879; most important contributions were withdrawal of support of federal troops from remaining carpetbag governments in South Carolina and Louisiana, use of federal troops in railway strike of 1877, order for troops to pursue marauding Mexicans across border, which resulted in American recognition of Díaz government, and beginning publication of *War of the Rebellion: Official Records*; was federal judge of 8th Judicial Circuit, 1880–1884; moved to Kansas City, Mo., 1884, and acted as general counsel for Atchison, Topeka and Santa Fe Railroad; member of firm of Pratt, McCrary, Hagerman and Pratt; died in St. Joseph, Mo., July 23, 1890; interment in Oakland Cemetery, Keokuk, Iowa. **References:** B.F. Gue, *History of Iowa* (1903); C.R. Williams, *The Life of Rutherford B. Hayes* (1914); Arthur Bishop, ed., *Rutherford B. Hayes, 1822–1893: Chronology, Documents, Bibliographical Aids* (1969).

McCULLOCH, Hugh

Born at Kennebunk, Me., December 7, 1808; son of Hugh and Abigail (Perkins) McCulloch; married Susan Mann in 1838; father of four children; educated at the academy at Saco, Me.; entered Bowdoin College but left in his sophomore year; Bowdoin subsequently gave him honorary A.M. degree; taught school at age 17; studied law in Boston; admitted to the bar in 1832; moved to Fort Wayne, Ind., in 1833, where he commenced the practice of law; appointed cashier and manager of the Fort Wayne branch of the State Bank of Indiana, holding that position until 1856; became president of the State Bank of Indiana from 1856 to 1863; though an opponent of the National Bank Act of 1863, which established federal control over the issue of currency by state banks, Secretary of the Treasury Chase invited him in April 1863 to assume the new office of federal comptroller of the currency, which the act had created to carry out its provisions; appointed SECRETARY OF THE TREASURY by President Lincoln on March 7, 1865, and served until March 4, 1869; labored to reduce the Civil War debt and advocated the retirement of legal tender (greenback) notes and return to specie payments, a program that Congress adopted on a limited scale in 1866 and abandoned again in 1868; advocated return to gold standard; at age 75, he was reappointed SECRETARY OF THE TREASURY by President Arthur, on October 28, 1884, a post he held until the incoming President Cleveland named a successor on March 4, 1885; became a partner in Jay Cook's Banking House in 1869, in charge of the London Branch; authored *Men and Measures of Half a Century* (1888); died at "Holly Hill," Prince Georges County, Md., on May 24, 1895. **References:** Jesse Burton Hendrick, *Lincoln's War Cabinet* (1946); George Frederick Howe, *Chester A. Arthur: A Quarter Century of Machine Politics* (1957).

McELROY, Neil Hosler

Born in Berea, Ohio, October 30, 1904; son of Malcolm Ross McElroy, teacher, and Susan Harriet (Hosler) McElroy; Episcopalian; married Mary Camilla Fry on June 29, 1929; father of Nancy Sue, Barbara Ellen, and Malcolm Neil; attended schools of Berea and Cincinnati, Ohio; received B.A. from Harvard, 1925; employed in advertising department of Procter and Gamble Co. in Cincinnati; became manager of promotion department in 1929, established new branch in England in 1930, was made advertising and promotion manager in 1940, and was chosen president of advertising and promotion in 1943; was president of Cincinnati Citizens Planning Board in 1946; made assistant to the president of Procter and Gamble in 1946, became vice-president and general manager, and was made president from 1948 to 1957; member of numerous Cincinnati civic organizations; trustee of Cincinnati Institute of Fine Arts; chairman of White House Conference on Education, 1955; chairman of National Industrial Conference Board in 1956; appointed SECRETARY OF DEFENSE in the cabinet of President Eisenhower and served from October 9, 1957, to December 1, 1959; most important contributions were appointment of director of guided missiles, establishment of Advanced Research Projects Agency, launching of first successful satellite, and passage of Department of Defense Reorganization Act of 1958; chairman of the board of Procter and Gamble, 1959–1972; director of General Electric Co., Chrysler Corp., and Equitable Assurance Society; member of National Council, United Negro College Fund; president of Commonwealth Commercial Club,

1960–1961; member of board of American Soap and Glycerine Producers, Inc.; died on November 30, 1972. **References:** Dean Albertson, *Eisenhower as President* (1963); Carl Borklund, *Men of the Pentagon* (1966).

McGRANERY, James Patrick

Born in Philadelphia, Pa., July 8, 1895; son of Patrick and Bridget (Gallagher) McGranery; Roman Catholic; married Regina T. Clark on November 29, 1939; father of James Patrick Jr., Clark, and Regina; after attending the parochial school in his native city and Maher Preparatory School, he entered Temple University in Philadelphia, where he studied law, graduating in 1928; admitted to the bar in 1928 and began practice in Philadelphia; served in the U.S. Army Air Corps as an observation pilot and as an adjutant in the 111th Infantry Division during World War I; worked briefly for the Curtis Publishing Co.; admitted to practice before the U.S. Supreme Court in 1939; member of the Democratic State Committee from 1928 to 1932; unsuccessful candidate for district attorney in 1931; unsuccessful candidate for the U.S. House of Representatives in 1934; served as chairman of the registration committee of Philadelphia in 1935; elected as a Democrat to the 75th through 78th Congresses, serving in all from January 3, 1937, until his resignation on November 17, 1943 to accept a presidential appointment in the Justice Department; appointed assistant U.S. attorney general in November 1943, serving until October 9, 1946, at which time he was sworn in as a U.S. district judge for the eastern district of Pennsylvania by appointment of President Truman; served in this capacity until May 26, 1952, when he resigned to accept the position of ATTORNEY GENERAL in the cabinet of President Truman; invited to join on May 21, 1952, he entered upon his duties on May 27, 1952, and served until the termination of the Truman administration on January 20, 1953; upon retirement, he returned to the general practice of law in Washington, D.C.; trustee of Immaculata College, Pa.; member of the Advisory Board of Temple University Law School and Villanova College; member of the American Judicature Society and of the American Catholic Historical Society; died on December 23, 1962. **References:** Alfred Steinberg, *The Man from Missouri: The Life and Times of Harry S. Truman* (1962); Cabell B.H. Phillips, *The Truman Presidency: The History of a Triumphant Succession* (1966).

McGRATH, James Howard

Born in Woonsocket, R.I., November 28, 1903; son of James J. and Ida E. (May) McGrath; Roman Catholic; married Estelle A. Cadorette on November 28, 1929; father of David; after receiving his primary education at the Woonsocket parochial school, he entered LaSalle Academy in Providence, R.I., graduating in 1922; matriculated at Providence College, receiving his Ph.B. in 1926; studied law at Boston University, graduating in 1928, admitted to the Rhode Island bar in 1929 and commenced practice in Providence; employed as assistant to Senator Gerry of Rhode Island; designated city solicitor of Central Falls, R.I., 1930–1934; vice-chairman of the Democratic State Committee; president of the Young Men's Democratic League, 1924–1938; chairman of the Rhode Island delegation to the Democratic National Convention in 1932; joined the law firm of Senator Green of Rhode Island in 1932; appointed U.S. district attorney for Rhode Island in 1934, serving until 1940; delegate to the Democratic National Conventions of 1936, 1944, 1948, 1952, and 1960; associated with J.J. McGrath and Sons, his father's real estate and insurance firm; elected governor of Rhode Island in 1940 and reelected in 1942 and 1944, serving until his resignation in October 1945 to accept the appointment of U.S. solicitor general; resigned his post in October 1946 to become the Democratic candidate for U.S. senator; elected to the U.S. Senate in November 1946 for the term commencing January 3, 1947, serving until his resignation on August 23, 1949; chairman of the Democratic National Committee from 1947 to 1949; selected ATTORNEY GENERAL in the cabinet of President Truman on August 19, 1949, entering upon his duties on August 24, 1949, and serving until his resignation on April 3, 1952; unsuccessful candidate for the nomination of U.S. senator in 1960; author of *The Power of the People* (1948) and *The Case for Truman* (1948); died on November 11, 1966. **References:** Alfred Steinberg, *The Man from Missouri: The Life and Times of Harry S. Truman* (1962); Cabell B. H. Phillips, *The Truman Presidency: The History of a Triumphant Succession* (1966).

McHENRY, James

Born in Ballymena, County Antrim, Ireland, on November 16, 1753; son of Daniel and Agnes McHenry; Roman Catholic; married Margaret Allison Caldwell on January 8, 1784; father of John; educated in Dublin; emigrated to Philadelphia in 1771; attended Newark Academy in Delaware in 1772 where he studied medicine, under Dr. Benjamin Rush, and poetry; volunteered for military service in Cambridge, Mass., 1775; assigned to medical staff of a Cambridge hospital in 1776; named surgeon of 5th Pennsylvania Battalion on August 10, 1776; discharged January 27, 1777, after the November capture of Fort Washington; became senior surgeon of the Flying Hospital, Valley Forge, and on May 15, 1778, he withdrew from medical practice upon appointment as Washington's secretary; transferred to Lafayette's staff in August 1780; commissioned major on May 30, 1781; resigned from active service upon election to the Maryland Senate in September 1781, where he served five years; appointed to Congress in May 1783, where he served until 1786; Maryland delegate to the 1787 Constitutional Convention; appointed SECRETARY OF WAR in the cabinet of President Washington in January 1796 and served until June 1, 1800, when he resigned at President Adams's request after political disagreements; in defense of his activities he read *A Letter to the Honorable Speaker of the House* on December 28, 1802 (published 1803); served as president of the Baltimore

Bible Society, 1813; died in Baltimore, Md., on May 3, 1816. **Reference:** B.C. Steiner, *The Life and Correspondence of James McHenry* (1907).

McKAY, Douglas James

Born in Portland, Ore., June 24, 1893; son of Edwin Donald and Minnie Adele (Musgrove) McKay; Presbyterian; married Mabel Christine Hill on March 31, 1917; father of Douglas, Shirley, and Mary Lou; after attending the public schools of Portland, he entered Oregon State College, graduating in 1917; worked in various positions for the Portland *Oregonian* and *Daily News*; served as a lieutenant with the American expeditionary forces in France and was severely injured during the Meuse-Argonne offensive during World War I; served as captain and then major at Camp Adair, Ore., during World War II; joined the Portland firm of Dooley and Co. as an insurance salesman in 1919; became an automobile salesman for the Francis Motor Co. of Portland, becoming manager in 1932; moved to Salem, Ore., in 1927, establishing his own automobile agency, the Douglas McKay Chevrolet Co., of which he was owner until 1955; became active in Republican Party politics in 1932; elected mayor of Salem, 1933–1934; elected senator in the Oregon state legislature from Marion County in 1934, serving in that capacity, except for his period of military service, until 1949; speaker of the House during 1947 and 1948; elected governor of Oregon in 1948 and reelected in 1950; invited to join the Eisenhower cabinet as SECRETARY OF THE INTERIOR on January 21, 1953, serving until his resignation to run for U.S. Senate on June 8, 1956; during his incumbency, he opposed the transfer of lands from the Wichita Wildlife Refuge for army use, added nine new wildlife areas, promulgated measures to govern oil and gas leasing on wildlife areas, and embarked on a long-range plan for the integration of Indians into American society, advancing a program of voluntary relocation from marginal economic areas to places where they could earn livelihoods; chairman of the President's Commission on Water Resources Policy; died in Salem, Ore., July 22, 1959. **References:** Robert J. Donovan, *Eisenhower, the Inside Story* (1956); Walter Bedell Smith, *Eisenhower's Six Great Decisions* (1956).

McKEAN, Thomas

Born in New London Township, Pa., March 19, 1734; son of William McKean, farmer and tavern keeper, and Letitia (Finney) McKean; married Mary Borden on July 21, 1763 and father of Joseph McKean, jurist; after death of first wife, married Sarah Armitage on September 3, 1774; attended the Rev. Francis Allison's academy, New London; studied law; engaged as a clerk to the prothonotary of the court of common pleas, 1750–1752; appointed deputy prothonotary and recorder for the probate of wills for New Castle County, Del., 1752; admitted to the bar in 1755 and began practice in New Castle; appointed deputy attorney general for Sussex County in 1756 and served until his resignation in 1758;

clerk of the Delaware House of Assembly, 1757 to 1759; went to England and continued law study at the Middle Temple in London; member of the Delaware House of Assembly, 1762–1775, serving as speaker in 1772; appointed a trustee of the New Castle County loan office in 1764 and served until 1776; member of the Stamp Act Congress, 1765; delegate from Delaware to the General Congress in New York City in 1765; appointed chief notary for the lower counties of Delaware on July 10, 1765; commissioned a justice of the peace of the court of common pleas and quarter sessions and of the orphan's court for New Castle County, 1765; appointed collector of the port of New Castle, 1771; member of the Continental Congress, 1774–1783; a signer of the Declaration of Independence; member of the Delaware House of Representatives in 1776 and 1777, serving as speaker in 1777; served in the Revolutionary War; commissioned chief justice of Pennsylvania on July 28, 1777, and served until 1799; PRESIDENT OF THE CONTINENTAL CONGRESS from July 10, 1781, to November 5, 1781; member of the convention of Pennsylvania that ratified the U.S. Constitution, December 12, 1787; elected governor of Pennsylvania and served from 1799 to 1808; retired from public life; compiled *The Acts of the General Assembly of Pennsylvania* (2 vols., 1782) and collaborated with Edmund Physick on *A Calm Appeal to the People of the State of Delaware* (1793); also coauthor, with James Wilson, of *Commentaries on the Constitution of the United States of America* (1792); died in Philadelphia, Pa., on June 24, 1817; interment in Laurel Hill Cemetery. **References:** J.H. Peeling, *The Public Life of Thomas McKean, 1734–1817* (1929); E.C. Burnett, *The Continental Congress* (1964).

McKENNA, Joseph

Born in Philadelphia, Pa., August 10, 1843; son of John and Mary (Johnson) McKenna; Roman Catholic; married Amanda F. Borneman in 1869; father of three girls; attended Catholic seminaries in Benicia, Calif.; graduated Benicia Collegiate Institute, 1865; turned to law after abandoning priesthood; admitted to bar, 1865; began practice in Fairfield, Solano County, Calif.; served as county attorney, 1866–1870; was representative in the state legislature, 1875–1876, and unsuccessful Republican candidate for speakership; defeated, due to religion, as candidate for U.S. House of Representatives in 1876, 1878, and 1880; elected to U.S. House, and served from March 4, 1885, until his resignation on March 28, 1892; appointed by President Benjamin Harrison as U.S. circuit court judge for the 9th circuit, 1892; appointed ATTORNEY GENERAL in the cabinet of President McKinley on March 5, 1897, and served until January 25, 1898; nominated, December 16, 1897, for associate justice of U.S. Supreme Court, confirmed January 21, 1898, and served until his resignation on January 25, 1925; died in Washington, D.C., November 21, 1926. **References:** O.T. Shuck, *History of the Bench and Bar of California* (1901); H.L. Carson, *The History of the Supreme Court of the United States* (1902); Margaret K. Leech, *In the Days of McKinley* (1959); Robert Dallek, *McKinley's Decision, War on Spain* (1970).

McKENNAN, Thomas McKean Thompson

Born in Dragon Neck, New Castle County, Del., March 31, 1794; son of Colonel William McKennan, soldier in the Revolutionary War, and Elizabeth (Thompson) McKennan; Presbyterian; married Matilda Lourie Bowman on December 6, 1815; father of William, Thomas, Isabella, Jacob Bowman, Thomas McKean Thompson, Anne Elizabeth, John Thompson, and Matilda Bowman; moved with family to western Virginia, 1797, and then to Washington, Washington County, Pa.; graduated Washington College (later Washington and Jefferson College) in 1810; tutor of ancient languages, 1813–1814; studied law in the office of Parker Campbell of Washington, Pa.; admitted to the bar, 1814; deputy attorney general for the county, 1815–1817; served as trustee of Washington College, 1818–1852; member of Washington town council, 1818–1831; became official of Washington (Pa.) and Pittsburgh Railroad Company, 1831; member of U.S. House of Representatives from March 4, 1831, to March 3, 1839; was presidential elector on Harrison–Tyler ticket, 1840; was member of Congress, May 3, 1842–March 3, 1843, completing an unexpired term; active Whig in tariff of 1842; headed Pennsylvania's presidential electors, 1848; appointed SECRETARY OF THE INTERIOR in the cabinet of President Fillmore and served from July 23, 1850, to August 14, 1850, leaving because of disagreement with administration; became first president of Hempfield Railroad Company, Inc., and remained so until death; founder of Washington Female Seminary; founder of Washington County Agricultural Society; died in Reading, Pa., July 9, 1852; interment in Washington Cemetery, Washington, Pa. **References:** Boyd Crumrine, *The Courts of Justice, Bench and Bar of Washington County* (1902); Robert J. Rayback, *Millard Fillmore* (1959).

McKINLEY, William, Jr.

Born in Neles, Ohio, January 29, 1843; son of William and Nancy Campbell (Allison) McKinley; Methodist Episcopalian; married Ida Saxton on January 25, 1871; father of Katherine and Ida; attended the public schools, Poland Academy, and Allegheny College in Meadville, Pa.; taught school near Poland, Ohio, in 1859; enlisted as a private in the 23d Regiment, Ohio Volunteer Infantry, on June 11, 1861; engaged in combat at the Battle of Carnifax Ferry on September 10, 1861; promoted to sergeant; commissioned second lieutenant in September 1862; promoted to first lieutenant, captain, and finally major, in 1865; discharged on July 26, 1865; studied law in Mahoning County, Ohio, and was admitted to the bar in 1867, commencing practice in Canton County, Ohio; elected prosecuting attorney of Stark County, Ohio, from 1869 to 1871; elected as a Republican to the U.S. House of Representatives, serving from March 4, 1877, until March 3, 1883; presented credentials as a member-elect to the 48th Congress but was unseated by Jonathan H. Wallace, who contested his election; reelected to the

U.S. House of Representatives in the 49th, 50th, and 51st Congresses, serving in all from March 4, 1885, to March 3, 1891; unsuccessful candidate for reelection to the 52d Congress in 1890; delegate to the Republican National Conventions of 1885, 1888, and 1892; unsuccessful candidate for the Republican presidential nomination in June 1892; elected governor of Ohio in 1891 and reelected in 1893, serving until January 13, 1896; elected PRESIDENT on the Republican ticket in November 1896 and reelected in November 1900; inaugurated on March 4, 1897, and served until he was shot by anarchist assassin Leon Czolgosz on September 6, 1901, while attending the Pan American Exposition in Buffalo, N.Y.; the third president to be assassinated; the fifth president to die in office; died in Buffalo, September 14, 1901; interment in the McKinley Monument in Canton, Ohio. **References:** Margaret K. Leech, *In the Days of McKinley* (1959); Paul W. Glad, *McKinley, Bryan, and the People* (1964).

William McKinley (Library of Congress)

McLANE, Louis

Born in Smyrna, Del., May 28, 1786; son of Allan McLane, Revolutionary War soldier and speaker of Delaware legislature, and Rebecca (Wells) McLane; married Catherine Mary Milligan in 1812; father of Robert Milligan, congressman and diplomat; attended private schools; served as midshipman in navy on USS *Philadelphia* from 1798 to 1799; entered Newark College in Delaware, 1801; but did not graduate; read law under James A. Bayard; was admitted to the bar in 1807; began practice in Smyrna; joined volunteer company in War of 1812 in defense of hometown and Baltimore; elected to Congress as a Jeffersonian Republican, 1816, took seat on March 4, 1817, and served until March 3, 1827; supported Crawford, 1824; was reelected to 20th Congress but resigned to take seat in Senate, March 4, 1827–March 16, 1829; supported Jackson, 1828; offered post of attorney general but refused; appointed envoy extraordinary and minister plenipotentiary to Great Britain and served from March 18, 1829, to July 6, 1831; appointed SECRETARY OF THE TREASURY in the cabinet of President Jackson and served from August 8, 1831, to May 28, 1833;

most important contribution was urging Congress to recharter the Bank of the United States, although President Jackson opposed it; appointed SECRETARY OF STATE in the cabinet of President Jackson and served from May 29, 1833, to June 26, 1834; most important contributions were firmness in dealings of claims and boundaries with Mexico, negotiation with Great Britain over Northeast boundary, pressure on France to pay spoliation claims, and introduction of orderly procedure into operation of department; president of Morris Canal and Banking Company; moved to Baltimore, 1837, to accept presidency of Baltimore & Ohio Railroad Company and remained in that capacity until his resignation in 1847; appointed U.S. minister to Great Britain by President Polk to negotiate Oregon question, June 1845–August 1846; offered position of commissioner to Mexico to gain ratification to Treaty of Guadalupe Hidalgo, 1848, but refused; member of Maryland constitutional convention, 1850–1851; died in Baltimore, Md., October 7, 1857; interment in Greenmount Cemetery. **References:** S.F. Bemis, *The American Secretaries of State and Their Diplomacy* (1928); Ronald Shaw, *Andrew Jackson, 1767–1845: Chronology, Documents, Bibliographical Aids* (1969).

McLAUGHLIN, Ann Dore

Born in Newark, N.J., November 16, 1941; daughter of Edward Joseph and Maria (Koellhofer) Lauenstein; Roman Catholic; married William Dore in 1963 and divorced in 1964; married John J. McLaughlin on August 23, 1975, and divorced in 1992; student, University of London, 1961–1962; B.A., Marymount College, 1963; postgraduate study, Wharton School, 1987; supervised network communications at ABC Television, New York City, 1963–1966; director, alumnae relations, Marymount College, Tarrytown, N.Y., 1966–1969; account executive, Myers-Infoplan International, New York City, 1969–1971; director of communications, Presidential Election Commission, Washington, 1971–1972; assistant to chairman and press secretary, Presidential Inauguration Committee, 1972–1973; director of office of public information, Environmental Protection Agency, 1973–1974; government relations and communications executive, Union Carbide Corp., 1974–1977; public affairs and issues management counseling, McLaughlin and Co., 1977–1981; assistant secretary for public affairs, U.S. Department of the Treasury, 1981–1984; undersecretary, U.S. Department of the Interior, 1984–1987; consultant, Center for Strategic and International Studies, Washington, 1987; appointed SECRETARY OF LABOR by President Reagan when William Brock resigned to manage the presidential bid of Senator Robert Dole; served from December 17, 1987, until the end of Reagan's term on January 20, 1989; opposed both increase in the minimum wage and organized labor's demand for plant closing notification, generally supporting Reagan-Bush policies toward unions and unionism; appointed a task force to study child care as a workforce issue, pressing businesses to expand their day-care facilities; visiting fellow, Urban Institute, 1989–1992; president and chief executive officer, New American Schools Development Corporation, 1992–1993; managed John McLaughlin's unsuccessful race for the Senate seat in Rhode Island, 1970; chair, President's Commission on Aviation Security and Terrorism, 1989–1990; member, American Council on Capital Formation, 1976–1978; member, Defense Advisory Committee of Women in the Services, 1973–1974; member, environmental education task force, U.S. Department of Health, Education, and Welfare, 1976–1977; member, board of directors, Fannie Mae, Kellogg Co., Nordstrom Co., Host Marriott Corp., Vulcan Materials Co., Donna Karan International, AMR Corp., Harman International Industries, Inc., Microsoft; chair, Aspen Institute, 1996–2000, vice-chair, 1996; president, Federal City Council, 1990–1995; member, board of overseers, Wharton School, University of Pennsylvania, board of directors, Charles A. Dana Foundation, The Conservation Fund, The Shakespeare Theatre, 1994, Public Agenda Foundation; trustee, Urban Institute, 1989–1996. **References:** *New York Times* (December 18, 1987); *Ms Magazine* (March 1988); *The New Republic* (May 9, 1988); *Who's Who in America, 1990–1991*.

McLEAN, John

Born in Morris County, N.J., March 11, 1785; son of Fergus McLean, weaver-turned-farmer, and Sophia (Blockford) McLean; married Rebecca Edwards in 1807; later married Sarah Bella (Ludlow) Garrard in 1843; moved with family to Morgantown, Va., 1789, then to Jessamine, Ky., and later to Maysville, Ky., and settled on a farm near Lebanon, now Warren County, Ohio, 1799; attended schools as opportunity permitted; worked; hired two private tutors at 16 years of age; indentured at 18 for 2 years to a clerk of Hamilton County court at Cinicinnati, worked, read law with Arthur St. Clair, and joined a debating club; was admitted to the bar, 1807, and began practice of law in Lebanon; founded weekly newspaper, the *Western Star*; elected as War Democrat to Congress from the district of Cincinnati in October 1812 and was reelected in 1814; declined candidacy for Senate, 1815; resigned seat in Congress, 1816, and became judge of Ohio Supreme Court, serving until 1822; appointed commissioner of land office by President Monroe, 1822; appointed POSTMASTER GENERAL in the cabinet of President Monroe, June 26, 1823, and continued under John Quincy Adams, serving from July 1, 1823, to March 9, 1829; most important contributions were removal of unfaithful and incompetent officials and holding of management contractors to agreements; declined cabinet portfolios of secretary of war and secretary of the navy in Jackson's administration; pursued interests in literary field; nominated associate justice of U.S. Supreme Court by President Jackson, confirmed by Senate on March 7, 1829, was assigned to 7th circuit, took seat in January 1830, and served until death; died in Cincinnati, Ohio, April 4, 1861; interment in Spring Grove Cemetery. **References:** Charles Warren, *The Supreme Court in United States History* (1922); H.F. Bremer, ed., *John Adams, 1735–1826: Chronol-*

ogy, Documents, Bibliographical Aids (1967); Ian Elliot, ed., *James Monroe, 1758–1831: Chronology, Documents, Bibliographical Aids* (1969).

McNAMARA, Robert Strange

Born in San Francisco, Calif., June 9, 1916; son of Robert James, wholesale shoe industry executive, and Clara Nell (Strange) McNamara; Presbyterian; married Margaret Craig on August 13, 1940; father of Margaret Elizabeth, Kathleen, and Robert; attended public schools of Piedmont, Calif.; A.B., University of California, Berkeley, 1937; M.B.A., Harvard, 1939; assistant professor of business administration, Harvard, 1940–1943; special consultant to U.S. Department of War, 1942; sent to England as civilian consultant in 1943; served to lieutenant colonel, U.S. Army Air Corps, 1943–1946; made colonel in Air Force Reserve; manager, Ford Motor Company, 1946–1949, comptroller, 1949–1953, assistant general manager, Ford division, 1953–1955, vice-president and general manager, Ford division, 1955–1957, director and group vice-president of car divisions, 1957–1960, and company president, 1960–1961; appointed SECRETARY OF DEFENSE by President Kennedy and continued under Lyndon B. Johnson, serving from January 21, 1961, until he resigned on February 29, 1968; most important contributions were new planning-programming-budget system, increase in nuclear defense bases, preparedness of forces during Berlin crisis, 1961, and Cuban Missile Crisis, 1962, establishment of Defense Supply Agency and Defense Intelligence Agency with Defense Intelligence School, formation of Office of Education and Manpower Resources; while he supported the escalation of American military involvement in Vietnam under President Kennedy and initially under President Johnson, his growing disillusionment with the course of the war led to his resignation; as secretary of defense, in 1967 he commissioned the study that became known upon its unauthorized release in 1971 as *The Pentagon Papers*; president, International Bank for Reconstruction and Development ("World Bank"), 1968–1981; during his tenure dealt with the growing inability of the Third World to pay back its debt and expanded the bank's daily loans in inflation-adjusted figures from less than $1 billion to nearly $12 billion; former director, Corning Glass Works, TWA, Royal Dutch Petroleum, Washington Post Company, Bank of America, 1981–1989; former trustee, Overseas Development Council, Urban Institute, Enterprise Foundation, Brookings Institution; author of *The Essence of Security: Reflections in Office* (1968), *One Hundred Countries—Two Billion People* (1973), *The McNamara Years at the World Bank* (1981), *Blundering into Disaster: Surviving the First Century of the Nuclear Age* (1986), *Out of the Cold: New Thinking for American Foreign and Defense Policy in the Twenty-first Century* (1989), *In Retrospect: The Tragedy and Lessons of Vietnam* (1995), and *Wilson's Ghost: Reducing the Risk of Conflict, Killing, and Catastrophe in the Twenty-first Century*

(2001); coauthor, with James G. Blight and Robert K. Brigham, of *Argument without End: In Search of Answers to the Vietnam Tragedy* (1999); recipient, Legion of Merit, Distinguished Service Medal, 1946, Presidential Medal of Freedom with distinction, Christian A. Herter Memorial award, Albert Pick, Jr., award, University of Chicago, 1979, Franklin D. Roosevelt Freedom from Want medal, 1983, Onassis Athinai prize, 1988, and honorary degrees from University of California, University of Michigan, Columbia University, Harvard University, George Washington University,

President Lyndon B. Johnson confers on November 23, 1963 with Secretary of Defense Robert McNamara. It was one of many conferences the new Chief Executive held with Cabinet members and high government officials. (AP/Wide World Photos)

Princeton University, Amherst College, Williams College, University of Alabama, Ohio State University, New York University, University of Notre Dame, University of Pennsylvania, University of St. Andrews, University of the Philippines, Aberdeen University, Oxford University, and University of Southern California; member, Phi Beta Kappa. **References:** Robert J. Art, *TFX Decision: McNamara and the Military* (1968); Vaughn Davis Bornet, *The Presidency of Lyndon B. Johnson* (1983); *Current Biography Yearbook 1987*; James N. Giglio, *The Presidency of John F. Kennedy* (1991); Richard Reeves, *President Kennedy: Profile of Power* (1993); Deborah Shapley, *Promise and Power: The Life and Times of Robert McNamara* (1993); Paul Hendrickson, *The Living and the Dead: Robert McNamara and Five Lives of a Lost War* (1996); H.R. McMaster, *Dereliction of Duty: Lyndon Johnson, Robert McNamara, the Joint Chiefs of Staff and the Lies That Led to Vietnam* (1997); *Who's Who in America, 2000.*

McREYNOLDS, James Clark

Born in Elkton, Ky., February 3, 1862; son of John Oliver McReynolds, surgeon and gynecologist, and Ellen (Reeves) McReynolds; never married; graduated Vanderbilt University in 1882 and received law degree at the University of Virginia in 1884; served briefly as private secretary to U.S. Senator (later Supreme Court Justice) Howell E. Jackson; began law practice in Nashville, Tenn.; in 1896, was unsuccessful candidate for Congress as a "gold" Democrat; professor of law at Vanderbilt University, 1900–1903; appointed assistant U.S. attorney general by President Theodore Roosevelt on June 1, 1903, to serve until January 1, 1907; appointed by the attorney general as special counsel for the government and from 1907 to 1912 was active in prosecuting violators of the Sherman Antitrust Act; appointed ATTORNEY GENERAL on March 5, 1913, in the cabinet of President Wilson; most important contributions were dissolving the Union Pacific–Southern Pacific railroad merger, initiating the government case against the alleged monopoly practices of the American Telephone & Telegraph Company, prohibiting price-fixing practices of the Elgin (Ill.) Board of Trade, helping to prepare the Covington Bill to create an Interstate Trade Commission, and prosecuting the monopolies of the National Wholesale Jewelers Association and the New York, New Haven, and Hartford Railroad Company; appointed asociate justice of the U.S. Supreme Court in August 1914 by President Wilson to succeed Justice Horace H. Lurton; confirmed by U.S. Senate, and took his seat on October 12, 1914, serving until his retirement on February 1, 1941; during the administration of President Franklin Roosevelt, became known as a staunch defender of states' rights and a literal interpretation of the Constitution, voting against more New Deal measures than any other justice; died in Washington, D.C., on August 24, 1946. **References:** Arthur S. Link, *Woodrow Wilson and the Progressive Era, 1910–1917* (1954) and *Woodrow Wilson: The New Freedom* (1965); Leon H. Canfield, *The Presidency of Woodrow Wilson* (1966).

MEESE, Edwin, III

Born in Oakland, Calif., December 2, 1931; son of Edwin Jr., treasurer and tax collector for Alameda County, and Leone Meese; Lutheran; married Ursula Herrick on September 6, 1959; father of Dana Lynne and Michael James; attended Oakland High School; B.A., Yale University, 1953; LL.B., Boalt Law School, University of California, Berkeley, 1958; lieutenant in military intelligence, U.S. Army; deputy district attorney, Alameda County, Calif., 1959–1967, where he supervised the arrests of hundreds of protesters in Berkeley in 1964 and opposed the Black Panther Party; secretary of legal affairs to California Governor Ronald Reagan, 1967–1969; executive assistant and chief of staff for Governor Reagan, 1969–1975; vice-president, Rohr Industries, Chula Vista, Calif., 1975–1976; sole legal practice, 1976–1980; founder, director, and professor of law, Center for Criminal Justice Policy and Management, University of San Diego Law School, 1977–1981; member, Ronald Reagan–George Bush Committee, 1980–1981, on Reagan's staff as a political adviser; counselor to President Reagan, 1981–1985; director of transition for President Reagan, 1981–1985; appointed ATTORNEY GENERAL by President Reagan and served from February 25, 1985, until he resigned on August 12, 1988; throughout the Reagan presidency, Meese served as spokesman for "law and order" policies; a Justice Department investigation found him guilty in January 1989 of violations of ethics rules for his involvement with the scandal-wracked Wedtech Corporation; though never charged with any crime, Meese was under three separate investigations while attorney general, and his reputation suffered greatly from the allegations of bribery, influence peddling, and involvement in a cover-up of the Iran-Contra affair; distinguished fellow, Heritage Foundation, Washington; fellow, Hoover Institution; recipient of honorary degrees from University of Delaware Law School, Widener University, University of San Diego, Valparaiso University, and California Lutheran College; vice-president of the First Lutheran Church in El Cajon, Calif.; author of *With Reagan: The Inside Story* (1992). **References:** *Current Biography Yearbook 1981; Who's Who, 1987; U.S. News & World Report* (January 30, 1989); *The New Republic* (September 10, 1990); James Traub, *Too Good to Be True* (1990); *National Review* (September 14, 1992); Douglas W. Kmiec, *The Attorney General's Lawyer: Inside the Meese Justice Department* (1992); Lawrence E. Walsh, *Firewall: The Iran-Contra Conspiracy and Cover-up* (1997).

MEIGS, Return Jonathan, Jr.

Born in Middletown, Conn., November 17, 1764; son of Return Jonathan Meigs, soldier and pioneer, and Joanna (Winborn) Meigs; married Sophia Wright in 1788; father of Mary; graduated Yale College in 1785; studied law, was admitted to the Ohio bar in 1788, and moved to Marietta, Ohio (then Northwest Territory), to practice law; fought in Indian wars of that area; appointed one of judges of territorial government, 1798; elected representative of Marietta region in territorial legislature, 1799; supported statehood in 1801; appointed chief justice of supreme court of new state of Ohio, 1803, and served until his resignation in October 1804; appointed commander of U.S. troops in St. Charles district of Louisiana, brevetted colonel, and served, 1804–1806; judge of supreme court of Louisiana, 1805–1806; returned to Ohio, 1806, and called to Richmond, Va., to participate in Burr's trial; was transferred to serve as U.S. district court judge for Michigan Territory, 1807–1808; resigned to become candidate for governor of Ohio and was elected but declared ineligible due to prolonged absence from state; elected U.S. senator to fill vacancy caused by resignation of John Smith, took seat on December 12, 1808, was reelected in 1809, and served until May 1, 1810; ran for governor in 1810, elected, reelected in 1812, and served until his resignation in 1814; appointed POSTMASTER GENERAL in the cabinet of President Madison on March 17, 1814, and continued under President Monroe, serving from April 11, 1814, to June 30, 1823, resigning due to ill health; deficits and irregularities in awarding of mail contracts led to investigations by Congress in 1816 and 1821, but neither resulted in more than charges of inefficiency; returned to Marietta, Ohio, and died there on March 29, 1824; interment in Mound Cemetery. **References:** F. B. Dexter, Biographical Sketches of the Graduates of Yale College (1907); Ian Elliot, ed., *James Madison, 1751–1836: Chronology, Documents, Bibliographical Aids* (1969) and *James Monroe, 1758–1831: Chronology, Documents, Bibliographical Aids* (1969).

MELLON, Andrew William

Born in Pittsburgh, Pa., March 24, 1855; son of Thomas, a banker, lawyer, and judge, and Sarah Jane (Negley) Mellon; Presbyterian; married Nora Mary McMullen on September 12, 1900 (divorced July 1912); father of Alisa and Paul; attended Western University of Pennsylvania (now University of Pittsburgh), 1868–1872, but left without taking a degree; started and operated a lumber and building business in Mansfield, Pa., 1872–1874; joined his father's banking firm, T. Mellon and Sons, 1874, becoming owner, 1882, and president when the firm incorporated as Mellon National Bank of Pittsburgh, 1902; leading organizer and first president, Union Trust Company, Pittsburgh, 1889; one of America's premier venture capitalists and the third richest man in the United States in his time, behind John D. Rockefeller and Henry Ford; helped found the Gulf Oil Corporation, Union Steel Company, and the Aluminum Company of America and served as an officer or member of the board of directors of over 60 corporations until 1921; appointed by President Warren Harding as SECRETARY OF THE TREASURY and served from March 4, 1921, through the administrations of Presidents Coolidge and Hoover, until February 12, 1932; instituted the "Mellon Plan" of tax reform, lowering tax rates on corporate profits and high personal incomes, and reduced both the overall federal budget and the post–World War I national debt significantly; his laissez-faire economic policies helped produce the general prosperity of the 1920s but could not counter the onset of the Great Depression in the wake of the stock market crash of 1929; U.S. ambassador to the Court of St. James, Great Britain, 1932–1933; returned to Mellon National Bank, 1933, and became involved in philanthropic efforts, including helping found the National Gallery of Art, Washington, D.C., in 1937 from his personal art collection; vice-president and treasurer, Carnegie Library, Pittsburgh; director, Carnegie Institute of Technology and Pittsburgh Maternity Hospital; trustee, University of Pittsburgh; established Mellon Institute of Industrial Research, University of Pittsburgh, 1913; author of *Taxation: The People's Business* (1924); died on August 26, 1937, at Southampton, Long Island, N.Y.; interment in Allegheny Cemetery, Pittsburgh. **References:** Philip H. Love, *Andrew W. Mellon: The Man and His Work* (1929); Harvey O'Connor, *Mellon's Millions: The Biography of a Fortune* (1933); William L. Mellon and Boyden Sparkes, *Judge Mellon's Sons* (1948); Joseph Brandes, *Herbert Hoover and Economic Diplomacy* (1962); Eugene P. Trani, *The Presidency of Warren Harding* (1977); Burton Hersh, *The Mellon Family* (1978); Martin L. Fausold, *The Presidency of Herbert C. Hoover* (1985); Michael E. Parrish, *Anxious Decades: America in Prosperity and Depression, 1920–1941* (1992); Robert H. Ferrell, *The Presidency of Calvin Coolidge* (1998).

—Jeffrey Coster

MEREDITH, Edwin Thomas

Born on a farm near Avoca, Iowa, December 23, 1876; son of Thomas Oliver and Minerva Jane (Marsh) Meredith; married Edna C. Elliott on January 8, 1896;

father of Edwin Thomas Jr. and Mildred Marie; attended the country schools until he was 16 years of age and then entered the business school of Highland Park College (later Des Moines University) in 1894; worked on the *Farmer's Tribune*, a family-operated farm newspaper devoted to Populism; received the *Farmer's Tribune* from his grandfather as a wedding gift, whereupon he turned it into an organ of statewide circulation; founded *Successful Farming* in 1902, selling his interest in the *Farmer's Tribune*; purchased the *Dairy Farmer* in 1922 and founded *Fruit, Gardens and Home* (later *Better Homes and Gardens*) that same year; an avant-garde believer in truth in advertising, he promised to reimburse any of his subscribers who were defrauded by any of his advertisers, promising to expose the malefactors; initially a Republican, he later became affiliated with the Democratic Party; became the Democratic candidate for U.S. senator in 1914 and Democratic candidate for governor in 1916 but was defeated in both contests; appointed director of the Chicago Federal Reserve Bank, 1918–1920; on February 2, 1920, he became SECRETARY OF AGRICULTURE in the cabinet of President Wilson, serving until March 4, 1921; a champion of "farm relief," tariff reform, adequate military preparedness, tax reform, the World Court, and the League of Nations; director of the U.S. Chamber of Commerce, 1915–1919 and 1923–1928; died in Des Moines, Iowa, on June 17, 1928. **References:** William Diamond, *The Economic Thought of Woodrow Wilson* (1943); John Morton Blum, *Woodrow Wilson and the Politics of Morality* (1956).

MEREDITH, William Morris

Born in Philadelphia, Pa., June 8, 1799; son of William Meredith, lawyer and bank president, and Gertrude Gouverneur (Ogden) Meredith; married Catherine Keppele on June 17, 1834; received B.A. from University of Pennsylvania in 1812 at the age of 13; admitted to Philadelphia bar in December 1817 but because of youth had to wait for successful practice; associated with John Sergeant and Horace Binney; served in the state legislature from 1824 to 1828; became president of select council of Philadelphia, 1834–1849; appointed U.S. attorney for eastern district of Pennsylvania by President William H. Harrison on March 15, 1841; candidate for U.S. Senate, 1849; appointed SECRETARY OF THE TREASURY in the cabinet of President Taylor, continued under Fillmore, and served from March 8, 1849, to July 22, 1850; most important contributions were argument for protective tariff in annual report and disapproval of compromise measures of 1850; returned to practice of law in Philadelphia; joined new Opposition or People's Party in Pennsylvania; delegate to Peace Convention of 1861; made attorney general of state by Governor Curtin, 1861–1867; first president of Union League Club in Philadelphia; appointed one of counsel of United States in *Alabama* claims case; president of state constitutional convention, November 1872–June 1873; died in Philadelphia, August 17, 1873. **References:** H.R. Mueller, *The Whig Party in Pennsylvania* (1922); Homan Hamilton, *Soldier in the White House* (1966); Robert J. Rayback, *Millard Fillmore* (1959).

METCALF, Victor Howard

Born in Utica, N.Y., October 10, 1853; son of William Metcalf and Sarah P. (Howard) Metcalf; married Emily Corrine Nicholsen on April 11, 1882; father of two children; attended public schools of Utica; went to Utica Free Academy; attended Russell's Military Institute at New Haven, Conn.; entered Yale College in 1872; graduated Yale Law School, 1876; graduated from law department of Hamilton College in 1877; during college vacations studied law in offices of Francis Kernan and Horatio and John F. Seymour; admitted to practice before supreme court of Connecticut, 1876; practiced in Utica, 1877–1879; moved to Oakland, Calif., in 1879; formed law partnership with George D. Metcalf; became prominent in Republican Party councils; elected to Congress on Republican ticket, 1898, and reelected, 1900 and 1902; served on committee of ways and means, 59th and 60th Congresses; appointed SECRETARY OF COMMERCE AND LABOR in the cabinet of President Theodore Roosevelt on July 1, 1904, and served until December 17, 1906; most important contributions were reduction of $300,000 in departmental expenses in one year, catching and breaking up of operations of Japanese trespassers upon Alaskan salmon fisheries, organization of bureau of manufacturers, investigations of exclusion of Japanese students from public schools by San Francisco school board in October 1906; appointed SECRETARY OF THE NAVY by President Theodore Roosevelt on December 17, 1906, and served until December 1, 1908; most important contribution was expansion of navy regarding number of ships and men; retired to private life; died February 20, 1936; interment in Mountain View Cemetery. **References:** James F. Rhodes, *McKinley and Roosevelt Administrations 1897–1909, in History of the United States*, vol. 9 (1922); George E. Mowry, *Era of Theodore Roosevelt, 1900–1912* (1958).

MEYER, George von Lengerke

Born in Boston, Mass., June 24, 1858; son of George A. Meyer, an East India merchant, and Helen (Parker) Meyer; Episcopalian; married Marion Alice Appleton on June 25, 1885; father of Julia, Alice, and George von Lengerke Jr.; attended Nobel's School in Boston; graduated Harvard College with B.A. in 1879; received LL.D. from Harvard, 1911; entered old mercantile house of Alpheus H. Hardy and Company and remained two years; became member of firm Linder and Meyer, established as East India merchant at India Wharf, Mass., by father in 1818; elected to Boston common council and served, 1889–1890; nominated by both parties for member of board of aldermen, 1901, and elected without opposition; Republican representative to state legislature, 1892–1897, and speaker of lower house, 1894–1897; appointed ambassador to Italy by President McKinley, 1900–1905; transferred by President Theodore Roosevelt to Russia in March 1905 and served as ambassador until 1907; appointed POSTMASTER GENERAL in the cabinet of President Roosevelt on March 4, 1907, and served until March 6, 1909; most important contributions were recommendation of the establishment of postal savings banks and putting into use experimentally a service of automobile mail collection; appointed SECRETARY OF THE NAVY in the cabinet of President Taft on March 6, 1909, and served until March 1913; trustee of Provident Institution for Savings; died March 9, 1918. **References:** James F. Rhodes, *McKinley and Roosevelt Administrations, 1897–1909,* in *History of the United States,* vol. 9 (1922); George E. Mowry, *Era of Theodore Roosevelt, 1900–1912* (1958); Norman M. Wilensky, *Conservatives in the Progressive Era* (1965).

MIDDLETON, Henry

Born near Charleston, S.C., in 1717; son of Arthur Middleton, acting colonial governor, and Sarah (Armory) Middleton; married to Mary Williams in 1741 and father of five sons and seven daughters, including Arthur Middleton, Revolutionary leader and signer of the Declaration of Independence, and Thomas Middleton, Revolutionary patriot; after death of first wife, married Maria Henrietta Bull in 1762; later married Lady Mary Mackenzie in January 1776; educated at home and in England; justice of the peace, 1742–1780; member of the provincial House of Commons, 1742–1755, and speaker, 1745–1747, 1754, and 1755; commissioned officer of the horse of the provincial forces in 1743; commissioner of Indian Affairs, 1755; also commissioner of the church act, of free schools, and internal improvements; member of His Majesty's Council for South Carolina from 1755 until his resignation in 1770; member of the provincial convention in 1774; chosen as a representative of the Continental Congress in July 1774; after the resignation of Peyton Randolph, elected second PRESIDENT OF THE CONTINENTAL CONGRESS and served from October 22, 1774, to May 10, 1775; president of the South Carolina Congress and a member of the Council of Safety in 1775 and 1776; appointed, along with his son Arthur, a member of the committee to frame a temporary constitution for the state, 1776; member of the legislative council under the transition government, 1776–1778; member of the state senate, 1778–1780; large landowner and planter; died on June 13, 1784, in Charleston, S.C.; interment at the Church of St. James Parish, Berkeley County, S.C. **References:** Edward McCrady, *The History of South Carolina in the Revolution* (1902); Edmund C. Burnett, *The Continental Congress* (1964).

MIFFLIN, Thomas

Born in Philadelphia, Pa., January 10, 1744; son of John Mifflin, merchant and public official, and Elizabeth (Bagnell) Mifflin; Quaker; married to Sarah Morris on March 4, 1767; attended a Quaker school; was graduated from the University of Pennsylvania in 1760; prepared for a mercantile career in the counting house of William Coleman for four years; went to Europe, 1764, returned to the colonies, 1765, and entered business as a merchant in partnership with his brother, George; member of the American Philosophical Society, 1765–1799; member of the colonial legislature, 1772–1774; member of the Continental

Congress, 1774–1776; assisted in the recruiting and training of troops for service in the Continental Army; major and chief aide-de-camp to General Washington, July 4, 1775; major and quartermaster general of the Continental Army, 1775; colonel, 1775; brigadier general, 1776; major general, 1777–1779; appointed a member of the board of war, November 7, 1777; trustee of the University of Pennsylvania, 1778–1791; member of the State Assembly, 1778–1779; again a member of the Continental Congress, 1782–1784; elected PRESIDENT OF THE CONTINENTAL CONGRESS on November 3, 1783, and served from December 13, 1783, until June 3, 1784; speaker of the state House of Representatives, 1785–1788; delegate to the federal Constitutional Convention, 1787; elected to the supreme executive council of Pennsylvania in 1788 and served as its president, 1788–1790; president of the state constitutional convention, 1790; elected governor of Pennsylvania and served three terms, 1790–1799; again a member of the state House of Representatives in 1799 and 1800; died on January 19, 1800, in Lancaster, Pa.; interment in the front yard of Trinity Lutheran Church. **References:** William Rawle, "Sketch of the Life of Thomas Mifflin," in *Memoirs of the Historical Society of Pennsylvania*, vol. 2 (1830); E.C. Burnett, *Letters of Members of the Continental Congress* (1921–1931) and *The Continental Congress* (1964).

MILLER, (George) William

Born in Sapulpa, Okla., March 9, 1925; son of James Dick, a furniture salesman, and Hazel Deane (Orrick) Miller; married Ariadna Rogojarsky on December 22, 1946; graduated from Borger High School, 1941; attended Amarillo Junior College, 1941; B.S. in marine engineering, U.S. Coast Guard Academy, 1945; J.D., University of California School of Law, Berkeley, 1952; U.S. Coast Guard officer, Pacific area, 1945–1949; admitted to the bars of California, 1952, and New York, 1953; attorney, Cravath, Swaine, and Moore, New York, 1952–1956; assistant secretary, Textron Inc., Providence, R.I., 1956–1957, vice-president, 1957–1960, president, 1960–1964, chief operating officer, 1960–1967, chief executive officer, 1967–1978; chairman, Federal Reserve Board, Washington, 1978–1979; appointed by President Carter as SECRETARY OF THE TREASURY and served from August 7, 1979, until the end of Carter's term on January 20, 1981; remained treasury secretary despite a Securities and Exchange Commission investigation that alleged that Miller knew of improper payments from his company to officials at the Department of Defense during his time as chairman of Textron; chairman, G. William Miller and Company, Inc., Washington, 1981– ; chairman and chief executive officer, Federated Department Stores, Inc., 1990–1992; chairman of the board, Waccamaw Corporation, 1995– ; vice-president and director, Agricole; president and director, TAG USA; member, board of directors, Repligen Corporation, GS Industries, Kleinwort Benson Australian Income Fund, Simon Property Group; past chairman, advisory council, President's Committee on Equal Employment Opportunity, 1963–1965;

member and consultant, National Foundation for the Humanities, 1966–1967; former member, board of directors, U.S. Coast Guard Academy, 1969–1978, president, 1973–1977, chairman, 1977–1978; chairman, U.S. Industrial Payroll Savings Bond Committee, 1977, President's Committee to HIRE, 1977; co chairman, Polish-U.S. Economic Council, 1977–1978, U.S.-USSR Trade and Economic Council, 1977–1978, President's Cir. NAS, 1989–1992, board of directors, H. John Heinz III Center for Science, Economics and the Environment, 2000, HomePlace of America, Inc., 1995–2000; campaign committee chairman for the reelection of U.S. Senator Claiborne Pell, 1966; Rhode Island delegate to the Democratic National Convention and national chairman of Businessmen for Hubert Humphrey–Edmund Muskie, 1968; chairman, Supervising Committee, Schroder Venture Trust, 1983– ; trustee, Marine Biological Laboratory, Woods Hole, Mass.; fellow, University of California, Berkeley; recipient of honorary degrees from Babson College, Boston University, Brown University, Bryant College, Fairfield University, Florida State University, Rhode Island University; member, board of directors, Washington Opera; member, State Bar of California, National Alliance of Businessmen (board of directors, 1968–1978, chairman, 1977–1978), Conference Board (trustee, 1972–1978, chairman, 1977–1978), Business Council, Phi Delta Phi. **References:** *Current Biography Yearbook 1979; Time* (February 11 and March 24, 1980); *Who's Who in America, 2000.*

MILLER, William Henry Harrison

Born in Augusta, N.Y., September 6, 1840; son of Curtis Miller, farmer, and Lucy (Duncan) Miller; married Gertrude A. Bunce in December 1863; father of Florence, Jessie, Samuel, and four other children; raised on father's farm; attended county schools; studied at Whitestown Seminary; graduated Hamilton College, Clinton, N.Y., in 1861; taught school in Maumee, Ohio; joined 84th Ohio Infantry in May 1862 and mustered out in September 1862 as second lieutenant; studied law with Morrison R. Waite in Toledo, Ohio; read law in Peru, Ind., while employed as superintendent of schools; admitted to the bar in 1865 and commenced practice; became county school examiner; moved to Fort Wayne and opened practice in partnership with William H. Coombs, 1866; went into law partnership with Benjamin Harrison and Hines at Indianapolis in 1874; received LL.D. from Hamilton College, 1889; was personal adviser to Harrison; appointed ATTORNEY GENERAL in the cabinet of President Harrison and served from March 5, 1889, to March 5, 1893; most important contributions were investigation of candidates for federal judicial positions, personal attention given to cases involving antilottery laws, Interstate Commerce Act, Sherman Antitrust Act, and constitutionality of McKinley tariff; practiced law in firm of Miller, Winter and Elam until 1910; died in Indianapolis on May 25, 1917. **Reference:** H.J. Sievers, ed., *Benjamin Harrison, 1833–1901: Chronology, Documents, Bibliographical Aids* (1969).

MILLS, Ogden Livingston

Born in Newport, R.I., August 23, 1884; son of Ogden and Ruth T. (Livingston) Mills; Episcopalian; married Margaret Stuyvesant Rutherford on September 20, 1911, the marriage ending in divorce in 1919; married Mrs. Dorothy (Randolph) Fell on September 2, 1924; no children from either marriage; after attending the Browning School in New York City, he entered Harvard University, graduating in 1904; entered Harvard Law School, graduating in 1907; admitted to the bar in 1908, commencing the practice of his profession in New York City; unsuccessful candidate for election to 63d Congress in 1912; delegate to the Republican National Conventions at Chicago in 1912, 1916, and 1920; elected to the New York State Senate from 1914 to 1917, when he resigned to enlist in the U.S. Army; served with the rank of captain until the close of hostilities; president of the New York Tax Association; elected to U.S. House of Representatives on the Republican ticket to the 67th, 68th, and 69th Congresses, serving in all from March 4, 1921, to March 3, 1927; unsuccessful candidate for the governorship of New York in 1926; appointed undersecretary of the treasury by President Coolidge on February 1, 1927, serving from March 4, 1927, until February 11, 1932; invited to join President Hoover's cabinet as SECRETARY OF THE TREASURY on February 12, 1932, serving until March 3, 1933; engaged as an author and a lecturer following his political career; authored *What of Tomorrow?* (1935), *Liberalism Fights On* (1936), and *The Seventeen Million* (1937); died in New York City on October 11, 1937; interment in St. James Churchyard, Staatsburg, N.Y. **References:** Eugene Lyons, *Our Unknown Ex-President: A Portrait of Herbert Hoover* (1948); Dorothy Horton McGee, *Herbert Hoover: Engineer, Humanitarian, Statesman* (1965).

MINETA, Norman Yoshio

Born in San Jose, Calif., November 12, 1931; son of Japanese immigrants Kay Kunisaku, an independent insurance agent, and Kane (Watanabe) Mineta; Methodist; married Danealia Darlene Hill ("Deni"); father of David K. and Stuart S. Mineta; stepfather of Robert M. and Mark Brantner; during World War II, he and his family were forced into an interment camp for Japanese Americans at Heart Mountain, Wyo.; graduated from San Jose High School, 1949; B.S., in business, University of California, Berkeley, 1953; intelligence officer, U.S. Army, Korea and Japan, 1953–1956; served to major, U.S. Army Reverse, 1956–1966; agent and broker, Mineta Insurance Agency, San Jose, 1956–1992; member, San Jose City Council, 1967–1971; vice-mayor, City of San Jose, 1969–1971, and mayor, 1971–1974, the first Asian Pacific American mayor of a major U.S. city; member, U.S. House of Representatives from 13th (now 15th) California district, 1975–1995; chairman, House Public Works and Transportation Committee, 1993–1995, ranking minority member, 1995; chairman, subcommittee on aviation, 1981–1988, surface transportation subcommittee, 1989–1991; in Congress, served as a deputy Democratic whip, was instrumental in supervising airline industry deregulation in the 1980s, was coauthor of the Intermodal Surface Transportation Efficiency Act of 1991, which shifted considerable public decision making on transportation infrastructure to state and local government and increased government funding for alternative and mass transit, and was largely responsible for Civil Liberties Act of 1988, the federal government's official apology and program of reparations for the Japanese American internment during World War II; senior vice-president and managing director of transportation systems and services, Lockheed Martin IMS, Bethesda, Md., 1995–1998, and vice-president, transportation business development, 1998–2000; appointed SECRETARY OF COMMERCE by President Clinton, serving from July 22, 2000, until the end of Clinton's term on January 20, 2001, becoming the first Asian Pacific American to hold a U.S. cabinet post; appointed SECRETARY OF TRANSPORTATION by President George W. Bush, taking office on January 25, 2001, as the only Democrat in a Republican administration; faced challenge of increasing security at U.S. airports and helping the declining fortunes of airline industries following the terrorist attacks on the World Trade Center and the Pentagon on September 11, 2001; former precinct chairman, Community Theater Bond Issue, 1964; secretary, Santa Clara County grand jury, 1964; member, board of directors, Wesley Foundation, San Jose State College, 1956–1958, Pacific Neighbors Community Council Center of Santa Clara County, Japan Society, San Francisco, National Conference of Christians and Jews, Santa Clara County chapter, Mexican American Community Services Agency; member, executive board, Northern California–Western Nevada district council, Japanese American Citizens League, 1960–1962, and president, San Jose chapter, 1957–1959; member, board of regents, Smithsonian Institution, 1979–1995, and Santa Clara University; former chairman, finance committee, Santa Clara County Council of Churches, 1960–1962, Smithsonian visiting committee for Freer Gallery, 1981–1995, National Civil Aviation Review ("Mineta") Commission, 1997; former member, Smithsonian National Board, 1996, advisory committee, President's Commission on Asian American and Pacific Islanders; former member, Greater San Jose Chamber of Commerce, the National and California Associations of Industrial Insurance Agents, San Jose Association of Independent Insurance Agents (director, 1960–1962), San Jose Human Relations Commission, 1962–1964, San Jose Housing Authority, 1966, advisory board, Bank of Tokyo in California, 1961–1975, North San Jose Optimists Club (president, 1956–1958), Jackson-Taylor Business and Professional Association (director, 1963), advisory committee, President's Commission on Critical Infrastructure Protection, 1997, Metropolitan Washington Airports Authority Board of Review, 1987–1995 (as chairman) and 2000, board of directors, Intelligent Transportation Society of America; cofounder and first chairman, Congressional Asian Pacific American caucus; former member, Democratic Congressional Campaign Committee, Santa Clara County United Democratic Committee, Democratic Central Committee, Santa Cruz County,

Democratic State Central Committee, California; former cochair, Dukakis for President Committee, 1988; recipient, Aviation Achievement award, Aero Club of Washington, 1985, Industry Public Service award, Air Transport World, 1987, Joseph P. Hartranft, Jr., "Doc Award," Aircraft Owners and Pilots Association, 1987, Award for Extraordinary Service, Federal Aviation Administration, 1989, Distinguished Service award, American Public Transit Association, 1993, Martin Luther King, Jr., Commemorative medal for contributions in the field of civil rights, George Washington University, 1995, Distinguished Service Medal, National Aeronautics and Space Administration, 1996, Hubert H. Humphrey award, Leadership Conference on Civil Rights, 1996, Public Service award, American Institute of Aeronautics and Astronautics, 1996, Glen A. Gilbert Memorial award, Air Traffic Control Association, 1996, and honorary degrees from Santa Clara University, 1989, and Rust College, 1993; honorary chairman, Americans for Democratic Action; honored as namesake of the Norman Y. Mineta International Institute for Surface Transportation Policy Studies, San Jose State University. **References:** *Business Journal* (May 2, 1994); *Newsweek* (March 8, 1999); *Who's Who in America, 2000; Washington Post* (January 4, 2001).

—Jeffrey Coster

MITCHELL, James Paul

Born in Elizabeth, N.J., November 12, 1900; son of Peter J. and Anna C. (Driscoll) Mitchell; Roman Catholic; married Isabelle Nulton on January 22, 1923; father of Elizabeth; attended St. Patrick's parochial school and Batten High School in Elizabeth, from which he graduated in 1917; worked in a grocery store and then opened a store of his own in Rahway, N.J.; became an expediter in the Western Electric Co. plant at Kearny, N.J., in 1926; assisted the New Jersey Relief Administration in directing the relief and work activities of Union County, 1931; took charge of labor relations in the New York City division of the Works Program Administration, 1936; director of industrial personnel for the War Department, 1941; member of the National Building Trades Stabilization Board; alternate for the undersecretary of war in the War Manpower Commission; director of personnel and industrial relations for R.H. Macy and Co. of New York City, 1945; vice-president in charge of labor relations and operations at Bloomingdale Brothers, New York City, in 1947; served on the personnel advisory board of the Hoover Commission on the organization of the executive branch of the government in 1948; chairman of the executive committee of the Retail Labor Standards Association of New York; designated assistant secretary of the army in charge of manpower and reserve forces affairs, July 1953; joined the Eisenhower cabinet as SECRETARY OF LABOR on January 20, 1954, serving until the termination of that administration on January 20, 1961; during his incumbency, he established the new career service position of deputy undersecretary of labor and three positions of deputy assistant secretary of labor, also adding an office of research and development to the department; he was the first secretary to determine prevailing minimum wages for the soft coal industry and later for other industries, under the provisions of the Walsh-Healey Act; died on October 19, 1964. **References:** Emmett John Hughes, *The Ordeal of Power: A Political Memoir of the Eisenhower Years* (1963); Arthur Larson, *Eisenhower: The President Nobody Knew* (1968).

MITCHELL, John Newton

Born in Detroit, Mich., September 15, 1913; son of Joseph Charles, businessman, and Margaret Agnes (McMahon) Mitchell; Presbyterian; married Elizabeth Katherine Shine (divorced 1957); married Martha (Beall) Jennings on December 30, 1957 (separated 1973); father of John Newton III and Jill Elizabeth Mitchell Reed by his first wife, and Martha by his second wife; raised on Long Island, N.Y., and graduated from Jamaica High School, Queens, N.Y., 1931; attended Fordham University, 1932–1934; LL.B., Fordham Law School, 1938; admitted to the New York state bar, 1938 (disbarred 1975); postgraduate study, St. John's University Law School, 1938–1939; served with U.S. Navy as torpedo boat squadron commander in the Pacific, 1943–1946; associate, Caldwell and Raymond, New York, 1938–1942; partner, Caldwell, Trimble, and Mitchell, 1942–1966; after a merger with the firm of former vice-president Richard Nixon, became partner, Nixon, Mudge, Rose, Guthrie, Alexander, and Mitchell, 1967–1968; campaign manager, Nixon for President, 1968; appointed ATTORNEY GENERAL by President Nixon and served from January 21, 1969, until resigning effective March 1, 1972, to serve as chairman of the Committee to Re-elect the President, Nixon's reelection campaign, 1972; the architect of Nixon's "law and order" campaign themes and an advocate of strong federal law enforcement powers, he sought the expansion of wiretapping authority and preventive detention and often prosecuted protestors; convicted of conspiracy, obstruction of justice, and perjury for his role in the Watergate affair coverup, 1975, and served 19 months in prison, 1977–1979; returned to private life as a business consultant; former member, American Bar Association; died on November 9, 1988, in Washington. **References:** *U.S. News & World Report* (December 23, 1968; July 28, 1969); *New York Times Magazine* (August 10, 1969); Winzola McLendon, *Martha: The Life of Martha Mitchell* (1979); John J. Sirica, *To Set the Record Straight* (1979); *New York Times* (November 10, 1988); Stanley I. Kutler, *The Wars of Watergate: The Last Crisis of Richard Nixon* (1992) and *Abuse of Power: The New Nixon Tapes* (1998); Melvin Small, *The Presidency of Richard Nixon* (1999); Richard Reeves, *President Nixon: Alone in the White House* (2001).

MITCHELL, William DeWitt

Born at Winona, Minn., September 9, 1874; son of William Mitchell, jurist, and Frances (Merritt) Mitchell; Presbyterian; married to Gertrude Bancroft on June

27, 1901; father of William and Bancroft; attended the Lawrenceville School, N.J.; studied electrical engineering at the Sheffield Scientific School of Yale University for two years; attended the University of Minnesota and was graduated in 1895; studied law and received his degree from the University of Minnesota in 1896; admitted to the bar and began practice with the firm of Stringer and Seymour; second lieutenant in the 15th Minnesota Volunteer Infantry during the Spanish-American War, also acting judge advocate for the 2d U.S. Army Corps, 1898, engineer officer, 1899, and captain and adjutant in the Minnesota National Guard, 1899–1901; resumed law practice in St. Paul and became partner in the firm of Butler, Mitchell, and Doherty; colonel in the Minnesota infantry during World War I; regional counsel for the U.S. Railroad Administration, 1919; resumed law practice and became head of the firm of Mitchell, Doherty, Rumble, Bunn, and Butler, 1922; appointed solicitor general on June 4, 1925, by President Coolidge; appointed ATTORNEY GENERAL in the cabinet of President Hoover on March 5, 1929; most important contributions were successfully arguing before the U.S. Supreme Court his contentions that the Jay Treaty of 1794 was abrogated by the War of 1812 and that in the case of a presidential "pocket veto" the bill in question does not become law, and supervising Prohibition legislation; served until the end of the Hoover administration, March 3, 1933; joined the New York law firm of Taylor, Capron, and Marsh, April 1933; headed the court cases against Germany in the Black Tom and Kingsland sabotage cases, 1939; special prosecutor in the federal grand jury investigation of publication of alleged confidential navy information; appointed chief counsel for the congressional Pearl Harbor investigating committee, 1945; member of a panel of jurists upholding the right of the United Nations secretary general to fire staff employees belonging to the American Communist Party, December 1952; died in Syosset, Long Island, N.Y., on August 24, 1955. **References:** Albert U. Romasco, *Poverty of Abundance: Hoover, the Nation, the Depression* (1965); Harris G. Warren, *Herbert Hoover and the Great Depression* (1967).

MONDALE, Walter Frederick

Born in Ceylon, Minn., January 5, 1928; son of Theodore Sigvaard, a minister, and Claribel Hope (Cowan) Mondale; Presbyterian; married Joan Adams, December 27, 1955; father of Theodore Adams, Eleanor Jane, and William Hall; attended public schools in Martin County and Macalester College in St. Paul, Minn.; B.A. cum laude, University of Minnesota, 1951, LL.B., 1956; served in U.S. Army as corporal, 1951–1953; admitted to the Minnesota bar, 1956; executive director, Students for Democratic Action, Washington, 1949–1950; law clerk, Minnesota Supreme Court; attorney in private practice, Minneapolis, 1956–1960; attorney general, State of Minnesota, 1960–1964; appointed as a Democrat to the U.S. Senate, December 30, 1964, to fill the vacancy caused by the resignation of Hubert H. Humphrey, elected to a full term in 1966, and reelected, 1972, serving in the Senate, 1964–1977; elected VICE-PRESIDENT OF

THE UNITED STATES on November 2, 1976, on the Democratic ticket with Jimmy Carter and served from January 20, 1977, until the end of Carter's term on January 20, 1981; was the most active vice-president up to that time and was fully briefed on all issues including being the first vice-president to be trained in how to respond in a nuclear war situation, should the president be incapacitated; he and Carter were defeated for reelection by the Republican ticket of Ronald Reagan and George H.W. Bush in 1980; attorney, Winston and Strawn, Washington, 1981–1987; unsuccessful Democratic candidate for president in 1984; partner, Dorsey and Whitney, Minneapolis, 1987–1993, 1996– ; U.S. ambassador to Japan, 1993–1996; member, board of directors, Northwest Airlines, Mayo Foundation, CAN Financial Group, Interra Financial, 1997– ; active in Democratic-Farmer-Labor politics in Minnesota, including on Humphrey's campaigns for mayor of Minneapolis, 1947, and for U.S. Senate, 1948, and as manager for Orville Freeman's gubernatorial reelection campaigns, 1956 and 1958; member, President's Consumer Advisory Council, 1960–1964; member, credentials committee, Democratic National Convention, 1964; former regent, Smithsonian Institution; member of American, Minnesota, and Hennepin County bar associations, Minnesota Safety Council, American Association for the United Nations, American Legion, and Democratic Farm Labor Party; on editorial board of *Minnesota Law Review*, 1955–1956; author of *The Accountability of Power: Toward a Responsible Presidency* (1976). **References:** Lewis Finlay, *Mondale: Portrait of an American Politician* (1980, 1984); Jimmy Carter, *Keeping Faith* (1982); Zbigniew Brzezinski, *Power & Principle: Memoirs of the National Security Adviser, 1977–1981* (1983); Tom Schneider, *Walter Mondale: Serving All the People* (1984); Peter Goldman and Tony Fuller, *The Quest for the Presidency 1984* (1985); Jules Witcover and Jack W. Germond, *Wake Us When It's Over: Presidential Politics of 1984* (1985); Burton I. Kaufman, *The Presidency of James Earl Carter, Jr.* (1993); *Who's Who in America, 2000.*

MONROE, James

Born in Westmoreland County, Va., April 28, 1758; son of Spence, a plantation owner, and Elizabeth (Jones) Monroe; Episcopalian; married Elizabeth Kortright (1768–1830) in 1785; father of James Spence, who died in infancy, Eliza Kortright, and Maria Hester; attended the College of William and Mary, 1774–1776, 1779; studied law with Virginia Governor Thomas Jefferson, 1780; admitted to the bar in Virginia, 1786; entered 3d Virginia Regiment as a cadet, eventually promoted to captain, and was wounded at the Battle of Trenton, 1776; aide-de-camp, with rank of major, to General William Alexander (Lord Stirling), 1777–1779, including the winter at Valley Forge, 1778–1779; promoted to lieutenant colonel and made military commissioner for Virginia, 1780; member, Virginia House of Delegates, 1782, 1787–1788, and 1810–1811; member, Virginia Governor's Council, 1782–1783; delegate from Virginia, Continental Congress, 1783–1786; delegate from Virginia, Annapolis Convention, 1786; law practice, Richmond,

James Monroe (Library of Congress)

1786–1787, 1789–1790; delegate, Virginia state convention to ratify the federal Constitution, 1788; originally an opponent of the U.S. Constitution because of its lack of a bill of rights; defeated by James Madison in election for U.S. representative to the 1st Congress, 1788; member from Virginia, U.S. Senate, 1790–1794; appointed by President Washington as U.S. minister to France, 1794–1796, but resigned over the apparent anti-French intentions of the Jay Treaty with Britain; Democratic-Republican governor of Virginia, 1799–1802 and January–April 1811; appointed by President Jefferson as envoy to France, 1803, to negotiate the purchase of New Orleans and eventually the Louisiana Territory; U.S. minister to Great Britain and envoy to Spain, 1803–1806; commissioner to Great Britain, 1806; appointed by President Madison as SECRETARY OF STATE and served from April 6, 1811, until September 30, 1814, and again from February 28, 1815, until March 3, 1817, the two stints separated by his appointment as SECRETARY OF WAR, where he served from October 1, 1814, until February 28, 1815; protested the British Navy's impressment of American sailors and supported, and for a time directed, the U.S. effort in the War of 1812; nominated for president by the Democratic-Republican Party in 1816, he won 183 electoral votes to defeat Federalist challenger Rufus King and became the fifth PRESIDENT OF THE UNITED STATES; inaugurated on March 4, 1817, he won reelection in 1820 with 231 of a possible 232 electoral votes and served for two full terms until March 4, 1825; inherited the nationalistic post–War of 1812 political climate known as the "Era of Good Feelings," but during his administration the sectional conflict over slavery arose, leading to the Missouri Compromise of 1820; aided by the diplomatic efforts of Secretary of State John Quincy Adams, he issued the Monroe Doctrine in 1823, warning Europe that the Western Hemisphere and the newly emerging independent countries in Latin America were off limits to further colonization; author of *A View of the Conduct of the Executive, in the Foreign Affairs of the United States* (1797); member, board of visitors, University of Virginia, 1828–1830; presiding officer, Virginia State Constitutional Convention, 1829; died on July 4, 1831, at his home in New York City; originally interred in Marble Cemetery, New York City; reinterred in 1858 in Hollywood Cemetery, Richmond, Va. **References:** George Dangerfield, *The Era of Good Feelings*

(1952); Stuart Gerry Brown, ed., *The Autobiography of James Monroe* (1959); Harry Ammon, *James Monroe: The Quest for National Identity* (1971, 1990); Ernest R. May, *The Making of the Monroe Doctrine* (1975); Robert Allen Rutland, *The Presidency of James Madison* (1990); Charles Seller, *The Market Revolution: Jacksonian America, 1815–1846* (1991); Noble E. Cunningham, *The Presidency of James Monroe* (1996).

—Jeffrey Coster

MOODY, William Henry

Born on a farm at Newbury, Mass., December 23, 1853; son of Henry L. and Melissa Augusta (Emerson) Moody; unmarried; graduated Phillips Andover Academy, 1872; received B.A. from Harvard College in 1876; studied law in office of Richard H. Dana of Boston; admitted to bar, 1878, and began practice in Haverhill; city solicitor, 1888–1890; elected U.S. district attorney for eastern district of Massachusetts in 1890 and served until 1895; elected to the 54th Congress and reelected in 1896, 1898, and 1900, serving in all from 1895 to 1902; appointed SECRETARY OF THE NAVY in the cabinet of President Theodore Roosevelt on May 1, 1902, and served until June 30, 1904; most important contributions were establishment of naval bases at Guantanamo, Cuba, and at Subic Bay in the Philippines, and establishment of first joint army and navy board to simplify and harmonize work; appointed ATTORNEY GENERAL by President Roosevelt on July 1, 1904, and served until December 16, 1906; most important contributions were securement of decision from U.S. Supreme Court to the effect that officers of a corporation cannot refuse to testify on a plea that they may incriminate the corporation nor withhold books and papers in proper legal proceedings, broke up "peonage," and instituted famous suit against the government by Standard Oil Company in 1906; became associate justice of the Supreme Court on December 17, 1906, and served until ill health forced his resignation on November 20, 1910; retired to Haverhill, Mass., where he died on July 2, 1917. **References:** George Whitelock, in *Green Bag* (June 1909); Theodore Roosevelt, in *Outlook* (November 5, 1910); James F. Rhodes, *McKinley and Roosevelt Administrations, 1897–1909*, in *History of the United States*, vol. 9 (1922); George E. Mowry, *Era of Theodore Roosevelt, 1900–1912* (1958).

MORGENTHAU, Henry, Jr.

Born in New York, N.Y., on May 11, 1891; son of Henry Morgenthau, ambassador to Turkey, and Josephine (Sykes) Morgenthau; Jewish; married Elinor Fatman on April 17, 1916; father of Henry, Robert, and Joan; married Marcelle Puthon on November 21, 1951; attended private schools; went to Exeter Academy; studied at Cornell University, 1909–1910, and 1912–1913; served in World War I as lieutenant in U.S. Navy; received LL.D. from Temple University in 1938; published *American Agriculturalist*, 1922–1933; chairman of Governor Roosevelt's Agricultural Advisory Commission, 1929; member, then chairman, of Taconic State Park Commission, 1929–1931; member of New York State Conservation Commission, 1931; member of Washington Farm Board; headed Farm Credit Administration in 1933; chosen acting secretary of the treasury in 1933; was undersecretary of the treasury in 1934; Secretary of the treasury *ad interim* from January 1, 1934, to January 8, 1934; appointed SECRETARY OF THE TREASURY in the cabinet of President Franklin Roosevelt on January 8, 1934, continued under Truman, and served until July 17, 1945; most important contributions were plan to transform Germany from an industrial power to an agricultural country, defense of dollar devaluation against competitive devaluation of foreign nations, and buying and selling foreign money to obtain monetary stabilization; general chairman of United Jewish Appeal, 1947–1950; member of American Financial and Development Corps for Israel from 1951 to 1954; died on February 6, 1967. **References:** John M. Blum, *From the Diaries of Henry Morgenthau, Jr.*, 3 vols. (1959–1967); H. F. Bremer, ed., *Franklin D. Roosevelt, 1882–1954: Chronology, Documents, Bibliographical Aids* (1969).

MORRILL, Lot Myrick

Born in Belgrade, Me., May 3, 1812; son of Peaslee and Nancy (Macomber) Morrill; Methodist; married Charlotte Holland Vance in 1845; father of four daughters; after attending the local schools and nearby academy, he taught school in order to obtain the tuition to attend Waterville (now Colby) College, 1830–1831; studied law in Readfield, Me.; admitted to the bar in 1839; moved to Augusta in 1841; became chairman of the state Democratic committee in 1849, retaining that office until 1856; elected to the Maine House of Representatives in 1854; elected to the state senate in 1856 and elected president of that body by the Democratic majority; converted to the Republican Party in 1856; elected Republican governor in 1858, 1859, and 1860; by appointment of the state legislature, he was sent to the U.S. Senate to succeed Hannibal Hamlin; popularly reelected to the Senate, he served from 1861 to 1869; member of the Peace Convention of 1861; led the debate that resulted in the act emancipating the slaves in the District of Columbia; advocate of an act giving suffrage to the black residents of the District; voted for the impeachment of President Andrew Johnson; reelected to the U.S. Senate in 1869, he resigned on July 7, 1876, to join the cabinet of President Grant as SECRETARY OF THE TREASURY, which post he held until March 9, 1877; appointed collector of customs in Portland, Me., by President Hayes on March 13, 1877; died in Augusta, Me., January 10, 1883; interment in Forest Grove Cemetery, Augusta. **References:** Allan Nevins, *Hamilton Fish: The Inner History of the Grant Administration* (1936); William Best Hesseltine, *Ulysses S. Grant, Politician* (1953).

MORTON, Julius Sterling

Born in Adams, N.Y., April 22, 1832; son of Julius Dewey and Emeline (Sterling) Morton; Episcopalian; married Caroline Joy French on October 30, 1854; father of four sons, one of whom, Paul, was secretary of the navy under Theodore Roosevelt; attended the University of Michigan, 1852–1853, and was expelled for his independence of constituted authorities; received B.A. from Union College in Schenectady, N.Y., in 1856; moved to Nebraska in 1854 and became editor of the *Nebraska City News*; member of Nebraska territorial legislature in the 2d Assembly, 1855–1856, and in the 4th Assembly, 1857–1858; served as acting governor; ran two times for territorial delegate to Congress; was four times Democratic nominee for governor; Nebraska legislature delegated April 22, his birthday, Arbor Day, for the purpose of encouraging tree planting; appointed SECRETARY OF AGRICULTURE in the cabinet of President Cleveland on March 6, 1893, and served in that office until March 4, 1897; most important contributions were emphasis on economy and temporary elimination of free distribution of seeds by congressmen as waste of money; undertook editorship of *The Illustrated History of Nebraska* in 1897; began publication of the *Conservative*, 1898; died in Lake Forest, Ill., April 27, 1902. **References:** J.M. Woolworth, *In Memory of Caroline Joy French Morton* (1882); R.W. Furnas, *Arbor Day* (1888); Henry J. Ford, *Cleveland Era* (1921); Margaret Leech, *In the Days of McKinley* (1959).

MORTON, Levi Parsons

Born in Shoreham, Vt., May 16, 1824; son of the Rev. Daniel Oliver and Lucretia (Parsons) Morton; Episcopalian; married Lucy Young Kimball on October 15, 1856; father of three children; attended public schools; studied at Shoreham Academy; was clerk in general store in Enfield, Mass., from 1838 to 1840; taught school in Boscawen, N.H., 1840 to 1841; pursued mercantile interests in Hanover, N.H., 1845; moved to Boston in 1850; dealt in dry goods in New York City in 1854; became head of Morton, Grinnell and Company on January 1, 1855; banker in New York City firm of Drexel, Morgan and Company in 1870; unsuccessful candidate for Congress in 1876; chosen commissioner to Paris Exposition in 1878; elected to U.S. House of Representatives in 1878, reelected 1880, and served from March 4, 1879, to March 21, 1881; made U.S. minister to France, August 5, 1881, to May 14, 1885; elected VICE-PRESIDENT in the administration of President Benjamin Harrison and served from March 4, 1889, to March 3, 1893; governor of New York, 1895–1897; founded Morton Trust Company in 1899; joined Guaranty Trust Company in 1909; traveled; died in Rhinebeck, N.Y., on May 16, 1920; interment in Rhinebeck Cemetery. **References:** J.G. Leach, *Memoranda Relating to the Ancestry and Family of Hon. Levi Parsons Morton, Vice President of the United States, 1889–93* (1894); H.J. Sievers, ed., *Benjamin Harrison, 1833–1901: Chronology, Documents, Bibliographical Aids* (1969).

MORTON, Paul

Born in Detroit, Mich., May 22, 1857; son of Julius Sterling Morton, secretary of agriculture under Cleveland, and Caroline Joy (French) Morton; Episcopalian, married Charlotte Goodridge on October 13, 1880; father of Caroline and Pauline; attended public schools in Nebraska City, Nebr.; clerk in land office of Burlington and Missouri River Railroad at Burlington, Iowa, for two years; moved to Chicago, where he became clerk in general freight office of Chicago, Burlington and Quincy Railroad and by 1890 had become general freight agent; became vice-president of Colorado Fuel and Iron Co., 1890; was president of Whitebreast Fuel Co., 1890–1896; became third vice-president of Atchison, Topeka and Santa Fe Railroad in 1896 and became second vice-president in 1898; originally a Democrat, he became a Republican in 1896; appointed SECRETARY OF THE NAVY in the cabinet of President Theodore Roosevelt on July 1, 1904, and served until July 1, 1905; devoted rest of life to rehabilitation of Equitable Co.; died in New York City, February 19, 1911. **References:** *Nation* (June 3, 1904; June 22, 1905); Edwin Lefevre, "Paul Morton—Human Dynamo," *Cosmopolitan Magazine* (October 1905); Obituary, *New York Evening Post* (January 20, 1911); James F. Rhodes, *McKinley and Roosevelt Administrations, 1897–1909*, in *History of the United States*, vol. 9 (1922); George E. Mowry, *Era of Theodore Roosevelt, 1900–1912* (1958).

MORTON, Rogers Clark Ballard

Born in Louisville, Ky., September 19, 1914; son of David Cummins, physician and milling business executive, and Mary Harris (Ballard) Morton; younger brother of Thruston B. Morton, U.S. congressman and senator from Kentucky; married Anne Prather Jones on May 27, 1939; father of David and Anne; graduated from Woodbury Forest (Va.) Preparatory School, 1933; B.A. in business and political science, Yale University, 1937; attended College of Physicians and Surgeons, Columbia University, 1937–1938; rose from private to captain, U.S. Army, 1941–1945, serving in Europe; with his father's firm, Ballard and Ballard, Louisville, 1938–1941, and president, 1946–1951; after the firm was bought, he became vice-president and director, Pillsbury Company, 1951–1963; independent operator of cattle-feeding business, Easton, Md., from the early 1950s; Republican member from Maryland's First District, U.S. House of Representatives, 1963–1971; served on House Interior and Insular Affairs and Merchant Marine and Fisheries Committees, 1963–1969, Select Committee on Small Business, 1963–1969, and Ways and Means Committee, 1969–1971; chairman, Republican National Committee, 1969–1970; appointed by President Nixon as SECRETARY OF THE INTERIOR and served from January 29, 1971, into the administration of President Gerald Ford, until April 30, 1975, when he resigned after Ford appointed him to be SECRETARY OF COMMERCE, in which capacity he served from May 1, 1975, until February 2, 1976; chairman of President Ford's reelection campaign, March–August 1976, and counselor to President Ford for economic and domestic policy matters until November 1976; retired from politics and returned to his farm and custom boat-building business, 1976; manager of the congressional campaigns of his brother and of Edward T. Miller, 1960; floor manager for the presidential nomination of Richard Nixon, Republican National Convention, 1968; former director and member, executive committee, Civil Advisory Board Air Training Command of the Air Force; former director, Atlas Chemical Industries, Inc.; died on April 19, 1979, in Easton, Md. **References:** *New York Times* (December 12–15, 1970; April 20, 1979); *Current Biography Yearbook 1971*; John Robert Greene, *The Presidency of Gerald R. Ford* (1995).

MOSBACHER, Robert Adam [Sr.]

Born in Mt. Vernon, N.Y., March 11, 1927; son of Emil Mosbacher, an investor and stock trader, and Gertrude (Schwartz) Mosbacher; Presbyterian; married Jane Pennybacker (died 1970); four children—Diane, Kathryn, Robert, and Lisa Mosbacher Mears; married Sandra Gerry Smith on March 4, 1973 (divorced in 1982); married Georgette Paulsin [divorced 1998?]; attended Choate School, Wallingford, Conn., 1939–1944; received B.A. from Washington and Lee University in 1947; served a 1-year apprenticeship under his father before beginning a 30-year career as an independent gas and oil producer based in Houston, Tex.; sole proprietor, 1948–1978; chairman and chief executive officer, Mosbacher Energy Company, 1978–1989; appointed SECRETARY OF COMMERCE in the cabinet of President George H.W. Bush January 31, 1989, and served until January 15, 1992; general chairman President Bush's reelection campaign, 1992; general chairman of finance, Republican National Committee, Washington, 1992– ; president, Mosbacher Energy Corp., Houston, 1995–present; director, Texas Commerce Bancshares, Houston, New York Life Insurance Co.; board of directors, Choate School; director, Aspen Institute, Center for Strategic and International Studies; chairman, board of visitors, M.D. Anderson Hospital; director, Texas Heart Institute; former director, Enron Corp.; member, American Petroleum Institute (director, executive committee), National Petroleum Council (chairman, 1984–1985), All American Wildcatters Association (past chairman), American Association of Petroleum Landmen (past president), Woodrow Wilson International Center for Scholars; chairman, board of directors, Council of the Americas; former member, Governor's Energy Council, State of Texas; political activity as Republican Party fund-raiser since 1960s: Harris County, Tex., chairman for Nixon for President campaign, 1968; George H.W. Bush for Senate committee, 1970; Republican Party national finance chairman for Texas, 1971–1972; Texas state chairman, business and industry, for reelection of the president, 1972; member Republican finance committee, 1975–1989; national finance chairman for President Ford, 1976, and Bush for President, 1980; member, finance committee Reagan-Bush campaign, 1980; executive committee of Republican finance committee, 1987; board of directors, Republican finance committee, 1988; recipient of honorary doctor of laws, Washington and Lee University, 1984, Man of Vision award, National Society to Prevent Blindness, 1984, Distinguished Service award, Texas Mid-Continent Oil and Gas Association, 1982, Distinguished Service award, Board of Visitors, University of Texas Cancer Foundation, Recognition for Exemplary Service, National Alliance of Businessmen, 1968, Leadership and Extraordinary Service award, Boy Scouts of America, 1985, Distinguished Service to the Community award, Houston Job Fair, 1972, Distinguished Service award, Greater Houston YMCA; medal winning Olympic class sailor, including winner of the 1958 Mallory Cup as the outstanding sailor in North America. **References:** *Who's Who in America, 1996; Who's Who in the World, 1999.*

— Jeffrey Coster

MUELLER, Frederick Henry

Born in Grand Rapids, Mich., November 22, 1893; son of John Frederick and Emma Matilde (Oesterle) Mueller; Episcopalian; married Mary Darrah on November 6, 1915; father of Marcia Joan and Frederick Eugene; while still attending the public schools, he began an apprenticeship at age 13 in his father's furniture-manufacturing company; entered Michigan State University in East Lansing, graduating with a B.S. in mechanical engineering in 1914; became a partner in his father's business in 1914, advancing to general manager in 1922, and later, president, which position he held until his retirement in 1955; president of the Furniture Mutual Insurance Company from 1936 to 1946; served as president and general manager of Grand Rapids Industries, Inc., from 1941 to 1946; president of the United Hospital Fund, Inc., from 1948 to 1955 and of Butterworth Hospital from 1945 to 1955; director of the People's National Bank of Grand Rapids; named assistant secretary of commerce for domestic affairs by President Eisenhower on November 22, 1958; promoted to undersecretary of commerce in November 1958; invited to join the Eisenhower cabinet as SECRETARY OF COMMERCE on August 6, 1959, serving until January 20, 1961; member of the governing board of Michigan State University; founder of the Grand Rapids Furniture Makers Guild, serving as its president from its inception until 1941; after leaving government became a member of the boards of directors of Fruehauf Trailer Co. and Detroit Edison Co.; retired 1974; died August 31, 1976. **References:** Emmett John Hughes, *The Ordeal of Power: A Political Memoir of the Eisenhower Years* (1963); Arthur Larson, *Eisenhower: The President Nobody Knew* (1968); *New York Times* (September 2, 1976).

MURPHY, Frank

Born in Harbor Beach, Mich., April 13, 1890; son of John T. and Mary (Brennan) Murphy; Roman Catholic; bachelor; after receiving his elementary and secondary education at Harbor Beach public schools, he entered the University of Michigan at Ann Arbor, graduating in 1912; studied law at the University of Michigan, receiving his LL.B. in 1914 and was admitted to the bar that same year; pursued graduate studies at Lincoln's Inn, London, and at Trinity College, Dublin; became clerk in law office of Monaghan and Monaghan of Detroit; enlisted in the U.S. Army during World War I, serving as a first lieutenant and then as a captain of the infantry with the American Expeditionary Forces in France and with the army of occupation in Germany following the Armistice; designated chief assistant U.S. attorney of the eastern district of Michigan, 1919–1920; resumed private practice, 1920–1923; instructor in law at the University of Detroit, 1923–1927; judge of the recorder's court of Detroit, 1923–1930; elected mayor of Detroit in 1930, resigning on May 1, 1933, to accept appointment as governor general of the Philippine Islands, serving during 1935 and 1936; appointed the first U.S. high commissioner to the Philippines; elected governor of Michigan, serving from 1936 to 1938; appointed ATTORNEY GENERAL by President Franklin D. Roosevelt on January 17, 1939, serving until January 17, 1940, when he joined the U.S. Supreme Court; while attorney general, he created a Civil Liberties Unit in the Criminal Division of the Justice Department; died while still a Supreme Court justice, in Detroit, on July 19, 1949. **References:** Leonard Baker, *Back to Back: The Duel between FDR and the Supreme Court* (1967); Paul K. Conkin, *The New Deal* (1967).

MUSKIE, Edmund Sixtus

Born in Rumford, Me., March 28, 1914; son of Stephen, a tailor, and Josephine (Czarnecki) Muskie; Roman Catholic; married Jane Frances Gray on May 29, 1948; father of Stephen Oliver, Ellen Muskie Allen, Melinda Muskie Stanton, Martha, and Edmund Sixtus Jr.; graduated from Stephens High School, 1932; B.A. cum laude, Bates College, 1936, and elected to Phi Beta Kappa and became class president; LL.B., Cornell University Law School, 1939; admitted to the bars of Massachusetts, 1939, Maine, 1940, U.S. District Court, 1941, New York, 1981, U.S. Supreme Court, 1981, District of Columbia, 1981; served to lieutenant, U.S. Naval Reserve, 1942–1945; attorney in private practice, Waterville, Me., 1940–1942, 1945–1955; member, Maine House of Representatives, 1947–1951, Democratic floor leader, 1949–1951; director, Maine Office of Price Stabilization, 1951–1952; executive director, American Veterans, 1951; city solicitor, Waterville, Me., 1954–1955; governor, State of Maine, 1955–1959; Democratic member from Maine, U.S. Senate, 1959–1980, assistant majority whip, 1966–1980; member, Senate Committees on Foreign Relations, Environment, Public Works, and Governmental Affairs and subcommittees on arms control and environmental pollution; chairman, Senate Budget Committee, 1974–1980, and subcommittee on intergovernmental relations; helped draft and lead floor passage of Clean Air Act of 1963, Water Quality Act of 1965, and over $400 million in appropriations for pollution control in 1967; unsuccessful Democratic candidate for vice-president on the ticket with Hubert H. Humphrey, 1968; unsuccessful candidate for Democratic nomination for president, 1972; chairman, Senate Budget Committee, 1975–1979; resigned from U.S. Senate when appointed SECRETARY OF STATE by President Carter and served from May 8, 1980, until January 18, 1981; his most important diplomatic contribution was helping to negotiate the release of 52 American hostages being held in Iran; partner, Chadbourne and Parke, Washington, D.C., 1982–1996; named director of Nestlé infant formula panel, May 4, 1982; named to National Security Council Review Board and Tower Commission to investigate the Iran-Contra affair, 1986; former member, Special Committee on Aging, Executive Committee of National Governors' Conference, Democratic National Committee, 1952–1955, advisory commission on intergovernmental relations; former member and chairman, Democratic Senatorial Campaign Committee, Roosevelt Campobello International Park Commission; recipient, Presidential Medal of Freedom, 1981, Notre Dame Laetre Medal, 1981, Congressional Distinguished Service award, 1981, and honorary degrees from University of New Brunswick, Middlebury College, St. Anselm's College, College of William and Mary, University of Maryland, Alliance College, University of New Hampshire, Northeastern University, John Carroll University, Providence College, Boston University, Syracuse University, University of Maine, Suffolk University, Bowdoin College, Colby College, Lafayette College, University of Notre Dame, Hanover College, George Washington University, University of Buffalo, Nasson College, and Husson College; former member, bar associations of Maine, Kennebec County, Waterville, and Massachusetts, Academy of Arts and Sciences, Lions, Amvets (national executive director, 1951), Veterans of Foreign Wars, American Legion, Phi Beta Kappa, and Phi Alpha Delta; author of *Journeys* (1972); coauthor, with McGeorge Bundy, of *Presidential Promises and Performances* (1980); died on March 26, 1996, in Washington, D.C. **References:** *Current Biography Yearbook 1968*; David Nevin, *Muskie of Maine* (1972); Bernard Asbell, *The Senate Nobody Knows* (1978); *Who's Who in America, 1988; New York Times* (March 27, 1996).

N

NAGEL, Charles

Born on a farm in Colorado County, Tex., August 9, 1849; son of Dr. Hermann F. and Friedericke (Litzmann) Nagel; married first to Fannie Brandeis, on August 4, 1876, and upon her death, to Anne Shepley on May 5, 1895; father of Hildegard, Mary Shepley, Edith, Charles Jr., and Anne Dorothea; educated in a boy's boarding school and a high school in St. Louis, Mo.; studied law at Washington University and graduated in 1872; traveled to Europe, where he pursued his education, studying Roman law and political economy at the University of Berlin in Germany; returning to St. Louis in 1873, he was admitted to the bar and commenced his practice there; elected to the Missouri state legislature in 1881; elected judge of the Supreme Court of Missouri in 1893; lecturer at the St. Louis Law School from 1886 until 1910; member of the Republican National Committee from 1908 to 1912; invited to join the cabinet of President Taft as SECRETARY OF COMMERCE AND LABOR on March 5, 1909, a position he held until March 1913; president of the Boy Scouts of St. Louis in 1918; died in St. Louis, Mo., on June 5, 1940. **References:** Henry Fowler Pringle, *The Life and Times of William Howard Taft* (1930); Norman M. Wilensky, *Conservatives in the Progressive Era: The Taft Republicans of 1912* (1965).

NELSON, John

Born in Fredericktown, Md., June 1, 1794; son of Roger Nelson, brigadier general in Revolutionary army and member of Congress; never married; graduated William and Mary College in 1811; admitted to bar in 1813 and began practice in Fredericktown; held local offices; elected to U.S. Congress and served from March 4, 1821, to March 3, 1823; made chargé d'affaires to the Two Sicilies,

October 24, 1831, to October 15, 1832; appointed ATTORNEY GENERAL in the cabinet of President Tyler and served from July 1, 1843, to March 5, 1845; while attorney general, served as secretary of state *ad interim*, February 29–March 6, 1844, following the death of Secretary Upshur in the USS *Princeton* disaster; died in Baltimore, Md., on January 28, 1860; interment in Greenmount Cemetery. **References:** Hugh R. Fraser, *Democracy in the Making: The Jackson-Tyler Era* (1938); Robert Seager, *And Tyler Too* (1963).

NEW, Harry Stewart

Born in Indianapolis, Ind., December 31, 1858; son of John Chalfont New, who held several important government positions under Presidents Grant, Arthur, and W.H. Harrison, and of Melissa New; member of the Central Christian Church; married first to Kathleen Virginia Mulligan on October 18, 1888, and after her death to Catherine McLaen on August 18, 1891; attended the public schools and, in 1880, Butler University in Indianapolis; served with the *Indianapolis Journal* as reporter, editor, part owner, and publisher, 1878–1903; member of the Indiana State Senate, 1896–1900; captain and assistant adjutant general in the army during the Spanish-American War; president of Bedford Stone and Construction Co., 1903; delegate to the Republican National Conventions of 1896, 1912, 1920, and 1924; member of the Republican National Committee, 1900–1912, and served as its chairman in 1907 and 1908; elected as a Republican to the U.S. Senate and served from March 4, 1917, to March 3, 1923; member of the Committee on Military Affairs and the Committee on Foreign Relations; unsuccessful candidate for renomination in 1922; first candidate to use radio in a political campaign; appointed POSTMASTER GENERAL in the cabinet of President Harding on February 27, 1923; reappointed by President Coolidge in 1925 and served until March 4, 1929; most important contributions were expanding the airmail service by substituting private airline contracts for government-owned planes and the establishment of a government-owned and -operated postal motor service; retired from active business pursuits and resided in Washington, D.C.; U.S. commissioner to the Century of Progress Exposition in Chicago, 1933; died in Baltimore, Md., on May 9, 1937; interment in Crown Hill Cemetery, Indianapolis, Ind. **References:** Edward Elwell Whiting, *President Coolidge: A Contemporary Estimate* (1923); Francis Russell, *The Shadow of Blooming Grove: Warren G. Harding and His Times* (1968).

NEWBERRY, Truman Handy

Born in Detroit, Mich., November 5, 1864; son of John Stoughton Newberry, elected to Congress in 1878, and Helen Parmelee (Handy) Newberry; married Harriet Josephine Bornes on February 7, 1888; father of Carol B. and Phelps; attended Michigan Military Academy at Orchard Lake; went to Charlie Institute in New York City; attended Reed's School at Lakeville, Conn.; graduated Yale

University, 1885; assisted in father's business and took over Newberry interests upon his death; superintendent of construction, payment, and freight and passenger agent of Detroit, Bay City, and Alpena Railroad, 1885–1887; succeeded his father as president of Detroit Steel Spring Company, 1887–1901; director of Union Trust Company, States Savings Bank, Union Elevator Company, Detroit Steel Casting Company, Parke, Davis, and Company, the Union Station and Depot Company, and Michigan State Telephone Company; vice-president of Grave Hospital; elected estimator-at-large for Detroit, 1891; undertook formation of naval militia in 1893; first landsman, then ensign on staff of 1st Battalion of Michigan state naval brigade, 1894; promoted to lieutenant and navigating and ordinance office in 1895; became lieutenant junior grade in U.S. Navy when Michigan reserves entered war with Spain, 1898; director of Packard Motor Car Company in 1903; appointed assistant secretary of the navy by President Theodore Roosevelt in 1905; appointed SECRETARY OF THE NAVY in the cabinet of President Theodore Roosevelt on December 1, 1908, and served until March 4, 1909; most important contributions were reorganization of the department and creation of general staff; member of the U.S. Senate from Michigan, 1919–1922; died on October 3, 1945. **References:** James F. Rhodes, *McKinley and Roosevelt Administrations 1897–1909*, in *History of the United States*, vol. 9 (1922).

NILES, John Milton

Born in Poquonnock, Conn., August 20, 1787; son of Moses and Naomi (Marshall) Niles; married Sarah Robinson on June 17, 1824, and following her death, married Jane Pratt on November 26, 1845; common school education; admitted to the Hartford bar in 1817 and began practice; founded and edited the Hartford *Times* in 1817; Republican and Tolerationist; supported General Jackson; judge for Hartford County, 1821–1829; ran for state legislature in 1826; appointed postmaster of Hartford in 1829; published *The Independent Whig* (1816), *Gazatteer of Connecticut and Rhode Island* (1819), *History of the Revolution in Mexico and South America with a View of Texas* (1829); chosen by Governor Henry W. Edwards to fill the U.S. Senate vacancy of Nathan Smith in 1835, reelected and served until March 1839; ran unsuccessfully in 1833 and 1840 for the governorship of Connecticut; appointed POSTMASTER GENERAL in the cabinet of Martin Van Buren on May 25, 1840, serving until March 3, 1841; elected to a second term as senator, 1843–1849; became a horticulturist; toured Europe, 1851–1852; died in Hartford, Conn., on May 31, 1856. **Reference:** Denis Tilden Lynch, *An Epoch and a Man: Martin Van Buren and His Times* (1941).

NIXON, Richard Milhous

Born in Yorba Linda, Calif., January 9, 1913; son of Francis Anthony, small merchant and farmer, and Hannah (Milhous) Nixon; Quaker; married Thelma Catherine ("Pat") Ryan (1912–1993) on June 21, 1940; father of Patricia Nixon

Richard Nixon (Library of Congress)

Cox and Julie Nixon Eisenhower; worked in father's gas station and general store; attended public schools in Whittier, Calif.; B.A., Whittier College, 1934; J.D., Duke University Law School, 1937, graduating second in his class; admitted to bar in California (1942) and in New York (disbarred in New York after Watergate); attorney, Kroop and Bewley, 1942; partner, Kroop, Bewley, and Nixon, 1942; attorney, Office of Emergency Management, Washington, January–August 1942; lieutenant (jg), U.S. Navy, 1942–1946, serving in the Pacific, 1943–1944; Republican member for California, U.S. House of Representatives, 1947–1950; member, House Committee on Labor, Select Committee on Foreign Aid, Committee on Un-American Activities (HUAC); subcommittee chairman, HUAC, 1948–1950; gained national prominence for his investigation of Alger Hiss's communist past; U.S. senator, 1950–1953; elected VICE-PRESIDENT OF THE UNITED STATES on the Republican ticket with Dwight D. Eisenhower in 1952, inaugurated on January 20, 1953, won reelection with Eisenhower in 1956, and served until the end of their second term on January 20, 1961; overcame allegations of personal use of secret campaign funds by detailing his finances in a televised special (the "Checkers" speech), September 1952; as vice-president, chaired various domestic policy subcommittees and made overseas trips, including a goodwill tour of Latin America, 1958, and a trip to Moscow, 1959, during which he engaged Soviet Premier Nikita Khrushchev in an impromptu debate over the merits of American consumer society (the "Kitchen Debate"); Republican candidate for president, 1960, but narrowly defeated by Democrat John F. Kennedy by only 120,000 votes and 303-219 in the electoral college; of counsel, Adams, Duque and Hazeltine, 1961–1963; unsuccessful candidate for governor of California, 1962; attorney, Mudge, Stern, Baldwin, and Todd (later, Nixon, Mudge, Rose, Guthrie, Alexander and Mitchell), 1963–1964; elected the thirty-seventh PRESIDENT OF THE UNITED STATES in 1968 on the Republican ticket with running mate Spiro T. Agnew, defeating Democratic candidate Hubert H. Humphrey with 43.4 percent of the popular vote and an electoral college margin of 301-191, in a race that also featured third-party challenger George C. Wallace; took office on January 20, 1969; with Agnew, won reelection in 1972, defeating Democratic candidate

George McGovern with 60.7 percent of the popular vote and 520-17 in the electoral college; despite campaigning on a promise to end the war in Vietnam, instead initiated the "Vietnamization" policy that, while gradually diminishing U.S. troop levels in Southeast Asia, contributed to four more years of fighting and the heaviest bombing campaigns of the war before a cease-fire in January 1973; greatest foreign policy achievement as president was opening diplomatic relations with People's Republic of China, following years of secret talks by his envoy and national security adviser, Henry Kissinger, and a presidential visit to Beijing, 1972; also moved toward détente with USSR with a 1972 visit to Moscow and the signing of arms limitation agreements; domestically, imposed wage and price controls in August 1971 to combat inflation but was ultimately unable to contain sharply rising prices after the Arab oil embargo in 1973–1974; participated in a cover-up of illegal activities in his administration following the arrest, and subsequent discovery of links to the White House, of five men for burglarizing offices in Democratic National Headquarters at the Watergate Hotel complex in Washington on June 17, 1972; a congressional investigation led to indictments against many of his aides, including Attorney General and campaign manager John Mitchell, the White House chief of staff, H.R. ("Bob") Haldeman, and Nixon's domestic policy adviser, John Ehrlichman, all of whom would be convicted; after the House Judiciary Committee recommended impeachment for obstruction of justice, abuse of presidential powers, and contempt of Congress, Nixon became the first person to resign the presidency, effective August 9, 1974; President Ford granted him a full pardon on September 8, 1974, to avoid the possibility of a trial; after leaving office, Nixon turned to writing, producing multiple volumes of memoirs and perspectives on international politics, and attempting to repair his reputation; became something of an "elder statesman," advising officials on foreign policy matters; author of *Six Crises* (1962), *RN: The Memoirs of Richard Nixon* (1978), *The Real War* (1980), *Leaders* (1982) *Real Peace* (1983), *No More Viet Nams* (1985), *1999: Victory without War* (1988), *In the Arena: A Memoir of Victory, Defeat, and Renewal* (1990), *Seize the Moment: America's Challenge in a One-Superpower World* (1992), and *Beyond Peace* (1994); died on April 22, 1994, in New York City; buried alongside his wife at Richard M. Nixon Library and Birthplace, Yorba Linda. **References:** Joe McGinnis, *The Selling of the President, 1968* (1969); Stephen Ambrose, *Nixon*, 3 vols. (1987–1991); Herbert Parmet, *Richard Nixon and His America* (1990); Stanley I. Kutler, *The Wars of Watergate: The Last Crisis of Richard Nixon* (1992); *U.S. News & World Report* (May 2, 1994); *National Review* (May 16, 1994); *Forbes* (May 23, 1994); *Current Biography Yearbook 1994*; Joan Hoff, *Nixon Reconsidered* (1994); Tom Wicker, *One of Us: Richard Nixon and the American Dream* (1995); William P. Bundy, *A Tangled Web: The Making of Foreign Policy in the Nixon Presidency* (1998); Jeffrey P. Kimball, *Nixon's Vietnam War* (1998); Stanley I. Kutler, ed., *Abuse of Power: The New Nixon Tapes* (1998); Greg Mitchell, *Tricky Dick and the Pink Lady: Richard Nixon vs. Helen Gahagan Douglas—Sexual Politics and the Red Scare, 1950*

(1998); Irwin F. Gellman, *The Contender: Richard Nixon, the Congress Years, 1946–1952* (1999); Melvin Small, *The Presidency of Richard Nixon* (1999); Anthony Summers, *The Arrogance of Power: The Secret World of Richard Nixon* (2000); Larry Berman, *No Peace, No Honor: Nixon, Kissinger and Betrayal in Vietnam* (2001); Richard Reeves, *President Nixon: Alone in the White House* (2001).

NOBLE, John Willock

Born in Lancaster, Ohio, October 26, 1831; son of John and Catherine (McDill) Noble; Presbyterian; married Lisabeth Halstead, February 8, 1864; attended Cincinnati public schools and University of Ohio for three years; graduated Yale College in 1851; graduated from Cincinnati Law School in 1852; studied in the offices of Henry Stanbery; moved to St. Louis in 1855, later moving to Keokuk, Iowa; practiced law in Keokuk, 1856–1861, sharing leadership of the Iowa state bar with Samuel Freeman Miller; enlisted as a private in the 3d Iowa Cavalry of the Union army in August 1861, commissioned brigadier general in 1865 when he resigned; following service in Civil War, served as judge advocate general of the Army of the Southwest; returned to St. Louis in 1865; appointed U.S. district attorney for the eastern district of Missouri in 1867; resumed private practice in 1870; appointed SECRETARY OF THE INTERIOR in the cabinet of President Benjamin Harrison on March 5, 1889, entering upon duties on March 7, 1889, and serving until his retirement on March 6, 1893; in this office he supported the tariff act of 1890, interpreted land laws in the settlers' favor, and most important, introduced forest reserve sections in the 1891 land laws, withdrawing millions of valuable acres for national forests; upon retirement, returned to St. Louis, where he died on March 22, 1912. **Reference:** Arthur W. Dunn, *From Harrison to Harding*, 2 vols. (1922).

NORTON, Gale Ann

Born in Wichita, Kans., March 11, 1954; daughter of Dale Bentsen, an aircraft mechanic, and Anna Jacqueline (Lansdowne) Norton; Methodist; raised in Thornton, Colo.; married and divorced; married second husband John Goethe Hughes, a real estate agent, on March 26, 1990; B.A. in political science, 1975, and J.D. with honors, 1978, from University of Denver; admitted to Colorado bar, 1978, and bar of U.S. Supreme Court, 1981; active in Libertarian Party politics, *ca.* 1980; judicial clerk, Colorado Court of Appeals, Denver, 1978–1979; senior attorney, Mountain States Legal Foundation, 1979–1983; national fellow, Hoover Institute, Stanford University, 1983–1984; assistant to deputy secretary, U.S. Department of Agriculture, 1984–1985; associate solicitor, United States Department of the Interior, 1985–1987; private legal practice in Denver, 1987–1990; attorney general, state of Colorado, 1991–1999; senior counsel, Brownstein, Hyatt & Farber, 1999–2000; appointed SECRETARY OF THE INTERIOR by President George W. Bush, taking office on January 30, 2001, as the first woman to head the department; her nomination was the target of considerable opposition by environmental groups for her libertarian outlook, history of pro-development positions, and advocacy of environmental protection through free market incentives rather than government regulations, and she was approved by the Senate by a vote of 75-24; immediately created controversy for supporting President Bush's proposal to open the Arctic National Wildlife Refuge in Alaska to exploratory oil drilling as the United States faced an energy crisis; Murdock fellow, Political Economy Research Center, Bozeman, Mont., 1984; senior fellow Independent Institute, Golden, Colo., 1988–1990; policy analyst, President's Commission on Environmental Quality, Washington, 1985–1988; lecturer, University of Denver Law School, 1989; transportation law program

Secretary of the Interior Gale Norton looks at a book titled *Too Many Pumpkins* with Isleta Elementary School fifth-grader Lia Sanchez, 11, on Isleta Pueblo, N.M., May 2002. Norton visited the school to promote the Family and Child Education Program, which was developed by the Bureau of Indian Affairs in 1990. (AP/Wide World Photos)

director, University of Denver, 1978–1979; participant in Republican Leadership Program, Colorado, 1988, and Colorado Leadership Forum, 1989; former member, Western Water Policy Commission; former general counsel, Colorado Civil Justice League; former chair, National Association of Attorneys General Environment Committee; cochair, National Policy Forum Environment Council; candidate for Republican nomination for U.S. Senate, 1996; national chair, Republican Environmental Advisers; chair of environment committee, Republican National Lawyers Association, 1999–2001; named Young Career Woman, Business and Professional Women, 1981, and Young Lawyer of the Year, National Federalist Society, 1991; recipient, Mary Lathrop Trailblazer award, Colorado Women's Bar Association, 1999; founder and former head of Council of Republicans for Environmental Advocacy, 1998; member, legal policy advisory board, Washington Legal Foundation, Federalist Society, Colorado Women's Forum, Order of St. Ives. **References:** *New York Times* (December 30, 2000); *Washington Post* (January 8, 2001); *Current Biography* (June 2001).

—Jeffrey Coster

O

O'BRIEN, Lawrence Francis, Jr.

Born in Springfield, Mass., July 7, 1917; son of Lawrence F. Sr., hotel owner and real estate dealer, and Myra (Sweeney); Roman Catholic; married Elva I. Brassard, an office clerk, May 30, 1944; father of Lawrence Francis III; graduated from Springfield Cathedral High School, 1934; tended bar and was active in Hotel and Restaurant Employees Union; LL.B., Northeastern University, Boston, 1942; served as sergeant, U.S. Army, 1943–1945; worked in real estate and public relations in Springfield, 1943–1960; directed U.S. Representative Foster Furcolo's congressional campaigns of 1946 and 1948 and worked in Washington as Furcolo's administrative assistant, 1948–1950; director of organization for John F. Kennedy's senatorial campaigns of 1952 and 1958 and presidential campaign, 1959–1960, for the Massachusetts Democratic Committee, 1956–1957, and for the Democratic National Committee, 1960; special assistant to Presidents Kennedy and Johnson in charge of White House Office of Congressional Relations, 1961–1965, successfully lobbying Congress to pass the Omnibus Housing Act (1961), Manpower Development and Training Act (1962), the Mental Retardation Facilities and Community Health Centers Act (1963), and in 1965, the Elementary and Secondary Education Act, the Voting Rights Act, Medicare, and the many measures associated with Johnson's War on Poverty; appointed POSTMASTER GENERAL by President Johnson and served from November 3, 1965, to April 26, 1968; most important contribution was proposal that post office department be replaced by a nonprofit government corporation; coordinator of Senator Robert F. Kennedy's campaign for the Democratic nomination for president, 1968; chairman, Democratic National Committee, 1968–1969, 1970–1972; founder and president, O'Brien Associates, public relations and management consultant firm, 1969; president, McDonnell and Company investment bankers, New York City, 1969; on June 17, 1972, police arrested five men for breaking into O'Brien's office in the Watergate complex, thus beginning the affair that would result in President Nixon's resignation in 1974; resigned as Democratic National Committee chairman to serve as presidential candidate George McGovern's national campaign chairman for the 1972 election; chairman, Democratic National Convention, 1972; commissioner, National Basketball Association, 1975–1984, senior adviser, 1984–1987; president, International Basketball Hall of Fame, Springfield, Mass., 1985–1987, board of trustees, 1987–1989; recipient, Special Victor award, 1977, Brotherhood award, National Conference of Christians and Jews, 1977, Israeli Prime Minister's medal in distinguished service to democracy, 1978, John W. Bunn award for outstanding contributions to basketball and to Basketball Hall of Fame, 1984, and of honorary degrees from Northeastern University, 1965, Villanova University, 1966, St. Anselm's College, 1966, Seton Hall University, 1967, Loyola University, 1967, Xavier University, 1971, American International College, 1971, Wheeling College, 1971, Bryant College, 1978, Springfield College, 1982; named Sportsman of the Year, *The Sporting News*, 1976, and Man of the Year, *Basketball Weekly*, 1978; honored as the namesake of the National Basketball Association's Larry O'Brien trophy, given annually to the champion team; elected to the Basketball Hall of Fame, 1991; former member, U.S. International Sports Committee, U.S. Information Agency; author of *No Final Victories: A Life in Politics—from John F. Kennedy to Watergate* (1974); died on September 26, 1990, in New York City. **References:** Patrick Anderson, *The President's Men* (1969); *Current Biography Yearbook 1977*; Vaughn Davis Bornet, *The Presidency of Lyndon B. Johnson* (1983); *New York Times* (September 29, 1990); James N. Giglio, *The Presidency of John F. Kennedy* (1991); Irving Bernstein, *Guns or Butter: The Presidency of Lyndon Johnson* (1996); Richard Reeves, *President Nixon: Alone in the White House* (2001).

O'LEARY, Hazel (Reid) Rollins

Born in Newport News, Va., May 17, 1937; daughter of Russell E. and Hazel (Palleman) Reid, both physicians; married Carl Rollins, a physician, *ca.* 1959 (divorced in early 1970s); mother of Carl G. Rollins; married John F. O'Leary, deputy secretary of energy under President Carter, on April 24, 1980 (died December 1987); raised in Newport News, Va., and Newark, N.J.; attended Arts High School, Essex County, N.J.; B.A. cum laude in history, Fisk University, 1959; J.D., Rutgers University, 1966; admitted to the bar in New Jersey, 1967, District of Columbia, 1985; certified financial planner; assistant prosecutor, Essex County, N.J. 1967; assistant attorney general, state of New Jersey, Trenton, 1967–1968; director, Community Action Legal Workshop, Newark, 1968; attorney in general practice, Orange, N.J., 1968–1969; assistant administrator,

Essex County Legal Services, East Orange, N.J., 1969–1970; attorney in private practice, Orange, 1971; director, public sector division, Cost of Living Council, Washington, 1972–1974; director, Office of Consumer Affairs/Special Impact, Federal Energy Administration (FEA), 1974–1976; general counsel, Community Services Administration, 1976–1977; assistant administrator for conservation and environment, FEA, 1977; deputy director, Economic Regulatory Administration, U.S. Department of Energy, 1977–1979, and director, 1979–1981; principal, Coopers and Lybrand, Washington, 1979; vice-president and general counsel, John F. O'Leary Associates, Morristown, N.J., an energy consulting firm, 1981–1989; director, Applied Energy Services and NRG Energy, 1989; senior vice-president for corporate affairs,

Energy Secretary Hazel O'Leary testifies on Capitol Hill, 1996, before the Senate Energy Committee hearing on the gasoline tax. (AP/Wide World Photos)

Northern States Power Company (NSP), Minneapolis, 1989–1990; executive vice-president for corporate affairs, 1990–1992, and president, NSP Gas Division, 1993; appointed by President Clinton as SECRETARY OF ENERGY and served from January 22, 1993, until the end of Clinton's first term on January 20, 1997; the first woman, the first African American, and the first energy executive to hold the post; promoted environmentally sound clean-energy technologies; president, O'Leary and Associates, Chevy Chase, Md., 1997–2000; chief operating officer, Blaylock and Partners, New York, investment firm, 2000– ; member, advisory committee, Hubert H. Humphrey Institute of Public Affairs, 1992– ; member, Governor's Commission on Long-Term Financial Planning and Management, 1991–1992; member, executive committee, United Federal Campaign, 1976; cochair, Combined Federal Campaign, Department of Energy, 1978; cochair, State Energy Advisory Board, U.S. Department of Energy, 1992–1993; member, board of directors, Greater Minneapolis Red Cross, 1990–1993, Turning Point, Minneapolis, 1990–1991, Penumbra Theatre Company, St. Paul, 1991–1992, Catholic Charities, 1990–1991, Executive Leadership Council, 1989–1993 (also former vice-president), Minnesota Center for Corporate Responsibility, 1992–1993, Northwest Area Foundation, 1992– , Minneapolis Foundation, 1992– , YMCA, Minneapolis, 1990–1991, UAL, Inc., AES Corporation, ICF Kaiser Group International, World Wildlife Fund; member, Governor's Commission on Long Term Financial Planning and Management, Minnesota;

trustee, Orange (N.J.) YMCA, 1964, William Mitchell College of Law, 1990–1993, St. Paul Chamber Orchestra, 1989–1993, Morehouse College, 1998– , University of Minnesota Foundation, 1992– , Africare, Center for Democracy, Andrew Young Center for International Development, Keystone Center, 1979–1993, Minnesota Zoological Society, 1991–1992; recipient, Outstanding Black Female Attorney, National Bar Association, Director's Distinguished Service award, Cost of Living Council, Trumpet Award, 1997, and honorary degree from Fisk University, 1994; member, Links, 1982– (former president), Girl Friends, Inc., 1982– , Committee of 200, 1992– , Business Council for a Sustainable Energy Future, Executive Women in Government, 1976– , Phi Beta Kappa. **References:** *New York Times* (December 22, 1992; January 9, 1993); *Washington Post* (January 19, 1993); *Current Biography Yearbook 1994; Ebony* (February 1995); *Jet* (December 2, 1996); *Contemporary Black Biography; Notable Black American Women; Who's Who among African Americans, 1998–99.*

—Phil Bagley

OLNEY, Richard

Born in Oxford, Mass., September 15, 1835; son of Wilson and Eliza L. (Butler) Olney; Presbyterian; married Agnes Thomas on March 6, 1861; father of two daughters; attended Leicester Academy; graduated from Brown University in 1856; received his law degree from Harvard Law School in 1858; admitted to the bar in 1859 and entered the law office of Benjamin F. Thomas, to whose practice he succeeded; in 1873 he was elected to the Massachusetts state legislature, but after repeated defeats in attempts at reelection, he temporarily gave up politics; appointed ATTORNEY GENERAL on March 6, 1893, by President Cleveland and served until June 9, 1895; in 1894 he prevented Coxey's "revolution" from assuming greater proportions by protecting the railroads from rebel takeover; in that same summer he thwarted a strike against the railroads by taking strict action against the American Railway Union, arresting union leader Eugene V. Debs and his lieutenants; afterward, he backed the Arbitration Act of 1898; appointed SECRETARY OF STATE on June 10, 1895; his major contributions in this office included arbitration of the Venezuela–British Guiana boundary dispute, which culminated in the award of 1899, and recommendations to Spain on how a revolution in Cuba might be avoided; retired from politics on March 5, 1897, and resumed his law practice; served on the boards of many foundations; died April 8, 1917. **References:** *Who Was Who in America*; Henry James, *Richard Olney and His Public Service* (1923).

O'NEILL, Paul Henry

Born in St. Louis, Mo., December 4, 1935; son of John Paul, an army sergeant, and Gaynald Elsie (Irvin) O'Neill; Methodist; married Nancy Jo Wolfe on September 4, 1955; father of Patricia, Margaret, Julie, and Paul Henry; B.A. in economics, Fresno State College, 1960; M.A. in public administration, Indiana University, 1966; graduate study, Claremont Graduate School, 1960–1961, and George Washington University, 1962–1965; site engineer, Morrison-Knudsen, Inc., Anchorage, Ala., 1955–1957; systems analyst, U.S. Veterans Administration, Washington, 1961–1966; budget examiner, Bureau of the Budget, Washington, 1967–1969; chief of human resources program division, Office of Management and Budget, Washington, 1969–1970, assistant director, 1971–1972, associate director, 1973–1974, and deputy director, 1974–1977; vice-president of planning and finance, International Paper Company, New York, 1977–1981, senior vice-president of planning and finance, 1981–1983, senior vice-president of paperboard and packaging division, 1983–1985, president and director, 1985–1987; chief executive officer, Alcoa, Incorporated, Pittsburgh, 1987–1989, and chairman of the board, 1987–2000; the first Alcoa head chosen from outside the aluminum industry, revitalizing the company to become the best-performing stock in the Dow Jones Industrial Average in 1999; as business executive, stressed importance of efficiency, competitiveness, and improved work processes and working conditions, and his tenure at Alcoa became the subject of a case study undertaken by Harvard University's John F. Kennedy School of Government; considering his experience in public policy (including his longtime personal friendships with Federal Reserve Board chairman Alan Greenspan and Vice-President Dick Cheney) and reputation as a successful business manager as compensation for his lack of experience on Wall Street, President George W. Bush appointed him SECRETARY OF THE TREASURY, and he took office on January 20, 2001; helped draft and lobby Congress to pass Bush's centerpiece economic legislation, a $1.35 trillion tax cut over ten years, that was signed into law on June 7, 2001; in the wake of the terrorist attacks on the World Trade Center and Pentagon on September 11, 2001, he was charged with organizing an international effort to eliminate access to cash by terrorist groups and revitalizing a sluggish U.S. economy; member, board of directors, Gerald R. Ford Foundation, 1981– , Rand Corporation (former chairman), Lucent Technologies, Eastman Kodak, Manpower Demonstration Research Corporation, 1981– , and Council for Excellence, board of trustees, American Enterprise Institute and H. John Heinz Center for Science, Economics and the Environment, board of governors, National Association of Securities Dealers; chair, President's Education Policy Advisory Commission, 1989–1992; recipient, Haynes Foundation fellowship, 1960–1961, Career Education Award, 1965, and fellowship, 1966, from National Institute for Public Affairs, William A. Jump Meritorious Service award, 1971, honorary degrees, Clarkson University, 1993, Edinboro University, 1997, California University, Pennsylvania, 1998, Duquesne University, 1999, and California State University, Fresno, 1999; member, Business Council, National Academy Social Ins., Institute for International Economics, Management Executives Society, International Primary Aluminum Institute. **References:** *Washington*

Post (December 21, 2000; October 7, 2001); *Who's Who in America, 2000; Forbes* (March 19, 2001); *Current Biography* (July 2001).

—Jeffrey Coster

OSGOOD, Samuel

Born in Andover, Mass., February 3, 1748; son of Peter and Sarah Osgood; Episcopalian; married Martha Brandon, January 4, 1775; remarried to Maria Bowne Franklin, May 24, 1786; graduated Harvard, 1770, studied theology; became merchant with his brother; at outbreak of Revolution joined army as captain of a company of Minute Men; became major and aide-decamp of General Artemis Ward; delegate to Essex County Convention, 1774; served in Provincial Congress, 1775; member of Massachusetts legislature; captain at Lexington and Cambridge, Mass., in April 1775; left army in 1776 with the rank of colonel and assistant assistant commissary; member, Massachusetts board of war, 1776; delegate to Constitutional Convention of 1779; member of Massachusetts legislature until 1780 entrance to state senate, where he served until 1781; Massachusetts delegate to Continental Congress, 1781–1784; appointed director of Bank of North America by Congress, December 1, 1781; chairman of delegation to Rhode Island to secure support for Hamilton's proposed import duty, 1782; first commissioner of the United States Treasury, 1785–1789; appointed POSTMASTER GENERAL in the cabinet of President Washington, September 26, 1789, serving until his resignation on August 12, 1791; continued living in New York when the government moved to Philadelphia; served in New York legislature, 1800–1803; founder of Society for Establishment of a Free School for the Education of Poor Children, and the American Academy of Fine Arts; supervisor of New York State, 1801–1803; appointed naval officer of the port of New York, May 10, 1803, serving until his death; died August 12, 1813, in New York City; interment in Brick Presbyterian Church, New York City. **References:** J.G. Wilson, *The Memorial History of the City of New York* (1893); Ira Osgood and Eben Putnam, *A Genealogy of the Descendents of John Christopher, and William Osgood* (1894).

P

PAIGE, Roderick

Born in Monticello, Miss., June 17, 1935; son of a school principal and a librarian; Baptist; divorced; father of Rod Jr.; graduated from Lawrence County Training School; B.S., Jackson State University, 1955; M.S., 1964, and Ph.D., 1969, both in physical education, Indiana University; head football coach, Utica (Miss.) Junior College, 1955–1962, and Jackson State University, 1962–1969; assistant football coach, University of Cincinnati, 1970–1971; affiliated with Texas Southern University (TSU), 1971–1994, as head football coach, 1971–1975, athletic director and assistant professor, 1971–1984, and dean, TSU College of Education, 1984–1994; member, board of education, Houston Independent School District, 1989–1994, and superintendent of schools, 1994–2001; pushed for closer ties between business community and schools, implemented a school voucher program, a system of charter schools, and performance contracts for teachers based on private sector model; appointed SECRETARY OF EDUCATION by President George W. Bush and took office on January 20, 2001; the first African American and the first local school superintendent to serve in that post; helped create and pass the "No Child Left Behind Act," signed on January 8, 2002, a reform of federal funding and supervision of public schools; member, National Commission for Employment Policy; raised a Democrat, he joined the Republican Party in the early 1970s, largely as a result of his acquaintance with the Bush family; recipient, Brentwood Dolphins Community Service award; named one of the top two educators in America, Council of Great City Schools, 1999. **References:** *Washington Post* (December 30, 2000); *Who's Who among African Americans, 2000; Washington Times* (January 2 and 16, 2001; January 9, 2002); *Newsweek* (February 5, 2001); *Current Biography* (July 2001); *Ebony* (October 2001).

—Herbert Brewer

PALMER, Alexander Mitchell

Born at Moosehead, Pa., May 4, 1872; son of Samuel Bernard Palmer, engineer; Quaker; married on November 23, 1898, to Roberta Bartlett Dixon; father of Mary; following death of first wife, married Margaret Fallon Burrall on August 29, 1923; attended public schools and the Moravian Parochial School, Bethlehem, Pa.; graduated from Swarthmore College in 1891; appointed official stenographer of the 43d judicial district of Pennsylvania, 1892; studied law under Judge John B. Strom of Stroudsburg, Pa., and admitted to the bar in 1893; began practice at Stroudsburg; director of various banks and public service corporations; member of the Democratic state executive committee of Pennsylvania; elected as a Democrat to the 61st, 62d, and 63d Congresses, serving from March 4, 1909, to March 3, 1915; cosponsored an anti–child labor bill and served on the Ways and Means Committee; delegate to the Democratic National Convention at Baltimore in 1912 and at St. Louis in 1916; ran unsuccessfully for the Senate in 1914; member of the Democratic National Committee, 1912–1920; appointed by President Wilson as alien property custodian on October 22, 1917, and served until his resignation on March 4, 1919; appointed ATTORNEY GENERAL in the cabinet of President Wilson on March 4, 1919; most important contributions were establishment of price-fixing committees and the use of antitrust laws to help combat inflationary trends and profiteering, dissolution of the "beef trust," prosecution of alleged radicals and anarchists and deportation of many to Russia, and usage of the injunction against striking mineworkers in 1919; left office with the outgoing administration on March 4, 1921; was a leading contender for the Democratic presidential nomination in 1920; retired from public life in 1921 and resumed law practice in Stroudsburg and Washington, D.C.; delegate to the 1932 Democratic National Convention, serving on the resolutions committee; died on May 11, 1936, in Washington; interment in Laurelwood Cemetery, Stroudsburg, Pa. **References:** J.M. Blum, *Joe Tumulty and the Wilson Era* (1951); Arthur S. Link, *Woodrow Wilson: The New Freedom* (1956); Leon H. Canfield, *The Presidency of Woodrow Wilson* (1966).

PATTERSON, Robert Porter

Born in Glens Falls, N.Y., February 12, 1891; son of Charles R. and Lodice E. (Porter) Patterson; Presbyterian; married Margaret Tarleton Winchester on January 3, 1920; father of Robert Porter, Aileen W., Susan Hand, and Virginia D.; after completing his preliminary and secondary education at the local schools, he entered Union College, graduating in 1912; studied law at Harvard, graduating in 1915; admitted to the bar in 1915, commencing practice in New York City; served as a private in the 7th Regiment of the New York National Guard; became a captain and then a major during World War I, serving in the 306th Infantry Division, U.S. Army; resumed his law practice in New York following the close of hostilities; became a member of the law firm of Webb, Patterson and

Hadley from 1920 to 1930; appointed judge of the U.S. district court, southern New York district, in 1930; appointed judge of the circuit court of appeals in 1939, resigning in July 1940 to accept a presidential appointment; named assistant secretary of war by President Franklin D. Roosevelt in December 1940; named SECRETARY OF WAR by President Truman on September 26, 1945, entering upon his duties on September 27, 1945, and serving until his resignation on July 1, 1947; director of the Federal Reserve Bank of New York; president of Practicing Law Institute; trustee of Union College; president of Harvard Law School Association, 1937–1949; president of Freedom House; chairman of the Commission on Organized Crime; recipient of the Distinguished Service Medal for his exemplary service to the nation; died in Elizabeth, N.J., on January 22, 1952; interment in Arlington National Cemetery, Arlington, Va. **References:** Alfred Steinber, *The Man from Missouri: The Life and Times of Harry S. Truman* (1962); Cabell B.H. Phillips, *The Truman Presidency: The History of a Triumphant Succession* (1966).

PAULDING, James Kirke

Born in Great Nine Partners, N.Y., August 22, 1778; son of William and Catherine (Ogden) Paulding; married Gertrude Kemble, sister of Governor Kemble, in 1818; educated in country schools in Westchester County; resided in Tarrytown; acquainted with Washington Irving through his brother-in-law, William Irving, and collaborated with the author on "Salamagundi" in 1807–1808; wrote *The Diverting History of John Bull and Brother Jonathan*, a comic treatment of early U.S. history (1812), *The Lay of the Scottish Fiddle*, a parody of Scott's "Lay of the Last Minstrel" (1813), and *The Backwoodsman* (1818); *The United States and England*, written in 1815, brought him an appointment by President Madison as secretary of the Board of Naval Commissioners; wrote three documentaries; *Letters from the South by a Northern Man*, written after an 1816 Virginia tour (1817), *A Sketch of Old England* (1822), and *John Bull in America*, a satire (1825); appointed naval agent for the port of New York in 1824; resided in New York until 1837; wrote *Konigsmarke* (1823), *The Dumb Girl* (1830), *The Dutchman's Fireside* (1831), *Westward Ho!* (1832), *The Old Continental* (1846), *The Puritan and His Daughter* (1846); appointed SECRETARY OF THE NAVY in the cabinet of President Van Buren on June 25, 1838, entering upon duties July 1, 1838, and serving until March 4, 1841, when the administration ended; during his period of service he sent a South Seas exploring expedition on a four-year mission to explore the Oregon coast and Antarctica and attempted to reform the Navy Department; following his wife's death, he toured the west with Van Buren in 1842; retired to his home, "Placentia," in Hyde Park, N.Y., in 1846 and died there on April 6, 1860; interment in Greenwood Cemetery, Brooklyn, N.Y. **References:** Denis Tilden Lynch, *An Epoch and a Man: Martin Van Buren and His Times* (1929); Robert V. Remini, *Martin Van Buren and the Making of the Democratic Party* (1951).

PAYNE, Henry Clay

Born in Ashfield, Mass., November 23, 1843; son of Orrin Pierre and Eliza Etta (Ames) Payne; Methodist; married Lydia Wood Van Dyke on October 15, 1869; childless; attended local schools at Ashfield, Mass.; went to Shelburne Falls Academy; moved to Milwaukee, Wisc., and entered wholesale dry goods house of Sherwin, Nowell and Pratt, 1863; took up insurance business in 1868; organized Young Men's Republican Club and took part in Grant-Greeley campaign, 1872; chairman, Republican State Central Committee; was postmaster of Milwaukee, 1875–1885; secretary and chairman of Republican state central committee; member of Republican National Committee, 1880–1904; became vice-president of Wisconsin Telephone Company, 1886, and president, 1889; became vice-president of Milwaukee Street Railway Company in 1890, and acting president, 1892–1895; elected president of Milwaukee Northern Railroad Company, 1890–1893; president of Chicago and Calumet Terminal Railway, 1893–1894; chairman of Republican county committee of Milwaukee County; organized Milwaukee Light, Heat and Traction Company; president of Fox River Electric Company; vice-president of Milwaukee Electric Railway and Light Company, 1896; in charge of Republican western headquarters in Chicago; supported Theodore Roosevelt for vice-president; appointed POSTMASTER GENERAL in the cabinet of President Theodore Roosevelt on January 9, 1902, and served until his death on October 4, 1904; most important contributions were concluding of parcel post conventions with Japan, Germany, and other foreign countries, organization of postal service into 15 "battalions" and rural free delivery into 8, free transmission of literature for the blind through the mails; died in Washington, D.C., October 4, 1904. **References:** *Railway Age* (October 7, 1904); W.W. Wright, *Henry Clay Payne, a Life* (1907); James F. Rhodes, *McKinley and Roosevelt Administrations 1897–1909*, in *History of the United States*, vol. 9 (1922).

PAYNE, John Barton

Born in Pruntytown, Va. (now W.Va.), January 26, 1855; son of Amos Payne, physician and farmer; Trinity Methodist Episcopalian; married on October 17, 1878, to Kate Bunker; after her death, married to Jennie Byrd Bryan on May 1, 1913; attended school and studied under tutors at Orleans, Va.; became clerk in general store in Warrentown in 1870; hired as manager of a general store, freight, and express office at Thoroughfare Gap, Prince William County, Va., in 1873; later that year entered the employ of Adolphus Armstrong, clerk of county and circuit courts at Pruntytown, and studied law; admitted to the bar in 1876 and began practice in Kingswood, W.Va.; published a newspaper, the *West Virginia Argus*; served as chairman of the Preston County Democratic Committee; in 1880, appointed special judge of the circuit court of Tucker County; elected mayor of Kingswood, 1882; moved to Chicago; president of Chicago Law Institute, 1889; elected judge of the superior court of Cook County in 1893, resigning in 1898 to become a trial lawyer; president of the board of South Park Commissioners, 1911–1924; offered the position of U.S. solicitor general by President Wilson in 1913 but declined; in 1917, accepted post of arbitrator in shipbuilding strikes on West Coast; moved to Washington, D.C.; appointed general counsel of the U.S. Shipping Board Emergency Fleet Corporation in 1917 and became its chairman in 1919; appointed SECRETARY OF THE INTERIOR in the cabinet of President Wilson on February 28, 1920, serving until the end of the Wilson administration on March 4, 1921; most important contributions were development of national parks and conservation of the navy's petroleum reserves; drafted the legislation under which the government took over the railroads and served as director general of railroads from May 1920 to April 1921; appointed chairman of the American Red Cross by President Harding on October 15, 1921, and reappointed by Presidents Coolidge, Hoover, and Roosevelt; chairman of the board of governors of the League of Red Cross Societies, 1922; appointed by President Harding commissioner for furthering better relations with Mexico, 1923; died on January 24, 1935; interment in Washington, D.C. **References:** *The Book of Chicagoans* (1905, 1911); *Red Cross Courier* (March 1935); Leon H. Canfield, *The Presidency of Woodrow Wilson* (1966).

PEÑA, Federico Fabian

Born in Laredo, Tex., March 15, 1947; son of Gustavo J., a cotton broker, and Lucia (Farias) Peña, the third of six children; Roman Catholic; married Ellen Hart, an attorney, May 1988; father of Nelia Joan and Cristina Lucila; raised in Brownsville, Tex., graduating from St. Joseph's Academy Catholic High School, 1964; attended University of Texas, Austin, receiving B.A., 1968, and J.D., 1972; passed Texas bar, 1972, Colorado bar, 1973; staff attorney, El Paso Legal Assistance, 1972, Mexican-American Legal Defense and Educational Fund, Denver, 1972–1974, Chicano Education Project, 1974–1977; partner with his brother, Alfredo, Peña, Peña and Nieto, Denver, 1978–1983; state representative, Colorado General Assembly, 1979–1982, serving on judiciary, legal services, rules, and finance committees, and as Democratic minority leader, 1981–1982; mayor, City and County of Denver, 1983–1991, strengthening Denver's position as major regional trade and cultural center through the construction of new transportation infrastructure, including the Denver International Airport, and major campaigns to revitalize historic city neighborhoods and diminish air pollution; president and chief executive officer, Peña Investment Advisors, Inc., Denver, 1992; counsel, Brownstein, Hyatt, Farber and Strickland, 1992; after heading the transition team on transportation issues, he was appointed SECRETARY OF TRANSPORTATION by President Clinton, serving there from January 21, 1993, until January 1997, when he accepted Clinton's appointment as SECRETARY OF ENERGY, where he served from March 12, 1997, until he resigned on April 6, 1998; was the first Hispanic American to head each of those departments; as secretary of transportation department, encouraged increased spending for mass transit and

Secretary of Transportation Frederico Peña at a news conference in Washington, 1996, where Amtrak announced it had selected a consortium of Bombardier and GEC Alsthom to build its new high-speed trains for the northeast corridor. (AP/Wide World Photos)

infrastructure, signed aviation agreements with over 40 countries, and helped open new markets for American airlines; as energy secretary, drafted comprehensive national energy strategy; joined Vestar Capital Partners, Denver, 1998, as senior adviser, 1998–2000, then as managing director, 2000– ; member, Alternative Fuels Council, 1990–1992, Metropolitan Transportation Development Committee, Denver, 1989–1990, Rocky Flats Long Term Utilization Committee, Denver, 1980–1983, Denver Regional Council of Governments, 1983–1991, National Democratic Platform Committee, 1984, Greater Denver Chamber of Commerce, 1983–1991, Hispanic Chamber of Commerce, 1983–1991; member, board of directors, Piton Foundation, 1991–1992, Multicultural Education and Training Advocacy Project, 1991–1992, Inter-American Dialogue, 1991–1992, Japan-Hispanic Institute, 1991–1992; recipient, Tree of Life award, Jewish National Fund, 1984, Boys Club of America award, 1986, Grateful Appreciation award, Colorado Coalition for Persons with Disabilities, 1988, National Image, Inc., award for outstanding contributions to the Hispanic community, 1989, Good Guy award, National Women's Political Caucus, 1990, Aviation award for excellence, Airport Consultants Council, 1991, Distinguished Alumni award, University of Texas, 1994, Person of the Year, American Association of Port Authorities, 1994, National Leadership and Service award, Travelers Aid Society of Washington, 1994, American Heritage award, Mountain State Anti-Defamation League, 1994, Señor Internacional award, LULAC Council 12, 1994, Man of the Year, American Subcontractors Association of Colorado, 1994, Father of the Year, National Father's Day Committee, 1995, honorary doctor of public service, Florida International University, 1995, Hispanic Heritage award for Leadership, 1996; named Outstanding House Democratic Legislator, Colorado General Assembly, 1981; member, North American Diversity Advisory Board, Toyota, 2002; associate, Harvard University Center for Law and Education; member, Colorado Board of Law Examiners, Texas Bar Association, Colorado Bar Association. **References:** *Current Biography Yearbook 1993; Washington Post* (December 20, 1996); *Who's Who in America, 2000.*

—Jeffrey Coster

PERKINS, Frances

Born in Boston, Mass., April 10, 1882; daughter of Frederick Winslow and Susan (Wright) Perkins; Episcopalian; married Paul Caldwell Wilson in 1913; mother of Susanna Perkins; after receiving her preliminary and secondary education at the local schools, she entered Mount Holyoke College, graduating in 1905; continued the study of sociology and economics at the Universities of Chicago, Pennsylvania, and Columbia, receiving an A.M. from Columbia University in 1910; worked at Hull House in Chicago; became secretary of the Research and Protective Association in Philadelphia, Pa.; moved to New York City in 1909; in 1912, became executive secretary of the Commission of Safety, which secured the adoption of some 30 bills designed to prevent sweatshop fires; executive director of the New York Council of Organization for War Service, 1917–1919; appointed commissioner of the New York State Industrial Commission in 1919, serving until 1921 and again from 1929 to 1933; member of the New York State Industrial Board from 1922 to 1933 and its chairman from 1926 to 1929; appointed by President Franklin D. Roosevelt as SECRETARY OF LABOR on March 4, 1933, and continued in office under President Truman, serving until May 31, 1945; she became the first woman ever to serve in a presidential cabinet; under her administration a public works program was begun, minimum wage standards and improved working conditions were provided in the Wages and Hours Act, and old-age insurance and unemployment compensation laws were enacted; civil service commissioner from 1945 to 1953; awarded the medal for eminent achievement by the American Women's Association; author of *Women as Employers* (1919), *A Social Experiment under the Workmen's Compensation Jurisdiction* (1921), *People at Work* (1934), *The Roosevelt I Knew* (1946); died in New York City, May 14, 1965; buried in Newcastle, Me. **References:** Rexford Guy Tugwell, *Democratic Roosevelt: A Biography of Franklin Delano Roosevelt* (1957); Don Lawson, *Frances Perkins: First Lady of the Cabinet* (1960).

PERRY, William James

Born in Vandergrift, Pa., October 11, 1927; son of Edward Martin, a grocer, and Mabelle Estelle (Dunlap) Perry; married Leonilla Mary Green ("Lee"), a certified public accountant, December 29, 1947; father of David Carter, William Wick, Rebecca Lynn, Robin Lee, and Mark Lloyd; raised in Butler, Pa.; B.S., 1949, and M.A., 1950, Stanford University, then Ph.D., Pennsylvania State University, 1957, all in mathematics; surveyor and noncommissioned officer, U.S. Army Corps of Engineers, stationed in Okinawa and Japan, 1946–1947; joined Reserve Officers' Training Corps, 1948, commissioned as second lieutenant, 1950; instructor of math, University of Idaho, 1950–1951, Penn State, 1951–1954; research engineer, Boeing Corporation, 1951; senior mathematician, HRB-Singer, State College, Pa., 1951–1954; director, electronic defense laboratory, GTE Sylvania, Mountain View, Calif., 1954–1964; cofounder, ESL, Inc., Sunnyvale, Calif., 1964, and president, 1964–1977, technical consultant, U.S. Department of Defense, Washington, 1967–1977; undersecretary of defense for research and engineering, 1977–1981, responsible for weapons system procurement and research and development, as well as chief adviser to Secretary of Defense Harold Brown on technology, communications, intelligence, and atomic energy; managing director, Hambrecht and Quist investment bankers, San Francisco, 1981–1985; founder, Technology Strategies and Alliances, Menlo Park, Calif., 1985, and chairman, 1985–1993; professor and codirector, Center for International Security and Arms Control, Stanford University, 1989–1993; deputy secretary of defense, 1993–1994; appointed SECRETARY OF DEFENSE by President Clinton, taking office on February 3, 1994, and serving until January 23, 1997; chief priorities during his tenure at the Defense Department were containing the international development and spread of weapons of mass destruction and maintaining a strong U.S. presence in the Persian Gulf, based on the strategy of prevention of potential threats to U.S. national security; also oversaw deployment of U.S. ground troops on NATO-sponsored peacekeeping mission to Bosnia in 1995; Michael and Barbara Berberian professor of engineering-economic systems and operations research, Stanford University, 1997– ; former member, President's Foreign Intelligence advisory board and technical review panel of the U.S. Senate's Select Committee on Intelligence; former member, board of directors, Atlantic Aerospace Electronics Corporation, Comtech Labs, FMS Corporation, Norden Systems, Science Applications International Corporation, United Technologies, Valisys Corporation; recipient, Outstanding Civilian Service medal, U.S. Army, 1962, Outstanding Service medal, Defense Intelligence Agency, 1977, Distinguished Public Service medal, U.S. Department of Defense, 1980 and 1981, Achievement medal, American Electronics Association, 1980, Distinguished Service medal, NASA, 1981, Knight Commander's Cross, Federal Republic of Germany, 1981, Grand Officer de l'Ordre National du Mérité, France, 1982, James Forrestal Memorial award, 1994, Henry Stimson Foundation award, 1994, Arthur Bueche medal, National Academy of Engineering, 1996, Eisenhower award, 1996, Presidential Medal of Freedom, 1997, and Outstanding Civilian Service medals from the U.S. Army, Navy, Air Force, Coast Guard, NASA, and Defense Intelligence Agency, 1997; senior fellow, Institute of International Studies, Stanford University, 1997– ; coordinator of policy on North Korea for the Clinton administration, 1998–1999; coauthor, with Ashton Carter, of *Preventive Defense: A New Security Strategy for America* (1999); coeditor, with Peter Wehner, of *The Latin American Policies of U.S. Allies: Balancing Global Interests and Regional Concerns* (1985); member, American Electronics Association, American Academy of Arts and Sciences, Aspen Institute for Humanistic Studies, Carnegie Commission on Science, Technology, and Government, Carnegie Endowment for International Peace, National Academy of Engineering, Committee on International Security and Arms Control of the National Academy of Science. **References:** *New York Times* (January 25, 1994); *Current Biography Yearbook 1995; Who's Who in America, 2000*; David Halberstam, *War in a Time of Peace: Bush, Clinton, and the Generals* (2001).

—Jeffrey Coster

PETERSON, Peter George

Born June 5, 1926, in Kearny, Nebr.; son of George and Venetia (Paul) Peterson; married Sally Hornbogen, May 9, 1953, divorced, 1979; father of John Scott, James, David, Holly and Michael; married Joan Ganz Cooney, April 26, 1980; attended Nebraska State Teachers College and Massachusetts Institute of Technology; B.S. summa cum laude, Northwestern University, 1947; M.B.A. with honors, University of Chicago, 1951; began working in 1947 for Market Facts, Inc., Chicago, executive vice-president, 1948–1952; vice-president, McCann-Erickson, Chicago, 1952–1958; president, Bell and Howell, Chicago, 1958–1971, executive vice-president, 1958–1961, chief executive officer, 1963–1971; assistant to President Nixon and head of the newly formed cabinet-level Council on International Economic Affairs, 1971–1973; appointed by Nixon as SECRETARY OF COMMERCE and served from February 29, 1972, until February 1, 1973, during which time he negotiated trade agreements with both Poland and the Soviet Union; called "the innovator" because he was "a reshaper of trade policies and initiator of new ways by which the government can spur productivity and technology"; chief executive officer and chairman, board of directors, Lehman Brothers and Lehman Brothers, Kuhn and Loeb, New York City, 1973–1984; chairman, The Blackstone Group, 1985– ; deputy chairman, Federal Reserve Bank of New York; chairman of the Planning Committee for the Illinois Citizens for Eisenhower, 1952; director, Minnesota Mining and Manufacturing Company, Rockefeller Center Properties Inc.; founding member, Bi-partisan Budget Appeal; cofounder in 1992, with Paul Tsongas and Warren Rudman, and president, The Concord Coalition; trustee, Commission for Economic Development, Museum of Modern Art, New York City; member, board of directors, Public Agenda; member, President's Bi-partisan Commission on Entitlement Reform, 1994; recipient, Outstanding Service award, Phoenix House, New York City, 1976, Stephen Wise award, American Jewish Congress, 1981, University of Chicago Alumni medal, 1983, Man of Vision award, 1994, Nebraskalander award, 1994, and of honorary degrees from Colgate University, George Washington University, Northwestern University, Georgetown University, University of Rochester, Southampton College at Long Island; named, one of the Ten Outstanding Young Men in the nation, U.S. Junior Chamber of Commerce, 1961, one of the 100 most important American men under 40, *Life* magazine, 1962; author of *Facing Up: How to Rescue the Economy from Crushing Debt and Restore the American Dream* (1993), *Will America Grow Up Before It Grows Old?* (1996), and *Gray Dawn: How the Coming Age Wave Will Transform America—and the World* (1999); coauthor, with Neil Howe, of *On Borrowed Time: How the Growth in Entitlement Spending Threatens America's Future* (1988); contributing editor, *Readings in Market Organizing and Price Policies*; member, Independent Committee on International Development Issues, Trilateral Commission, Council on Foreign Relations (chairman, 1985–), Institute for International Economics (chairman, 1980), National Bureau of Economic Research (trustee), Japan Society, Atlantic Club, Economic Club of Chicago, Beta Gamma Sigma, Alpha Tau Omega. **References:** *Current Biography Year-*

book 1972; Time (January 8, 1973; August 13, 1973); *New York Times* (January 26, 1971; September 3, 1972; May 23, 1976; April 14, 1984; February 24, 1985; October 22, 1985; November 13, 1987); *Business Week* (April 25, 1994); *Who's Who in America, 2000*; Richard Reeves, *President Nixon: Alone in the White House* (2001).

PICKERING, Timothy

Born in Salem, Mass., July 17, 1745; son of Timothy and Mary (Wingate) Pickering; Puritan; married Rebecca White on April 8, 1776; father of John, Henry, and Octavius; graduated Harvard in 1763; appointed registrar of deeds for Essex; commissioned lieutenant in militia, 1766; admitted to bar in 1768; elected colonel in 1775; appointed judge of Essex court of common pleas and judge of the district maritime court including Boston and Salem in 1775; published "An Essay of Discipline for the Militia" in 1775; became representative to general court in May 1776; commanded Essex regiment and joined Washington at Morristown in February 1777; made adjutant general and member of the board of war; succeeded General Greene as quartermaster general in August 1780, held post until resigning in 1785 when the post was abolished; member of the Pennsylvania constitutional convention in 1789; concluded treaty with the six Indian Nations in 1791; appointed POSTMASTER GENERAL in the cabinet of President Washington, serving from August 12, 1791, to February 24, 1795, when he succeeded General Knox as SECRETARY OF WAR, serving from January 2, 1795, to January 26, 1796; aided in organization of West Point and supervised the building of frigates *Constitution, Constellation,* and *United States*; placed in charge of the Department of State following Edmund Randolph's resignation on August 19, 1795; appointed SECRETARY OF STATE in the cabinet of President Washington on December 10, 1795, and served until removed from office by President Adams on May 12, 1800; settled as a farmer in Danvers, Mass.; appointed chief justice of court of common pleas at Essex in 1802; elected to the U.S. Senate in 1803, where he served until 1811; retired from the Senate in 1811 to a farm in Wentham, Mass.; wrote "Political Essays: A Series of Letters Addressed to the People of the United States" in 1812; elected member of Congress, serving from 1813 to 1817; elected member of the Massachusetts executive council in 1817; wrote *A Review of the Correspondence between Honorable John Adams...and the Late William Cunningham, Esq.* in 1824; died in Salem, Mass., on January 29, 1829. **References:** Octavius Pickering, *The Life of Timothy Pickering* (1867–1873); Ellery Harrison and C.P. Bowditch, *The Pickering Genealogy* (1897).

PIERCE, Franklin

Born in Hillsborough (now Hillsboro), N.H., November 23, 1804; son of General Benjamin and Elizabeth (Andrews) Pierce; Episcopalian; married Jane Means Appleton on November 10, 1834; father of Franklin, Robert, Frank, and

Benjamin; attended the academies of Hancock and Francestown, N.H., and the preparatory school at Exeter, N.H.; entered Bowdoin College, Brunswick, Me., graduating in 1824; studied law and was admitted to the bar in 1827, commencing the practice of his profession in Hillsborough; elected to the New Hampshire House of Representatives, serving from 1829 to 1833; speaker of the House from 1832 and 1833; elected as a Democrat to the U.S. House of Representatives in the 23d and 24th Congresses, serving in all from March 4, 1833, until March 3, 1837; elected to the U.S. Senate, serving from March 4, 1837, until February 28, 1842, when he resigned to resume the practice of law at Concord, N.H.; declined the appointment of attorney general tendered by President Polk in 1846; enlisted as a private in the Mexican War, rising to the rank of brigadier general on March 3, 1847; resigned from army on March 20, 1848; member of the New Hampshire

Franklin Pierce (Library of Congress)

constitutional convention held in 1850, serving as its president; elected PRESIDENT on the Democratic ticket in November 1852; inaugurated on March 4, 1853, serving until March 3, 1857; unsuccessful candidate for the Democratic nomination for the presidency in 1856; upon his retirement he made a European tour, 1857, and then returned to Concord, N.H., and resumed the practice of law; died on October 8, 1869, in Concord; interment in Old North Cemetery, Concord. **Reference:** Roy F. Nichols, *Franklin Pierce: Young Hickory of the Granite Hills* (1969).

PIERCE, Samuel Riley, Jr.

Born in Glen Cove, N.Y., September 8, 1922; son of Samuel R. Sr., an independent small business owner, and Hettie Elenor (Armstrong) Pierce; Methodist; married Barbara Penn Wright, a physician, on April 1, 1948; father of Victoria Wright; A.B. with honors, Cornell University, 1947, and J.D., 1949; postgraduate study, Yale University Law School, 1957–1958; LL.M. in taxation, New York University, 1952; admitted to the bar of New York, 1949, and the U.S. Supreme Court, 1956; served with Criminal Investigation Division, U.S. Army,

1943–1946, in North Africa and Italy; first lieutenant, Judge Advocate General Corps, U.S. Army Reserves, 1950–1952; attorney in private practice, 1957–1959; adjunct professor, New York University School of Law, 1957–1970; partner, Battle, Fowler, Stokes and Kheel, 1961–1970, and Battle, Fowler, Joffin, Pierce, and Kheel, 1973–1981, 1989–2000; the first African American partner in a major New York law firm; assistant district attorney, County of New York, 1949–1953; assistant U.S. attorney, Southern District, New York, 1953–1955; assistant to the undersecretary of labor, Washington, 1955–1956; appointed to the Supreme Court in 1956; associate counsel, Judicial Subcommittee on Antitrust, U.S. House of Representatives, 1956–1957; judge, New York Court of General Sessions, 1959–1961; member, council on Fundamental International and Social Economic Education, 1961–1967; chairman, Impartial Disciplinary Review Board, New York City Transit System, 1968–1981; general counsel and head legal director, Department of the Treasury, Washington, 1970–1973; appointed by President Reagan as SECRETARY OF HOUSING AND URBAN DEVELOPMENT and served through both of Reagan's terms, from January 23, 1981, until January 20, 1989; accepted Reagan's budget cuts in the department but fought to keep key programs for public housing and urban rehabilitation; after leaving office, an investigation into misuse of funds at HUD during his tenure resulted in convictions of several of his aides, but he was never charged himself; consultant, The Turner Corporation, 1989–2000; treasurer for U.S. Representative Kenneth Keating's Senate campaign, 1958; became the first African American director of a Fortune 500 company when he was chosen to sit on the board of U.S. Industries in 1964; cofounder, Freedom National Bank, 1964, the first bank in New York state that was predominantly managed by African Americans; member, Committee of Black Americans for Nixon and Agnew, 1968; chairman, New York state Minimum Wage Board, Hotel Industry, 1961; member, New York state Banking Board, 1961–1970, New York City Board of Education, 1961, Administrative Conference, U.S., 1968–1970, Battery Park City Authority, 1968–1970, New York City Special Commission Inquiry into Energy Failures, 1977, national advisory committee, Comptroller of Currency, 1975–1980, advisory group, commissioner of the IRS, 1974–1976, National Wiretapping Commission, 1973–1976, board of governors, American Stock Exchange, 1977–1980; director, New York World's Fair Corporation, 1964–1965; trustee, Institute for Civil Justice, Mt. Holyoke College, 1967–1975, Hampton Institute, Institute for International Education, Cornell University, Howard University, 1976–1981; member, board of directors, Tax Foundation, Prudential Insurance Company of America, 1964–1970, 1973–1981, U.S. Industries, 1964–1970, 1973–1979, International Paper Company, 1973–1981, General Electric Corporation, 1974–1981, International Basic Economics Corporation, 1973–1980; U.S. delegate, Conference on Cooperation, Georgetown, British Guiana, 1956; fraternal delegate, All-African People's Conference, Accra, Ghana, 1958; member, National Defense Exec. Res., 1957–1970, national executive board, Boy Scouts of America, 1969–1975, New York City, United Service Organization, 1959–1961, panel of arbitrators, American

Arbitration Association and Federal Mediation and Conciliation Service, 1957–2000, board of directors, Louis T. Wright Memorial Fund, National Parkinson Foundation, 1959–1961; secretary-director, YMCA of Greater New York, 1969–1970; staff member, New York State Republican Campaign Headquarters, 1952, 1958; governor, New York Young Republican Club, 1951–1953; former member, commission on interjurisdictional relations, United Methodist Church; chairman, Urban Affairs Ministers Conference, Organization for Economic Cooperation and Development, 1983–1989; recipient, Ford Foundation Fellowship, 1957–1958, Distinguished Service Award, New York City Junior Chamber of Commerce, 1958, Alexander Hamilton award, Treasury Department, 1973, Distinguished Alumnus award, Cornell University Law School, 1988, Distinguished Service medal, Nassau County Bar Association, 1988, Reagan Revolution Medal of Honor, 1989, Presidential Citizens Medal, 1989, Salute to Greatness award, Martin Luther King, Jr., Center, 1989, and of many honorary degrees; selected as member, Long Island Sports Hall of Fame, 1988; fellow, American College of Trial Lawyers; former member, American Bar Association, Association of the Bar of the City of New York, Cornell Association of Class Secretaries, Telluride Association Alumni, Cornell University Alumni Association of New York City, C.I.D. Agents Association, New York County Lawyers Association, Institute of Judicial Administration; Phi Beta Kappa, Phi Kappa Phi, Alpha Phi Alpha, and Alpha Phi Omega; died on October 31, 2000, in a hospital in a suburb of Washington, D.C. **References:** *Newsweek* (January 5, 1971); *Time* (January 5, 1981); *Current Biography Yearbook 1982; National Review* (December 9, 1988); *New York Times* (November 3, 2000); *Who's Who in America, 2000.*

PIERREPONT, Edwards

Born at North Haven (now New Haven), Conn., March 4, 1817; son of Giles and Eunice (Munson) Pierpont; married Margaretta Willoughby on May 27, 1846; educated at the schools of his native town and graduated from Yale College in 1837; studied law at the New Haven Law School; admitted to the bar in 1840; tutored at Yale College in 1840 and 1841; moved to Columbus, Ohio, and pursued the practice of law there; moved to New York City in 1846; became active in the campaigns of the Democratic Party; elected judge of the superior court of the city of New York in 1857 but resigned in 1860 to resume his law practice; helped organize the War Democrats in support of the reelection of President Lincoln in 1864; approved President Andrew Johnson's policies of Reconstruction; appointed U.S. district attorney for the southern district of New York in 1869 and 1870, by President Grant; became director, counsel, and treasurer of the Texas and Pacific Railroad in 1871; appointed minister to Russia in 1873 but declined to serve; invited to serve in the cabinet of President Grant as ATTORNEY GENERAL on April 26, 1875, took office on May 15, 1875, and served until May 31, 1876; during his incumbency, he prosecuted members of the "Whiskey Ring"; appointed minister to Great

Britain in 1876 by President Grant, serving until December 1877; member of the state constitutional convention of 1867 and 1868 and one of the Committee of Seventy in 1870 that assisted in ridding New York of the "Tweed Ring"; died in New York City, March 6, 1892. **References:** Courtlandt Canby, ed., *Lincoln and the Civil War: A Profile and a History* (1960); John Y. Simon, ed., *The Papers of Ulysses S. Grant* (1967).

PINKNEY, William

Born in Annapolis, Md., March 17, 1764; son of Jonathan and Ann (Rind) Pinkney; married Maria Rodgers on March 16, 1789; father of ten children, among them Edward Coate, author; entered office of Judge Samuel Chase in 1783 at Baltimore, after attending the King William School; admitted to bar in 1786; began practice in Hartford County, Md., practiced two years; elected to the U.S. constitutional convention in 1788, voted against ratification; representative to the Maryland House of Delegates, 1788–1792; resisted antislavery legislation; in 1792 elected member of the executive council of Maryland, serving until his resignation in 1795; Anne Arundel County delegate to the state legislature, 1795; appointed commissioner of the United States under the seventh article of Jay's Treaty to settle United States' claims against Great Britain in 1796; returned to the United States in 1804, moving from Annapolis to Baltimore; appointed attorney general of Maryland in 1805; sent to London with Minister James Monroe in 1806 regarding reparations and impressment, retained in 1807 when Monroe resigned, returned in 1811; elected to the state senate in September 1811; appointed ATTORNEY GENERAL in the cabinet of President Madison on December 11, 1811, resigned on February 10, 1814; while in office he advocated the War of 1812; commanded a battalion in the War of 1812; congressional representative of Baltimore, March 4, 1815, to April 18, 1816, when he resigned to accept an appointment as minister plenipotentiary to Russia and special envoy to Naples to negotiate compensation for United States' losses in 1809; returned to the United States, 1818; elected U.S. senator to fill a vacancy, serving from 1819 to 1822; pro-slavery attitudes instrumental in the Missouri Compromise; died in Washington, D.C., February 25, 1822; interment in the Congressional Cemetery. **References:** Abbot Emerson Smith, *James Madison, Builder: A New Estimate of a Memorable Career* (1937); Irving Brant, *James Madison: The President 1809–1812* (1956); Irving Brant, *James Madison: Commander in Chief, 1812–1836* (1961); Gaillard Hunt, *The Life of James Madison* (1968).

POINSETT, Joel Roberts

Born in Charlestown (now Charleston), S.C., March 2, 1779; son of Dr. Elisha and Ann (Roberts) Poinsett; Baptist; married Mrs. Mary (Izard) Pringle on October 24, 1833; spent his early childhood in England, returning to the United

States in 1788; attended private schools at Greenfield Hill, Conn., and, later, in Wandsworth, near London, England; studied medicine at St. Paul's School in Edinburgh, Scotland; attended the military academy at Woolwich, England; studied law briefly; traveled extensively in Europe from 1801 to 1809; sent to South America by President Madison in 1809 to investigate revolutionary struggles for independence from Spain; returned to Charleston in 1816; elected to the state House of Representatives from 1816 to 1820; served as president of the Board of Public Works; elected as a Democrat to the 17th, 18th, and 19th Congresses, serving from 1821 to 1825, when he resigned to enter the diplomatic service; appointed minister to Mexico from 1825 to 1829; invited to join the cabinet of President Martin Van Buren as SECRETARY OF WAR on March 7, 1837, entering upon his duties on March 14, 1837, and serving until March 4, 1841; during his secretaryship, he improved the status of the regular army, proposed a plan for universal training and frontier defense, organized a general staff, improved the artillery, broadened the course of study at the West Point Military Academy, moved more than 40,000 Indians west of the Mississippi River, and directed the war against the Seminoles in Florida; retired to his South Carolina plantation in 1841; opposed the Mexican War and the secessionist movement of 1847–1852; the *Poinsettia pulcherina*, an indigenous Mexican flower, was named for him on his introducing it to the United States; founded the Academy of Fine Arts in Charleston, S.C.; authored *Notes on Mexico, Made in 1822, with an Historical Sketch of the Revolution* (1824); died near what is now Statesburg, S.C., on December 12, 1851; interment in the Church of the Holy Cross (Episcopal) Cemetery, Statesburg, S.C. **References:** Robert Vincent Remini, *Martin Van Buren and the Making of the Democratic Party* (1959); Edwin Palmer Hoyt, *Martin Van Buren* (1964).

POLK, James Knox

Born near Little Sugar Creek, N.C., November 4, 1795; son of Samuel and Jane (Knox) Polk; Presbyterian; married Sarah Childress on January 1, 1824; no children; moved to Tennessee with his family in 1806, settling in what is now Maury County; attended the common schools and was privately tutored briefly; entered the University of North Carolina at Chapel Hill, graduating in 1818; studied law at Portsmouth, N.H., and Northampton, Mass., and was admitted to the bar in 1820, commencing practice in Columbia, Tenn.; became chief clerk of the Tennessee Senate from 1821 to 1823; served in the Tennessee House of Representa-

James K. Polk (Library of Congress)

tives from 1823 to 1825; elected as a Democrat to the U.S. House of Representatives in the 19th through 25th Congresses, serving in all from March 4, 1825, until March 3, 1839; served as speaker of the House during the sessions of the 24th and 25th Congresses; did not seek renomination in 1838, having become a candidate for governor; elected governor of Tennessee from 1839 to 1841; elected PRESIDENT on the Democratic ticket, November 1844; inaugurated on March 4, 1845, serving until March 3, 1849; he did not seek a second term; upon retiring from the White House, he returned to Nashville, where he died on June 15, 1849; interment within the grounds of the State Capitol, Nashville, Tenn. **Reference:** Charles Allan McCoy, *Polk and the Presidency* (1960).

PORTER, James Madison

Born in Selma, Pa., January 6, 1793; son of Andrew and Elizabeth (Parker) Porter and brother of David Rittenhouse Porter and Robert Porter; married Eliza Michler on September 18, 1821; studied law in Lancaster, Pa., in 1809 and later with his brother Robert in Reading, Pa.; in 1812 served as a clerk in a prothonotary's office in Philadelphia; organized a volunteer force to fight the British and served as second lieutenant; discharged with the rank of colonel; admitted to the bar on April 23, 1813, and began his own law practice; in 1818 moved to Easton to serve as deputy attorney general of Northampton County; he returned to private practice in 1821 and maintained one of the largest practices in that vicinity; active member of the founding committee of Lafayette College, chartered in 1826; served as president of the board of trustees of Lafayette from 1826 to 1852 and as professor of jurisprudence and political economy from 1837 to 1852; appointed in June 1839 to serve as presiding judge of the 12th district; resigned in 1840 to resume his legal practice; in 1843, President Tyler appointed him SECRETARY OF WAR; he was to assume the duties of that office on March 8, 1843, but Congress rejected his nomination on January 30, 1844, after he had served almost ten months; in 1847 he became the first president of the Schuylkill and Susquehanna Railroad, and when its name was changed in 1853 to Lehigh Valley Railroad he became president of the new company; in 1849 he was elected to the state legislature where he became chairman of the judiciary committee; elected president judge of the 22d judicial district, 1853, and served until March 1855, when he was forced to resign following a stroke; died on November 11, 1862; interment in Easton, Pa. **References:** *Dictionary of American Biography*; Charles H. Hart, *James Madison Porter* (1856); *Who Was Who in American Politics.*

PORTER, Peter Buell

Born in Salisbury, Conn., August 14, 1773; son of Colonel Joshua and Abigail Buell Porter; married to Letitia Breckinridge in 1818; was graduated from Yale College in 1791; studied law in Litchfield, Conn.; admitted to the bar and began practice in Canandaigua, N.Y., in 1795; appointed clerk of Ontario County, 1797, serving until 1805 when he was removed by Governor Morgan Lewis because of his identification with the Burr faction of the Republican Party; member of the New York State Assembly in 1802 and again in 1828; removed to Black Rock, N.Y., in 1809 and engaged in transportation enterprises; elected as a Democrat to the 11th and 12th Congresses, serving from March 4, 1809, until March 3, 1813; appointed canal commissioner by the New York state legislature in 1811; served in the War of 1812 as major general of New York Volunteers, 1812–1815; elected to the 14th Congress and served from March 4, 1815, to January 23, 1816; secretary of state of New York, 1815–1816; appointed member of the Northwestern Boundary Commission, 1816; unsuccessful candidate for governor of New York, 1817; regent of the University of the State of New York, 1824–1830; appointed SECRETARY OF WAR in the cabinet of President John Quincy Adams on June 21, 1828; most important contribution was advocating moving all Indians residing in the eastern states to west of the Mississippi; served until March 3, 1829; moved to Niagara Falls, N.Y., in 1836, where he died on March 20, 1844; interment in Oakwood Cemetery. **References:** D.S. Alexander, *A Political History of the State of New York*, vol. 1 (1906); Robert A. East, *John Q. Adams: The Critical Years* (1962); F. Clarke, *John Quincy Adams* (1966).

POWELL, Colin Luther

Born in New York City, N.Y., April 5, 1937; son of Luther, a shipping clerk, and Maud Ariel (McKoy) Powell, garment worker; both parents were immigrants from Jamaica; Episcopalian; married Alma Vivian Johnson, a speech pathologist, on August 25, 1962; father of Michael, Linda, and Annemarie; raised in South Bronx and attended New York City public schools; graduated from Morris High School, 1954; B.S. in geology, City College of New York, 1958; M.B.A., George Washington University, 1971; attended National War College, Fort McNair, Washington, D.C., 1975–1976; a Reserve Officers Training Corps (ROTC) cadet in college, he was commissioned a second lieutenant, U.S. Army, 1958, and advanced through grades to rank of general, 1989; served in West Germany, Fort Benning, Ga., and Fort Owens, Mass., 1958–1963; served in Vietnam, as a military adviser to a South Vietnamese infantry battalion, 1962–1963, and as battalion executive officer and division operations officer, 23rd Division, 1968–1969; wounded on each tour; White House fellow and assistant to the deputy director, Office of Management and Budget, 1972–1973; battalion commander in South Korea, 1973–1974; staff officer, U.S. Department of Defense, 1974–1976; commander, Second Brigade, 101st Airborne Division, Fort Campbell, Ky., 1976–1977; executive assistant to secretary, U.S. Department of Energy, 1979; senior military assistant to the secretary, U.S. Department of Defense, 1979–1981; assistant division commander, 4th Infantry Division, Ft. Carson, Colo., 1981–1983; deputy commander, Fort Leavenworth, Kans., 1983; military assistant to secretary, Department of Defense, 1983–1986; commander,

Colin Powell (National Archives)

U.S. V Corps, Frankfurt, West Germany, 1986–1987; deputy assistant to President Ronald Reagan for national security affairs, 1987; assistant to the president for national security affairs, 1987–1989; commander-in-chief, U.S. Forces Command, Fort McPherson, Ga., 1989–1994; chairman, Joint Chiefs of Staff (JCS), Department of Defense, Washington, 1989–1993, the youngest person and the first African American to hold that position; responsible for coordination of U.S. and allied military operations against Iraq in the Persian Gulf, 1990–1991, convincing President Bush to authorize a ground campaign on February 23, 1991, after Iraq's rejection of an allied ultimatum to withdraw from Kuwait; credited with the "Powell Doctrine" as a guideline for U.S. military operations, calling for decisive force deployed for clearly winnable objectives; retired from the army upon completion of his term as JCS chairman, September 1993; despite efforts to draft him as a nominee, he refused to become a candidate for U.S. president in either 1996 or 2000; founding chairman, The President's Summit for America's Future, 1997; chairman, America's Promise—The Alliance for Youth, 1997–2001; appointed by President George W. Bush as SECRETARY OF STATE and took office on January 20, 2001, the first African American to serve in that position; at the center of the administration's efforts to broker agreements amidst growing tensions in the Israeli-Palestinian situation and the India-Pakistan crisis in late 2001, as well as gain diplomatic support for the war on terrorism in the wake of the September 11, 2001, attacks on the World Trade Center and the Pentagon; recipient, Purple Heart, 1963, Bronze Star, 1963, Legion of Merit Award, 1969 and 1971, Air Medal, Distinguished Service Medal, Presidential Medal of Freedom, 1991 and 1993, President's Citizens Medal, Congressional Gold Medal, Secretary of State's Distinguished Service Medal, 1988, Secretary of Energy's Distinguished Medal, and Living Legend award; commencement speaker, Harvard University, 1993; named honorary knight commander, Most Honorable Order of the Bath, Queen Elizabeth II of the United Kingdom, 1993; author of the memoir *My American Journey* (1995); member, board of trustees, Howard University, board of directors, United Negro College Fund, board of governors, The Boys and Girls Clubs of America, advisory board, Children's

Health Fund; member, Association of the U.S. Army. **References:** *Current Biography Yearbook 1988*; Bob Woodward, *The Commanders* (1991); Howard Means, *Colin Powell: Soldier/Statesman, Statesman/Soldier* (1992); David Roth, *Sacred Honor: A Biography of Colin Powell* (1993); *Newsweek* (October 10, 1994; December 25, 2000; March 5, 2001; December 3, 2001); *Time* (March 13 and July 10, 1995); James A. Baker, with Thomas M. DeFrank, *The Politics of Diplomacy: Revolution, War and Peace, 1989–1992* (1995); George H.W. Bush and Brent Scowcroft, *A World Transformed* (1998); *Washington Post* (December 16, 2000); John Robert Greene, *The Presidency of George Bush* (2000); *The Economist* (December 24, 2001); David Halberstam, *War in a Time of Peace: Bush, Clinton, and the Generals* (2001).

—Robert T. Chase

PRESTON, William Ballard

Born in Smithfield, Va., November 29, 1805; son of James Patton Preston, governor of Virginia, and Ann (Taylor) Preston; married to Lucinda Staples Redd on November 21, 1839; father of Walter, Nannie, James, Lucy, Jane, and Keziah; attended the common schools; attended William and Mary College, Williamsburg, Va., and graduated in 1823; studied law at the University of Virginia at Charlottesville in 1825; admitted to the bar and began practice in 1826; member of the Virginia House of delegates, 1830–1832 and 1844–1845; served in the state senate from 1840 until 1844; elected in 1846 as a Whig to the 30th Congress, serving from March 4, 1847, until March 3, 1849; appointed SECRETARY OF THE NAVY in the cabinet of President Taylor to serve from March 7, 1849, until July 19, 1850, when the cabinet was reorganized by President Fillmore; resumed law practice; sent to France in 1858 to negotiate the establishment of a commercial steamship line between Virginia and France but was unsuccessful due to the outbreak of the Civil War; opposed Virginia's secession from the Union but defended its right to secede and thus was elected from Montgomery County to the secession convention of Virginia in February 1861; elected senator from Virginia to the Confederate Congress and served in that body until his death on November 16, 1862, in Smithfield, Va.; interment probably in the cemetery of the Old Brick Church, Smithfield. **References:** L.A. Wilson, ed., *The Preston Genealogy* (1900); Holman Hamilton, *Zachary Taylor: Soldier in the White House* (1966); Brainerd Dyer, *Zachary Taylor* (1967).

PRINCIPI, Anthony Joseph

Born in New York City, N.Y., April 16, 1944; son of Antonio Joseph, an immigrant and owner of an electrical supply company, and Theresa (Princiotta) Principi; Roman Catholic; married Elizabeth Ann Ahlering, nurse and navy lawyer, on June 26, 1971; father of Anthony III, Ryan, and John; grew up in New York

City; graduated from Mount Saint Michael Academy, 1962; attended New Mexico Military Institute, 1962–1963; B.S., U.S. Naval Academy, 1967; J.D., Seton Hall University School of Law, 1975; admitted to the bar in Pennsylvania, 1975, California, 1978; after receiving commission, 1967, advanced through grades to commander, U.S. Navy, 1984; ensign, USS *J.P. Kennedy*, Newport, R.I., 1967–1969; lieutenant, river patrol squadron, Vietnam, 1969–1970, and Naval Education Training Center, Newport, 1970–1972; legislative assistant to New Jersey state senator A. Scardino, 1973–1975; lieutenant commander and attorney, Legal Service Office, Judge Advocate General Corps, San Diego, 1975–1977; commander and attorney, Training Command, U.S. Pacific Fleet, San Diego, 1977–1979; commander, Office of Legislative Affairs, U.S. Department of the Navy, Washington, 1979–1981; counsel, Armed Services Committee, U.S. Senate, 1981–1983; associate deputy administrator for congressional and public affairs, Veterans Administration, 1983–1984; Republican chief counsel and staff director, Veterans Affairs Committee, U.S. Senate, 1984–1988; staff director and majority chief counsel, Office of Republican Senator from Wyoming Alan Simpson, 1984–1986; general counsel, Navy Broadway Complex Office, San Diego, 1988–1989; deputy secretary, U.S. Department of Veterans Affairs, 1989–1992, and acting secretary, 1992–1993; aide to Republican Senator Strom Thurmond, Republican chief counsel and minority staff director, U.S. Senate Armed Services Committee, 1993; partner, Luce, Forward, Hamilton & Scripps, San Diego, 1990–1995; partner, Principi & McCain, La Jolla, Calif., 1994–2001; senior vice-president and chief executive officer, Lockheed Martin IMS Integrated Solutions, Santa Clara, Calif., 1995–1996; president and chairman, Federal Network Telecommunications Company, 1996–1997; chairman, Congressional Commission on Service Members and Veterans Transition Assistance ("Principi Commission") to review the effectiveness of services and benefits for current and former military personnel, 1998–1999; president, QTC Medical Services, Inc., 1999–2000; appointed by President George W. Bush as SECRETARY OF VETERANS AFFAIRS and took office on January 20, 2001; California chairman, Veterans for Bush, 2000; decorated Bronze Star with Combat V, Vietnamese Cross of Gallantry, three Navy Commendation medals with Combat V, Meritorious Service medals, and Navy Combat Action Ribbon; member, American Bar Association (chairman, military law section of legislation subcommittee, 1983–1986, and subcommittee on general practice, 1985), American Legion, Veterans of Foreign Wars. **References:** *Washington Post* (December 29, 2000; January 5, 2001); *New York Times* (January 19, 2001); *Who's Who, 2001.*

—Rachel Ban

PROCTOR, Redfield

Born in Proctorsville, Vt., July 1, 1831; son of Jabez Proctor, farmer, merchant, and manufacturer, and Betsey (Parker) Proctor; married Emily J. Dutton on May 26, 1858; father of five children; was graduated from Dartmouth College in 1851; studied law at the Albany Law School, graduating in 1859; admitted to the bar and began practice in Boston, Mass., in 1860; during the Civil War, attained the rank of major in the 5th Vermont Regiment; discharged due to ill health in 1863 but later returned as colonel of the 15th Vermont Regiment and participated in the Battle of Gettysburg; returned to Vermont and the practice of law; pursued business interests in the marble industry and became president of the Vermont Marble Company in 1880; member of the Vermont House of Representatives, 1867–1868; served in the state senate and was president *pro tempore* in 1874 and 1875; lieutenant governor of Vermont, 1876–1878; governor of Vermont, 1878–1880; delegate to the Republican National Conventions of 1884, 1888, and 1896; reelected to the state House of Representatives in 1888; appointed SECRETARY OF WAR in the cabinet of President Benjamin Harrison on March 5, 1889; most important contributions were revision of court-martial system, institution of system of efficiency records and examinations for officers' promotions, organization of a record and pension division in the department, all of which influenced the decline in the rate of desertions; resigned on November 2, 1891, to enter the U.S. Senate; subsequently reelected in 1892, 1898, and 1904, serving in all from 1891 to 1908; in 1904, edited from the original manuscripts in the Library of Congress the *Records of Conventions in the New Hampshire Grants for the Independence of Vermont*; died in Washington, D.C., on March 4, 1908; interment in the City Cemetery, Proctor, Vt. **References:** F.C. Partridge, "Redfield Proctor," *Vermont Historical Society, 1913–1914* (1915); Harry J. Sievers, *Benjamin Harrison: Hoosier President*, vol. 3 (1966).

Q

QUAYLE, James Danforth ("Dan"), III

Born in Indianapolis, Ind., February 4, 1947; oldest son of James C., newspaper publisher, and Corinne (Pulliam) Quayle; grandson of newspaper baron Eugene C. Pulliam; Presbyterian; married Marilyn Tucker, lawyer, on November 18, 1972; father of Tucker Danforth, Benjamin Eugene, and Mary Corinne; family moved to Phoenix, Ariz., 1955, and to Huntington, Ind., 1963, following his father's work; graduated from Huntington High School, 1965; B.A. in political science, DePauw University, 1969; J.D., Indiana University Law School, 1974; admitted to the bar in Indiana, 1974; served as a welder, clerk-typist, and military journalist in the Indiana National Guard, 1969–1975; court reporter, Huntington *Herald-Press*, 1965–1969; investigator, consumer protection division, Indiana Attorney General's Office, 1971; administrative assistant to Indiana Governor Edgar Whitcomb, 1971–1973; director, inheritance tax division, Indiana Department of Revenue, 1973–1974; established law practice with his wife, Quayle and Quayle, Huntington, 1974–1976; associate publisher and general manager of his family's newspaper, the Huntington *Herald-Press*, 1974–1976; teacher of business law, Huntington College, 1975; Republican member representing Indiana's 4th congressional district, U.S. House of Representatives, 1977–1980, winning his first election over eight-term incumbent Democrat Edward Roush in 1976 with 54 percent of the vote and winning reelection in 1978 with 64 percent; served on House government operations, foreign affairs, and small business committees and gained reputation as a staunch conservative; Republican member from Indiana, U.S. Senate, 1981–1989; defeated three-term incumbent Democrat Birch Bayh in 1980 with 54 percent of the vote and won reelection in 1986 with 61 percent; served on Senate armed services, budget, and labor and human resources committees, chaired the defense acquisition and employment and productivity subcommittees, 1985–1987, coauthored, with Democratic Senator Edward Kennedy, the Job Training Partnership Act of 1986, and advocated federal tax reform and the creation of the Strategic Defense Initiative, President Reagan's national missile defense system; chosen by Republican presidential nominee George H.W. Bush to be his running mate, and on November 8, 1988, was elected the forty-fourth VICE-PRESIDENT OF THE UNITED STATES, taking office on January 20, 1989, and serving until the end of Bush's term on January 20, 1993; as vice-president, served as the Bush administration's chief congressional liaison, was a member of the National Security Council, the first chairman of the National Space Council, and head of the Council of Competitiveness; visited 47 countries promoting a variety of issues including U.S. trade interests and free enterprise; along with Bush, was defeated for reelection in 1992 by the Democratic ticket of Bill Clinton and Al Gore; chairman, Competitiveness Center, Hudson Institute, 1993– ; founder and chairman, Campaign America, Republican fund-raising political action committee, 1995–1999; distinguished visiting professor of international studies at the American Graduate School of International Management, 1997–1999; unsuccessfully sought Republican nomination for president, 1999; writer of nationally syndicated newspaper column; member, board of trustees, Hudson Institute; member, board of directors, American Standard Inc., Central Newspapers Inc., BTC Inc., AMTRAM Inc, Vice President's Residence Foundation; former director and vice-president, Huntington Newspapers Inc., 1974–1989, and Sunland Publications, 1978–1983; former trustee, Franklin College, 1986–1989; honorary trustee, Huntington College, 1983–1987; recipient, Taxpayers' Best Friend award, National Taxpayers Union, Golden Bulldog award, Watch Dog of the Treasury, Guardian of Small Businesses, National Federation of Independent Business, National Security Leadership award, Coalition for Peace through Strength, 1985, and honorary degrees from Tri-State University, Indiana Institute of Technology, Vincennes University, and DePauw University; named one of Ten Outstanding Young Men in America, U.S. Jaycees; author of *Standing Firm* (1994), *The American Family: Discovering The Values That Make Us Strong* (1996), and *Worth Fighting For* (1999); member, Rotary, Huntington Chamber of Commerce, Hoosier State Press, and Huntington Bar Association; resides in Arizona. **References:** *Time* (August 29, 1988); *New York Times* (November 20, 1988); *Current Biography Yearbook 1989*; Richard F. Fenno, *The Making of a Senator: Dan Quayle* (1989); Bob Woodward and David S. Broder, *The Man Who Would Be President: Dan Quayle* (1992); Charles Kolb, *White House Daze: The Unmaking of Domestic Policy in the Bush Years* (1994); John Robert Greene, *The Presidency of George Bush* (2000); *Who's Who in America, 2000.*

—William J. Lombardo

R

RAMSEY, Alexander

Born near Harrisburg, Pa., September 8, 1815; son of Thomas and Elizabeth (Kelker) Ramsey; Methodist; married to Anna Earl Jenks on September 10, 1845; father of three children; worked as a store clerk and carpenter while attending the common schools; studied law at Lafayette College, Easton, Pa.; admitted to the bar in 1839 and began practice in Harrisburg; became active in the Whig Party; secretary of the Pennsylvania electoral college, 1840; chief clerk of the Pennsylvania House of Representatives in 1841; elected as a Whig to the 28th and 29th Congresses, serving from March 4, 1843, until March 3, 1847; chairman of the Whig central committee of Pennsylvania, 1848; commissioned governor of the Minnesota territory by President Taylor on April 2, 1849 and served until 1853; pursued real estate interests in St. Paul, Minn.; mayor of St. Paul in 1855; unsuccessful Republican candidate for governor of Minnesota in 1857; secured governorship in 1859 and was reelected in 1861; elected in 1863 to the U.S. Senate as a Republican and reelected in 1869, serving until 1875; appointed SECRETARY OF WAR in the cabinet of President Hayes on December 10, 1879, and served until the close of the Hayes administration, March 4, 1881; appointed by President Arthur as chairman of the commission to carry out the provisions of the Edmunds bill dealing with Mormonism in Utah and served in this capacity until 1886; first president of the Minnesota Historical Society from 1849 to 1863; was author of several papers in the Minnesota Historical Collections, 1891–1903; delegate to the centennial celebration of the adoption of the federal Constitution in 1887; died in St. Paul, Minn., on April 22, 1903; interment in Oakland Cemetery. **References:** J.H. Baker, *Lives of the Governors of Minnesota* (1908); T. Harry Williams, ed., *Hayes: The Diary of a*

President, 1875–1881 (1964); Arthur Bishop, ed., *Rutherford B. Hayes, 1822–1893: Chronology, Documents, Bibliographical Aids* (1969).

RANDALL, Alexander Williams

Born at Ames, N.Y., October 31, 1819; son of Phineas Randall, lawyer, and Sarah (Beach) Randall; married to Mary C. Van Vechten in 1842; after death of first wife, married Helen M. Thomas in 1863; attended Cherry Valley Academy; studied law; admitted to the bar in 1840 and began practice in the new village of Prairieville in Wisconsin Territory; formerly a Whig, became a Democrat by 1845; appointed by President Polk as postmaster of Prairieville; delegate to the Wisconsin constitutional convention, 1846; member of the Wisconsin Assembly, 1848; associate justice of the Milwaukee circuit court, 1855–1857; elected governor of Wisconsin as a Republican in 1857 and reelected in 1859; appointed minister to Italy by President Lincoln, serving from 1862 to 1863; appointed first assistant postmaster general in 1863 in the cabinet of President Lincoln; appointed POSTMASTER GENERAL in the cabinet of President Andrew Johnson on July 25, 1866, and remained in that post until the close of that administration, March 3, 1869; settled in Elmira, N.Y., and resumed law practice; died on July 26, 1872. **References:** H.A. Tenney and David Atwood, *Memorial Record of the Fathers of Wisconsin* (1880); "Reminiscences of Alex W. Randall," *Milwaukee Sentinel* (November 14, 1897); Eric L. McKitrick, *Andrew Johnson and Reconstruction* (1960).

RANDOLPH, Edmund Jennings

Born in Williamsburg, Va., August 10, 1753; son of John Randolph, King's attorney for Virginia, and Ariana (Jennings) Randolph; nephew of Peyton Randolph, president of the Continental Congress in 1774 and 1775; married Elizabeth Nicholas in 1776; father of Lucy and Peyton; attended William and Mary College; studied law in his father's office, 1773; became an aide-de-camp to George Washington in 1775; elected to Virginia convention in 1776, assisted in writing of Virginia constitution and bill of rights; elected attorney general of state of Virginia, 1776–1782; member of Continental Congress 1779–1782; governor of Virginia, 1786–1788; delegate to 1787 Constitutional Convention; wrote "Letter...on the Federal Constitution" in 1787; entered the Virginia Assembly in 1788; appointed ATTORNEY GENERAL in the cabinet of President Washington on February 2, 1790, and served until January 28, 1794; reported on the judiciary system and defended foreigners' right to sue the state; appointed SECRETARY OF STATE in the cabinet of President Washington on January 2, 1794; instrumental in developing Jay Treaty with England while maintaining relations with France and the 1795 Treaty of San Lorenzo (Pinckney Treaty) with Spain regarding free navigation of the Mississippi River; resigned from office on August 19, 1795; wrote "Democratic Societies," 1795, and "Political Truth,"

1796; resumed law practice, acting as senior counsel at Aaron Burr's trial for treason in 1807; died in Millwood, Va., September 13, 1813. **References:** Robert Wirt, *British Spy* (1803); Jonathan Eliot, *The Debates in the Several States on the Adoption of the Federal Constitution* (1836); M.D. Conoway, *Omitted Chapters of History* (1888); S.F. Bemis, "Edmund Randolph," in *The American Secretaries of State and Their Diplomacy* (1927); H.J. Eckenrode, *The Randolphs: The Story of a Virginia Family* (1928); Nathan Schachner, *The Founding Fathers* (1954).

RANDOLPH, Peyton

Born in Williamsburg, Va., in September 1721; son of Sir John Randolph, King's attorney of Virginia, diplomat, and speaker of the House of Burgesses, and Susanna (Beverly) Randolph; uncle of Edmund Randolph, attorney general and secretary of state under Washington; member of Bruton Parish Church; married to Elizabeth Harrison on March 8, 1745; no children; studied under private tutors; attended the College of William and Mary; began study of law at the Inner Temple, London, 1739, and admitted to the bar in February 10, 1744; appointed King's attorney for the province in 1748; member of the House of Burgesses representing Williamsburg, 1748–1749 and 1758–1775, and representing the College of William and Mary, 1752–1758; elected speaker of the House of Burgesses in November 1766 and reelected in successive assemblies until the Revolution; member of the Virginia Committee of Correspondence, 1759–1767; chairman of the Committee of Correspondence, 1773; president of the Virginia revolutionary conventions in 1774 and 1775; appointed by the Virginia convention to the first session of the Continental Congress; elected first PRESIDENT OF THE CONTINENTAL CONGRESS on September 5, 1774; resigned on October 22, 1774, to attend the state legislature; reelected PRESIDENT OF THE CONTINENTAL CONGRESS in Philadelphia and served from May 10 to May 24, 1775; resigned on account of ill health; died in Philadelphia on October 22, 1775; interment in the chapel of the College of William and Mary, Williamsburg, Va. **References:** H.J. Eckenrode, *The Revolution in Virginia* (1916); *Virginia Magazine of History and Biography* (January 1924); Edmund C. Burnett, *The Continental Congress* (1964).

RAWLINS, John Aaron

Born in Galena, Ill., February 13, 1831; son of James Dawson Rawlins, farmer, and Lovisa (Collier) Rawlins; married to Emily Smith on June 5, 1856; after death of first wife married Mary E. Hurlburt on December 23, 1863; father of three children; attended local schools and the Rock River Seminary at Mount Morris, Ill.; studied law in Galena; admitted to the bar in 1854; elected attorney for Galena in 1857; nominated for the electoral college on the Douglas ticket; at the start of the Civil War, played an active part in the organization of the 45th Illinois Infantry, becoming a major in that regiment in 1861; aide-de-camp to

General Ulysses S. Grant; commissioned a lieutenant, August 1861; became captain and assistant adjutant general of U.S. Volunteers as a member of General Grant's staff, August 30, 1861; editor of Grant's papers; promoted to brigadier general of the Volunteers, August 11, 1863; became brigadier general and chief of staff of the army following the creation of that permanent position by Congress on March 3, 1865; promoted to major general on April 9, 1865; appointed SECRETARY OF WAR in the cabinet of President Grant on March 11, 1869; attempted to annex Cuba to the United States; after five months in office, died in Washington on September 6, 1869. **References:** Ulysses Simpson Grant, *Personal Memoirs of U.S. Grant* (1885); J.H. Wilson, *The Life of John A. Rawlins* (1916); John Y. Simon, ed., *The Papers of Ulysses S. Grant* (1967); Philip R. Moran, ed., *Ulysses S. Grant, 1822–1885: Chronology, Documents, Bibliographical Aids* (1968).

Ronald Reagan (Library of Congress)

REAGAN, Ronald Wilson

Born in Tampico, Ill., February 6, 1911; second of two sons of John Edward, a shoe salesman, and Nelle Clyde (Wilson) Reagan; Presbyterian; married Jane Wyman (1914–), actress, on January 26, 1940 (divorced, 1948); married Nancy Davis (1921–), actress, on March 4, 1952; father of Maureen Elizabeth by first wife, Michael Edward (adopted, 1945), and Patricia Ann and Ronald Prescott by second wife; grew up in Dixon, Ill., and was credited with saving 77 lives over seven summers as a lifeguard there; graduated from Dixon High School, 1928, where he was student body president and played his first acting part; A.B. in economics and sociology, Eureka (Ill.) College, 1932; enlisted with U.S. Army Reserve and promoted to second lieutenant, 1937–1942, then served to captain on active duty making training films, First Motion Picture Unit, Culver City, Calif., 1942–1945; broadcaster, WOC radio station, Davenport, Iowa, and WHO, Des Moines, 1932–1937; signed first acting contract with Warner Brothers Studios, 1937; later signed with Universal Studios and continued his acting career until 1965, making 53 motion pictures and one television movie; president, Screen Actors

Guild, Hollywood, 1947–1952, 1959–1960; host and production supervisor, *General Electric Theater* television series, 1954–1962; host and part-time performer, *Death Valley Days* television series, 1962–1966; originally a Democrat and supporter of Presidents Roosevelt and Truman, he campaigned as a Democrat for Eisenhower, 1952 and 1956, and formally switched parties in 1962; gained national attention for a televised speech, "A Time for Choosing," endorsing Barry Goldwater for president, October 1964, and became the figurehead for the growing conservative political movement in United States from that point; Republican governor, state of California, 1967–1975; achieved budget surpluses large enough to institute income tax rebates and property tax relief in 1973 and to establish the California Welfare Reform Act of 1971; businessman, rancher, syndicated columnist, and radio commentator on public policy, 1975–1980; unsuccessful candidate for the Republican nomination for president, 1976; nominated for president at the Republican National Convention on July 16, 1980, and chose former Congressman and CIA director George H.W. Bush as his running mate; on November 4, 1980, was elected the fortieth PRESIDENT OF THE UNITED STATES, defeating the reelection bid of Democratic President Jimmy Carter with 50.7 percent of the popular vote and a 489-49 electoral margin in a race that also featured independent candidate John Anderson; along with Bush, reelected on November 6, 1984, defeating Democratic candidate Walter Mondale with 58.4 percent of the popular vote and 525-13 in the electoral college; inaugurated on January 20, 1981; the oldest president ever to be elected in U.S. history; shortly after his inaugural address on January 21, 1981, Iran released 52 American hostages who had been held for 444 days; wounded by a gunshot in an assassination attempt in Washington, March 30, 1981; important elements of his presidency include comprehensive income tax cut, 1982; significant increases in military and defense spending throughout his presidency, including for research and development on the Strategic Defense Initiative (SDI, or "Star Wars") missile shield project; signed into law federal budgets with the largest annual deficits in U.S. history, tripling the national debt during the course of his eight years in office; virulent rhetorical denunciations of the Soviet Union during his first term, softening in his second as new Soviet Premier Mikhail Gorbachev moved toward reform of the communist system; signed Intermediate-Range Nuclear Forces (INF) reduction treaty, December 1987; supported anticommunist forces in Central America and Afghanistan; launched invasion of Grenada, 1983, and authorized bombings of military targets in Libya, 1986, in retaliation for recent terrorist attacks; credibility damaged by revelations of Iran-Contra arms-for-hostages scandal, 1986–1987, but left office at the end of his second term on January 20, 1989, enormously popular and widely credited with renewing American confidence about its government and its role in the world and praised for his anticommunist efforts when the Soviet Union and its domination of eastern Europe collapsed during the administration of his successor, President George H.W. Bush; on November 5, 1994, he acknowledged that he had been diagnosed with Alzheimer's disease and has made few public appearances in the following years as his condition deteriorated; member, California state Republican Central Committee, 1964–1966; state cochairman, California Citizens for Goldwater-Miller, 1964; delegate, Republican National Convention, 1968, 1972; chairman, Republican Governor's Association, 1968–1973; member, Presidential Commission on CIA Activities within the U.S., 1975; member, board of directors, Committee on the Present Danger, Washington, 1977; became the longest-living former U.S. president in October, 2001; recipient, honorary M.A., Eureka College, 1957, Great American of the Decade Award, Virginia Young Americans for Freedom, 1960–1970, Man of the Year Free Enterprise Award, San Fernando Valley Business and Professional award, 1964, American Legion award, 1965, Horatio Alger Award, 1969, George Washington Honor Medal Award, Freedoms Foundation, Valley Forge, Pa., 1971, Distinguished American award, Gold Medal, U.S. Congress, 2000; inducted into National Football Foundation Hall of Fame and American Patriots Hall of Fame; honored as namesake of the second largest federal building in the United States, the Ronald Reagan Building and International Trade Center, Washington, 1998, and of the renamed Ronald Reagan Washington National Airport, 1998; author of *Where's the Rest of Me* (1965), *Speaking My Mind: Selected Speeches* (1989), and *An American Life* (1990); coauthor of *Reagan, in His Own Hand: The Writings of Ronald Reagan That Reveal His Revolutionary Vision for America* (2001); former member, American Federation of Radio and Television Artists, Screen Actors Guild, Lions, Friars, Tau Kappa Epsilon. **References:** *Current Biography Yearbook 1982*; Nancy Reagan and William Novak, *My Turn* (1989); Paul Boyer, ed., *Reagan as President: Contemporary Views of the Man, His Politics, and His Policies* (1990); Lou Cannon, *President Reagan: The Role of a Lifetime* (1991); Michael Schaller, *Reckoning with Reagan: America and Its President in the 1980s* (1992); Lawrence E. Walsh, *Firewall: The Iran-Contra Conspiracy and Cover-up* (1997); Edmund Morris, *Dutch: A Memoir of Ronald Reagan* (1999); Matthew Dallek, *The Right Moment: Ronald Reagan's First Victory and the Decisive Turning Point in American Politics* (2000); Frances FitzGerald, *Way Out There in the Blue: Reagan, Star Wars, and the End of the Cold War* (2000); *Who's Who in America, 2000.*

—Jeffrey Coster

REDFIELD, William Cox

Born in Albany, N.Y., June 18, 1858; son of Charles Bailey Redfield; Episcopalian; married to Elise Mercein Fuller on April 8, 1885; father of Elsie and Humphrey; moved with his parents to Pittsfield, Mass, in 1867; attended the public schools and received home instruction; worked in the Pittsfield post office and as a traveling salesman for a paper company; went to New York City in 1877 and was employed in the stationery and printing business; in

1883 began work with J.H. Williams and Company of Brooklyn, making steel and iron forgings, becoming treasurer and later president of the firm; elected to the board of the Equitable Life Insurance Company, through the influence of Grover Cleveland, in 1905, and served as director until 1913; delegate to the Gold Democrat National Convention at Indianapolis in 1896; unsuccessful candidate as Gold Democrat for election to Congress in 1896; appointed commissioner of public works for Brooklyn in 1902 and 1903; elected as a Democrat to the 62d Congress, serving from March 4, 1911, until March 3, 1913; appointed SECRETARY OF COMMERCE in the cabinet of President Wilson on March 4, 1913; most important contributions were reorganization and enlargement of the Bureau of Foreign and Domestic Commerce, institution of the commercial attaché service, strengthening of the Bureau of Standards; resigned on November 1, 1919; engaged in banking and insurance concerns in New York City; active in civic organizations and philanthropic enterprises; author of *The New Industrial Day* (1912), *With Congress and Cabinet* (1924), *Dependent America* (1926), *We and the World* (1927), and an extended series of articles, "Glimpses of Our Government," appearing in the *Saturday Evening Post* (May 1924–January 1925); died in New York City on June 13, 1932; interment in the Albany Rural Cemetery, Albany, N.Y. **References:** William C. Redfield, *With Congress and Cabinet* (1924); R.S. Baker and W.E. Dodd, *The Public Papers of Woodrow Wilson*, vol. 2 (1925); Arthur S. Link, *Woodrow Wilson: The New Freedom* (1956); Leon H. Canfield, *The Presidency of Woodrow Wilson* (1966).

REGAN, Donald Thomas

Born in Cambridge, Mass., December 21, 1918; son of William F., a policeman and railroad worker, and Kathleen (Ahern) Regan; Catholic; married Ann G. Buchanan on July 11, 1942; father of Donna, Donald, Richard, and Diane; attended Cambridge Latin School; B.A. in English, Harvard University, 1940; served to lieutenant colonel, U.S. Marine Corps, 1940–1946; graduated from Merrill Lynch Company's course for stockbrokers, 1946; with Merrill Lynch, Pierce, Fenner, and Smith, Inc., 1946–1981, becoming partner in 1952, the youngest ever at that firm, and serving as director, administrative division, 1960–1964, executive vice-president, 1964–1968, president, 1968–1970, chairman of the board and chief executive officer, 1971–1980; chairman and chief executive officer, Merrill Lynch and Co., Inc., 1973–1981; appointed by President Reagan as SECRETARY OF THE TREASURY and served from January 22, 1981, until February 1, 1985, when he and James A. Baker switched positions and Regan became White House chief of staff during Reagan's second term, 1985–1987; vice-chairman, board of directors, New York Stock Exchange, 1972–1975; chairman, board of trustees, University of Pennsylvania, 1974–1979, life trustee, 1978–1981; member, Council on Foreign Relations and Policy Commission, Business Roundtable, 1978–1980; trustee, Commission for Economic Development, 1978–1980; named Laureat, Business

Hall of Fame, 1981; commander, Legion of Honor; recipient of honorary degrees from Hahnemann Medical College and Hospital, 1968, Tri-State College, 1969, University of Pennsylvania, 1972, Pace University, 1973, Colgate University, 1984, and Middlebury College, 1999; author of *A View from the Street* (1972) and *For the Record* (1988); member, Army-Navy Club of Washington, Metropolitan Club of Washington, Economic Club of New York City. **References:** *U.S. News & World Report* (December 22, 1980); *Fortune* (March 23, 1981); *Current Biography Yearbook 1981*; Ronald Brownstein and Nina Easton, *Reagan's Ruling Class* (1982); Lou Cannon, *President Reagan: The Role of a Lifetime* (1991); Lawrence E. Walsh, *Firewall: The Iran-Contra Conspiracy and Cover-up* (1997); *Who's Who in America, 2000.*

REICH, Robert Bernard

Born in Scranton, Pa., June 24, 1946; son of Edwin Saul, clothing store owner, and Mildred Dorf (Freshman) Reich; married Clare Dalton, a law professor, on July 7, 1973; father of Adam and Samuel; grew up in South Salem, N.Y.; A.B. summa cum laude, Dartmouth College, 1968; M.A., Oxford University, England, 1970; J.D., Yale University, 1973; law clerk, Judge Frank M. Coffin, U.S. Court of Appeals, Boston, 1973–1974; assistant solicitor general, U.S. Department of Justice, 1974–1976; director of policy planning, Federal Trade Commission, 1976–1981; professor of business and public policy, John F. Kennedy School of Government, Harvard University, 1981–1992; appointed SECRETARY OF LABOR by President Bill Clinton and served from January 22, 1993, until January 10, 1997; contributions include overseeing the enactment and implementation of the Family and Medical Leave Act, the Pension Protection Act, the first increase in minimum wage in nearly a decade, the School-to-Work Apprenticeship Act, and a national crackdown on sweatshops; university professor and Maurice B. Hexter Professor of Social and Economic Policy, Heller Graduate School, Brandeis University, 1997– ; summer intern for Senator Robert Kennedy, 1967; regional student coordinator of Minnesota Senator Eugene McCarthy's campaign for the Democratic presidential nomination, 1968; adviser to the presidential campaigns of Democratic candidates Walter Mondale, 1984, Michael Dukakis, 1988, and Bill Clinton, 1992; announced he would seek the Democratic nomination for governor of Massachusetts in 2002, his first bid for elected office; corporate consultant, 1981–1992; chairman, biotechnology section, U.S. Office of Technological Assessment, Washington, 1990–1991; chairman, economic policy transition team, President-elect Clinton, 1992–1993; former member, board of directors, Economic Policy Institute, Business Enterprise Trust, 1989–1993; member, governing board, Common Cause, 1981–1985; trustee, Dartmouth College, 1989–1993; coauthor of *Minding America's Business: The Decline and Rise of the American Economy* (with Ira Magaziner, 1982) and *New Deals: The Chrysler Revival and the American*

System (with John D. Donahue, 1985); author of *The Next American Frontier* (1983), *Tales of a New America* (1987), *The Power of Public Ideas* (1988), *The Resurgent Liberal* (1989), *Public Management in a Democratic Society* (1990), *The Work of Nations: Preparing Ourselves for 21st Century Capitalism* (1991), *Locked in the Cabinet* (1997), *The Future of Success: Working and Living in the New Economy* (2001), and *I'll Be Short: Essential Ideas for Getting America to Work* (2002); former editor, *Yale Law Review*; contributing editor, *The New Republic*; founder and chairman, editorial board, *The American Prospect*, 1990– ; Rhodes scholar, 1968; recipient, Louis Brownlow Book award, National Academy of Public Administration, 1984. **References:** *Current Biography Yearbook 1993*; Elizabeth Drew, *On the Edge: The Clinton Presidency* (1994); Bob Woodward, *The Agenda* (1994).

—Edmund Wehrle

RENO, Janet

Born in Miami, Fla., July 21, 1938; daughter of Henry and Jane (Wood) Reno, both reporters for Miami newspapers; graduated from Coral Gables High School; B.A. in chemistry, Cornell University, 1960; LL.B., Harvard University Law School, 1963; admitted to the bar in Florida, 1963; associate, Brigham and Brigham, Miami, 1963–1967; partner, Lewis and Reno, Miami, 1967–1971; staff director, Judiciary Committee, Florida House of Representatives, 1971–1972; counsel, Criminal Justice Committee for

Former U.S. Attorney General and Florida Democratic gubernatorial hopeful Janet Reno talks with host Jay Leno during the taping of *The Tonight Show with Jay Leno*, March 26, 2002. (AP/Wide World Photos)

Revision of the Criminal Code, Florida Senate, 1973; assistant state attorney, 11th Judicial Circuit, Fla., 1973–1976; partner, Steel, Hector and Davis, Miami, 1976–1978; state attorney, Dade County, Fla., 1978–1993; the first female state attorney in Florida history, she was initially appointed to the post and later won reelection, 1978, 1982, 1986, and 1990; appointed by President Bill Clinton as ATTORNEY GENERAL and served from March 12, 1993, until the end of Clinton's second term on January 20, 2001; the first woman to hold the post; faced criticism for her handling of an FBI raid on Branch Davidian compound in Waco, Tex., April 1993, as well as her reluctance to investigate allegations of campaign finance law violations by President Clinton and Vice-President Gore; unsuccessful Democratic candidate for state legislature, 1972; consultant, Florida Senate Criminal Justice Committee for Revision of Florida's Criminal Code, 1973; member, judicial nominating commission, 11th Judicial Circuit, Florida,

1976–1978; chair, Governor's Council for the Prosecution of Organized Crime, 1979–1980; president, Florida Prosecuting Attorney's Association, 1984–1986; announced she would be a candidate for the Democratic nomination for governor of Florida, 2002; recipient, Herbert Harley award, American Judicature Society, 1981, Women First award, YWCA, 1993, Spirit of Crazy Horse award, Reclaiming Youth International, 2001; named to National Women's Hall of Fame, 2000; member, American Bar Association, American Law Institute, American Judicature Society, Dade County Bar Association. **References:** *Current Biography Yearbook 1993*; Paul Anderson, *Janet Reno: Doing the Right Thing* (1994); Elizabeth Drew, *On the Edge: The Clinton Presidency* (1994).

—Jeremy Brett

RIBICOFF, Abraham Alexander

Born in New Britain, Conn., April 9, 1910; son of Samuel and Rose (Sable) Ribicoff; Jewish; married Ruth Siegel (died 1971) on June 28, 1931; married Lois Mell Mathes ("Casey") on August 4, 1972; father of Peter and Jane Bishop; stepfather of Peter Mathes; attended public schools in New Britain; studied at New York University, 1928–1929; LL.B. cum laude, University of Chicago Law School, 1933; headed Chicago office of G.E. Prentice Company, 1920–1931; admitted to the bars of Connecticut, 1933, New York, 1981, U.S. Supreme Court, 1981, and U.S. Court of Appeals, District of Columbia Circuit, 1982; attorney, A.S. Bordon, 1933–1938; partner, Bordon and Ribicoff, 1938–1941; member, Connecticut House of Representatives, 1939–1942; municipal judge, Hartford, Conn., 1942–1943, 1945–1947; partner and cofounder with his brother, Ribicoff, Ribicoff and Kotkin, 1941–1954; Democratic member from Connecticut, U.S. House of Representatives, 1949–1953; unsuccessful Democratic candidate for U.S. Senate, 1952; governor, state of Connecticut, 1955–1961; appointed SECRETARY OF HEALTH, EDUCATION, AND WELFARE by President Kennedy and served from January 21, 1961, to July 13, 1962; most important contributions were proposal for federal funds to better educational resources and offer educational opportunities to larger numbers of people, appropriations for dental research, licensing and use of Sabin oral polio vaccine, increase in radiation screening of milk, water, air, and other foodstuffs, and liberalization of Social Security legislation; Democratic U.S. senator from Connecticut, 1963–1981; special counsel, Kaye, Scholer, Fireman, Hays, and Handler, 1981–1998; member, American Arbitration Association, 1941; chairman, Connecticut assembly of municipal court judges, 1941–1942; chairman, Commission for the Study of Alcoholism and Crime, 1943; member, Bi-partisan Hartford Charter Revision Committee, 1945–1947; hearing examiner, Connecticut Interracial Commission, 1947–1948; delegate to San Francisco Peace Conference, 1951; received considerable publicity for his criticism of the police methods authorized by Chicago Mayor Richard J. Daley in quelling protestors outside the Democratic National Convention, 1968; chairman, Senate Governmental Affairs

Committee, 1975–1981; member, Senate Rules and Administration Commission, 1983, charged with studying the ways the Senate passes legislation and develops recommendations for change; headed a bipartisan commission to determine which military bases should be closed, 1988; former director, Hartford Insurance Group; namesake of the Abraham A. Ribicoff Federal Building and U.S. Courthouse in Hartford; author of *Politics: The American Way* (1967), *America Can Make It* (1972), *The American Military Machine* (1972); coauthor of *American Hostages in Iran: The Conduct of a Crisis* (1980); contracted Alzheimer's disease late in life; died on February 22, 1998, in Riverdale, the Bronx, New York. **References:** *Current Biography Yearbook 1955*; New York Times, *The Kennedy Years* (1964); *New York Times* (November 20, 1980; April 8, 1983; June 6, 1985; July 13, 1988; February 23, 1998).

RICHARDSON, Elliot Lee

Born in Boston, Mass., July 20, 1920; son of Dr. Edward P. and Clara (Shattuck) Richardson; Episcopalian; married Anne Francis Hazard on August 2, 1952; father of Henry, Nancy, and Michael; A.B. cum laude, Harvard University, 1941, LL.B. cum laude, 1947; admitted to the bars of Massachusetts, 1949, and District of Columbia, 1980; first lieutenant, 4th Infantry Division, U.S. Army, 1942–1945; law clerk, Judge Learned Hand, U.S. Court of Appeals, Second Circuit, New York, 1947–1948, Justice Felix Frankfurter, U.S. Supreme Court, 1948–1949; associate, Ropes, Gray, Best, Coolidge, and Rugg, Boston, 1949–1953, 1954–1956; law lecturer at Harvard, 1952; assistant to U.S. Senator Leverett Saltonstall of Massachusetts, 1953–1954; acting counsel to Massachusetts Governor Christian A. Herter, 1956; assistant secretary for legislation, U.S. Department of Health, Education, and Welfare, Washington, 1957–1959, acting secretary, April–July 1958; U.S. attorney for Massachusetts, 1959–1961; special assistant to the U.S. attorney general, 1961; partner, Ropes and Gray, Boston, 1961–1964; Republican lieutenant governor of Massachusetts, 1965–1967; attorney general of Massachusetts, 1967–1969; undersecretary, U.S. Department of State, 1969–1970; appointed SECRETARY OF HEALTH, EDUCATION, AND WELFARE by President Nixon and served from June 24, 1970, until January 29, 1973; while head of HEW, sought to simplify the processing of grants, consolidate existing programs, and transfer greater administrative responsibility to state and local governments; in August 1970 he announced an end to the policy of cutting off federal funds to school districts that refused to desegregate; left HEW when Nixon appointed him as SECRETARY OF DEFENSE, where he served from January 30, 1973, until May 24, 1973, leaving the Defense Department when Nixon named him ATTORNEY GENERAL; served as the head of the Justice Department from May 25, 1973, until October 20, 1973, when he resigned rather than carry out Nixon's order to fire Archibald Cox, director of the Office of the Watergate Special Prosecuting Force; fellow, Woodrow Wilson International Center for Scholars, Washington, 1974–1975; U.S. ambassador to the Court of

St. James, London, United Kingdom, 1975–1976; appointed by President Ford as SECRETARY OF COMMERCE and served from February 2, 1976, until the end of Ford's term on January 20, 1977, while secretary of commerce, he headed the probe of alleged payoffs by American corporations to secure foreign contracts; the only person to head four different federal cabinet department; U.S. ambassador-at-large, special representative of President Carter, United Nations Law of the Sea Conference, Washington, 1977–1980; senior partner to retired partner, Milbank, Tweed, Hadley, and McCloy, Washington, 1980–1992, 1993–1999; unsuccessful Republican candidate for U.S. Senate from Massachusetts, 1984; appointed personal representative of the secretary-general of the United Nations for Nicaraguan Elections, 1989–1990; appointed special representative of Presidents George H.W. Bush and Bill Clinton for multilateral assistance in the Philippines, 1989–1994; member, Chatam House Foundation to improve Anglo-American relations, 1985; appointed by the government of the People's Republic of China to conduct a comprehensive study of China's commercial relations with the United States, 1986; named to special UN Crisis Panel to discover how the United Nations could increase its authority during international crises, 1987; cofounder, Council for Excellence in Government, 1983; former member, board of directors, EcuMed, Oak Industries, John Hancock Life Insurance Company, BNFL Inc., U.S. Council of International Business, Urban Institute, Inter-American Dialogue, advisory board, American Flywheel Systems, Inc., board of overseers, Harvard College, overseers committee to visit Harvard University Law School, comptroller general's consulting panel; former chairman, Council on Ocean Law, Quality Review Board, General Accounting Office, overseers committee to visit John F. Kennedy School of Government, Harvard University, and to visit Harvard Medical School and School of Dental Medicine, Hitachi Foundation, Japan-American Society of Washington; former trustee, Public International, National Public Radio (NPR) Satellite Equipment, Radcliffe College, Massachusetts General Hospital, Roger Tory Peterson Institute; former president, World Affairs Council, Boston; former director, Massachusetts Bay United Fund; former chairman, Greater Boston United Fund Campaign; former vice-chairman, Citizens Network for Foreign Affairs; recipient, Bronze Star, Purple Heart with oak leaf cluster, Legion d'Honneur, Jefferson award, American Institute of Public Service, Thomas Hart Benton award, Kansas City Art Institute, Emory R. Buckner medal, Federal Bar Council, Penn Club award, Albert Lasker Special Public Service award, 1978, Neptune award, Meritorious Public Service award, U.S. Coast Guard, Harry Truman Good Neighbor award, Speaker Thomas P. O'Neill, Jr., award for public service, Sam Rayburn award, Franklin D. Roosevelt Freedom medal, Presidential Medal of Freedom, 1999, Harvard Law School Association award, and honorary degrees from many schools, including Harvard University, 1971; namesake of the Elliot L. Richardson Prize for Excellence in Government Service and Public Management, Council for Excellence in Government, beginning in 2000; author of *The Creative Balance* (1976) and *Reflections of a Radical Moderate* (1996); former fellow, AAAS, American Bar Foundation, Massachusetts Bar Foundation; former member,

American Bar Association, ASPA, District of Columbia Bar Association, Massachusetts Bar Association, Harvard University Alumni Association, Council on Foreign Relations, American Law Institute, American Society for International Law, Bretton Woods Committee, American Academy of Diplomacy, American Academy for Social Insurance, International Law Association, National Academy of Public Administrators, Council on Excellence in Government, Veterans of Foreign Wars, and American Legion; died on December 30, 1999, in Boston. **References:** *Newsweek* (June 15, 1970); *Time* (June 15, 1970); *Current Biography Yearbook 1971; New York Times* (February 12, March 20, September 16, and December 13, 1984; March 12, 1985; February 2 and November 13, 1986; January 24, 1987; January 1, 2000); Kenneth W. Thompson, ed., *The Nixon Presidency: Twenty-two Intimate Perspectives* (1987); James Cannon, *Time and Chance: Gerald Ford's Appointment with History* (1994); Melvin Small, *The Presidency of Richard Nixon* (1999); *Who's Who in America, 2000*; Richard Reeves, *President Nixon: Alone in the White House* (2001).

RICHARDSON, William Adams

Born in Tyngsborough, Mass., November 2, 1821; son of Daniel and Mary (Adams) Richardson; Unitarian; married Anna Maria Marston on October 29, 1849; father of one daughter; received his preparatory education at Pinkerton Academy in Derry, N.H., and at Lawrence Academy in Groton, Mass.; graduated Harvard in 1843; studied law at the Harvard Law School and was admitted to the bar in July 1846, commencing his legal practice in Lowell, Mass.; initially a Whig, he became a Republican in 1855; appointed to compile and index the statute laws of Massachusetts, 1856; became judge of probate for Middlesex County in 1856; appointed assistant secretary of the treasury by President Grant on March 20, 1869, at the recommendation of Treasury Secretary Boutwell; tendered a full cabinet portfolio as SECRETARY OF THE TREASURY by President Grant on March 17, 1873, and served until June 3, 1874; appointed to the Massachusetts Court of Appeals in June 1874 and was elevated to chief justiceship in 1885; overseer of Harvard University, 1863 to 1875; lecturer and professor at Georgetown Law School in Washington, D.C.; authored *The Banking Laws of Massachusetts* (1855), *Practical Information Covering the Debt of the United States* (1872), *National Banking Laws* (1872), *History, Jurisdiction and Practice of the Court of Claims* (1885); died in Washington, D.C., on October 19, 1896. **References:** Louis Arthur Coolidge, *Ulysses S. Grant* (1917); William Best Hesseltine, *Ulysses S. Grant, Politician* (1953).

RICHARDSON, William Blaine

Born in Pasadena, Calif., November 15, 1947; son of William, a bank executive, and Maria Luisa (Zubiran) Richardson; married Barbara Flavin, an antiques restorer, 1972; grew up mainly in Mexico City, Mexico; attended Middlesex prep school in Massachusetts; B.A. in political science, Tufts University, 1970; M.A., Fletcher School of Law and Diplomacy, Tufts University, 1971; staff member, U.S. House of Representatives, 1971–1972; member, congressional liaison office, U.S. Department of State, 1973–1975; staff member, Foreign Relations Committee, U.S. Senate, 1975–1978; executive director, New Mexico State Democratic Committee and Bernalillo County Democratic Committee, 1978; trade consultant and businessman, Santa Fe, N.M., 1978–1982; Democratic member from New Mexico's 3d district, U.S. House of Representatives, 1983–1997; member, House Energy and Commerce Committee, Select Committee on Intelligence, Helsinki Commission, and Congressional Hispanic Caucus (chairman, 1985); chairman, Native American Affairs Subcommittee, 1993–1995; ranking minority member, subcommittee on National Parks, Forests and Lands; one of four chief deputy Democratic House whips, 1993–1997; while in Congress took several trips as unofficial diplomatic envoy for the U.S. government, including monitoring elections in Nicaragua, meeting with Nobel Peace Prize winner Aung San Suu Kyi of Myanmar and calling for her release from prison in 1994, encouraging Haitian General Raoul Cedras to step down from power in 1994, traveling to North Korea in 1994 to discuss the issue of nuclear disarmament and negotiating for the release of hostages and captives in Iraq, Cuba, the Sudan, North Korea, and Bangladesh; U.S. ambassador to the United Nations, 1997–1998; appointed by President Bill Clinton as SECRETARY OF ENERGY and served from August 18, 1998, until the end of Clinton's term on January 20, 2001; faced major controversy stemming from security lapses at U.S. nuclear laboratories leading to the obtaining of nuclear weapons secrets by China; visiting professor, John F. Kennedy School of Government, Harvard University, 2001– ; associate, Kissinger McLarty Associates, 2001– ; consultant, global energy and power group, Citigroup's Salomon Smith Barney, 2001– ; unsuccessful Democratic candidate for Congress, 1980; former vice-chairman, Democratic National Committee; former member, NATO 2000 Board, American G.I. Forum; member, board of directors, Valero Energy Corporation, 2001– ; member, Big Brothers–Big Sisters, Santa Fe, Santa Fe Hispanic Chamber of Commerce, Santa Fe Chamber of Commerce, Council on Foreign Relations. **References:** *New York Times* (July 18, 1995); *Washington Post* (December 14, 1996); *Current Biography Yearbook 1996.*

—Jeremy Brett

RILEY, Richard Wilson

Born in Greenville County, S.C., January 2, 1933; son of Edward Patterson, a lawyer and assistant U.S. attorney, and Martha Elizabeth (Dixon) Riley; Methodist; married Ann Osteen Yarborough on August 23, 1957; father of Richard Wilson, Anne Y., Hubert D, Theodore D.; B.A. cum laude, Furman University, 1954; LL.B., University of South Carolina, 1959; served from ensign to lieutenant (jg), U.S. Naval Reserve, 1954–1956; in 1955 he contracted rheumatoid spondylitis, a degenerative bone disease, which stabilized in the early 1970s but left him with a curvature in his spine and an inability to turn his neck; partner, Riley and Riley, Greenville, 1959–1978; legal counsel, Judiciary Committee, U.S. Senate, 1960; Democratic member, South Carolina House of Representatives, 1963–1966, and state senate, 1966–1976; a progressive liberal who supported school desegregation; governor of South Carolina, 1979–1987; established a nationally recognized statewide education program in which school attendance and test scores in basic skills increased significantly; cofounder and senior partner, Nelson, Mullins, Riley, and Scarborough, Greenville and Columbia, S.C., 1987–1993; appointed by President Bill Clinton as SECRETARY OF EDUCATION and served from January 22, 1993, until the end of Clinton's second term on January 20, 2001; focused on improving academic standards and educational opportunities for the poor, expanded grants and loans for college, helped create the Partnership for Family Involvement in Education, helped public schools and libraries gain greater Internet access, and helped to amend the Individuals with Disabilities Education Act; former chairman, South Carolina State Planning Council on Nuclear Waste Management; vice-president, Young Lawyers Club, Greenville, 1961; unsuccessful candidate for the Democratic nomination for governor, 1974; headed the South Carolina presidential campaign of Jimmy Carter, 1975; personnel director, Clinton-Gore transition team, 1992–1993; recipient, Outstanding Young Man of Greenville award, Junior Chamber of Commerce, Friend of Education Award, South Carolina Education Association, Connie Award for special conservation achievement, National Wildlife Federation, 1981, Government Responsibility Award, Martin Luther King, Jr., Center, 1983, Distinguished Service award, Council of Chief State School Officers, 1994, James Bryant Conant Award, Education Commission of the States, 1995, T.H. Bell award for Outstanding Education Advocacy, Committee for Education Funding, 1996, Distinguished Service award, American Council on Education, 1998; former member, National Assessment Governing Board, Carnegie Foundation Task Force of Meeting the Needs of Young Children; fellow, John F. Kennedy School of Government, Harvard University; member, South Carolina and Greenville Bar Associations, Furman University Alumni Association (president, 1968–1969), Phi Beta Kappa. **References:** *Current Biography Yearbook 1993; Almanac of the Executive Branch, 1999; Federal Yellow Book, 2000; Who's Who, 2001.*

—Robert T. Chase

ROBESON, George

Born at Oxford Furnace, N.J., March 16, 1829; son of William Penn Robeson, iron manufacturer, and Ann (Maxwell) Robeson; married to Mary Isabelle (Ogston) Aulick in 1872; father of one daughter; graduated from Princeton College in 1847; studied law with Chief Justice Hornblower; admitted to the bar in 1850; licensed as a counselor, 1854; practiced in Newark, N.J., and later in Camden; appointed prosecuting attorney for Camden County in 1858; during the Civil War was commissioned a brigadier general and took an active part in the organization of the state troops; attorney general of New Jersey from 1867 until his resignation in 1869; appointed SECRETARY OF THE NAVY in the cabinet of President Grant on June 25, 1869, to fill the vacancy caused by the resignation of A.E. Borie; most important contribution was securing the federal appropriation for the ill-fated North Polar Expedition of Captain C.F. Hall, who named Robeson Channel in northern Greenland after the secretary; served until the end of President Grant's second term, resigning on March 12, 1877; resumed practice of law; unsuccessful candidate for U.S. senator in 1877; elected as a Republican to the 46th and 47th Congresses from the 1st New Jersey district and served from March 4, 1879, until March 3, 1883; unsuccessful candidate for reelection in 1882 to the 48th Congress; resumed practice of law in Trenton, N.J.; died in Trenton on September 27, 1897; interment in Belvidere Cemetery, Belvidere, N.J. **References:** Adam Badeau, *Grant in Peace* (1888); William Best Hesseltine, *Ulysses S. Grant, Politician* (1957); John Y. Simon, ed., *The Papers of Ulysses S. Grant* (1967).

ROCKEFELLER, Nelson Aldrich, Sr.

Born in Bar Harbor, Me., July 8, 1908; son of John Davison, Jr., and Abby Greene (Aldrich) Rockefeller; grandson of John D. Rockefeller, Sr., founder of Standard Oil Company, and Nelson Aldrich, U.S. senator from Rhode Island; married Mary Todhunter Clark, June 23, 1930 (divorced, 1962); married Margaretta ("Happy") Fitler Murphy on May 4, 1963; father of Rodman, Ann Coste, Steven, Michael, and Mary Morgan, by his first wife, and Nelson Aldrich Jr. and Mark Fitler, by his second wife; attended the Lincoln School of Teachers College at Columbia University, New York City, 1917–1926; A.B. in economics, cum laude and Phi Beta Kappa, Dartmouth College, 1930; employed at London and Paris branches, Chase National Bank, 1931; member, board of directors, Rockefeller Center, Inc., 1931–1958, and president, 1938–1945 and 1948–1951, chairman, 1945–1953 and 1956–1958; member, board of directors, Creole Petroleum Company, Venezuelan subsidiary of Standard Oil of New Jersey, 1935–1940; coordinator, Office of Inter-American Affairs, Washington, 1940–1944; chairman, Inter-American Development Commission, 1940–1947; assistant secretary for American Republic Affairs, U.S. Department of State, Washington, 1944–1945; founder and president, American International Association for Economic and Social Development, 1946–1953, and International Basic Economy Corporation, 1947–1953; undersecretary, U.S. Department of Health, Education, and Welfare, 1953–1955; special assistant for foreign affairs to President Eisenhower, 1954–1955; Republican governor, state of New York, 1959–1973; an activist, progressive governor, he promoted state funding for education, transportation, and social welfare projects; regarded as the leader of the eastern, more liberal wing of the national Republican Party throughout the 1960s;

Nelson A. Rockefeller, right, and Joseph C. Rovensky (Library of Congress)

special envoy to Latin America for President Nixon, 1969; appointed by President
Gerald Ford as forty-first VICE-PRESIDENT OF THE UNITED STATES and served from
December 19, 1974, until the end of Ford's term on January 20, 1977; the first
unelected vice-president, he was confirmed by Congress under the terms of the
Twenty-fifth Amendment; did not run with Ford for reelection in 1976 campaign; founder, Nelson Rockefeller Collection, Inc., an art reproduction business, 1978; unsuccessful candidate for the Republican presidential nomination,
1960, 1964, and 1968; trustee, Museum of Modern Art, New York City,
1932–1979, and treasurer, 1935–1939, president, 1939–1941 and 1946–1953;
cofounder and trustee, Rockefeller Brothers Fund, 1940–1975 and 1977–1979,
and president, 1956; member, Westchester County (N.Y.) Board of Health,
1933–1953, Mayor's Business Advisory Committee, New York City, 1940–1947,
Mexican-American Commission for Economic Cooperation, 1943–1945, U.S.
delegation to the United Nations Conference on Organization, San Francisco,
1945, Mayor's Committee for the United Nations, New York City, 1946, President's Advisory Commission on Intergovernmental Relations, 1965–1969,
President's Foreign Intelligence Advisory Board, 1969–1974; founder, president, and trustee, Museum of Primitive Art, New York City, 1954–1975; chairman, International Development Advisory Board, 1950–1951, President's
Advisory Committee on Government Organization, 1953–1958, Special Com-
mittee on Defense Organization, 1953, Special Studies Project, Rockefeller
Brothers Fund, 1956–1958, Temporary State Commission on the Constitutional
Convention, New York, 1956–1958, Special Legislative Committee on the
Revision and Simplification of the Constitution, New York, 1958, Committee
on Civil Defense and Post-Attack Recovery, National Governor's Conference
(NGC), 1959–1966, Conference on Public Safety, NGC, 1966, Commission on
Human Resources, NGC, 1968, National Commission on Critical Choices for

Americans, 1973–1974, National Commission on Water Quality, 1973–1976, Commission on CIA Activities within the United States, 1975, National Commission on Productivity and Work Quality, 1975, President's Panel on Federal Compensation, 1975; consultant to Secretary of Defense on the organization of the Defense Department, 1958; former trustee, Dartmouth College; recipient, Order of Merit, Chile, 1945, National Order of the Southern Cross, Brazil, 1946, Order of the Aztec Eagle, Mexico, 1949, citations by National Conference of Christians and Jews for work in field of human relations, 1948 and 1950, Thomas F. Cunningham Award for contributions toward betterment of Inter-American Relations, 1964, Gold Medal, National Institution of Social Sciences, 1967, and honorary degrees from Fordham University, 1941, Dartmouth College, 1942, and Jewish Theological Seminary, 1950; author of *The Future of Federalism* (1962), *Unity, Freedom and Peace* (1968), and *Our Environment Can Be Saved* (1970); died of a heart attack on January 26, 1979, in New York City. **References:** Stewart Alsop, *Nixon & Rockefeller: A Double Portrait* (1960); Joe Alex Morris, *Nelson Rockefeller: A Biography* (1960); James Poling, *The Rockefeller Record* (1960); James Desmond, *Nelson Rockefeller: A Political Biography* (1964); Frank H. Gervasi, *The Real Rockefeller* (1964); William Rodgers, *Rockefeller's Follies: An Unauthorized View* (1966); Gary Allen, *The Rockefeller File* (1976); Michael Kramer and Sam Roberts, *"I Never Wanted to Be Vice-President of Anything": An Investigative Biography of Nelson Rockefeller* (1976); *New York Times* (January 2, May 10, and October 27, 1977; January 27 and 28, 1979); Robert H. Connery and Gerald Benjamin, *Rockefeller of New York: Executive Power in the Statehouse* (1979); Joseph E. Persico, *The Imperial Rockefeller* (1982); Michael Turner, *The Vice President as Policy Maker: Rockefeller in the Ford White House* (1982); Bernard J. Firestone and Alexej Ugrinsky, eds., *Gerald Ford and the Politics of Post-Watergate America*, vol. 1 (1993); Gerald Colby and Charlotte Dennett, *Thy Will Be Done: The Conquest of the Amazon: Nelson Rockefeller and Evangelism in the Age of Oil* (1995); John Robert Greene, *The Presidency of Gerald R. Ford* (1995); Cary Reich, *The Life of Nelson A. Rockefeller, 1908–1958: Worlds to Conquer* (1996); Darlene Rivas, *Missionary Capitalist: Nelson Rockefeller in Venezuela* (2002).

—Jeffrey Coster

RODNEY, Caesar Augustus

Born in Dover, Del., January 4, 1772; son of Thomas and Elizabeth (Fisher) Rodney; married Susan Hunn; father of ten daughters and five sons; family settled in Wilmington, Del., in 1780; after completing preparatory studies, he entered the University of Pennsylvania, graduating in 1789; studied law, was admitted to the bar, and commenced practice in Wilmington in 1793; elected as a Democrat to the 8th Congress, serving from March 4, 1803, to March 3, 1805; one of managers appointed in January 1804 to conduct impeachment proceedings against

Judges John Pickering and Samuel Chase; invited to join the cabinet of President Jefferson as ATTORNEY GENERAL on January 20, 1807, and was continued in that office by President Madison, serving until his resignation on December 5, 1811; served in the War of 1812 and was commissioned as captain on April 7, 1813; member of the Delaware Committee of Safety in 1813; elected to the state senate in 1815; was sent to South America by President Monroe as one of the commissioners to investigate and report on the propriety of recognizing the independence of the Spanish-American republics, 1817; elected as a Democrat to the 17th Congress, serving from March 4, 1821, to January 24, 1822, when he resigned; elected to the U.S. Senate, serving from January 24, 1822, to January 29, 1823, when he resigned; appointed minister plenipotentiary to Argentina on January 27, 1923, and served until his death in Buenos Aires on June 10, 1824; interment in the English Churchyard, Buenos Aires, Argentina. **References:** Max Beloff, *Thomas Jefferson and American Democracy* (1949); Leonard Patrick O'Connor Wibberly, *Time of the Harvest: Thomas Jefferson, the Years 1801–1826* (1966).

ROGERS, William Pierce

Born in Norfolk, N.Y., June 23, 1913; son of Harrison Alexander and Myra (Beswick) Rogers; married Adele Langston on June 27, 1936; father of Dale, Anthony Wood, Jeffrey Langston, and Douglas Langston; attended high school in Canton, N.Y.; A.B., Colgate University, 1934; LL.B., Cornell University Law School, 1937; admitted to the bars of New York, 1937, and the District of Columbia, 1950; served to lieutenant commander, U.S. Navy, 1942–1946; assistant district attorney, New York, 1938–1942, 1946–1947; chief counsel, U.S. Senate Special Committee investigating the national defense program, 1947, U.S. Senate Investigations Subcommittee to the Committee on Executive Expenditures, 1948–1950; advised then-Congressman Richard Nixon to pursue allegations against Alger Hiss that led to his conviction for perjury; attorney, Dwight, Royall, Harris, Koegel and Caskey, New York City and Washington, 1950–1953; deputy attorney general, U.S. Department of Justice, 1953–1957; appointed by President Eisenhower as ATTORNEY GENERAL on November 8, 1957, serving until the end of Eisenhower's term on January 20, 1961; he advocated a constitutional amendment to deal with the question of presidential disability or inability to perform the functions of the office, sent a group of deputy U.S. marshals to Little Rock, Ark., to ensure enforcement of the desegregation orders of the federal courts, and created a special unit to fight syndicated crime and racketeering in 1958; partner, Royall, Koegel, Rogers and Wells, 1961–1969; appointed by President Nixon as SECRETARY OF STATE on January 22, 1969, and resigned that post effective September 3, 1973, having been continually frustrated by Nixon's preference for conducting foreign policy through his national security adviser, Henry Kissinger, rather than the State Department; senior partner, Rogers and Wells LLP, New York City and Washington, 1973–2001; as adviser to Dwight Eisenhower's 1952 presidential campaign, advised Nixon to resist calls to leave the ticket amid allegations that prominent businessmen had created a "slush fund" for the vice-presidential candidate; U.S. representative to the 20th General Assembly, United Nations, 1965; member, UN Ad Hoc Committee on Southwest Africa, 1967, President's Commission on Law Enforcement and Administration, 1965–1967; chairman, Presidential Commission to Investigate Space Shuttle *Challenger* Accident, 1986, which panel charged that NASA officials had abandoned good judgment in handling safety problems with the space shuttle; editor, *Cornell Law Quarterly*, 1935–1937; recipient, Presidential Medal of Freedom, 1973; died on January 2, 2001, in Bethesda, Md. **References:** Emmett John Hughes, *The Ordeal of Power: A Political Memoir of the Eisenhower Years* (1963); Arthur Larson, *Eisenhower: The President Nobody Knew* (1968); *Current Biography Yearbook 1969*; James Cannon, *Time and Chance: Gerald Ford's Appointment with History* (1994); Melvin Small, *The Presidency of Richard Nixon* (1999); *New York Times* (January 4, 2001); Richard Reeves, *President Nixon: Alone in the White House* (2001).

ROMNEY, George Wilcken

Born in Chihuahua, Mexico, on July 8, 1907; son of Gaskell, a contractor, and Anna (Pratt) Romney; Mormon; married to Lenore La Fount on July 2, 1931; father of Lynn Romney Keenan, Jane Romney Robinson, Scott, and Willard Mitt; began work at age 11 as a sugar harvester and then as a lath and plaster workman; attended Latter-Day Saints High School and Junior College, Salt Lake City, Utah, 1922–1926; Mormon missionary in Scotland and England, 1927–1928; attended the University of Utah, 1929, and George Washington University, 1929–1930; tariff specialist for U.S. Senator David I. Walsh, 1929–1930; apprentice, Aluminum Company of America, Los Angeles, 1930, and salesman, 1931; Washington representative, Aluminum Company of America and Aluminum Wares Association, 1932–1938; manager, Automobile Manufacturers Association, Detroit, 1939–1941, and general manager, 1942–1948; vice-president, Nash-Kelvinator Corporation, 1950–1953, and executive vice-president and director, 1953–1954; after Nash merged with Hudson Motor Car and became American Motors Corporation, he served as president, chairman of the board, and general manager, 1954–1962; responsible for putting the first compact car model, the Rambler, on the U.S. market; Republican governor, state of Michigan, 1963–1968; briefly a candidate for the Republican presidential nomination in 1968 until his withdrawal early that year; appointed SECRETARY OF HOUSING AND URBAN DEVELOPMENT by President Nixon and served from January 2, 1969, until February 2, 1973; most important contributions were reorganizing the Model Cities program and initiating "Operation Breakthrough" to help secure mass housing for the poor; returned to private business interests in Michigan; founder, chairman, and chief executive officer, National Center for Voluntary Action, 1973–1979, before retiring from public life; management member, Detroit-Area War Manpower Commission and Labor-Management Commission; president, Washington Trade Association, 1937–1938, Detroit

Trade Association, 1941; director, American Trade Association Executives, 1944–1947, National Automobile Golden Jubilee Committee, 1946; managing director, Automotive Council War Production, 1942–1945; U.S. employer delegate to Metal Trades Industry Conferences, 1946–1949; chairman, Citizens for Michigan, 1959–1962; named A.P. Industry Man of the Year, 1958–1961; past member, board of directors, National Conference of Christians and Jews, United Fund, Cranbrook School, Points of Light Foundation, National and Community Commission; past president, Detroit Stake Church of Jesus Christ of Latter-Day Saints, regional representative, 1973–1980; died on July 26, 1995, in Bloomfield Hills, Mich. **References:** *Current Biography Yearbook 1958*; D. Duane Angel, *Romney: A Political Biography* (1967), G. Harris, *Romney's Way* (1967); Gerald O. Plas, *Romney Riddle* (1967); Clark Mollenhoff, *George Romney, Mormon in Politics* (1968); *New York Times* (July 27, 1995); Richard Reeves, *President Nixon: Alone in the White House* (2001).

ROOSEVELT, Franklin Delano

Born near Hyde Park, N.Y., January 30, 1882; son of James, lawyer, financier, and railroad executive, and Sara (Delano) Roosevelt; Episcopalian; married (Anna) Eleanor Roosevelt (1884–1962), niece of President Theodore Roosevelt and a distant cousin, on March 17, 1905; father of Anna Eleanor, James, Franklin Delano Jr., Elliott, and John Aspinwall; educated mainly by private tutors; graduated from the Groton School, 1900; B.A., Harvard University, 1903; attended Columbia Law School, 1904–1907; admitted to the New York bar, 1907; attorney, Carter, Ledyard and Milburn, New York; Democratic member from Dutchess County, New York State Senate, 1911–1913, when he resigned to accept an appointment from President Wilson to be assistant secretary of the navy, where he served until 1920; unsuccessful Democratic candidate for vice-president as running mate of James M. Cox, 1920; attorney, Emmet, Marvin and Roosevelt, 1920; vice-president, Fidelity and Deposit Company of Maryland, 1920–1928; stricken with infantile paralysis at his summer home in Campobello, New Brunswick, Canada, in August 1921; attorney, Roosevelt and O'Connor, 1924; Democratic governor of New York, 1929–1933; elected thirty-second PRESIDENT OF THE UNITED STATES in November 1932, defeating the reelection bid of President Herbert Hoover with 57.4 percent of the national popular vote and by 472-59 in the electoral college; inaugurated on March 4, 1933; reelected in 1936, with 60.8 percent of the popular vote and an electoral margin of 523-8 over challenger Alfred Landon; reelected in 1940, defeating Wendell Wilkie with 54.8 percent of the popular vote and by 449-82 in the electoral college; reelected in 1944, defeating Thomas Dewey with 53.5 percent of the popular vote and by 432-99 in the electoral college; served until his death in office on April 12, 1945; accomplishments as president include the ambitious agenda of the first hundred days, including shoring up the national banking system, aiding farmers and manufacturers, and offering relief for the unemployed; the "New Deal," a series of federal government measures intended to counter the national economic

Franklin Roosevelt (Library of Congress)

depression and dealing with agriculture, banking and finance, labor relations, social welfare, environmental conservation, and public works construction; gave a series of radio addresses known as "fireside chats" to inform the American public of his initiatives and to bolster their confidence; used executive authority to assist Great Britain in spite of Congressional Neutrality Acts; reorganized the executive branch of the federal government, which greatly expanded in size and scope with the twin crises of depression and war; and served as commander-in-chief during World War II, effectively mobilizing the American people on the home front and working closely with Allied leaders, especially British Prime Minister Winston Churchill, to direct the war effort; former president of the Woodrow Wilson Foundation, the Boy Scouts Foundation, and the Seaman's Institute; former chairman, Taconic Park Commission; former trustee, Vassar College; author of *Government, Not Politics* (1932), *Looking Forward* (1933), and *On Our Way* (1934); he was the seventh president to die in office, the fourth of these to die of natural causes; died in Warm Springs, Ga., on April 12, 1945; interment in the family plot at Hyde Park, N.Y. **References:** James MacGregor Burns, *Roosevelt: The Soldier of Freedom* (1970) and *Roosevelt: The Lion and the Fox* (1984); Frank Freidel, *Franklin D. Roosevelt: A Rendezvous with Destiny* (1990); Patrick J. Maney, *The Roosevelt Presence* (1992, 1998); Doris Kearns Goodwin, *No Ordinary Time: Franklin and Eleanor Roosevelt: The Home Front in World War II* (1994); William Leuchtenberg, *The FDR Years: On Roosevelt and His Legacy* (1995); George T. McJimsey, *The Presidency of Franklin Delano Roosevelt* (2000).

ROOSEVELT, Theodore

Born in New York City, N.Y., October 27, 1858; son of Theodore, banker and merchant, and Martha (Bulloch) Roosevelt; Dutch Reformed Church; married Alice Hathaway Lee (1861–1884) on October 27, 1880; married Edith Kermit Carow (1861–1948) on December 2, 1886; father of Alice Lee (Mrs. Nicholas Longworth) by his first wife and, by his second wife, Theodore Jr. and Kermit, both of whom were killed in action in World War II, Ethel Carow, Archibald Bulloch, and Quentin, who was killed in action in World War I; graduated from Harvard College, 1880; studied law at Columbia University, 1882; representative from Manhattan, New York State Assembly, 1882–1884; after his first wife's death, in childbirth, on the same day as the death of his mother, he moved to North Dakota and managed a cattle ranch, 1884–1886; unsuccessful candidate for mayor of New York City, 1886; appointed by President Benjamin Harrison as head commissioner, U.S. Civil Service Board, 1889–1895, where he fought the "spoils system" and revised civil service exams; president, Board of Police Commissioners, New York City, 1895–1897; assistant secretary, U.S. Department of the Navy, Washington, 1897–1898, where he ordered the U.S. fleet in the Pacific to prepare for war with Spain's naval forces in Manila, Philippines;

Theodore Roosevelt (Library of Congress)

organizer, and commander, as colonel, of the 1st U.S. Volunteer Cavalry Regiment ("Rough Riders"), fighting in Cuba during the Spanish-American War and gaining a national reputation, 1898; Republican governor of New York, 1899–1901; chosen by incumbent Republican President McKinley as his running mate and elected VICE-PRESIDENT OF THE UNITED STATES in 1900; inaugurated on March 4, 1901, and served until the death of McKinley from wounds suffered by an assassin's bullet, whereby he became the twenty-sixth PRESIDENT OF THE UNITED STATES on September 14, 1901; elected to a full term in 1904, defeating Democratic challenger Alton B. Parker with 57.4 percent of the popular vote and 336 electoral votes; remained in office until March 4, 1909; at age 42, is the youngest person to have served as president; operated as a conservative reformer through much of his presidency, using socially progressive legislation such as the Pure Food and Drug Act of 1906 and prosecutions of high-profile antitrust cases to alleviate public anxiety about corporate power; after 1906, began to argue more strongly that the rights of the public welfare justified government regulation of private property; issued the "Roosevelt Corollary" to the Monroe Doctrine, justifying U.S. actions in Latin America as the "policeman of the Western Hemisphere," and helped arrange the construction of the Panama Canal; won the Nobel Peace Prize in 1906 for his role in the Portsmouth (N.H.) Conference that ended the Russo-Japanese War; organized a scientific expedition to Africa under the auspices of the Smithsonian Institution, to gather materials for the new National Museum of Natural History, 1909–1910; an unsuccessful candidate for the Republican nomination for president in 1912, he organized and became the candidate of the Progressive, or "Bull Moose," Party, finishing second in the election of 1912 behind Democrat Woodrow Wilson; survived an assassination attempt, October 14, 1912; headed an exploring party to South America, 1914; was rejected by Wilson as a volunteer for military duty, 1917; at the time of his death, was considered a strong candidate for the upcoming Republican presidential nomination for 1920; author of over 40 books, on topics ranging from politics, biography, and history to hunting, sports, and the outdoors, including *The Naval War of 1812* (1882), *Hunting Trios of a Ranchman* (1885), *Life of Thomas Hart Benton* (1886), *Winning of the West* (4 vols., 1889–1896), *The Rough Riders* (1899), *The Strenuous Life* (1901), *The New Nationalism* (1910), *Theodore Roosevelt, an Autobiography* (1913), and *History as Literature, and Other Essays* (1914); president, American Historical Association, 1912; member, Phi Beta Kappa; died on January 6, 1919, at Oyster Bay, N.Y.; interment in Young's Memorial Cemetery there. **References:** Richard Hofstadter, *The American Political Tradition* (1948); Howard K. Beale, *Theodore Roosevelt and the Rise of America to World Power* (1956); George E. Mowry, *The Era of Theodore Roosevelt* (1958); John Morton Blum, *The Republican Roosevelt* (1977); Edmund Morris, *The Rise of Theodore Roosevelt* (1979) and *Theodore Rex* (2001); David McCullough, *Mornings on Horseback* (1981); John Milton Cooper, Jr., *The Warrior and the Priest: Woodrow Wilson and Theodore Roosevelt* (1983) and *Pivotal Decades: The United States, 1900–1920* (1990); Lewis L. Gould, *The Presidency of Theodore Roosevelt* (1991); Nathan Miller, *Theodore Roosevelt: A Life* (1992); H.W. Brands, *T.R.: The Last Romantic* (1997); Louis Auchincloss, *Theodore Roosevelt* (2002).

—Jeffrey Coster

ROOT, Elihu

Born in Clinton, N.Y., February 15, 1845; son of Oren Root, professor at Hamilton College, and Nancy Whitney (Buttrick) Root; married Clara Wales on January 8, 1878; father of Edith, Elihu, and Edward Wales; graduated from Hamilton College in 1864; taught at the Rome Academy in 1865; received LL.B. from New York University Law School in 1867 and was admitted to the bar that same year; began practicing as corporation lawyer in New York; U.S. district attorney for southern district of New York, 1883–1885; chairman of the judiciary committee in the New York constitutional convention of 1894; appointed SECRETARY OF WAR in the cabinet of President McKinley on August 1, 1899, and continued in President Theodore Roosevelt's cabinet until February 1, 1904; most important contributions were reorganization of the administration of the army and establishment of governments in territories newly acquired from Spain; appointed SECRETARY OF STATE in the cabinet of President Roosevelt on July 1, 1905, and served until his resignation on January 27, 1909; most important contributions were efforts to improve deteriorating relations with Latin America and obtainment of Japanese adherence to the Open Door Policy; elected U.S. senator from

New York in January 1909, and served until March 4, 1915; acted as U.S. counsel in North Atlantic fisheries dispute in 1910; sat on the Hague Tribunal, 1910; headed the Carnegie Endowment for International Peace, 1910; won Nobel Peace Prize in 1912; headed U.S. diplomatic mission to Russia in an attempt to keep Russia fighting for the Allies, 1917; work on Permanent Court of International Justice plans led to its establishment; author of *Experiment in Government and the Essentials of the Constitution* (1913), *Russia and the United States* (1917), and other books; U.S. commissioner plenipotentiary at Washington Conference on Limitations of Armaments, 1921–1922; received doctorate degrees in law and political sciences from 20 colleges and universities, 1894–1929; died in New York, N.Y., February 7, 1939. **References:** P.C. Jessup, *Elihu Root* (1938); Richard William Leopold, *Elihu Root* (1954).

ROPER, Daniel C.

Born in Marlboro County, S.C., April 1, 1867; son of John Wesley Roper, farmer, merchant, and Confederate officer during the Civil War, and Henrietta Virginia (McLaurin) Roper; member of the Methodist Episcopal Church; married to Lou McKenzie in 1889; father of Margaret May, James Hunter, Daniel Calhoun, Grace Henrietta, John Wesley, Harry McKenzie, and Richard Frederick; attended Wofford College, Spartansburg, S.C., and then Trinity College, from which he was graduated in 1888; taught school, worked as a farmer, and wrote life insurance, 1888–1892; elected to the state House of Representatives, 1892; appointed clerk of the U.S. Senate Committee on Interstate Commerce in 1893 and served for three years; engaged in private business in New York City, 1896–1898; life insurance agent in Maryland and Washington, D.C., studied law at the National Law School, Washington, D.C., and received his degree in 1901; special agent of the federal Bureau of the Census, 1900–1911; appointed clerk of the U.S. House of Representatives Ways and Means Committee, 1911; appointed first assistant postmaster general, 1913, and served until 1916; chairman of the organization bureau of the Democratic National Committee, 1916; appointed vice-chairman of the U.S. Tariff Commission, 1917; appointed by President Wilson as commissioner of Internal Revenue in 1917 and served until his resignation in 1920; president of the Marlin-Rockwell Corporation, 1920–1921; engaged in law practice in Washington, D.C., 1921–1933, as head of the firm of Roper, Hagerman, Hurrey, and Parks, and later of Roper, Hurrey, and Dudley; appointed SECRETARY OF COMMERCE in the cabinet of President Franklin D. Roosevelt on March 4, 1933; most important contributions were establishing a business advisory council, helping to organize and administer many early reform measures of the New Deal, and reorganizing the department to reduce expenditures; resigned on December 23, 1938, and resumed law practice in Washington; appointed temporary U.S. minister to Canada by President Roosevelt in May 1939 and resigned from that post after four months of service; director of the Atlantic Coast Line Railroad; author of *The United States Post Office* (1917) and an autobiography; died in Washington, D.C., on April 11, 1943. **References: Daniel C. Roper, *Fifty Years of Public Life* (1942); Barry Karl, *Executive Reorganization and Reform in the New Deal* (1963).

ROYALL, Kenneth Claiborne

Born in Goldsboro, N.C., July 24, 1894; son of George and Clara Howard (Jones) Royall; Episcopalian; married Margaret Best on August 18, 1917; father of Kenneth Claiborne Jr., Margaret, and George Pender; attended Episcopal High School, Alexandria, Va.; B.A., University of North Carolina, 1914; J.D., Harvard University, 1917; associate editor, *Harvard Law Review*, 1915–1917; admitted to the North Carolina bar in 1917 and began practice in Goldsboro and Raleigh; elected state senator, 1927; author of the North Carolina bank liquidation statute; second lieutenant in the field artillery, 1917–1918, and first lieutenant in France, 1918–1919; served in the U.S. Army during World War II, rising from colonel to brigadier general; special assistant to the Secretary of War, 1944–1945; appointed by President Truman as SECRETARY OF WAR on July 19, 1947, and served until September 17, 1947, when the military structure of the U.S. government was reorganized and the War Department merged with the Department of the Navy to form the new Department of Defense; appointed the first secretary of the army under the unification of the armed forces, 1947–1949; senior partner, Royall, Koegel and Rogers, 1949–1967; delegate-at-large to the Democratic National Convention in 1964; member, Presidential Racial Commission, Birmingham, Ala., 1963; national chairman, Lawyer's Committee for the Johnson and Humphrey national ticket in 1964; trustee, John Fitzgerald Kennedy Memorial Library; member, General Alumni Association, University of North Carolina (president, 1959–1960); died on May 25, 1971. **References:** *Current Biography Yearbook 1947*; Alfred Steinberg, *The Man from Missouri: The Life and Times of Harry S. Truman* (1962); Cabell B.H. Phillips, *The Truman Presidency: The History of a Triumphant Succession* (1966); *New York Times* (May 27, 1971).

RUBIN, Robert Edward

Born in New York City, N.Y., August 29, 1938; son of Alexander, a lawyer, and Sylvia (Seiderman) Rubin; Jewish; married Judith Leah Oxenberg, New York City commissioner of protocol, on March 27, 1963; father of James Samuel and Philip Matthew; raised in Miami Beach, Fla.; A.B. summa cum laude in economics, Harvard University, 1960; LL.B., Yale University Law School, 1964; attended the London School of Economics, 1960–1961; admitted to the bar in New York, 1965; associate, Cleary, Gottlieb, Steen & Hamilton, NYC, 1964–1966; associate, Goldman Sachs & Company, NYC, 1966–1970, general partner, 1971–1992, member, management committee, 1980–1992, co-vice-chairman and chief operating officer, 1987–1990, co-senior partner and cochairman,

1990–1992; assistant to President Bill Clinton for Economic Policy and director, National Economic Council, 1993–1995; one of the leading forces in the creation of the North American Free Trade Agreement (NAFTA); appointed by President Clinton as SECRETARY OF THE TREASURY and served from January 10, 1995, until July 2, 1999; handled several international economic crises, including Mexico, 1994–1995, and Southeast Asia, 1997, and the weakening of the dollar in 1995; along with Federal Reserve Chairman Alan Greenspan, was one of the major figures credited for government fiscal and monetary policies that enabled and supported the economic prosperity and stock market boom of the second half of the 1990s; chairman, executive committee, board of directors, Citigroup, 1999– ; member, President's Advisory Committee for Trade Negotiations, 1980–1982, investment advisory council, NYC Pension Fund, 1980–1989, committee to visit economics department, board of overseers, Harvard University, 1981–1987, committee on university resources, 1987–1992, advisory committee on tender offers, Securities and Exchange Commission (SEC), 1983, Governor's Commission on Trade Competitiveness, 1987, regulatory advisory committee, New York Stock Exchange, 1988–1990, advisory committee, international capital markets, Federal Reserve Bank of New York, 1989–1993, Mayor's Council of Economic Advisors, 1990, Governor's Council on Fiscal and Economic Priorities, 1990–1992, SEC Market Oversight and Financial Services Advisory Committee, 1991–1993, Governor's Advisory Panel on Financial Services, 1988–1989, Commission on National Elections; partner and member, board of directors, NYC Partnership Inc., 1991–1993; member, board of directors, Chicago Board of Options Exchange, 1972–1976, New York Futures Exchange, 1979–1985, Center for National Policy, 1982–1993 (vice-chairman, 1984), New York Stock Exchange, Harvard Management Company, New York City Partnership, Ford Motor Company, 2000– ; trustee, American Ballet Theatre Foundation, 1969–1993, Mt. Sinai Hospital, 1977–1992 (vice-chairman, 1986), Collegiate School, 1978–1984, Station WNET-TV, 1985–1993, Carnegie Corporation of New York, 1990–1993; fund-raiser for Democratic political candidates since 1972; political adviser, strategist, and member, New York finance committee, Walter Mondale for President, 1983–1984; informal economic adviser to the presidential campaigns of Michael Dukakis, 1988, and Bill Clinton, 1992; chairman, Democratic Congressional Dinner, Washington, 1982, Democrats for the 80s, 1985–1989, Democrats for the 90s, 1989–1990, NYC host committee, 1992 Democratic National Convention, 1989–1992; recipient, National Association of Christians and Jews award, NYC, 1977, Distinguished Leadership in Government award, Columbia Business School, 1996, *Euromoney* Magazine award, 1996, Medal for High Civic Service, Citizens' Budget Committee, 1997, Foreign Policy Association medal, 1998, "Chairman" award, Greater Washington Boys/Girls Clubs, 1998, Intrepid Museum award, 1998, Jefferson award, American Institute of Public Service, 1998, Award of Merit, Yale University, 1998, Global Leadership award, UN Association, 1998, Paul Tsongas award, 1998, EQUITIES Achiever award, 1999; member, Phi Beta Kappa. **References:** Bob

Woodward, *The Agenda* (1994); *Current Biography Yearbook 1997; Newsweek* (November 8, 1999); *Who's Who, 2001.*

—*Robert T. Chase*

U.S. Secretary of Defense Donald Rumsfeld shakes hands with pin trader Riley Jensen after trading a dove and two delicate arch pins for two silver cowboy hat pins, following a visit to the Olympic village in Salt Lake City, February 19, 2002. Rumsfeld toured the village during a visit to troops helping in the $310 million security operation at the 2002 Winter Olympic Games. Joyce Rumsfeld is with him. (AP/World Wide Photos)

RUMSFELD, Donald H.

Born in Chicago, Ill., July 9, 1932; son of George Donald and Jeannette (Husted) Rumsfeld; married Joyce Pierson on December 27, 1954; father of Valerie Jeanne, Marcy Kay, and Donald Nicholas; raised and attended public schools in Winnetka, Ill.; A.B. in political science, Princeton University, 1954; served as an aviator in the U.S. Navy, 1954–1957, rising from rank of ensign to lieutenant (jg); administrative assistant, U.S. Representative David S. Dennison (Republican, Ohio), 1957–1959, and U.S. Representative Robert P. Griffin (Republican, Michigan), 1959; investment broker, A.G. Becker and Company, Chicago, 1960–1962; Republican member from the 13th district of Illinois, U.S. House of Representatives, 1963–1969; served on the House Science and Astronautics and Government Operations Committees, the Joint Economic Committee, and the House Republican Policy Committee, earning a reputation as a staunch conservative; won reelection in 1968 but resigned when appointed director, Office of Economic Opportunity, and assistant to President Nixon with cabinet status, and member, President's Urban Affairs Council, 1969–1970; counselor to the president and director of the economic stabilization program, 1971–1972; U.S. ambassador and permanent representative to NATO, Brussels, Belgium, 1973–1974; chairman, transition team for President Gerald Ford, 1974; White House chief of staff for President Ford, 1974–1975; appointed by President Ford as SECRETARY OF DEFENSE, he became the youngest person to hold that position when sworn in at age 43 on November 20, 1975, and served until the end of Ford's administration on January 20, 1977; an ardent proponent of maintaining U.S. military strength vis-à-vis the Soviet Union; president, chief executive officer, and then chairman, G.D. Searle and Company, Skokie, Ill., 1977–1985; senior adviser, William Blair and Company, Chicago,

1985–1990; chairman and chief executive officer, General Instrument Corporation, 1990–1993; national chairman, Dole for President, 1996; chairman, board of directors, Gilead Sciences Incorporated, Foster City, Calif., 1997–2001; appointed by President George W. Bush as SECRETARY OF DEFENSE, becoming at age 68 the oldest person to hold that post when sworn in on January 20, 2001; a strong advocate of a national missile defense system and the modernization of the U.S. military; became prominent as one of the architects and spokesmen for the Bush administration's war on terrorism, especially U.S. military operations in Afghanistan, following the September 11, 2001, terrorist attacks on the Pentagon and the World Trade Center; former visiting professor, Graduate School of Management, Northwestern University, and Woodrow Wilson School of International Affairs, Princeton University; former member, Rural Affairs Council, Cabinet Commission on Civil Rights and Education, U.S-Russia Business Forum, President Reagan's General Advisory Committee on Arms Control, 1982–1986, U.S. Joint Advisory Commission on U.S.-Japan Relations, 1983–1984, National Commission on the Public Service, 1987–1990, National Economic Commission, 1988–1989, board of visitors, National Defense University, 1988–1992, Commission on U.S.-Japan Relations, 1989–1991, High Definition Television advisory committee, Federal Communications Commission, 1992–1993, U.S. Federal Trade Deficit Review Commission, 1999–2000; special envoy of President Reagan, first on the Law of the Sea Treaty, 1982–1983, then to the Middle East, 1983–1984; senior adviser, President Reagan's panel on strategic systems, 1983–1984; former chairman, Congressional Leadership's National Security Advisory Group, Property Reevaluation Board, 1971–1973, Rand Corporation, 1981–1986 and 1995–1996, Commission to Assess the Ballistic Missile Threat to the U.S., 1998–1999, U.S. Commission to Assess National Security Space Management and Organization, 2000; recipient, Distinguished Eagle Scout award, 1975, Presidential Medal of Freedom, 1977, Outstanding Chief Executive Officer in the Pharmaceutical Industry, *Wall Street Transcript*, 1980, and *Financial World*, 1981, George Catlett Marshall award, 1984, Woodrow Wilson award, 1985, Shelby Davis award, 1985, Dwight D. Eisenhower medal, 1993, and honorary degrees from DePaul University College of Commerce, Illinois College, Lake Forest College, Park College, Tuskegee Institute, National College of Education, Bryant College, Claremont Graduate School, Illinois Wesleyan University, Rand Graduate School, and Hampden-Sydney College; former member, board of directors, Amylin Pharmaceuticals, Asea Brown Boverit Limited, Tribune Company; former member, advisory board, Forstmann Little and Company and TIS Worldwide, 2000; former chairman, international advisory board, Salomon Smith Barney; member, board of trustees, Gerald R. Ford Foundation, Eisenhower Exchange Fellowships, Hoover Institution, National Park Foundation; member, National Academy of Public Administration. **References:** *Current Biography Yearbook 1970; Forbes* (October 26, 1992; March 19, 2001); Bernard J. Firestone and Alexej Ugrinsky, eds., *Gerald R. Ford and the Politics of Post-Watergate America*, vol.

1 (1993); James Cannon, *Time and Chance: Gerald Ford's Appointment with History* (1994); John Robert Greene, *The Presidency of Gerald R. Ford* (1995); *Washington Post* (December 29, 2000); *Who's Who in America, 2000; U.S. News & World Report* (January 8, August 13, and December 17, 2001); *Time* (May 14, August 27, and October 15, 2001); *Newsweek* (October 15, 2001); Richard Reeves, *President Nixon: Alone in the White House* (2001).

—Jeffrey Coster

RUSH, Richard

Born in Philadelphia, Pa., August 29, 1780; son of Dr. Benjamin and Julia (Stockton) Rush; married Catherine E. Murray on August 29, 1809; father of ten children; raised in a cultured home, he entered the College of New Jersey (now Princeton) at the age of 14 in 1794, graduating in 1797; studied law and was admitted to the bar in December 1800; appointed attorney general of Pennsylvania in January 1811; became comptroller of the treasury in November 1811, by appointment of President Madison; invited to join the cabinet of President Monroe on February 10, 1814, as ATTORNEY GENERAL and served until November 12, 1817; during his incumbency, he superintended the publication of *The Laws of the United States from 1789 to 1815* (1815); appointed secretary of state, *ad interim*, on October 30, 1817, by President Monroe, pending the return of John Quincy Adams from Europe to assume that office; during his secretaryship, he negotiated the Rush–Bagot Convention on April 28, 1817, establishing a limitation of naval armaments on the Great Lakes; appointed minister to Great Britain on October 31, 1817; appointed SECRETARY OF THE TREASURY by President John Quincy Adams on March 7, 1825, serving until March 3, 1829; unsuccessful candidate for vice-president on Adams's ticket in 1828; appointed by President Jackson to adjust the dispute concerning the boundaries between Ohio and Michigan in 1835; sent to England in 1836 by President Jackson to obtain the legacy bequeathed the United States by the late James Smithson, which legacy resulted in the erection in Washington, D.C., of the Smithsonian Institution in August 1846; appointed minister to France on March 3, 1847, by President Polk; author of *Memoranda of a Residence at the Court of London* (1833) and *Occasional Productions, Political, Diplomatic and Miscellaneous* (1860); died in Philadelphia, Pa., July 30, 1859. **References:** John William Ward, *Andrew Jackson, Symbol for an Age* (1955); Irving Brant, *James Madison and American Nationalism* (1968).

RUSK, (David) Dean

Born in Cherokee County, Ga., February 9, 1909; son of Robert Hugh, farmer and minister, and Frances Elizabeth (Clotfelter) Rusk, a teacher; Presbyterian; married Virginia Foisie on June 19, 1937; father of David Patrick, Richard Geary, and Margaret Elizabeth; attended public schools in Atlanta; worked two years in Atlanta law office; B.A., Davidson College, 1931; B.S., 1933, and M.A., 1934, St. Johns College, Oxford University; associate professor of government and international relations, Mills College, Oakland, Calif., 1934–1938, dean of faculty, 1938; studied law at University of California, Berkeley, 1937–1940; infantry reserve officer, 1931–1940, commissioned as captain and called to active duty in 1940, working for Army Intelligence in Washington before being sent to China-Burma-India Theater of Operations as part of war plans department of general staff; deputy chief of staff to General Joseph W. Stilwell; assistant chief, operations division of U.S. War Department general staff; attained rank of colonel; assistant chief, division of international security affairs, U.S. Department of State, 1946; special assistant to the secretary of war, 1946–1947; director, Office of Special Political Affairs and Office of United Nations Affairs, 1947–1949; assistant secretary of state, 1949; deputy undersecretary of state, 1949–1950; assistant secretary of state for Far Eastern affairs, 1950–1951; president, Rockefeller Foundation, 1952–1961; appointed SECRETARY OF STATE by President Kennedy and continued under President Johnson, serving from January 21, 1961, to January 20, 1969; most important contributions were negotiations for test ban treaty, conferences on Berlin situation and support of United Nations action in Congo, economic and military aid to Republic of Korea, and defending an interventionist and virulently anticommunist American policy in Vietnam; Samuel H. Sibley professor of international law, University of Georgia, 1969–1994; testified before the U.S. National Bipartisan Commission on Central America, on September 1, 1983, advocating economic and social aid to Central American countries; member of a group organized to save the ABM (antiballistic missile) treaty, June 19, 1984; recipient, Cecil Peace Prize, 1933, Legion of Merit with oak leaf cluster, honored as namesake of the Dean Rusk Center for International and Comparative Law and Institute for Continuing Judicial Education, University of Georgia; Rhodes scholar; author of *The Winds of Freedom* (1963) and *As I Saw It* (1990); former member, American Society for International Law, Phi Beta Kappa; died on December 20, 1994, at his home in Athens, Ga. **References:** *Current Biography Yearbook 1961*; Warren I. Cohen, *Dean Rusk* (1980); Vaughn Davis Bornet, *The Presidency of Lyndon B. Johnson* (1983); Thomas J. Schoenbaum, *Waging Peace and War: Dean Rusk in the Truman, Kennedy, and Johnson Years* (1988); James N. Giglio, *The Presidency of John F. Kennedy* (1991); Richard Reeves, *President Kennedy: Profile of Power* (1993); *New York Times* (December 22, 1994); Thomas W. Zeiler, *Dean Rusk: Defending the American Mission Abroad* (2000).

RUSK, Jeremiah McLain

Born on a farm at Malta, Ohio, June 17, 1830; son of Daniel and Jane (Faulkner) Rusk; married to Mary Martin on April 5, 1849, and after her death, to Elizabeth M. Johnson in 1856; father of five children; received a limited education at the local schools; moved to Vernon County, Wisc., in 1853 and engaged in agricultural pursuits; became owner of a stagecoach line and part owner of a bank; became sheriff of Viroqua, Wisc., 1855–1857; became coroner in 1857; elected to the State Assembly in 1862; served as a combatant in the Civil War, rising to the rank of major in the 28th Regiment of the Wisconsin Volunteer Infantry, advanced to lieutenant colonel, to colonel, and finally to brigadier general on March 13, 1856; mustered out on June 7, 1865; bank comptroller of Wisconsin, 1866–1869; elected as a Republican to the 42d, 43d, and 44th Congresses, serving from 1871 to 1877; declined the appointment of minister to Uruguay and Paraguay tendered by President Garfield; elected governor of Wisconsin, 1882–1889; in connection with his orders to shoot strikers in Milwaukee in May 1866, he remarked, "I seen my duty and I done it"; appointed to the cabinet of President Benjamin Harrison as SECRETARY OF AGRICULTURE on March 5, 1889, serving until March 5, 1893; died in Viroqua, Wisc., November 21, 1893; interment in Viroqua Cemetery. **References:** Theodore Clarke Smith, *The Life and Letters of James Abram Garfield* (1925); Robert Granville Caldwell, *James A. Garfield, Party Chieftain* (1931).

S

ST. CLAIR, Arthur

Born in Thurso, Caithness, Scotland, on March 23, 1734; probably the son of William Sinclair, merchant, and Elizabeth (Balfour) Sinclair; married to Phoebe Bayard on May 15, 1760; father of seven children; attended the University of Edinburgh; studied medicine; became an ensign in the British Army, May 13, 1757; resigned on April 16, 1762, with the commission of lieutenant; purchased an estate and settled in Ligonier Valley, Pa., 1764; erected mills; surveyor of the district of Cumberland, 1770; justice of the court of quarter sessions and of common pleas; member of the proprietary council, justice, recorder, and clerk of the orphans' court; prothonotary of Bedford and Westmoreland counties; colonel of the Pennsylvania Militia, 1775; became brigadier general in the Continental Army, August 9, 1776; became major general on February 19, 1777; recalled from service by Congress after his evacuation of Fort Ticonderoga; exonerated of charges by court-martial, September 1778, and served until the end of the Revolutionary War; member of the military tribunal that tried Major André, 1780; member of the Pennsylvania council of censors, 1783; member of the Continental Congress from November 2, 1785, to November 28, 1787; elected PRESIDENT OF THE CONTINENTAL CONGRESS and served from February 2, 1787, to January 21, 1788; appointed governor of the Northwest Territory in 1787 and served until 1802; major general and commander of the U.S. Army, March 4, 1791, to March 5, 1792; retired to his home, "Hermitage," near Ligonier, Pa.; author of *A Narrative of the Manner in Which the Campaign against the Indians in... [1791] was Conducted Under the Command of Major General St. Clair...*, died near Youngstown, Pa., on August 31, 1818; interment in General St. Clair Cemetery, Greensburg, Pa. **References:** W.H. Smith, *The St. Clair Papers* (1882); E.C. Burnett, *The Continental Congress* (1964).

SARGENT, John Garibaldi

Born in Ludlow, Vt., October 13, 1860; son of John Henmon and Ann Eliza (Hanley) Sargent; Universalist; married Mary Lorraine Gordon on August 4, 1887; father of Gladys Gordon; attended the Vermont Liberal Institute, Plymouth, Vt., and the Black River Academy, Ludlow, Vt., graduating the latter in 1883; entered Tufts College, receiving an A.B. degree in 1887; studied law and was admitted to the Vermont bar in 1890; became a member of the law firm of Stickney, Sargent and Skeels; state's attorney of Windsor County, Vt., from 1898 to 1900; appointed secretary of civil and military affairs of Vermont by Governor Stickney from 1900 to 1902; returned to private practice from 1902 to 1908; attorney general of Vermont from 1908 to 1912; invited to join the Coolidge cabinet as ATTORNEY GENERAL on March 17, 1925, entering upon his duties on March 18, 1925, and serving until March 4, 1929; during his incumbency, he vigorously supported enforcement of Prohibition and upheld the validity of evidence secured by wiretapping; resumed private practice after his retirement; appointed referee in the reorganization of the railroads of Vermont in 1935; director of the Vermont Valley, Boston and Maine Railroad and the Central Vermont Railroad from 1935 until his death; served as president of the Ludlow Savings Bank and Trust Company; chairman of the Vermont Commission on Uniform State Laws; trustee of the Black River Academy; member of the Vermont Historical Society; died in Ludlow, Vt., on March 5, 1939. **References:** Donald R. McCoy, *Calvin Coolidge: The Quiet President* (1967); Jules Abel, *In the Time of Silent Cal* (1969).

SAWYER, Charles

Born in Cincinnati, Ohio, February 10, 1887; son of Edward Milton and Caroline (Butler) Sawyer; Episcopalian; married to Margaret Sterrett on July 15, 1918, and after her death married Elizabeth De Veyrac on June 10, 1942; father of Anne Johnston, Charles, Jean Johnston, John, and Edward; after receiving his education at the local public schools, he entered Oberlin College in Ohio, graduating in 1908; studied law at the University of Cincinnati, graduating in 1911; admitted to the bar in 1911, commencing practice in Cincinnati; elected to the Cincinnati city council in 1911; delegate to the Democratic National Convention in 1912; reelected in 1913; enlisted in the U.S. Army as a private in 1917; subsequently commissioned a captain and promoted to major; delegate to the Democratic National Convention in 1932 and again in 1936, at Philadelphia, at which time he was elected the Democratic national committeeman from Ohio; elected lieutenant governor of Ohio in 1933 and 1934; unsuccessful Democratic nominee for the office of governor in 1938; appointed U.S. ambassador to Belgium and Luxembourg in 1944 by President Franklin D. Roosevelt, serving until his resignation in 1946; named SECRETARY OF COMMERCE by President Truman on May 6, 1948, serving until January 20, 1953; during his tenure, he broadened the activities of the department by the addition of the Bureau of Public Roads to its jurisdiction and the creation of a new agency, the Maritime Administration; trustee of Oberlin College; member of the National Council of Boy Scouts of America; recipient of the Freedom Foundation Award in 1949; upon retiring from public service, he resumed the practice of law in Glendale, Ohio; chairman, Cincinnati Community Chest, 1954; Cincinnati United Fund, 1955–1960; in 1955, appointed to the Overseas Economic Operations Task Force of the Hoover Commission and charged with recommending policy changes concerning foreign aid; served on the Commission on Money and Credit, created by the Committee for Economic Development, between May 1958 and June 1961; upon retirement from government service, practiced law as a senior partner for the law firm of Taft, Stettinius, and Hollister; wrote autobiography *Concerns of a Conservative Democrat* (1968); died on April 7, 1979, in Palm Beach, Fla. **References:** William Hillman, *Mr. President* (1952); *New York Times* (January 29, 1953; June 18, 1961; April 9, 1979); Cabell B.H. Phillips, *The Truman Presidency: The History of a Triumphant Succession* (1966); *Who's Who in America, 1976–1977*; Maeva Marius, *Truman and the Steel Seizure Case* (1977); Eleanora W. Schoenebaum, ed., *Facts on File: Political Profiles: The Truman Years* (1978).

SAXBE, William Bart

Born in Mechanicsburg, Ohio, on June 24, 1916; son of Bart Rockwell and Faye Henry (Carey) Saxbe; Episcopalian; married Ardath Louise ("Dolly") Kleinhans on September 14, 1940; father of William Bart, Juliet Louise Saxbe Blackburn, and Charles Rockwell; A.B., Ohio State University, 1940, LL.B., 1948; served with 107th Cavalry, U.S. Army, 1940–1942, and U.S. Army Air Corps, 1942–1945, achieving the rank of colonel in the reserves; member, Ohio General Assembly, 1947–1954, majority leader, 1951–1952, speaker, 1953–1954; partner, Saxbe, Boyd and Prine, 1955–1958; attorney general, state of Ohio, 1957–1958, 1963–1968; partner, Dargusch, Saxbe and Dargusch, 1960–1963; Republican U.S. senator from Ohio, 1969–1974; appointed ATTORNEY GENERAL by Richard Nixon and served from January 4, 1974, until February 3, 1975; took over Justice Department in wake of Nixon's firing Attorney General Elliot Richardson in a dispute over the investigation of the Watergate incident; despite attempts to repair administration relations with the press, made several embarrassing public statements in his first months in office; eventually sided with Watergate special prosecutor Leon Jaworski in demanding that Nixon turn over the White House tapes as evidence and investigated Cointelpro, the FBI's counterintelligence program and declared that it had been used in "reprehensible" fashion to harass left-wing groups, black leaders, and campus radicals; presided over federal antitrust suits against IBM and AT&T; left Justice Department to serve as U.S. ambassador to India, 1975–1977; partner, Chester, Saxbe, Hoffman, and Wilcox, Columbus, Ohio, 1977–1981; of counsel, Jones, Day Reavis, and Pogue, Cleveland, 1981–1984; of counsel, Pearson, Ball, and Dowd, Washington, 1984–1993; independent special counsel, Central States Teamsters Pension Fund, 1982; of counsel, Chester Willcox and Saxbe, Columbus, 1994– ; recipient of honorary degrees from Central State University, Findlay College, Ohio Wesleyan University, Wilmington College, Walsh College, Ohio State University, Capital University, and Bowling Green State University; member, American Bar Association, Ohio Bar Association, American Judicature Society, Masons, Chi Phi, Phi Delta Phi. **References:** *New York Times Magazine* (May 5, 1974); *New York Times* (December 5, 1982); *Who's Who in America, 1988–1989*; *Newsweek* (December 23, 1974); *Current Biography Yearbook 1974.*

SCHLESINGER, James Rodney

Born on February 15, 1929, in New York City; son of Julius and Rhea (Rogen) Schlesinger; Lutheran; married Rachel Mellinger on June 19, 1954; father of Cara K., Charles L., Ann R., William F., Emily, Thomas S., Clara, and James Rodney; A.B. summa cum laude, Harvard, 1950, A.M. in economics, 1952, Ph.D. in economics, 1956; assistant professor, then associate professor of economics, University of Virginia, 1955–1963; senior staff member, Rand Corporation, 1963–1967, and director of strategic studies, 1967–1969; assistant director, Bureau of the Budget, 1969, acting deputy director, 1969–1970; assistant director, Office of Management and Budget, 1970–1971; chairman, Atomic Energy Commission, 1971–1973; director, Central Intelligence Agency, February–July 1973; appointed by President Nixon as SECRETARY OF DEFENSE and continued into the administration of President Ford, serving from July 2, 1973, until November 19, 1975; as head of the Defense Department, directed U.S. airlifts of supplies to Israel after Egypt and Syria invaded in October 1973, oversaw the evacuation of all remaining U.S. personnel from Saigon in April 1975, and directed the U.S. military response to the capture by Cambodian forces of the USS *Mayaguez* in May 1975; was an opponent of budget cuts and critical of arms reduction treaties, fearing the Soviet Union would gain in superiority from American disarmament; visiting scholar, Johns Hopkins University School for Advanced International Studies, 1976–1977; assistant to the president, 1977; appointed by President Carter as the first SECRETARY OF ENERGY for the newly created federal Department of Energy and served from August 6, 1977, until he resigned on August 23, 1979, at Carter's request; counselor, Center for Strategic and International Studies, Georgetown University, 1979– ; senior adviser, Lehman Brothers, 1979– ; academic consultant, Naval War College, 1957; consultant to board of governors, Federal Reserve Board, 1962–1963; former consultant, Bureau of Budget, 1965–1969, board of governors, Federal Reserve System; member, board of directors, BNFL Inc.; trustee, Atlantic Council, Center for Global Energy Studies, and Henry M. Jackson Foundation; fellow, National Academy of Public Administration; member, America's Academy of Diplomacy, President's Commission on Strategic Forces, 1982–1983, Governor's Commission on Virginia's Future, 1982–1984; vice-chairman, President's Blue Ribbon Task Group on Nuclear Weapons Program Management, 1984–1985; recipient, Frederick Sheldon prize fellow, Harvard University, 1950–1951, Distinguished Intelligence Service Medal, 1975, Distinguished Public Service Medal, Department of the Navy, 1976, Exceptional Citizen Service Medal, Department of the Air Force, 1976, National Security Medal, 1979, Dwight D. Eisenhower Distinguished Service medal, George Catlett Marshall medal, H.H. Arnold award, National Merit citation, Navy League, Military Order of the World Wars, Jimmy Doolittle award, William Oliver Baker award, Henry M. Jackson award for Distinguished Public Service, and 11 honorary doctorates; author of *The Political Economy of National Security: A Study of the Economic Aspects of the Contemporary Power Struggle* (1960) and *America at Century's End* (1989); coauthor of *Issues in Defense Economics* (1967); member, Phi Beta Kappa. **References:** *Current Biography Yearbook 1973*; Burton I. Kaufman, *The Presidency of James Earl Carter, Jr.* (1993); James Canon, *Time and Chance: Gerald Ford's Appointment with History* (1994); Gary M. Fink and Hugh Davis Graham, eds., *The Carter Presidency: Policy Choices in the Post–New Deal Era* (1998); *Who's Who in America, 2000.*

SCHOFIELD, John McAllister

Born in Gerry, N.Y., September 29, 1831; son of James Schofield, Baptist clergyman, and Caroline (McAllister) Schofield; married Harriet Bartlett in June 1857; father of two sons and one daughter; married Georgia Kilbourne in 1891; moved with family to Freeport, Ill., in 1843; attended public schools; was surveyor of public lands in northern Wisconsin during summers; taught district school; appointed cadet at West Point, 1849–1853; brevetted second lieutenant of 2d Artillery at Fort Moultrie, S.C.; commissioned second lieutenant of 1st Artillery in Florida and dealt with Seminole Indian troubles; made first lieutenant in 1855, then sent to West Point as assistant professor of philosophy; took leave of absence, 1860, and was professor of physics at Washington University, Mo.; became mustering officer for Missouri in 1861; made major in 1st Missouri Volunteer Infantry; chosen chief of staff to General Nathaniel Lyon in June 1861 and assumed command upon Lyon's death, August 10, 1861; made captain, and later brigadier general, of volunteers; headed "Army of the Frontier," October 1862 to April 1863; appointed major general and took command of Department of the Missouri in St. Louis; commanded 23d Corps of Department of Army of the Ohio, February 1864; made brigadier general in regular army in November 1864 and brevetted major general in March 1865; headed Department of North Carolina; went on mission to France, 1865–1866; commanded Department of Potomac; appointed SECRETARY OF WAR in the cabinet of President Andrew Johnson on May 28, 1868, and served from July 1, 1868, to March 10, 1869; most important contributions were organization of light artillery school at Fort Riley, Mounted Service School, and U.S. Cavalry

School; commanded Department of the Missouri from March 20, 1869, to May 3, 1870; went on mission to Hawaii in 1872; superintendent of U.S. Military Academy, 1876–1881; spent one year in Europe; took command of Division of Pacific on October 15, 1882, Division of Missouri on November 1, 1883, and Division of Atlantic on April 2, 1886; made commanding general of the army on August 14, 1888; became lieutenant general in February 1895; retired in September 1895; wrote *Forty-six Years in the Army* (1897); died in St. Augustine, Fla., on March 4, 1906. **Reference:** J.D. Cox, *The March to the Sea* (1906).

SCHURZ, Carl

Born in Liblar-am-Rhein, near Cologne, Germany, March 2, 1829; son of Christian Schurz, village schoolmaster and businessman, and Marianne (Jussen) Schurz; married Margarethe Meyer on July 6, 1852; father of two sons and two daughters; attended gymnasium at Cologne, 1839–1846; was candidate for doctorate at University of Bonn in 1847; took part in revolution of 1848; became lieutenant and staff officer in revolutionary army; fled Germany and joined refugees in Switzerland; was newspaper correspondent in Paris in 1851; taught in London; moved to United States in August 1852 and settled in Philadelphia until 1855; bought farm in Watertown, Wisc., 1856; admitted to bar, 1856, and began practice in Milwaukee; was antislavery Republican; unsuccessful candidate for lieutenant governor in 1857; spoke for Lincoln against Douglas in Illinois, 1858; unsuccessful candidate for governor of Wisconsin; chairman of Wisconsin delegation to Chicago Republican Convention in 1860; appointed minister to Spain in 1862; made brigadier general in charge of a division in Frémont's Army on June 10, 1862; became major general on March 14, 1863; was chief of staff to Major General Slocum in Sherman's army; Washington correspondent for *New York Tribune*, 1865–1866; became editor-in-chief of Detroit *Post* in 1866; made joint editor with Emil Pretorius on St. Louis *Westliche Post*, 1867; delegate to Republican National Convention of 1868; elected U.S. senator from Missouri in 1868 and served from March 4, 1869, to March 3, 1875; was permanent president of Cincinnati convention to form Liberal Republican Party in 1872; appointed SECRETARY OF THE INTERIOR in the cabinet of President Hayes and served from March 12, 1877, to March 4, 1881; most important contributions were use of merit system in department, development of national parks, enlightened treatment of Indians, and preservation of public domain; published *The New South* (1885) and *Life of Henry Clay* (1887); became counselor for *Evening Post*; wrote essay on Lincoln in *Atlantic Monthly* (June 1891); president of National Service Reform League, 1892–1900; contributed articles to *Harper's Weekly* from 1892 to 1898; president of Civil Service Reform Association of New York, 1893–1906; died in New York City on May 14, 1906; interment in Sleepy Hollow Cemetery, Tarrytown, N.Y. **References:** C.R. Goedsche and Walter E. Glaettle, *Carl Schurz* (1963); James P. Terzian, *Defender of Human Rights: Carl Schurz* (1965).

SCHWEIKER, Richard Schultz

Born in Norristown, Pa., June 1, 1926; son of Malcolm Alderfer and Blanche (Schultz) Schweiker; married Claire Joan Coleman on September 10, 1955; father of Malcolm C., Lani, Kyle, Richard S. Jr., and Lara Kristi; B.A., Pennsylvania State University, 1950; served with U.S. Naval Reserve in World War II; business executive, 1950–1960; Republican member from the 13th district of Pennsylvania, U.S. House of Representatives, 1961–1969; member, House Armed Services and Government Operations Committees; U.S. senator from Pennsylvania, 1969–1981; member, Senate Appropriations and Health and Human Resources Committees; ranking Republican member, Health and Labor–HEW Subcommittees; appointed SECRETARY OF HEALTH AND HUMAN SERVICES by President Ronald Reagan and served from January 22, 1981, until February 3, 1983; as secretary he strengthened the Social Security system, put more emphasis on preventative medicine, cut Medicare and food stamp grants to the states, and tightened welfare eligibility rules; president, American Council of Life Insurance, Washington, 1983–1994; alternate delegate, Republican National Convention, 1952 and 1956, and delegate, 1972 and 1980; while running, ultimately unsuccessfully, for the Republican nomination for president in 1976, Ronald Reagan designated Schweiker as his vice-presidential candidate; member, board of directors, Tenet Healthcare Corporation, LabOne Inc; chairman, Partnership for Prevention, 1991–1997; recipient, Outstanding Young Man of the Year award, Junior Chamber of Commerce, 1960, Distinguished Alumnus award, Pennsylvania State University, 1970, Dr. Charles H. Best award, American Diabetes Association, 1974, Outstanding Alumnus of the Year award, Phi Kappa Sigma, 1982, Gold medal, Pennsylvania Association of Broadcasters, 1982, National Outstanding Service award, Headstart, 1983, Public Service Gold medal, U.S. Surgeon General, 1988, Government Achievement award, Juvenile Diabetes Foundation, 1990, Distinguished Achievement award, National Council on Aging, 1991, John Newton Russell award, National Association of Life Underwriters, 1992, and honorary degrees from Temple University, 1970, and Georgetown University, 1981; member, Phi Beta Kappa. **References:** *New York Times* (January 7, 1981; January 13, 1983); *Who's Who in America, 2000.*

SCHWELLENBACH, Lewis Baxter

Born in Superior, Wisc., September 20, 1894; son of Francis William and Martha (Baxter) Schwellenbach; Episcopalian; married Anne Duffy on December 30, 1935; no children; moved to Spokane, Wash., with his parents in 1902; after attending the public schools of Spokane, he entered the University of Washington at Seattle and was graduated with a law degree in 1917; assistant instructor at the University of Washington in 1916 and 1917; during World War I, he served as a private in the 1st Regiment, U.S. Infantry, and then as a corporal, being discharged on February 2, 1919; was admitted to the bar in 1919 and commenced the practice of his profession in Seattle; state commander of the American Legion in 1922; member of the Board of Regents of the University of Washington during 1933 and 1934, serving as president in 1933; chairman of the Democratic state convention in 1924; chairman of the King County Democratic Committee from 1928 to 1930; unsuccessful candidate for nomination for governor in 1932; delegate to the Interparliamentary Union at The Hague in 1936; elected as a Democrat to the U.S. Senate, serving from January 3, 1935, to December 6, 1940, when he resigned to enter the judiciary; appointed U.S. district judge for the eastern district of Washington, in which capacity he served until tendered a cabinet portfolio; invited to join the Truman cabinet as SECRETARY OF LABOR on June 1, 1945, entering upon his duties on July 1, 1945, serving continuously until his death; during his incumbency, he helped to end the wartime government controls over management-labor relations and to restore free bargaining between management and labor and was a vigorous foe of the Taft-Hartley Law; died in Washington, D.C., on June 10, 1948; interment in Washelli Cemetery, Seattle, Wash. **References:** Alfred Steinberg, *The Man from Missouri: The Life and Times of Harry S. Truman* (1962); Cabell B.H. Phillips, *The Truman Presidency: The History of a Triumphant Succession* (1966).

SEATON, Frederick Andrew

Born in Washington, D.C., December 11, 1909; son of Fay Noble and Dorothea Elizabeth (Schmidt) Seaton; Methodist; married Gladys Hope Dowd on January 23, 1931; father of Donald Richard, Johanna Christine, Monica Margaret, and Alfred Noble; moved with his family to Manhattan, Kans., in 1915; after attending the local public schools, he entered the Kansas State Agricultural College in Manhattan, Kans., graduating in 1931; while in college, he became a sports announcer over radio stations KSAC and WIBW, continuing until 1937; became associated with his father's newspaper business in 1931; wire news editor on the Manhattan *Morning Chronicle* in 1932; city editor of the *Mercury* in 1933; associate editor of Seaton Publications in 1933, remaining in that capacity until 1937; elected chairman of the Young Republicans, becoming national committeeman for Kansas in 1935; vice-chairman of the Kansas Republican National Convention delegation in 1936; vice-chairman of the Kansas Republican state committee from 1934 to 1937; secretary to Alfred M. Landon, the Republican presidential candidate in 1936; member of the Republican National Speakers Bureau from 1936 to 1940; moved to Hastings, Nebr. in 1937, where he became publisher of the *Daily Tribune* and president of the Seaton Publishing Company; named a director of the Nebraska State Grain Improvement Association in 1945; served for two terms, from 1945 to 1949, in Nebraska's legislature; chairman of the Nebraska Legislative Council from 1947 to 1949; manager of Harold E. Stassen's presidential primary campaign in Nebraska; appointed to the U.S. Senate by Governor Peterson to fill a vacancy on December 10, 1951, serving until January 3, 1953; appointed assistant secretary of defense for legislative affairs in September 1953; promoted to presidential administrative assistant for congressional liaison on February 19, 1955, rising to deputy assistant to President Eisenhower on June 15, 1955; invited to join the Eisenhower cabinet as SECRETARY OF THE INTERIOR on June 6, 1956, entering upon his duties on June 8, 1956, and serving until the close of that administration on January 20, 1961; during his secretaryship, he engaged in a program to extract drinking water from the sea via a saline water conversion program; considered for Richard Nixon's vice-presidential running mate in 1960; ran unsuccessfully for governor of Kansas in 1962, defeated by incumbent Frank B. Morrison; member, board of directors, Investors Life Insurance Co., Omaha, Nebr., 1961–1974; member, board of directors, First National Bank, Hastings, Nebr., 1961–1974; worked for Seaton Publishing Co., 1962–1974; served as Kansas state chairman, Radio Free Europe Fund, 1965; served as chairman of the Senior Advisors to the Nixon Campaign, 1968; chairman, President Nixon's Committee on Timber and the Environment, 1973; director of the Nebraska State Reclamation Association; trustee of the University of Nebraska Foundation and of Hastings College; member of the National Editorial Association and the American Academy of Political and Social Science; upon his retirement from government service, he resumed his interest in the Seaton Publishing Company; died January 16, 1974, in Minneapolis. **References:** Robert J. Donovan, *Eisenhower: The Inside Story* (1956); Arthur Larson, *Eisenhower: The President Nobody Knew* (1968); *New York Times* (January 18, 1974); Eleanora W. Schoenebaum, ed., *Facts on File: Political Profiles: The Eisenhower Years* (1977).

SEWARD, William Henry

Born in Florida, N.Y., May 16, 1801; son of Dr. Samuel S. and Mary (Jennings) Seward; married Frances Miller, daughter of his law partner Judge Elijah Miller, on October 20, 1824; father of Augustus Henry, Frederick William, William Henry, Fanny, and Cornelia, who died in infancy; attended Farmer's Hall Academy, Goshen, N.Y.; graduated from Union College, 1820; read law and admitted to bar in New York, 1822; taught at Union Academy, Eatonville, Ga., 1819–1820; practiced law, Auburn, N.Y., 1823–1839 and 1843–1849; entered politics as the protégé of Thurlow Weed, leader of New York state's Anti-Masonic Party in the 1820s, then of the Whig Party in the 1830s; member, New York State Senate, Albany, 1830–1834; unsuccessful Whig Party candidate for governor of New York, 1834, though winning elections in 1838 and 1840 and serving as New York governor, 1839–1843; member from New York, U.S. Senate, 1849–1861; the leader of the antislavery wing of the national Whig Party until its demise in the mid-1850s, he joined the Republican Party in 1855; famous for a speech declaring slavery and freedom to be in "irrepressible conflict," Rochester, N.Y., October 25, 1858; unsuccessful candidate for the Republican nomination for president, 1860; member of the Senate Committee of Thirteen organized to address the secession crisis, 1860–1861; appointed by President Abraham Lincoln as SECRE-

William Seward (Library of Congress)

TARY OF STATE and served for two full terms, from March 6, 1861, through the administration of President Andrew Johnson until March 4, 1869; a leading adviser to Lincoln, his diplomacy helped prevent British and French recognition of the Confederacy, especially his negotiations with Great Britain to settle the *Alabama* claims; wounded during an attempt on his life the night Lincoln was assassinated, April 14, 1865; negotiated the purchase of Alaska from Russia in March 1867 (nicknamed "Seward's Folly" by its detractors); promoted U.S. trade expansion in Asia and the Caribbean; made an around-the-world tour, 1870–1871; author of *William Henry Seward's Travels around the World* (1873), *Autobiography of William Henry Seward, from 1801 to 1834, with a Memoir of His Life, and Selections from His Letters, from 1831 to 1846* (1877) and *The Life of John Quincy Adams* (1886); died on October 16, 1872, in Auburn; interment in Fort Hill Cemetery. **References:** Jesse Burton Hendrick, *Lincoln's War Cabinet* (1946); Glyndon G. Van Deusen, *William Henry Seward* (1967); Eric Foner, *Free Soil, Free Labor, Free Men: The Ideology of the Republican Party before the Civil War* (1970); Ernest N. Paolino, *The Foundations of the American Empire: William Henry Seward and U.S. Foreign Policy* (1973); Albert E. Castel, *The Presidency of Andrew Johnson* (1979); William E. Gienapp, *The Origins of the Republican Party, 1852–1856* (1987); John M. Taylor, *William H. Seward: Lincoln's Right Hand* (1991); Phillip Shaw Paludan, *The Presidency of Abraham Lincoln* (1994); Michael F. Holt, *The Rise and Fall of the American Whig Party: Jacksonian Politics and the Onset of the Civil War* (1999).

—Jeffrey Coster

SHALALA, Donna Edna

Born in Cleveland, Ohio, February 14, 1941; daughter of James Abraham, real estate salesman and leader of Cleveland's Syrian-Lebanese community, and Edna (Smith) Shalala, nationally ranked tennis player, physical education teacher, and lawyer; attended West Tech High School, Cleveland; A.B. in urban studies, Western College for Women, Oxford, Ohio, 1962; M.S. in social science, Syracuse

University, 1968; Ph.D. in political science, Maxwell Graduate School of Citizenship and Public Affairs, Syracuse University, 1970; volunteer, Peace Corps, Iran, 1962–1964, teaching social science and serving as dean of women at the agricultural college of the University of Ahwaz; while in graduate school, worked summers for the U.S. Information Agency in Lebanon and Syria, instructing teachers of English as a second language; assistant to the director, metropolitan studies program, Syracuse University, 1965–1969; assistant to the dean, Maxwell Graduate School, Syracuse University, 1969–1970; assistant professor of political science, Bernard Baruch College, City University of New York (CUNY), 1970–1972; associate professor, politics and education, Teachers College, Columbia University, 1972–1979; visiting professor, Yale University Law School, 1972–1979; member, board of directors, and treasurer, Municipal Assistance Corporation, NYC, 1975–1977, which rescued the city from financial collapse; assistant secretary for policy development and research, U.S. Department of Housing and Urban Development (HUD), Washington, 1977–1980, where she promoted women's issues such as the creation of shelters for battered women, the Women and Mortgage Credit project, and antidiscrimination measures; professor of political science and president, Hunter College, CUNY, 1980–1987; chancellor and professor of political science and educational policy studies, University of Wisconsin, Madison, 1988–1993; only the second woman to head a major research university, and the first to lead a Big Ten school, she administered America's largest public research university and used state-private funding partnerships to improve research facilities, undergraduate education, and campus opportunities for women and minorities; appointed by President Clinton as SECRETARY OF HEALTH AND HUMAN SERVICES and served from January 22, 1993, until the end of Clinton's second term on January 20, 2001; the longest-serving HHS secretary, her policy initiatives included revision of health-care financing, expansion of the Head Start program for preschool children, universal childhood immunizations, expansion of AIDS research, and welfare reform; cochair, Advisory Commission on Consumer Protection and Quality in the Health Care Industry, 1996–2001; visiting distinguished fellow, Center for Public Service, Brookings Institution, Washington, 2001; president, University of Miami (Fla.), 2001– ; assistant director, Peace Corps Training Project for Peru, 1966; assistant to the chairman, New York State Constitutional Convention's Committee on Local Government and Home Rule, 1967; cofounder, Washington Women's Network, 1977, a support group for female government officials; member, board of directors, Children's Defense Fund, 1980–1993, Institute for International Economics, 1981–1993, American Ditchley Foundation, 1981–1993, Spencer Foundation, 1988–1993, M&I Bank, Madison, 1991–1993, NCAA Foundation, 1991, Lennar Corporation, 2001– ; member, board of governors, American Stock Exchange, 1981–1987; trustee, Committee on Economic Development, 1981–1993, TIAA, 1985–1989, Brookings Institute, 1989–1993; member, Trilateral Commission, 1988–1993, Knight Commission on Intercollegiate Sports, 1990–1993; Trustee scholar, Western College, 1958–1962, Carnegie fellow, 1966–1968, National Academy of Education Spencer fellow, 1972–1973, and Guggenheim fellow, 1975–1976; recipient, Ohio Newspaper Women's Scholar award, 1958, Distinguished Service Medal, Columbia University Teacher's College, 1989, National Public Service Award, 1992, Career Achievement Award for Distinguished Scholarship in Urban Politics, American Political Science Association, Ballington and Maud Booth award, Volunteers of America, 2000, and over 30 honorary degrees; named one of the top five managers in higher education, *Business Week*, 1992, and Woman of the Year, *Glamour Magazine*, 1994; author of *Neighborhood Governance* (1971), *The City and the Constitution* (1972), *The Property Tax and the Votes* (1973), and *The Decentralization Approach* (1974); member, ASPA, American Political Science Association, National Academy of Arts and Sciences, National Academy of Public Administration, National Academy of Education, Council on Foreign Relations. **References:** *Current Biography Yearbook 1991; Who's Who, 2001.*

—William J. Lombardo

SHAW, Leslie Mortier

Born in Morristown, Vt., November 2, 1848; son of Boardman O. and Louise (Spaulding) Shaw; Methodist; married Alice Crenshaw on December 6, 1877; father of one son and two daughters; attended village academy in Stowe; taught school; went to uncle's farm in Iowa, 1869; graduated Cornell College in 1874; completed course at Iowa College of Law, Des Moines, 1876, and started practice at Dennison, Iowa; organized bank and mortgage loan business, 1880; champion of gold standard in campaign of 1896; elected governor of Iowa and served two terms, 1898–1902; became permanent chairman of International Monetary Convention, 1898; campaigned for Theodore Roosevelt, 1900; appointed SECRETARY OF THE TREASURY in the cabinet of President Theodore Roosevelt on January 9, 1902, and served until March 3, 1907; most important contributions were liberalizing security and waiving reserve requirements for government bank deposits, withholding funds for deposit in time of need, artificially stimulating gold importation, and regulating note issues by executive decree; head of Carnegie Trust Company of New York, 1907–1908; head of First Mortgage Guarantee and Trust Company of Philadelphia, 1909–1913; moved to Washington to write and lecture, 1913; published *Current Issues* (1908) and *Vanishing Landmark: The Trend toward Bolshevism* (1919); died in Washington, D.C., March 28, 1932. **References:** *Annual Reports of the Secretary of the Treasury* (1902–1906); B.F. Shambaugh, *The Messages and Proclamations of the Governors of Iowa* (1905); James F. Rhodes, *McKinley and Roosevelt Administrations, 1897–1909*, in *History of the United States*, vol. 9 (1922).

SHERMAN, James Schoolcraft

Born in Utica, N.Y., October 24, 1855; son of Richard U. Sherman, newspaper editor, Democratic politician, and member of the state legislature, and Mary

Frances (Sherman) Sherman; Dutch Reformed; married on January 26, 1881, to Carrie Babcock; father of Sherrill, Richard, and Thomas; attended the public schools of New Hartford, Utica Academy, and Whitestone Seminary; was graduated from Hamilton College in 1878; studied law and received his degree from Hamilton College in 1879; admitted to the bar and began practice with his brother-in-law, Henry J. Cookinham; elected as a Republican mayor of Utica in 1884, serving until 1886; elected to the U.S. House of Representatives in 1886 and served until 1891, and again from 1893 to 1909; in 1895 became president of the New Hartford Canning Company; helped form the Utica Trust and Deposit Company, becoming its president in 1900; presided over three New York state Republican conventions and chairman of the congressional campaign committees in 1906; nominated for the vice-presidency at the Republican National Convention in Chicago, June 1908, and elected VICE-PRESIDENT with President Taft on November 3, 1908, taking office on March 4, 1909; renominated in 1912 but died before the close of the campaign on October 30, 1912, in Utica, N.Y.; interment in Utica. **References:** Henry F. Pringle, *Life and Times of William H. Taft* (1939); Norman M. Wilensky, *Conservatives in the Progressive Era* (1965).

SHERMAN, John

Born in Lancaster, Ohio, May 10, 1823; son of Charles Robert and Mary (Hoyt) Sherman; younger brother of William Tecumseh Sherman; Methodist; married Margaret Sarah Cecelia Stewart on August 31, 1848; father of an adopted daughter; after attending the common schools, he entered Horner Academy in Lancaster, Ohio, from 1835 to 1837; became junior rodman of an Engineers Corps in 1839; studied law and was admitted to the bar in 1844, commencing his practice at Mansfield, Ohio; delegate to the Whig National Conventions at Philadelphia in 1848 and at Baltimore in 1852, serving as secretary to the 1848 convention; moved to Cleveland, Ohio, in 1853; president of the first Ohio Republican state convention in 1855; elected as a representative to the 34th through 37th Congresses, serving from March 4, 1855, to March 21, 1861, when he resigned; elected as a Republican to the U.S. Senate in 1861 and was reelected in 1866 and 1872, serving from March 21, 1861, until his resignation on March 8, 1877; was president *pro tempore* in the Senate from 1885 to 1887; invited to join the cabinet of President Hayes as SECRETARY OF THE TREASURY on March 8, 1877, and served until March 3, 1881; as secretary, his main objectives were the resumption of specie payments and the funding of the public debt and settling the silver question without banishing gold or displacing paper; elected to the U.S. Senate in the place of James A. Garfield, who had been elected president, on March 4, 1881, reelected in 1886 and 1892, and served until his resignation on March 4, 1897; appointed SECRETARY OF STATE in the cabinet of President McKinley, serving from March 5, 1897, until his resignation on April 25, 1900; retired to private life; died in Washington, D.C., on October 22, 1900; interment in Mansfield Cemetery, Mansfield, Ohio. **References:** Richard Shuster, *The Selfish and the Strong* (1958); T. Harry Williams, ed., *Hayes, the Diary of a President, 1875–1881* (1964).

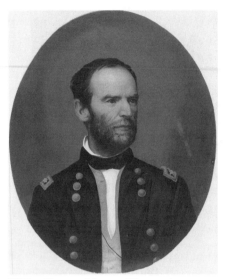

William Sherman (Library of Congress)

SHERMAN, William Tecumseh

Born in Lancaster, Ohio, on February 8, 1820; son of Charles Robert Sherman, lawyer and state supreme court judge, and Mary (Hoyt) Sherman; Methodist; married Eleanor Boyle Ewing on May 1, 1850; father of eight children; after death of father in 1829, raised by Thomas Ewing; attended local academy; received appointment to West Point in 1836, graduated in 1840, and appointed second lieutenant, 3d Artillery, in Florida; became first lieutenant in 1841; studied law while stationed at Fort Moultrie, S.C.; aide to Philip Kearney, adjutant to Richard Barnes Mason, and then adjutant general to Persifer Frazer Smith in Mexican War; made captain of subsistence department until resignation on September 6, 1853; became partner in branch bank in San Francisco; bank representative in New York, 1857; law partnership with Thomas and Hugh Boyle Ewing in Leavenworth, Kans.; was superintendent of military college at Alexandria, La., from October 1859 to January 18, 1861; president of Louisiana street railway, named colonel of 13th Infantry in 1861; fought on Union side in Civil War; named major general of volunteers in May 1862; became major general in 1864 and lieutenant general in 1866; temporarily put in command of army; sent on mission to Mexico, 1866; made general in command of army on March 4, 1869; appointed SECRETARY OF WAR in the cabinet of President Grant on September 9, 1869, and served from September 11, 1869, to October 25, 1869; toured Europe, 1871–1872; established school at Fort Leavenworth; retired from active duty on November 1, 1883; settled in St. Louis; moved to New York, 1889; died in New York City on February 14, 1891. **References:** Henry Hitchcock, *Marching with Sherman* (1927); E.S. Miers, ed., *The General Who Marched to Hell* (1965).

SHULTZ, George Pratt

Born in New York, N.Y., December 13, 1920; son of Birl E., personnel director and founder of the New York Stock Exchange Institute, and Margaret Lennox (Pratt) Shultz; Episcopalian; married Helena Maria O'Brien on February 16,

1946; father of Margaret Ann Shultz Tilsworth, Kathleen Pratt Shultz Jorgensen, Peter Milton, Barbara Lennox Shultz White, and Alexander George; married Charlotte Mailliard on August 15, 1997; graduated from Loomis Institute, Windsor, Conn., 1938; B.A. in economics, Princeton University, 1942; Ph.D. in industrial economics, Massachusetts Institute of Technology (MIT), 1949; served to captain, U.S. Marine Corps, 1942–1945; teaching assistant in economics, MIT, 1946–1947, instructor, 1948–1949, assistant professor of industrial relations, 1949–1954, and associate professor, 1955–1957; professor of industrial relations, Graduate School of Business, University of Chicago, 1957–1968, dean of school, 1968–1969; appointed by President-elect Nixon as chairman of a task force to study manpower, labor-management relations, and wage-price policy in 1968; appointed SECRETARY OF LABOR by President Nixon and served from January 22, 1969, until July 1, 1970; most important contributions were opposing an increase in the minimum wage rate, helping to avert a national rail strike in April 1969, ordering into effect the "Philadelphia Plan" to increase minority group employment, and helping to negotiate a settlement during the postal workers' strike in 1970; first director of the federal Office of Management and the Budget, 1970–1972; appointed SECRETARY OF THE TREASURY by Nixon and served from June 12, 1972, until May 8, 1974; helped formulate Nixon and Ford responses to inflationary pressures and unemployment; professor of management and public policy, Graduate School of Business, Stanford University, 1974–1982; executive vice-president, Bechtel Corporation, San Francisco, 1974–1975, president, 1975–1977, vice-chairman, 1977–1981; president, Bechtel Group Inc., 1981–1982; appointed SECRETARY OF STATE by President Reagan and served from July 16, 1982, until the end of Reagan's second term on January 20, 1989; as secretary of state, handled plans to end conflicts in Central America and the Middle East, supported President Reagan's strong national defense policy, and led arms limitation negotiations with the Soviet Union; survived an assassination attempt in South America, August 1988; professor of international economics, Stanford University, 1989–1991, professor emeritus, 1991– ; distinguished fellow, Hoover Institution, Stanford University, 1989– ; began to serve on arbitration panels for labor-management disputes, 1953; senior staff economist, President's Council of Economic Advisors, 1955; consultant to the Office of Secretary of Labor, 1960; consultant, President's Advisory Committee on Labor-Management Policy, 1961–1962; member, Governor's Committee on Unemployment in Illinois, 1961–1962; chairman, task force of the U.S. Employment Service, 1962; member, National Manpower Policy task force, 1963; fellow, Center for Advanced Study in the Behavioral Sciences, University of Chicago, 1968–1969; former chairman, Council on Economic Policy, East-West Trade Policy committee; member, Treasury Advisory Committee on reform of the international monetary system, 1975; chairman, President's Economic Policy advisory board, 1981–1982; member, board of directors, Borg-Warner Corp., Stein, Roe, and Farnham, General Transportation Company, Charles Schwab and Company, Bechtel Group,

Inc., Infrastructureworld.com, G.M. Corporation, Gilead Sciences, Unext.com, Dillon, Read, and Co., Inc., Boeing Co.; chairman, J.P. Morgan International Council and advisory council, Institute for International Studies, 1990–1998, California Governor's Economic Policy Advisory Board, 1995–1998; recipient of honorary degrees from Yeshiva University, University of Tel Aviv, Technion-Israel Institute of Technology, Keio University, Tokyo, Brandeis University, University of Notre Dame, Princeton University, Loyola University, University of Pennsylvania, University of Rochester, Carnegie-Mellon University, Baruch College, Northwestern University, and Tblisi State University; author of *Leaders and Followers in an Age of Ambiguity* (1975) and *Turmoil and Triumph: My Years as Secretary of State* (1993); coauthor of *Pressures on Wage Decisions* (with Charles A. Myers, 1951), *The Dynamics of a Labor Market* (with John R. Coleman, 1951), *Labor Problems: Cases and Readings* (with T.L. Whisler, 1953), *Management Organization and the Computer* (with Arnold A. Weber, 1960), *Strategies for the Displaced Worker* (with Robert Z. Aliber, 1966), *Workers and Wages in the Urban Labor Market* (with Albert Rees, 1970), and *Economic Policy beyond the Headlines* (with Kenneth W. Dam, 1977, 1998); coeditor, with Robert Z. Aliber, of *Guidelines, Informed Controls, and the Market Place* (1966); member, American Economic Association, Industrial Relations Research Association (president, 1968), National Academy of Arbitrators. **References:** *U.S. News & World Report* (December 23, 1968); Earl Mazo and Stephan Hess, *Nixon: A Political Portrait* (1969); Dan Rather and Gary Paul Gates, *The Palace Guard* (1974); *Current Biography Yearbook 1988; Who's Who, 1989*; Lou Cannon, *President Reagan: The Role of a Lifetime* (1991); Michael Schaller, *Reckoning with Reagan: America and Its President in the 1980s* (1992); Lawrence E. Walsh, *Firewall: The Iran-Contra Conspiracy and Cover-up* (1997); Melvin Small, *The Presidency of Richard Nixon* (1999); Richard Reeves, *President Nixon: Alone in the White House* (2001).

SIMON, William Edward

Born in Paterson, N.J., November 27, 1927; son of Charles and Eleanor (Kearns) Simon; married Carol Girard (died 1995) on September 9, 1950; father of William E. Jr., John Peter, Mary Beth Simon Streep, Carol Leigh Simon Porges, Aimee Simon Bloom, Julie Ann Simon Munro, Johanna Katrina Morris; married Tonia Adams Donnelley on July 2, 1996; attended schools in Spring Lake, N.J.; graduated from Newark Academy, 1946; B.A. in government and law, Lafayette College, 1952; U.S. Army, 1946–1948; with Union Securities Co., New York City, 1952–1957, assistant vice-president and manager, municipal trading department, 1955–1957; vice-president, Weeden and Company, New York City, 1957–1964; joined Salomon Brothers, New York City, 1964, senior partner and member, executive committee, 1964–1973; deputy secretary, U.S. Department of the Treasury, 1973–1974; director, Federal Energy Office,

December 1973–April 1974, a period coinciding with the Arab oil embargo and consequent U.S. oil shortage; appointed SECRETARY OF THE TREASURY by President Nixon and continued under President Ford, serving from May 8, 1974, until January 20, 1977; as secretary, faced a growing economic slump characterized by inflation and a recession; senior consultant, Booz Allen and Hamilton, 1977–1979; senior adviser, Blyth Eastman Dillon and Co. Inc., 1977–1980; deputy chairman, Olayan Investments Company Establishment, 1980–1982; chairman, Crescent Diversified Ltd., 1980–1982; chairman, Wesray Corporation, 1981–1986; chairman, Wesray Capital Corporation, 1984–1986; chairman emeritus, Wesray Corporation and Wesray Capital Corporation, 1987; founder in 1988 and former chairman, William E. Simon and Sons, Morristown, N.J., and Los Angeles; founder of the philanthropic William E. Simon Foundation, Inc., in the early 1980s; founder and former cochairman, WSGP International Inc., Los Angeles, 1986–1992; first president of the newly formed Association of Primary Dealers in U.S. Government Securities, 1969; treasurer, U.S. Olympic Committee, 1977–1980, president, 1981–1984, with key roles in the U.S. boycott of the 1980 Summer Games in Moscow and the planning of the 1984 Summer Games in Los Angeles; an important figure in the creation of the U.S. Olympic Foundation as a financial source for U.S. amateur sports; former president, John M. Olin Foundation; founding president, Richard Nixon Presidential Library and Birthplace; chairman, investment committee, U.S. Air Force Academy, USAF Academy Academic Development Fund; former trustee Heritage Foundation; trustee emeritus, Lafayette College; trustee and member, investment committee, executive advisory council, Simon School, University of Rochester; former chairman, board of trustees, U.S. Olympic Foundation; former member, board of directors, Sequoia Institute, Kissinger Associates, National Football Foundation and Hall of Fame Inc.; former director emeritus, International Foundation for Education and Self Help, Citizens Network for Foreign Affairs, Atlantic Council of U.S., Target; board of directors, cochairman, and endowment committee, Covenant House; honorary director, Gerald R. Ford Foundation; board of advisers, Catholic League for Religious and Civil Rights; member, advisory board, Jesse Owens Foundation; member, board of overseers, Hoover Institution on War, Revolution and Peace, Stanford University; member, advisory board, Pacific Security Research Institute, Sydney, Australia, University of Southern California School of Business Administration, Private Sector Initiatives Foundation, Women's Sports Foundation, U.S. Association of Blind Athletes, Catholics Committed to Support the Pope, Acton Institute, Center for International Management Education, University of Dallas, Center for Christianity and the Common Good; member, national advisory board, Sudden Infant Death Syndrome Alliance; honorary board of governors, Tel Aviv University; member, board of advisers, William J. Casey chair geopolitical studies, John M. Ashbrook Center for Public Affairs; member, advisory council, Consumer Alert, International Center for the Disabled; member, board of governors, Hugh O'Brian Youth Foundation, New York Hospital, Ronald

Reagan Presidential Foundation; member, President's Committee on Arts and Humanities; member, visiting committee, Marine Science Research Center, SUNY, Stony Brook; member, international councilors, Center for Strategic and International Studies; member, executive committee, Bretton Woods Committee; member, policy council, Tax Foundation; member, national planning board, Morality in Media Inc.; member, chairman's council, National Council on Alcoholism and Drug Dependence Inc.; member, advisory council, William J. Donovan Memorial Foundation Inc.; member, board of advisers, Center for Military Readiness; former consultant, W.R. Grace and Company, Brazilinvest, Allstate Insurance Company, Calvin Bullock Limited, Johnson and Johnson; member, public review board, Arthur Andersen and Company; past chairman, World Trade Bancorp.; member, advisory board, Classics of Liberty Library (Gryphon Editions Inc.), Corporation for Development and Commerce, *The Papers of Albert Gallatin*; adjunct faculty member and distinguished visiting professor, U.S. Air Force Academy, 1995; recipient, Decorated Order of the Nile, Government of Egypt, Investment Bankers Association of America award, 1970, Small Business Administration citation, 1971, Youth Services award, Wall Street division, B'nai B'rith, 1971, Outstanding Service to His Country award, Port Authority of New York, 1973, Merit award, Securities Industry Association, 1973, Outstanding Citizen of New Jersey award, Advertising Club of New Jersey, 1974, Financial World award, 1974, Good Scout award Boy Scouts of America, 1974, Executive Government award, OIC Government Relations Service, 1974, Outstanding Citizen of the Year award, 1974, U.S. Industrial Payroll Savings Bonds award, 1974, Civic Leadership award, American Jewish Committee, 1975, Dean's citation, American University, 1975, Trustees medal, Fairleigh Dickinson University, 1975, Gold medal, National Institute of Social Sciences, 1975, American Eagle award, National Invest in America Council, 1975, Achievement award, Newark Academy Alumni Association, 1975, Bicentennial award, U.S. Citizen's Congress, 1975, Young Americans for Freedom citation, 1975, American Institute for Public Service award, 1976, Business in Public Affairs award, Chamber of Commerce of Maryland, 1976, Flame of Truth award, Fund for Higher Education in Israel, 1976, Distinguished Achievements award, Money Marketers of NYU, 1976, Pennsylvania Society medal, 1976, NYU College of Business and Public Administration medal, 1976, Government Service award, Public Relations Society of America, 1976, Carnauba Palm award, S.C. Johnson and Son Inc., 1976, President's Award for Outstanding Achievement, 1976, Economic Forum citation, Chapman College, 1977, Alexander Hamilton award, Department of the Treasury, 1977, American Legion award, 1977, Brotherhood award, National Conference of Christians and Jews, 1977, Outstanding Achievement award, Freedoms Foundation at Valley Forge, 1978, Order of Anthony Wayne citation, Valley Forge Military Academy and Junior College, 1978, Distinguished Patriot award, SAR, 1979, George Washington Kidd award, Lafayette College Alumni Association, 1979, George Washington Honor medal, Valley Forge

Freedom Foundation, 1979, Eastside Conservative Club, 1980, Service Above Self award, Easton Rotary Club, 1980, Charles Edison Memorial award, Leadership award, Columbia Business School, 1982, Catholic Big Brothers of the Year award, Lotus Club, 1982, Hall of Fame award, Tri-County Scholarship, 1983, Distinguished Service award, The Liberty Bowl, 1983, Jesse Owens International Amateur Athletic award, 1984, Reed K. Swenson Leadership award, National Junior College Athletic Association, 1984, Governor's Committee on Scholastic Achievement award, 1985, Golden Medallion award, International Swimming Hall of Fame, 1985, International Executive of the Year award, American Graduate School of International Management, 1985, Humanitarian award, American Sportscaster Association, 1985, Man of the Year award, Morristown Rotary Club, 1986, Distinguished Citizen award, Greater New York Council of the Boy Scouts of America, 1986, Sportsman of the Year award, All-American Collegiate Golf Foundation, 1986, Golden Plate award, American Academy of Achievement, 1986, Société d'Honneur award, Lafayette College, 1986, Kriendler award, Marine Corps School, 1986, Reunion Alumni Achievement award, Newark Academy, 1986, Covenant House award, 1988, First Annual award, Mid-Atlantic Legal Foundation, 1988, President's medal, Adelphi University, 1989, Entrepreneur of the Year award, Henry Bloch School of Business and Professional Administration, University of Missouri, Kansas City, 1989, Jesse Owens International award, U.S. Olympic Committee, 1990, Ellis Island Medal of Honor award, 1990, Club of Champions Gold medal, Catholic Youth Organization of Archdiocese of New York, 1991, Robert S. Brookings award, Washington University, St. Louis, 1993, Humanitarian award, St. Leo College, Tampa, Fla., 1995, Louis C. Wills award for Excellence, Helen Keller Services for the Blind, New York City, 1995, Blessed Hyacinth Cormier award for Outstanding Catholic Leadership, 1996, and honorary degrees from over 20 colleges and universities; namesake of William E. Simon Residence Hall at U.S. Olympic Training Center, Colorado Springs, Colo., 1995, and William E. Simon Graduate School of Business Administration, University of Rochester; named to l'Ordre Olympique by le Comité Internat. Olympique, 1987, U.S. Olympic Committee Hall of Fame, 1991; author of *A Time for Truth* (1978) and *A Time for Action* (1980); former member, Pilgrims of U.S., National Federation of State High School Administrators (chairman emeritus), Mont Pelerin Society, Asia Society (former trustee), Explorers Club, American Association of Master Knights of Sovereign Military Order of Malta, American Association of Retired Persons, Arctic Institute of North America, American Australian Association, Author's Guild, New Jersey Farm Bureau, Pennsylvania Society, Royal Geographical Society, Kappa Beta Phi; died on June 3, 2000, in Santa Barbara, Calif. **References:** *Time* (January 21, 1974); *Current Biography Yearbook 1974; Who's Who in America, 1976–1977; International Who's Who, 1988–1989*; John Robert Greene, *The Presidency of Gerald R. Ford* (1995); *New York Times* (June 5, 2000).

SKINNER, Samuel Knox

Born in Chicago, Ill., June 10, 1938; son of Vernon Orlo and Imelda Jane (Curran) Skinner; Presbyterian; married Susan Thomas, 1960; married Mary Jacobs, 1989; father of Thomas, Steven, and Jane; B.S., University of Illinois, 1960; J.D., DePaul University, 1966; first lieutenant, U.S. Army, 1960–1961; admitted to the bar in Illinois, 1966; assistant U.S. attorney, 1968–1974, first assistant U.S. attorney, 1974–1975, and U.S. attorney, 1975–1977, Northern District of Illinois, Chicago; partner, Sidley and Austin, Chicago, 1977–1989; appointed by President George H.W. Bush as SECRETARY OF TRANSPORTATION, serving from February 6, 1989, until December 16, 1991; White House chief of staff for Bush, December 1991–August 1992; general chairman, Republican National Committee, Washington, 1992–1993; president and director, Commonwealth Edison Company, Chicago, and its holding company, Unicom Corporation, 1993–1998; partner and cochairman, Hopkins and Sutter, Chicago, 1998–2000; director, USFreightways Corporation, 1999– , president and chief executive officer, 2000– , and chairman, 2001– ; chairman, Illinois Capitol Development Board, 1977–1984, and Regional Transportation Authority, Chicago, 1984; member, board of directors, ANTEC Corporation, EVEREN Capital, LTV Corporation (including board affairs and audit committees), 1993– , Midwest Express Holdings, Transportation.com, Union Pacific Resources Group, NAVIGANT Consulting, 1999– , Odetics ITS, 1999– ; member, American Bar Association, Chicago Bar Association. **References:** *Current Biography Yearbook 1989*; Michael Duffy and Dan Goodgame, *Marching in Place: The Status Quo Presidency of George Bush* (1992); Charles Kolb, *White House Daze: The Unmaking of Domestic Policy in the Bush Years* (1994); John Robert Greene, *The Presidency of George Bush* (2000).

SLATER, Rodney Earl

Born in Tutwyler, Miss., February 23, 1955; son of Velma Brewer; stepson of Earl Brewer, mechanic and maintenance man; married Cassandra Wilkins; father of Bridgette Josette; grew up in public housing in Marianna, Ark., in one of the ten poorest counties in the United States; attended Lee High School; B.S., Eastern Michigan University, 1977; on football scholarship, he was team captain and star running back; J.D., University of Arkansas Law School, 1980; assistant attorney general, state of Arkansas, 1980–1982; special assistant to Governor Bill Clinton for community and minority affairs, 1983–1985; executive assistant to Governor Clinton for economic and community programs, 1985–1987; member, Arkansas State Highway and Transportation Commission, 1987–1993, and chairman, 1992–1993; director of intergovernmental relations, Arkansas State University, 1987–1993; head administrator, Federal Highway Administration, U.S. Department of Transportation, Washington, 1993–1997; appointed by President Clinton as SECRETARY OF TRANSPORTATION and served from February 14, 1997, until the end of Clinton's second term on January 20, 2001; vital in promoting President Clinton's Africa Initiative, launched in 1997 to promote economic development in Africa, in passing the federal highway bill providing for new roads, 1998, and in promoting high standards for safety and education; worked on Bill Clinton's gubernatorial campaigns, 1980–1990; Arkansas liaison, Martin Luther King, Jr., Federal Holiday Commission, 1983–1987; member, Arkansas Sesquicentennial Commission, 1986; deputy campaign manager and senior traveling adviser, Bill Clinton for President, 1992; deputy to the chairman, Clinton-Gore transition team, 1992–1993; considered a candidate for the Democratic nomination for governor of Arkansas, 2002; named 1 of the 100 most influential African Americans, *Ebony* magazine, 1997; member, Arkansas Bar Association (secretary-treasurer, 1989–1993), W. Harold Flowers Law Society (president, 1985–1992). **References:** *New York Times* (December 21, 1996); *Ebony* (July 1997); *Current Biography Yearbook 1999; Who's Who among African Americans*, 2000.

—Herbert Brewer

SMITH, Caleb Blood

Born in Boston, Mass., April 16, 1808; son of Blood Smith; married Elizabeth B. Walton on July 18, 1831; father of three children; moved with his parents to Cincinnati, Ohio, in 1814; attended the College of Cincinnati, 1823–1825, and Miami University, Oxford, Ohio, 1825–1826, but did not graduate; studied law in Cincinnati and in Connorsville, Ind.; admitted to the bar and began practice in 1828 in Connorsville; founded and edited the *Indiana Sentinel* in 1832; elected as a Whig to the state House of Representatives in 1832; reelected each year until 1837 and elected again in 1840 and 1841; served as Speaker of the House in 1836; presidential elector on the Whig ticket of 1840; elected as a Whig to the 28th, 29th, and 30th Congresses, serving from March 4, 1843, to March 3, 1849; appointed by President Taylor as member of the board investigating American claims against Mexico and served until 1851; moved to Cincinnati and resumed law practice; president of the Cincinnati and Chicago Railroad Company, 1854; presidential elector on the Republican ticket of 1856; moved to Indianapolis, Ind., in 1859; delegate to the Republican National Convention in Chicago in 1860; Indiana delegate to the peace convention held in Washington in 1861 to attempt to avert war; appointed SECRETARY OF THE INTERIOR in the cabinet of President Lincoln and served from March 5, 1861, until January 1, 1863, when he resigned; appointed judge of the U.S. District Court for Indiana, serving from 1863 until his death; died in Indianapolis, Ind., on January 7, 1864; interment in the City Cemetery, Connorsville, Ind. **References:** L.J. Bailey, "Caleb Blood Smith," *Indiana Magazine of History* (September 1933); Burton J. Hendrick, *Lincoln's War Cabinet* (1946); Noah Brooks, *Mr. Lincoln's Washington* (1967).

SMITH, Charles Emory

Born in Mansfield, Conn., February 18, 1842; son of Emory Boutelle and Arvilla Topliff (Royce) Smith; married Ella Huntly on June 3, 1863; married Nettie Nichols on October 3, 1907; childless; moved to Albany, N.Y., at age 7, attended public schools of Albany; graduated from Albany Academy at age 16; began journalistic career while still in school by writing for *Albany Evening Transcript*; entered Union College as a junior, graduating in 1861; received LL.D. from Union College, 1889; granted LL.D. from Lafayette, 1900; received LL.D. from Wesleyan, 1901; became military secretary to Brigadier General John F. Rathbone at beginning of Civil War and resigned, 1862; became instructor in Albany Academy, 1862; joined staff of *Albany Express* in 1865; became associate editor of leading Republican newspaper, the *Albany Evening Journal*, 1870, served as editor, 1874–1880; president of New York State Press Association, 1874; wrote nearly all state Republican platforms, 1874–1880, and most of national, 1876; chairman of committee on resolutions of the Republican state conventions, 1874–1880; president of Republican state convention, 1879; elected member of board of regents of the University of the State of New York, 1879–1880; became editor of *Philadelphia Press* in 1880; trustee of Union College, 1881; U.S. minister to Russia, 1890–1892; appointed POSTMASTER GENERAL in the cabinet of President McKinley on April 21, 1898, continued under Theodore Roosevelt, and served until his resignation on January 15, 1902; most important contributions were advice on political problems of Spanish-American War period, prevention of use of mails for fraudulent purposes, extension and popularization of rural free delivery service, and elimination of corruption in postal service established by his department in Cuba; died in Philadelphia, Pa., January 19, 1908. **References:** S.W. Pennypacker, *The Autobiography of a Pennsylvanian* (1894); *New York Times* (January 20, 1908); Dorothy G. Fowler, *The Cabinet Politician: The Postmasters General, 1829–1900* (1943); Margaret K. Leech, *In the Days of McKinley* (1959); H. Wayne Morgan, *William McKinley and His America* (1963).

SMITH, C(yrus) R(owlett)

Born in Minerva, Tex., September 9, 1899; son of Roy Edgerton and Marion (Burck) Smith; Baptist; married Elizabeth L. Manget (divorced) on December 29, 1934; father of Douglas Manget; attended School of Business Administration, University of Texas, but left without receiving a degree, 1924; served from colonel to major general, U.S. Army Air Corps, 1942–1945; deputy commander, Air Transport Command, 1942–1945; worked in franchise-tax department of Office of Texas Secretary of State and was a part-time examiner for the Federal Reserve Bank of Houston; public accountant, Peat, Marwick, Mitchell and Company, Dallas, 1924–1926; assistant treasurer, Texas-Louisiana Power Company, Fort Worth, Tex., 1926–1928; vice-president, Texas Air Transport,

Inc., Fort Worth, 1929–1930; vice-president, American Airways, Inc., Fort Worth and St. Louis, 1930–1933; vice-president, American Airlines, Inc., Fort Worth, 1934; president, American Airlines, Inc., Chicago and New York City, 1934–1942; chairman of the board, American Airlines, 1946–1968; appointed SECRETARY OF COMMERCE by President Johnson and served from March 6, 1968, to January 19, 1969; partner, Lazard Freres and Company, New York, 1969–1973; chief executive officer, American Airlines, 1973–1974; decorated D.S.M. Legion of Merit, Air Medal U.S.; honorary Commander of the Order of the British Empire; named to Aviation Hall of Fame, 1974, and Business Hall of Fame, 1975; recipient, Wright Brothers award, Billy Mitchell award; former member, Metropolitan Club; died on April 4, 1990, in Annapolis, Md. **References:** *Current Biography Yearbook 1945*; *Chemical Week* (March 2, 1968); *U.S. News & World Report* (March 22, 1968); Hugh Sidney, *A Very Personal Presidency: Lyndon Johnson in the White House* (1968); *Who's Who in America, 1984*; Robert J. Serling, *Eagle: The Story of American Airlines* (1985); *New York Times* (April 6, 1990); William M. Leary, ed., *The Airline Industry* (1992).

SMITH, Hoke

Born in Newton, N.C., September 2, 1855; son of Professor H.H. Smith, educator, and Mary Brent (Hoke) Smith; Presbyterian; married Birdie Cobb on December 19, 1885; father of one son and three daughters; married Mazie Crawford on August 27, 1924; tutored by his father; read law in offices of Collier, Mynatt, and Collier in Atlanta, Ga., while teaching in Waynesboro, Ga., 1872; admitted to the bar at the age of 17, in 1873; began practice; chairman of Fulton County Democratic executive committee, 1876; delegate to state Democratic convention, 1882; president of Young Men's Library, 1881, 1882, and 1883; organized and became president of Atlanta *Evening Journal* in June 1887; delegate to Democratic National Convention in 1892; appointed SECRETARY OF THE INTERIOR in the cabinet of President Cleveland on March 6, 1893, and served until resignation on September 1, 1896; most important contributions were furthering the cause of conservation, purging the pension list of fraud, and upholding Cleveland's effort to maintain the gold standard; offered himself as candidate for governor of Georgia, 1906; served as governor from July 1907 to July 1909, and July 1911 to November 1911; elected by the legislature to fill unexpired term of U.S. Senator A.S. Clay, 1911; reelected to U.S. Senate in 1914 and served until 1921; chairman of commission on national aid to vocational education created by a joint resolution of Congress on January 20, 1914; responsible for Smith-Hughes bill, which provided for studies of agriculture, home economics, trade, and industry in public schools and vocational education of the disabled, February 23, 1917; chairman of Board of Education in Atlanta; organized Piedmont Hotel and Fulton National Bank; died on November 27, 1931. **References:** A.D. Candler and C.A. Evans, eds., *Georgia* (1906); Clark

Howell, *History of Georgia* (1926); Dewey Grantham, *Hoke Smith and the Politics of the New South* (1958); Robert L. Vexter, ed., *Grover Cleveland, 1837–1908: Chronology, Documents, Bibliographical Aids* (1968).

SMITH, Robert

Born in Lancaster, Pa., November 3, 1757; married distant cousin Margaret Smith on December 7, 1790; father of eight children; graduated from the College of New Jersey in 1781; studied law in Baltimore, Md., and was admitted to bar in 1786; served in Maryland Senate from 1793 until 1795; member of Maryland House of Delegates, 1796–1800; served on Baltimore City Council from 1798 until 1801; accepted appointment by President Jefferson as SECRETARY OF THE NAVY on July 15, 1801, served July 27, 1801, until March 8, 1809; confirmed as ATTORNEY GENERAL in 1805, only to return to navy secretary position after a few months and served out his term without recommission; accomplishments include maintenance of blocking squadron in Mediterranean during war on Barbary States, conscientiously enforcing Embargo despite personal disapproval; appointed SECRETARY OF STATE by President Madison, served March 6, 1809, until his resignation under pressure from President Madison on April 1, 1811; declined President Madison's offer of the position of minister to Russia in March 1811; published *Robert Smith's Address to the People of the United States* in June 1811, as an attempted defense of the actions that had caused President Madison to seek his resignation; retired to private business in Baltimore; died November 26, 1842. **References:** G.E. Davies, "Robert Smith and the Navy," *Maryland Historical Magazine* (December 1919); C.C. Tansill, "Robert Smith," in S.F. Bemis, *The American Secretaries of State and Their Diplomacy*, vol. 3 (1927).

SMITH, William French

Born in Wilton, N.H., August 26, 1917; son of William French, president of the Mexican Telephone and Telegraph Company, and Margaret (Dawson) Smith; married Marion Hannah on March 5, 1943, divorced, 1958; married Jean Webb Vaughan on November 6, 1964; father of William French, Stephanie Oakes, Scott Cameron, and Gregory Hale; A.B. summa cum laude, University of California, Berkeley, 1939; LL.B., Harvard Law School, 1942; served to lieutenant, U.S. Naval Reserve, 1942–1946; admitted to the California bar in 1942; senior partner, Gibson, Dunn, and Crutcher, Los Angeles, 1946–1981; became Ronald Reagan's personal lawyer in 1966 and served as an informal adviser to him as governor of California; appointed as ATTORNEY GENERAL by President Reagan and served from January 23, 1981, until February 24, 1985; major contributions were supporting Reagan's welfare reform program, adopting a more lenient attitude toward corporate mergers in order to make government more responsive to the concerns of business, selecting appointees to the federal bench who believed in judicial restraint, and recommending a comprehensive crime package of more than 150 administrative and legislative initiatives, including a federal death penalty, the denial of bail for certain types of crime, modification of the rule barring the use of illegally seized evidence in criminal trials, mandatory prison sentences for crimes involving the use of guns, and the use of private Internal Revenue Service information in combating organized crime; U.S. delegate, The East-West Center for Cultural and Technical Interchange, Hawaii, 1975–1977; member, U.S. Advisory Commission on International Educational and Cultural Affairs, 1971–1978, Stanton Panel on International Information, Education, and Cultural Relations, 1974–1975, President's Foreign Intelligence Advisory Board, 1985–1989, President's Drug Advisory Commission, 1989–1990; member, advisory council, School of Government, Harvard University, 1977–1990, visiting committee, Center for International Affairs, Harvard, 1986–1990, advisory board, Center for Strategic and International Studies, Georgetown University, 1978–1982, 1985–1990, national board of advisers, Federation for American Immigration Reform, 1985–1990, national advisory committee, International Tennis Foundation and Hall of Fame, Inc., 1985–1990, National Legal Center for the Public Interest, 1985–1990, executive committee, The California Roundtable, 1976–1981, and board of directors, 1985–1990, California Community Foundation, 1980–1981, 1985–1990, board of regents, University of California, 1968–1990, and chairman, 1970–1972, 1974–1975, 1976; member, board of directors, Legal Aid Foundation, Los Angeles, 1963–1972, Los Angeles World Affairs Council, 1970–1990, and president, 1975–1978; director, America-China Society, 1987–1990; trustee, Claremont McKenna College, 1967–1990, Independent Colleges of Southern California, 1969–1974, Center Theatre Group, Los Angeles Music Center, 1970–1981, Henry E. Huntington Library and Art Gallery, 1971–1990, The Cate School, 1971–1978, Northrop Institute of Technology, 1973–1975; chairman, board of trustees, Ronald Reagan Presidential Library Foundation, 1985–1990; national trustee, National Symphony Orchestra, Washington, 1974–1990; member, board of fellows, The Institute for Judicial Administration, Inc., 1981–1990; chairman, California Delegation to Republican National Convention, 1968, and vice chairman, 1971, 1976, 1980, 1988; member, board of directors, Crocker National Bank, San Francisco, 1971–1981, Pullman, Inc., 1979–1981, Pacific Mutual Life Insurance Co., 1970–1981, RCA, 1985–1986, Pacific Enterprises, 1967–1981, NBC Corp., 1985–1990, American International Group Inc., 1985–1990, Pacific Telesis Group, Pacific Bell, 1974–1981, 1985–1990, General Electric Company, 1986–1990, H.F. Ahmanson & Co., 1974–1981, 1985–1990, Earle M. Jorgensen Co., Fisher Scientific Group Inc., 1986–1989, Weintraub Entertainment Group Inc., 1987–1990, Spectradyne, Inc., 1989–1990; recipient, American Jewish Committee Human Relations award, University of California Outstanding University Service award, University of California Alumnus of the Year award, Golden Plate award, American Academy of Achievement, 1984, Franklin Social Award, Federation for American Immigration Reform, 1986, and honorary degrees from Pepperdine University, DePaul University, and University of San Diego; author of *Law and Justice in the Reagan Administration: The Memoirs of an Attorney General* (1991); fellow, American Bar Foundation; former member, American Bar Association, Los Angeles County Bar Association, California Chamber of Commerce (board of directors, 1963–1980, president, 1974–1975), American Law Institute, American Judicature Society, Phi Beta Kappa, Pi Gamma Mu, Pi Sigma Alpha, Phi Delta Phi; died on October 29, 1990, in Los Angeles. **References:** *Current Biography Yearbook 1982; New York Times* (October 30, 1990); Lou Cannon, *President Reagan: The Role of a Lifetime* (1991).

SNYDER, John Wesley

Born in Jonesboro, Ark., June 21, 1895; son of Jesse Hartwell and Ellen (Hatcher) Snyder; Episcopalian; married Evlyn Cook on January 5, 1920; father of Edith Drucie; after receiving his early education in the local public schools, he entered Vanderbilt University in 1914; joined the U.S. Army in World War I and was commissioned a second lieutenant in the Field Artillery; subsequently promoted to the rank of captain; served with Army of Occupation until June 1919; served in various banks in Arkansas and Missouri from 1919 to 1930; national bank receiver from 1930 to 1936, in the office of the Comptroller of Currency, Washington, D.C.; manager of the St. Louis branch of the Reconstruction Finance Corp. from 1937 to 1943; special assistant to the board of directors of the Reconstruction Finance Corp. and director of Defense Plants Corp., a subsidiary of RFC, from 1940 to 1944; vice-president of the First National Bank of St. Louis, Mo., in 1943; appointed Federal Loan Administrator by President Truman in April 1945, and in July 1945, he was promoted to director of war mobilization and reconversion, playing a leading part in the transition of the nation's economy from a wartime to a peacetime basis; joined the Truman cabinet as SECRETARY OF THE TREASURY on June 12, 1946, entering upon his duties on June 25, 1946, serving until the termination of the Truman administration on January 20, 1953; during his tenure the national debt was reduced by approximately $15 billion; he instituted a vigorous campaign for the sale of U.S. savings bonds; chairman of the board of trustees of the endowment fund of the American or National Red Cross, and Library of Congress fund board, and the National Advisory Council on International Monetary and Financial Problems; U.S. governor of the International Monetary Fund and the International Bank for Reconstruction and Development; trustee of the Federal old age and survivors insurance trust fund; trustee of the postal savings system, the National Gallery of Art, the National Archives Council, and the Franklin Delano Roosevelt Library; director of the Federal Farm Mortgage Corporation; member of the National Park Trust Fund Board, Defense Mobilization Board, Smithsonian Institution, and the National Securities Resources Board; colonel in the U.S. Army field artillery reserve; died on October 8, 1985, on Seabrook Island, S.C., at the age of 90. **References:** Alfred Steinberg, *The Man from Missouri: The Life and Times of Harry S. Truman* (1962); Cabell B.H. Phillips, *The Truman Presidency: The History of a Triumphant Succession* (1966); *Facts on File Yearbook* (1985).

SOUTHARD, Samuel Lewis

Born in Basking Ridge, N.J., June 9, 1787; son of Henry Southard, congressman, and Sarah (Lewis) Southard; married Rebecca Harrow in 1811; attended the school conducted by the Rev. Robert Finley at Basking Ridge; entered the College of New Jersey (now Princeton), graduating in 1804; engaged as a private tutor by a family near Fredericksburg, Va., in 1805; studied law and was admitted to the bar in Virginia in 1809; returned to New Jersey and commenced practice in Flemington in 1811; appointed law reporter of the Supreme Court by the state legislature in 1814; elected to the New Jersey General Assembly in 1815, resigning upon his designation to the state Supreme Court bench; associate justice of the New Jersey Supreme Court from 1815 to 1820; moved to Trenton, N.J., becoming city recorder; was a presidential elector on the Democratic ticket of Monroe and Tompkins in 1820; appointed and subsequently elected to the U.S. Senate, serving from January 26, 1821, to March 3, 1823, when he resigned, having been tendered a cabinet portfolio; appointed SECRETARY OF THE NAVY by President Monroe, September 6, 1823, holding the office until the close of President John Quincy Adams's administration on March 3, 1829; during his incumbency, he began the program of building naval hospitals in 1828 and also advocated the construction of a naval academy, a thorough charting of the American coastline, a naval criminal code, a reorganization and increase of the Marine Corps, and the establishment of regular communication across Panama; he and his father both served in the 16th Congress; appointed secretary of the treasury, *ad interim*, by President John Quincy Adams on March 7, 1825; appointed secretary of war, *ad interim*, by President Adams on May 26, 1828; attorney general of New Jersey from 1829 to 1833; elected governor of New Jersey on October 26, 1832, serving until February 23, 1833, when he resigned to become a senator; elected as a Whig to the U.S. Senate in 1833 and reelected in 1839, serving from March 4, 1833, until his death; was president *pro tempore* of the Senate from March 4, 1841, to May 31, 1842, when he resigned; died in Fredericksburg, Va., on June 26, 1842; interment in the Congressional Cemetery, Washington, D.C. **References:** Arthur Styron, *The Last of the Cocked Hats: James Monroe and the Virginia Dynasty* (1945); Robert Abraham East, *John Quincy Adams: The Critical Years, 1785–1794* (1962).

SPEED, James

Born in Farmington, Ky., March 11, 1812; son of John and Lucy Gelmer (Fry) Speed; married Jane Cochran in 1841; father of seven sons; attended local schools and St. Joseph College in Bardstown, Ky., graduating in 1828; clerk in the circuit

James Speed (Library of Congress)

and county courts, 1828–1830; studied law at Transylvania University in Lexington, Ky.; admitted to the bar and began practice in Louisville in 1833; elected to the Kentucky state legislature in 1847; defeated as delegate to the state constitutional convention in 1849; staunch advocate of Negro emancipation; taught law at the University of Louisville, 1856–1858; elected in 1861 to the state senate and continued in that capacity until July 1863; appointed ATTORNEY GENERAL in the cabinet of President Lincoln on December 2, 1864, and continued under Andrew Johnson; most important contributions were advocating Negro suffrage, supporting the Fourteenth Amendment; resigned on July 17, 1866, as a result of policy disagreement with President Johnson; returned to Louisville; chairman of the Southern Radical convention in Philadelphia in 1866; defeated in contests for vice-president in 1868 and for congressman in 1870; delegate to the Republican National Conventions of 1872 and 1876; continued law practice and taught law again at the University of Louisville from 1872 to 1879; died in Louisville, Ky., on June 25, 1887; interment in Cave Hill Cemetery, Louisville. **References:** James Speed, *James Speed, a Personality* (1914); Burton J. Hendrick, *Lincoln's War Cabinet* (1946); James G. Randall, *Constitutional Problems under Lincoln* (1964); Ernest S. Cox, *Lincoln's Negro Policy* (1968).

SPENCER, John Canfield

Born in Hudson, N.Y., January 8, 1788; son of Ambrose and Laura (Canfield) Spencer; Methodist; married Elizabeth Scott Smith in 1809; father of three children; after attending the common schools, he entered Williams College at Williamstown, Mass., remained there a year, and then transferred to Union College, Schenectady, N.Y., graduating in 1806; studied law and was admitted to the bar in 1809, commencing his legal practice in Canandaigua, N.Y.; served as a combatant in the War of 1812; appointed judge advocate general in 1813; appointed postmaster of Canandaigua, 1814; designated assistant attorney general for western New York in 1815; elected as a Democrat to the 15th Congress, serving from March 4, 1817, to March 3, 1819; elected to the New York State

Assembly in 1820 and 1821, serving one year as Assembly speaker; elected to the New York State Senate from 1824 to 1828; charged by Governor De Witt Clinton with the task of revising the statutes of New York State, his efforts culminating in *The Revised Statutes of the State of New York*, 3 vols. (1829); reelected to the New York State Assembly in 1831 and 1832; appointed special attorney general to prosecute the abductors of Morgan, 1839; designated secretary of state of New York in 1839; invited to join the cabinet of President Tyler as SECRETARY OF WAR on October 12, 1841, serving until March 3, 1843; assigned a new cabinet portfolio by President Tyler, that of SECRETARY OF THE TREASURY, serving from March 3, 1843, to May 2, 1844, when, because of his opposition to the annexation of Texas, he resigned; nominated by President Tyler to become associate justice of the U.S. Supreme Court in January 1844, a position subsequently denied him by the U.S. Senate; died in Albany, N.Y., on May 18, 1855; interment in the Rural Cemetery, Albany, N.Y. **References:** Oscar Doane Lambert, *Presidential Politics in the United States 1840–1844* (1936); Robert J. Morgan, *A Whig Embattled: The Presidency under John Tyler* (1954).

STANBERY, Henry

Born in New York, N.Y., February 20, 1803; son of Dr. Jonas and Ann Lucy (Seaman) Stanbery; Presbyterian; married to Frances E. Beecher in 1829, and upon her death in 1840, married Cecelia Bond; father of five children; moved with his family to Ohio in 1814, settling in Zanesville; graduated from Washington College (now Washington and Jefferson College), Pa., at the age of 16; studied law and was admitted to the bar in 1824, commencing the practice of law at Lancaster, Ohio; elected the first attorney general of Ohio, 1846; a member of the state constitutional convention of 1850; transferred his law office to Cincinnati in 1853; invited to join the cabinet of President Andrew Johnson on July 23, 1866, as ATTORNEY GENERAL; a moderate, he interpreted the Reconstruction legislation as liberally as the language of the acts permitted; with the initiation of proceedings against President Johnson, he resigned on March 12, 1868, to serve as the president's chief counsel; at the close of the trial, President Johnson renominated him attorney general, but the Senate refused to confirm his appointment; resumed his law practice in Cincinnati; became president of the Law Association of Cincinnati; retired from active practice in 1878; died in New York City on June 26, 1881. **References:** Eric L. McKitrick, *Andrew Johnson and Reconstruction* (1960); Margaret Green, *Defender of the Constitution: Andrew Johnson* (1962).

STANS, Maurice Hubert

Born in Shakopee, Minn., March 22, 1908; son of J. Hubert and Mathilda (Nyseen) Stans; Roman Catholic; married Kathleen Carmody (died 1984) on September 7, 1933; father of Steven, Maureen, Theodore, and Terrell; attended

Shakopee High School; student, Northwestern University, 1925–1928, Columbia University, 1928–1930; certified public accountant; after starting as an office boy in 1928, became partner, Alexander Grant and Company accountants, 1931–1938, executive partner, 1940–1955; president and director, Moore Corporation, Joliet, Ill., stove manufacturers, 1938–1945; director and member of executive committee, James Talcott, Inc., New York City, 1941–1955; financial consultant to U.S. postmaster general, 1953–1955; deputy postmaster general, 1955–1957; deputy director, U.S. Bureau of the Budget, 1957–1958, director, 1958–1961; president, Western Bancorp., Los Angeles, 1961–1962; senior partner, William R. Staats & Co., 1963–1964, president, 1964–1965; vice-chairman, United California Bank, 1961–1962; president, Glore Forgan, William R. Staats & Co., Inc., New York, 1965–1969; appointed SECRETARY OF COMMERCE by President Nixon and served from January 21, 1969, until resigning, effective February 15, 1972, to take charge of Committee to Re-Elect the President; most important contribution as commerce secretary was heading a U.S. trade mission to Europe in April 1969; indicted for involvement in the Watergate affair, acquitted of perjury and conspiracy, but pled guilty to five nonwillful violations of campaign finance laws and paid a $5,000 fine; business consultant in Los Angeles, 1975–1992; founder, Stans Foundation, 1940; consultant, U.S. House of Representatives Appropriations Committee, 1953; syndicated columnist, 1961–1962; chairman, Nixon Finance Committee, 1968, Republican National Finance Committee, 1968–1969, 1972–1973, Finance Committee to Re-Elect the President, 1972–1973; finance chairman and board of directors, Nixon Presidential Library, 1985; named director of the Overseas Private Investment Corporation, 1981; trustee, Pomona College, 1962–1969; former member, board of directors, Uniglobe Travel, Vancouver, Huntington Medical Research Institute, Arnold and Mabel Beckman Foundation, Irvine, Calif., 1988–1992, Eisenhower World Affairs Institute, Washington, 1991–1993; former president, board of directors, Farmont Corp. L.A.; board of directors and treasurer, Electronic Town Hall Meetings, Inc., 1992–1993; chairman, board of directors, AT&D Inc., 1992–1993, Weatherby, Inc., 1986–1991, Minority Enterprise Development Advisory Council, Washington, 1989–1991; founding director, African Wildlife Foundation, Washington, 1958; recipient, National Alpha Kappa Psi award, American Accounting Association, 1952, Public Service award, AICPA, 1954, Great Living American award, Tax Foundation award, 1960, U.S. Chamber of Commerce, 1961, Free Enterprise award, International Franchise Association, 1988, and honorary degrees from Wesleyan University, Northwestern University, DePauw University, Parsons College, Grove City College, St. Anselm's College, University of San Diego, Gustavus Adolphus College, Pomona College, Maryville College, Rio Grande College, National University, and Pepperdine University; named to the Accounting Hall of Fame, 1968; creator, Stans African Halls section, Museum of York County, Rock Hill, South Carolina, 1980; financed and constructed Stans Historical Center, Shakopee, Minn., and deeded it to Scott County Historical Society; author of *The Terrors of Justice: The*

Untold Side of Watergate (1978) and *One of the President's Men: Twenty Years with Eisenhower and Nixon* (1995); member, National Association of Manufacturers (director, 1968–1969), American Institute of Certified Professional Accountants (president, 1954–1955), Illinois Society of CPAs (director, 1944–1946), American Accounting Association, Federal Government Accountants Association, Union League, Adventurers Club of Chicago, California Club of Los Angeles, Explorers Club of New York, Athenaeum of Pasadena, Shikar-Safari Club International (founding trustee, 1952), African Safari Club (founding board of directors, 1957); honorary member, D.C. Society of CPAs, Hawaii Society of CPAs, National Association of Postmasters, Iron Molders and Foundry Workers Union; died on April 14, 1998, in Pasadena, Calif. **References:** *U.S. News & World Report* (March 21, 1958); *Time* (March 24, 1958; December 20, 1968); *Current Biography Yearbook 1958*; Earl Mazo and Stephan Hess, *Nixon: A Political Portrait* (1969); Kenneth W. Thompson, ed., *The Nixon Presidency: Twenty-two Intimate Perspectives* (1987); *New York Times* (April 15, 1998); Richard Reeves, *President Nixon: Alone in the White House* (2001).

STANTON, Edwin McMasters

Born in Steubenville, Ohio, December 19, 1814; son of Dr. David and Lucy (Norman) Stanton; Quaker; married to Mary Ann Lamson on December 31, 1834, and upon her death, married Ellen M. Hutchinson on June 25, 1856; father of six children; he was obliged to withdraw from school due to lack of funds; clerked in a local bookstore, studying in his spare time; entered Kenyon College in 1831, but his funds ran out and he was unable to complete his academic career; studied law and was admitted to the bar in 1836, commencing his practice in Cadiz, Ohio; moved to Steubenville in 1839 and then to Pittsburgh, Pa., in 1847; moved to Washington, D.C., in 1856, where he won a national reputation by his astute handling of the fraudulent land claims in California, serving as special counsel for the U.S. government; invited to join

Edwin Stanton (Library of Congress)

the cabinet by appointment of President Buchanan as ATTORNEY GENERAL on December 20, 1860, entering upon his duties on December 22, 1860, and serving until March 3, 1861; though a staunch Unionist, and averse to the institution of slavery, he contended that all laws constitutionally enacted for the protection of slavery should be rigidly enforced; though an outspoken critic of President Lincoln and of his administration, he was invited to join the Lincoln cabinet as SECRETARY OF WAR on January 15, 1862, entering upon his duties on January 20, 1862; during his secretaryship, he scrutinized all War Department contracts, prosecuting those tainted with fraud; persuaded Congress to authorize the taking over of the railroads and telegraph lines where necessary; continued in office by President Andrew Johnson, he directed the demobilization of the Union armies; on August 5, 1867, President Johnson requested his resignation; when that request by the president was ignored, he was suspended forthwith, and General Grant was appointed secretary of war, *ad interim*; Stanton resigned May 26, 1868; gave active support to Grant's candidacy in 1868 and subsequently was nominated and confirmed for a justiceship on the U.S. Supreme Court on December 20, 1869, but died before he could occupy his seat, in Washington, D.C., on December 24, 1869. **References:** William Severn, *In Lincoln's Footsteps: The Life of Andrew Johnson* (1960); Benjamin Platt Thomas and Harold M. Hyman, *Stanton: The Life and Times of Lincoln's Secretary of War* (1962).

STETTINIUS, Edward Reilley, Jr.

Born in Chicago, Ill., October 22, 1900; son of Edward Reilley and Judith (Carrington) Stettinius; Episcopalian; married Virginia Gordon Wallace on May 15, 1926; father of Edward Reilley III, Wallace, and Joseph; attended the Pomfret School in Connecticut, 1907–1919; entered University of Virginia in 1919; briefly studied law and considered the clergy; elected president of Young Men's Christian Society in 1921; organized an employment agency and paid needy students' tuition; left University of Virginia in 1924 and became a stock-boy for Hyatt Roller Bearing Works; became assistant to the vice-president of General Motors Corp. in 1926, and in 1931 was appointed vice-president in charge of industrial and public relations; named vice-president of United States Steel Corp. in 1934 and in 1938 became chairman of the board; left United States Steel in the same year to chair President Franklin Roosevelt's War Resources Board, and on May 28, 1940, he resigned all business affiliations and entered government service; appointed director of the Office of Production Management under President Roosevelt and served from January to September 1941; special assistant to the president, October 1941–September 1943, and chief legislator of the Lend-Lease Policy; played a vital role at the Dumbarton Oaks Conference, August 1944; appointed undersecretary of state and served in that position from September 25, 1943, to November 30, 1944; named SECRETARY OF STATE in Roosevelt's cabinet on November 30, 1944; chief adviser to President Roosevelt at the Yalta Conference, January 1945, and continued under Harry Truman, serving until July 2, 1945; chairman of the U.S. delegation to the United Nations Conference on International Organization at San Francisco, April–June

Edward Stettinius with FDR. (Library of Congress)

1945; resigned his post as secretary of state in December 1945 to serve as first U.S. delegate to the United Nations, a post held until 1946; became rector of the University of Virginia, 1946; was also director of the Foreign Policy Administration, Thomas Jefferson and Patrick Henry Memorial Organization, General Electric, and the Federal Reserve Bank of Richmond, Va.; member of the governing board of the Pan American Union and the American Red Cross; died in Greenwich, Conn., October 31, 1949; interment in Locust-Valley Cemetery, Locust Valley, N.Y. **References:** *New York Times*, Obituary (November 1, 1949); *Who Was Who in America*.

STEVENSON, Adlai Ewing

Born in Christian County, Ky., October 23, 1835; son of John Turner Stevenson, small planter, and Ann Eliza (Ewing) Stevenson; married Letitia Grenn on December 20, 1866; father of Louis Green, Mary, Julia, and Letitia; attended local schools and was preparatory student for two years at Illinois Wesleyan University; attended Centre College for two years; taught; read law under Judge Davis and Robert E. Williams; admitted to the bar, 1857; opened law office at Metamora, Ill., 1858; was master in chancery, 1860–1864; was state district attorney of Illinois and master of circuit court, 1865–1869; elected to U.S. Congress in 1874 and served from 1875 to 1877; candidate for reelection in 1876 but was defeated; member of board to inspect military academy at West Point, 1877; reelected to Congress with Greenback support in 1878 and served from 1879 to 1881; appointed assistant postmaster general under Cleveland in 1885, serving until 1889; headed Illinois delegation to Democratic National Convention in 1892 and helped nominate Cleveland for president; elected VICE-PRESIDENT under Grover Cleveland, serving from March 4, 1893, to March 3, 1897; appointed member of monetary commission to Europe, 1897; was Bryan's running mate in 1900; ran unsuccessfully for governor of Illinois in 1908; published *Something of Men I Have Known* (1909); died in Chicago, Ill., June 14, 1914; interment in Bloomington, Ill. **References:** Henry J. Ford, *Cleveland Era* (1921); Robert L. Vexter, *Grover Cleveland, 1837–1908: Chronology, Documents, Bibliographical Aids* (1968).

STIMSON, Henry Lewis

Born in New York City, N.Y., September 21, 1867; son of Lewis Atterbury, a surgeon, and Candace (Wheeler) Stimson; Presbyterian; married Mabel Wellington White on July 6, 1893; graduated from Phillips Academy, Andover, Mass., 1883, and spent a postgraduate semester there, 1884; graduated from Yale University, 1888; M.A., Harvard Law School, 1890; admitted to the bar in New York, 1891; joined New York National Guard, 1898; commissioned lieutenant colonel and promoted to colonel, Field Artillery, U.S. Army, serving in France during World War I, 1917–1918; lawyer in New York City, 1890–1892; partner, Root and Clark, 1893–1897, Root, Howard, Winthrop, and Stimson, 1897–1901, and Winthrop and Stimson, New York, 1901–1906, 1913–1917, 1918–1926, and 1933–1940; appointed by President Theodore Roosevelt as U.S. attorney for the southern district of New York, 1906–1909; appointed by President Taft as special counsel for federal antitrust prosecution, 1909–1910, then as SECRETARY OF WAR, and served from May 22, 1911, until the end of Taft's term on March 4, 1913; reorganized the U.S. Army to a more efficient grouping of its forces; appointed by President Coolidge as special peace envoy, first to arbitrate a territorial dispute between Chile and Peru, 1926, and then to end a civil war in Nicaragua, 1927, and as governor-general, Philippine Islands, 1927–1929; appointed by President Hoover as SECRETARY OF STATE and served from March 28, 1929, until the end of Hoover's term on March 4, 1933; supported international armaments limitations and was chairman of the American delegation, London Naval Conference, 1930, and General Conference for the Reduction and Limitation of Armaments, Geneva, 1932; issued the "Stimson Doctrine" condemning Japan's occupation of Manchuria and all territorial gains by force, January 1932; despite being a Republican, he was a critic of isolationism and was appointed by President Franklin Roosevelt to the International Court of Arbitration, The Hague, Netherlands, 1938–1940, then as SECRETARY OF WAR, where he served from July 10, 1940, into the administration of President Truman, until September 21, 1945; he advocated compulsory military training and conscription even before the United States entered World War II, helped establish the autonomy of the U.S. Air Corps, supported the Lend-Lease Act, participated in Allied conferences, reorganized the army command, advised the presidents on atomic energy, and recommended the use of the first atomic bomb against Japan; retired from office shortly after Japan officially surrendered on September 2, 1945, ending World War II; unsuccessful Republican candidate for governor of New York, 1910; delegate to New York State Constitutional Convention, 1915; recipient of Distinguished Service Medal from President Truman, 1945; author of *American Policy in Nicaragua* (1927), *Democracy and Nationalism in Europe* (1934), and *The Far Eastern Crisis* (1936); coauthor, with McGeorge Bundy, of autobiography, *On Active Service in Peace and War* (1948); member, editorial board, *Foreign Affairs*; died on October 20, 1950, at his home in Huntington, N.Y. **References:** Richard Nelson, *Secretary Stimson: A Study in Statecraft* (1954, 1970); Elting E. Morison, *Turmoil and Tradition: A Study of the Life and Times of Henry L. Stimson* (1960, 1963); Armin Rappaport, *Henry L. Stimson and Japan, 1931–1933* (1963); Paolo Enrico Coletta, *The Presidency of William Howard Taft* (1973); Martin L. Fausold, *The Presidency of Herbert C. Hoover* (1985); Godfrey Hodgson, *The Colonel: The Life and Wars of Henry Stimson, 1867–1950* (1990); George T. McJimsey, *The Presidency of Franklin Delano Roosevelt* (2000); Margot Louria, *Triumph and Downfall: America's Pursuit of Peace and Prosperity, 1921–1933* (2001); David F. Schmitz, *Henry L. Stimson: The First Wise Man* (2001).

STODDERT, Benjamin

Born in Charles County, Md., in 1751; son of Captain James Stoddert, officer in French and Indian War, and Sarah (Marshall) Stoddert; married Rebecca Lowndes on June 17, 1781; educated as a merchant; joined Pennsylvania regiment at outbreak of Revolution, became cavalry captain, gained rank of major; wounded in Battle of Brandywine and forced to retire; unanimously elected secretary of the Board of War on September 1, 1779, serving until 1781; settled in Georgetown, District of Columbia, as a merchant; organizer and later president of Bank of Columbia in January 1794; appointed SECRETARY OF THE NAVY in the cabinet of President John Adams on May 21, 1798, entering upon duties June 1, 1798, and serving until March 1, 1801, when he retired to private life; during period of cabinet service, faced war with France, built up naval forces and recommended them reduced following the war, drafted bill for government of Marine Corps, and began construction of a naval hospital at Newport, R.I.; died in Bladensburg, Md., on December 18, 1813. **References:** Manning J. Daver, *The Adams Federalists* (1953); Stephen G. Kurtz, *The Presidency of John Adams* (1957).

Harlan Stone (Library of Congress)

STONE, Harlan Fiske

Born in Chesterfield, N.H., October 11, 1872; son of Frederick Lauson and Ann Sophia (Butler) Stone; married Agnes Harvey on September 7, 1899; father of Marshall Harvey and Lauson Harvey; after attending the local school and Amherst High School, he entered the Massachusetts Agricultural College in Amherst and later enrolled at Amherst College, receiving a B.S. in 1894 and an M.A. in 1897; entered Columbia University School of Law in New York City, graduating in 1898; taught at Adelphi Academy in Brooklyn, N.Y.; admitted to the bar in 1898; lecturer on law at Columbia University, 1899–1902, and professor of law, 1902–1905; dean of the Columbia University School of Law, 1910–1923; member of the law firm of Sullivan and Cromwell of New York City; invited to join the Coolidge cabinet as ATTORNEY GENERAL on April 7, 1924, entering upon his duties on April 9, 1924, and serving until March 2, 1925; during his incumbency, he created a precedent by taking personal charge of many of the more important cases; appointed associate justice of the U.S. Supreme Court by President Coolidge on March 2, 1925, serving in that capacity until June 1941, when he was named chief justice by President Franklin D. Roosevelt; vice-president of the American Red Cross and of the Washington Monument Society; honorary president of the National Association of Legal Aid Organizations in 1941; trustee of Amherst College; chairman of the board of trustees of the National Gallery of Art; chancellor of the Smithsonian Institution; president of the Association of American Law Schools; fellow of the American Academy of Arts and Sciences; died in Washington, D.C., on April 22, 1946. **References:** Edward Connery Latham, ed., *Meet Calvin Coolidge: The Man behind the Myth* (1960); Leonard Baker, *Back to Back: The Duel between FDR and the Supreme Court* (1967).

STRAUS, Oscar Solomon

Born in Otterberg, Rhenist Bavaria, Germany, December 23, 1850; son of Lazarus and Sara (Straus) Straus; Jewish; married Sarah Lavanburg on April 19, 1882; father of three children; family migrated to the United States in 1854, first settling in Talbotton and Columbus, Ga., and later in New York City; studied at private schools preparatory to his attendance at Columbia College, where he graduated in 1871; entered Columbia Law School, graduating in 1873; admitted to the bar and commenced practice in New York City; abandoned the law and became a partner in L. Straus and Sons, merchants in china and glassware; a progressive Democrat in politics, he drew the notice of President Cleveland, who, in 1887, appointed him minister to Turkey, a post he held until 1889; reappointed minister to Turkey by President McKinley in 1898, resigning in 1900; appointed a member of the Permanent Court of Arbitration at The Hague, Netherlands, in 1902, and was subsequently reappointed in 1908, 1912, and 1920; invited to join the cabinet of President Theodore Roosevelt as SECRETARY OF COMMERCE AND LABOR on December 12, 1906, serving until March 4, 1909; again designated minister to Turkey by President William Howard Taft in 1909, this time as the first American ambassador to the Ottoman Empire; his service under both Republican and Democratic administrations made him one of the earliest American career diplomats; resigned his mission to Turkey in December 1910; unsuccessful candidate for the governorship of New York on the Theodore Roosevelt Progressive ticket in 1912; appointed chairman of the New York Public Service Commission by Governor Whitman, 1915–1918; member of the League to Enforce Peace; authored *The Origin of the Republican Form of Government in the United States* (1885), *Reform in the Consular Service* (1894), *The American Spirit* (1913), and his autobiographical memoirs, *Under Four Administrations: From Cleveland to Taft* (1922); died in New York City on January 11, 1931. **References:** Norman M. Wilensky, *Conservatives in the Progressive Era: The Taft Republicans of 1912* (1965); James L. Penick, Jr., *Progressive Politics and Conservatives* (1968).

STUART, Alexander Hugh Holmes

Born in Staunton, Va., April 2, 1807; son of Archibald and Eleanor (Briscoe) Stuart; Episcopalian; married Frances Cordelia Baldwin on August 1, 1833; father of nine children; after attending Staunton Academy, he entered William and Mary College, Williamsburg, Va., and later the University of Virginia at Charlottesville, graduating in 1828; studied law and was admitted to the bar in 1828, commencing his practice in Staunton; became a Whig and a champion of Henry Clay; elected to the Virginia House of Delegates, 1836–1839; elected as a Whig to the 27th Congress, serving from March 4, 1841, to March 3, 1843; presidential elector on the Whig ticket of Clay and Freylinghuysen in 1844, and of Taylor and Fillmore in 1848; invited to join the cabinet of President Fillmore as SECRETARY OF THE INTERIOR, serving from September 16, 1850, to March 6, 1853; elected to the state senate from 1857 to 1861; member of the state secession convention in 1861; delegate to the national convention of conservatives, held in Philadelphia in 1866; presented credentials as a member-elect to the

39th Congress in 1865 but was not seated; chairman of the Committee of Nine, which was responsible for the restoration of Virginia to the Union in 1870; again elected to the Virginia House of Delegates from 1874 to 1877; rector of the University of Virginia from 1874 to 1882; president of the Virginia Historical Society; resumed the practice of law; authored *The Recent Revolution, Its Causes and Its Consequences* (1866); died in Staunton, Va., on February 13, 1891; interment in Thornrose Cemetery, Staunton. **References:** Robert J. Rayback, *Millard Fillmore: Biography of a President* (1959); Philip Shriver Klein, *President James Buchanan, a Biography* (1962).

SULLIVAN, Louis Wade

Born in Atlanta, Ga., November 3, 1933; youngest son of Walter Wade, undertaker, and Lubirda Elizabeth (Priester) Sullivan, teacher; parents were civil rights activists and founders of the Blakely, Ga., chapter of the NAACP; Episcopalian; married Eve Williamson, September 30, 1955; father of Paul, Shanta, and Halsted; B.S. magna cum laude, Morehouse College, 1954; M.D. cum laude, Boston University Medical School, 1958, the only African American member of his graduating class; received American Board of Internal Medicine, diploma, 1966; intern, New York Hospital–Cornell Medical Center, New York City, 1958–1959, and resident in internal medicine, 1959–1960; fellow in pathology, Massachusetts General Hospital, 1960–1961; research fellow of medicine, Thorndike Memorial Lab, Boston City Hospital and Harvard Medical School, 1961–1963; resident associate, Thorndike Memorial lab, Boston City Hospital, 1963–1964; instructor, Harvard Medical School, 1963–1964; assistant professor, New Jersey College of Medicine, 1964–1966; codirector of hematology, Boston University Medical Center, and assistant professor of medicine, Boston University Medical School, 1966–1968, then associate professor of medicine, 1968–1974, and professor of medicine and physiology, 1974–1975; director of hematology and project director, Boston Sickle Cell Center, 1973–1975; founding dean and director of Medical Education Program, Morehouse College, 1975–1981, only the third predominantly black medical school in the United States; dean and first president of the independent Morehouse School of Medicine (MSM), 1981–1989; appointed by President George H.W. Bush as SECRETARY OF HEALTH AND HUMAN SERVICES and served from March 10, 1989, until the end of Bush's term on January 20, 1993; the highest-ranking African American in the Bush administration and only black member of the Bush cabinet; at HHS, pursued agenda of improving health care among minorities and the poor; evoked controversy during confirmation process over contradictory public statements on abortion issue; later took a stand on community needle exchange programs to fight the AIDS epidemic that was at odds with the Bush administration's opposition to such programs; returned as president of MSM, 1993– ; member, medical advisory board, National Leukemia Association, 1968–1970 (chairman, 1970), ad hoc panel on blood diseases, National Heart, Lung, and

Blood Disease Bureau, 1973, sickle cell anemia advisory commission, National Institutes of Health, 1974–1975, National Advisory Research Council, 1977; founding member, National Association of Minority Medical Educators; member, board of directors, CIGNA, Bristol-Myers Squibb, 3M Corporation, Household International, Georgia Pacific, Equifax, the Boy Scouts of America, Little League, United Way of America, The Ida Cason Callaway Foundation, the Woodruff Arts Center, Medical Education for South African Blacks, Africare, the International Foundation for Education and Self Help, the Southern Center for International Studies, the Association of Minority Health Professions Schools, Association for Academic Health Centers; associate editor, *Nutrition Reports International*, 1969–1973; member, editorial board, *American Journal of Hematology*, 1975–1977, *Journal of Medical Education*, 1977–1978, and *Minority Health Today*; recipient, John Hay Whitney Foundation Opportunity fellowship, 1960–1961, Outstanding Alumnus award, New York University's Cornell Medical Center, 1984, Boston University Alumni award for Distinguished Public Service, 1985, the first Martin Luther King Visiting Professorship, University of Michigan, 1986, Equitable Southeastern Regional Black Achievement Award for Education, 1986, Honor medal, American Cancer Society, 1991, and 49 honorary degrees; member, American Medical Association, National Medical Association, Atlanta Medical Association, Medical Association of Atlanta, Medical Association of Georgia, Georgia State Medical Association, Institute of Medicine of the National Academy of Sciences, Society for the Exploration of Biology and Medicine, American Federation for Clinical Research, American Association for the Advancement of Science, Federation of American Societies for Experimental Biology, American Society of Hematology, American Society for Clinical Investigation, Alpha Omega Alpha, Phi Beta Kappa. **References:** *Washington Post* (December 22 and 23, 1988; February 23, 1989); *New York Times* (December 23, 1988; January 24, 1989; April 25, 1989); *Current Biography Yearbook 1989*; Charles Kolb, *White House Daze: The Unmaking of Domestic Policy in the Bush Years* (1994).

—William J. Lombardo

SUMMERFIELD, Arthur Ellsworth

Born in Pinconning, near Bay City, Mich., March 17, 1899; son of William Henry and Cora Edith (Ellsworth) Summerfield; married Miriam W. Graim on July 22, 1918; father of Gertrude Miriam and Arthur E. Jr.; after completing grammar school, worked on a factory production line, followed by a job as inspector in the ammunition department of the Chevrolet plant in Flint, Mich.; entered the real estate business in 1919; became distributor for the Pure Oil Co. in Flint, developing his company into the largest distributorship in Michigan; launched the Summerfield Chevrolet Co. in September 1929 and remained the company's president since its establishment; president of the Bryant Properties

Corp.; member of the board of directors of the American Motorists Insurance Co. as well as of the Lumbermen's Mutual Insurance Co.; entered politics to aid the presidential aspirations of Wendel Willkie in 1940; Michigan director of the National Dealers Association from 1942 to 1949 and its onetime regional vice-president; chairman of the National Auto Dealers of America Postwar Planning Committee during 1943 and 1944; appointed finance director of the Republican state central committee in 1943; elected committeeman from Michigan at the 1944 Republican National Convention; regional vice-chairman of the Republican Party's national finance committee in 1946; organized the Michigan Republicans for Vandenberg for President in 1946; chairman of the Republican strategy committee in July 1949; succeeded in keeping the Michigan delegation to the 1952 Republican National Convention uncommitted and was thus instrumental in throwing the eventual nomination to General Eisenhower; joined the Eisenhower cabinet as POSTMASTER GENERAL on January 21, 1953, and was recommissioned on February 4, 1957, serving until the termination of the Eisenhower administration on January 20, 1961; during his incumbency, rural mail delivery services were extended to an additional 300,000 farm families, and the first large-scale automation and mechanization program to modernize the post office system was initiated; director of the Boys Club of America; member of the board of trustees of Cleary College, Ypsilanti, Mich.; upon his retirement from political service, he resumed his interests in the automobile business; died on April 26, 1972. **References:** Emmett John Hughes, *The Ordeal of Power: A Political Memoir of the Eisenhower Years* (1963); Arthur Larson, *Eisenhower: The President Nobody Knew* (1968).

SUMMERS, Lawrence Henry

Born in New Haven, Conn., November 30, 1954; son of Robert and Anita (Arrow) Summers, both economists and professors at University of Pennsylvania; nephew of Kenneth J. Arrow and Paul A. Samuelson, both Nobel Prize winners in economics; married Victoria Perry, a tax attorney, in 1985; father of twin daughters, Pamela M. and Ruth P., and a son, Harry C.; raised in Penn Valley, Pa., a suburb of Philadelphia; attended public schools in Lower Merion, Pa., graduating from Harriton High School, 1971; S.B., Massachusetts Institute of Technology (MIT), 1975; Ph.D. in economics, Harvard University, 1982; assistant professor of economics, MIT, 1979–1982; research fellow, National Bureau of Economic Research, Cambridge, Mass., 1979–1991; domestic policy economist, Council of Economic Advisors (CEA), Washington, 1982–1983; Nathaniel Ropes Professor of Political Economy, Harvard, 1983–1993 (on leave 1991–1993); vice-president and chief economist, The World Bank, Washington, 1991–1993; senior deputy assistant secretary for international economic policy, U.S. Department of the Treasury, Washington, 1993; undersecretary for international affairs, 1993–1995, the fourth-ranking position in the Treasury Department; deputy secretary, 1995–1999, the second-ranking post; appointed SECRETARY OF THE TREASURY by President Clinton to replace Robert Rubin and served from

July 2, 1999, until the end of Clinton's term on January 20, 2001; major contributions as treasury secretary include financial deregulation, plans for federal government to pay down a significant portion of the national debt with budget surpluses, and efforts to ensure the long-term viability of the Social Security and Medicare trust funds; Arthur Okun distinguished fellow in economics, globalization, and governance, Brookings Institution, Washington, January–June 2001; became president of Harvard University on July 1, 2001, and is expected to overhaul the undergraduate program there; served on President Reagan's CEA under his former dissertation adviser Martin Feldstein; at age 28, was the youngest person ever to receive tenure at Harvard, 1983; survived treatment for cancer and Hodgkin's disease, 1983–1984; economic adviser to Democratic candidate for president, Michael Dukakis, 1987–1988; director, Thermo Energy Systems, Waltham, Mass., 1989–1993; consultant, American Express, Goldman Sachs, Kodak, National Broadcasting Corporation, 1989–1990; fellow, Econometric Society, American Academy of Arts and Sciences; member, Council of Foreign Relations, American Economic Association; recipient, David Wells prize for outstanding doctoral thesis from Harvard University, Outstanding Thesis award, National Tax Association, Alan T. Waterman award for outstanding scientific achievement, National Science Foundation (the first social scientist ever to win an NSF grant), 1987, John Bates Clark Medal for outstanding economist under age 40 from American Economic Association, 1993, Distinguished Achievement award, Boys' and Girls' Club of Greater Washington, 2000, Distinguished Service award, Golden Slipper Club and Charities, 2000, Economic Patriot award, Concord Coalition, 2000, Stephen P. Guggan award, Institute for International Economics, 2000, and Alexander Hamilton medal, U.S Department of the Treasury, 2001; author of *Understanding Unemployment* (1990); coauthor of *Reform in Eastern Europe* (1991); editor of MIT Press series *Tax Policy and the Economy*, 1987–1990; former editor, *Quarterly Journal of Economics*; gave Ely Lectures, American Economics Association, 2000. **References:** *Fortune* (June 7, 1999; May 29, 2000); *The New Republic* (June 7, 1999); *Who's Who in America, 2000.*

—Jeffrey Coster

SWANSON, Claude Augustus

Born in Swansonville, near Danville, Va., March 31, 1862; son of John Muse Swanson, farmer and tobacco manufacturer, and Catherine (Pritchett) Swanson; married to Lizzie Deane Lyons on December 11, 1894, and after her death married Lulie (Lyons) Hall on October 27, 1923; no children; attended the public schools; worked on farm; taught school; attended the Virginia Agricultural and Mechanical College at Blacksburg; worked as grocer's clerk; was graduated from Randolph-Macon College in 1885; received law degree from the University of Virginia in 1886; admitted to the bar and began practice in 1886 in

Chatham, Va.; elected as a Democrat to the 53d through 59th Congresses, serving from March 4, 1893, until his resignation on January 30, 1906; unsuccessful candidate for governor in 1901; elected governor of Virginia to serve from 1906 until 1910; appointed on August 1, 1910, to the U.S. Senate to fill the vacancy caused by the death of Senator John W. Daniel; reappointed on February 28, 1911, and subsequently reelected as senator in 1916, 1922, and 1928, serving until March 3, 1933; appointed by President Hoover as delegate to the General Disarmament Conference in Geneva, 1932; appointed SECRETARY OF THE NAVY in the cabinet of President Franklin Roosevelt on March 4, 1933; most important contribution was urging expansion of the navy to the limits established by the London Naval Treaty of 1930; died in office while on a visit to Rapidan Camp in the Blue Ridge Mountains, near Criglersville, Va., on July 7, 1939; funeral services held in the Senate Chamber; interment in Hollywood Cemetery, Richmond, Va. **References:** C.P. Hill, *Franklin Roosevelt* (1966); A.J. Wann, *The President as Chief Administrator: A Study of Franklin D. Roosevelt* (1968).

T

TAFT, Alphonso

Born at Townshend, Vt., November 5, 1810; son of Peter Rawson Taft, member of the Vermont legislature and judge, and Sylvia (Howard) Taft; married to Fanny Phelps on August 29, 1841; father of five children, the eldest being Charles Phelps, lawyer, publisher, and philanthropist; after death of first wife, married Louisa Torrey on December 26, 1853; father of William Howard Taft, U.S. president and chief justice, and of Henry, Horace, Fanny, and Alphonso; attended local schools; taught school; studied at Amherst Academy; entered Yale College in 1829, graduating in 1833; taught in the high schools of Ellington, Conn., 1833–1835; studied law and admitted to the bar in 1838; moved to Cincinnati, Ohio, and there began law practice; became member of the city council; connected with railroad development; appointed to the superior court of Cincinnati to fill a vacancy in 1865 and was elected to the bench for two terms, resigning to resume law practice on January 1, 1872; appointed SECRETARY OF WAR in the cabinet of President Grant on March 8, 1876; served until May 22, 1876, when he was appointed ATTORNEY GENERAL in Grant's cabinet; most important contribution was assisting in drafting a bill that established the commission to settle the Hayes-Tilden election; continued in this post until the end of the Grant administration, March 3, 1877; resumed law practice; appointed minister to Austria-Hungary by President Arthur; transferred to St. Petersburg, Russia, on July 4, 1884, where he remained until August 1885; died in San Diego, Calif., on May 21, 1891. **References:** Mabel T.R. Washburn, *Ancestry of William Howard Taft* (1908); L.A. Leonard, *The Life of Alphonso Taft* (1920); Ishbel Ross, *American Family: The Tafts, 1678–1964* (1964).

William Taft (Library of Congress)

TAFT, William Howard

Born in Cincinnati, Ohio, September 15, 1857; son of Alphonso Taft, secretary of war and attorney general in Grant's cabinet, and Louisa Maria (Torrey) Taft; Unitarian; married Helen Herron on June 19, 1886; father of Robert Alphonso Taft, U.S. senator, and two other children; attended local schools and Woodward High School; entered Yale, 1874, and graduated, 1878; received law degree from Cincinnati Law School and was admitted to the bar, 1880; while studying, served as court reporter for *Cincinnati Commercial*; appointed prosecuting attorney of Hamilton County, 1881; appointed collector of internal revenue for Cincinnati in 1882; resumed practice of law; toured Europe; appointed judge of superior court of Ohio in March 1887; elected judge of superior court for five-year term in April 1888; received post of U.S. solicitor general from President Benjamin Harrison, 1890; became federal circuit court judge on March 17, 1892, and served until March 1900; became president of Philippine Commission in March 1900; appointed SECRETARY OF WAR in the cabinet of President Theodore Roosevelt on February 1, 1904, and served until June 28, 1908; most important contributions were trip to Canal Zone to investigate start of construction of Panama Canal, trip to Cuba to effect peace when revolution threatened; elected PRESIDENT OF THE UNITED STATES on November 1, 1908, on the Republican ticket; nominated to run for a second term in 1912 but lost to Wilson; returned to Yale as Kent Professor of Constitutional Law in March 1913; served as joint chairman of National War Labor Board, 1918–1919; named by President Harding chief justice of the U.S. Supreme Court on June 3, 1921; served until ill health forced his retirement on February 3, 1930; died in Washington, D.C., March 8, 1930; interment in Arlington National Cemetery. **References:** Henry F. Pringle, *William Howard Taft* (1939); William Smith, *The Taft Story* (1954); Ishbel Ross, *American Family: The Tafts, 1678–1964* (1964); Norman M. Wilensky, *Conservatives in the Progressive Era* (1965).

TANEY, Roger Brooke

Born in Calvert County, Md., March 17, 1777; son of Michael and Monica (Brooke) Taney; Roman Catholic; married Anne P.C. Key, sister of Francis

Scott Key, on January 7, 1806; father of six daughters and one son; graduated from Dickinson College in 1795; studied law under Judge Jeremiah Townley Chase; admitted to practice in 1799; elected to state legislature in 1799; moved in 1801 to Frederick, Md., where he established a law practice; elected in 1816 to a five-year term in the state senate; moved to Baltimore in 1823; appointed attorney general of Maryland in 1827; appointed chairman of the state committee for the election of Andrew Jackson in 1828; accepted recess appointment from President Jackson in 1831 as ATTORNEY GENERAL, took oath on July 20, 1831, was confirmed in December 1831, and served until September 23, 1833; most important contributions include advising President Jackson to veto proposed law that would grant a charter to the Second Bank of the United States, aiding him in redrafting this veto message when all others refused, and advising President Jackson to withdraw government deposits from the Second Bank of the United States; accepted recess appointment from President Jackson as SECRETARY OF THE TREASURY on September 23, 1833; most important contribution was the withdrawal of federal funds from the Second Bank of the United States and redistributing them in specified state banks; confirmation of his appointment was rejected by a hostile Senate on June 24, 1834; nomination for associate justice of the Supreme Court was defeated on March 3, 1835; nominated for chief justice of the Supreme Court on December 28, 1835, to fill vacancy left by Chief Justice Marshall; appointment was confirmed on March 15, 1836; most significant ruling was in connection with *Dred Scott v. Sandford*, when he proposed that Congress had no power to ban slavery from the territories; died in Washington, D.C., on October 12, 1864. **References:** Walker Lewis, *Without Fear or Favor* (1965); J. Herman Schauinger, *Profiles in Action* (1966).

TAYLOR, Zachary

Zachary Taylor (Library of Congress)

Born in Montebello, Va., November 24, 1784; son of Lieutenant Colonel Richard and Sarah Dabney (Strother) Taylor; Episcopalian; married Margaret Mackall Smith on June 21, 1810; father of Anne Margaret Mackall, Sarah, Knox, Octavia Pannel, Margaret Smith, Mary Elizabeth, and Richard; moved with his family to Muddy Fork in Jefferson County, Ky., in 1785; received his only formal education from a tutor; assisted his father on the family plantation during his formative years; appointed first lieutenant in the 7th Infantry in 1806 and promoted to captain in 1810; advanced to the rank of major; transferred to the 26th Infantry Division on May 15, 1814; commanded the 3d Infantry Division at Green Bay, Wisc.; also in command of Fort Winnebago; appointed lieutenant colonel of the 4th Infantry Division on April 20, 1819; commanded Fort Snelling in the unorganized Territory of Minnesota in 1828; commanded Fort Crawford in the Michigan Territory (now the state of Wisconsin) in 1829; promoted to full colonel of the 1st Regiment on April 4, 1832; advanced to brigadier general for his distinguished service during the Battle of Okeechobee against the Seminole Indians on August 21, 1832; assumed full command of Fort Jesup on June 17, 1844; promoted to major general during the Mexican campaigns, on May 28, 1846; established his residence at Baton Rouge, La., in 1840; defeated Santa Anna at the Battle of Buena Vista on February 23, 1847; nominated for the presidency by the Whigs on July 18, 1848, and subsequently resigned from the U.S. Army on January 31, 1849; elected PRESIDENT in November 1848; inaugurated on March 4, 1849, serving until his death in office on July 9, 1850; the first president representing a state west of the Mississippi River; the second president to die in the White House; died in Washington, D.C., on July 19, 1850; interment in Springfield, Ky. **Reference:** Holman Hamilton, *Zachary Taylor: Soldier in the White House* (1960).

TELLER, Henry Moore

Born on a farm in Granger, N.Y., May 23, 1830; son of John and Charlotte (Moore) Teller; Methodist; married Harriet M. Bruce on June 7, 1862; father of three children; after attending the rural schools and the academy at Rushford, he entered Alfred University at Alfred, N.Y., graduating in 1852; taught school; studied law at Angelica, N.Y., and was admitted to the bar in 1858; moved to Morrison, Ill., in 1858 and then to Central City, Colo., in 1861; major general of the Colorado militia from 1862 to 1864; upon the admission of Colorado to the Union, he was elected to the U.S. Senate, serving from November 15, 1876, until his resignation on April 17, 1882, to accept a cabinet portfolio; appointed SECRETARY OF THE INTERIOR by President Arthur, serving from April 17, 1882, to March 4, 1885; elected as a Republican to the U.S. Senate in 1885 and reelected in 1891; elected to the Senate again as an Independent Republican in 1897 and as a Democrat in 1903, serving in all from March 4, 1885, to March 3, 1909; secured the adoption of the Teller Resolution, which pledged the United States to an independent Cuba in 1898; appointed a member of the U.S. Monetary Commission in 1908; resumed the private practice of law until his death in Denver, Colo., February 23, 1914; interment in Fairmount Cemetery, Denver. **References:** Allan Nevins, *Grover Cleveland, a Study in Courage* (1932); George Frederick Howe, *Chester A. Arthur: A Quarter Century of Machine Politics* (1957).

THOMAS, Philip Francis

Born in Easton, Md., September 12, 1810; son of Dr. Tristam and Maria (Francis) Thomas; married Sarah Maria Kerr on February 5, 1835, and upon her death, married Mrs. Clintonia (Wright) May in 1876; father of 13 children; attended the Easton Academy and then entered Dickinson College, Carlisle, Pa., graduating in 1830; studied law and was admitted to the bar in 1831, commencing his legal practice in Easton, Md.; delegate to the state constitutional convention in 1836; elected to the Maryland House of Delegates in 1838, 1843, and 1845; elected as a Democrat to the 26th Congress, serving from March 4, 1839, to March 3, 1841; declined renomination in 1840, resuming the practice of law; judge of the Land Office Court of eastern Maryland, 1841; elected governor of Maryland from 1848 to 1851; declined the governorship of the Utah Territory offered by President Buchanan; comptroller of the U.S. Treasury from 1851 to 1853; collector of the Port of Baltimore from 1853 to 1860; declined the position of treasurer of the United States tendered to him by President Buchanan; U.S. commissioner of patents from February 16, 1860, until December 10, 1860, resigning to accept a cabinet portfolio; appointed SECRETARY OF THE TREASURY by President Buchanan on December 10, 1860, serving until his resignation on January 11, 1861, because of his Southern sympathies; again elected to the Maryland House of Delegates in 1863; presented credentials as a senator-elect to the U.S. Senate for the term beginning March 4, 1867, but was not seated on the grounds of disloyalty, because of his earlier Confederate sympathies; elected as a Democrat to the 44th Congress, serving from March 4, 1875, to March 3, 1877; unsuccessful candidate for election to the U.S. Senate in 1878; elected a member of the Maryland House of Delegates from 1878 to 1883; delegate to the Democratic state convention in 1883; resumed the practice of law in Easton, Md.; died in Baltimore, Md., on October 2, 1890; interment in Spring Hill Cemetery, Easton, Md. **References:** Philip Gerald Auchampaugh, *James Buchanan and His Cabinet on the Eve of Secession* (1926); Philip Shriver Klein, *President James Buchanan, a Biography* (1962).

THOMPSON, Jacob

Born in Leasburg, N.C., May 15, 1810; son of Nicholas and Lucretia (Van Hook) Thompson; married Catherine Jones; father of one son; attended the public schools and Bingham Academy in Orange County; entered the University of North Carolina, at Chapel Hill, graduating in 1831; member of the faculty of the University of North Carolina in 1831 and 1832; studied law and was admitted to the bar in 1834; commenced the practice of law in Pontatoc, Miss., in 1835; elected as a Democrat to the 26th through 31st Congresses, serving from March 4, 1839, to March 3, 1851; appointed SECRETARY OF THE INTERIOR by President Buchanan, serving from March 6, 1857, until his resignation on January 8, 1861; served as inspector general for the Confederate army during the Civil War; confidential agent of the Confederacy to Canada in 1864 and 1865; traveled throughout Europe in 1866 and 1867; settled in Memphis, Tenn., in 1868 and died there on March 24, 1885; interment in Elmwood Cemetery, Memphis. **References:** Philip Gerald Auchampaugh, *James Buchanan and His Cabinet on the Eve of Secession* (1926); Philip Shriver Klein, *President James Buchanan, a Biography* (1962).

THOMPSON, Richard Wigginton

Born in Culpeper County, Va., June 9, 1809; son of William and Catherine Wigginton (Broadus) Thompson; married Harriet Eliza Gardiner on May 5, 1836; father of eight children; pursued classical studies; moved to Louisville, Ky, in 1831; clerked in a store; moved to Lawrence County, Ind., in 1831; taught school; studied law and was admitted to the bar in 1834, commencing his legal practice in Bedford, Ind.; elected to the Indiana House of Representatives, 1834–1836; elected to the state senate, 1836–1838, serving as president *pro tempore* for a short time; elected as a Whig to the 27th Congress, serving from March 4, 1841, to March 3, 1843; moved to Terre Haute, Ind., in 1843; Terre Haute city attorney in 1846 and 1847; elected as a Whig to the 30th Congress, serving from March 4, 1847, to March 3, 1849; declined several presidential appointments; commander of Camp Thompson, Ind., and provost marshal, 1861–1865; appointed collector of internal revenue by President Lincoln for the seventh district of Indiana, serving one term; presidential elector on the Republican ticket of Lincoln and Johnson in 1864; delegate to the Republican National Convention of Chicago in 1868 and of Cincinnati in 1876; judge of the fifth Indiana circuit court, 1867–1869; joined the cabinet of President Hayes as SECRETARY OF THE NAVY, serving from March 12, 1877, until his forced resignation on November 21, 1880, because of an economic "conflict of interests"; chairman of the American committee of the Panama Canal Company in 1881; director of the Panama Railroad from 1881 to 1888; author of *The Papacy and the Civil Power* (1876), *The History of Protective Tariff Laws* (1888), *Recollections of Sixteen Presidents* (1894), and *The Footprints of the Jesuits* (1894); died in Terre Haute, Ind., February 9, 1900; interment in High Lawn Cemetery, Terre Haute. **References:** George Frederick Howe, *Chester A. Arthur: A Quarter Century of Machine Politics* (1957); Courtlandt Canby, ed., *Lincoln and the Civil War: A Profile and a History* (1960).

THOMPSON, Smith

Born in Dutchess County, N.Y., January 17, 1768; son of Ezra and Rachel (Smith) Thompson; Presbyterian; married Sarah Livingston in 1794; father of two sons and two daughters; remarried to Eliza Livingston in 1836; father of one son and two daughters; graduated from the College of New Jersey (now Princeton) in 1788; studied law in Poughkeepsie, N.Y., under James Kent while teaching school; admitted to the bar in 1792 and began law practice in Troy, N.Y.; returned to Poughkeepsie in 1793 and practiced there; elected to the state legislature in 1800; represented Dutchess County in constitutional convention of 1801; appointed district attorney for the middle district, 1801, but did not serve; appointed associate justice of the New York Supreme Court on January 8, 1802, and served until 1814; made chief justice on February 25, 1814; became regent of the University of the State of New York in 1813; appointed SECRETARY

OF THE NAVY in the cabinet of President Monroe on November 9, 1818, and served from January 1, 1819, until August 31, 1823; accepted appointment of associate justice in New York State Supreme Court left vacant by the death of Henry Livingston and served from 1823 to 1843; received honorary LL.D.s from Yale and Princeton, 1824; ran unsuccessfully for governor of New York in 1828; received honorary LL.D. from Harvard, 1835; was vice-president of the American Bible Society; died in Poughkeepsie, N.Y., December 18, 1843. **References:** Charles Warren, *The Supreme Court in United States History* (1922); Ian Elliot, *James Monroe, 1758–1831: Chronology, Documents, Bibliographical Aids* (1969).

THOMPSON, Tommy George

Born in Elroy, Wisc., November 19, 1941; son of Allan, a teacher and grocery store owner, and Julie (Dutton) Thompson, a teacher; Roman Catholic; married Sue Ann Mashak, a teacher, in 1969; father of Tommi, Kelli Sue, and Jason; attended a two-room public elementary school and Elroy High School; B.S. in political science and history, University of Wisconsin, Madison, 1963, and J.D., 1966; participated in Reserve Officer Training Corps in college and served in Wisconsin National Guard and U.S. Army Reserve; intern, U.S. Representative Thomson, Washington, 1963; legislative messenger, Wisconsin State Senate, 1964–1966; independent law practice, Elroy and Mauston, Wisc., 1966–1987; self-employed real estate broker, Mauston, 1970– ; Republican representative, District 87, Wisconsin State Assembly, 1966–1987; assistant minority leader, 1972–1981, and minority leader, 1981–1987; governor, state of Wisconsin, 1987–2001; the first Wisconsin governor to be reelected to a third term, 1994, and a fourth term, 1998; a critic of government bureaucracy, he initiated reforms of the state welfare system that drastically reduced the number of families receiving state aid, imposed strict standards and time limits on recipients, and became models for federal reforms enacted by the Republican-controlled Congress in the 1990s; appointed by President George W. Bush as SECRETARY OF HEALTH AND HUMAN SERVICES and took office on February 2, 2001; administration coordinator and spokesman for treatment and investigations of anthrax poisonings in Washington following the September 11, 2001, terrorist attacks; founder, University of Wisconsin chapter, Collegians for Barry Goldwater, 1964; alternate delegate, Republican National Convention, 1976; former chairman, Intergovernmental Policy Advisory Commission to U.S. Trade Representative; former member, executive committee, National Governors Association (NGA); chairman, NGA, 1995–1996, Education Commission of the States, and Midwestern Governors Conference; chairman, platform committee, Republican National Convention, 2000; member, board of directors, Amtrak, 1998–1999; recipient, medal award for Legislation, Wisconsin Academy of General Practice, Thomas Jefferson Freedom award, American Legislative Exchange Council, 1991, Most Valuable Public Official award, *City and State* magazine, 1991,

Governance award, Free Congress Foundation, 1992, Public Official of the Year award, *Governing* magazine, 1997, Horatio Alger Award, 1998, Good Neighbor award, U.S.A.-Mexico Chamber of Commerce, 1999; author of the autobiography *Power to the People: An American State at Work* (1996); member, American Bar Association, Wisconsin Bar Association, Republican Governors Association, Phi Delta Phi. **References:** *Washington Post* (December 5, 1993; December 30, 2000); *New York Times Magazine* (January 15, 1995); *Current Biography Yearbook 1995; Time* (October 29, 2001); *Who's Who, 2001.*

—*Matt Wasniewski*

THORNBURGH, Richard Lewis

Born in Pittsburgh, Pa., July 16, 1932; son of Charles Garland, an engineer, and Alice (Sanborn) Thornburgh; Episcopalian; married Virginia Hooton (died 1960) in 1955; married Virginia Walton Judson, author and advocate for people with disabilities, on October 12, 1963; father of John, David, Peter, William; attended Mercersburg Academy; B.S. in engineering, Yale University, 1954; LL.B. with high honors, University of Pittsburgh, 1957; admitted to the bars of Pennsylvania, 1958, U.S. Supreme Court, 1965, District of Columbia, 1998; legal counsel, Aluminum Corporation of America, Pittsburgh, 1958; attorney, Kirkpatrick, Lockhart, and Johnson, Pittsburgh, 1959–1969; unsuccessful Republican candidate for the U.S. House of Representatives, 1966; U.S. attorney for western Pennsylvania, Pittsburgh, 1969–1975; assistant attorney general, criminal division, U.S. Department of Justice, Washington, 1975–1977; partner, Kirkpatrick, Lockhart, Johnson, and Hutchinson, 1977–1979; governor, Commonwealth of Pennsylvania, 1979–1987; praised by President Carter for his leadership after the accident at the Three Mile Island Nuclear Power Plant, 1979; first Republican to serve two successive terms as Pennsylvania governor; director, Institute of Politics, John F. Kennedy School of Government, Harvard University, 1987–1988; appointed by President Ronald Reagan as ATTORNEY GENERAL and served from August 12, 1988, into the administration of President George H.W. Bush until August 9, 1991; was instrumental in the passage of the Americans with Disabilities Act in July 1990; for his efforts to combat international drug trafficking and strengthen the U.S. Drug Enforcement Administration was named an honorary special agent of the Federal Bureau of Investigation; served as chairman *pro tempore* of President Bush's Domestic Policy Council; unsuccessful Republican candidate for U.S. Senate, 1991; undersecretary-general for administration and management, United Nations, New York, 1992–1993; international observer to legislative and presidential elections in Russia, 1993 and 1996; counsel, Kirkpatrick and Lockhart, 1994– ; visiting lecturer, George Washington University School of Law, 1995; delegate, Pennsylvania Constitutional Convention, 1967–1968; former member, board of directors, Urban League of Pittsburgh, American Civil Liberties Union of Pittsburgh, Investors Security Corporation, and Neighborhood Legal Services Association, 1967–1969; former chairman, Republican Governors Association; member, board of directors, Elan Corporation, University of Pittsburgh, The Urban Institute, the National Museum of Industrial History, and the DeWitt Wallace Fund for Colonial Williamsburg; former member, board of directors, Merrill Lynch Incorporated, Rite-Aid Corporation, ARCO Chemical Corporation, and the National Academy of Public Administration; chairman, State Science and Technology Institute; vice-chairman, World Committee on Disability; member, board of advisers, Russian American Institute for Law and Economics; chair, Legal Policy Advisory Board, Washington Legal Foundation, and U.S. Committee for Hong Kong; recipient, Distinguished Service medal, American Legion, and 30 honorary degrees; he and his family were named Family of the Year, Pennsylvania Association of Retarded Citizens, 1985; he and his wife were featured speakers at the Vatican Conference on Disabilities, 1992; former editor, *University of Pittsburgh Law Review*; fellow, American Bar Foundation; member, American Bar Association, American Judicature Society, American Law Institute, Council on Foreign Relations. **References:** *Current Biography Yearbook 1988*; Cornell W. Clayton, *The Politics of Justice* (1992); Charles Kolb, *White House Daze: The Unmaking of Domestic Policy in the Bush Years* (1994); John Robert Greene, *The Presidency of George Bush* (2000); *Who's Who in America, 2000*.

—*Johnathan O'Neill*

TOBIN, Maurice Joseph

Born in Boston, Mass., May 22, 1901; son of James Tobin, carpenter, and Margaret M. (Daly) Tobin; Roman Catholic; married Helen M. Noonan on November 19, 1932; father of Helen Louise, Carol Ann, and Maurice Joseph; attended Our Lady of Perpetual Help elementary school and High School of Commerce in Boston; studied at Boston College; worked for Conway Leather Company, 1919–1922; became district traffic manager of New England Telephone and Telegraph Co., 1928–1937; elected to Massachusetts House of Representatives for a two-year term in 1926; member of Boston School Committee, 1931–1934 and 1935–1937; elected mayor of Boston in 1937 and reelected 1942; chosen governor of Massachusetts in 1944 and took office in January 1945; appointed SECRETARY OF LABOR in the cabinet of President Truman on February 1, 1949, having previously served in the interim of August 13, 1948, to February 1, 1949, and served until January 20, 1953; most important contributions were establishment of Federal Safety Council in Bureau of Labor Standards, increase in minimum wage through Fair Labor Standards Amendment of 1949, and extension of Wagner-Peysen Act to Puerto Rico and Virgin Islands; died in Jamaica Plain, Mass., July 19, 1953; interment in Holyhood Cemetery. **References:** Barton J. Bernstein and A.J. Matusow, *Truman Administration: A Documentary History* (1966); Howard Furrer, ed., *Harry S. Truman 1884– : Chronology, Documents, Bibliographical Aids* (1969).

TOMPKINS, Daniel D.

Born in Scarsdale N.Y., June 21, 1774; son of Jonathon G. Tompkins, Revolutionary patriot, and Sarah (Hyatt) Tompkins; brother of Caleb Tompkins, member of Congress; Presbyterian; married Hannah Minthorne about 1797; father of seven children; completed preparatory studies; was graduated from Columbia College in 1795; studied law and was admitted to the bar in 1797; began practice in New York City; member of the state constitutional convention in 1801; member of the State Assembly in 1803; elected as a Democrat to the 9th Congress in 1804 but resigned before the beginning of his term to accept appointment as an associate justice of the New York State Supreme Court, serving from 1804 to 1807; elected governor of New York in 1807 and reelected in 1810, 1813, and 1816; as governor, was responsible for the passage of a law ending slavery in the state and also urged improvements in the state school system, liberalization of its criminal code, and reform of the militia system; declined an appointment as secretary of state in 1814; elected VICE-PRESIDENT under President Monroe in 1816 and reelected with Monroe in 1820, serving from March 4, 1817, to March 3, 1825; president of the New York state constitutional convention of 1821; one of the founders of the New York Historical Society; died in Tompkinsville, Staten Island, N.Y., on June 11, 1825; interment in the Minthorne vault in St. Mark's Churchyard, New York City. **References:** P.J. Van Pelt, *An Oration Containing Sketches of the Life, Character, and Services of the Late Daniel D. Tompkins* (1843); J.L. Jenkins, *Lives of the Governors of New York State* (1851).

TOUCEY, Isaac

Born in Newtown, Conn., November 5, 1796; son of Zalmon and Phebe (Booth) Toucey; married Catherine Nichols on October 28, 1827; childless; educated by private tutors; studied law in office of Asa Chapman; admitted to the bar in Hartford in 1818 and began the practice of law; became state attorney for Hartford County, 1822–1835; elected to the 24th and 25th Congresses, serving from March 4, 1835, to March 3, 1839; unsuccessful candidate for reelection in 1838; made state attorney, 1842–1844; unsuccessful Democratic candidate for governor in 1845; elected governor of Connecticut, 1846–1847, but failed to be reelected; appointed ATTORNEY GENERAL in the cabinet of President Polk on June 21, 1848, and served from June 29, 1848, to March 7, 1849; acting secretary of state, 1849–1850; member of Connecticut Senate in 1850; elected to state House of Representatives in 1852; became member of U.S. Senate in 1852 and served from May 12, 1852, to March 3, 1857; appointed SECRETARY OF THE NAVY in the cabinet of President Buchanan and served from March 6, 1857, to March 3, 1861; most important contribution was supervision of expedition to Paraguay; returned to law practice in Hartford; benefactor of Trinity College; died in Hartford, Conn., July 30, 1869; interment in Cedar Hill Cemetery. **Ref-**

erences: Irving J. Sloan, ed., *James Buchanan, 1791–1868: Chronology, Documents, Bibliographical Aids* (1968).

TRACY, Benjamin Franklin

Born in Oswego, N.Y., April 26, 1830; son of Benjamin Franklin Tracy; married Delinda E. Catlin in 1851; attended common schools of Oswego; went to Oswego Academy; studied in law office of N.W. Davis; admitted to the bar in May 1851; elected district attorney of Tioga County as Whig in November 1853, reelected in 1856; chosen member of New York State Assembly as Republican and War Democrat, 1861; recruited two regiments of state volunteers in 1862 and became colonel of 109th Regiment; fought in Battle of the Wilderness, 1864; became colonel of 127th U.S. Negro troops; commanded military post at Elmira, N.Y., and was in charge of prison camps; brevetted brigadier general; discharged on June 3, 1865; entered law firm of Benedict, Burr and Benedict in New York City; appointed U.S. district attorney for eastern district of New York, 1866–1873; returned to practice in Brooklyn, N.Y., 1873; made associate justice of state court of appeals, December 1881 to January 1883; went into law partnership with his son, F.B. Tracy, and with William C. DeWitt; appointed SECRETARY OF THE NAVY in the cabinet of President Benjamin Harrison and served from March 5, 1889, to March 5, 1893, most important contributions were plans for rehabilitation and increase of naval force; was counsel for Venezuela in boundary arbitration; chairman of commission that formed charter of Greater New York, 1896; bred trotters on Tioga County farm; died August 6, 1915. **References:** D.S. Alexander, *Four Famous New Yorkers* (1923); H.J. Sievers, ed., *Benjamin Harrison, 1833–1901: Chronology, Documents, Bibliographic Aids* (1969).

TROWBRIDGE, Alexander Buel, Jr.

Born in Englewood, N.J., December 12, 1929; son of Alexander, college history professor, and Julie (Chamberlain) Trowbridge; Presbyterian; married Nancy Horst on July 2, 1955; father of Stephen C., Corrin S., and Kimberley; married Eleanor Hutzler on April 18, 1981; graduated from Philips Academy, Andover, Mass., 1947; A.B. cum laude, Princeton University, 1951; with U.S. Marine Corps Reserves, 1951–1953, served in Korea, attained rank of major; volunteered for reconstruction work in western Europe after World War II; member of International Intern Program of United Nations headquarters in Lake Success, N.Y., 1948; assistant to Congressman Franklin D. Roosevelt, Jr., 1950; employed by Central Intelligence Agency, 1951; joined California Texas Oil Company and became marketing assistant for petroleum products, 1954–1959; operations manager, Esso Standard Oil, S.A., Ltd., Panama Canal Zone, 1959–1961, then division manager, El Salvador, 1961–1963, president, Puerto Rico, 1963–1965; assistant secretary, U.S. Department of Commerce, Washington, 1965–1967, and acting secretary, January–June 1967; appointed SECRETARY OF COMMERCE by President Lyndon Johnson and served from June 14, 1967, to March 1, 1968; most important contribution was organization of Office of Foreign Direct Investment to curb deficit in balance of payments; president, American Management Association, New York, 1968–1970; president, The Conference Board, Inc., New York, 1970–1976; vice-chairman, board of directors, Allied Chemical Corporation, 1976–1980; board of directors, National Association of Manufacturing, Washington, 1978–, president, 1980–1990; member, President's Task Force on Private Sector Initiatives, National Commission on Social Security Reform, 1982, National Commission on Executive, Legislative, and Judicial Salaries, 1985, National Commission on Public Services, Competitiveness Policy Council, 1991; member, board of directors, New England Insurance Company, Federation of YMCA, Better Business Bureau, Warburg Pincus Funds, Sunoco, ICOS Corporation, Rouse Company, Harris Corporation, Gillette Company, IRI International Corporation; decorated Bronze Star with combat V; recipient, Arthur Flemming award, 1966, President's Certificate for Export Service, 1968, Bryce Harlow award for Business-Government Relations, 1988, and honorary degrees from D'Youville College, Hofstra University, Hobart College, and William Smith College; coauthor, with H. Cleveland et al., of *The Overseas Americans* (1960) and aided in preparation of *Spearheads of Democracy—Labor in the Developing Countries* (1962); member, Council on Foreign Relations, Metropolitan Club, Georgetown Club, University Club. **References:** *New York Times* (June 9, 1967); *Newsweek* (February 26, 1968); *Who's Who in America, 2000.*

TRUMAN, Harry S

Born in Lamar, Mo., May 8, 1884; son of John Anderson, farmer and livestock dealer, and Martha Ellen (Young) Truman; Baptist; married Elizabeth ("Bess") Virginia Wallace (1885–1982) on June 28, 1919; father of (Mary) Margaret; moved with family to Harrisonville, Mo., 1886, to a farm in Grandview, Mo., 1888, and to Independence, Mo., 1890; attended public schools; worked in mail room of Kansas City *Star*; became timekeeper for contractor of Santa Fe Railroad, 1902; employed by National Bank of Commerce in Kansas City, 1903–1905; worked at Union National Bank of Kansas City in 1905; joined Missouri National Guard as a corporal, 1905; worked on family farm as a partner, 1906–1917; commissioned as first lieutenant, 1917, and served to major, 1919, U.S. Army, commanding a field artillery battery in France, July 1918–April 1919; went into haberdashery business in Kansas City, 1919–1921; administrative judge, Jackson County Court, Mo., 1922–1924; attended Kansas City Law School, 1923–1925; presiding judge, Jackson County Court, 1926–1934; Democratic member from Missouri, U.S. Senate, 1935–1945; chairman of Senate Committee ("Truman Committee") investigating war profiteering; elected VICE-

PRESIDENT OF THE UNITED STATES on Democratic ticket with President Franklin D. Roosevelt in November 1944 and was inaugurated on January 20, 1945, serving until April 12, 1945, when he became the thirty-third PRESIDENT OF THE UNITED STATES upon the death of Roosevelt; reelected in 1948, defeating Republican candidate Thomas E. Dewey and third-party challengers with 49.6 percent of the popular vote and a 303-189 margin in the electoral college; chose not to run for reelection in 1952 and served until the end of his term on January 20, 1953; during his presidency he authorized the use of two atomic bombs against Japan to end World War II, issued the "Truman Doctrine" declaring U.S. support for governments resisting subversion or external aggression, 1947, established the doctrine of containment that would characterize American foreign policy throughout the Cold War, set up the European Recovery Plan ("Marshall Plan"), ordered the Berlin Airlift of supplies over a Soviet blockade of the city, 1948–1949, issued an executive order desegregating the

Harry Truman (Library of Congress)

U.S. military, 1948, promoted the formation of NATO, became the first head of state to officially recognize the creation of Israel, commissioned a national civil rights study, established a United Nations coalition, consisting mainly of U.S. troops, to aid South Korea against invasion from communist North Korea, 1950–1953, and outlined the "Fair Deal," an extension of New Deal social welfare policies that failed to pass during his administration but would become the basis for liberal Democratic social policies in the decades to come; was later honored by President Johnson when the latter traveled to Independence, Mo., to sign Medicare into law, 1965, in recognition of Truman's efforts to establish a national health-care program; author of three-volume autobiography, *Years of Decisions* (1955); *Years of Trial and Hope* (1956), and *Mr. Citizen* (1960); died in Kansas City, Mo., on December 26, 1972; buried at the Truman Library, Independence. **References:** Robert H. Ferrell, ed., *The Autobiography of Harry S. Truman* (1980) and *Dear Bess: The Letters from Harry to Bess Truman, 1910–1959* (1983); Donald R. McCoy, *The Presidency of Harry S. Truman* (1984); Michael J. Lacey, ed., *The Truman Presidency* (1989); Robert H. Ferrell, *Harry S. Truman: A Life* (1994) and *Truman and Pendergast* (1999); David McCullough, *Truman* (1994); Alonzo Hamby, *Man of the People: A Life of Harry S. Truman* (1995); Michael T. Benson, *Harry S. Truman and the Founding of Israel* (1997); J. Samuel Walker, *Prompt and Utter Destruction: Truman and the Use of Atomic Bombs against Japan* (1997); Harold I. Gullan, *The Upset That Wasn't: Harry S. Truman and the Crucial Election of 1948* (1998); Michael Hogan, *A Cross of Iron: Harry S. Truman and the Origins of the National Security State, 1945–1954* (1998); Dennis Wainstock, *Truman, MacArthur, and the Korean War* (1999); Zachary Karabell, *The Last Campaign: How Harry Truman Won the 1948 Election* (2000).

John Tyler (Library of Congress)

TYLER, John

Born at Greenway, Va., March 29, 1790; son of John Tyler, judge, member and speaker of the Virginia House of Delegates, and fourteenth governor of Virginia, and Mary Marot (Armstead) Tyler; Episcopalian; married to Letitia Christian on March 29, 1813, and father of seven children; after death of first wife in 1842, married Julia Gardiner on June 26, 1844, and was father of seven more children, including David Gardiner Tyler, member of Congress; attended private schools; graduated from William and Mary College in 1807; studied law; admitted to the bar in 1809 and began practice in Charles City County, Va.; captain of a military company, 1813; elected to the Virginia House of Delegates and served from 1811 to 1816; member of Virginia executive council, 1815–1816; elected in 1816 as a Democratic-Republican to the 14th Congress to fill a vacancy; reelected to the 15th and 16th Congresses and served from December 16, 1817, until March 3, 1821; member of the Virginia House of Delegates, 1823–1825; elected governor of Virginia in 1825 and served until 1827; elected to the U.S. Senate in 1827 and reelected in 1833, serving from March 4, 1827, until his resignation on February 29, 1836; elected president *pro tempore* of the Senate on March 3, 1835; member of the state constitutional convention, 1829 and 1830; nominated for U.S. vice-president, 1835; again elected to the state House of Delegates, 1838; elected VICE-PRESIDENT on the Whig ticket with William H. Harrison in 1840 and took office on March 4, 1841; upon the death of President Harrison, took the oath of office as PRESIDENT on April 6, 1841, becoming the first vice-president to assume the presidency by right of succession; served until March 3, 1845; chairman of the Washington, D.C., peace convention in February 1861; member of the Virginia secessional convention, 1861; member of the Confederate provisional congress in 1861; elected to the House of Representatives of the Confederate congress but died before serving; died in Richmond, Va., on January 18, 1862; interment in Hollywood Cemetery, Richmond, where a monument has been erected by the U.S. Congress. **References:** Hugh Russell Fraser, *Democracy in the Making: The Jackson-Tyler Era* (1938); Robert J. Morgan, *A Whig Embattled: The Presidency under John Tyler* (1954); Robert Seager, *And Tyler Too* (1963).

TYNER, James Noble

Born in Brookville, Ind., January 17, 1826; pursued academic studies and graduated from Brookville Academy, 1844; went into business with father, 1846–1854; studied law, was admitted to the bar in 1857, and began practice in Peru, Ind.; secretary of Indiana State Senate; presidential elector on Lincoln-Hamlin Republican ticket, 1860; special agent for post office department, 1861–1866; chosen member of Congress to fill vacancy and served from March 4, 1869, to March 3, 1875; appointed second assistant postmaster general and served from February 26, 1875, to July 11, 1876; appointed POSTMASTER GENERAL in the cabinet of President Grant and continued under the administration of President Hayes, serving from July 12, 1876, to March 11, 1877; was first assistant postmaster general from April 1877 to October 1881; delegate from U.S. to International Postal Congresses of 1878 in Paris; assistant attorney general for post office department, March 21, 1889–May 27, 1893, and May 6, 1897–April 27, 1903; died in Washington, D.C., December 5, 1904; interment in Oak Hill Cemetery. **Reference:** Allan Nevins, *Hamilton Fish: The Inner History of the Grant Administration* (n.d.).

U

UDALL, Stewart Lee

Born in St. Johns, Ariz., January 31, 1920; son of Levi Stewart, chief justice of Supreme Court of Arizona, and Louise (Lee) Udall; brother of former U.S. Congressman Morris Udall; Mormon; married Irma Lee ("Lee") Webb on August 1, 1947; father of Thomas (Democratic U.S. representative from New Mexico), Scott, Lynn, Lori, Denis, and James; attended public schools in St. Johns and Eastern Arizona Junior College; LL.B., University of Arizona, 1948; served in U.S. Army Air Corps in Italy, 1944; admitted to the Arizona bar in 1948; partner, with his brother Morris, Udall and Udall, Tucson, 1948–1954; Democratic member from 2d Arizona district, U.S. House of Representatives, 1955–1961; served on House Committee on the Interior and Insular Affairs, Committee on Education and Labor, and Joint Committee on Navajo-Hopi Indian Administration; appointed SECRETARY OF THE INTERIOR by President Kennedy, continued under President Johnson, and served from January 21, 1961, to January 20, 1969; most important contributions were 18-month moratorium on sale of public lands, study of Bureau of Indian Affairs, establishment of manufacturing plants to provide employment for Indians; adjunct professor of environmental humanism, Yale University, 1969; chairman, board of directors, Overview Corp., Washington, 1969– ; headed Overseer Group at New School for Social Research in New York City; brought several lawsuits against the U.S. government on behalf of Nevada residents, including the widows of Navajo uranium miners, suffering from the effects of nuclear tests in the 1950s, 1978–1990; helped create the Radiation Exposure Compensation Act of 1990; author of *The Quiet Crisis* (1963, 1988), *1976: Agenda for Tomorrow* (1968), *Natural Wonders of America* (1971), *America's Natural Treasures: National Nature Monuments and Seashores* (1971), *The National Parks* (1974), *To the Inland Empire:*

Coronado and Our Spanish Legacy (1987), *Arizona, Wild and Free* (1993), and *The Myths of August: A Personal Exploration of Our Tragic Cold War Affair with the Atom* (1994); coauthor of *The Energy Balloon* (1974) and *National Parks of America* (1966, 1972); recipient of honorary degrees from Syracuse University, 1961, Dickinson College, 1963, and Colby College, 1963; conferred a knighthood by King Juan Carlos of Spain, 1987, in appreciation of his book *To the Inland Empire*; member, American Bar Association. **References:** Hugh Sidey, *John F. Kennedy, President* (1963); New York Times, *The Kennedy Years* (1964); *Who's Who in America, 1988–1989.*

UPSHUR, Abel Parker

Born in Northampton County, Va., June 17, 1790; son of Littlejohn Upshur, planter, Federalist member of Virginia legislature in 1809, and captain in the War of 1812, and Ann (Parker) Upshur; married Elizabeth Dennis, February 26, 1817; after her death in childbirth in October 1817, remarried to Elizabeth Ann Brown Upshur, his second cousin, March 24, 1824; father of one daughter; received classical education under tutors; attended Yale and Princeton; studied law and was admitted to the bar in 1810; began practice in Richmond, Va.; elected to the Virginia House of Delegates in 1812 and served until 1813; served as commonwealth attorney for Richmond from 1816 until his resignation in 1823; was also elected to the Common Hall (city council) and continued his law practice; retired to "Vaucluse," his plantation in Northampton County; elected again to the House of Delegates in 1824, to serve there until 1827; justice in the General Court of Virginia, 1826 to 1841; member of the Virginia constitutional convention from 1829 to 1830; a former Federalist, he supported the Whig Party in the election of 1840; appointed SECRETARY OF THE NAVY on September 13, 1841, in the cabinet of President Tyler and served until July 23, 1843; most important contributions were reorganization of the department into bureaus to promote efficiency, initiation of expansion and modernization measures, the construction of the first iron-hulled steamship in the U.S. Navy, and reform of some disciplinary abuses; appointed SECRETARY OF STATE by Tyler on June 23, 1843; most important contributions were urging of the annexation of Texas as a slaveholding state and authorizing negotiations for that purpose in October 1843, and opening up negotiations with Britain to solve Oregon dispute, efforts eventually leading to the acquisition of both territories by the United States; wrote many essays, addresses, and pamphlets, including "A Brief Inquiry into the True Nature and Character of Our Federal Government: A Review of Judge Joseph Story's Commentaries on the Constitution" (Petersburg, Va., 1840); killed February 28, 1844, along with several other cabinet members when a gun of the new steamer *Princeton* exploded upon being fired during a demonstration cruise on the Potomac River; interment in Congressional Cemetery, Washington, D.C. **References:** *Cyclopedia of American Biog-*

raphy, vol. 6 (1899); R.G. Adams, "Abel Parker Upshur," in S.F. Bemis, ed., *The American Secretaries of State*, vol. 5 (1928); *Dictionary of American Biography*, vol. 10 (1936); Claude H. Hall, *Abel Parker Upshur: Conservative Virginian* (1964); *Who Was Who in America*, Historical Volume (1967).

USERY, William Julian, Jr.

Born in Hardwick, Ga., December 21, 1923; son of Willie J. Sr. and Effie Mae (Williamson) Usery; Baptist; married Gussie Mae Smith on June 14, 1942; father of Melvin J.; attended Midway High School in Hardwick, 1937–1938, Georgia Military College, Milledgeville, Ga., 1938–1941, Mercer University, Macon, Ga., 1948–1949; welder, naval shipyards, Brunswick, Ga., 1941–1942; served as welder in U.S. Navy in the Pacific, 1943–1946; welder-steamfitter, Georgia State Hospital, Milledgeville, 1946–1948; machinist, Armstrong Cork Company, Macon, 1948–1956; founding member, Local 8, International Association of Machinists and Aerospace Workers (IAM), Macon, 1952; special representative for IAM, Cape Canaveral Air Force Test Facilities, Florida, 1954–1956; IAM Grand Lodge representative, AFL-CIO, 1956–1969; assistant secretary for labor-management relations, U.S. Department of Labor, 1969–1973; as assistant labor secretary, helped negotiate the first collective bargaining agreement for the U.S. Postal Service; director, Federal Mediation and Conciliation Service, 1973–1976; special assistant to President Nixon for labor-management affairs, January–August 1974; special assistant to President Ford for labor-management negotiations, 1975–1977; appointed SECRETARY OF LABOR by President Ford and served from February 10, 1976, until the end of Ford's term on January 20, 1977; during his administration the nation continued its slow recovery from the economic recession, prompting many unions to renegotiate contracts to increase wages and offset the effects of inflation; founder, Bill Usery Associates, consultants on employer-employee relations, Washington, 1977– ; founder, Bill Usery Labor-Management Relations Foundation, 1985; member, Advisory Commission on United Mine Workers of America Retiree Health Benefits, 1989–1990; founder, Partners in Economic Reform, 1991, promoting free collective bargaining in the states of the former Soviet Union; founder, W.J. Usery Center for the Workplace, Georgia State University, 1997; industrial union representative, President's Missile Sites Labor Commission, Cape Canaveral/Kennedy Space Center and Marshall Space Flight Center, Huntsville, Ala., 1961–1967; member, Cape Kennedy Labor-Management Relations Council, 1967–1968, chairman, 1968; was offered, but declined, position of director, department of organization and field services, AFL-CIO, 1973; member, Commission on the Future of Worker-Management Relations, 1993–1995; appointed by President Clinton as special mediator for major league baseball strike, 1994–1995; Mason, Elk. **References:** National Journal, *Ford's Presidency; Who's Who in America, 1976.*

USHER, John Palmer

Born in Brookfield, N.Y., January 9, 1816; son of Dr. Nathaniel and Lucy (Palmer) Usher; married Margaret Patterson on January 26, 1844; father of four sons; attended the common schools; studied law in the office of Henry Bennett of New Berlin, N.Y.; was admitted to the bar in 1839; moved to Terre Haute, Ind., 1840, and began practice of law; served in the Indiana legislature, 1850–1851; appointed attorney general of Indiana in November 1861 and resigned four months later; became assistant secretary of the interior at Washington in 1862; appointed secretary of the interior *ad interim* in the cabinet of President Lincoln, January 1, 1863, to January 7, 1863; appointed SECRETARY OF THE INTERIOR by President Lincoln, and continued under Johnson, serving from January 8, 1863, to May 14, 1865, most important contributions were recommendation of small tax on net profits of larger Indian reservations and silver and gold mines, request for greater appropriations for Indians, and report on public lands; resumed practice of law; moved to Lawrence, Kans., and accepted appointment as chief counsel for Union Pacific Railroad; died in Philadelphia, Pa., April 13, 1889. **References:** A.T. Rice, *President Lincoln's Cabinet* (1925); Elmo R. Richardson and Alan W. Farley, *John Palmer Usher, Lincoln's Secretary of the Interior* (1960).

V

VAN BUREN, Martin

Born in Kinderhook, N.Y., December 5, 1782; son of Abraham Van Buren, farmer and innkeeper, and Maria Goes Hoes (Van Allen) Van Buren; Dutch Reformed; married Hannah Hoes on February 21, 1807; father of Abraham, John, Martin, and Smith Thompson; attended local schools; went to Kinderhook Academy; worked in law office of Francis Sylvester, 1796–1802; studied law in New York City with William P. Van Ness in 1802; admitted to bar in 1803 and began practice in Kinderhook; counselor for Superior Court of New York, 1807; appointed surrogate of Columbia County, N.Y., on February 20, 1808, and remained in that capacity until 1813; moved to Hudson, N.Y., 1809; member of New York State Senate from 1813 to 1820; was attorney general of New York State, 1815–1819;

Martin Van Buren (Library of Congress)

elected U.S. senator from New York and served from March 4, 1821, to December 20, 1828; delegate to third New York State constitutional convention, August 28, 1821; served as governor of New York from January 1, 1829, until his resignation on March 12, 1829; appointed SECRETARY OF STATE in the cabinet of President Jackson on March 6, 1829, and served from March 28, 1829, to

May 23, 1831; commissioned minister to Great Britain on January 25, 1831, but returned after January 25, 1832, when Senate rejected the nomination; elected VICE-PRESIDENT in the administration of President Jackson and served from March 4, 1833, to March 3, 1837; elected PRESIDENT and served from March 4, 1837, to March 3, 1841; was unsuccessful Democratic nominee for reelection in 1840 and 1844; unsuccessful Free Soil nominee for presidential election in 1848; returned to Lindewald, Kinderhook, N.Y., and retired; died in Kinderhook, July 24, 1862; interment in Kinderhook Cemetery. **References:** Robert V. Remini, *Martin Van Buren and the Making of the Democratic Party* (1959); Irving J. Sloan, ed., *Martin Van Buren, 1782–1862: Chronology, Documents, Bibliographical Aids* (1969).

VANCE, Cyrus Roberts

Born in Clarksburg, W.Va., March 27, 1917; son of John Carl and Amy (Roberts) Vance; Episcopalian; married Grace Elsie Sloane, a painter, on February 15, 1947; father of Elsie Nicoll, Amy Sloane, Grace Roberts, Camilla, and Cyrus Roberts Jr.; attended Kent School, Kent, Conn.; B.A. in economics, Yale, 1939; LL.B. with honors, Yale Law School, 1942; admitted to the bars of New York, 1947, and U.S. Supreme Court, 1970; served to lieutenant, U.S. Navy, 1942–1946; assistant to the president, Mead Corp., 1946–1947; associate, Simpson, Thacher and Bartlett, New York, 1947–1956; partner, 1956–1961, 1967–1977, 1980–1998; special counsel, preparedness investigating subcommittee, U.S. Senate Armed Services Committee, 1957–1960; general counsel, U.S. Department of Defense, 1961–1962; secretary, U.S. Army, 1962–1963; deputy secretary of defense, 1964–1967; special representative of President Johnson on peacemaking missions during international crises in Cyprus, 1967, and Korea, 1968; U.S. negotiator, and deputy ambassador to Averell Harriman, Paris Peace Conference on Vietnam, 1968–1969; selected to be SECRETARY OF STATE by President Carter and served from January 23, 1977, until April 28, 1980; dealt with Iranian hostage crisis, Strategic Arms Limitation Talks (SALT) II with the Soviet Union, Camp David Accords that led to the Israeli-Egyptian peace treaty, Panama Canal treaties, and the deployment of the neutron bomb in Europe; resigned in protest of Carter's decision to attempt a military rescue of the hostages in Iran, which failed and in which eight U.S. servicemen were killed, April 1980; returned to New York law practice, 1980–1998; personal envoy for the UN secretary-general on Yugoslavia crisis, 1991–1992, and on South Africa and Nagorno-Karabakh, 1992; cochairman, United Nations–European Community International Conference on the Former Yugoslavia, 1992–1993; special envoy for the UN secretary-general, Greece–Former Yugoslavian Republic of Macedonia Negotiations, 1993; consulting counsel, Special Committee on Space and Astronautics, U.S. Senate, 1958; chairman, committee on adjudication of claims, Administrative Conference of the United States, United Nations Development Corporation, 1976, International Commission on Missing Persons in the

Former Yugoslavia, 1995; member, Committee to Investigate Alleged Police Corruption in New York City, 1970–1972, Independent Committee on Disarmament and Security Issues, New York State Commission on Government Integrity, New York State Judicial Commission on Minorities in the Court; member, board of directors, Federal Reserve Bank of New York, 1989–1993, chairman, 1989–1991; member board of directors, IBM, Pan American World Airways and the *New York Times*; trustee, Yale Corporation, 1968–1978, 1980–1987, Rockefeller Foundation, 1970–1977, 1980–1982; chairman, Rockefeller Foundation, 1975–1977, American Ditchley Foundation, 1981–1994; recipient, Medal of Freedom, 1969, Grand Cordon Order of Rising Sun, Government of Japan, 1990, Legion of Honor, French Republic, 1993; appointed Honorary Knight Commander, Most Excellent Order of the British Empire, 1994, and honorary degrees from over 20 colleges and universities, including Yale, 1968, and Harvard, 1981; fellow, American College of Trial Lawyers; author of *Hard Choices: Critical Years in America's Foreign Policy* (1983), *Common Security: A Blueprint for Survival* (1982), and *Building the Peace: US Foreign Policy for the Next Decade (Alternatives for the 1980's)* (1982); member, American Bar Association, Association of the Bar of the City of New York (president, 1974–1976), Council on Foreign Relations (director and vice-chairman, 1985–1987), Japan Society (chairman, 1985–1993); died on January 12, 2002, in New York City. **References:** *New York Times* (December 4, 1976); *Time* (December 13, 1976); *U.S. News & World Report* (December 13, 1976); *New Republic* (December 18, 1976); Jimmy Carter, *Keeping Faith* (1982); Zbigniew Brzezinski, *Power and Principle: Memoirs of the National Security Advisor, 1977–1980* (1983); Davis S. McLellan, *Cyrus Vance* (1985); Burton I. Kaufman, *The Presidency of James Earl Carter, Jr.* (1993); *Who's Who in America, 2000; Washington Post* (January 13, 2002).

VENEMAN, Ann Margaret

Born in Modesto, Calif., June 29, 1949; daughter of John G. ("Jack") Veneman, a California state politician and deputy undersecretary of health, education, and welfare in the administration of President Nixon; received B.A. in political science, University of California, Davis, 1970; M.A. in public policy, University of California, Berkeley, 1971; J.D., University of California's Hastings College of the Law, San Francisco, 1976; legislative intern for California state assemblyman and future governor Pete Wilson, 1970; summer intern for the White House Conference on Children and Youth, 1970; worked for Ross Wurm & Associates, Modesto, 1971–1972, then for the Office of Economic Opportunity in San Francisco for a short time in 1972; served as an equal opportunity specialist for the U.S. Department of Health, Education, and Welfare in San Francisco, 1972–1973, then for the Office for Civil Rights, 1974–1975; law clerk, Public Advocates, Inc., San Francisco, 1975; law clerk, municipal court Judge Mary Moran Pajalich, San Francisco, 1976; member of the bar for the state of California, the federal district court of the eastern and central districts of California, and the U.S.

Supreme Court; associate attorney, Office of the General Counsel, San Francisco Bay Area Rapid Transit District, Oakland, 1976–1978; deputy public defender, Stanislaus County Public Defender's Office, Modesto, 1978–1980; partner, Damrell, Damrell & Nelson, Modesto, 1980–1986; administrator with the Foreign Agricultural Service, U.S. Department of Agriculture (USDA), Washington, 1986–1989, first as assistant to the administrator, 1986–1987, then as associate administrator for trade policy, 1987–1989; deputy undersecretary, International Affairs and Commodity Programs, USDA, 1989–1991; deputy secretary, USDA, 1991–1993; helped negotiate Uruguay Round of General Agreement on Tariffs and Trade and North American Free Trade Agreement while serving in the administration of President George H.W. Bush; attorney, Patton Boggs, LLP, Washington, 1993–1995; appointed by Governor Pete Wilson to be secretary of California Department of Food and Agriculture, 1995–1999, the first woman to head the agency; attorney, Nossaman, Guthner, Knox & Elliott, Sacramento, 1999–2001, specializing in agriculture, environment, technology, and trade-related issues; state cochair of George W. Bush's presidential campaign in California in 2000 and Republican state elector; appointed SECRETARY OF AGRICULTURE by President George W. Bush, taking office on January 20, 2001, the first woman to head the department and an advocate of big agribusiness, biotechnology, and expanded international trade; member, board of directors, Calgene, Inc., 1993–1995; member emeritus, International Policy Council on Agriculture, Food and Trade. **Reference:** *Washington Post* (December 22, 2000).

—Jeffrey Coster

VERITY, C(alvin) William, Jr.

Born in Middletown, Ohio, January 26, 1917; son of Calvin W. Verity and Elizabeth (O'Brien) Verity; Episcopalian; married Margaret (Peggy) Burnley Wymond on April 19, 1941; father of Jonathan George, Peggy Wymond, and William Wymond; student at the Choate School in Wallingford, Conn.; graduated from Phillips Academy, Exeter, N.H., 1935; B.A. in economics, Yale University, 1939; worked in New York City for advertising firm of Young and Rubican and then for the Hapsburg House restaurant as a manager; returned to Ohio and Armco, the business founded by his grandfather, as a laborer in the Hamilton plant, then in the public relations department in Middletown; lieutenant, U.S. Navy, 1942–1946; returned to Armco as an assistant safety adviser at Middletown, 1946–1948, assistant to the plant officer in charge of personnel, grievances, and labor relations, 1948–1950, head of personnel and labor negotiations at Ashland, Ky., plant, 1950–1953, assistant to the works manager responsible for all staff operations, 1953–1957, director of organizational planning and development, Armco, Middletown, 1957–1961, director of public relations, 1961–1964, vice-president and general manager of steel, 1964–1965, and president and chief executive officer, Armco Inc., Middletown, 1965–1971, at a time when Armco was the fourth largest steel company in the United States; during the 1970s he became a spokesman to make U.S. businesses more competitive abroad; chairman of the board, Armco, 1971; chairman, U.S. Chamber of Commerce, 1980–1981; chairman, President's Bipartisan Task Force on Private Sector Initiatives, Washington, 1981–1983; cochairman of the U.S.-USSR Trade Economic Council, 1979–1984; appointed by President Reagan as SECRETARY OF COMMERCE and served from October 19, 1987, until the end of Reagan's term on January 20, 1989. **References:** *Current Biography Yearbook 1988; Who's Who in America, 1988–1989*; Kenneth W. Thompson, ed., *The Reagan Presidency: Ten Intimate Perspectives* (1997).

VILAS, William Freeman

Born in Chelsea, Vt., July 9, 1840; son of Levi B. and Esther G. (Smilie) Vilas; married Anna M. Fox on January 3, 1866; father of Mary Esther, moved with his parents to Madison, Wisc., in 1851; attended the common schools; entered the University of Wisconsin, at Madison, graduating in 1858; graduated from the University of Albany School of Law, Albany, N.Y., in 1860; was admitted to the bar and commenced his legal practice in Madison on July 9, 1860; enlisted in the Union army during the Civil War; captain of Company A, 23d Regiment, Wisconsin Volunteer Infantry; later promoted to major and then lieutenant colonel; professor of law at the University of Wisconsin; regent of the University of Wisconsin from 1880 to 1885; appointed by the Wisconsin Supreme Court to prepare a revised body of the statute law that was subsequently adopted in 1878; elected to the Wisconsin State Assembly in 1885; delegate to the Democratic National Convention in 1876, 1880, 1884, 1892, and 1896; invited to join the cabinet as POSTMASTER GENERAL by appointment of President Cleveland on March 7, 1885, serving until January 16, 1888, when President Cleveland commissioned him SECRETARY OF THE INTERIOR, a portfolio he held until March 6, 1889; elected as a Democrat to the U.S. Senate from Wisconsin on January 28, 1891, serving from March 4, 1891, to March 3, 1897; again designated regent of the University of Wisconsin, a position he held from 1896 to 1905, whereupon he resumed the practice of law; died in Madison, Wisc., on August 28, 1908; interment in Forest Hills Cemetery, Madison. **References:** Allan Nevins, *Grover Cleveland: A Study in Courage* (1932); Horace Samuel Merrill, *Bourbon Leader: Grover Cleveland and the Democratic Party* (1957).

VINSON, Frederick Moore

Born in Louisa, Ky., January 22, 1890; son of James Vinson, county jailer, and Virginia (Ferguson) Vinson; Methodist; married to Roberta Dixon on January 24, 1923; father of Frederick Moore and James Robert; attended the local schools; was graduated from Kentucky Normal College in Louisa in 1908; graduated from the law department of Centre College, Danville, Ky., in 1911;

admitted to the bar in 1911 and began practice in Louisa; city attorney of Louisa, 1914 and 1915; also engaged in grocery, milling, and banking enterprises; served in the U.S. Army during World War I; elected commonwealth attorney for the 32d judicial district of Kentucky in 1921 and served until January 1924; elected as a Democrat to the 68th Congress in 1924 to fill a vacancy; reelected to the 69th and 70th Congresses and served until March 3, 1929; resumed law practice in Ashland, Ky.; elected to the 72d through 75th Congresses, serving from March 4, 1931, until May 12, 1938; appointed associate justice of the U.S. Circuit Court of Appeals for the District of Columbia by President Franklin Roosevelt in December 1937; subsequently appointed on March 2, 1942, as chief judge of the U.S. Emergency Court of Appeals by Chief Justice Harlan Stone; served in each capacity until his resignation on May 27, 1943, to accept an appointment by the president as director of the Office of Economic Stabilization and in that capacity was vice-chairman of the U.S. delegation to the United Nations Monetary and Financial Conference in July 1944; served until March 5, 1945, when he became federal loan administrator; appointed director of War Mobilization and Reconversion and served from April 4 to July 22, 1945; appointed SECRETARY OF THE TREASURY in the cabinet of President Truman on July 18, 1945; most important contributions were supervising the last of the great war bond drives, recommending the Revenue Act of 1945 to relieve tax burdens, serving as the first chairman of the boards of governors of both the International Monetary Fund and the International Bank for Reconstruction and Development, serving as chairman of the National Advisory Council on International Monetary and Financial Problems, and urging the extension of credit to Great Britain; served until June 23, 1946, when he resigned following his appointment by President Truman as chief justice of the United States to succeed Harlan F. Stone; received the Medal of Merit of the United States in 1947; died in Washington, D.C., on September 8, 1953. **References:** Glendon Schubert, *Judicial Mind: Attitudes and Ideologies of Supreme Court Justices, 1946–1963* (1965); Barton J. Bernstein and A.J. Matusow, *The Truman Administration: A Documentary History* (1966); Cabell Phillips, *The Truman Presidency* (1966).

VOLPE, John Anthony, Sr.

Born in Wakefield, Mass., December 8, 1908; son of Vito and Filomena (Benedetto) Volpe, both Italian immigrants; Roman Catholic; married Jennie Benedetto on June 18, 1934; father of Loretta Jean (Mrs. Roger Rotondi) and John Anthony Jr.; attended Malden High School in Boston; worked as a journeyman plasterer, 1926–1928; graduate in architectural construction, Wentworth Institute, Boston, 1930; lieutenant, Civil Engineer Corps, U.S. Navy during World War II; retired from navy as lieutenant commander, 1946; timekeeper of a residential and commercial construction firm and assistant superintendent of construction, 1930–1932; founder and president, John A. Volpe Construction Company, 1933; deputy chairman, Republican state committee,

1950–1953; alternate delegate to the Republican National Convention, 1952; member, Massachusetts commission of public works, 1953–1956; appointed by President Eisenhower the first federal highway administrator, 1956–1957; Republican governor of Massachusetts, 1961–1963, 1965–1967; defeated for reelection, 1962; appointed SECRETARY OF TRANSPORTATION by President Nixon and served from January 22, 1969, until February 1, 1973; attempted without success to prevent Penn Central bankruptcy; U.S. ambassador to Italy, 1973–1977; publisher, Malden (Mass.) *News* and Medford *Daily Mercury*; president, Greater Boston Chamber of Commerce, 1958–1959; former chairman, Greater Boston Community Fund; former trustee, Wentworth Institute; chairman, Presidential Commission on Drunk Driving, 1983; named Grand Officer, Order of Merit, Republic of Italy, 1957; recipient of honorary degrees from St. Michael's College, 1954, and Northeastern University, 1956; former member, Knights of Malta, Knights of Columbus, American Legion; died on November 11, 1994, in Nahant, Mass. **References:** *Current Biography Yearbook 1962*; Earl Mazo and Stephen Hess, *Nixon: A Political Portrait* (1969); *New York Times* (November 13, 1994); Richard Reeves, *President Nixon: Alone in the White House* (2001).

W

WALKER, Frank Comerford

Born in Plymouth, Pa., May 30, 1886; son of David Walker, merchant and copper mine operator, and Ellen (Comerford) Walker; Roman Catholic; married on November 11, 1914, to Hallie Victoria Boucher; father of Thomas Joseph and Laura Hallie; attended parochial schools in Butte, Mont.; attended Gonzaga University, 1903–1906; studied law at the University of Notre Dame, graduating in 1909; admitted to the bar in 1909 and began practice in Butte with his brother Thomas Joseph; assistant district attorney of Silver Bow County, 1909–1912; member of the Montana legislature, 1913; first lieutenant in the U.S. Army during World War I; moved to New York City, 1925; became vice-president and general counsel of Comerford Theaters, Inc., and general counsel of the Meco Realty Co. and the Comerford Publix Corp., all of Scranton, Pa.; treasurer of the Democratic National Committee, 1932–1933; appointed executive secretary of President Franklin Roosevelt's Executive Council in 1933; appointed executive director of the National Emergency Council and served, 1933–1935; engaged in business pursuits; named chairman of the finance committee of the Democratic campaign of 1938; appointed POSTMASTER GENERAL in the cabinet of President Roosevelt on September 10, 1940, continued under President Truman, and served until May 8, 1945; most important contributions were establishing the V-mail system to reduce weight and bulk of mail to U.S. servicemen abroad and initiating helicopter and bus delivery of mail in rural areas; chairman of the Democratic National Committee, 1943–1944; attended the first session of the United Nations General Assembly as an alternate U.S. delegate in 1946 and served as a U.S. representative on the Assembly's legal committee; served as director of the First National Bank, Scranton, and the Grace National Bank, New York; died in New York City on September 13, 1959. **References:** Rexford G.

Tugwell, *FDR: Architect of an Era* (1967); A.J. Wann, *The President as Chief Administrator: A Study of Franklin D. Roosevelt* (1968).

WALKER, Robert James

Born in Northumberland, Pa., July 19, 1801; son of Jonathan Hoge Walker, a jurist, and Lucretia (Duncan) Walker; married Mary Blechynder Bacle, granddaughter of Benjamin Franklin, on April 4, 1825; father of eight children; attended town schools; studied under private tutors; graduated University of Pennsylvania in 1819; was admitted to the bar in 1821; moved to Natchez, Miss., in 1826 and entered law practice with Duncan Walker, his brother; elected judge of state supreme court, 1828, but declined to serve; became member of U.S. Senate on February 22, 1835, was reelected, and served from March 4, 1835, to March 5, 1845; appointed SECRETARY OF THE TREASURY in the cabinet of President Polk on March 5, 1845, and served from March 8, 1845, to March 5, 1849; most important contributions were establishment of independent treasury system to deal with public funds, favoring of free trade, and financing of Mexican War; attended to business interests and lands in Mississippi, Louisiana, and Wisconsin, 1849–1857; sold securities of Illinois Central Railroad in England, 1851–1852; appointed governor of Kansas Territory, serving from April 10, 1857, to his resignation in December 1857; part owner of and contributor to *Continental Monthly* with F.P. Stanton in 1862; went to Europe as U.S. financial agent, 1863 and 1864; acted as lobbyist of Russian minister and Seward in passing bill of Alaskan purchase; wrote on advantages of annexation of Nova Scotia; died in Washington, D.C., November 11, 1869; interment in Oak Hill Cemetery. **References:** G.W. Brown, *Reminiscences of Governor R.J. Walker* (1902); W.E. Dodd, *Robert J. Walker: Imperialist* (1914).

WALLACE, Henry Agard

Born on a farm near Orient, Iowa, October 7, 1888; son of Henry Cantwell, agricultural scientist, farm journalist, and U.S. secretary of agriculture, 1921–1924, and May (Brodhead) Wallace; Presbyterian; married Ilo Browne on May 20, 1914; father of Henry B., Robert B., and Jean B.; graduated from West Des Moines (Iowa) High School, 1906; B.S. in animal husbandry, Iowa State College, 1910; writer and member of the editorial staff of the newspaper run by his grandfather and father, *Wallaces' Farmer*, Des Moines, 1910–1916, associate editor (upon his grandfather's death), 1916–1924, and editor (upon his father's death), 1924–1929; editor, *Wallaces' Farmer and Iowa Homestead*, 1929–1932; experimented with high-yielding strains of corn, 1913–1933, founded the Hi-Bred Corn Company (after 1935, the Pioneer Hi-Bred Corn Company) to market seed, 1926, and was company president, 1926–1933; raised a Republican, but dissatisfied with the GOP's farm policies, he joined the Democratic Party after

his father's death in 1924; appointed by President Franklin Roosevelt as SECRE-
TARY OF AGRICULTURE and served there for most of Roosevelt's first two terms,
from March 4, 1933, until September 9, 1940; helped draft and win congressional approval for the Agricultural Adjustment Act to create a national farm support program to counter the effects of the Great Depression, 1933; advocated
expanding international markets for American farm products; chosen by Roosevelt as his running mate and elected VICE-PRESIDENT OF THE UNITED STATES in
1940; inaugurated on January 20, 1941, and served until January 20, 1945;
headed the Economic Defense Board (later the Board of Economic Warfare),
1941–1943, made a wartime goodwill tour to China, the Soviet Union, and Latin
America, 1943, and advocated planning for an internationalist postwar foreign
policy; replaced by Senator Harry Truman on the Democratic presidential ticket,
1944; appointed by Roosevelt as SECRETARY OF COMMERCE and served from
March 2, 1945, into the administration of President Truman, until September 20,
1946, when he resigned after publicly criticizing the administration's policy
toward the Soviet Union; he broke with the Democratic Party and ran as the presidential candidate of the Progressive Party in 1948, winning over 1 million votes,
but was smeared as a communist sympathizer; he left the party in 1950 because
it refused to endorse the U.S. war effort in Korea and later admitted he had
wrongly interpreted Soviet intentions in the 1940s; retired to his farm in South
Salem, N.Y., 1948, where he spent the remainder of his life in agricultural study
and experimentation; member, American Farm Economists Association; delegate, International Conference of Agricultural Economics, England, 1929, and
Democratic National Conventions, 1940, 1944; author of *Agricultural Prices*
(1920), *America Must Choose* (1934), *New Frontiers* (1934), *Statesmanship and
Religion* (1934), *Technology, Corporations, and the General Welfare* (1937), *The
Century of the Common Man* (1943), *Democracy Reborn* (1944), *Sixty Million
Jobs* (1945), *Toward World Peace* (1948), and the posthumously published diary,
edited by John Morton Blum, *The Price of Vision: The Diary of Henry A. Wal-
lace, 1942–1946* (1973); coauthor, with William L. Brown, of *Corn and Its Early
Fathers* (1956); editor, *The New Republic*, 1946–1948; recipient of honorary
doctor of science degree from Iowa State College, 1934; died on November 18,
1965, in Danbury, Conn.; interment in Des Moines. **References:** Dwight Mac-
donald, *Henry Wallace: The Man and the Myth* (1948); Richard S. Kirkendall,
Social Scientists and Farm Politics in the Age of Roosevelt (1966); Edward L.
Schapsmeier and Frederick H. Schapsmeier, *Henry A. Wallace of Iowa: The
Agrarian Years, 1910–1940* (1968) and *Prophet in Politics: Henry A. Wallace
and the War Years, 1940–1965* (1970); Van L. Perkins, *Crisis in Agriculture: The
Agricultural Adjustment Administration and the New Deal, 1933* (1969); Nor-
man D. Markowitz, *The Rise and Fall of the People's Century: Henry A. Wallace
and American Liberalism, 1941–1948* (1973); J. Samuel Walker, *Henry A. Wal-
lace and American Foreign Policy* (1976); Richard J. Walton, *Henry Wallace,
Harry Truman, and the Cold War* (1976); Donald R. McCoy, *The Presidency of
Harry S Truman* (1984); Graham J. White and John Maze, *Henry A. Wallace: His*

Search for a New World Order (1995); George T. McJimsey, *The Presidency of Franklin Delano Roosevelt* (2000).

—*Jeffrey Coster*

WALLACE, Henry Cantwell

Born in Rock Island, Ill., May 11, 1866; son of Henry and Nannie (Cantwell) Wallace; Presbyterian; married Carrie May Broadhead; father of Henry Agard Wallace, vice-president under Franklin Roosevelt, and five other children; learned the printer's trade in the newspaper offices in Winterset; attended the Iowa State Agricultural College (now the Iowa State College of Agriculture) from 1885 to 1887; returned to college in 1891, graduating in 1892; became part owner and publisher of the *Farm and Dairy* in Ames, Iowa; purchased the publication outright with his father and brother, moving the plant to Des Moines and changing the name to *Wallaces' Farm and Dairy* and later to *Wallaces' Farmer*; this farm journal eventually became one of the leading agricultural periodicals in the United States; secretary of the Cornbelt Meat Producers Association for 14 years; invited to join the cabinet of President Harding as SECRETARY OF AGRICULTURE on March 5, 1921, and was continued in office by President Coolidge, remaining in that post until his death; during his incumbency, he urged the Department of Agriculture not only to assist the farmer in increasing the efficiency of production but also to develop improved systems of marketing, emphasized the adjustment of production to the needs of consumption as a proper function of the department, established the Bureau of Agricultural Economics and the Bureau of Home Economics, and inaugurated the radio service for market reports; authored *Our Debt and Duty to the Farmers* (1925); died in Washington, D.C., on October 25, 1924; funeral services held at the White House; interment in Des Moines, Iowa. **References:** Harold Underwood Faulkner, *From Versailles to the New Deal: A Chronicle of the Harding, Coolidge, Hoover Era* (1958); Edward Connery Latham, ed., *Meet Calvin Coolidge: The Man behind the Myth* (1960).

WANAMAKER, John

Born in Philadelphia, Pa., July 11, 1838; son of Nelson, a brickmaker, and Elizabeth Deshong (Kochersperger) Wanamaker; Presbyterian; married Mary Erringer Brown in 1860; father of Lewis Podman and Thomas B., and two daughters; worked as an errand boy for a publisher, then in the men's clothing business, eventually as a salesman, 1851–1857; became the first paid secretary of a Young Men's Christian Association, Philadelphia, 1857; founded Bethany (N.Y.) Sunday School, 1858; first invested in men's clothing business, 1861, and opened a series of Philadelphia stores, starting with "Oak Hall," which would become the largest retail men's clothing store in the United States by the

1870s, then John Wanamaker and Company, 1869, the Grand Depot dry goods and clothing store, 1876, and a new type of store that became the forerunner of the modern department store, featuring various specialty shops under one roof, March 12, 1877; a constant business innovator, he began the money-back guarantee in 1865 and started an employees' mutual benefit association in 1881 to train clerks; an important fund-raiser for the Republican Party, he was appointed POSTMASTER GENERAL by President Benjamin Harrison and served from March 6, 1889, until March 7, 1893; experimented with rural free delivery, advocated parcel post and postal savings, favored government ownership of telegraph and telephone utilities, established sea post offices, and improved the efficiency of the mail delivery system; began John Wanamaker Commercial Institute, 1896, and trained employees for military duty, 1898–1917; used store editorials to support U.S. entry into World War I; died on December 12, 1922, at his home at Lindenhurst in Philadelphia. **References:** H.A. Gibbons, *John Wanamaker*, 2 vols. (1926; reprinted 1971); Homer E. Socolofsky, *The Presidency of Benjamin Harrison* (1987); Walter Licht, *Getting Work: Philadelphia, 1840–1950* (1992); William Leach, *Land of Desire: Merchants, Power, and the Rise of a New American Culture* (1993).

WASHBURNE, Elihu Benjamin

Born in Livermore, Me., September 23, 1816; son of Israel Washburn, farmer and small storeowner, and Martha (Benjamin) Washburn; brother of Israel Washburn, governor of Maine, and Cadwallader Washburn, governor of Wisconsin; Presbyterian; married Adele Gratiot on July 31, 1845; father of seven children; left home at age 14; added "e" to surname; worked on a farm; taught school for three months; was apprentice for newspaper publisher; became typesetter; decided to study law; attended Maine Wesleyan Seminary at Kent's Hill; apprenticed in law office in Boston; was admitted to Massachusetts bar in 1840 and settled in Galena, Ill.; went into a quasi-partnership with Charles S. Hempstead to practice law, then practiced alone, 1841–1845; entered into actual partnership with Hempstead, 1845; invested in western lands; supported Whigs; unsuccessful candidate for Congress, 1848; elected to 33d through 41st Congresses, serving from March 4, 1853, to March 6, 1869; supported Lincoln during the Civil War but was kept out of army because of health; supported Grant in campaign of 1868; appointed SECRETARY OF STATE in the cabinet of President Grant, serving from March 5, 1869, until his resignation on March 16, 1869, after serving only 11 days (resignation was tendered on March 10); became minister of France on March 17, 1869, and served until 1877; almost nominated for presidency in 1880; member of Chicago Historical Society; published *Recollections of a Minister to France 1869–1877* (1877); wrote and published articles in *Scribner's Magazine* and *The Edwards Papers*; died in Chicago, Ill., October 22, 1887; interment in Greenwood Cemetery, Galena, Ill. **References:** Gaillard Hunt, *Israel, Elihu and Cadwallader Washburn* (1925); S.F. Bemis,

The American Secretaries of State (1928); Allan Nevins, *Hamilton Fish: The Inner History of the Grant Administration* (n.d.).

George Washington (Library of Congress)

WASHINGTON, George

Born at Wakefield, his father's estate near Pope's Creek, Westmoreland County, Va., February 22 (February 11, old style), 1732; son of Augustine, a plantation owner, and Mary (Ball) Washington; Episcopalian; married Mrs. Martha (Dandridge) Custis (1731–1802) on January 6, 1759; stepfather of Martha ("Patsy") Parke Custis and John Parke Custis and custodian of the latter's two sons after his death in 1781; raised in Stafford County, Va., in the custody of his older half brother Lawrence after their father died in 1743; self-educated in surveying; surveyed lands of Lord Fairfax, 1748; county surveyor for Culpeper County, Va., 1749–1751; traveled to Barbados with Lawrence and contracted smallpox, 1751–1752; district adjutant, with the rank of major, of the Virginia militia, 1752–1753; commander of an expedition in the Ohio Valley that eventually engaged French troops in combat, 1753–1754, considered as one of the opening incidents of the French and Indian War; aide-de-camp to General Braddock, 1755; promoted to colonel and commander-in-chief of all Virginia forces, 1755–1758; wheat and tobacco planter at Mount Vernon from 1759; member from Fairfax, Virginia House of Burgesses, 1759–1767; justice of the peace, Fairfax County, Va., 1760–1774; vestryman, Truro Parish; delegate from Virginia, Continental Congress, 1774–1775; appointed by Congress as commander-in-chief, Continental Army, 1775–1783, and led American troops in the campaigns in New York, New Jersey, and Pennsylvania, 1776–1778, and at the Battle of Yorktown, 1781; resigned his commission and retired to Mount Vernon, 1783; delegate and presiding officer, Constitutional Convention, Philadelphia, 1787; received votes from all 69 electors in 1789 and became the first PRESIDENT OF THE UNITED STATES; inaugurated on April 30, 1789, in New York City; reelected in 1792, with votes from all 132 electors, he served two full terms until leaving office on March 4, 1797; his presidency was marked by the creation of a federal civil service and federal judiciary system, the establishment of financial policies by Secretary of the Treasury Alexander Hamilton, the maintenance of U.S. neutrality in the Anglo-French conflict after 1793, the suppression of the Whiskey Rebellion in 1794, the normalization of diplomatic relations with Great Britain,

1795, and the consolidation of rival factions under Hamilton and Secretary of State Thomas Jefferson into the first two-party system of Federalists and Democratic-Republicans; appointed lieutenant general and commander, U.S. Army, 1798–1799; died on December 14, 1799, at his home in Mount Vernon and is interred there. **References:** James Thomas Flexner, *George Washington*, 4 vols. (1965–1972) and *George Washington: The Indispensable Man* (1974); Marcus Cunliffe, *George Washington and the Making of a Nation* (1966); Forrest McDonald, *The Presidency of George Washington* (1974); Richard Norton Smith, *Patriarch: George Washington and the New American Nation* (1993); Richard Brookhiser, *Founding Father: Rediscovering George Washington* (1996); Willard Sterne Randall, *George Washington: A Life* (1997).

—Jeffrey Coster

WATKINS, James David

Born in Alhambra, Calif., March 7, 1927; son of Edward Francis, utility company executive, and Louise Whipple (Ward) Watkins, politician; Roman Catholic; married Sheila Jo McKinney (died, 1996) on August 19, 1950; father of Katherine Marie, Laura Jo, Charles Lancaster, Susan Elizabeth, James David, and Edward Francis; B.S., U.S. Naval Academy, 1949; M.S. in mechanical engineering, Naval Postgraduate School, Monterey, Calif., 1958; commissioned as ensign, 1949, en route to a career as an officer in the U.S. Navy; administrative assistant to Admiral Hyman G. Rickover, 1962; commanding officer, nuclear attack submarine USS *Snook*, 1964–1966; executive officer, USS *Long Beach*, 1967–1969; head of submarine and nuclear power distribution control branch, Bureau of Naval Personnel (BNP), Department of the Navy, Washington, 1969–1971; director of enlisted personnel division, BNP, 1971–1972; assistant chief of naval personnel for enlisted personnel control, BNP, 1972–1973; commander, Cruiser-Destroyer Group One, 1973–1975; deputy chief, naval operations manpower, 1975–1978; chief, BNP, 1975–1978; commander, U.S. Sixth Fleet, 1978–1979; promoted to admiral, 1979; vice-chief of naval operations, 1979–1981; commander-in-chief, U.S. Pacific Fleet, 1981–1982; appointed by President Ronald Reagan as chief of naval operations and member of the Joint Chiefs of Staff, 1982–1986, where he was an important advocate of Reagan's Strategic Defense Initiative, or "Star Wars" missile defense program; retired from navy on June 20, 1986; appointed by President Reagan as chairman of Presidential Commission on Acquired Immune Deficiency Syndrome (AIDS), 1987, where he helped focus national attention on the emerging epidemic of human immunodeficiency virus (HIV); appointed by President George H.W. Bush as SECRETARY OF ENERGY and served from March 9, 1989, until the end of Bush's term on January 20, 1993; major contributions include overseeing a program to clean up nuclear arms plants, the development of a comprehensive National Energy Strategy, and passage of Energy Policy Act of 1992; while in office, he weathered a scandal involving illegal spending at the Energy Department's nuclear weapons plants; president, Consortium for Oceanographic Research and Education, 1993– , and Joint Oceanographic Institution, 1993– ; director and chairman, Eurotech Ltd., 1998– ; recipient, Chairman's Award, American Association of Engineering Societies, 1991, and honorary degrees from Dowling College, 1983, Catholic University, 1985, New York Medical College, 1988, University of Alabama, 1991, Mt. Sinai School of Medicine, 1993, California University of Pennsylvania, 1994, and the College of William and Mary, 1999; decorated, Distinguished Service Medal with one gold star, Legion of Merit with two gold stars, Bronze Star medal with Combat V; member, Knights of Malta, U.S. Naval Academy Alumni Association. **References:** *Current Biography Yearbook 1989; Who's Who in America, 2000.*

—Edmund Wehrle

WATSON, William Marvin, Jr.

Born in Oakhurst, Tex., June 6, 1924; son of William Marvin Sr. and Lillie Mae (Anderson) Watson; married Marion Baugh; father of Winston Lee, Kimberly Baugh Watson Rathmann, and William Marvin III; graduated from Huntsville (Tex.) High School; B.A. in business administration, Baylor University, 1949, M.A. in economics, 1950; served from private to sergeant, U.S. Marine Corps, during World War II; instructor in economics, Baylor University; manager, Chamber of Commerce, Daingerfield, Tex., 1951–1954; Daingerfield city secretary, 1954, and city judge, 1956; executive assistant to the president, Lone Star Steel, Dallas and Daingerfield, 1956–1965; chairman, Texas state Democratic executive committee, 1964–1965; special assistant to President Lyndon Johnson and administrative chief of staff, 1965–1968; appointed POSTMASTER GENERAL by President Johnson and served from April 26, 1968, to January 20, 1969; co-owner, Watson Investments, Inc., 1969–1986; president and chief executive officer, Occidental International Corporation, 1969–1976; member, board of directors, Occidental Petroleum Corporation, 1971–1976, and executive vice-president for corporate affairs, 1972–1976; resigned after pleading guilty to helping Occidental chairman Armand Hammer cover up illegal contributions made to President Nixon's 1972 reelection campaign; co-owner, Wyatt C. Hendrick Corporation, 1972–1975, and owner, 1975– ; professor, president and chief executive officer, Dallas Baptist University, 1979–1987; president and chairman, board of directors, Independent Refinery group, 1979; vice-chairman, Mutuus Corporation, 2000; member, Texas State Democratic Executive Committee, 1958–1964, and chairman, 1964; director and coordinator, Democratic National Convention, Atlantic City, N.J., 1964, and Chicago, 1968; former member, Texas Civil Judicial Council, Texas Industrial Development Council, state board of directors, Texas United Fund, executive board, Texas Law Enforcement Foundation, governmental affairs committee, East Texas Chamber of Commerce and West Texas Chamber of Commerce, U.S. Chamber of Commerce, and government operations and management committee, U.S. Chamber of Commerce; chairman, Governor's Committee on Medicaid, 1977; former president, Alumni Association, Hankamer School of Business, Baylor University; member, board of directors, Matrix Energy, 1981–1985, Gold Crown Resources, 1981–1985, Xenerex Corporation, National Liberty Corporation, Friends of the LBJ Library, 1971– ; trustee, Mount Vernon College, 1967–1973, Barrington College, 1974–1976, Scott and White Memorial Hospital, and Scott, Sherwood and Brindley Foundation; former member, board of development, Hardin-Simmons University; member, Council for Institutional Development, Baylor University, 1972; member, school board, Daingerfield–Lone Star Independent School District, 1977; member, advisory council, Southwestern Baptist Theological Seminary, 1974– , Texas Baptist School Administrators Association, 1979– (president, 1985–1986), Association for Higher Education of North Texas, 1979– (president, 1986–1987); chairman, appeals committee, Southern Association of Colleges and Schools, 1986–1987, Private Schools and Universities Division, United Way of Metropolitan Dallas, 1980, and Public Schools Division, 1981–1982; secretary, Northeast Texas Municipal Water District, 1951, and president, 1953–1965; state vice-president, Red River Valley Association, Shreveport, La., 1955; chairman, Governor's Statewide Water Recreation Study Committee, 1964; member, Texas Water Development Council; former member, board of directors, Rose Capitol Bank, Central National Bank of Woodway-Hewitt, Sam Houston National Bank, East Texas National Bank; member, board of directors, Billy Graham Evangelistic Association, 1971– , World Impact Inc., 1974– (executive board, 1975–), World Wide Pictures Inc., 1974– (executive committee, 1974–1986), World Evangelism and Christian Education Fund, 1978– , Religious Heritage of America, 1980–1984, Foundation for Creative Television Programming, 1982– ; chief executive officer, Old-Time Gospel Hour, Jerry Falwell Ministries, 1979; vice-president and director, Dallas Council on World Affairs, 1980, first vice-president, 1981–1986, and president, 1986–1987; recipient of honorary degrees from Ouachita University, 1968, and Hardin-Simmons University, 1972. **References:** Rowland Evans and Robert Novak, *Lyndon B. Johnson: The Exercise of Power* (1965); Patrick Anderson, *The Presidents' Men* (1968); Ronnie Dugger, *Johnson: From Poverty to Power* (1968); *Who's Who in America, 1975–1976*.

WATT, James Gaius

Born in Lusk, Wyo., January 31, 1938; son of William G., attorney, and Lois M. (Williams) Watt, manager of the Globe Hotel in Wheatland, Wyo.; affiliated with the Assemblies of God; married Leilani Bomgardner, November 2, 1957; father of Erin Gaia and Eric Gaius; B.S., University of Wyoming, 1960, J.D., 1962; admitted to the Wyoming bar, 1962, and the bar of the U.S. Supreme Court, 1966; assistant counsel to Republican U.S. Senator Simpson of

Wyoming, 1962–1966; secretary to the Natural Resources Committee and Environmental Pollution Advisory Panel, U.S. Chamber of Commerce, 1966–1969; special assistant and consultant to former Alaska Governor Walter J. Hickel, 1968–1969; deputy assistant secretary with special responsibility for water and power development, U.S. Department of the Interior, 1969–1972; U.S. delegate, Economic Commission for Europe, Geneva, 1971; director, Bureau of Outdoor Recreation, Interior Department, 1972–1975; member and vice-chairman, Federal Power Commission, 1975–1977; president and chief legal officer, Mountain States Legal Foundation, Denver, Colo., 1977–1980; appointed by President Reagan as SECRETARY OF THE INTERIOR and served from January 23, 1981, until he resigned on November 8, 1983; chairman, Cabinet Council on Natural Resources and Environment and Advisory Commission of Intergovernment Relations; from the beginning of his tenure, Watt was embroiled in controversy; in February 1982, he was cited for contempt by the House Energy and Commerce Committee after he had invoked executive privilege in refusing to supply the committee with documents concerning Canadian energy policy; the charges were later dropped when the White House agreed to make the documents available to the committee; in July 1982, he went under fire because of a letter he had sent to the Israeli ambassador in Washington, warning that opposition by "liberal Jews" to the administration's energy policy could weaken the U.S.'s "ability to be a good friend to Israel"; angry reactions from Jewish leaders and members of Congress prompted Watt to issue an apology; business consultant, Washington, 1983–1986, Jackson Hole, Wyo., 1986– ; instructor, College of Commerce and Industry, University of Wyoming; chairman, board of directors, Environmental Diagnostics, 1984–1987, Disease Detection International, 1986–1990; sentenced to community service and a $5,000 fine after pleading guilty to attempting to influence a grand jury investigation of his lobbying activities, 1996; coauthor, with Doug Wead, of *The Courage of a Conservative* (1985); former editor, *Wyoming Law Journal*; member, Phi Kappa Phi, Delta Theta Phi. **References:** *New York Times* (December 23, 1980); *Current Biography Yearbook 1982; Who's Who in America, 1982–1983*; Jonathan Lasch, *Season of Spoils* (1984).

WEAVER, Robert Clifton

Born in Washington, D.C., December 29, 1907; son of Mortimer G., a postal clerk, and Florence (Freeman) Weaver; grandson of Robert Mortimer Freeman, a Harvard graduate and the first African American to earn a degree in dentistry; Methodist; married Ella V. Hiath (died 1991) on July 19, 1935; father of Robert (died 1962); attended schools in Washington; B.A. in economics, Harvard University, 1929, M.A., 1931, Ph.D., 1934; adviser on Negro affairs, Department of the Interior, 1933–1937, a member of President Franklin Roosevelt's "Black Cabinet"; special assistant to the administrator, U.S. Housing Authority, 1937–1940; administrative assistant, OPM, WPB, Washington, 1940–1944;

director, Negro Manpower Service, War Manpower Commission; visiting professor, Columbia Teacher's College, New York City, 1947, New York University School of Education, 1947–1949; director of opportunity fellowships, J.H. Whitney Foundation, 1949–1954; deputy commissioner, New York State Division of Housing, 1954–1955; rent administrator, state of New York, 1955–1959; consultant, Ford Foundation, 1959–1960; vice-chairman, Housing and Redevelopment Board of New York City, 1960–1961; administrator, Housing and Home Finance Agency, 1961–1966; appointed SECRETARY OF HOUSING AND URBAN DEVELOPMENT by President Lyndon Johnson and served from January 18, 1966, to December 3, 1968; most important contribution was lobbying for "demonstration cities" bill; the first African American to hold a cabinet position in a presidential administration; president, Bernard M. Baruch College, New York City, 1969–1970; distinguished professor of urban affairs, Hunter College, 1970–1978, distinguished professor emeritus, 1978–1997; became director, Urban Programs, Brookdale Center on Aging, Hunter College, 1978; president, National Commission against Discrimination in Housing, Inc., 1973–1987; executive secretary, Mayor's Commission on Race Relations, Chicago, 1944–1945; member, UN Relief and Rehabilitation Administration mission in Ukraine, 1946; chairman of the board, NAACP, 1960–1961, chairman emeritus, 1978–1997; member, board of directors, National Academy of Public Administration, 1969, Metropolitan Life Insurance Company, 1969–1980, Mount Sinai Hospital and Medical School, 1970–1997, board of overseers, School of Fine Arts, University of Pennsylvania, 1962; trustee, Bowery Savings Bank, 1969–1980; vice-chairman, New York State Temporary Commission on Powers of Local Governments, 1970–1973; member, New York City Conciliation and Appeals Board for rent control, 1973–1984, visiting commission of the Harvard University School of Design, 1978–1983, School of Urban and Public Affairs, Carnegie-Mellon University, 1984–1985; member, executive committee, board of directors, NAACP Legal Defense Fund, 1978–1997; recipient, Springarn medal, NAACP, 1962, Russwurm Award, 1963, Albert Einstein Commemorative Award, 1968, Merrick Moore Spaulding Achievement Award, 1968, Public Service award, U.S. General Accounting Office, 1975, Frederick Douglass award, New York City Urban League, 1977, M. Justice Herman Memorial award, National Association of Housing and Redevelopment Officials, 1986, Equal Opportunity Day award, National Urban League, 1987, and of honorary degrees from Harvard University, Temple University, Pratt Institute, Howard University, Morehouse College, Amherst College, Boston College, Rutgers University, Southern Illinois University, University of Michigan, University of Pennsylvania, University of Illinois, Duquesne University, and Columbia University; named to the National Association of Homebuilders Hall of Fame, 1982; author of *Negro Labor: A National Problem* (1946), *The Negro Ghetto* (1948), *The Urban Complex* (1964), and *The Dilemmas of Urban America* (1965); former fellow emeritus, American Academy of Arts and Sciences; former member, National Academy of Public Administration, Omega Psi Phi; died on July 17,

1997, at his home in Manhattan. **References:** Richard Bardolph, *The Negro Vanguard* (1959); *Current Biography Yearbook 1961*; Rowland Evans and Robert Novak, *Lyndon B. Johnson: The Exercise of Power* (1966); Hugh Sidey, *A Very Personal Presidency: Lyndon Johnson in the White House* (1968); Mark I. Gelfand, *A Nation of Cities: The Federal Government and Urban America, 1933–1965* (1975); Harvard Sitkoff, *A New Deal for Blacks: The Emergence of Civil Rights as a National Issue* (1978); *Who's Who in America, 1988–1989; New York Times* (July 19, 1997).

WEBSTER, Daniel

Born in Salisbury (now Franklin), N.H., January 18, 1782; son of Ebenezer, a militia captain in the Revolutionary War, state legislator, and farmer, and Abigail (Eastman) Webster; Presbyterian; married Grace Fletcher (died 1828) on May 29, 1808; father of Daniel Fletcher, Julia, Edward, who died while serving in the Mexican War, and two children who died in infancy, Grace Fletcher and Charles; married Caroline Le Roy on December 12, 1829; attended Phillips Academy, Exeter, N.H., 1796; graduated from Dartmouth College, 1801; taught school, Fryeburg (Me.) Academy, 1802; studied law in Salisbury and Boston, 1802–1805; admitted to the bar in Massachusetts, 1805, and New Hampshire, 1807; practiced law in Boscawen, Mass., 1805–1807, and Portsmouth, N.H., 1807–1813 and 1817–1822; became a leading Federalist during the War of 1812; argued before the U.S. Supreme Court and won the *Dartmouth College v. Woodward*, 1818–1819, *McCulloch v. Maryland*, 1819, and *Gibbons v. Ogden*, 1824, all of which strengthened the federal government's powers in the realm of commerce; Federalist member, U.S. House of Representatives, representing New Hampshire, 1813–1817, then Massachusetts, 1823–1827; member, Massachusetts General Court, 1822; member from Massachusetts, U.S. Senate, 1827–1841 and 1845–1850, as a Federalist to 1834, then as a Whig; one of the most prominent orators in U.S. history; argued against John C. Calhoun's theories on states' rights and nullification and defended the inviolability of the union in his debate with Senator Robert Hayne, 1830, denounced nullification during the sectional crisis over the tariff, 1832, opposed the expansion of slavery into western territories, and supported the Compromise of 1850; appointed SECRETARY OF STATE by President William Henry Harrison and took office on March 6, 1841, serving into the administration of President John Tyler, until May 8, 1843; negotiated the Webster-Ashburton Treaty, improving relations with Britain and establishing the boundary between Maine and Canada, 1842, and initiated diplomatic steps toward a commercial treaty with China, 1843; appointed to a second stint as SECRETARY OF STATE by President Millard Fillmore and served from July 23, 1850, until his death on October 24, 1852; supported Commodore Matthew Perry's mission to Japan, 1851–1852; delegate to Massachusetts state constitutional convention, 1820; director, Bank of the United States, 1827; unsuccessful candidate for the Whig nomination for president, 1848 and 1852; died on October 24, 1852, in Marshfield, Mass.; interment in Winslow Cemetery, Marshfield.

References: Howard Jones, *To the Webster-Ashburton Treaty: A Study in Anglo-American Relations, 1783–1843* (1977); Maurice G. Baxter, *One and Inseparable: Daniel Webster and the Union* (1984); Merrill Peterson, *The Great Triumvirate: Webster, Clay, and Calhoun* (1987); Elbert B. Smith, *The Presidencies of Zachary Taylor and Millard Fillmore* (1988); Norma Lois Peterson, *The Presidencies of William Henry Harrison and John Tyler* (1989); Kenneth Shewmaker, ed., *Daniel Webster: "The Completest Man"* (1990); Robert Remini, *Daniel Webster: The Man and His Times* (1997); Herman Belz, ed., *The Webster-Hayne Debate on the Nature of the Union* (2000).

—Jeffrey Coster

WEEKS, (Charles) Sinclair

Born in West Newton, Mass., June 15, 1893; son of John Wingate Weeks, secretary of war under Presidents Harding and Coolidge, and Martha Aroline (Sinclair) Weeks; married Beatrice Dowse on December 4, 1915; father of Frances Lee, John Wingate, Sinclair, Beatrice, and William Dowse; married Jane (Tompkins) Rankin on January 3, 1948; attended Newton public schools; received B.A. from Harvard University in 1914; served in World War I as lieutenant and later captain; lieutenant colonel in National Guard, 1918; vice-president, president, and later chairman of the board of Reed and Barton Corp., 1923–1953; president and chairman of the board of United Carr Fastener Corp., director of Gillette Safety Razor Co., Prellman Co., and First National Bank of Boston; served as alderman of Newton, 1923–1929; mayor of Newton, 1930–1935; chairman of Republican state committee, 1936–1938; member of national committee, 1940–1953; treasurer of Republican National Committee, 1941–1942; appointed U.S. senator from Massachusetts to fill seat vacated by Henry Cabot Lodge in February 1944, serving until December 1944; did not seek reelection to the vacancy; chairman of finance committee, 1949–1952; appointed SECRETARY OF COMMERCE in cabinet of President Eisenhower and served from January 21, 1953, to November 12, 1958; most important contributions were expansion of services of department while decreasing budget, increased interest and defense highways, largest peacetime shipbuilding program of merchant ships, increased safety of jet age travel; director of Wentworth Institute; trustee of Fessenden School in West Newton, Mass.; was director and honorary vice-president of National Association of Manufacturers; died on February 7, 1972. **References:** David A. Frier, *Conflict of Interest in the Eisenhower Administration* (1959); Dean Albertson, ed., *Eisenhower as President* (1963).

WEEKS, John Wingate

Born near Lancaster, N.H., April 11, 1860; son of William Dennis Weeks, farmer and county probate judge; married on October 7, 1885, to Martha A. Sinclair; father of Katherine and Charles Sinclair (secretary of commerce under

President Eisenhower); attended local schools; received appointment to the U.S. Naval Academy in 1877 and graduated in 1881; continued in the navy until 1883; engaged in land surveying in Florida and served as assistant land commissioner of the Florida Southern Railway until 1888; removed to Boston, Mass., and formed a banking and brokerage firm, Hornblower and Weeks; served in Massachusetts naval brigade, 1890–1900, and was commanding officer for last six years; lieutenant in the Volunteer Navy during Spanish-American War and later rear admiral in Massachusetts naval reserve; alderman of Newton, Mass., 1900–1902; elected mayor of Newton in 1903 and served for two terms; chairman of the Republican state convention, 1905; elected to Congress as a Republican from the 12th Massachusetts district and reelected four times, serving from 1905 until 1913; named to the U.S. Senate in 1913 by the Massachusetts legislature to succeed Winthrop Murray Chase and served until 1919; candidate for presidential nomination at the 1916 Republican National Convention; member of Republican National Committee in 1920 and a manager of the Harding presidential campaign; appointed SECRETARY OF WAR in the cabinet of President Harding on March 4, 1921, continuing under Coolidge until his resignation on October 13, 1925, due to ill health; most important contributions were contradicting charges of Brigadier Gen. William Mitchell concerning the adequacy of the nation's air defenses, putting into effect the National Defense Act of 1920, disposing of war equipment, and establishing in 1924 a National Defense Day; attacked Prohibition, women's suffrage, and the primary election system; died at Mount Prospect near Lancaster, N.H., on July 12, 1926; ashes interred in Arlington National Cemetery, Fort Myer, Va. **References:** Jacob Chapman, *Leonard Weeks and His Descendants* (1889); C.G. Washburn, *The Life of John W. Weeks* (1928); Samuel Hopkins Adams, *The Incredible Era* (1939); Donald R. McCoy, *Calvin Coolidge, the Quiet President* (1967).

WEINBERGER, Caspar Willard

Born in San Francisco, Calif., August 18, 1917; son of Herman and Cerise Carpenter (Hampson) Weinberger; Episcopalian; married Jane Dalton on August 16, 1942; father of Arlin Cerise and Caspar Willard; A.B. magna cum laude, Harvard University, 1938, LL.B., 1941; admitted to the bars of California, 1941, and the U.S. Supreme Court of Appeals, District of Columbia circuit, 1990; entered U.S. Army as private in 1941 and left the service as captain in 1945, serving in the Pacific Theater during World War II; law clerk, U.S. Judge William E. Orr, 1945–1947; attorney, Heller, Ehrman, White and McAuliffe, 1947–1969, as partner, 1959–1969; member, California state legislature, 1952–1958; vice-chairman, California Republican Central Committee, 1960–1962, and chairman, 1962–1964; chairman, Committee on California Government Organization and Economics, 1967–1968; director of finance, state of California, 1968–1969;

Caspar Weinberger (AP/Wide World Photos)

chairman, Federal Trade Commission, 1970; deputy director, Office of Management and Budget, 1970–1972, then director, 1972–1973; counselor to President Nixon, 1973; appointed SECRETARY OF HEALTH, EDUCATION, AND WELFARE by President Nixon and served from February 12, 1973, into the administration of President Ford, until he resigned, effective August 8, 1975; while HEW secretary, Congress blocked his proposed cuts in the department's programs; when Nixon created his "Super Cabinet" to oversee the actions of the ordinary cabinet, Weinberger joined Secretary of Housing and Urban Development James Lynn and Secretary of Agriculture Earl L. Butz as presidential counselors on human resources; general counsel, vice-president, and director, Bechtel Power Corp., Bechtel Inc., and Bechtel Corp., San Francisco, 1975–1980; appointed by President Reagan as SECRETARY OF DEFENSE and served from January 21, 1981, until he resigned, effective November 21, 1987, to spend more time with his wife, who was battling cancer; as defense secretary, pushed Congress for, and presided over, the largest peacetime military spending increase in U.S. history, advocated the strategic defense initiative (SDI, or "Star Wars") space-based missile-defense system, favored building up the U.S. nuclear arsenal and new weapons systems such as the MX missile and B-l bomber; also oversaw removal of U.S. troops from multinational peacekeeping force in Lebanon, 1983, invasion of Grenada, 1983, and air attacks on military targets in Libya, 1986; second longest tenure, behind Robert McNamara, of any defense secretary; sparred frequently with Secretary of State George Schultz over arms control policies; counsel, Rogers and Wells, Washington and New York, 1988–1994; chairman, Forbes Magazine, New York, 1989– ; in 1992, was indicted on charges of lying to Congress during the investigation of the "Iran-Contra" affair but was granted a full pardon by President George H.W. Bush in December 1992 before any trial could be held, all the while maintaining his innocence; moderator of weekly television program *Profile, Bay Area* and columnist, San Francisco, 1959–1968; cohost, *World Business Review*, 1996–1999; former chairman, President's Committee on Mental Retardation, 1973–1975; former member, Trilateral Commission, advisory council, American Ditchley Foundation; former treasurer, Episcopal Church Diocese of California; former member, board of directors, the J.F. Kennedy Center for the Performing Arts, San Francisco Symphony, Yosemite Institute, Chatham House Foundation, 1996; former trustee, St. Luke's Hospital, Mechanics Institute, Winston Churchill Memorial Trust, 1994; former chairman, national board of trustees, National Symphony, Washington; former chairman, USA-ROC Economic Council, 1991–1994; cochairman, Winston Churchill Travelling Fellowships Foundation, 1989–1999; decorated Bronze Star; recipient, Grand Cordon of Order of the Rising Sun, Government of Japan, Honor Knight Grand Cross Order of the British Empire, Order of Brilliant Star with Grand Cordon, Government of Taiwan, 1999, Presidential Medal of Freedom with distinction, 1987, Mérito First Class, Mexico, 1987, George Catlett Marshall medal, 1988, Civil award, Hilal-i-Pakistan, 1989, Keeper of the Flame award, Center for Security Policy, 1990, and honorary degrees from University of Leeds, England, University of Buckingham, Rennselear Polytechnic Institute, and University of San Francisco; editor, Harvard *Crimson*, 1937–1938; author of *Fighting for Peace: Seven Critical Years in the Pentagon* (1990); coauthor, with Peter Schweizer, of *The Next War* (1996); coauthor, with Gretchen Roberts, of *In the Arena: A Memoir of the Twentieth Century* (2002); member, American Bar Association, State Bar of California, District of Columbia Court of Appeals, Council on Foreign Relations, Century Club of New York, Pacific Union Club of San Francisco, and Harvard Club of Washington. **References:** *New York Times* (November 29, 1972; December 12, 1980; November 3, 4, and 6, 1987; March 1, 1988); *Time* (December 11, 1972; February 11, 1985); A. James Reichley, *Conservatives in an Age of Change: The Nixon and Ford Administrations* (1981); Lou Cannon, *President Reagan: The Role of a Lifetime* (1991); Michael Schaller, *Reckoning with Reagan: America and Its President in the 1980s* (1992); *National Review* (February 1, 1993); Lawrence E. Walsh, *Firewall: The Iran-Contra Conspiracy and Cover-up* (1997); *Who's Who in America, 2000*; Richard Reeves, *President Nixon: Alone in the White House* (2001).

WELLES, Gideon

Born in Glastonbury, Conn., July 1, 1802; son of Samuel and Ann (Hale) Welles; Episcopalian; married to Mary Jane Hale on June 16, 1835; father of nine children; attended the Episcopalian academy at Cheshire, Conn., 1819–1821, and the American Literary, Scientific, and Military Academy at Norwich, Vt., 1823–1825; studied law and was admitted to the bar in 1834; part owner and editor of the *Hartford Times*, 1826–1836; member of the Connecticut legislature, 1827–1835; elected state comptroller of public accounts in 1935, 1842, and 1843; appointed postmaster of Hartford by President Jackson in 1836 and served until 1841; chief of the Bureau of Provisions and Clothing for the U.S. Navy, 1846–1849; left the Democratic Party on the slavery issue and helped organize the Republican Party in 1855 when the Democrats supported the Kansas-Nebraska bill; helped establish and was a contributor to the *Hartford Evening Press*, a Republican organ, in 1856; member of the Republican National Committee and the National Executive Committee, 1856–1864; chairman of the Connecticut delegation to the Chicago convention of 1860; appointed SECRETARY OF THE NAVY in the cabinet of President Lincoln on March 5, 1861, and continued in that office in the cabinet of President Andrew Johnson, serving until March 3, 1869; most important contributions were reorganizing the navy upon the outbreak of the Civil War, sponsoring the construction of the first ironclad ships, supervising experiments in guns and naval tactics, ordering naval commanders to give protection to runaway slaves, issuing orders to enlist former slaves in the navy, and urging enlargement and modernization of navy yards after the war; in 1868 returned to the Democratic Party; became a Liberal Republican in 1872; author of a diary, several articles, and *Lincoln and Seward* (1874); died in Hartford, Conn., on February 11, 1878. **References:** J.C. Nicolay and John Hay, *Abraham Lincoln: A History*, vol. 3 (1897); Gideon Welles, *Diary of Gideon Welles* (1911); H.K. Beale, *The Critical Year: A Study of Andrew Johnson and Reconstruction* (1930); Noah Brooks, *Mr. Lincoln's Washington* (1967).

WEST, Roy Owen

Born in Georgetown, Ill., October 27, 1868; son of Pleasant and Helen Anna (Yapp) West; member of the Methodist Episcopal Church; married to Louisa Augustus on June 11, 1898, and upon her death, married Louise McWilliams on June 8, 1904; father of two children; after receiving his preliminary education in the public schools at Georgetown, he entered DePauw University, graduating in 1890; studied law and was admitted to the bar in 1890, commencing his practice in Chicago; became a leader in state and national Republican Party affairs; served as assistant attorney of Cook County in 1893; elected city attorney of Chicago from 1895 to 1897; elected a member of the Cook County board of review of assessments from 1898 to 1914; member of the Cook County Republican committee from 1900 to 1928; chairman of the Illinois Republican state central committee from 1904 to 1914; secretary of the Republican state central committee from 1924 to 1928; western treasurer of the Republican National Committee in 1928; delegate to the Republican National Convention in 1908, 1912, 1916, and 1928; appointed SECRETARY OF THE INTERIOR, *ad interim*, by President Calvin Coolidge on July 25, 1928; elevated to full cabinet status by President Coolidge on January 21, 1929, serving until March 3, 1929; became head of the national Republican Party, a conservative group, which opposed the progressive Republicans of 1932; alumni trustee of DePauw University in 1914; president of the board of trustees of DePauw University in 1928; special assistant to the U.S. attorney general in 1941, a position he held continuously until 1953; died in Chicago, Ill., on November 29, 1958. **References:** Edward Connery Latham, ed., *Meet Calvin Coolidge: The Man behind the Myth* (1960); Jules Abel, *In the Time of Silent Cal* (1969).

WEST, Togo Dennis, Jr.

Born in Winston-Salem, N.C., June 21, 1942; son of Togo Dennis Sr., a high school principal, and Evelyn (Carter) West; Episcopalian; married Gail Estelle Berry, attorney and former deputy assistant secretary of the U.S. Air Force, on June 18, 1966; father of Tiffany Berry and Hilary Carter; B.S. in electrical engineering, Howard University, 1965, and J.D. cum laude, 1968; admitted to the bars of District of Columbia, 1968, New York, 1969, U.S. Court of Military Appeals, 1969, U.S. Supreme Court, 1978, U.S. Court of Claims, 1981; served to captain, Judge Advocate General Corps and Office of the Assistant Secretary of the Army for Manpower and Reserve Affairs, U.S. Army, 1969–1973; electrical engineer, Duquesne Light and Power Company, 1965; patent researcher, Sughrue, Rothwell, Mion, Zinn and McPeak, 1966–1967; legal intern, U.S. Equal Employment Opportunity Commission, 1967; law clerk, Covington and Burling, Washington, 1967–1968, summer associate, 1968, associate, 1973–1975 and 1976–1977; law clerk, Judge Harold Tyler, U.S. District Court for Southern District of New York, 1968–1969; associate deputy attorney general, U.S. Department of Justice, 1975–1976; general counsel, U.S. Department of the Navy, 1977–1979, the first African American to hold that position; special assistant to secretary and deputy secretary, U.S. Department of Defense, 1979–1980, and general counsel, 1980–1981; managing partner, Patterson, Belknap, Webb and Tyler, Washington, 1981–1990; senior vice-president for government relations, Northrop Corporation, Arlington, Va., 1990–1993; U.S. secretary of the army, 1993–1998; appointed by President Clinton as SECRETARY OF VETERANS AFFAIRS and served from May 5, 1998, until the end of Clinton's second term on January 20, 2001; member, National Council of Friends of John F. Kennedy Center for the Performing Arts, 1984–1991 (treasurer, 1987–1991), D.C. Commission on Public Education, 1988–1993 (chairman, 1990–1991), national advisory committee, UN Association USA, 1991–1993; commissioner, D.C. Law Review Commission, 1982–1989 (chairman, 1985–1989); member, board of governors, Antioch University School of Law, 1983–1987 (vice-chairman, 1986–1987), board of visitors, Wake Forest University School of Law, 1991–1994; chairman, Greater Washington Board of Trade, and member, legislative bureau, 1987–1989, board of directors, 1987–1993, executive committee, 1987–1992, federal legislative committee, 1990–1993; chairman, Kennedy Center Community and Friends Board, 1991; trustee, The Aerospace Corporation, 1983–1990, Center for Strategic and International Studies, 1987–1990, National Lawyers Commission for Civil Rights under Law, 1987–1993, Institute for Defense Analyses, 1989–1991, Protestant Episcopal Cathedral Foundation, 1989, Shakespeare Theatre at The Folger, 1990–1993, North Carolina School of Arts, 1990, Aerospace Education Foundation of Air Force Association, 1991–1993; member, board of directors, D.C. Law Students in Court Program, 1986–1992, World Affairs Council, 1991–1993, Atlantic Council,

1991–1993; member, finance committee, Episcopal Diocese of Washington, 1989, and standing committee, 1990–1992; senior warden, St. John's Church, Lafayette Square, Washington; chairman, trustee council, YMCA of Metropolitan Washington, 1990–1992; D.C. Court of Appeals Admissions Committee, 1990–1993; adjunct professor, Duke University School of Law, 1980–1981; member, board of consultants, Riggs National Bank, Washington, 1990–1993; chairman, Panama Canal Commission, 1997; decorated Legion of Merit; recipient, Eagle Scout award with Bronze Palm, Boy Scouts of America, 1957, Service to Howard University award, 1965, Distinguished Public Service medal, Department of Defense, 1981, Distinguished Eagle Scout award, 1995, and honorary degrees from Winston-Salem University, 1996, and Gannon University, 1998; managing editor, *Howard Law Journal*, 1968; member, American Bar Association, National Bar Association, Washington Council of Lawyers (director, 1973–1975), Sigma Pi Phi, Phi Alpha Delta, Omega Psi Psi, Alpha Phi Omega. **References:** *New York Times* (September 18, 1993; May 29, 1994); *Washington Post* (November 22–23, 1996); *Howard University 2000 Alumni Directory; Who's Who among African-Americans, 2000; Department of Veterans Affairs* (2001).

—Herbert Brewer

WHEELER, William Almon

Born in Malone, N.Y., June 30, 1819; son of Almon Wheeler, lawyer, and Eliza (Woodworth) Wheeler; Presbyterian; married Mary King on September 17, 1845; no children; attended Franklin Academy; taught school; attended the University of Vermont, 1838–1840; studied law in Malone, 1840–1844, and admitted to the bar in 1845; while studying law was elected town clerk, then appointed school commissioner and school inspector; elected district attorney, serving from 1846 to 1849; member of the State Assembly in 1850 and 1851; appointed trustee for mortgage holders of the Northern Railway, 1853; state senator and president *pro tempore* of the state senate, 1858–1860; elected as a Republican from New York to the 37th Congress, serving from March 4, 1861, to March 3, 1863; president of the state constitutional conventions in 1867 and 1868; elected to the 41st through 44th Congresses, serving from March 4, 1869, to March 3, 1877; nominated as the Republican candidate for vice-president in 1876; elected VICE-PRESIDENT in 1876 under President Hayes and took the oath of office on March 5, 1877; left office with the outgoing administration on March 3, 1881; retired from public life and active business pursuits due to ill health; died in Malone, N.Y., June 4, 1887; interment in Morningside Cemetery. **References:** A.G. Wheeler, *The Genealogical and Encyclopedic History of the Wheeler Family in America* (1914); C.R. Williams, ed., *Diary and Letters of Rutherford Birchard Hayes*, vols. 3 (1924) and 4 (1925); E.P. Myers, *Rutherford B. Hayes* (1969).

WHITING, William Fairfield

Born at Holyoke, Mass., July 20, 1864; son of William Whiting, U.S. congressman (1883–1889) and paper manufacturer, and Anne Maria (Fairfield) Whiting; Congregationalist; married to Anne Chapin on October 19, 1892; father of William, Edward, Fairfield, and Ruth; attended the Holyoke schools and Williston Academy, Easthampton, Mass.; graduated from Amherst College in 1886; worked in father's paper business; served as president of the Whiting Paper Company, 1911–1928; delegate to the Republican National Conventions of 1920, 1924, 1928, and 1932; appointed SECRETARY OF COMMERCE in the cabinet of President Coolidge on August 21, 1928, to fill the vacancy caused by the resignation of Herbert Hoover; served until the end of the Coolidge administration, March 3, 1929; in this post, he served as chairman of the U.S. section, Inter-American High Commission; member of the Federal Narcotics Control Board, the Federal Oil Conservation Board, the U.S. Council of National Defense, the National Board for Vocational Education, and the Foreign Service Buildings Commission; died on August 31, 1936; interment in Holyoke, Mass. **References:** Donald R. McCoy, *Calvin Coolidge* (1967); Jules Abel, *In the Time of Silent Cal* (1969).

WHITNEY, William Collins

Born in Conway, Mass., July 5, 1841; son of Brigadier General James Scollay and Laurinda (Collins) Whitney; married Flora Payne on October 13, 1869, and after her death, married Mrs. Edith Sibyl (May) Randolph sometime between 1893 and 1899; father of four children; after being educated by private tutors, he entered Yale, graduating in 1863; attended Harvard Law School in 1863 and 1864 and was admitted to the bar in 1865; took part in the action against the "Tweed Ring" in New York City; became corporation counsel in New York City, 1875–1882; supported Grover Cleveland in 1884 and was subsequently appointed SECRETARY OF THE NAVY by President Cleveland, serving from March 6, 1885, to March 4, 1889; during his incumbency, he inaugurated the Naval War College at Newport, R.I.; supported Cleveland again in 1892; fought free silver ideology at the Democratic convention of 1896; declined to accept further public office; became a horse-breeder in Lexington, Ky., operating a racing stable in 1898; director of Consolidated Gas Co. of New York, Fifth Avenue Trust Co., and Mutual Life Insurance Co. of New York; author of *The Whitney Stud* (1902); died in New York City, February 2, 1902. **References:** Horace Samuel Merrill, *Bourbon Leader: Grover Cleveland and the Democratic Party* (1957); Allan Nevins, *Grover Cleveland, a Study in Courage* (1932).

WICKARD, Claude Raymond

Born on a farm in Carroll County, Ind., February 28, 1893; son of Andrew Jackson and Iva Lenora (Kirkpatrick) Wickard; member of the United Brethren

Church; married to Louise Eckert in 1918; father of Betty Jane and Ann Louise; was graduated from the agricultural college of Purdue University in 1915; elected to the Indiana Senate, 1932; gave up his office to work for the Agricultural Adjustment Administration in 1933, becoming chief of its corn-hog section; also served as assistant director of the administration's central division in 1937 and as its director from 1937 to 1940; undersecretary of agriculture from February to August 1940; appointed SECRETARY OF AGRICULTURE in the cabinet of President Franklin Roosevelt on August 27, 1940, and continued under President Truman, serving until June 2, 1945; most important contributions were offering many proposals for conservation and restoration of farm and forests to be put into effect after the war and urging that the United States develop export markets for its agricultural products while retaining price supports; administrator of the Rural Electrification Administration under President Truman, 1945–1953; headed an executive committee of farmers supporting Senator John. F. Kennedy in the 1960 presidential election; member of the Indiana Farm Bureau Federation and the national Farm Bureau Federation; received Master Farmer of Indiana award; killed in an automobile accident in Delphi, Ind., on April 29, 1967; interment in Deer Creek, Ind. **References:** Dean Albertson, *Roosevelt's Farmer: Claude R. Wickard in the New Deal* (1961); A.J. Wann, *President as Chief Administrator: A Study of Franklin D. Roosevelt* (1968).

WICKERSHAM, George

Born in Pittsburgh, Pa., September 19, 1858; son of Samuel Morris Wickersham, inventor in the iron and steel industry, and Elizabeth Cox (Woodward) Wickersham; Quaker as a youth but later Episcopalian; married Mildred Wendell on September 19, 1883; father of Cornelius Wendell, Mildred, Gwendolyn, and Constance; studied civil engineering at Lehigh University, 1873–1875; studied law at the University of Pennsylvania, graduating in 1880; admitted to the bar in 1880 and began practice in Philadelphia; editor of "The Weekly Notes of Cases" of Pennsylvania; moved to New York City in 1882; became managing clerk in the law firm of Strong and Cadwallader in 1883 and became a partner in 1887; appointed ATTORNEY GENERAL in the cabinet of President Taft on March 5, 1909, serving until March 5, 1913; most important contributions were initiating many suits against monopolistic practices of corporations, proposing the creation of a body similar to the Interstate Commerce Commission, drawing up the original draft of the Mann-Elkins Railroad Act (1910), and assisting with the corporation tax provision in the Payne-Aldrich Tariff Act; retired with the outgoing administration and resumed law practice; floor leader of the New York State Constitutional Convention in 1915 and chairman of the judiciary committee; commissioner of the War Trade Board to Cuba, August–September 1918, by appointment of President Wilson; special correspondent for the *New York Tribune* in Paris, 1919, to cover the Peace Conference; American member of the League of Nations committee to codify international law; president of the international arbitral tribunal under the Young Plan; president of the American Law Institute; member of the commission for the reorganization of the New York State government, 1925; appointed head of the National Commission on Law Observance and Enforcement by President Hoover in 1929; author of *The Changing Order* (1914) and *Some Legal Phases of Corporate Financing, Re-organization and Regulation* (1917); died in New York City, January 26, 1936; interment in Rockside Cemetery, Englewood, N.J. **References:** Robert C. McManus, "Unhappy Warrior: A Portrait of George Wickersham," *Outlook and Independent* (September 17, 1930); Henry F. Pringle, *The Life and Times of William H. Taft* (1939); Norman M. Wilensky, *Conservatives in the Progressive Era* (1965).

WICKLIFFE, Charles Anderson

Born near Springfield, Ky., June 8, 1788; son of Charles and Lydia (Hardin) Wickliffe; married Margaret Crepps in 1813; father of eight children; after completing preparatory education, studied law and was admitted to the bar in 1809, commencing practice in Bardstown, Ky.; served in the War of 1812; elected to the Kentucky House of Representatives in 1812 and 1813; again entered the army as an aide to General Caldwell; reelected to the state legislature in 1822, 1823, 1833, and 1835, serving as speaker of the House in 1834; elected as a Democrat to the 18th through 22d Congresses, serving in all from March 4, 1823, to March 3, 1833; chosen to conduct impeachment proceedings against Judge James H. Peck, 1830; elected lieutenant governor of Kentucky in 1836 and, upon the death of Governor Clark, succeeded to the governorship, serving from March 5, 1839, to September 1840; invited to join the cabinet of President Tyler as POSTMASTER GENERAL on September 13, 1841, entering upon his duties on October 13, 1841, and serving until March 6, 1845; was the first postmaster general to appoint a woman to office in the postal service; sent on a secret mission by President Polk to the Republic of Texas in 1845, in connection with the annexation of Texas to the Union; delegate to the Kentucky constitutional convention in 1849; member of the Peace Conference of 1861; opposed the movement for the secession of Kentucky in 1861; elected as a Union Whig to the 37th Congress, serving from March 4, 1861, to March 3, 1863; delegate to the Democratic National Convention at Chicago in 1864; died near Ilchester, Md., October 31, 1869; interment in Bardstown Cemetery, Bardstown, Ky. **References:** Charles Allan McCoy, *Polk and the Presidency* (1960); Robert Seager, *And Tyler Too: A Biography* (1963).

WILBUR, Curtis Dwight

Born in Boonesboro, Iowa, May 10, 1867; son of Dwight Locke and Edna Maria (Lyman) Wilbur; brother of Ray Lyman Wilbur, secretary of the interior under Hoover; Congregationalist; married to Ella T. Chilson on November 9,

1893, and upon her death to Olive Doolittle on January 13, 1898; father of Edna May, Lyman Dwight, Paul Curtis, and Leonard Fiske; after completing his preliminary and secondary education at rural schools, he entered the U.S. Naval Academy at Annapolis, graduating in 1888; resigned his commission and moved to Los Angeles, Calif.; studied law and was admitted to the bar in 1890; designated chief deputy district attorney of Los Angeles County, serving from 1899 to 1903; appointed judge of the Superior Court of California, serving from 1919 to 1921; became chief justice of the Supreme Court of California in 1922, serving until his resignation in 1927; joined the Coolidge cabinet as SECRETARY OF THE NAVY on March 18, 1924, serving until March 4, 1929; during his secretaryship he advocated a larger navy and greater use of heavier-than-air craft; judge of the 9th U.S. Circuit Court of Appeals in 1929; senior circuit judge from 1931 to 1945, when he retired to his estate. "Pine Lane," Los Altos, Calif.; organized the Juvenile Court of Los Angeles and drafted several juvenile laws in California; died in Los Altos on September 8, 1954. **References:** Edward Latham, ed., *Meet Calvin Coolidge: The Man behind the Myth* (1960); Jules Abel, *In the Time of Silent Cal* (1969).

WILBUR, Ray Lyman

Born in Boonesboro, Iowa, April 13, 1875; son of Dwight Locke and Edna Maria (Lyman) Wilbur; brother of Curtis Dwight, secretary of the navy under Coolidge; Congregationalist: married Marguerite May Blake on December 5, 1898; father of three sons; moved to California, where he graduated from Riverside High School in 1892; attended Stanford University, earning his B.A. in 1896 and his M.A. in 1897; received his M.D. from Cooper Medical College in 1899; served as dean of the Stanford University medical school, 1911–1916; served as president of Stanford University, 1916–1943; elected lifetime chancellor of Stanford in 1943; served as chief of the Conservation Division of the Food Administration in 1917; U.S. delegate to the 6th Pan-American Congress in Havana in 1928; headed committee on the costs of medical care, 1928; appointed SECRETARY OF THE INTERIOR by President Hoover, serving from March 5, 1929, to March 4, 1933; accomplishments include announcement that no new leases for naval oil reserves would be awarded, the allocation of 36 percent of the power of the projected Hoover Dam to Arizona and 64 percent to California for the period 1930–1980, advocating the return of public land to state control, reorganization of Indian Affairs favoring freedom from the restriction of reservation life in order to foster a more self-supporting citizenry; served as chairman of the White House Conferences on Child Health and Protection, 1929–1931; served as cochairman of the Conference on Home Building and Home Ownership, 1931; chairman of the National Advisory Commission on Illiteracy, 1930–1931; chairman of the federal Oil Conservation Board, 1929–1933; elected president of the American Social Hygiene Association, 1936; received the Dr. William F. Snow medal for distinguished service to humanity, 1943; returned to Stanford University to continue work in the field of medicine; died on June 26, 1949, in Stanford, Calif. **References:** A. Guerard, "Ray Lyman Wilbur," *Nation* (June 30, 1949); Edgar Eugene Robinson and Paul Carrol Edwards, eds., *Ray Lyman Wilbur* (1960).

WILKINS, William

Born in Carlisle, Pa., December 20, 1779; son of John and Catherine (Rowan) Wilkins; married to Catherine Holmes in 1815 and, after her death, to Matilda Dallas on October 1, 1818; father of four daughters and three sons; after attending the local schools, he entered Dickinson College in Carlisle; studied law and was admitted to the bar on December 28, 1801, commencing the practice of law in Pittsburgh; president of the Pittsburgh Common Council, 1816–1819; elected to the Pennsylvania House of Representatives in 1820, resigning on December 18, 1820; president judge of the 5th judicial district of Pennsylvania, 1821–1824; judge of the U.S. district court for western Pennsylvania, 1824–1831; elected to the 21st Congress but resigned before qualifying; elected as a Democrat and Anti-Mason to the U.S. Senate, serving from March 4, 1831, to June 30, 1834, when he resigned upon being tendered a diplomatic post; appointed U.S. minister to Russia, serving from June 1834 to December 1835; received the Pennsylvania electoral vote for vice-president in 1833; elected as a Democrat to the 28th Congress, serving from March 4, 1843, to February 14, 1844, when he resigned to accept a cabinet portfolio; appointed SECRETARY OF WAR by President Tyler on February 14, 1844, entering upon his duties on February 20, 1844, and serving until March 6, 1845; Pennsylvania state senator, 1855–1857; major general of the Pennsylvania Home Guards in 1862; one of the founders and first president of the Bank of Pittsburgh; died at "Homewood," near Pittsburgh, Pa., June 23, 1865; interment in Homewood Cemetery, Wilkinsburgh, Pa. **References:** Robert J. Morgan, *A Whig Embattled: The Presidency under John Tyler* (1954); Oliver Perry Chitwood, *John Tyler, Champion of the Old South* (1964).

WILLIAMS, George Henry

Born in New Lebanon, N.Y., March 23, 1823; son of Taber and Lydia (Goodrich) Williams; Episcopalian; married to Kate Van Antwerp in 1850 and, after her death, to Kate (Hughes) George in 1867; father of one daughter and two adopted children; attended the district schools and Pompey Academy at Pompey Hills, N.Y., until the age of 17; studied law and was admitted to the bar in 1844; moved to Iowa Territory and commenced the practice of law in Fort Madison in 1844; after the admission of Iowa to the Union, he was elected a district judge, serving from 1847 to 1852; presidential elector on the Democratic ticket of Pierce and King, 1852; appointed chief justice of the Oregon Territory by President Pierce, 1853–1857; member of the state constitutional convention of Oregon in 1858; elected as a Union Republican to the U.S. Senate, serving from March 4, 1865, to March 3, 1871; voted "guilty" in the impeachment trial of President Andrew Johnson; appointed a member of the Joint High Commission in February 1871, which negotiated the Treaty of Washington with Great Britain; invited to join the cabinet as ATTORNEY GENERAL by President Grant on December 14, 1871, entering upon his duties on January 10, 1872, and serving until May 15, 1875; nominated as chief justice of the U.S. Supreme Court by President Grant but asked that his name be withdrawn in face of protest from the opposition; twice elected mayor of Portland, Ore., serving from 1902 to 1905; president of Boys' and Girls' Aid Society and of the Patton Home for the Aged; died in Portland, Ore., April 4, 1910; interment in Riverview Cemetery, Portland. **Reference:** William Best Hesseltine, *Ulysses S. Grant, Politician* (1957).

WILSON, Charles Erwin

Born in Minerva, Ohio, July 18, 1890; son of Thomas E. Wilson, principal of a local school, and Rosilynd (Unkfer) Wilson; married Jessie Ann Curtis in 1912; father of Edward, Thomas Erwin, Charles Erwin Jr., and three daughters; moved to Mineral City with family at the age of four; graduated Carnegie Institute of Technology in 1909; worked for Westinghouse Corp. and designed first motor for auto starters; went to Washington on a series of special assignments for army, navy, and air corps during World War I; became chief engineer for Remy Electric Co.; moved to Detroit, 1919, and later to Anderson, Ind.; became president of Delco-Remy Corp., 1926; vice-president of General Motors Corp., 1929–1939; appointed SECRETARY OF DEFENSE in the cabinet of President Eisenhower and served from January 28, 1953, to October 8, 1957; most important contributions were narrow-base defense plans; returned to business interests; member of board of trustees of General Motors; chairman of Michigan advisory committee to U.S. Commission of Civil Rights; died in Norwood, La., on September 26, 1961; interment in Acadia Park Cemetery. **References:** Dean Albertson, ed., *Eisenhower as President* (1963); Carl W. Borklund, *Men of the Pentagon* (1966).

WILSON, Henry

Born in Farmington, N.H., February 16, 1812; son of Winthrop and Abigail (Witham) Colbaith; originally named Jeremiah Jones Colbaith, he changed his name legally upon attaining his majority; Congregationalist; married Harriet Malvina Howe in 1840; father of one son; attended the common schools; soon after his tenth birthday, he was bound by indenture to work for a neighboring farmer; moved to Natick, Mass., in 1833, where he learned the shoemaker's trade; traveled through the South in 1836; returned to New Hampshire where he attended the Strafford, Wolfsboro, and Concord Academies for short periods;

taught school in Natick; elected to the Massachusetts House of Representatives in 1841 and 1842; served in the state senate, 1844–1846 and 1850–1852; delegate to the Whig convention in Philadelphia in 1848 but withdrew from the party upon its rejection of the antislavery resolutions; owner and editor of the *Boston Republican*, 1848–1851; delegate to the Free Soil convention in Pittsburgh, 1852; delegate to the state constitutional convention in 1852; elected to the U.S. Senate in 1854 and reelected in 1859, 1865, and 1871, serving from January 31, 1855, to March 3, 1873; elected VICE-PRESIDENT under President Grant, serving from March 4, 1873, until his death; authored *History of the Anti-Slavery Measures of the Thirty-seventh and Thirty-eighth United States Congresses* (1864), *History of the Reconstruction Measures of the Thirty-ninth and Fortieth Congress* (1868), and *History of the Rise and Fall of the Slave Power in America* (3 vols., 1872–1877); died in Washington, D.C., November 22, 1875; interment in Old Dell Park Cemetery, Natick, Mass. **References:** Louis Arthur Coolidge, *Ulysses S. Grant* (1917); William Best Hesseltine, *Ulysses S. Grant, Politician* (1957).

WILSON, James

Born on a farm in Ayrshire, Scotland, August 16, 1835; son of John and Jean (McCosh) Wilson; married Esther Wilbur on May 7, 1863; father of eight children; immigrated to the United States in 1852, settling in Norwich, Conn.; moved to Iowa in 1855, locating in Traer, Tama County; attended the public schools and Grinnell College, Grinnell, Iowa; engaged in agricultural pursuits; taught school; elected to the Iowa House of Representatives from 1867 to 1871, serving as speaker in 1870 and 1871; designated regent of the State University from 1870 to 1874; elected as a representative on the Republican ticket to the 43d and 44th Congresses, serving in all from March 4, 1873, until March 3, 1877; member of the Iowa Railway Commission from 1878 to 1883; presented credentials as a member-elect to the 48th Congress and served from March 4, 1883, until March 3, 1885; director of the Agricultural Experiment Station and professor of agriculture at the Iowa Agricultural College at Ames, Iowa, from 1891 to 1897; invited to join the cabinet as SECRETARY OF AGRICULTURE by President McKinley on March 5, 1897, and subsequently retained in that capacity by President Theodore Roosevelt and President Taft, serving for 16 years, until March 3, 1913; during his incumbency, the department extended its activities into many fields: experiment stations were established in all parts of the United States, farm demonstration work was inaugurated in the South, cooperative extension work in agriculture and home economics was begun, experts and scientists were enlisted to obtain information from all over the world for the promotion of agriculture; editor of the *Agricultural Digest*; died in Traer, Iowa, on August 26, 1920; interment in Buckingham Cemetery, Buckingham, Iowa. **References:** William Henry Harbaugh, *Power and Responsibility: The Life and Times of Theodore Roosevelt* (1961); Norman M. Wilensky, *Conservatives in the Progressive Era: The Taft Republicans of 1912* (1965).

WILSON, (Thomas) Woodrow

Born in Staunton, Va., December 28, 1856; son of Joseph Ruggles, a minister and chief executive of the Southern Presbyterian Church, and Janet ("Jessie") Woodrow Wilson; Presbyterian; married Ellen Louise Axson (1860–1914) on June 24, 1885; father of Margaret Woodrow, Jessie Woodrow (Mrs. Francis B. Sayre), and Eleanor Randolph (Mrs. William G. McAdoo); married Edith Bolling Galt (1872–1961) on December 18, 1915; raised and educated in Augusta, Ga., and Columbia, S.C.; attended Davidson College, 1873–1874, withdrawing for health reasons; B.A., College of New Jersey (now Princeton University), 1879, where he was managing editor of the daily *Princetonian*; graduated from University of Virginia Law School, 1881; Ph.D. in political science, Johns Hopkins University, 1886; admitted to the bar in Georgia, 1882; partner in law practice, Atlanta, 1882–1883; professor of history and political science, Bryn Mawr College, 1885–1988, and Wesleyan University, 1888–1890; an important theme in his early scholarship was a critique of the relative powerlessness of the U.S. federal executive branch compared to the British system; professor and chairman of department of jurisprudence and political economy, Princeton University, 1890–1902, and university president, 1902–1910, where he reorganized the structure of academic and social life based on the model of the English university system; Democratic governor of New Jersey, 1911–1913, earning a national reputation as a progressive; at the Democratic National Convention in Baltimore in 1912 was a compromise candidate nominated on the forty-sixth ballot to head the presidential ticket; he chose Indiana Governor Thomas R. Marshall as his running mate and was elected the twentieth-eighth PRESIDENT OF THE UNITED STATES by winning 41.9 percent of the popular vote and 435 electoral votes in a four-person race, defeating Progressive Party candidate Theodore Roosevelt, Republican William H. Taft, and Socialist Eugene V. Debs; inaugurated on March 4, 1913; won reelection in 1916, defeating Republican challenger Charles E. Hughes with 49.4 percent of the popular vote and 277 electoral votes; while president, he promoted tariff reductions, antitrust legislation, and the creation of the Federal Reserve System, 1913, and the Federal Trade Commission, 1914; cam-

Woodrow Wilson (Library of Congress)

paigned for reelection on the slogan "He kept us out of war" but requested and received a congressional declaration of war in April 1917 in response to over two years of German violations of American neutrality and unrestricted submarine warfare; created and led a "war cabinet" of chairs of central committees charged with mobilizing and coordinating resources for the war effort, including food, shipping, industrial production, labor, and public information; after the November 11, 1918, armistice, led a U.S. delegation to the Peace Conference, where he put forth his Fourteen Points program, calling for "peace without victory" and the establishment of a League of Nations; suffered a great personal and political defeat when the Republican-led U.S. Senate refused to ratify the Treaty of Versailles in November 1919; suffered a severe stroke that left him paralyzed and partially brain damaged in late 1919; after two full terms, he left office on March 4, 1921; formed a law practice with his former secretary of state, Bainbridge Colby, but his physical condition permitted little activity, and he lived in retirement in Washington, D.C., in the early 1920s; author of *Congressional Government* (1885), *The State* (1889), *Division and Reunion, 1829–1889* (1893), *An Old Master and Other Political Essays* (1893), *George Washington* (1896), *History of the American People* (5 vols., 1902), and *Constitutional Government in the United States* (1908); recipient of the Nobel Peace Prize, 1919; died on February 3, 1924, in Washington, D.C.; interment in the National Cathedral, Washington. **References:** Edith Bolling Wilson, *My Memoir* (1918); Ray Stannard Baker, *Woodrow Wilson: Life and Letters*, 8 vols. (1927–1939); Arthur S. Link, *Wilson*, 5 vols. (1947–1965); Arthur S. Link et al., eds., *The Papers of Woodrow Wilson*, 69 vols. (1966–1993); John Milton Cooper, *The Warrior and the Priest: Woodrow Wilson and Theodore Roosevelt* (1983), *Pivotal Decades: The United States, 1900–1920* (1990), and *Breaking the Heart of the World: Woodrow Wilson and the Fight for the League of Nations* (2001); Kendrick Clements, *Woodrow Wilson: World Statesman* (1987, 1999) and *The Presidency of Woodrow Wilson* (1992); August Hecksher, *Woodrow Wilson* (1991); Louis Auchincloss, *Woodrow Wilson* (2000).

—Jeffrey Coster

WILSON, William Bauchop

Born in Blantyre, Scotland, on April 2, 1862; son of Adam Wilson, miner; married on June 7, 1883, to Agnes Williamson; father of 11 children; emigrated with his parents to Arnot, Pa., in 1870; attended the common schools until the age of nine, when he began work in Pennsylvania coal mines; president of the district miners' union, 1888–1890; member of the national executive board of the miners' union that organized the United Mine Workers of America in 1890; secretary-treasurer of that body from 1900 until 1908 and was prominently connected with coal strikes of 1899 and 1902; appointed member of a Pennsylvania commission in 1891 to revise state laws relating to coal mining; elected to the 60th Congress and served three successive terms from 1907 to 1913; appointed the first SECRETARY OF LABOR on March 5, 1913, in the cabinet of President Wilson; most important contributions were reorganization of the Bureau of Immigration and Naturalization, the development of agencies to mediate in industrial disputes, and the formation of the U.S. Employment Service to handle the problems of wartime employment and transfer of workers; resigned with outgoing administration on March 5, 1921; during World War I, member of the Council for National Defense; president of the International Labor Conference, 1919; member, Federal Board for Vocational Education, 1914–1921, and chairman, 1920–1921; appointed member of the International Joint Commission, 1921; engaged in mining and agricultural pursuits near Blossburg, Pa.; died on a train near Savannah, Ga., on May 25, 1934; interment in Arbon Cemetery, Blossburg, Pa. **References:** Chris Evans, *History of the United Mine Workers of America*, 2 vols. (1918, 1920); R.W. Babson, *William B. Wilson and the Department of Labor* (1919); Ray Stannard Baker, *Woodrow Wilson, Life and Letters–President, 1913–1914* (1931); Arthur S. Link, *Woodrow Wilson: The New Freedom* (1956).

WILSON, William Lyne

Born at Middleway, Jefferson County, Va. (now W.Va.), May 3, 1843; son of Benjamin and Mary Whiting (Lyne) Wilson; married Nannine Huntington on August 6, 1868; father of six children; attended Charles Town Academy and then entered Columbian College (now George Washington University), Washington, D.C., graduating in 1860; also studied at the University of Virginia at Charlottesville; served in the Confederate army as a private during the Civil War, in the 12th Virginia Cavalry; taught for several years at Columbian College, during which time he was graduated from its school; was admitted to the bar in 1869 and commenced the practice of law in Charles Town, W.Va.; delegate to the Democratic National Convention at Cincinnati in 1880; presidential elector on the Democratic ticket of Hancock and English in 1880; elected president of the University of West Virginia, at Morgantown, in 1882; elected as a Democrat to the 48th Congress and to the five succeeding Congresses, serving from March 4, 1883, until March 3, 1895; invited to join the cabinet as POST-MASTER GENERAL by President Cleveland, serving from April 4, 1895, until March 5, 1897; during his secretaryship inaugurated the rural free delivery and enlarged the classified civil service; president of Washington and Lee University, Lexington, Va.; permanent chairman of the Democratic National Convention in 1892; died in Lexington, Va., on October 17, 1900; interment in Edgehill Cemetery, Charles Town, W.Va. **References:** Allan Nevins, *Grover Cleveland: A Study in Courage* (1932); Horace Samuel Merrill, *Bourbon Leader: Grover Cleveland and the Democratic Party* (1957).

WINDOM, William

Born in Belmont County, Ohio, May 10, 1827; son of Hezekiah and Mary (Spencer) Windom; Quaker; married Ellen P. Hatch on August 20, 1856; father of three children; pursued an academic course at Martinsburg, Ohio, and at the academy at Mount Vernon, Ohio; studied law and was admitted to the bar in 1850, commencing the practice of his profession in Mount Vernon; elected prosecuting attorney of Knox County in 1852, on the Whig ticket; moved to Winona, Minn., in 1855; elected as a Republican to the 36th through 40th Congresses, serving from March 4, 1859, until March 3, 1869; appointed to the U.S. Senate to fill a vacancy, serving from July 15, 1870, to January 22, 1871; popularly elected to full six-year term in the Senate in 1871 and was reelected in 1877, serving until March 7, 1881, when he resigned to accept a cabinet portfolio; appointed SECRETARY OF THE TREASURY by President Garfield on March 5, 1881, entered upon his duties on March 8, 1881, and was continued in office by President Arthur, serving until he resigned on November 14, 1881, having been reelected U.S. senator on October 26, 1881; served from November 15, 1881, until March 3, 1883; moved to New York City where he resumed the practice of law; invited to join the cabinet of President Benjamin Harrison as SECRETARY OF THE TREASURY on March 5, 1889, serving from March 7, 1889, until his death; he was a high tariff man and generally an advocate of sound money, although he was a believer in international bimetallism; died in New York City on January 29, 1891; interment in Rock Creek Cemetery, Washington, D.C. **References:** George Frederick Howe, *Chester A. Arthur: A Quarter Century of Machine Politics* (1957); Richard Shuster, *The Selfish and the Strong* (1958).

WIRT, William

Born at Bladensburg, Md., November 8, 1772; son of Jacob and Henrietta Wirt; Presbyterian; married to Mildred Gilmer on May 28, 1795, and upon her death, married Elizabeth Washington, on September 7, 1802; father of 12 children; attended school at Georgetown, District of Columbia, and then at the academy operated by the Rev. James Hunt in Montgomery County, Md.; acted as a private tutor while he pursued his studies; studied law and was admitted to the bar in 1792, opening a law office at the Court House, Culpeper, Va.; moved to Richmond in 1799; designated clerk of the House of Delegates; became chancellor of the eastern district of Virginia in 1802; by appointment of President Jefferson, was named prosecuting attorney in the trial of Aaron Burr in 1807; appointed U.S. district attorney for Virginia by appointment of President Madison in 1816; invited to join the cabinet of President Monroe as ATTORNEY GENERAL on November 13, 1817, entering upon his duties on November 15, 1817, and was continued in that office by President John Quincy Adams, serving until March 3, 1829; moved to Baltimore, Md., in 1829; he was the first attorney general to organize the work of the office and to make a systematic practice of preserving his official opinions so that they might serve as precedents for his successors; he took an active part in the U.S. Supreme Court cases of *McCulloch v. Maryland* and the Dartmouth College Case, both landmark decisions; authored *Letters of a British Spy* (1803), *The Rainbow* (1808), *The Old Bachelor* (1812); died in Washington, D.C., on February 18, 1834; interment in the National Cemetery, Washington, D.C. **References:** Merrill D. Peterson, *The Jefferson Image in the American Mind* (1960); John Dos Passos, *The Shackles of Power: Three Jeffersonian Decades* (1966); Irving Brant, *James Madison and American Nationalism* (1968).

WIRTZ, William Willard

Born in DeKalb, Ill., March 14, 1912; son of William Willard, educator and businessman, and Alpha Belle (White) Wirtz; Methodist; married Mary Jane Quisenberry on September 8, 1936; father of Richard and Philip; attended public schools of DeKalb; studied at Northern Illinois State Teachers College, DeKalb, 1928–1930, and University of California at Berkeley, 1930–1931; A.B., Beloit College, 1933; LL.B., Harvard, 1937; admitted to bar in 1939; taught at Kewanee (Ill.) High School, 1933–1934; assistant professor, University of Iowa School of Law, 1937–1939, Northwestern University School of Law, 1939–1942; assistant general counsel, Board of Economic Warfare, 1942–1943; with War Labor Board, 1943–1945, as general counsel and public member, 1945; chairman, National Wage Stabilization Board, 1946; professor, Northwestern University School of Law, 1946–1954; adviser to Illinois Governor Adlai Stevenson during presidential campaign of 1952; cofounder, Stevenson and Wirtz, Chicago, 1955, and partner, Stevenson and Wirtz (later, Paul, Weiss, Rifkind, Wharton and Garrison), 1955–1961; undersecretary, U.S. Department of Labor, 1961–1962; appointed SECRETARY OF LABOR by President Kennedy, continued under Johnson, and served from September 25, 1962, to January 20, 1969; most important contributions were backing of trade expansion bill, Manpower Development and Training Act, and the fight against public apathy regarding the unemployed; partner, Wirtz and Gentry, Washington, 1970–1978, Wirtz and Lapointe, Washington, 1979–1986; professor of law, University of San Diego, 1986–1998; member, Illinois Liquor Commission, 1949–1953; author of *Labor and the Public Interest* (1964) and *The Boundless Resource: A Prospectus for an Education Work Policy* (1975); member, American, D.C., and Illinois Bar Associations, Phi Beta Kappa, Beta Theta Pi, Delta Sigma Rho. **References:** New York Times, *The Kennedy Years* (1964); Hobart Rowen, *The Free Enterprisers: Kennedy, Johnson and the Business Establishment* (1964); *Who's Who in America, 2000.*

WOLCOTT, Oliver

Born in Litchfield, Conn., January 11, 1760; son of General and Governor Oliver Wolcott and Laura (Collins) Wolcott; Congregationalist; married Elizabeth Stoughton on June 1, 1785; father of five sons and two daughters; entered Litchfield Grammar School at age 11, leaving at age 13 to enter Yale, from which he graduated in 1778; studied law under Judge Tapping Reeve at Litchfield; served as aide-de-camp to his father in 1779; admitted to the bar in January 1781; moved to Hartford and became a clerk in the financial office of the Connecticut department of state; appointed member of central board of accountants, January 1782, serving until the office was abolished in May 1788; member of the literary circle of John Trumbull and Joel Barlow; assisted in organization of the Hartford County bar, November 1783; commissioned with Oliver Ellsworth in May 1784 to settle claims of Connecticut against the federal government; headed office of comptroller of public accounts until September 1789, when the new national constitution became effective; appointed auditor of the U.S. Treasury, 1789–1791; became comptroller of the Treasury in the spring of 1791 after refusing the presidency of the United States Bank; appointed SECRETARY OF THE TREASURY in the cabinet of President Washington on February 2, 1795, continuing in office under President John Adams; accused with other Federalists, by Republicans, of setting fire to the State Department, he resigned on November 8, 1800, in protest against the investigation; appointed by President Adams as judge of the U.S. Supreme Court for the second district, including Vermont, New York, and Connecticut; served until 1802 when the judiciary act under which he was appointed was repealed; moved to New York City in 1802 and entered mercantile business; became president of the Merchant's Bank in 1803; founder and president of the Bank of North America, 1812–1814; returned to Litchfield in 1815 as a gentleman farmer and began manufacturing textiles with his brother, Frederick, in Wolcottville; defeated for the governorship of Connecticut in 1816; presided over convention for constitutional revisions on August 26, 1818; conferred honorary LL.D. degrees by Yale, Princeton, and Brown; died in New York City, June 1, 1833; interment in Litchfield, Conn. **References:** George Gibbs, *Memoirs of the Administrations of Washington and John Adams, Edited from the Papers of Oliver Wolcott* (1846); Samuel Wolcott, *Memorial of Henry Wolcott* (1881).

WOOD, Robert Coldwell

Born in Saint Louis, Mo., September 16, 1923; son of Thomas Frank and Mary (Bradshaw) Wood; married Margaret Byers on March 22, 1952; father of Frances, Margaret, and Frank Randolph; A.B. summa cum laude, Princeton, 1946; M.A., 1947, M.B.A., 1948, Ph.D, 1950, all from Harvard; served with U.S. Army in Europe during World War II and became sergeant; associate director, Florida Legislative Reference Bureau, Tallahassee, 1949–1951; management organization expert, U.S. Bureau of the Budget, Washington, 1951–1954; lecturer in government, Harvard, 1953–1954, then assistant professor, 1954–1957; assistant professor of political science, Massachusetts Institute of Technology,

1957–1959, associate professor, 1959–1962, professor, 1962–1966, head of department, 1965–1966, 1969–1970; undersecretary, U.S. Department of Housing and Urban Development, 1966–1968; appointed SECRETARY OF HOUSING AND URBAN DEVELOPMENT by President Johnson and served from January 2, 1969, until the end of Johnson's term on January 20, 1969; chairman, Massachusetts Bay Transportation Authority, Boston, 1969–1970; director, Harvard University–MIT Joint Center for Urban Studies, Cambridge, Mass., 1969–1970; president, University of Massachusetts, Boston, 1970–1977; superintendent, Boston Public Schools, 1978–1980; professor of political science, University of Massachusetts, Boston, 1980–1983; Henry Luce Professor of Democratic Institutions and the Social Order, Wesleyan University, Middletown, Conn., 1983–1993, John E. Andrus Professor of Government, 1993; professor emeritus, University of Massachusetts, 1994– ; fellow, McCormack Institute for Public Affairs, University of Massachusetts; chairman, Twentieth Century Task Force on Federal Educational Policy, 1983; member, Commission on Academic Health Centers and the Economy in New England; board of directors, Lincoln Institute of Land Policy, 1976–1980, chairman, Institute for Resource Management, 1982–1984, 20th Century Task Force for Federal Educational Policy, 1983, Connecticut Governor's Coalition on Adult Literacy, 1989–1990; member, Governor's Commission on Quality and Integrated Education; decorated Bronze Star; recipient, Fruin Colnon award in urban affairs, National Municipal League, 1960, public administrator of the year, Massachusetts chapter, American Society for Public Administration, 1969, Mayor's Jubilee Bostonian award in education, 1980, Hubert Humphrey award, American Political Science Association (APSA), 1985, Literacy Volunteers of Connecticut award, 1986, Career Achievement award, APSA, 1989, Humphrey Award, Public Policy Association, 1991, and honorary degrees from St. Bonaventure College, 1965, University of Pittsburgh, 1965, Brooklyn Polytechnic Institute, 1966, Princeton University, 1969, Rhode Island College, 1970, University of Massachusetts, 1970, Worcester Polytechnic Institute, 1971, University of Maine, 1972, Hokkaido University, Japan, 1975, North Adams College, 1977, Boston University, 1978, and Stonehill College, 1979; author of *Suburbia—Its People and Their Politics* (1958), *Metropolis against Itself* (1959), *The Necessary Majority: Middle America and the Urban Crisis* (1972), and *Whatever Possessed the President? Academic Experts and Presidential Policy, 1960–1988* (1993); coauthor of *1400 Governments: The Political Economy of the New York Region* (1960), *Schoolmen and Politics* (1962), and *Government and Politics of the United States* (1965); editor, *Remedial Law: When Courts Become Administrators* (1990), *Turnabout Time: Public Higher Education in the Commonwealth* (1995); trustee, Kettering Foundation, 1971–1976; College Board, 1979–1983; fellow, American Academy of Arts and Sciences; member, American Political Science Association, American Society of Public Administration, American Antiquarian Society, National Municipal League, Cosmos Club of Washington, Phi Beta Kappa. **References:** Rowland Evans and Robert Novak, *Lyndon B. Johnson: The Exercise of Power* (1966);

Hugh Sidney, *A Very Personal Presidency: Lyndon Johnson in the White House* (1968); *Who's Who in America, 2000.*

WOODBURY, Levi

Born in Francestown, N.H., December 22, 1789; son of Peter and Mary (Woodbury) Woodbury; married Elizabeth Williams Clapp in June 1819; father of five children; after attending the village schools, he entered Dartmouth College, graduating in 1809; studied law and was admitted to the bar in 1812 and practiced his profession in Francestown from 1813 to 1816; appointed judge of the Superior Court of New Hampshire in 1816; moved to Portsmouth, N.H., in 1819; designated governor of New Hampshire in 1823 and 1824; elected to the state House of Representatives in 1825, where he served as speaker of the House; elected as a Democrat to the U.S. Senate for the term beginning March 4, 1825, serving until March 3, 1831; invited to join the cabinet of President Jackson as SECRETARY OF THE NAVY on May 23, 1831, serving until June 30, 1834, when President Jackson appointed him SECRETARY OF THE TREASURY, a post he held until March 3, 1841; during his administration, he favored the independent treasury, maintaining that the government needed no banks to care for its funds; believed that Congress had no power to recharter the bank; again elected to the U.S. Senate, serving from March 4, 1841, to November 20, 1845, when he resigned; appointed associate justice of the U.S. Supreme Court, serving from November 20, 1845, until his death; died in Portsmouth, N.H., on September 4, 1851; interment in Harmony Grove Cemetery, Portsmouth. **References:** Harold Coffin Syrett, *Andrew Jackson: His Contributions to the American Tradition* (1953); John William Ward, *Andrew Jackson—Symbol for an Age* (1955).

WOODIN, William Hartman

Born in Berwick, Pa., May 27, 1868; son of Clemuel Ricketts and Mary Louise (Dickerman) Woodin; Presbyterian; married Annie Jessup on October 9, 1899; father of Mary, Anne Jessup, William Hartman Jr., and Elizabeth Foster; after attending the New York Latin School and the Woodbridge School, he attended the School of Mines of Columbia University in 1890; entered the plant of the Jackson and Woodin Manufacturing Co., makers of railroad cars and railroad equipment, working as a day laborer for one year; became general superintendent of the company in 1892, vice-president in 1895, and upon his father's death, president in 1899; after a merger with the American Car and Foundry Co., became district manager in charge of the Berwick plant; advanced to president and member of the executive board of the American Car and Foundry Co. in 1916; president of the American Locomotive Company during 1925 and 1926 and from 1927 to 1929; chairman of the board of the Brill Co., the Montreal Locomotive Works, and the Railway Steel Co.; director of the Cuba Railroad Company, Compañía Cubana, and the Remington Arms Company; trustee of the American Surety Co.; appointed New York State fuel administrator in 1922; though nominally a Republican, he supported the candidacy of Al Smith for the presidency in 1928, on the Prohibition issue; appointed a member of a committee to study and revise the banking laws of New York in 1929 by Governor Roosevelt; supported Franklin Roosevelt for the presidency in 1932; joined the Roosevelt cabinet as SECRETARY OF THE TREASURY on March 4, 1933, serving until illness forced his resignation on January 1, 1934; during his incumbency, he played a conspicuous part in formulating and putting into effect the measures adopted to meet the financial crisis of 1933; devised and promulgated the regulations permitting the banks to resume operations following the banking moratorium and also undertook to prevent the hoarding of gold; trustee of the Georgia Warm Springs Foundation and of Lafayette College, Easton, Pa.; studied music in Vienna, Berlin, and Paris and became a composer; among his works was the "Franklin D. Roosevelt March," which was played at the presidential inauguration in 1933; authored *The United States Pattern—Trial and Experimental Pieces* (1913), a standard work on American coinage; died in New York City, May 3, 1934. **Reference:** Paul K. Conkin, *The New Deal* (1967).

WOODRING, Henry H.

Born in Elk City, Kans., May 31, 1890; son of Hines Woodring, farmer and soldier in the Union army during the Civil War; Congregationalist; married to Helen Coolidge in 1933; father of two children; attended the high schools of Elk City and Independence but did not graduate; completed one-year business and commerce course at Lebanon University, Lebanon, Ind.; worked in an Elk City bank and later as a bookkeeper; removed to Neodesha and became a bank cashier; served as a second lieutenant in the U.S. Tank Corps during World War I; resumed banking career in Kansas City; bought a controlling interest in the Neodesha bank and sold it in 1929; served as state commander of the American Legion, 1929; elected Democratic governor of Kansas, 1930; appointed assistant secretary of war in the cabinet of President Franklin Roosevelt, 1932; took over duties of assistant secretary of war for air when that cabinet post was abolished in 1933; appointed SECRETARY OF WAR in the cabinet of President Roosevelt on September 25, 1936; most important contributions were opposing the draft and any commitment of American troops to Europe, instituting competitive bidding as the new policy for government airplane purchases, and recommending the appointment of General George C. Marshall as Army Chief of Staff over the objections of prominent congressmen; resigned from office on June 19, 1940; opposed Roosevelt's fourth presidential campaign and headed the American Democratic National Committee; died in Topeka, Kans., on September 9, 1967. **References:** A.J. Wann, *President as Chief Administrator: A Study of Franklin D. Roosevelt* (1968); Robert A. Divine, *Roosevelt and World War II* (1969).

WORK, Hubert

Born at Marion Center, Pa., July 3, 1860; son of Moses Thompson Work; Presbyterian; married in 1887 to Laura M. Arbuckle, who died in 1924; father of Philip, Doris, and Robert; married in December 1933 to Ethel Reed Gano; studied at the Pennsylvania State Normal School, the Medical School of the University of Michigan, 1882–1884, and the University of Pennsylvania, receiving M.D. degree in 1885 from the latter institution; began medical practice in 1885 in Greeley, Colo.; moved to Pueblo, Colo., in 1896 and there founded the Woodcroft Hospital for Mental and Nervous Diseases; delegate-at-large to the Republican National Convention of 1908; chairman of the Colorado Republican state central committee, 1912; during World War I, served in the U.S. Army Medical Corps; commissioned as a major by President Wilson and assigned to the staff of the provost marshal; later promoted to colonel; president of the American Medical Association, 1920; served as Colorado member of the Republican National Committee, 1920; became the first assistant postmaster general of the United States on March 4, 1921, in the cabinet of President Harding, serving until March 4, 1922; appointed POSTMASTER GENERAL by President Harding on March 4, 1922; served until March 4, 1923; appointed SECRETARY OF THE INTERIOR on March 5, 1923, in the cabinet of President Harding; continued to serve under President Coolidge until his resignation on July 24, 1928; most important contributions were reorganization of the department, decreasing its budget by $129 million, and granting citizenship to noncitizen American Indians born in the United States; chairman of the Republican National Committee, 1928–1929; died in South Denver, Colo., on December 14, 1942. **References:** Samuel Hopkins Adams, *The Incredible Era* (1939); Francis Russell, *The Shadow of Blooming Grove: Warren G. Harding and His Times* (1968).

WRIGHT, Luke Edward

Born in Memphis, Tenn., August 29, 1846; son of Archibald and Mary Elizabeth (Elderidge) Wright; married Kate Semmes on December 15, 1869; father of Elderidge, Anna, Luke E., Semmes, and Katrina; attended local schools; attended University of Mississippi, 1867–1868; enlisted in Confederate army at outset of Civil War and eventually became captain; admitted to Tennessee bar in 1870; opened office in Memphis; attorney general of Tennessee, 1870–1878; appointed member of U.S. Philippine commission in 1900 and served as president until 1904; appointed vice-governor of Philippine Islands by President Theodore Roosevelt on October 29, 1901; governor general, 1904–1906; became American ambassador to Japan on March 30, 1906, and served until resignation on September 1, 1907; returned to law practice; appointed SECRETARY OF WAR in the cabinet of President Theodore Roosevelt on July 1, 1908, and served until March 5, 1909; died November 17, 1922. **References:** J.M. Keating, *History of Memphis* (1888); James F. Rhodes, *McKinley and Roosevelt Administrations,*

1897–1909, in *History of the United States*, vol. 9 (1922); J.T. Moore, *Tennessee, the Volunteer State* (1923); George E. Mowry, *Era of Theodore Roosevelt, 1900–1912* (1958).

WYNNE, Robert John

Born in New York, N.Y., November 18, 1851; son of John and Mary Wynne; married Mary McCabe on July 7, 1875; attended public schools in New York City; moved to Philadelphia, Pa., and learned telegraphy; employed by Bankers and Brokers Telegraph Co., 1870; went to Washington, D.C., to become assistant correspondent of Cincinnati *Gazette*, 1880; private secretary to Charles Foster, secretary of the treasury under Benjamin Harrison, 1891–1893; at accession of Cleveland, returned to journalism as Washington correspondent of Cincinnati *Tribune* and Philadelphia *Bulletin*; became Washington correspondent for New York *Press*: appointed POSTMASTER GENERAL in the cabinet of President Theodore Roosevelt on October 4, 1904, and served until March 4, 1905; became consul-general to Great Britain, 1905; president of First National Fire Insurance Company in 1915; died March 11, 1922. **References:** James F. Rhodes, *McKinley and Roosevelt Administrations, 1897–1909*, in *History of the United States*, vol. 9 (1922); George E. Mowry, *Era of Theodore Roosevelt, 1900–1912* (1958).

Y

YEUTTER, Clayton Keith

Born in Eustis, Nebr., December 10, 1930; son of Reinhold F. and Laura P. Yeutter; married Lillian Jeanne Vierk, 1952; father of Brad, Gregg, Kim, and Van; graduated from Eustis High School, 1948; B.S., University of Nebraska, 1952; J.D., University of Nebraska Law School, 1963, ranked first in graduating class; Ph.D. in agricultural economics, University of Nebraska, 1966; admitted to the bars in Nebraska, 1963, and the District of Columbia, 1977; served with United States Air Force (USAF), 1952–1957, and USAF Reserve, 1957–1987, first enlisted as a basic airman, later receiving a direct commission in medical administration, and retiring as a lieutenant colonel; farmer and rancher, Nebraska, 1957–1975; law practice in Lincoln, Nebr., 1963–1968; faculty member, department of agricultural economics, University of Nebraska, 1960–1966; executive assistant to the governor of Nebraska, 1966–1968; director, University of Nebraska mission in Colombia, South America, 1968–1970; administrator, consumer and marketing service, U.S. Department of Agriculture (USDA), Washington, 1970–1971; regional director, committee for the reelection of the president, 1972; assistant secretary of agriculture for marketing and consumer services, USDA, 1973–1974; assistant secretary of agriculture for international affairs and commodity programs, USDA, 1974–1975; deputy special trade representative, Executive Office of the President, 1975–1977; senior partner, Nelson, Harding, Yeutter & Leonard, Lincoln, 1977–1978; president and chief executive officer, Chicago Mercantile Exchange, 1978–1985; appointed by President-elect Ronald Reagan as chairman of the administration's Transition Task Force on Agricultural Policy and later as head of the Agricultural Development Task Force to Peru; became the first American businessman invited to Japan in 1982 under Japanese government program to improve trade relations with the United

States; appointed by President Reagan as U.S. trade representative, 1985–1989, during which time he led U.S. negotiations with Canada that established the precursor to the North Atlantic Free Trade Agreement (NAFTA), as well as helping inaugurate the Uruguay Round of talks within the General Agreement on Tariffs and Trade that led to the creation of the World Trade Organization; appointed by President George H.W. Bush as SECRETARY OF AGRICULTURE and served from February 16, 1989, until March 1, 1991; chairman, Republican National Committee, Washington, 1991–1992; White House counselor to President Bush for domestic policy and chairman *pro tempore* of the White House Policy Coordinating Group, 1992; of counsel, Hogan and Hartson L.L.P., Washington, 1993– ; member, board of directors, Caterpillar, FMC Corporation, Oppenheimer Funds; member, board of advisors, Stonebridge International LLC; former trustee, Garrett-Evangelical Theological Seminary, Evanston, Ill.; former member, board of directors, Chicago Council on Foreign Relations, board of visitors, Georgetown University School of Business Administration; former trustee and member of executive committee, Farm Foundation, Oak Brook, Ill.; former editor, *Nebraska Law Review*; recipient, Israel Prime Minister's medal, Master Builder of Men award, FarmHouse Leadership award, Fowler-McCracken Commission, Consumers for World Trade award, and honorary degrees from University of Nebraska, Clemson University, Georgetown University, Santa Clara University, Nebraska Wesleyan University, University of Maryland, and DePaul University; member, Nebraska Bar Association. **References:** *New York Times* (December 15, 1988); *Current Biography Yearbook 1988*; Charles Kolb, *White House Daze: The Unmaking of Domestic Policy in the Bush Years* (1994); Kenneth W. Thompson, ed., *The Reagan Presidency: Ten Intimate Perspectives* (1997) and *The Bush Presidency: Ten Intimate Perspectives* (1997); John Robert Greene, *The Presidency of George Bush* (2000).

Appendixes

Other Federal Government Service

U.S. SENATE

Name	State	Dates
Abraham, Spencer	Mich.	1995–2001
Adams, Brockman	Wash.	1987–93
Adams, John Q.	Mass.	1801–08; 1831–48
Alger, Russell A.	Mich.	1902–07
Anderson, Clinton P.	N.M.	1948–50; 1954–67
Armstrong, John	N.Y.	1800–02; 1803–04
Ashcroft, John	Mo.	1995–2001
Badger, George E.	N.C.	1846–55
Barbour, James	Va.	1815–25
Barkley, Alben W.	Ky.	1927–49; 1955–56
Bayard, Thomas F.	Del.	1869–85
Bell, John	Tenn.	1947–59
Bentsen, Lloyd	Tex.	1971–93
Berrien, John M.	Ga.	1825–29; 1841–52
Bibb, George M.	Ky.	1811–14; 1828–34
Blaine, James G.	Me.	1876–81
Boutwell, George S.	Mass.	1873–77
Brady, Nicholas F.	N.J.	1982
Branch, John	N.C.	1823–29
Breckinridge, John	Ky.	1801–05
Breckinridge, John C.	Ky.	1861

Browning, Orville H.	Ky.	1861–63
Buchanan, James	Pa.	1835–45
Burr, Aaron	N.Y.	1791–97
Byrnes, James F.	S.C.	1931–41
Calhoun, John C.	S.C.	1832–43; 1845–50
Cameron, James D.	Pa.	1877–97
Cameron, Simon	Pa.	1845–49; 1857–61; 1867–77
Campbell, George W.	Tenn.	1811–14; 1815–18
Carlisle, John G.	Ky.	1890–93
Cass, Lewis	Mich.	1845–48; 1849–57
Chandler, William E.	N.H.	1887–91; 1895–1901
Chandler, Zachariah	Mich.	1857–75; 1879
Chase, Salmon P.	Ohio	1849–55; 1861*
Clay, Henry	Ky.	1806–07; 1810–11; 1831–42; 1849–52
Clayton, John M.	Del.	1829–36; 1845–49; 1853–56
Cohen, William	Me.	1979–97
Collamer, Jacob	Vt.	1855–65
Conrad, Charles M.	La.	1842–43
Corwin, Thomas	Ohio	1845–50
Crawford, William H.	Ga.	1807–13
Creswell, John A.J.	Md.	1865–67
Crittenden, John J.	Ky.	1817–19; 1835–41; 1843–48; 1855–61
Curtis, Charles	Kans.	1907–13; 1915–29
Dallas, George M.	Pa.	1831–33
Davis, James J.	Pa.	1930–45
Davis, Jefferson	Miss.	1847–51; 1857–61
Dexter, Samuel	Mass.	1799–1800
Dickerson, Mahlon	N.J.	1817–29; 1829–33
Dix, John A.	N.Y.	1845–49
Dulles, John F.	N.Y.	1949
Eaton, John H.	Tenn.	1818–29
Elkins, Stephen B.	N.M.	1895–1911
Evarts, William M.	N.Y.	1885–91
Everett, Edward	Mass.	1853–54
Ewing, Thomas	Ohio	1831–37; 1850–51
Fairbanks, Charles W.	Ind.	1897–1905

---

*Resigned after two days.

Fall, Albert B.	N.M.	1912–21
Fessenden, William P.	Me.	1854–64; 1865–69
Fish, Hamilton	N.Y.	1851–57
Forsyth, John	Ga.	1818–19; 1823–27
Frelinghuysen, Frederick T.	N.J.	1866–69; 1871–77
Gallatin, Albert	Pa.	1795–1801
Garland, Augustus H.	Ark.	1877–85
Glass, Carter	Va.	1920–46
Goff, Nathan	W.Va.	1913–19
Gore, Albert, Jr.	Tenn.	1985–93
Graham, William A.	N.C.	1840–43
Grundy, Felix	Tenn.	1829–38; 1839–40
Guthrie, James	Ky.	1865–68
Hamlin, Hannibal	Me.	1848–56; 1857–61; 1869–81
Harding, Warren G.	Ohio	1915–21
Harlan, James	Iowa	1855–57; 1857–65; 1867–73
Harrison, Benjamin	Ind.	1881–87
Harrison, William H.	Ohio	1825–28
Hendricks, Thomas A.	Ind.	1863–69
Howe, Timothy O.	Wisc.	1861–79
Hull, Cordell	Tenn.	1930–33
Humphrey, Hubert H.	Minn.	1948–64
Jackson, Andrew	Tenn.	1797–98; 1823–25
Johnson, Andrew	Tenn.	1857–62; 1875
Johnson, Lyndon B.	Tex.	1948–61
Johnson, Reverdy	Md.	1845–49; 1863–68
Johnson, Richard M.	Ky.	1819–29
Kellogg, Frank B.	Minn.	1917–23
Kennedy, John F.	Mass.	1953–65
Kennedy, Robert F.	N.Y.	1965–68
Key, David M.	Tenn.	1875–77
King, William R. de V.	Ala.	1819–44; 1848–52
Kirkwood, Samuel J.	Iowa	1866–67; 1877–81
Knox, Philander C.	Pa.	1904–09; 1917–21
Lamar, Lucius Q.C.	Miss.	1877–85
Lee, Richard H.	Va.	1789–92
Livingston, Edward	La.	1829–31
Marcy, William L.	N.Y.	1831–32

McAdoo, William G.	Calif.	1933–39
McGrath, James H.	R.I.	1947–49
McLane, Louis	Del.	1827–29
Meigs, Return J., Jr.	Ohio	1808–10
Mills, Ogden L.	N.Y.	1921–27
Mondale, Walter F.	Minn.	1964–76
Monroe, James	Va.	1790–94
Morrill, Lot M.	Me.	1861–76
Muskie, Edmund S.	Me.	1959–80
New, Harry S.	Ind.	1917–23
Niles, John M.	Conn.	1835–39; 1843–49
Nixon, Richard M.	Calif.	1950–53
Pickering, Timothy	Mass.	1803–11
Pierce, Franklin	N.H.	1837–42
Pinkney, William	Md.	1819–22
Proctor, Redfield	Vt.	1891–1908
Quayle, Danforth	Ind.	1981–89
Ramsey, Alexander	Minn.	1863–75
Ribicoff, Abraham A.	Conn.	1963–89
Rodney, Caesar A.	Del.	1822–23
Root, Elihu	N.Y.	1910–15
Saxbe, William	Ohio	1969–74
Schurz, Carl	Mo.	1869–75
Schweiker, Richard	Pa.	1969–81
Schwellenbach, Lewis B.	Wash.	1935–40
Seaton, Frederick A.	Nebr.	1951–53
Seward, William H.	N.Y.	1850–61
Sherman, John	Ohio	1881–97
Smith, Hoke	Ga.	1911–21
Southard, Samuel L.	N.J.	1821–23; 1834–42
Swanson, Claude	Va.	1910–33
Teller, Henry M.	Colo.	1876–82; 1885–1909
Toucey, Isaac	Conn.	1852–57
Truman, Harry S	Mo.	1935–45
Tyler, John	Va.	1827–36
Van Buren, Martin	N.Y.	1821–28
Vilas, William F.	Wisc.	1891–97
Walker, Robert J.	Miss.	1835–45
Webster, Daniel	Mass.	1827–41; 1845–50

Weeks, John W.	Mass.	1913–19
Weeks, Sinclair	Mass.	1944
Wilkins, William	Pa.	1831–34
Williams, George H.	Ore.	1865–71
Wilson, Henry	Mass.	1855–73
Windom, William	Minn.	1870–81; 1881–83
Woodbury, Levi	N.H.	1825–31; 1841–45

U.S. HOUSE OF REPRESENTATIVES

Name	State	Dates
Adams, Brockman	Wash.	1965–77
Alexander, Joshua W.	Mo.	1907–19
Anderson, Clinton P.	N.M.	1941–45
Aspin, Les	Wisc.	1971–93
Barkley, Alben W.	Ky.	1913–27
Bates, Edward	Mo.	1827–29
Bell, John	Tenn.	1827–41
Bentsen, Lloyd	Tex.	1949–55
Bergland, Robert S.	Minn.	1970–77
Blaine, James G.	Me.	1863–69
Boudinot, Elias	N.J.	1789–95
Boutwell, George S.	Mass.	1863–69
Branch, John	N.C.	1831–33
Breckinridge, John	Va.	1792
Breckinridge, John C.	Ky.	1851–55
Brock, William E., III	Tenn.	1963–71
Brown, Aaron V.	Tenn.	1839–45
Bryan, William J.	Nebr.	1891–95
Buchanan, James	Pa.	1821–31
Burleson, Albert S.	Tex.	1899–1913
Bush, George H.W.	Tex.	1967–71
Byrnes, James F.	S.C.	1911–25
Calhoun, John C.	S.C.	1811–17
Campbell, George W.	Tenn.	1803–09
Carlisle, John G.	Ky.	1877–90
Cheney, Richard B.	Wyo.	1979–89
Clay, Henry	Ky.	1811–14; 1815–21; 1823–25

Clifford, Nathan	Me.	1839–43
Cobb, Howell	Ga.	1843–51; 1855–57
Cohen, William	Me.	1973–79
Colfax, Schuyler	Ind.	1855–69
Collamer, Jacob	Vt.	1843–49
Conrad, Charles M.	La.	1849–50
Corwin, Thomas	Ohio	1831–40; 1859–61
Crawford, George W.	Ga.	1843 (Jan. 7–Mar. 4)
Creswell, John A. J.	Md.	1863–65
Crittenden, John J.	Ky.	1861–63
Crowninshield, Benjamin W.	Mass.	1823–31
Curtis, Charles	Kans.	1893–1907
Cushing, Caleb	Mass.	1835–43
Davis, Jefferson	Miss.	1845–46
Dearborn, Henry	Me.	1793–97
Delano, Columbus	Ohio	1845–47
Denby, Edwin	Mich.	1905–11
Derwinski, Edward J.	Ill.	1959–83
Dexter, Samuel	Mass.	1793–95
Elkins, Stephen B.	N.M.	1873–77
Espy, Michael	Miss.	1987–93
Eustis, William	Mass.	1801–05; 1820–23
Fessenden, William P.	Me.	1841–43
Fillmore, Millard	N.Y.	1833–35; 1837–43
Fish, Hamilton	N.Y.	1843–45
Ford, Gerald R., Jr.	Mich.	1949–73
Forsyth, John	Ga.	1813–18
Forward, Walter	Pa.	1822–25
Foster, Charles	Ohio	1871–79
Garner, John N.	Tex.	1903–33
Glass, Carter	Va.	1902–18
Glickman, Daniel	Kans.	1977–95
Goff, Nathan	W.Va.	1883–89
Good, James W.	Iowa	1909–21
Gore, Albert, Jr.	Tenn.	1977–85
Granger, Francis	N.Y.	1835–37; 1839–41; 1841–43
Grundy, Felix	Tenn.	1811–14
Harrison, William H.	Ohio	1816–19
Hayes, Rutherford B.	Ohio	1865–67

Heckler, Margaret M.	Mass.	1967–83
Hendricks, Thomas A.	Ind.	1851–54
Herter, Christian A.	Mass.	1942–53
Hoar, Ebenezer R.	Mass.	1973–75
Hull, Cordell	Tenn.	1906–21; 1923–31
Ingham, Samuel D.	Pa.	1822–29
Jackson, Andrew	Tenn.	1796–97
Johnson, Andrew	Tenn.	1843–53
Johnson, Cave	Tenn.	1829–37; 1839–45
Johnson, Lyndon B.	Tex.	1937–48
Johnson, Richard M.	Ky.	1807–19; 1829–37
Jones, William	Pa.	1801–03
Kemp, Jack	N.Y.	1971–89
Kennedy, John F.	Mass.	1947–53
Kennedy, John P.	Md.	1838–40; 1841–45
King, William R. de V.	N.C.	1811–16
Kleppe, Thomas S.	N.D.	1967–71
Knebel, John A.	D.C.	1968–71
Laird, Melvin R.	Wisc.	1952–69
Lamar, Lucius Q.C.	Miss.	1857–60; 1873–77
Legaré, Hugh S.	S.C.	1837–39
Lincoln, Abraham	Ill.	1847–49
Lincoln, Levi	Mass.	1800–01
Livingston, Edward	N.Y.	1794–1801
Livingston, Edward	La.	1823–29
Long, John D.	Mass.	1883–89
Lujan, Manuel, Jr.	N.M.	1969–89
Madison, James	Va.	1789–97
Madigan, Edward	Ill.	1973–91
Marshall, John	Va.	1799–1800
Martin, Lynn	Ill.	1981–91
Mason, John Y.	Va.	1831–37
Maynard, Horace	Tenn.	1857–63; 1866–75
McClelland, Robert	Mich.	1843–49
McCrary, George W.	Iowa	1869–77
McGranery, James P.	Pa.	1937–49
McKenna, Joseph	Calif.	1885–92
McKennan, Thomas M.T.	Pa.	1831–39
McKinley, William, Jr.	Ohio	1877–83; 1885–91

McLane, Louis	Del.	1817–27
McLean, John	Ohio	1813–16
Metcalf, Victor H.	Calif.	1899–1904
Mineta, Norman	Calif.	1975–95
Moody, William H.	Mass.	1895–1902
Morton, Levi P.	N.Y.	1879–81
Morton, Rogers C.B.	Md.	1963–69
Nelson, John	Md.	1821–23
Nixon, Richard M.	Calif.	1947–50
Palmer, Alexander M.	Pa.	1909–15
Pickering, Timothy	Mass.	1813–17
Pierce, Franklin	N.H.	1833–37
Pinkney, William	Md.	1815–16
Poinsett, Joel R.	S.C.	1821–25
Polk, James K.	Tenn.	1825–39
Porter, Peter B.	N.Y.	1809–13; 1815–16
Preston, William B.	Va.	1847–49
Quayle, Danforth	Ind.	1977–81
Ramsey, Alexander	Pa.	1843–47
Redfield, William C.	N.Y.	1911–13
Ribicoff, Abraham A.	Conn.	1949–53
Richardson, William B.	N.M.	1983–97
Robeson, George	N.J.	1879–83
Rodney, Caesar A.	Del.	1803–05; 1821–22
Rumsfeld, Donald	Ill.	1963–69
Rusk, Jeremiah M.	Wisc.	1871–77
Schweiker, Richard	Pa.	1961–69
Sherman, James S.	N.Y.	1887–97; 1893–1909
Sherman, John	Ohio	1855–61
Smith, Caleb	Ind.	1843–49
Spencer, John C.	N.Y.	1817–19
Stevenson, Adlai E.	Ill.	1875–77; 1879–81
Stuart, Alexander H.H.	Va.	1841–43
Swanson, Claude	Va.	1893–1906
Thomas, Philip F.	Md.	1839–41; 1975–77
Thompson, Jacob	Miss.	1839–51
Toucey, Isaac	Conn.	1835–39

Tyler, John	Va.	1817–21
Tyner, James N.	Ind.	1869–75
Udall, Stewart L.	Ariz.	1955–61
Vinson, Frederick M.	Ky.	1924–29
Washburne, Elihu B.	Ill.	1853–59
Webster, Daniel	N.H.	1813–17
Webster, Daniel	Mass.	1823–27
Weeks, John W.	Mass.	1905–13
Wheeler, William A.	N.Y.	1861–63; 1869–77
Wickliffe, Charles A.	Ky.	1823–33; 1861–63
Wilkins, William	Pa.	1843–44

U.S. SUPREME COURT

Name	Dates
Byrnes, James F.	1941–42
Chase, Salmon P.	1864–73 (Chf. Justice)
Clark, Tom C.	1949–67
Clifford, Nathan	1858–81
Day, William R.	1903–22
Goldberg, Arthur J.	1962–65
Hughes, Charles E.	1910–16
Hughes, Charles E.	1930–41 (Chf. Justice)
Jackson, Robert H.	1941–54
Jay, John	1789–95 (Chf. Justice)
Marshall, John	1801–35
McKenna, Joseph	1898–1925
McLean, John	1830–61
McReynolds, James C.	1914–41
Moody, William H.	1906–10
Stone, Harlan F.	1925–46 (Chf. Justice, 1941–46)
Taft, William H.	1921–30 (Chf. Justice)
Taney, Roger B.	1836–64 (Chf. Justice)
Vinson, Frederick M.	1946–53
Wolcott, Oliver, Jr.	1800–02
Woodbury, Levi	1845–51

OTHER FEDERAL JUDICIAL SERVICE

Name	Office	Dates
Akerman, Amos T.	Dist. Atty.	1867–70
Alexander, Joshua W.	Judge, Circ. Ct.	1901–07
Barry, William T.	Judge, Circ. Ct.	1816–17
Bates, Edward	Cir. Pros. Atty.	1818–20
Bates, Edward	Dist. Atty.	1821–26
Bayard, Thomas F.	Dist. Atty.	1853–54
Bell, Griffin B.	Judge, Circ. Ct. of Appeals	1961–76
Biddle, Francis B.	Chf. Counsel to Investigate TVA	1938–39
Biddle, Francis B.	Judge. Circ. Ct. of Appeals	1939–40
Biddle, Francis B.	Solicitor Gen.	1940–41
Black, Jeremiah	Judge, Dist. Ct.	1842
Blair, Montgomery	Dist. Atty.	1839
Blair, Montgomery	First Solicitor Ct. of Claims	1855
Brannan, Charles F.	Asst. Reg. Atty., U.S. Dept. of Agricult. Resettlement Admin.	1935
Brannan, Charles F.	Reg. Atty., U.S. Dept. of Agricult. Resettlement Admin.	1937
Bristow, Benjamin H.	Dist. Atty.	1866–70
Bristow, Benjamin H.	Solicitor Gen.	1870–72
Butler, Benjamin	Dist. Atty.	1838–41
Campbell, George W.	Judge, Dist. Ct.	*ca.* 1821–30
Chandler, William E.	Solicitor, Navy Dept.	1865
Civiletti, Benjamin R.	Judge, Dist. Ct.	1961
Collamer, Jacob	Judge, Circ. Ct.	1850–54
Connor, John T.	Gen. Counsel, Ofc. of Scientif. Rsch. and Devel.	1942
Connor, John T.	Counsel, Ofc. of Naval Rsch.	1946
Crawford, William H.	Judge, Circ. Ct.	1827–34
Crittenden, John J.	Dist. Atty.	1827–29
Dallas, Alexander	Dist. Atty.	1801–04
Dallas, George M.	Solicitor, U.S. Bank	1815–17
Dallas, George M.	Dist. Atty.	1829–31
Day, William R.	Judge, Circ. Ct. of Appeals	1899–1903
Dickerson, Mahlon	Judge, Dist. Ct.	1840
Elkins, Stephen B.	Dist. Atty.	1867–70

Evarts, William M.	Asst. Atty.	1849–53
Fowler, Henry	Counsel for Fed. Power Comm.	1941
Fowler, Henry	Counsel for Ofc. of Prod. Mgmt.	1941
Gilpin, Henry D.	Solicitor, U.S. Treas.	1837
Goff, Nathan	Dist. Atty.	1868–81; 1881–82
Gresham, Walter Q.	Dist. Judge	1869–82
Gresham, Walter Q.	Circ. Judge	1884–93
Griffin, Cyrus	Judge, Dist. Ct.	1789–1810
Hall, Nathan K.	Dist. Judge	1852–74
Hills, Carla A.	Asst. Atty. Gen.	1974–75
Hufstedler, Shirley M.	Ct. of Appeals	1968–79
Hunt, William H.	Judge, Ct. of Claims	1878–81
Jackson, Robert H.	Gen. Counsel, Bur. of Internal Rev.	1933
Jackson, Robert H.	Spec. Counsel, Sec. & Exch. Comm.	1935
Jackson, Robert H.	Solicitor Gen.	1938
Johnson, Cave	Circ. Judge	1850–51
Kellogg, Frank B.	Federal Prosecutor	1905
Kellogg, Frank B.	Spec. Counsel to Interstate Commerce Comm.	1906
Kellogg, Frank B.	Govt. Counsel	1909
Kennedy, Robert F.	Atty., Justice Dept.	1951–52
Kennedy, Robert F.	Asst. Counsel, Sen. Investig. Subcomt.	1953
Kennedy, Robert F.	Minority Counsel, Sen. Subcomt.	1953
Kennedy, Robert F.	Chf. Counsel, Sen. Investig. Subcomt.	1955
Kennedy, Robert F.	Chf. Counsel, Sen. Subcomt. to Investig. Labor–Mgmt. Relations	1957–59
Knox, Philander C.	Asst. Dist. Atty.	1876
Lansing, Robert	Counselor, Dept. State	1914–15
Lee, Charles	Circ. Judge	1801–02
Livingston, Edward	Dist. Atty.	1800–03
Mason, John Y.	Dist. Judge	1837
McCrary, George W.	Circ. Judge	1880–84
McGranery, James P.	Dist. Judge	1946–52
McGrath, James H.	Dist. Atty.	1934–40
McGrath, James H.	Solicitor Gen.	1945–46
McKenna, Joseph	Circ. Judge	1892–97
McReynolds, James C.	Spec. Counsel for U.S. Govt.	1907–12
Meigs, Return J.	Dist. Judge	1807–08

Meredith, William M.	Dist. Atty.	1841–49
Mitchell, William D.	Solicitor Gen.	1925–29
Mitchell, William D.	Spec. Pros. Fed. Grand Jury	1929–33
Mitchell, William D.	Chf. Counsel, Cong. Pearl Harbor Investig. Comt.	1945
Moody, William H.	Dist. Atty.	1890–95
Murphy, Frank	Asst. Dist. Atty.	1919–20
Noble, John W.	Dist. Atty.	1867–70
Patterson, Robert P.	Dist. Judge	1930–39
Patterson, Robert P.	Circ. Judge	1939–40
Pierce, Samuel R., Jr.	Asst. Dist. Atty.	1949–52
Pierce, Samuel R., Jr.	U.S. Atty.	1953–55
Pierrepont, Edwards	Dist. Atty.	1869–70
Richardson, Elliot L.	U.S. Atty.	1959–61
Rogers, William P.	Counsel. Sen. Comt. to Investig. Natl. Defense	1947
Root, Elihu	Dist. Atty.	1838–85
Saxbe, William	Atty. Gen.	1974–75
Schwellenbach, Lewis B.	Dist. Judge	1940–45
Skinner, Samuel K.	Asst. U.S. Atty.	1968–74
Skinner, Samuel K.	1st Asst. U.S. Atty.	1974–75
Skinner, Samuel K.	U.S. Atty.	1975–77
Smith, Caleb	Dist. Judge	1863–64
Stanton, Edwin McM.	Spec. Counsel for U.S. Govt.	1856
Stimson, Henry L.	U.S. Atty.	1906–09
Taft, William H.	Solicitor Gen.	1890–92
Taft, William H.	Judge, Circ. Ct.	1892
Thornburgh, Richard L.	U.S. Atty.	1969–75
Tracy, Benjamin F.	Dist. Atty.	1866–73
Vinson, Frederick M.	Judge, Circ. Ct.	1937–43
Vinson, Frederick M.	Judge, Emerg. Ct. of Appeals	1942–43
Wilbur, Curtis D.	Judge. Circ. Ct. of Appeals	1929–31
Wilbur, Curtis D.	Senior Cir. Judge	1931–35
Wilkins, Wilbur	Judge, Dist. Ct.	1824–31
Wirt, William	Pros. Atty., Aaron Burr Trial	1807
Wirt, William	Dist. Atty.	1816–17
Wirtz, William W.	Assoc. Gen. Counsel. Bd. of Econ. Warfare	1942–43
Wirtz, William W.	Gen. Counsel. War Labor Bd.	1943–45

OTHER EXECUTIVE BRANCH SERVICE

Name	Office	Dates
Abraham, Spencer	Dep. Chief of Staff to Vice-Pres.	1990–91
Acheson, Dean	Undersecy. Treas.	1933
	Asst. Secy. State	1941–45
	Undersecy. State	1945–47
Albright, Madeleine	Leg. Asst., Nat. Security Coun.	1978–81
Alexander, Lamar	Exec. Asst., White House	1969–70
Aspin, Les	Asst. to Chair, Coun. of Econ. Adv.	1963–66
	Asst. to Secy. Defense	1966–68
Babbitt, Bruce	Asst. to Dir., VISTA	1965–67
Bacon, Robert	Asst. Secy. State	1905–09
Baker, James	Undersecy. Commerce	1975–76
	White House Chief of Staff	1981–85
		1992–93
Barr, Joseph	Undersecy. Treas.	1965–68
Barr, William	Staff Officer, CIA	1973–77
	Asst. Atty. Gen.	1989–90
Bennett, William	Chair, Nat. Endowment for Humanities	1981–85
	Dir., Ofc. of Nat. Drug Control Policy	1989–90
Blumenthal, Michael	Dep. Asst. Secy. State	1961–63
Boutwell, George	Comr. of Int. Revenue	1862–63
Boyd, Alan	Undersecy. Commerce	1965–67
Brannan, Charles	Reg. Dir., Farm Security Admin.	1941–45
	Asst. Secy. Agri.	1944–48
Brock, William	U.S. Trade Rep.	1981–85
Brown, Harold	Sec. A.F.	1965–69
Brown, Jesse	Nat. Service Officer, Disabled Am. Vets (DAV)	1967–73
	Supervisor, DAV	1973–81
	Chief of Claims, DAV	1981–83
	Dep. Dir., DAV	1983–89
	Exec. Dir., DAV	1989–93
Brown, Walter	Asst. Secy. Commerce	1927–29
Burnley, James	Dir., VISTA	1981–82
Bush, George H.W.	Dir., CIA	1976–77
Butz, Earl	Asst. Secy. Agric.	1954–57
Card, Andrew	Spec. Asst. to Pres.	1983–87

	Asst. to Pres.	1988
	Dep. White House Chief of Staff	1989–92
	White House Chief of Staff	2001–
Carlucci, Frank	Dir., Ofc. of Econ. Opportunity	1971–72
	Dep. Dir., CIA	1978–81
Chandler, William	Asst. Secy. Treas.	1865–67
Chao, Elaine	Asst., White House Ofc. of Policy Dvlpmt.	1983
	Dep. Admin., Dept. of Transportation	1986–88
	Dep. Secy. Transportation	1989–91
Chapman, Oscar	Asst. Secy. Interior	1933–46
	Undersecy. Interior	1946–49
	Secy. Interior *ad int.*	1949–50
Cheney, Dick	Asst. to Dir., Ofc. of Econ. Opportunity	1969–70
	Dep. to White House Counselor	1970–71
	Asst. Dir., Cost of Living Coun.	1971–73
	Asst. to Pres.	1974–75
	White House Chief of Staff	1975–77
Christopher, Warren	Dep. Atty. General	1967–69
	Dep. Secy. State	1977–81
Cisneros, Henry	Asst. to Secy. HEW	1971–72
Clark, Tom C.	Asst. Atty. Gen.	1943–45
Clark, W. Ramsey	Asst. Atty. Gen.	1961–65
	Acting Atty. Gen.	1966–67
Clifford, Clark	Pres. Naval Aide	1946
	Spec. Counsel to Pres.	1946–50
	Adv. to Pres.	1963–65
Cohen, Wilbur	Bur. Dir., Soc. Sec. Admin.	1953–56
	Consultant to White House Conf. on Aging	1959–60
	Asst. Secy. HEW	1961–65
	Undersecy. HEW	1965–67
	Acting Secy. HEW	1968
Colby, Bainbridge	Spec. Asst. to Atty. Gen.	1917
	Comr., U.S. Shipping Bd. Emer. Fleet	1917–19
Colman, Norman	U.S. Comr. Agric.	1885–89
Connally, John	Secy. of the Navy	1961–62
Connor, John	Head, Ofc. of Sci. Research & Dvlpmt.	1942–44
	Counsel, Ofc. of Naval Research	1946

	Spec. Asst. to Secy. Navy	1946–47
Cuomo, Andrew	Asst. Secy. HUD	1993–96
Daley, William	Spec. Counsel to Pres.	1993
Daniels, Josephus	Chf. Clerk, U.S. Dept. Interior	1893–95
Davis, Dwight	Mbr., War Finance Corp.	1921–23
	Asst. Secy. War	1923–25
	Acting Secy. War	1925
	Gov. Gen., Philippines	1929–32
	Dir. Gen., Army Spec. Corps	1942
Dawes, Charles	Comp. of the Currency	1898–1901
	Dir., Bureau of Budget	1921–23
	Recon. Finance Corp.	1932
Delano, Columbus	Comr. of Int. Revenue	1869–70
Derwinski, Edward	Counselor, State Dept.	1983–87
	Undersecy. State	1987–89
	Dir., Veterans Admin.	1989
Devens, Charles	U.S. Marshal	1849–53
Dillon, Douglas	Dep. Undersecy. State	1957–58
	Undersecy. State for Econ. Affairs	1958–59
	Undersecy. State	1959–60
Dole, Elizabeth	Asst. to Asst. Secy. HEW	1966–67
	Dep. Dir., Ofc. of Consumer Affairs	1971
	Dep. Asst. to Pres.	1971–73
	Asst. to Pres.	1981–83
Donaldson, Jesse	Dep. Asst. Postm. Gen.	1933–45
	Chf. Post Ofc. Inspector	1945–46
	Asst. Postm. Gen.	1946–47
Dulles, John Foster	Spec. Agt., Dept. of State	1917
	Consultant to Secy. State	1951–52
Duncan, Charles	Dep. Secy. Defense	1977–79
Eagleburger, Lawrence	Foreign Service Officer, State Dept.	1957–69
		1975–84
	Asst. to Nat. Security Adviser	1969–71
	Dep. Asst. Secy. Defense	1971–73
	Acting Asst. Secy. Defense	1973
	Exec. Asst. to Secy. Defense	1973–75
	Dep. Undersecy. Defense	1975–77
	Asst. Secy. State	1981–82

	Undersecy. State	1982–84
	Dep. Secy. State	1989–92
Edison, Charles	Natl. Recovery Bd.	1935
	Asst. Secy. Navy	1936–39
	Acting Secy. Navy	1939
Eisenhower, Dwight	Asst. Exec. to Asst. Secy. War	1929–33
	Spec. Asst. to Army Chief of Staff	1933–39
	Commander, NATO	1951–52
Fairchild, Charles	Asst. Secy. Treas.	1885–86
	Acting Secy. Treas.	1886–87
Forrestal, James	Admin. Asst. to Pres.	1940
	Undersecy. Navy	1940–44
	Acting Secy. Navy	1944
Fowler, Henry	Undersecy. Treas.	1961–64
Franklin, Barbara H.	White House Asst.	1971–73
Gates, Thomas	Undersecy. of Navy	1955–57
	Secy. of Navy	1957–59
	Undersecy. of Defense	1959–60
Gilpin, Henry	Dir. Bank of U.S.	1833–37
	Solicitor, Dept. of Treasury	1837–40
Gore, Howard	Asst. of U.S. Food Admin.	1917
	Chf. of Trade Practices, Dept. of Agric.	1921–23
	Asst. Secy. Agric.	1923–24
Gregory, Thomas W.	Spec. Asst. to U.S. Atty. Gen.	1912–14
Griffin, Cyrus	Comr. to Creek Nation	1789
Haig, Alexander	White House Chief of Staff	1973–74
Hannegan, Robert	Dist. Collector of Int. Revenue	1942–43
	Comr. of Int. Revenue	1943–44
Harriman, Averell	Business Adv. Coun., Dept. Commerce	1933–39
	Asst. Admin., National Recovery Admin.	1934–35
	Ofc. of Prod. Mgmt.	1940–41
	Spec. Asst. to Pres.	1950–51
	Dir., Mutual Security Agency	1951–53
	Asst. Secy. State	1961–63
	Undersecy. State	1963–65
	Asst. to Pres.	1968–69
Harrison, William H.	Comr. of Indian Affairs	1801–13
Hatton, Frank	Asst. Postm. Gen.	1881–82
Hendricks, Thomas	Comr. of Gen. Land Office	1855–59

Herman, Alexis	Dir., Women's Bureau, Labor Dept.	1977–81
	Asst. to Pres.	1993–96
Herrington, John	Dep. Asst. to Pres.	1981
	Asst. Secy. Navy	1981–83
	Asst. to Pres.	1983–85
Herter, Christian	Amer. Relief Admin.	1919
	Asst. Secy. Commerce	1919–24
	Undersecy. State	1957–59
	Negotiator on Foreign Trade	1962–65
Hitchcock, Frank	Chf. Clerk, Dept. Commerce and Labor	1903–04
	Asst. Postm. Gen.	1905–08
Hobby, Oveta	Section Chief, War Dept.	1941–42
	Dir., Women's Auxiliary Army Corp	1942–45
	Admin., Federal Security Agency	1953
Hodel, Donald	Dep. Dir., Bonneville Power Admin.	1969–72
	Undersecy. Interior	1981–82
Hodges, Luther	Ofc. of Price Admin.	1944
	Consultant to Secy. Agric.	1945
Hodgson, James	Undersecy. Labor	1969–70
Holt, Joseph	Comr. of Patents	1857–59
Hoover, Herbert	U.S. Food Admin.	1917–19
Hughes, Charles	Spec. Asst. to Atty. Gen.	1906
Hurley, Patrick	Asst. Secy. War	1928–29
Jackson, Robert	Counsel, SEC	1935
	Asst. Atty. Gen.	1937–38
	Solicitor General	1938–40
Johnson, Louis	Aide to Secy. War	1933–37
	Asst. Secy. War	1937–40
Kantor, Mickey	U.S. Trade Rep.	1993–96
Katzenbach, Nicholas	Asst. Atty. Gen.	1961–62
	Dep. Atty. Gen.	1962–64
	Acting Atty. Gen.	1964–65
	Undersecy. State	1966–69
Kendall, Amos	Aud. of the Treas.	1832–35
Kennedy, David	Bd. of Gov., Fed. Reserve System	1930–46
	Spec. Asst. to Secy. Treas.	1953–54
King, Horatio	Clerk, U.S. Post Office	1839–41
	Dept. Head, U.S. Post Office	1841–50
	Supt., U.S. Post Office	1850–54

	First Asst. Postm. Gen.	1854–61
	Acting Postm. Gen.	1861
Kleppe, Thomas	Head, Small Bus. Admin.	1971
Klutznick, Philip	Federal Housing Comm.	1944–46
Knebel, John	Undersecy. Agric.	1975–76
Krug, Julius	Public Utilities Expert, FCC	1935–37
	Chf. Power Engineer, TVA	1938–43
	Head of Power Branch, Ofc. of Prod. Mgmt.	1943–44
	Head of Ofc. of War Utilities	1943–44
Lamont, Daniel	Private Secy. to Pres. Cleveland	1885
Lamont, Robert	Procurement Div., Army Ordnance Dept.	1918–19
Levi, Edward	Spec. Asst. to Atty. Gen.	1940–45
Lovett, Robert	Asst. Secy. War	1941–45
	Undersecy. Defense	1947–51
	Consultant to Pres. Kennedy	1961–63
Lyng, Richard	Dir. Commodity Credit Corp.	1969–73
	Dep. Secy. Agriculture	1981–86
Lynn, James	Undersecy. Dept. Comm.	1971–72
Marshall, James	Asst. Postm. Gen.	1869–74
McAdoo, William	Dir. Gen., U.S. Railroads	1917–19
McCulloch, Hugh	Comp. of the Currency	1863–65
McGranery, James	Asst. Atty. Gen.	1943–46
McLaughlin, Ann	Dir. EPA Office of Public Info.	1973–74
	Asst. Secy. Public Affairs, Treasury	1981–84
	Undersecy. Interior	1984–87
McNamara, Robert	Consultant, War Dept.	1942–43
McReynolds, James	Asst. Atty. Gen.	1903–07
	Spec. Counsel	1907–12
Meese, Edwin	Counselor to Pres.	1981–85
Mills, Ogden	Undersecy. Treas.	1927–32
Mitchell, James	Admin., WPA	1936–41
	Dir. of Indus. Personnel, War Dept.	1941–45
	Asst. Secy. Army	1953–54
Morgenthau, Henry	Farm Credit Admin.	1933
	Acting Secy. Treas.	1933–34
	Undersecy. Treas.	1934
	Secy. Treas. *ad int.*	1934
Mueller, Frederick	Asst. Secy. Commerce	1958

	Undersecy. Commerce	1958–59
Murphy, Frank	Gov. Gen. Philippines	1935–36
Newberry, Truman	Asst. Secy. Navy	1905–08
Norton, Gale	Asst. to Dep. Secy. Agri.	1984–85
	Assoc. Solicitor, Interior	1985–87
O'Brien, Lawrence	Asst. to Pres. for Nat. Security	1961–65
O'Leary, Hazel	Dir., Cost of Living Coun.	1972–74
	Dir., Fed. Energy Admin.	1974–76
	Asst. Admin., Fed. Energy Admin.	1977
	Dep. Dir., Econ. Reg. Adm., Energy Dept.	1977–79
	Dir., Econ. Reg. Adm., Energy Dept.	1979–81
O'Neill, Paul	Systems Analyst, Veterans Admin.	1961–66
	Examiner, Bur. of Budget	1967–69
	Div. Chief, OMB	1969–70
	Asst. Dir., OMB	1971–72
	Assoc. Dir., OMB	1973–74
	Dep. Dir., OMB	1974–77
Osgood, Samuel	Comr., U.S. Treas.	1785–89
Palmer, Alexander	Alien Property Custodian	1917–19
Patterson, Robert	Asst. Secy. War	1940–45
Paulding, James	Secy., Bd. of Naval Comrs.	1815
Perkins, Frances	Civil Service Comr.	1945–53
Perry, William	Undersecy. Defense	1977–81
	Dep. Secy. Defense	1993–94
Pierce, Samuel	Asst. Undersecy. Labor	1955–56
	Gen. Counsel, Treasury	1970–73
Powell, Colin	Asst. to Dep Dir., Ofc. Management & Budget	1972–73
	Staff Officer, Defense Dept.	1974–76
	Exec. Asst. to Secy. Energy	1979
	Sr. Milit. Asst. to Secy. Defense	1979–81
	Milit. Asst. to Secy. Defense	1983–86
	Dep. Asst. to Pres. for Nat. Security	1987
	Asst. to Pres. for Nat. Security	1987–89
	Army Chief of Staff & Chair, Jt. Chiefs of Staff	1989–93
Principi, Anthony	Ofc. of Leg. Affairs, Dept. of Navy	1981–83
	Assoc. Dep. Admin., Veterans Admin.	1983–84

	Dep. Secy. Veterans Admin.	1989–92
	Acting Secy. Veterans Admin.	1992–93
Randall, Alexander	Asst. Postm. Gen.	1863–66
Reich, Robert	Asst. Solicitor Gen., Justice Dept.	1974–76
	Dir., Federal Trade Commission	1976–81
	Section Chief, Ofc. of Technological Assmt.	1990–91
Richardson, Elliot	Asst. Secy., Dept. of HEW	1957–59
	Acting Secy., Dept. of HEW	1958
	Spec. Asst. to U.S. Atty. Gen.	1961
	Undersecy. State	1969–70
Richardson, William A.	Asst. Secy. Treas.	1869–73
Richardson, William B.	Staff, Dept. of State	1973–75
Rockefeller, Nelson	Asst. Secy. State	1944–45
	Undersecy. HEW	1953–54
Rogers, William	Dep. Atty. Gen.	1952–58
Roosevelt, Franklin	Asst. Secy. Navy	1913–20
Roosevelt, Theodore	U.S. Civil Service Bd.	1889–95
	Asst. Secy. Navy	1897–98
Roper, Daniel	Spec. Agt., Fed. Bureau of Census	1900–11
	Asst. Postm. Gen.	1913–16
	Comr. of Int. Revenue	1917–20
Royall, Kenneth	Spec. Asst. to Secy. War	1944–45
Rubin, Robert	Asst. to Pres.; Dir., Nat. Econ. Coun.	1993–95
Rumsfeld, Donald	Dir., OEO	1969–70
	Dir., Cost of Living Coun. & Couns. to Pres.	1971–72
	White House Chief of Staff	1974–75
Rush, Richard	Comp. of the Treas.	1811–14
Rusk, Dean	Staff, War Dept.	*ca.* 1945
	Asst. Chf., Intl. Security Affairs, Dept. State	1946
	Spec. Asst. to Secy. War	1946–47
	Dir., Off. of Spec. Pol. Affairs & UN Affairs	1947–49
	Asst. Secy. State	1949
	Dep. Undersecy. State	1949–50
	Asst. Secy. State	1950–51
Seaton, Frederic	Asst. Secy. Defense	1953–55

	Asst. to Pres.	1955–56
Schlesinger, James	Consultant, Bur. of Budget	1965–69
	Asst. Dir. Bur. of Budget	1969
	Acting Dep., Dir., Bur. of Budget	1969–70
	Asst. Dir., OMB	1970–71
	Dir., CIA	1973
	Asst. to Pres.	1977
Shalala, Donna	Asst. Secy. HUD	1977–80
Shultz, George	Consultant to Ofc. of Secy. Labor	1960
	Dir., OMB	1970–72
Simon, William	Dep. Secy. Treasury	1973–74
Skinner, Samuel	White House Chief of Staff	1991–92
Slater, Rodney	Admin., Fed. Highway Admin., Dept. Transportn.	1993–97
Snyder, John	Natl. Bank Receiver	1930–36
	Fed. Loan Admin.	1945
	Dir., War Mobilization & Reconversion	1945–46
Stans, Maurice	Financial Cons. to Postm. Gen.	1953–55
	Dep. Postm. Gen.	1955–57
	Dep. Dir., Bureau of Budget	1957–58
	Dir., Bureau of Budget	1958–61
Stettinius, Edward	Dir., Ofc. of Prod. Mgmt.	1941
	Spec. Asst. to Pres.	1941–43
	Undersecy. State	1943–44
	Pres. Adv. at Yalta Conference	1945
Stevenson, Adlai	Asst. Postm. Gen.	1885–89
Stimson, Henry	Gov. Gen. Philippines	1927–29
Summers, Lawrence	Staff, Coun. of Econ. Advisers	1982–83
	Dep. Asst. Secy. Treasury	1993
	Undersecy. Treasury	1993–95
	Dep. Secy. Treasury	1995–97
Thomas, Philip	Comp. of U.S. Treas.	1851–53
	Comr. of Patents	1860
Thompson, Richard	Collector of Int. Revenue	1861–65
Thornburgh, Richard	Asst. Atty. Gen.	1975–77
Toucey, Isaac	Acting Secy. State	1849–50
Trowbridge, Alexander	Employee of CIA	1951
	Asst. Secy. Commerce	1965–67

	Acting Secy. Commerce	1967
Tyner, James	Spec. Agt. for Post Ofc. Dept.	1861–66
	Second Asst. Postm. Gen.	1875–76
	First Asst. Postm. Gen.	1877–81
	Del. to Intl. Postal Congresses	1878; 1897
	Asst. Atty. Gen.	1889–93; 1897–1903
Usery, Willie	Secy. of Labor	1976–77
Usher, John	Asst. Secy. Interior	1862–63
Vance, Cyrus	General Counsel, Dept. of Army	1961–62
	Secy. Army	1962–63
	Dep. Secy. Defense	1964–67
	Secy. State	1977–80
Veneman, Ann	Admin., Dept. of Agri.	1985–89
	Dep. Undersecy. Agri.	1989–91
	Dep. Secy. Agri.	1991–93
Vinson, Frederick	Dir., Ofc. of Econ. Stabilization	1943–45
	Fed. Loan Admin.	1945
Volpe, John	Fed. Highway Admin.	1956–57
Walker, Frank	Exec. Dir., Natl. Emer. Council	1933–35
Watkins, James	Branch Head, Bur. of Naval Personnel (BNP)	1969–71
	Div. Dir., BNP	1971–72
	Asst. Chief, BNP	1972–73
	Dep. Chief and Chief, BNP	1975–78
	Chief of Naval Ops. & Jt. Chiefs of Staff	1982–86
Watson, Marvin	Spec. Asst. to Pres.	1965–68
Watt, James	Undersecy. Interior	1969–72
	Bur. of Outdoor Recreation, Interior Dept.	1972–75
	Federal Power Comm.	1975–77
Weaver, Robert	Adv. of Negro Affairs, Dept. of Interior	1933–37
Weeks, Sinclair	Chmn. of Finance Comt.	1949–52
Weinberger, Caspar	Dep. Dir., Off. Mgmt. and Budget	1972–73
	Secy. HEW	1973–75
West, Roy	Spec. Asst. to U.S. Atty. Gen.	1941–53
West, Togo	Assoc. Dep Atty. Gen.	1975–76
	General Couns., Dept. of Navy	1977–79

	Dep. Secy. Defense	1979–80
	General Couns., Dept. of Defense	1980–81
	Secy. Army	1993–98
Wickard, Claude	Agric. Adjust. Admin.	1933–37
	Asst. Div. Dir., Agric. Adjust. Admin.	1937
	Dir., Agric. Adjust. Admin.	1937–40
	Undersec. Agric.	1940
	Admin., Rural Electrification Admin.	1945–53
Wilbur, Ray	Conservation Div., Food Admin.	1917
Wirtz, William	Undersec. Labor	1961–62
Wolcott, Oliver	Aud., U.S. Treas.	1789–91
	Comp. of U.S. Treas.	1791–95
Wood, Robert	Mgmt. Org. Expert, Bureau of Budget	1951–54
	Undersec. HUD	1966–68
Woodring, Henry	Asst. Secy. War	1932–33
	Asst. Secy. War for Air	1933–36
Work, Hubert	Asst. Postm. Gen.	1921–22
Yeutter, Clayton	Admin., Dept. of Agri.	1970–71
	Asst. Secy. Agriculture	1973–75
	Dep. Spec. Trade Rep.	1975–77
	U.S. Trade Rep.	1985–89
	Counsel to Pres.	1992

FEDERAL COMMISSIONS AND COMMITTEES

Name	Commission or Committee	Dates
Acheson, Dean	Exec. Admin. Investig. Comm.	1939
	Comm. for Org. of Exec. Branch	1947–49
	U.S.-Canadian Defense Bd.	1947–48
Alexander, Joshua	Comm. of U.S. to Intl. Conf. on Safety at Sea	1913–14
Alexander, Lamar	Pres.'s Cmsn. to Celebrate the Great Outdoors	1985–87
	Natl. Cmsn. on Philanthropy	1996–97
Anderson, Clinton	U.S. Coronado Exposition Comm.	1939–40
Aspin, Les	Pres.'s Foreign Intell. Adv. Bd.	1994–95
Babbitt, Bruce	Pres.'s Cmsn. on the Accident at Three Mile Island	1979–80

	Adv. Cmsn. on Intergovernmental Relations	1980–84
	Nuclear Safety Oversight Cmsn.	1980–81
Baker, Newton	Natl. Comm. on Law Enforcemt. and Observ.	1929
Ballinger, Richard	Commr., Gen. Land Office	1907
Bayard, Thomas	Chf. Counsel to Investig. TVA	1938–39
Biddle, Francis	Chmn., Natl. Labor Relations Bd.	1934–35
Bonaparte, Charles	Bd. of Indian Cmsnrs.	1902–04
Boutwell, George	Comm. to Edit Statutes at Large	1877
Boyd, Alan	Civil Aero. Bd.	1959–61
Brady, Nicholas	National Bipartisan Comm. on Central America	1983
	Comm. on Executive, Legislative & Judicial Salaries	1985
	Stock Market Crisis Comm.	1987–88
Brewster, Benjamin	Commr. for Cherokee Indians	1846
Brown, Harold	Air Force Adv. Bd.	1956–61
	Congrl. Technology Assessment Adv. Council	1974–77
	Cmsn. on Roles & Capabilities of U.S. Intell. Cmmty.	1995–96
Brown, Jesse	Pres.'s Health Care Reform Committee	1993
Brown, Ronald H.	Natl. Adv. Cmsn. on Criminal Justice	1973
	Natl. Cmsn. for UNESCO	1977–79
Burleson, Albert	U.S. Comm. to Intl. Wire Communications Conf.	1920
Carter, Jimmy	Hon. Co-chair, Natl. Cmsn. on Federal Election Reform	2001
Chao, Elaine	Chair, Fed. Maritime Cmsn.	1988–89
Chapman, Oscar	Comm. to Coord. Health and Welfare Svcs.	1935
	Comm. on Voc. Education	1936
	Comm. to Review Charges of Subversion…	1941–42
Cisneros, Henry	Natl. Bipartisan Cmsn. on Central America	1983
Clifford, Clark	Comm. on Defense Estab.	1960
	Foreign Adv. Bd.	1961
	Foreign Intel. Adv. Bd.	1963–68
Creswell, John	Counsel for U.S. to *Alabama* Claims Comm.	1874–76
Cushing, Caleb	Counsel for U.S. to Geneva to settle *Alabama* claims	1872–74

Dawes, Charles	Reparations Comt.	1923
Day, William	Mixed Claims Comm.	1922
Dole, Elizabeth	Exec. Dir., Pres. Comm. on Consumer Interest	1969–71
	Commissioner, Federal Trade Cmsn.	1973–79
Dulles, John F.	Asst. to Chair, War Labor Bd.	1917–18
	War Trade Bd.	1918
Durkin, Martin	Defense Mobil. Bd.	1953
	Natl. Security Resources Bd.	1953
	Natl. War Labor Bd.	ca. 1950
Espy, Michael	Adv. Bd. to Secy. Energy	1999–2001
Farley, James	Comm. on Org. of Exec. Branch	1953
Fish, Hamilton	Comm. for Relief of Civil War Pris.	1867–69
Flemming, Arthur	Civil Service Comm.	1939–48
	War Manpower Comm.	1942–45
	Comm. for Org. of Exec. Branch	1947
	Atomic Energy Comm.	1948
	Asst. to Dir., Defense Mobil.	1951
	Pres. Adv. Comm. on Govt. Org.	1953
	Dir., Ofc. of Defense Mobil.	1953
	Natl. Security Council	1953
	Natl. Adv. Comm. on Peace Corps	1961
Folsom, Marion	Business Adv. Council	1936–48
	Adv. Council on Social Security	1937–38
	Reg. War Manpower Comt.	1942–45
	Adv. Comm. on Merchant Marine	1947–48
Ford, Gerald R.	Warren Cmsn. to Investigate Death of Pres. Kennedy	1963–64
	Hon. Co-chair, Natl. Cmsn. on Federal Election Reform	2001
Fowler, Henry	War Prod. Bd.	1942–44
	Nat. Prod. Auth.	1951–52
	Defense Prod. Admin.	1952–53
	Natl. Comm. on Money and Credit	n. a.
Franklin, Barbara	Consumer Product Safety Cmsn.	1973–79
	U.S.-Russia Bus. Development Comm.	ca. 1992
	Pres.'s Adv. Coun. for Trade Policy & Negots.	1982–86, 1989–92

Gardner, John	Adv. Comm. on Intl. Educ. and Cultural Affairs	1962–64
	White House Conf. on Ed.	1965
Garfield, James	Civil Service Comm.	1902–03
	Commr. of Corporations	1903
Griffin, Cyrus	Commr. to Creek Nation	1789
Hardin Clifford M.	Foreign Aid Review Comt.	1962
	Agricul. Dept. Task Force	1968
Harrison, William	Commr., Ofc. of Indian Affairs	1800–13
Hendricks, Thomas	Commr., General Land Ofc.	1855–59
Herrington, John	Reserve Forces Policy Bd.	1981–83
	Per Diem Cmsn., Dept. of Defense	1982–83
Hoar, Ebenezer	Comm. on *Alabama* Claims	1871–72
Hobby, Oveta	Comm. for Org. of Exec. Branch (Hoover Comm.)	1948
	Security Admin.	1953
Hodges, Luther	Intl. Mgmt. Conf.	1951
Hoover, Herbert	Indust. Conf.	1920
Hopkins, Harry	Fed. Emer. Relief Admin.	1933
	Adm., Lend-Lease Prog.	1940–41
	War Prod. Bd.	1942–44
	War Resources Bd.	1942–45
Humphrey, Hubert	WPA Admin. Staff	1941–43
	Asst. Reg. Dir., War Manpower Comm.	1943
Jackson, Robert	Spec. Counsel, Sec. & Exch.	1935
Jones, Jesse	War Prod. Bd.	1942–44
Kantor, Mickey	Nat. Adv. Cmsn. on Criminal Justice Goals & Standards	1972
Kendall, Amos	Indian Agt. for Collections of Claims	1843
Kennedy, David	Comm. on Fed. Budget Drafting	1967
Krug, Julius	War Prod. Bd.	1942–44
	Dir., Ofc. of War Utilities	1943
	Acting Head, War Prod. Bd.	1944
	Permanent Chmn., War Prod. Bd.	1944–45
Lane, Franklin	Member, Interstate Commerce Comm.	1906–13
	Chmn., Interstate Commerce Comm.	1913
Marcy, William	Commr. on Mexican Claims	1839–42
Marshall, F. Ray	Chmn., Comm. on Apprenticeships	n.a.
Marshall, Thomas	Fed. Coal Comm.	1922–23

McElroy, Neil	Chmn., White House Conf. on Ed.	1955
McLean, John	Commr., Land Ofc.	1822–23
Miller, G. William	Chmn., Federal Reserve Bank	1978–79
Mitchell, James	Comm. for Org. of Exec. Branch (Hoover Comm.)	1948
Muskie, Edmund	Tower Cmsn. to Investigate Iran-Contra	1986
Perry, William	Pres. Foreign Intell. Adv. Bd.	n.a.
Peterson, Peter	Chmn., Council on Int'l. Econ. Affairs	1971
Porter, Peter	Northwestern Boundary Comm.	1816
Powell, Colin	Chair, Pres.'s Summit for America's Future	1997
Principi, Anthony	Chair, Congrl. Cmsn. on Veteran Transition Assistance.	1998–99
Ramsey, Alexander	Chmn., Edmunds Comm.	1882–86
Roper, Daniel	Clerk, Sen. Comm. on Interstate Comm.	1893–96
	Clerk, House Ways and Means Commt.	1911
	Tariff Comm.	1917
Royall, Kenneth	Pres. Race Comm.	1963
Rubin, Robert	Pres.'s Adv. Comm. for Trade Negotiations	1980–82
	Adv. Comm., Securities & Exchange Cmsn.	1983
Rumsfeld, Donald	Pres.'s Adv. Comm. on Arms Control	1982–86
	U.S. Jt. Adv. Cmsn. on U.S.-Japan Relations	1983–84
	Pres.'s Panel on Strategic Systems	1983–84
	Natl. Cmsn. on the Public Service	1987–90
	Natl. Economic Cmsn.	1988–89
	Cmsn. on U.S.-Japan Relations	1989–90
	Adv. Comm., Federal Communications Cmsn.	1992–93
	Chair, Cmsn. to Assess Ballistic Missile Threat	1998–99
	U.S. Federal Trade Deficit Review Cmsn.	1999–2000
	Chair, U.S. Cmsn. to Assess Natl. Sec.	2000
Schlesinger, James	Chmn., Atomic Ener. Comm.	1971–73
Shalala, Donna	Co-chair, Adv. Cmsn. on Health Care Industry	1996–2000
Shultz, George	Cons., Pres. Cmsn. on Labor-Mngt. Policy	1961–62
Simon, William	Dir., Fed. Energ. Off.	1973–74
Smith, Caleb	Mexican Claims Bd.	1849–51
Smith, Hoke	Jt. Comm. on Natl. Aid to Voc. Ed.	1914
Snyder, John	Dir., War Mobil. and Reconversion	1945–46

Stans, Maurice	Consultant, House Approp. Comt.	1953
Stettinius, Edward	War Resources Bd.	1938–51
Summers, Lawrence	Pres.'s Council of Economic Advisers	1982–83
Taft, William H.	Jt. Chmn., Natl. War Labor Conf. Bd.	1918–19
Teller, Henry	Monetary Comm.	1908
Trowbridge, Alexander	Pres.'s Task Force on Private Sector Initiatives	n.a.
	Natl. Cmsn. on Social Security Reform	1982
	Natl. Cmsn. on Exec., Leg., and Judicial Salaries	1985
	Natl. Cmsn. on the Public Services	*ca.* 1987
Usery, Willie	Dir., Med. and Concil. Serv.	1973–76
Verity, C. William	Bipartisan Task Force on Private Sector Initiatives	1981
	U.S.-U.S.S.R. Trade Council	1979–84
Vinson, Frederick	Dir., War Mobil. and Reconversion	1945
Watkins, James	Chairman, Pres.'s Cmsn. on AIDS	1987
Weaver, Robert	Housing & Home Finance Comm.	1961–66
Weinberger, Caspar	Chmn., FTC	1970
West, Togo	Natl. Adv. Comm., UN Association USA	1991–93
Wickersham, George	War Trade Bd. to Cuba	1918
	Natl. Comm. on Law Observ. Enforcemt.	1929
Wilson, William B.	Intl. Jr. Comm.	1921
Wirtz, William	Assoc. Gen. Counsel, Bd. of Economic Warfare	1942–43
	Gen. Counsel, War Labor Bd.	1943–45
	Chairman, Natl. Wage Stabilization Bd.	1946
Wright, Luke	Member, Philippine Comm.	1900
	Pres., Philippine Comm.	1900–04

DIPLOMATIC CORPS

Name	Office	Dates
Acheson, Dean G.	Del. to U.N. Monetary and Financial Conference	1944
Adams, John Q.	Min. to Netherlands	1794
Adams, John Q.	Min. to Russia	1808
Albright, Madeleine	Amb. to U.N.	1993–97
Armstrong, John	Min. to France	1804–10

Armstrong, John	Acting Min. to Spain	1806
Bacon, Robert	Amb. to France	1909–12
Baker, Newton D.	Del. Permanent Court of Arbitration, The Hague	1928
Bancroft, Robert	Min. to Great Britain	1846
Barbour, James	Min. to Great Britain	1828–29
Barry, William T.	Min. to Spain	1835
Bayard, Thomas F.	Amb. to Great Britain	1893–97
Biddle, Francis B.	Del., Permanent Court of Arbitration, The Hague	n.a.
Blumenthal, W. Michael	Sp. Rep. for Trade	1963–67
Borie, Adolph	Consul to Belgium	1843
Buchanan, James	Min. to Russia	1832–34
Buchanan, James	Min. to Great Britain	1853–56
Bush, George H.W.	Amb. to U.N.	1971–73
Bush, George H.W.	Liaison Office to China	1974–75
Cameron, Simon	Min. to Russia	1862–63
Campbell, George W.	Min. to Russia	1818–20
Carlucci, Frank C., III	Vice Consul, Union of South Africa	1956–60
Carlucci, Frank C., III	Vice Consul, Congo	1960–62
Carlucci, Frank C., III	Head, Congo Desk	1962–65
Carlucci, Frank C., III	Amb. to Brazil	1965–69
Carlucci, Frank C., III	Amb. to Portugal	1974–77
Carlucci, Frank C., III	Deputy Dir. CIA	1978–81
Cass, Lewis	Min. to France	1836–42
Clifford, Nathan	Min. to Mexico	1848–53
Cohen, Wilbur J.	Consultant to U.N.	1956–57
Corwin, Thomas	Min. to Mexico	1861–64
Crawford, William H.	Min. to France	1813–15
Cushing, Caleb	Min. to China	1843–45
Cushing, Caleb	Min. to Spain	1874–77
Dallas, George M.	Min. to Russia	1837–39
Dallas, George M.	Min. to Great Britain	1856–61
Daniels, Josephus	Amb. to Mexico	1933–41
Davis, Dwight F.	Gov.-Gen., Philippines	1929–32
Dawes, Charles G.	Amb. to Great Britain	1929–32
Dawes, Charles G.	Del. to London Naval Conf.	1930
Dearborn, Henry	Min. to Portugal	1822–24
Derwinski, Edward	Del. to U.N.	1971

Dickinson, Donald McD.	Counsel to Comm. on Bering Sea Claims	1896
Dickinson, Donald McD.	U.S.-El Salvador Court of Arbitration	1902
Dickinson, Jacob McG.	U.S. Counsel to Alaskan Boundary Tribunal	1903
Dillon, C. Douglas	Amb. Extraordinary Plenipot. to France	1953–57
Dix, John A.	Min. to France	1866–69
Dulles, John F.	Amer. Comt. to Negotiate Peace	1918–19
Dulles, John F.	Reparations Comt.	1919
Dulles, John F.	Supreme Economic Council	1919
Dulles, John F.	Berlin Dept. Conference	1933
Dulles, John F.	San Fran. Conference on World Organization	1945
Dulles, John F.	Adviser, Council of Foreign Ministers, London	1945
Dulles, John F.	U.N. Representative	1946–49
Dulles, John F.	Adviser, Council of Foreign Ministers, Moscow and London	1947
Dulles, John F.	U.S. Del. to France	1948; 1950
Dulles, John F.	Council of Foreign Ministers, Paris	1949
Dulles, John F.	Amb. to Peace Treaty Negotiations	1950–51
Eagleburger, Lawrence	Amb. to Yugoslavia	1977–81
Eaton, John H.	Min. to Spain	1836–40
Evarts, William M.	Envoy to Great Britain	1863–64
Evarts, William M.	Del. to International Monetary Conference, Paris	1881
Everett, Edward	Min. to Great Britain	1841–45
Fairbanks, Charles W.	U.S.-British Joint High Comm.	1898
Folsom, Marion B.	Del. to International Labor Conference, Geneva	1936
Forsyth, John	Min. to Spain	1819–23
Forward, Walter	Chargé d'affaires. Denmark	1849–51
Foster, John W.	Min. to Mexico	1873
Foster, John W.	Min. to Russia	1880–81
Foster, John W.	Min. to Spain	1883
Foster, John W.	Agent to Madrid Treaty Negotiations	1890
Foster, John W.	Agent to Bering Sea Arbitration	n.a.
Foster, John W.	Second Hague Conference	1907
Fowler, Henry H.	U.S. Mission of Economic Affairs in London	1944
Fowler, Henry H.	Foreign Economic Admin.	1945

Francis, David R.	Amb. to Russia	1916
Franklin, Barbara H.	Publ. Del. to U.N.	1989–93
Gallatin, Albert	Negotiator for Treaty of Ghent	1814
Gallatin, Albert	Min. to France	1815–23
Goldberg, Arthur J.	U.N. Representative	1965–68
Gregory, Thomas W.	Adviser to Versailles Peace Conference	*ca.* 1917
Griggs, John W.	Permanent Court of Arbitration, The Hague	1901–02
Hamlin, Hannibal	Min. to Spain	1881–82
Hardin, Clifford M.	Del. to International Conference of Agricultural Economists	1947
Harriman, William A.	Amb. to U.S.S.R.	1943–46
Harriman, William A.	Amb. to Great Britain	1946
Harriman, William A.	U.S. Representative in Europe	1946
Harriman, William A.	Amb. Extraordinary	1948–50
Harriman, William A.	NATO Defense Representative	1951
Harriman, William A.	Amb.-at-Large	1961; 1965
Harriman, William A.	Peace Talks Representative on Vietnam	1968–69
Harris, Patricia R.	Amb. to Luxembourg	1965–67
Harrison, William H.	Min. to Colombia	1828–29
Hay, John M.	Min. to Great Britain	1897–98
Herter, Christian A.	Del. in Brussels	1917
Herter, Christian A.	American Comm. for Peace with Germany	1918
Hitchcock, Ethan A.	Min. to Russia	1897
Hoover, Herbert C.	American Relief Comt., London	1914–15
Hoover, Herbert C.	Comm. for Relief of Belgium	1915–19
Hoover, Herbert C.	Supreme Economic Conference, Paris	1919
Hopkins, Harry L.	Del. to London	1940; 1941
Hopkins, Harry L.	Del. to U.S.S.R.	1941
Hughes, Charles E.	Del., Permanent Court of Arbitration, The Hague	1926–30
Hughes, Charles E.	Del. to Pan-American Conference	1928
Hull, Cordell	Pan-American Conference	1940
Hull, Cordell	Del. to U.N. Conf., San Francisco	1945
Humphrey, Hubert	Del. to U.N.	1956–58
Hunt, William H.	Min. to Russia	1882–84
Hurley, Patrick J.	Min. to New Zealand	1942
Hurley, Patrick J.	Presidential Rep. to U.S.S.R.	n.a.
Hurley, Patrick J.	Amb. to China	1944–45
Jardine, William M.	Min. to Egypt	1930–33

Jay, John	Min. to Spain	1780
Jay, John	British Peace Negotiations	1782
Jay, John	Envoy to Great Britain	1794
Jefferson, Thomas	Min. Plenipot. to France	1784–87
Jewell, Marshall	Min. to Russia	1873
Johnson, Cave	Commr., U.S.-Paraguay Dispute	1860
Johnson, Louis A.	Rep. to India	1942
Johnson, Reverdy	Min. to Great Britain	1868–69
Kantor, Michael	U.S. Trade Rep.	1993–96
Kellogg, Frank B.	Del. to International Conference on American States	1923
Kellogg, Frank B.	Min. to Great Britain	1923–25
Kellogg, Frank B.	Del., Permanent Court for International Justice	1930–35
King, William R. deV.	Secy. of U.S. Legation, Naples	1816
King, William R. deV.	Secy. of U.S. Legation, Russia	1818
King, William R. deV.	Min. to France	1844–46
Klutznick, Philip M.	U.N. Delegate	1957
Klutznick, Philip M.	U.N. Amb.	1961–63
Lansing, Robert	Anglo-American Claims Arbitration	1912–14
Lansing, Robert	American Comm. to Negotiate Peace	1918–19
Legaré, Hugh S.	Chargé d'affaires, Belgium	1832–36
Lincoln, Robert T.	Min. to Great Britain	1889–93
Livingston, Edward	Min. to France	1833–35
MacVeagh, Wayne	Min. to Turkey	1870–72
MacVeagh, Wayne	Amb. to Italy	1893–97
MacVeagh, Wayne	Counsel to Venezuela Arb.	1903
Marshall, James W.	Consul at Leeds, England	1861–65
Marshall, John	Min. to France	1797
Mason, John Y.	Min. to France	1854–59
Maynard, Horace	Min. to Turkey	1875–80
McLane, Louis	Min. to Great Britain	1829–31; 1845–46
Mellon, Andrew W.	Amb. to Great Britain	1932–33
Meyer, George von L.	Amb. to Italy	1900–05
Meyer, George von L.	Amb. to Russia	1905–07
Mondale, Walter	Amb. to Japan	1993–96
Monroe, James	Min. to France	1794–99
Monroe, James	Min. to Great Britain	1803–07

Morton, Levi P.	Commr. to Paris Exhibition	1878
Morton, Levi P.	Min. to France	1881–85
Murphy, Frank	Gov.-Gen. of Philippines	1935–36
Nelson, John	Chargé d'affaires, Two Sicilies	1831–32
Payne, John B.	Commr. to Mexico	1923
Pierrepont, Edward S.	Min. to Great Britain	1876–77
Pinkney, William	Commr. to Great Britain	1796
Pinkney, William	Min. to London	1807–11
Pinkney, William	Min. to Russia	1816–18
Pinkney, William	Spec. Envoy to Naples	1816–18
Poinsett, Joel R.	Min. to Mexico	1825–29
Preston, William B.	Envoy to France	1858
Randall, Alexander W.	Min. to Italy	1862–63
Richardson, William B.	Amb. to U.N.	1997–98
Rodney, Caesar A.	Commr. to South America	n.a.
Rodney, Caesar A.	Min. to Argentina	1823–24
Root, Elihu	U.S. Counsel, North Atlantic Fisheries Dispute	1910
Root, Elihu	Envoy to Russia	1917
Root, Elihu	Commr. at Washington Conf. on Armaments Limitations	1921–22
Roper, Daniel C.	Min. to Canada	1839
Rumsfeld, Donald	Amb. to NATO	1973–74
Rush, Richard	Min. to Great Britain	1817
Rush, Richard	Min. to France	1847
Sawyer, Charles	Amb. to Belgium and Luxembourg	1944–46
Saxbe, William	Amb. to India	1975–77
Schofield, John McA.	Mission to France	1865–66
Schofield, John McA.	Mission to Hawaii	1872
Schurz, Carl	Min. to Spain	1862
Schwellenbach, Lewis B.	Del. to Interparliamentary Union, The Hague	1936
Sherman, William T.	Envoy to Mexico	1866
Smith, Charles Emory	Min. to Russia	1890–92
Stettinius, Edwin R., Jr.	Chief U.S. Del. to U.N. Conf., San Francisco	1945
Stettinius, Edwin R., Jr.	Del. to U.N.	1945–46
Stimson, Henry L.	Envoy to Nicaragua	1927
Stimson, Henry L.	Gov.-Gen., Philippines	1927–29

Stimson, Henry L.	Del., Intl. Ct. of Arbitration, The Hague	1938–40
Straus, Oscar S.	Min. to Turkey	1887–89; 1898–1900; 1902; 1908; 1909–10
Straus, Oscar S.	Del., Permanent Ct. of Arbitration, The Hague	1912; 1920
Strauss, Lewis L.	Del. to Armistice Convention, Brussels	1919
Swanson, Claude	Del. to Gen. Disarmament Conference	1932
Taft, Alphonso	Min. to Austria-Hungary	n.a
Taft, Alphonso	Min. to Russia	1884–85
Thornburgh, Richard	U.N. Undersecretary General	1992–93
Van Buren, Martin	Min. to Great Britain	1831–32
Walker, Frank C.	Alt. Del. to U.N.	1946
Walker, Frank C.	Rep. to U.N. Legal Comt.	1946
Walker, Robert J.	Financial Agt. to Europe	1863–64
Washburne, Elihu B.	Min. to France	1869–72
Wickersham, George	League of Nations Comt. to Codify Internatl. Law	n.a.
Wickersham, George	Pres., Internatl. Arbitral Tribunal, Young Plan	n.a.
Wickliffe, Charles A.	Envoy to Repub. of Texas	1845
Wilbur, Ray L.	Del. to Pan-American Conf.	1928
Wilkins, William	Min. to Russia	1834–35
Williams, George H.	Joint High Comm.	1871
Wright, Luke E.	Vice-Gov., Philippines	1901–04
Wright, Luke E.	Gov.-Gen., Philippines	1904–06
Wright, Luke E.	Amb. to Japan	1906–07
Wynne, Robert J.	Consul-Gen. to Great Britain	1905
Yeutter, Clayton	U.S. Trade Rep.	1985–89

State, County, and Municipal Government Service

STATE ADMINISTRATIVE SERVICE

Name	Office	State	Dates
Agnew, Spiro T.	Governor	Md.	1967–69
Alexander, Lamar	Governor	Tenn.	1979–87
Alger, Russell A.	Governor	Mich.	1885–87
Anderson, Clinton	Treasurer	N.M.	1933–34
Anderson, Robert	Asst. Atty. Gen.	Tex.	1933–34
Andrus, Cecil D.	Governor	Ida.	1970–77
Armstrong, John	Secy.	Pa.	1783–87
Ashcroft, John	Atty. Gen.	Mo.	1977–84
Ashcroft, John	Governor	Mo.	1985–92
Babbitt, Bruce	Atty. Gen.	Az.	1975–78
Babbitt, Bruce	Governor	Az.	1978–87
Barbour, James	Governor	Va.	1813–15
Barry, William T.	Lt. Governor	Ky.	1820–22
Barry, William T.	Secy. of State	Ky.	1824–25
Bates, Edward	State's Atty.	Mo.	1820–22
Bell, Griffin B.	Chf. of Staff	Ga.	1959–61
Bell, Terrel H.	Comm. of Education	Utah	1976–80
Block, John R.	Dir. Dept. of Agric.	Ill.	1977–80
Boutwell, George	Governor	Mass.	1851–52
Bowen, Otis R.	Governor	Ind.	1973–81
Bradford, William	Atty. Gen.	Pa.	1780–91

Branch, John	Governor	N.C.	1817–20
Branch, John	Territorial Governor	Fla.	1844–45
Breckinridge, John	Atty. Gen.	Ky.	1795–97
Brewster, Benjamin	Atty. Gen.	Pa.	1867–68
Brown, Aaron	Governor	Tenn.	1845–47
Burleson, Albert	Dist. Atty.	Tex.	1891–98
Burr, Aaron	Atty. Gen.	N.Y.	1789–90
Bush, George W.	Governor	Tex.	1995–2000
Byrnes, James F.	Solicitor of 2d Judicial Court	S.C.	1908
Byrnes, James	Governor	S.C.	1950–53
Campbell, James	Atty. Gen.	Pa.	1852
Carlisle, John	Lt. Governor	Ky.	1871–75
Carter, Jimmy	Governor	Ga.	1971–74
Chase, Salmon	Governor	Ohio	1855–59
Clayton, John	Secy. of State	Del.	1826–28
Cleveland, Grover	Governor	N.Y.	1883–85
Clifford, Nathan	Atty. Gen.	Me.	1834–38
Clinton, George	Governor	N.Y.	1777–97
Clinton, William J.	Atty. Gen.	Ark.	1977–79
Clinton, William J.	Governor	Ark.	1979–81; 1983–92
Connally, John B.	Governor	Tex.	1962–69
Coolidge, Calvin	Lt. Governor	Mass.	1916–18
Coolidge, Calvin	Governor	Mass.	1919–20
Corwin, Thomas	Governor	Ohio	1840–42
Cox, Jacob Dolson	Governor	Ohio	1866–68
Crawford, G. W.	Atty. Gen.	Ga.	1827–31
Crittenden, John	Territorial Atty. Gen.	Ill.	1809–10
Crittenden, John	Governor	Ky.	1848–50
Dallas, Alexander	Secy. of State	Pa.	1791–1801
Dern, George	Governor	Utah	1924–32
Dickerson, Mahlon	Adj. Gen.	Pa.	1805–08
Dickerson, Mahlon	Governor	N.J.	1815–17
Dix, John	Adj. Gen.	N.Y.	1830
Dix, John	Secy. of State	N.Y.	1833–39
Dix, John	Postmaster	N.Y.	1860–61
Dix, John	Governor	N.Y.	1872–74
Eaton, John	Territorial Governor	Fla.	1834–36
Edison, Charles	Governor	N.J.	1940–44

Edwards, James	Governor	S.C.	1975–78
Epsy, Michael	Asst. Secy. State	Miss.	1978–84
Epsy, Michael	Asst. Atty. Gen.	Miss.	1984 85
Eustis, William	Governor	Mass.	1823–25
Everett, Edward	Governor	Mass.	1836–40
Fairchild, Charles	Dep. Atty. Gen.	N.Y.	1874–75
Fairchild, Charles	Atty. Gen.	N.Y.	1875–77
Fillmore, Millard	Comptroller	N.Y.	1847–49
Finch, Robert	Lt. Governor	Calif.	1966–68
Fish, Hamilton	Lt. Governor	N.Y.	1847
Fish, Hamilton	Governor	N.Y.	1849–51
Floyd, John B.	Governor	Va.	1850–52
Forsyth, John	Atty. Gen.	Va.	1808
Forsyth, John	Governor	Ga.	1827–29
Foster, Charles	Governor	Ohio	1879–81
Francis, David	Governor	Mo.	1888–93
Freeman, Orville	Governor	Minn.	1955–61
Frelinghuysen, Frederick	Atty. Gen.	N.J.	1861–66
Garland, Augustus	Acting Secy. of State	Ark.	1874
Garland, Augustus	Governor	Ark.	1875–77
Gerry, Elbridge	Governor	Mass.	1810–12
Gilmer, Thomas	Governor	Va.	1840–41
Gore, Howard	Governor	W.Va.	1925–29
Graham, William	Governor	N.C.	1845–49
Griggs, John	Governor	N.J.	1896–98
Guthrie, James	Commonwealth Atty.	Ky.	1820
Hamilton, Paul	Comptroller	S.C.	1799–1804
Hamilton, Paul	Governor	S.C.	1804–06
Hamlin, Hannibal	Governor	Me.	1856–57
Hancock, John	Governor	Mass.	1780–85; 1787–93
Harding, Warren	Lt. Governor	Ohio	1904–05
Harmon, Judson	Governor	Ohio	1908–13
Hathaway, Stanley	Governor	Wyo.	1962–64
Hayes, Rutherford	Governor	Ohio	1868–77; 1876–77
Hendricks, Thomas	Governor	Ind.	1873–77
Herter, Christian	Governor	Mass.	1953–57
Hickel, Walter J.	Governor	Alaska	1966–68

Hodges, Luther H.	Lt. Governor	N.C.	1952–54
Hodges, Luther H.	Governor	N.C.	1954–61
Hughes, Charles	Governor	N.Y.	1906–10
Hunt, William H.	Atty. Gen.	La.	1876
Huntington, Samuel	Lt. Governor	Conn.	1785
Huntington, Samuel	Governor	Conn.	1786–96
Hyde, Arthur M.	Governor	Mo.	1921–25
Ingham, Samuel	Secy. of Commonwealth	Pa.	1819–20
Jardine, William	Treasurer	Kans.	1933–34
Jay, John	Governor	N.Y.	1795–1801
Jefferson, Thomas	Governor	Va.	1779–81
Jewell, Marshall	Governor	Conn.	1869–74
Johnson, Andrew	Governor	Tenn.	1853–57
Johnson, Reverdy	Dep. Atty. Gen.	Md.	1816–17
Key, David McK.	Chancellor	Tenn.	1870–75
Kirkwood, Samuel	Governor	Iowa	1859–63; 1875–77
Landrieu, Moon E.	House of Rep.	La.	1959–53; 1966–70
Legaré, Hugh S.	Atty. Gen.	S.C.	1830–32
Lincoln, Levi	Governor's Council	Mass.	1806; 1810–12
Lincoln, Levi	Lt. Governor	Mass.	1807–08
Lincoln, Levi	Governor	Mass.	1808–09
Long, John D.	Lt. Governor	Mass.	1879
Long, John D.	Governor	Mass.	1880–82
Lyng, Richard E.	Dir. Dept. of Agric.	Calif.	1967–69
Marcy, William L.	Comptroller	N.Y.	1823
Marcy, William L.	Governor	N.Y.	1833–39
Marshall, Thomas	Governor	Ind.	1908–13
Maynard, Horace	Atty. Gen.	Tenn.	1863–65
McClelland, Robert	Governor	Mich.	1850–54
McGrath, James	Governor	R.I.	1940–45
McKay, Douglas	Governor	Ore.	1948–52
McKean, Thomas	Governor	Pa.	1799–1808
McKennan, Thomas M. T.	Dep. Atty. Gen.	Pa.	1815–17
McKinley, William	Governor	Ohio	1892–96
Meese, Edwin, III	Chf. of Staff	Calif.	1975–76

Meigs, Return J.,	Governor	Ohio	1808*; 1810–14
Meredith, William	Atty. Gen.	Pa.	1861–67
Mifflin, Thomas	Governor	Pa.	1790–99
Monroe, James	Governor	Va.	1799–1802; 1811
Morrill, Lot M.	Governor	Me.	1858–61
Morton, Julius S.	Secy. of the Territory	Nebr.	1858–61
Muskie, Edmund	Governor	Me.	1955–59
Norton, Gale	Atty. Gen.	Colo.	1991–99
O'Leazy, Hazel	Asst. Atty. Gen.	N.J.	1967–68
Osgood, Samuel	State Supervisor	N.Y.	1801–03
Pinkney, William	Exec. Council	Md.	1792–95
Polk, James K.	Governor	Tenn.	1839–41
Porter, Peter B.	Secy. of State	N.Y.	1815–16
Proctor, Redfield	Lt. Governor	Vt.	1876–78
Proctor, Redfield	Governor	Vt.	1878–80
Quayle, Danforth	Consumer Protect. Agency	Ind.	1970–71
	Dir., Dept. of Revenue	Ind.	1973–74
Quayle, Danforth	Admin. Assist. to Governor	Ind.	1971–73
	Admin. to Atty. Gen.	Ind.	1971
Ramsey, Alexander	Territorial Governor	Minn.	1849–53
Ramsey, Alexander	Governor	Minn.	1859–63
Randall, Alexander	Governor	Wisc.	1857–61
Randolph, Edmund	Atty. Gen.	Va.	1776–82
Randolph, Edmund	Governor	Va.	1786–88
Reagan, Ronald	Governor	Calif.	1967–75
Reno, Janet	Asst. St. Atty.	Fla.	1973–76
Reno, Janet	State Atty.	Fla.	1978–93
Richardson, Elliot	Lt. Governor	Mass.	1965–67
Richardson, Elliot	Atty. Gen.	Mass.	1967–69
Riley, Richard	Governor	S.C.	1979–87
Robeson, George	Atty. Gen.	N.J.	1867–69
Rockefeller, Nelson	Governor	N.Y.	1959–73
Romney, George	Governor	Mich.	1963–68
Roosevelt, Franklin D.	Governor	N.Y.	1928–33
Rush, Richard	Atty. Gen.	Pa.	1811
Rusk, Jeremiah	Bank Comptroller	Wisc.	1866–69

*Elected but never served.

Rusk, Jeremiah	Governor	Wisc.	1882–89
St. Clair, Arthur	Territorial Governor N.W. Terr.	N.W.	1787–1802
Sargent, John G.	Secy. of Civil and Military Affairs	Vt.	1900–02
Sawyer, Charles	Lt. Governor	Ohio	1933–34
Seward, William	Governor	N.Y.	1838–42
Slater, Rodney	Asst. Atty. Gen.	Ark.	1980–82
Slater, Rodney	Asst. to Governor	Ark.	1983–87
Smith, Hoke	Governor	N.C.	1907–09; 1911
Southard, Samuel	Atty. Gen.	N.J.	1829–33
Southard, Samuel	Governor	N.J.	1832–33
Spencer, John C.	Asst. Atty. Gen.	N.Y.	1815
Spencer, John C.	Secy. of State	N.Y.	1839
Stanbery, Henry	Atty. Gen.	Ohio	1846
Stevenson, Adlai	Dist. Atty.	Ill.	1865–69
Swanson, Claude	Governor	Va.	1906–10
Taney, Roger	Atty. Gen.	Md.	1827
Thomas, Philip	Governor	Md.	1848–51
Thompson, Tommy	Governor	Wisc.	1987–2001
Thornburgh, Richard	Governor	Pa.	1979–87
Tobin, Maurice J.	Governor	Mass.	1945–48
Tompkins, Daniel	Governor	N.Y.	1807–16
Toucey, Isaac	State Atty.	Conn.	1842–44
Toucey, Isaac	Governor	Conn.	1846–47
Tyler, John	Exec. Council	Va.	1815–16
Tyler, John	Governor	Va.	1825–27
Van Buren, Martin	Atty. Gen.	N.Y.	1815–19
Van Buren, Martin	Governor	N.Y.	1829
Veneman, Ann	Secy. Agri.	Calif.	1995–99
Vinson, Frederick	Dist. Atty.	Ky.	1921–24
Volpe, John A.	Governor	Mass.	1960–62; 1967–68
Walker, Robert J.	Territorial Governor	Kans.	1857
Welles, Gideon	Comptroller of Public Accounts	Conn.	1835; 1842; 1843
Wheeler, William	Dist. Atty.	N.Y.	1846–49
Wickliffe, Charles	Lt. Governor	Mo.	1836–39
Wickliffe, Charles	Governor	Mo.	1839–40
Wilson, Woodrow	Governor	N.J.	1911–13

Wirt, William	Chancellor	Va.	1802
Woodbury, Levi	Governor	N.H.	1823–24
Woodring, Henry	Governor	Kans.	1930–32
Wright, Luke E.	Atty. Gen.	Tenn.	1870–78
Yeutter, Clayton	Asst. to Governor	Nebr.	1966–68

STATE LEGISLATIVE SERVICE

Name	Office	State	Dates
Alexander, Joshua	House	Mo.	1883–87
Barbour, James	House	Va.	1798–1812
Barry, William T.	House	Ky.	1809–12; 1814–15
Barry, William T.	Senate	Ky.	1817–20
Bates, Edward	House	Mo.	1822; 1834
Bates, Edward	Senate	Mo.	1830–34
Belknap, William	House	Iowa	1857–58
Bell, John	Senate	Tenn.	1817
Berrien, John M.	Senate	Ga.	1822–23
Bibb, George M.	House	Ky.	1817
Blaine, James G.	House	Me.	1859–62
Boutwell, George	House	Mass.	1842–50
Branch, John	Senate	N.C.	1811; 1813–17
Breckinridge, John	House	Ky.	1798–1800
Breckinridge, John	House	Ky.	1849–51
Bristow, Benjamin	Senate	Ky.	1863–65
Brown, Aaron V.	Senate	Tenn.	1821–25; 1826–27
Brown, Aaron V.	House	Tenn.	1831
Brownell, Herbert.	Assembly	N.Y.	1933–37
Browning, Orville	Senate	Ill.	1836–43
Buchanan, James	House	Pa.	1814–15
Burr, Aaron	Assembly	N.Y.	1784
Butler, Benjamin	Assembly	N.Y.	1827–33
Calhoun, John C.	House	S.C.	1808
Card, Andrew	House	Mass.	1975–82
Carlisle, John G.	House	Ky.	1859–61
Carlisle, John G.	Senate	Ky.	1867–71
Carter, Jimmy	Senate	Ga.	1962–66

Cass, Lewis	House	Ohio	1806
Celebrezze, Anthony	Senate	Ohio	1951–53
Chandler, William	House	N.H.	1863–67
Clay, Henry	House	Ky.	1803; 1808–09
Clayton, John M.	House	Del.	1824
Clifford, Nathan	House	Me.	1830–34
Colby, Bainbridge	Assembly	N.Y.	1901
Collamer, Jacob	House	Vt.	1821–22; 1827–28
Colman, Norman	House	Mo.	1865
Conrad, Charles	House	La.	1830–42
Coolidge, Calvin	House	Vt.	1907–08
Coolidge, Calvin	Senate	Mass.	1912–15
Corwin, Thomas	House	Ohio	1821; 1822; 1829
Cox, Jacob D., Jr.	Senate	Ohio	1858
Crawford, George	House	Ohio	1837–42
Crawford, William	House	Ga.	1803–07
Creswell, John	House	Md.	1861–62
Crittenden, John	House	Ky.	1811–17; 1825; 1829
Crowninshield, Benjamin	House	Mass.	1811; 1833
Crowninshield, Benjamin	Senate	Mass.	1812; 1822
Cushing, Caleb	House	Mass.	1825; 1850
Cushing, Caleb	Senate	Mass.	1826
Daugherty, Harry	House	Ohio	1890–94
Davis, Dwight F.	House	Mo.	1907–09
Delano, Columbus	House	Ohio	1863
Denby, Edwin	House	Mich.	1903
Dennison, William	Senate	Ohio	1848
Dern, George H.	Senate	Utah	1914–23
Derwinski, Edward	House	Ill.	1957–58
Devens, Charles	Senate	Mass.	1848–49
Dexter, Samuel	House	Mass.	1788–90
Dickerson, Mahlon	Assembly	N.J.	1811–13
Dix, John A.	Assembly	N.Y.	1841
Dobbin, James C.	House	N.C.	1848; 1850; 1852
Duane, William J.	House	Pa.	1809; 1819
Eaton, John H.	House	Tenn.	1815; 1816
Edwards, James	Senate	S.C.	1972–74
Eustis, William	House	Mass.	1788–94

Fessenden, William P.	House	Me.	1831; 1839
Fillmore, Millard	Assembly	N.Y.	1829–31
Floyd, John B.	House	Va.	1847–49
Folger, Charles J.	Senate	N.Y.	1861–69
Gallatin, Albert	House	Pa.	1790–92
Garfield, James R.	Senate	Ohio	1896–99
Garner, John N.	House	Tex.	1898–1902
Gerry, Elbridge	House	Mass.	1786
Gilmer, Thomas	House	Va.	1829–36; 1838–39
Glass, Carter	Senate	Va.	1889; 1901
Goff, Nathan	House	Va.	1867
Graham, William	House	N.C.	1833–40; 1854
Granger, Francis	Assembly	N.Y.	1826–28; 1830–32
Granger, Gideon	House	Conn.	1792–1801
Granger, Gideon	Senate	N.Y.	1820–21
Gresham, Walter	House	Ind.	1860
Griggs, John W.	Assembly	N.J.	1876–78
Griggs, John W.	Senate	N.J.	1882–86
Grundy, Felix	House	Ky.	1800–05
Grundy, Felix	House	Tenn.	1819–25
Gorham, Nathaniel	Senate	Mass.	1780–81
Gorham, Nathaniel	House	Mass.	1781–87
Guthrie, James	House	Ky.	1827–29
Guthrie, James	Senate	Ky.	1831–40
Habersham, Joseph	House	Ga.	1785; 1790
Hall, Nathan K.	Assembly	N.Y.	1846
Hamilton, Alexander	Assembly	N.Y.	1787
Hamilton, Paul	House	S.C.	1787–89
Hamilton, Paul	Senate	S.C.	1794; 1798–99
Hamlin, Hannibal	House	Me.	1836–41; 1847
Hannegan, Robert	House	Mo.	1935
Hanson, John	Assembly	Md.	1756–77
Hanson, John	Senate	Md.	n.a.
Harding, Warren	Senate	Ohio	1899–1903
Hendricks, Thomas	House	Ind.	1848
Henshaw, David	House	Mass.	1826; 1830; 1839
Herter, Christian	House	Mass.	1931–43
Hoar, Ebenezer R.	Senate	Mass.	1846
Hobart, Garret A.	Assembly	N.J.	1872–76

Hobart, Garret A.	Senate	N.J.	1876–82
Hobby, Oveta C.	House	Tex.	1925–31; 1939–41
Howe, Timothy O.	House	Me.	1845
Hull, Cordell	House	Tenn.	1893–97
Ingham, Samuel	House	Pa.	1806
Johnson, Andrew	House	Tenn.	1835–37; 1838–41
Johnson, Louis A.	House	W.Va.	1916–24
Johnson, Reverdy	Senate	Md.	1824–28
Johnson, Richard	House	Ky.	1804–07; 1819; 1841–42; 1850
Kennedy, John P.	House	Md.	1821–23
King, William R.	House	N.C.	1807–09
Kirkwood, Samuel	Senate	Iowa	1856–59
Kleindienst, Richard G.	House	Ariz.	1953–54
Laird, Melvin R.	Senate	Wisc.	1946–50
Lee, Charles	Assembly	Va.	1793–95
Legaré, Hugh S.	House	S.C.	1820–22; 1824–29
Lincoln, Abraham	House	Ill.	1834–42
Lincoln, Levi	House	Mass.	1796
Lincoln, Levi	Senate	Mass.	1797–98
Livingston, Edward	House	La.	1820
Long, John D.	House	Mass.	1875–77
Madigan, Edward	House	Ill.	1967–72
Madison, James	House	Va.	1783–86
Marshall, John	Assembly	Va.	1782–87; 1788–91; 1797
Martin, Lynn	House	Ill.	1977–79
Martin, Lynn	Senate	Ill.	1979–81
Mason, John Y.	Assembly	Va.	1823–31
McCrary, George	House	Iowa	1857–59
McCrary, George	Senate	Iowa	1861–65
McHenry, James	Senate	Md.	1781–86
McKay, Douglas	Senate	Ore.	1934–49
Meigs, Return J.,	Rep. to Terr. Legislature	Ohio	1799
Meredith, William	House	Pa.	1824–28
Meyer, George von L.	House	Mass.	1892–97
Middleton, Henry	Congress	S.C.	1775–76
Middleton, Henry	Senate	S.C.	1778–80

Mifflin, Thomas	House	Pa.	1785–88; 1799–1800
Mills, Ogden L.	Senate	N.Y.	1914–17
Monroe, James	Assembly	Va.	1782; 1786; 1810–11
Morrill, Lot M.	House	Me.	1854–56
Morrill, Lot M.	Senate	Me.	1856–58
Morton, Julius S.	Territorial Legislature	Nebr.	1855–56; 1857–58
Muskie, Edmund	House	Me.	1947–51
Nagel, Charles	Legislature	Mo.	1881
New, Harry S.	Senate	Ind.	1896–1900
Olney, Richard	Legislature	Mass.	1873
Osgood, Samuel	Legislature	Mass.	*ca.* 1775–80
Osgood, Samuel	Senate	Mass.	1780–81
Osgood, Samuel	House	Mass.	1784
Osgood, Samuel	Assembly	N.Y.	1800–03
Peña, Federico	House	Colo.	1979–82
Pierce, Franklin	House	N.H.	1829–33
Pinkney, William	House of Delegates	Md.	1788–92
Pinkney, William	Legislature	Md.	1795
Pinkney, William	Senate	Md.	1811
Poinsett, Joel R.	House	S.C.	1816–20
Polk, James K.	House	Tenn.	1823–25
Porter, James M.	House	Pa.	1849–53
Porter, Peter B.	Assembly	N.Y.	1802; 1828
Preston, William	House of Delegates	Va.	1830–32; 1844–45
Preston, William	Senate	Va.	1840–45
Proctor, Redfield	House	Vt.	1867–68; 1888–89
Proctor, Redfield	Senate	Vt.	1874–75
Randolph, Edmund	Assembly	Va.	1888–89
Randolph, Peyton	Legislature	Va.	1774–75
Ribicoff, Abraham	House	Conn.	1938–42
Riley, Richard	House	S.C.	1963–66
Riley, Richard	Senate	S.C.	1966–76
Rodney, Caesar A.	Senate	Del.	1815
Roosevelt, Franklin D.	Senate	N.Y.	1911–13
Roosevelt, Theodore	Assembly	N.Y.	1882–84
Roper, Daniel C.	House	S.C.	1892–93

Royall, Kenneth C.	Senate	N.C.	1927
Rusk, Jeremiah McL.	Assembly	Wisc.	1862
Saxbe, William	House	Ohio	1947–54
Seaton, Frederick	Legislature	Nebr.	1945–49
Seward, William	Senate	N.Y.	1830–34
Smith, Caleb	House	Ind.	1832–37; 1840–41
Smith, Robert	Senate	Md.	1793–95
Smith, Robert	House of Delegates	Md.	1796–1800
Southard, Samuel	General Assembly	N.J.	1815
Speed, James	Legislature	Ky.	1847
Speed, James	Senate	Ky.	1861–63
Spencer, John C.	Assembly	N.Y.	1820–21; 1830–31
Spencer, John C.	Senate	N.Y.	1824–28
Stuart, Alexander	House of Delegates	Va.	1836–39; 1847–82
Taney, Roger	Legislature	Md.	1799–1801
Taney, Roger	Senate	Md.	1816–21
Thomas, Philip F.	House	Md.	1838; 1843; 1845; 1863; 1878–83
Thompson, Richard	House	Ind.	1834–36
Thompson, Richard	Senate	Ind.	1836–38
Thompson, Smith	Legislature	N.Y.	1800
Thompson, Tommy	Assembly	Wisc.	1966–87
Tobin, Maurice J.	House	Mass.	1926–28
Tompkins, Daniel	Assembly	N.Y.	1803
Toucey, Isaac	Senate	Conn.	1850–52
Toucey, Isaac	House	Conn.	1852–57
Tracy, Benjamin	Assembly	N.Y.	1861
Tyler, John	House of Delegates	Va.	1811–16; 1823–25; 1838–40
Upshur, Abel P.	House of Delegates	Va.	1812–13; 1824–27
Upshur, John P.	Legislature	Ind.	1850–51
Van Buren, Martin	Senate	N.Y.	1813–20
Vilas, William F.	Assembly	Wisc.	1885
Walker, Frank C.	Legislature	Mont.	1913
Weinberger, Caspar W.	Legislature	Calif.	1952–58
Welles, Gideon	Legislature	Conn.	1827–35
Wheeler, William	State Assembly	N.Y.	1850–51
Wheeler, William	Senate	N.Y.	1858–60
Wickliffe, Charles	House	Ky.	1812–13; 1822; 1823; 1833; 1835

Wilkins, William	House	Pa.	1820
Wilkins, William	Senate	Pa.	1855–57
Wilson, Henry	House	Mass.	1841–42
Wilson, Henry	Senate	Mass.	1844–46; 1850–52
Wilson, James	House	Iowa	1867–71
Woodbury, Levi	House	N.H.	1825

STATE JUDICIAL SERVICE

Name	Office	State	Dates
Badger, George E.	Superior Ct.	N.C.	1820–25
Barry, William T.	Ct. of Appeals (Chf. Justice)	Ky.	1825–29
Berrien, John M.	Supreme Ct.	Ga.	1845
Bibb, George M.	Ct. of Appeals (Chf. Justice, 1809–10)	Ky.	1808–10
Bibb, George M.	Ct. of Appeals (Chf. Justice)	Ky.	1828
Black, Jeremiah	Supreme Ct. (Chf. Justice, 1851–54)	Pa.	1851–57
Bradford, William	Supreme Ct.	Pa.	1791–94
Branch, John	Territorial Judge	Fla.	1822
Campbell, George W.	Supreme Ct. of Errors and Appeals	Tenn.	1809–11
Campbell, James	Ct. of Common Pleas	Pa.	1842–52
Clayton, Henry M.	Chf. Justice	Del.	1837–39
Collamer, Jacob	Supreme Ct.	Vt.	1833–42
Day, William R.	Ct. of Common Pleas	Ohio	1886
Devens, Charles	Superior Ct.	Mass.	1867–73
Devens, Charles	Supreme Ct.	Mass.	1873–77; 1881–91
Dickinson, Jacob M.	Supreme Ct.	Tenn.	1891–93
Endicott, William C.	Supreme Ct.	Mass.	1873–82
Folger, Charles S.	State Ct. of Appeals	N.Y.	1870
Garrison, Lindley M.	Vice-Chancellor	N.J.	1904–13
Grundy, Felix	Supreme Ct. of Errors and Appeals	Ky.	1806
Grundy, Felix	Supreme Ct. (Chf. Justice)	Ky.	1807
Hall, Nathan K.	Master in Chancery	N.Y.	1839
Harlan, James	2d Ct. of Claims	Ala.	1882–86

Hoar, Ebenezer	Ct. of Common Appeals	Mass.	1849–55
Hoar, Ebenezer	Supreme Judicial Ct.	Mass.	1859–69
Howe, Timothy	4th Circ. and Supreme Ct.	Wisc.	1850–53
Hufstedler, Shirley	Los Angeles Superior Ct.	Calif.	1961–66
Hufstedler, Shirley	Calif. Ct. of Appeals	Calif.	1966–68
Hull, Cordell	5th State Judicial Ct.	Tenn.	1903–07
Jackson, Andrew	Supreme Ct.	Tenn.	1798–1804
Jay, John	Supreme Ct.	N.Y.	1877–78
Johnson, Cave	Circ. Ct.	Tenn.	1820–29
Lincoln, Levi	Probate Ct.	Mass.	1771–81
Marcy, William L.	Supreme Ct.	N.Y.	1829–31
McLean, John	Supreme Ct.	Ohio	1816–22
Meigs, Return J.,	Territorial Judge	Ohio	1798
Meigs, Return J.,	Supreme Ct. (Chf. Justice)	Ohio	1803–04
Meigs, Return J.,	Supreme Ct.	La.	1805–06
Nagel, Charles	Supreme Ct.	Mo.	1893
Pierce, Samuel R.,	Court of General Sessions	N.Y.	1959–61
Porter, James M.	Dist. Ct.	Pa.	1839–40; 1853–55
Richardson, William A.	Ct. of Appeals	Mass.	1874
Southard, Samuel	Supreme Ct.	N.J.	1915–20
Spencer, John C.	Judge Advocate General	N.Y.	1813
Taft, William H.	Superior Ct.	Ohio	1887–90
Thomas, Philip F.	Land Office Ct.	Md.	1841
Thompson, Smith	Supreme Ct.	N.Y.	1802–19; 1823–43
Tompkins, Daniel	Supreme Ct.	N.Y.	1804–07
Tracy, Benjamin	Ct. of Appeals	N.Y.	1881–83
Upshur, Abel P.	General Ct.	Va.	1826–41
Wilbur, Curtis D.	Superior Ct.	Calif.	1919–21
Wilbur, Curtis D.	Supreme Ct.	Calif.	1922–27
Wilkins, William	Dist. Ct.	Pa.	1824
Williams, George	Dist. Ct.	Iowa	1847–52
Williams, George	Territorial Chf. Justice	Ore.	1853–57
Woodbury, Levi	Superior Ct.	N.H.	1816

STATE COMMISSIONS AND COMMITTEES

Name	Commission or Committee	State	Dates
Adams, John	Const. Convention	Mass.	1780

Alexander, Joshua	Bd. of Mgrs., State Hospital	Mo.	1893–96
Alexander, Joshua	State Const. Conv.	Mo.	1922
Anderson, Clinton	Relief Admin.	N.M.	1935–36
Anderson, Clinton	Dir., Unemployment Compensation Comm.	N.M.	1936–38
Anderson, Robert	State Tax Comm.	Tex.	1934
Anderson, Robert	Dir., Unemployment Comm.	Tex.	1936
Anderson, Robert	Economy Comm.	Tex.	1938
Anderson, Robert	Chmn., Bd. of Education	Tex.	1949
Ashcroft, John	Bd. of Buildings Records Cmsn. Housing Dvlpmt. Cmsn. Bd. of Fund Cmsnrs.	Mo.	n.a.
Baldrige, Malcolm	Comm. on Status of Women	Conn.	1968
Bates, Edward	State Const. Conv.	Mo.	1820
Bell, Griffin	Chmn., Comm. on Crime Delinq.	Ga.	1965–66
Bell, Terrel H.	Textbook Consn. Bd. of Educ.	Utah	n.a.
Bergland, Robert	Chmn., Agric. Stabil. and Cons. Serv. Comm.	Minn.	1963–68
Boutwell, George	State Bank Comm.	Mass.	1849–51
Bowen, Otis	Public Health	Ind.	1961–65
Boyd, Alan	Railroad and Public Util. Comm.	Fla.	1957–58
Cavazos, Lauro	Higher Ed. Mgmt. Coun.	Tex.	1980–82
Christopher, Warren	Coord. Coun. for Higher Educ.	Calif.	1960–67
Christopher, Warren	Cmsn. on L.A. Riots	Calif.	1965
Christopher, Warren	Cmsn. on L.A.P.D.	Calif.	1991
Conrad, Charles	State Const. Conv.	La.	1844
Day, James E.	Comm. on Intergov. Cooperation	Ill.	1949–53
Day, James E.	Insurance Comm.	Ill.	1950–53
Day, James E.	Gov.'s Comm. on Metropolitan Area Problems	Calif.	1959–61
Dickerson, Mahlon	Comm. on Bankruptcy	Pa.	1802
Dickerson, Mahlon	State Const. Conv.	N.J.	1844
Dix, John A.	Supt. of Common Schools	N.Y.	1833–39
Edison, Charles	State Recovery Bd.	N.J.	1933
Edwards, James	Comm. for Health Care Planning	S.C.	1968–72
Fall, Albert B.	State Const. Conv.	N.M.	1911
Franklin, Barbara H.	State Bd. of Ed.	Pa.	1980–81
Gallatin, Albert	State Const. Conv.	Pa.	1790
Glass, Carter	State Const. Conv.	Va.	1901–02
Gore, Howard	Bd. of Education	W.Va.	1920–25

Gore, Howard	Commr. of Agriculture	W.Va.	1931–33
Gorham, Nathaniel	Bd. of War	Mass.	1778–81
Gronouski, John	Commr. of Taxation	Wisc.	1960–63
Grundy, Felix	State Const. Conv.	Ky.	1799
Hancock, John	State Const. Conv.	Mass.	1780
Hendricks, Thomas	State Const. Conv.	Ind.	1850
Hodges, Luther H.	Vocational Ed. Bd.	N.C.	1929–33
Hodges, Luther H.	State Highway Comm.	N.C.	1933–37
Hopkins, Harry L.	Depty. Chmn./Chmn., Temp. Emergency Relief Admin.	N.Y.	1931–33
Jackson, Andrew	State Const. Conv.	Tenn.	1796
Jones, Jesse H.	Tex. Cent. Celeb.	Tex.	1926–34
Jones, Jesse H.	Tex. Comm. for N.Y. World's Fair	Tex.	1939
Key, David McK.	State Const. Conv.	Tenn.	1870
Kirkwood, Samuel	State Const. Conv.	Ohio	1850–51
Knox, W. Frank	State Publicity Comm.	N.H.	1922–24
Krug, Julius A.	Public Util. Comm.	Wisc.	1932
Krug, Julius A.	Public Serv. Comm.	Ky.	1937
Lincoln, Levi	State Const. Conv.	Mass.	1779
MacVeagh, Wayne	State Const. Conv.	Pa.	1872–73
Madison, James	Exec. Council	Va.	1778
Madison, James	State Const. Conv.	Va.	1829
Marshall, John	State Const. Conv.	Va.	1788; 1829
Martinez, Mel	Growth Management Cmsn.	Fla.	1999
Mason, John Y.	State Const. Conv.	Va.	1850
McClelland, Robert	State Const. Conv.	Mich.	1835; 1850; 1967
McLane, Louis	State Const. Conv.	Md.	1850–51
Meredith, William	State Const. Conv.	Pa.	1872–73
Middleton, Henry	Const. Comt.	S.C.	1776
Middleton, Henry	Leg. Council	S.C.	1776–78
Mitchell, James P.	Relief Admin.	N.J.	1931
Monroe, James	State Const. on Fed. Conv.	Va.	1788
Monroe, James	State Const. Conv.	Va.	1829
Morgenthau, Henry	Agricult. Adv. Comm.	N.Y.	1929
Morgenthau, Henry	Taconic State Park Comm.	N.Y.	1929–31
Morgenthau, Henry	Conservation Comm.	N.Y.	1931
Osgood, Samuel	Bd. of War	Mass.	1776
Peña, Federico	Alternative Fuels Council	Colo.	1990–92

Peña, Federico	Denver Regional Council of Governments	Colo.	1983–91
Peña, Federico	Metrop. Transp. Dvlpmt. Comt.	Colo.	1989–90
Perkins, Frances	Comm. of Safety	N.Y.	1912
Perkins, Frances	Council of Org. for War Serv.	N.Y.	1917–19
Perkins, Frances	Indust. Comm.	N.Y.	1919–21; 1929–33
Perkins, Frances	Indust. Bd.	N.Y.	1922–33
Pickering, Timothy	Const. Conv.	Pa.	1789
Pierce, Franklin	Const. Conv.	N.H.	1850
Pierrepont, Edwards	Const. Conv.	N.Y.	1867–68
Porter, Peter B.	Canal Comm.	N.Y.	1811
Ribicoff, Abraham	Comm. on Alcoholism and Crime	Conn.	1943
Ribicoff, Abraham	Inter-racial Comm.	Conn.	1947–48
Rodney, Caesar A.	Comt. of Safety	Del.	1813
Roosevelt, Theodore	Bd. of Police Comm.	N.Y.	1895–97
Root, Elihu	State Const. Conv.	N.Y.	1894
Shultz, George P.	Gov.'s Comt. on Unemployment	Ill.	1961–62
Slater, Rodney	Highway and Transp. Cmsn.	Ark.	1987–93
Stanbery, Henry	State Const. Conv.	Ohio	1850
Stimson, Henry L.	State Const. Conv.	N.Y.	1915
Straus, Oscar S.	Public Serv. Comm.	N.Y.	1915–18
Thomas, Philip F.	State Const. Conv.	Md.	1836
Thompson, Smith	State Const. Conv.	N.Y.	1801
Tompkins, Daniel	State Const. Conv.	N.Y.	1801
Tyler, John	State Const. Conv.	Va.	1829–30
Upshur, Abel	State Const. Conv.	Va.	1829–30
Van Buren, Martin	State Const. Conv.	N.Y.	1821
Volpe, John A.	Public Wks. Comm.	Mass.	1953–56
Weaver, Robert	Dpty. Comm., Div. of Housing	N.Y.	1954–55
Weaver, Robert C.	Rent Admin.	N.Y.	1955–59
Webster, Daniel	State Const. Conv.	N.H.	1820
Weinberger, Caspar	Chmn., Comm. on Govt. Org. and Econ.	Calif.	1967–68
Weinberger, Caspar	Dir. of Fin.	Calif.	1968–69
Wheeler, William	State Const. Conv.	N.Y.	1867–68
Wickersham, George	State Const. Conv.	N.Y.	1915
Wickersham, George	Govt. Reorg. Comm.	N.Y.	1925
Wickliffe, Charles	State Const. Conv.	Ky.	1849

Williams, George	State Const. Conv.	Ore.	1858
Wilson, Henry	State Const. Conv.	Mass.	1853
Wilson, James	Railway Comm.	Iowa	1878–83
Wilson, William	Coal Laws Comm.	Pa.	1891
Wirtz, William W.	Liquor Control Comm.	Ill.	1950–56
Wolcott, Oliver,	State Const. Conv.	N.Y.	1818
Wood, Robert C.	Assoc. Dir., Legisl. Bureau	Fla.	1949–51
Woodin, William	Fuel Administrator	N.Y.	1922
Woodin, William	Banking Laws Comt.	N.Y.	1929

COUNTY SERVICE

Name	Office	County & State	Dates
Agnew, Spiro T.	Chmn., Zoning Bd. of Appeals	Balt., Md.	1957–61
Agnew, Spiro T.	Chf. Exec.	Balt., Md.	1962–67
Alexander, Joshua	Pub. Admin.	Davies, Mo.	1877–81
Barkley, Alben W.	Pros. Atty. for County Ct.	McCracken, Ky.	1905–09
Barkley, Alben W.	Judge, County Ct.	McCracken, Ky.	1909–13
Bentsen, Lloyd	Judge, County Ct.	Hidalgo Cty., Tex.	1946–48
Black, Jeremiah S.	Dep. Atty. Gen.	Somerset, Pa.	1831
Carter, Jimmy	School Bd.	Sumter Cty. Ga	1955–62
Clark, Tom C.	Civ. Dist. Atty.	Dallas, Tex.	1927–32
Cleveland, Grover	Asst. Dist. Atty.	Erie, N.Y.	1863–65
Cleveland, Grover	Sheriff	Erie, N.Y.	1871–73
Collamer, Jacob	State Atty.	Windsor, Vt.	1822–24
Corwin, Thomas	Pros. Atty.	Warren, Ohio	1818–28
Cummings, Homer	State Atty.	Fairfield, Conn.	1914–24
Curtis, Charles	Pros. Atty.	Shawnee, Kans.	1885–89
Davis, James J.	Recorder	Madison, Ind.	1903–07
Delano, Columbus	Pros. Atty.	Knox, Ohio	1832
Folger, Charles J.	Judge, Ct. of Common Pleas	Ontario, N.Y.	1844
Folger, Charles J.	County Judge	Ontario, N.Y.	1851–55
Garner, John N.	County Judge	Uvalde, Tex.	1893–96
Hall, Nathan K.	Judge, Ct. of Common Pleas	Erie, N.Y.	1841
Harding, Warren	Auditor	Marion, Ohio	1895
Hays, William H.	City Atty.	Sullivan, Ind.	1910–13
Johnson, Cave	County Pros. Atty.	Montgomery, Tenn.	1817–20
Kellogg, Frank B.	City Atty.	Olmstead, N.Y.	1882–87

Kirkwood, Samuel J.	Pros. Atty.	Richland, Ohio	1845–49
Lane, Franklin K.	County Atty.	San Fran. Calif.	1899–1904
Lincoln, Abraham	Dep. County Surveyor	Hardin, Ill.	1834–36
Martin, Lynn	County Board	Winnebago Cty., Ill.	1972–76
Martinez, Mel	Chairman	Orange Cty., Fla.	1998–2001
MacVeagh, Wayne	Dist. Atty.	Chester, Pa.	1859–64
McKenna, Joseph	County Atty.	Solano, Calif.	1866–70
McKinley, William	Pros. Atty.	Stark, Ohio	1869–71
Meese, Edwin, III	Dep. Dist. Atty.	Alameda Cty., Calif.	1958–67
O'Leary, Hazel	Asst. Admin.	Essex Cty., N.J.	1969–70
Payne, John B.	Special Judge, Circ. Ct.	Tucker, W.Va.	1880–82
Payne, John B.	Judge, Superior Ct.	Cook, Ill.	1893–98
Porter, James	Dep. Atty. Gen.	Northampton, Pa.	1818–21
Richardson, William A.	Probate Judge	Middlesex, Mass.	1856
Robeson, George	Pros. Atty.	Camden, N.J.	1858
Sargent, John G.	State Atty.	Windsor, Vt.	1898–1900
Taft, William	Pros. Atty.	Hamilton, Ohio	1881–82
Toucey, Isaac	State Atty.	Hartford, Conn.	1822–35
Truman, Harry	Judge, County Ct.	Jackson, Mo.	1922–24; 1926–34
Van Buren, Martin	Surrogate Ct.	Columbia, N.Y.	1808–13
Walker, Frank	Asst. Dist. Atty.	Silver Bow, Mont.	1909–12
West, Roy	Asst. Atty.	Cook, Ill.	1893
Wilbur, Curtis	Dep. Dist. Atty.	Los Angeles, Calif.	1899–1903
Windom, William	Pros. Atty.	Knox, Ohio	1852

MUNICIPAL SERVICE

Name	Office	City & State	Dates
Adams, Charles F.	Councilman	Quincy, Mass.	*ca.* 1895
Adams, Charles F.	Mayor	Quincy, Mass.	1896–97
Alexander, Joshua	Secy. and Pres., Board of Ed.	Gallatin, Mo.	1882–1901
Alexander, Joshua	Mayor	Gallatin, Mo.	1891–92
Arthur, Chester A.	Port Collector	New York, N.Y.	1871–78
Baker, Newton D.	Asst. Dir., Law Dept.	Cleveland, Ohio	1902
Baker, Newton D.	City Solicitor	Cleveland, Ohio	1903–12
Baker, Newton D.	Mayor	Cleveland, Ohio	1912–16
Ballinger, Richard	City Atty.	Kankakee, Ill.	1888

Ballinger, Richard	Judge, Superior Ct.	Port Townsend, Wash.	1894–97
Ballinger, Richard	Mayor	Seattle, Wash.	1904–06
Bancroft, George	Port Collector	Boston, Mass.	1832–34
Bates, Edward	Judge, Land Ct.	St. Louis, Mo.	1853–56
Bibb, George	Chancellor, Chancery Ct.	Louisville, Ky.	1835–44
Blair, Montgomery	Mayor	St. Louis, Mo.	1842–43
Blair, Montgomery	Judge, Common Pleas Ct.	St. Louis, Mo.	1843–49
Burleson, Albert	Asst. City Atty.	Austin, Tex.	1885–90
Butler, Benjamin	Dist. Atty.	Albany, N.Y.	1821–24
Celebrezze, Anthony	Mayor	Cleveland, Ohio	1950–62
Chandler, Zachariah	Mayor	Detroit, Mich.	1851–52
Chapman, Oscar	Chf. Probation Officer, Juvenile Ct.	Denver, Colo.	1921–29
Cisneros, Henry	Mayor	San Antonio, Tex.	1981–89
Cleveland, Grover	Mayor	Buffalo, N.Y.	1882
Cohen, William	Mayor	Bangor, Me.	1971–72
Colman, Norman	Dist. Atty.	New Albany, Ind.	1852
Coolidge, Calvin	City Council	Northampton, Mass.	1899
Coolidge, Calvin	City Solicitor	Northampton, Mass.	1900–01
Coolidge, Calvin	Clerk of the Cts.	Northampton, Mass.	1904
Coolidge, Calvin	Mayor	Northampton, Mass.	1910–11
Cummings, Homer	Mayor	Stamford, Conn.	1900–02; 1904–06
Cuomo, Andrew	Asst. Dist. Atty.	New York, N.Y.	1984–85
Cushing, Caleb	Mayor	Newburyport, Mass.	1851–52
Dallas, George M.	Dep. Atty. Gen.	Philadelphia, Pa.	1817
Dallas, George M.	Mayor	Philadelphia, Pa.	1829
Daugherty, Harry	Town Clerk	Washington Ct. House, Ohio	1882
Davis, Dwight F.	Public Rec. Comm.	St. Louis, Mo.	1906–07
Davis, Dwight F.	Park Comm.	St. Louis, Mo.	1911–15
Davis, James J.	City Clerk	Elwood, Ind.	1898–1902
Dearborn, Henry	Port Collector	Boston, Mass.	1809
Devens, Charles	City Solicitor	Worcester, Mass.	1856–58
Dickerson, Mahlon	City Recorder	Philadelphia, Pa.	1808–10
Duane, William J.	Pros. Atty., Mayor's Ct.	Philadelphia, Pa.	1820
Duane, William J.	Select Council	Philadelphia, Pa.	1829
Endicott, William	Common Council	Salem, Mass.	1857–58
Endicott, William	City Solicitor	Salem, Mass.	1858–63

Farley, James	Town Clerk	Stony Point, N.Y.	n.a.
Fisher, Walter	Special Assessment Atty.	Chicago, Ill.	1889
Fisher, Walter	Special Transportation Counsel	Chicago, Ill.	1907
Francis, David	Mayor	St. Louis, Mo.	1885
Frelinghuysen, Frederick	City Atty.	Newark, N.J.	1849
Frelinghuysen, Frederick	City Council	Newark, N.J.	1850–61
Glass, Carter	City Council Clerk	Lynchburg, Va.	1881–1901
Glickman, Daniel	Board of Educ.	Wichita, Kans.	1975–76
Goldschmidt, Neil	Mayor	Portland, Ore.	1973–79
Good, James W.	City Atty.	Cedar Rapids, Iowa	1906–08
Gregory, Thomas	Asst. City Atty.	Austin, Tex.	1891–94
Griggs, John	City Counsel	Paterson, N.J.	1879–82
Hall, Nathan K.	City Atty.	Buffalo, N.Y.	1833–34
Hall, Nathan K.	Mbr., Bd. of Aldermen	Buffalo, N.Y.	1837
Hamlin, Hannibal	Port Collector	Boston, Mass.	1865
Harmon, Judson	Mayor	Wyoming, Ohio	1875–76
Harmon, Judson	Judge, Superior Ct.	Wyoming, Ohio	1877–87
Hatton, Frank	Postmaster	Burlington, Iowa	1879–81
Hayes, Rutherford	City Solicitor	Cincinnati, Ohio	1857–59
Henshaw, David	Port Collector	Boston, Mass.	1827–30
Hobart, Garret A.	City Counsel	Paterson, N.J.	1871
Humphrey, Hubert	Mayor	Minneapolis, Minn.	1945–48
Hyde, Arthur M.	Mayor	Princeton, Mo.	1908–12
James, Thomas L.	Insp. of Customs	New York, N.Y.	1864–70
James, Thomas L.	Dep. Collector of Port	New York, N.Y.	1870–73
James, Thomas L.	Mayor	Tenafly, N.J.	1896
Johnson, Andrew	Alderman	Greenville, Tenn.	1828–30
Johnson, Andrew	Mayor	Greenville, Tenn.	1830–33
Jones, William	Collector of Customs	Philadelphia, Pa.	1827–29
Kellogg, Frank B.	City Atty.	Rochester, N.Y.	1878–81
King, William R.	City Solicitor	Wilmington, N.C.	1810–11
Landrieu, Moon E.	Mayor	New Orleans, La.	1970–78
Lane, Franklin K.	City Atty.	San Fran., Calif.	1899–1904
Lee, Charles	Collector of Port	Alexandria, Va.	1789–93
Lincoln, Abraham	Postmaster	New Salem, Ill.	1833–36
Livingston, Edward	Mayor	New York, N.Y.	1800–03
Marcy, William L.	Recorder	Troy, N.Y.	1816–18

Martinez, Mel	Board of Commissioners, Orlando, Fla. Housing Authority		1983–80
McGrath, James	City Solicitor	Central Falls, R.I.	1930–34
McKay, Douglas	Mayor	Salem, Ore.	1933–34
Meredith, William	Select Council	Philadelphia, Pa.	1834–49
Meyer, George	Common Council	Boston, Mass.	1889–90
Meyer, George	Bd. of Aldermen	Boston, Mass.	1891
Mineta, Norman	City Council	San Jose, Calif.	1967–71
Mineta, Norman	Mayor	San Jose, Calif.	1971–74
Moody, William	City Solicitor	Haverhill, Mass.	1888–90
Murphy, Frank	Judge, Recorder's Ct.	Detroit, Mich.	1923–30
Murphy, Frank	Mayor	Detroit, Mich.	1930–33
Muskie, Edmund	City Solicitor	Waterford, Me.	1954–55
Paige, Rod	Supt. of Schools	Houston, Tex.	1994–2001
Paulding, James	Naval Agent	New York, N.Y.	1824
Payne, Henry C.	Postmaster	Milwaukee, Wisc.	1875–85
Payne, John B.	Mayor	Kingswood, W.Va.	1889
Peña, Federico	Mayor	Denver, Colo.	1983–91
Pickering, Timothy	Judge, Ct. of Common Pleas	Essex, Mass.	1802–03
Pierrepont, Edwards	Superior Ct.	New York, N.Y.	1857–60
Ramsey, Alexander	Mayor	St. Paul, Minn.	1855
Randall, Alexander	Postmaster	Prairieville, Wisc.	1845
Randall, Alexander	Judge, Circuit Ct.	Milwaukee, Wisc.	1855–57
Redfield, William	Comm. of Public Wks.	Brooklyn, N.Y.	1902–03
Ribicoff, Abraham	Judge, Municipal Ct.	Hartford, Conn.	1941–43; 1945–47
Ribicoff, Abraham	Charter Revision Comt.	Hartford, Conn.	1945–47
Rusk, Jeremiah	Sheriff	Viroqua, Wisc.	1855–57
Rusk, Jeremiah	Coroner	Viroqua, Wisc.	1857
Sawyer, Charles	City Council	Cincinnati, Ohio	1911–15
Shalala, Donna	Dir., MAC	New York, N.Y.	1975–77
Sherman, James S.	Mayor	Utica, N.Y.	1884–86
Smith, Robert	City Council	Baltimore, Md.	1798–1801
Spencer, John C.	Postmaster	Canandaigua, N.Y.	1814
Taft, Alphonso	Judge, Superior Ct.	Cincinnati, Ohio	1865–72
Taft, William H.	Collector of Int. Revenue	Cincinnati, Ohio	1882
Thomas, Philip F.	Collector of Port	Baltimore, Md.	1853–60
Thompson, Richard	City Atty.	Terre Haute, Ind.	1846–47

Tobin, Maurice J.	Mayor	Boston, Mass.	1938–46
Tracy, Benjamin	Charter Comm.	New York, N.Y.	1896
Upshur, Abel P.	City Council	Richmond, Va.	1816
Upshur, Abel P.	Atty.	Richmond, Va.	1816–23
Vinson, Frederick	City Atty.	Louisa, Ky.	1914–15
Watson, William	City Secy.	Daingerfield, Tex.	1954
Watson, William	City Judge	Daingerfield, Tex.	1958
Weaver, Robert C.	Vice-Chmn., Housing and Redevelopment of Board	New York, N.Y.	1960–61
Weeks, John W.	Alderman	Newton, Mass.	1900–02
Weeks, John W.	Mayor	Newton, Mass.	1903–05
Weeks, Sinclair	Alderman	Newton, Mass.	1923–29
Weeks, Sinclair	Mayor	Newton, Mass.	1930–35
Welles, Gideon	Postmaster	Hartford, Conn.	1836–41
West, Roy O.	City Atty.	Chicago, Ill.	1895–97
Wilkins, William	Common Council	Pittsburgh, Pa.	1816–19
Williams, George	Mayor	Portland, Ore.	1902–05

Military Service by Branch

ARMY

Name	War or Dates Served	Highest Rank Attained
Agnew, Spiro T.	World War II	co. combat cmdr.
Alger, Russell A.	Civil War	maj. gen.
Armstrong, John	War of 1812	brig. gen.
Aspin, Les	1966–68	capt.
Bacon, Robert	World War I	lt. col.
Baldrige, Malcolm	World War II	capt.
Barry, William T.	War of 1812	ADC
Bates, Edward	War of 1812	sgt.
Belknap, William W.	Civil War	brig. gen.
Bell, Griffin B.	1941–46	maj.
Berrien, John MacP.	War of 1812	capt.
Blair, Montgomery	1835–36	lt.
Block, John R.	1957–60	capt.
Blount, Winton M.	World War II	lt.
Boudinot, Elias	Revolutionary War	commissary gen.
Bowen, Otis R.	World War II	capt.
Boyd, Alan S.	World War II	maj.
Bradford, William	Revolutionary War	col.
Breckinridge, John C.	Mexican War	maj.
Bristow, Benjamin H.	Civil War	maj. gen.
Brown, Ronald H.	1963–67	capt.

Browning, Orville H.	1832	n.a.
Bryan, William J.	1898	col.
Buchanan, James	War of 1812	n.a.
Burr, Aaron	Revolutionary War	lt. col.
Cass, Lewis	War of 1812	brig. gen.
Cavazos, Lauro	1945–46	n.a.
Clark, Tom C.	World War I	sgt.
Coleman, William T., Jr.	World War II	n.a.
Cox, Jacob D., Jr.	Civil War	maj. gen.
Crittenden, John J.	War of 1812	ADC
Cushing, Caleb	Mexican War	brig. gen.
Davis, Dwight F.	World War I	col.
Davis, Jefferson	1828–35; Mexican War	col.
Dawes, Charles G.	World War I	brig. gen.
Dearborn, Henry	Revolutionary War	maj.
Dearborn, Henry	War of 1812	maj. gen.
Derwinski, Edward J.	1944–46	sgt.
Devens, Charles	Civil War	maj. gen.
Dix, John A.	War of 1812	maj.
Dix, John A.	Civil War	maj. gen.
Dulles, John F.	World War I	maj.
Durkin, Martin P.	World War I	pvt.
Eagleburger, Lawrence	1952–54	1st lt.
Eisenhower, Dwight D.	1915–48	chief of staff
Elkins, Stephen B.	Civil War	capt.
Eustis, William	Revolutionary War	physician
Fall, Albert B.	Spanish-American War	capt.
Folsom, Marion B.	World War I	capt.
Foster, John W.	Civil War	brig. gen.
Garfield, James A.	1861–70	maj. gen.
Goff, Nathan	Civil War	maj.
Gore, Albert	1969–71	pvt.
Grant, Ulysses S.	1843–54; 1861–67	general of the army
Gresham, Walter Q.	Civil War	maj. gen.
Gronouski, John A.	World War II	1st lt.
Habersham, Joseph	Revolutionary War	lt. col.
Haig, Alexander M., Jr.	1947–79	gen.
Hamilton, Alexander	Revolutionary War	capt.
Harrison, Benjamin	Civil War	brig. gen.

Harrison, William H.	1791–98; 1811–14	maj. gen.
Hathaway, Stanley K.	1943–45	n.a.
Hatton, Frank	Civil War	1st lt.
Hayes, Rutherford B.	Civil War	maj. gen.
Hobby, Oveta C.	World War II	maj. (WAAC)
Hodges, Luther H.	1919	2d lt.
Hull, Cordell	Spanish-American War	capt.
Hurley, Patrick J.	World War I	col.
Hurley, Patrick J.	World War II	brig. gen.
Jackson, Andrew	1814–16	maj. gen.
Johnson, Andrew	Civil War	brig. gen.
Johnson, Louis A.	World War I	maj.
Johnson, Richard M.	War of 1812	col.
Jones, William	Revolutionary War	pvt.
Katzenbach, Nicholas	World War II	navigator, army air corps
Kemp, Jack	1958	pvt.
Kennedy, John P.	War of 1812	n.a.
Kissinger, Henry A.	1943–46	st. sgt.
Kleindienst, Richard G.	World War II	lt.
Kleppe, Thomas S.	1942–46	war. off.
Knox, Henry	Revolutionary War	maj. gen.
Landrieu, Moon E.	1955–57	capt.
Lincoln, Robert T.	Civil War	capt.
Livingston, Edward	War of 1812	ADC
MacVeagh, Wayne	Civil War	capt.
Marcy, William L.	War of 1812	adj. gen.
Marshall, George C.	1901–45	gen. & chief of staff
Marshall, John	Revolutionary War	capt.
Matthews, Forrest D.	1958–59	n.a.
McHenry, James	Revolutionary War	maj.
McKay, Douglas J.	World War I	maj.
McKay, Douglas J.	World War II	maj.
McKinley, William, Jr.	Civil War	maj.
McNamara, Robert S.	World War II	col.
Meese, Edwin, III	1956–57	lt.
Meigs, Return J., Jr.	1804–06	cmdr.
Mifflin, Thomas	Revolutionary War	maj. gen.
Miller, William H. H.	Civil War	2d lt.
Mills, Ogden L.	World War I	capt.

Mineta, Norman	1953–56	maj.
Mitchell, William D.	Spanish-American War	2d lt.
Mondale, Walter F.	1951–53	cpl.
Monroe, James	Revolutionary War	lt. col.
Morton, Rogers C. B.	World War II	capt.
Murphy, Frank	World War I	capt.
Noble, John W.	Civil War	brig. gen.
O'Brien, Lawrence F.	World War II	sgt.
Osgood, Samuel	Revolutionary War	col.
Patterson, Robert P.	World War I	maj.
Perry, William	1946–47	sgt.
Pickering, Timothy	Revolutionary War	quartermaster gen.
Pierce, Franklin	1846–48	brig. gen.
Pierce, Samuel R., Jr.	World War II	lt.
Porter, James M.	War of 1812	col.
Powell, Colin	1958–94	gen.
Proctor, Redfield	Civil War	col.
Randolph, Edmund J.	Revolutionary War	ADC
Rawlins, John A.	Civil War	maj. gen.
Reagan, Ronald W.	World War II	capt.
Richardson, Elliot L.	World War II	1st lt.
Robeson, George	Civil War	brig. gen.
Roosevelt, Theodore	Spanish-American War	col.
Royall, Kenneth C.	World War I	brig. gen.
Royall, Kenneth C.	World War II	brig. gen.
Rusk, D. Dean	1931–41	infantry res. off.
Rusk, D. Dean	World War II	col.
Rusk, Jeremiah McL.	Civil War	brig. gen.
St. Clair, Arthur	Revolutionary War	maj. gen.
Sawyer, Charles	World War I	maj.
Saxbe, William	World War II	n.a.
Schofield, John McA.	Civil War	maj. gen.
Schurz, Carl	Civil War	maj. gen.
Schwellenbach, Lewis B.	World War I	cpl.
Sherman, William T.	1840–69	general in command
Simon, William E.	1946–48	n.a.
Skinner, Samuel K.	1960–61	lt.
Smith, Cyrus R.	World War II	maj. gen.
Snyder, John W.	World War I	capt.

Spencer, John C.	War of 1812	brigade judge advocate
Stoddert, Benjamin	Revolutionary War	maj.
Taylor, Zachary	1806–49	maj. gen.
Thompson, Richard W.	Civil War	camp cmdr.
Tracy, Benjamin F.	Civil War	brig. gen.
Truman, Harry S	World War I	maj.
Udall, Stewart L.	World War II	gunner, army air corps
Vilas, William F.	Civil War	lt. col.
Vinson, Frederick M.	World War I	pvt.
Walker, Frank C.	World War I	1st lt.
Washington, George	Revolutionary War	lt. gen. & comdr.
Weeks, Sinclair	World War I	capt.
West, Togo	1969–73	capt.
Weinberger, Caspar W.	World War II	capt.
Wolcott, Oliver, Jr.	Revolutionary War	ADC
Wood, Robert C.	World War II	gen.
Woodring, Henry H.	World War I	2d lt.
Work, Hubert	World War I	col.

NAVY

Name	War or Dates Served	Highest Rank Attained
Acheson, Dean G.	World War I	ens.
Adams, Brockman	World War II	n.a.
Andrus, Cecil D.	1951–55	n.a.
Brennan, Peter J.	1943–53	lt. comdr.
Brock, William E., III	Korean War	lt. (jg)
Bush, George H.W.	1942–45	lt.
Califano, Joseph Anthony	1955–58	lt.
Carter, Jimmy	1946–53	lt.
Celebrezze, Anthony J.	World War II	seaman
Chapman, Oscar L.	World War I	pharm. mate
Christopher, Warren	1943–46	lt. (jg)
Clifford, Clark McA.	World War II	capt.
Connally, John B.	World War II	en., res.
Day, James E.	World War II	lt.
Denby, Edwin	Spanish-American War	gunner's mate, 3rd c.
Dent, Frederick B.	1943–46	n.a.

Dillon, C. Douglas	World War II	lt. cmdr.
Ford, Gerald R., Jr.	1942–46	lt. cmdr.
Forrestal, James V.	World War I	lt.
Gates, Thomas S., Jr.	World War II	comdr., res.
Hodgson, James D.	World War II	intell. ofcr.
Johnson, Lyndon B.	1941–48	cmdr.
Kantor, Rickey	1961–65	lt.
Kennedy, John F.	World War II	lt.
Laird, Melvin R.	World War II	n.a.
Lovett, Robert A.	World War I	lt.
Lynn, James T.	1945–46	ETM 2nd cl.
Marshall, Freddie R.	World War II	n.a.
McLane, Louis	1798–99	midshipman
Mitchell, John N.	World War II	cmdr.
Morgenthau, Henry	World War I	lt.
Muskie, Edmund S.	World War II	lt.
Newberry, Truman H.	1894–99	lt. (jg)
Nixon, Richard M.	World War II	lt. (jg)
Principi, Anthony	1967–84	cmdr.
Riley, Richard	1954–56	lt. (jg)
Rogers, William P.	World War II	lt. cmdr.
Rumsfeld, Donald	1954–57	lt. (jg)
Strauss, Lewis L.	World War II	rear adm.
Usery, Willie J., Jr.	1943–46	n.a.
Vance, Cyrus R.	1942–46	lt. (jg)
Verity, C. William, Jr.	World War II	lt.
Volpe, John A.	World War II	lt.
Watkins, James D.	1949–86	adm.
Weeks, John W.	1881–83	midshipman

MARINE CORPS

Name	War or Dates Served	Highest Rank Attained
Baker, James A., III	1952–54	capt.
Bell, Terrel H.	World War II	sgt.
Brown, Jesse	Vietnam/1963–66	cpl.
Clark, W. Ramsey	1945–46	cpl.
Connor, John T.	World War II	2d lt.

Denby, Edwin	World War I	maj.
Finch, Robert H.	World War II	1st lt.
Finch, Robert H.	Korean War	1st lt.
Freeman, Orville L.	World War II	maj.
Gardner, John W.	World War II	capt.
Regan, Donald T.	World War II	lt. col.
Shultz, George P.	World War II	capt.
Trowbridge, Alexander B.	Korean War	2d lt.
Watson, William M., Jr.	World War II	sgt.

AIR FORCE

Name	War or Dates Served	Highest Rank Attained
Bentsen, Lloyd	1942–45	maj.
Brinegar, Claude Stout	1945–47	n.a.
Knebel, John A.	1959–62	1st lt.
McGranery, James P.	World War I	adj.
Yeutter, Clayton K.	1952–57	lt. col.

COAST GUARD

MILITIA/NATIONAL GUARD

Name	War or Dates Served	Highest Rank Attained
Arthur, Chester A.	1857–62	brig. gen.
Badger, George E.	1814–16	maj.
Bush, George W.	1968–74	1st lt.
Clinton, George	Revolutionary War	brig. gen.
Collamer, Jacob	War of 1812	lt.
Colman, Norman J.	Civil War	lt. col.
Dearborn, Henry	Revolutionary War	maj. gen.
Edwards, James	World War II	deck off.
Eustis, William	Revolutionary War	surgeon
Fillmore, Millard	Civil War	cmdr., Home Guard
Hamilton, Paul	Revolutionary War	n.a.
Hurley, Patrick J.	1902–07	capt.
Hyde, Arthur M.	1904–05	capt.

Jackson, Andrew	1812–14	cmdr.
Knox, W. Frank	World War I	col.
Lee, Richard H.	1781	col.
Lincoln, Abraham	1832	capt.
Marcy, William L.	1821	adj. gen.
Miller, G. William	1945–49	lt. (jg)
Mitchell, William D.	1899–1901	capt. & adj.
Patterson, Robert P.	World War I	maj.
Porter, James M.	War of 1812	2d lt.
Quayle, Danforth	1969–75	cpl.
Rodney, Caesar A.	1813–14	capt.
St. Clair, Arthur	1775	col.
Teller, Henry M.	Civil War	maj. gen.
Thompson, Tommy	*ca.* 1963–66	n.a.
Truman, Harry S	1905–11	cpl.
Weeks, Sinclair	1918	lt. col.

Education

Name	Graduated? (degree)	Institution	Year Completed
Abraham, Spencer	B.A.	Michigan St. U.	1974
	J.D.	Harvard U.	1979
Acheson, Dean	B.A.	Yale U.	1915
	LL.B.	Harvard U.	1918
Adams, Brock	B.A.	U. of Washington, Seattle	*ca.* 1950
	LL.B.	Harvard U.	1952
Adams, Charles F.	B.A.	Harvard Coll.	1888
	grad.	Harvard Law Sch.	1892
Adams, John	B.A.	Harvard Coll.	1755
Adams, John Quincy	B.A.	Harvard Coll.	1787
Agnew, Spiro	LL.B.	U. of Baltimore	1947
Akerman, Amos	grad.	Dartmouth Coll.	1842
Albright, Madeleine	B.A.	Wellesley Coll.	1959
	M.A.	Columbia U.	1968
	Ph.D.	Columbia U.	1976
Alexander, Joshua	grad.	Christian U. (now Culver-Stockton Coll.)	1872
Alexander, Lamar	B.A.	Vanderbilt U.	1962
	J.D.	New York U.	1965
Alger, Russell	no deg.	read law	
Anderson, Clinton	no deg.	Dakota Wesleyan U.	1915
	no deg.	U. of Michigan	1916
Anderson, Robert	B.A.	Weatherford Coll./ Southwestern U.	1927

	LL.B.	U. of Texas	1932
Andrus, Cecil	no deg.	Oregon St.	1949
Armstrong, John	no deg.	Princeton Coll.	1775
Arthur, Chester	B.A.	Union Coll.	1848
Ashcroft, John	B.A.	Yale U.	1964
	J.D.	U. of Chicago	1967
Aspin, Les	B.A.	Yale U.	1960
	M.A.	Oxford U. (England)	1962
	Ph.D.	Mass. Inst. of Tech.	1965
Babbitt, Bruce	B.S.	U. of Notre Dame	1960
	M.S.	U. of Newcastle (England)	1962
	LL.B.	Harvard U.	1965
Bacon, Robert	grad.	Harvard U.	1880
Badger, George	no deg.	Yale U.	1811
Baker, James	B.A.	Princeton U.	1952
	LL.B.	U. of Texas	1957
Baker, Newton	B.A.	Johns Hopkins U.	1892
	law deg.	Washington & Lee U.	1894
Baldrige, Malcolm	B.A.	Yale U.	1944
Ballinger, Richard	grad.	Williams Coll.	1884
Bancroft, George	grad.	Harvard U.	1817
	Ph.D.	U. of Göttingen (Germany)	1820
Barbour, James	no deg.	read law	
Barkley, Alben	B.A.	Marvin Coll.	1897
	no deg.	Emory Coll.	1898
	no deg.	U. of Virginia Law Sch.	1902
Barr, Joseph	A.B.	DePauw U.	1939
	M.A.	Harvard U.	1941
Barr, William	A.B.	Columbia U.	1971
	M.A.	Columbia U.	1973
	J.D.	George Washington U.	1977
Barry, William	grad.	Coll. of William & Mary	1803
	no deg.	Transylvania Coll. of Law	*ca.* 1805
Bates, Edward	no deg.	read law	
Bayard, Thomas	no deg.	read law	
Belknap, William	B.A.	Princeton U.	1852
Bell, Griffin	LL.B.	Mercer U.	1948

Bell, John	grad.	Cumberland Coll. (now U. of Nashville)	1814
Bell, Terrel	B.A.	Southern Idaho Coll. of Educ.	1946
	M.S.	U. of Idaho	1953
	Ed.D.	U. of Utah	1961
Bennett, William	B.A.	Williams Coll.	1965
	Ph.D.	U. of Texas	1970
	J.D.	Harvard U.	1971
Benson, Ezra	B.S.	Brigham Young U.	1926
	M.S.	Iowa St. Coll.	1927
Bentsen, Lloyd	J.D.	U. of Texas	1942
Bergland, Robert	no deg.	U. of Minnesota	1948
Berrien, John	grad.	Princeton Coll.	1796
Bibb, George	grad.	Coll. of William & Mary	1792
Biddle, Francis	grad.	Harvard U.	1908
	law deg.	Harvard U. Law Sch.	1911
Bissell, Wilson	grad.	Yale U.	1869
Black, Jeremiah	no deg.	read law	
Blaine, James G.	grad.	Washington Coll.	1847
Blair, Montgomery	grad.	U.S. Military Academy	1835
	no deg.	Transylvania Coll. of Law	*ca.* 1836
Bliss, Cornelius	no deg.	no college	
Block, John	B.S.	U.S. Military Academy	1957
Blount, Winton	no deg.	U. of Alabama	1941
Blumenthal, Michael	B.S.	U. of California, Berkeley	1951
	M.A.	Princeton U.	1953
	Ph.D.	Princeton U.	1956
Bonaparte, Charles	grad.	Harvard U.	1872
	law deg.	Harvard U. Law Sch.	1874
Boric, Adolph	grad.	U. of Pennsylvania	1825
Boudinot, Elias	no deg.	read law	
Boutwell, George	no deg.	read law	
Bowen, Otis	A.B.	Indiana U.	1939
	M.D.	Indiana U.	1942
Boyd, Alan	LL.B.	U. of Virginia	1948
Bradford, William	grad.	Princeton Coll.	1772
Brady, Nicholas	B.A.	Yale U.	1952
	M.B.A.	Harvard U.	1954
Branch, John	grad.	U. of North Carolina	1801

Brannan, Charles	LL.B.	U. of Denver	1929
Breckinridge, John	no deg.	Augusta Acad. (now Washington & Lee U.)	*ca.* 1780
	no deg.	Coll. of William & Mary	*ca.* 1781
Breckinridge, John C.	grad.	Centre (Ky.) Coll.	1839
	no deg.	Coll. of New Jersey (now Princeton)	1840
	no deg.	Transylvania Coll.	1841
Brennan, Peter	no deg.	City Coll. of New York	*ca.* 1928
Brewster, Benjamin	grad.	Princeton Coll.	1834
Brinegar, Claude	B.A.	Stanford U.	1950
	M.A.	Stanford U.	1951
	Ph.D.	Stanford U.	1954
Bristow, Benjamin	grad.	Jefferson Coll.	1851
Brock, William	B.S.	Washington & Lee U.	1953
Brown, Aaron	grad.	U. of North Carolina	1814
Brown, Harold	A.B.	Columbia U.	1945
	M.A.	Columbia U.	1946
	Ph.D.	Columbia U.	1949
Brown, Jesse	A.A.	Kennedy-King Jr. Coll.	1972
Brown, Ronald	B.A.	Middlebury Coll.	1962
	J.D.	St. John's U.	1970
Brown, Walter	A.B.	Harvard U.	*ca.* 1891
	law deg.	Harvard U. Law Sch.	1894
Brownell, Herbert	B.A.	U. of Nebraska	1924
	LL.B.	Yale U.	1927
Browning, Orville	no deg.	Augusta Coll.	*ca.* 1830
Bryan, William Jennings	grad.	Illinois Coll.	1881
	grad.	Union Coll. of Law	1883
Buchanan, James	grad.	Dickinson Coll.	1809
Burleson, Albert	no deg.	Texas A&M U.	*ca.* 1880
	grad.	Baylor U.	1881
	law deg.	U. of Texas	1884
Burnley, James	B.A.	Yale U.	1970
	J.D.	Harvard U.	1973
Burr, Aaron	grad.	Coll. of New Jersey (now Princeton)	1772
Bush, George H.W.	B.A.	Yale U.	1948
Bush, George W.	B.A.	Yale U.	1968

	M.B.A.	Harvard U.	1975
Butler, Benjamin	no deg.	read law	
Butz, Earl	B.A.	Purdue U.	1932
	Ph.D.	Purdue U.	1937
Byrnes, James	no deg.	read law	
Calhoun, John C.	grad.	Yale U.	1804
Califano, Joseph	A.B.	Holy Cross Coll.	1952
	LL.B.	Harvard U.	1955
Cameron, James	grad.	Princeton Coll.	1852
Cameron, Simon	no deg.	no college	
Campbell, George	grad.	Princeton Coll.	1794
Campbell, James	no deg.	read law	
Card, Andrew	B.S.	U. of South Carolina	1971
Carlisle, John	no deg.	read law	
Carlucci, Frank	A.B.	Princeton U.	1952
	no deg.	Harvard U. Bus. Sch.	1956
Carter, Jimmy	B.S.	U.S. Naval Academy	1946
	no deg.	Union Coll.	1952
Cass, Lewis	no deg.	read law	
Cavazos, Lauro	B.A.	Texas Tech. U.	1949
	M.A.	Texas Tech. U.	1951
	Ph.D.	Iowa St. U.	1954
Celebrezze, Anthony	LL.B.	Ohio Northern U.	1936
Chandler, William	law deg.	Harvard U.	1854
Chandler, Zachariah	no deg.	no college	
Chao, Elaine	A.B.	Mount Holyoke Coll.	1975
	M.B.A.	Harvard U. Bus. Sch.	1979
Chapin, Roy	no deg.	U. of Michigan	1901
Chapman, Oscar	no deg.	U. of Denver	1924
	no deg.	U. of New Mexico	1928
	grad.	Westminster Law Sch.	1929
Chase, Salmon P.	grad.	Dartmouth Coll.	1826
Cheney, Dick	B.A.	U. of Wyoming	1965
	M.A.	U. of Wyoming	1966
	no deg.	U. of Wisconsin	1968
Christopher, Warren	B.S.	U. of Southern California	1945
	LL.B.	Stanford U.	1949
Cisneros, Henry	B.A.	Texas A&M U.	1968
	M.A.	Texas A&M U.	1970

	M.A.	Harvard U.	1973
	Ph.D.	George Washington U.	1975
Civiletti, Benjamin	A.B.	Johns Hopkins U.	1957
	LL.B.	U. of Maryland	1961
Clark, Tom	B.A.	U. of Texas	1921
	LL.B.	U. of Texas	1922
Clark, William P.	no deg.	Stanford U.	1951
	no deg.	Loyola U.	1958
Clark, W. Ramsey	B.A.	U. of Texas	1949
	M.A.	U. of Chicago	1950
	J.D.	U. of Chicago	1950
Clay, Henry	no deg.	read law	
Clayton, John	grad.	Yale U.	1815
	no deg.	Litchfield Law Sch.	*ca.* 1819
Cleveland, Grover	no deg.	read law	
Clifford, Clark	LL.B.	Washington U.	1928
Clifford, Nathan	no deg.	read law	
Clinton, George	no deg.	read law	
Clinton, Bill	B.A.	Georgetown U.	1968
	no deg.	Oxford U. (England)	1970
	J.D.	Yale U.	1973
Cobb, Howell	grad.	Franklin Coll. (now part of U. of Georgia)	1834
Cohen, Wilbur	Ph.B.	U. of Wisconsin	1934
Cohen, William	A.B.	Bowdoin Coll.	1962
	LL.B.	Boston U.	1965
Colby, Bainbridge	B.A.	Williams Coll.	1890
	no deg.	Columbia U.	1891
	LL.B.	New York Law Sch.	1892
Coleman, William	A.B.	U. of Pennsylvania	1941
	LL.B.	Harvard U.	1946
Colfax, Schuyler	no deg.	no college	
Collamer, Jacob	grad.	U. of Vermont	1810
Colman, Norman	LL.B.	U. of Louisville	1851
Connally, John	J.D.	U. of Texas	1941
Connor, John	A.B.	Syracuse U.	1936
	J.D.	Harvard U.	1939
Conrad, Charles	no deg.	read law	
Coolidge, Calvin	B.A.	Amherst Coll.	1895

Cortelyou, George	LL.B.	Georgetown U.	1895
	LL.M.	George Washington U.	1896
Corwin, Thomas	no deg.	read law	
Cox, Jacob	grad.	Oberlin Coll.	1851
Crawford, George	grad.	Coll. of New Jersey (now Princeton)	1820
Crawford, William	no deg.	read law	
Creswell, John	grad.	Dickinson Coll.	1848
Crittenden, John	no deg.	Washington Coll. (now Washington & Lee U.)	*ca.* 1803
	grad.	Coll. of William & Mary	1806
Crowninshield, Benjamin	no deg.	no college	
Cummings, Homer	Ph.B.	Yale U.	1891
	LL.B.	Yale U.	1893
Cuomo, Andrew	B.A.	Fordham U.	1979
	J.D.	Albany Law Sch.	1982
Curtis, Charles	no deg.	read law	
Cushing, Caleb	grad.	Harvard U.	1817
Daley, William	B.A.	Loyola U., Chicago	1970
	LL.B.	John Marshall Law Sch.	1975
Dallas, Alexander	no deg.	read law	
Dallas, George	grad.	Princeton	1810
Daniels, Josephus	no deg.	U. of North Carolina Law Sch.	1885
Daugherty, Harry	law deg.	U. of Michigan	1881
Davis, Dwight	grad.	Harvard U.	1900
	law deg.	Washington U.	1903
Davis, James	no deg.	Sharon Bus. Coll.	*ca.* 1890
Davis, Jefferson	grad.	U.S. Military Academy	1828
Dawes, Charles	grad.	Marietta Coll.	1884
	LL.B.	Cincinnati Law Sch.	1886
Day, James	A.B.	U. of Chicago	1935
	LL.B.	Harvard U.	1938
Day, William	grad.	U. of Michigan	1870
Dearborn, Henry	no deg.	studied medicine independently	*ca.* 1772
Delano, Columbus	no deg.	read law	
Denby, Edwin	law deg.	U. of Michigan	1896
Dennison, William	grad.	Miami (Ohio) U.	1835
Dent, Frederick	B.A.	Yale U.	1943

Dern, George	no deg.	U. of Nebraska	1894
Derwinski, Edward	B.S.	Loyola U., Chicago	1951
Devens, Charles	grad.	Harvard U.	1838
Dexter, Samuel	grad.	Harvard U.	1781
Dickerson, Mahlon	grad.	Princeton	1789
Dickinson, Donald	law deg.	U. of Michigan	1867
Dickinson, Jacob	grad.	U. of Nashville	1872
	no deg.	Columbia U. Law Sch.	*ca.* 1873
Dillon, C. Douglas	A.B.	Harvard U.	1931
Dix, John	no deg.	read law	
Doak, William	no deg.	business college	*ca.* 1900
Dobbin, James	grad.	U. of North Carolina	1832
Dole, Elizabeth	B.A.	Duke U.	1958
	M.A.	Harvard U.	1960
	J.D.	Harvard U.	1965
Donaldson, Jesse	no deg.	Teacher's Normal Coll.	*ca.* 1901
	no deg.	Sparks Business Coll.	*ca.* 1903
Donovan, Raymond	B.A.	Notre Dame Seminary	1952
Duane, William	no deg.	read law	
Dulles, John Foster	grad.	Princeton	1908
	no deg.	Sorbonne (France)	1909
	law deg.	George Washington U.	1911
Duncan, Charles	B.S.	Rice U.	1947
	no deg.	U. of Texas	1949
Dunlop, John	A.B.	U. of California, Berkeley	1935
	Ph.D.	U. of Chicago	1968
Durkin, Martin	no deg.	no college	
Eagleburger, Lawrence	B.S.	U. of Wisconsin	1952
	M.A.	U. of Wisconsin	1957
Eaton, John	no deg.	U. of North Carolina	1804
Edison, Charles	grad.	Mass. Inst. of Tech.	1913
Edwards, James	B.S.	Charleston Coll.	1950
	D.M.D.	U. of Louisville	1955
	no deg.	U. of Pennsylvania Med. Sch.	1958
Eisenhower, Dwight	B.S.	U.S. Military Academy	1915
Elkins, Stephen	B.A.	U. of Missouri	1860
	M.A.	U. of Missouri	1868
Endicott, William	grad.	Harvard U.	1847

	no deg.	Harvard U. Law Sch.	1850
Espy, Michael	B.A.	Howard U.	1975
	LL.B.	Santa Clara U.	1978
Eustis, William	grad.	Harvard U.	1772
		studied medicine independently	*ca.* 1772
Evans, Donald	B.S.	U. of Texas	1969
	M.B.A.	U. of Texas	1973
Evarts, William	B.A.	Yale U.	1833
	M.A.	Yale U.	1837
Everett, Edward	grad.	Harvard U.	1811
	no deg.	studied theology independently	*ca.* 1814
Ewing, Thomas	B.A.	Ohio U.	1815
Fairbanks, Charles	grad.	Ohio Wesleyan U.	1872
Fairchild, Charles	grad.	Harvard U.	1863
	grad.	Harvard U. Law Sch.	1865
Fall, Albert	no deg.	read law	
Farley, James	no deg.	Packard Commercial Sch.	*ca.* 1906
Fessenden, William	grad.	Bowdoin Coll.	1823
Fillmore, Millard	no deg.	read law	
Finch, Robert	B.A.	Occidental Coll.	1947
	J.D.	U. of Southern Calif.	1951
Fish, Hamilton	grad.	Columbia Coll.	1827
Fisher, Walter	grad.	Hanover Coll.	1883
Flemming, Arthur	A.B.	Ohio Wesleyan U.	1927
	M.A.	American U.	1928
	LL.B.	George Washington U.	1932
Floyd, John	grad.	South Carolina Coll.	1829
Folger, Charles	grad.	Geneva Coll. (now Hobart)	1836
Folsom, Marion	A.B.	U. of Georgia	1912
	M.B.A.	Harvard U.	1914
Ford, Gerald	A.B.	U. of Michigan	1935
	LL.B.	Yale U.	1941
Forrestal, James	no deg.	Dartmouth	1912
	no deg.	Princeton U.	1915
Forsyth, John	no deg.	read law	
Forward, Walter	no deg.	read law	
Foster, Charles	no deg.	no college	

Foster, John	grad.	Indiana St. U.	1855
	no deg.	Harvard U. Law Sch.	*ca.* 1856
Fowler, Henry	B.A.	Roanoke Coll.	1929
	LL.B.	Yale U.	1932
	J.S.D.	Yale U.	1933
Francis, David	B.A.	Washington U.	1870
Franklin, Barbara H.	B.A.	Pennsylvania St. U.	1962
	M.B.A.	Harvard U.	1964
Freeman, Orville	B.A.	U. of Minnesota	1940
	LL.B.	U. of Minnesota	1946
Frelinghuysen, Frederick	grad.	Rutgers Coll.	1836
Gage, Lyman	no deg.	no college	
Gallatin, Albert	grad.	Acad. of Geneva (Switz.)	1779
Gardner, John	B.A.	Stanford U.	1935
	M.A.	Stanford U.	1936
	Ph.D.	U. of California, Berkeley	1938
Garfield, James A.	grad.	Williams Coll.	1858
Garfield, James R.	grad.	Williams Coll.	1885
	no deg.	Columbia U. Law Sch.	*ca.* 1886
Garland, Augustus	no deg.	read law	
Garner, John Nance	no deg.	Vanderbilt U.	*ca.* 1886
Garrison, Lindley	law deg.	U. of Pennsylvania	1886
Gary, James	B.A.	Allegheny Coll.	1854
Gates, Thomas	B.A.	U. of Pennsylvania	1928
Gerry, Elbridge	grad.	Harvard U.	1762
Gilmer, Thomas	no deg.	read law	
Gilpin, Henry	grad.	U. of Pennsylvania	1819
Glass, Carter	no deg.	no college	
Glickman, Daniel	B.A.	U. of Michigan	1966
	J.D.	George Washington U.	1969
Goff, Nathan	no deg.	Georgetown U.	*ca.* 1860
	LL.B.	New York U. Law Sch.	1866
Goldberg, Arthur	B.S.L.	Northwestern U.	1929
	J.D.	Northwestern U.	1930
Goldschmidt, Neil	A.B.	U. of Oregon	1963
	LL.B.	U. of California, Berkeley	1967
Good, James	B.S.	Coe Coll.	1892
	LL.B.	U. of Michigan	1893
Gore, Albert, Jr.	B.A.	Harvard U.	1969

	no deg.	Vanderbilt U.	1976
Gore, Howard	grad.	West Virginia U.	1900
Gorham, Nathaniel	no deg.	no college	
Graham, William	grad.	U. of North Carolina	1824
Granger, Francis	grad.	Yale Coll.	1811
Granger, Gideon	grad.	Yale Coll.	1787
Grant, Ulysses	grad.	U.S. Military Academy	1843
Gregory, Thomas	grad.	Southwestern Presbyterian U.	1883
	no deg.	U. of Virginia Law Sch.	1884
	LL.B.	U. of Texas	1885
Gresham, Walter	no deg.	Indiana U.	1852
Griffin, Cyrus	no deg.	U. of Edinburgh (Scotland)	*ca.* 1770
	no deg.	Middle Temple (England)	*ca.* 1774
Griggs, John	no deg.	Lafayette Coll.	1868
Gronouski, John	B.A.	U. of Wisconsin	1942
	M.A.	U. of Wisconsin	1947
	Ph.D.	U. of Wisconsin	1955
Grundy, Felix	no deg.	read law	
Guthrie, James	no deg.	read law	
Habersham, Joseph	no deg.	no college	
Haig, Alexander	B.S.	U.S. Military Academy	1947
	M.A.	Georgetown U.	1961
Hall, Nathan	no deg.	read law	
Hamilton, Alexander	no deg.	King's Coll. (now Columbia U.)	1776
Hamilton, Paul	no deg.	no college	
Hamlin, Hannibal	no deg.	read law	
Hancock, John	grad.	Harvard Coll.	1754
Hannegan, Robert	LL.B.	St. Louis U.	1925
Hanson, John	no deg.	no college	
Hardin, Clifford	B.A.	Purdue U.	1937
	M.A.	Purdue U.	1939
	Ph.D.	Purdue U.	1941
Harding, Warren	no deg.	read law	
Harlan, James	grad.	Indiana Asbury U.	1845
Harmon, Judson	B.A.	Dennison U.	1866
	LL.B.	Cincinnati Law Sch.	1869
Harriman, W. Averell	B.A.	Yale U.	1913
Harris, Patricia	A.B.	Howard U.	1945
	M.A.	U. of Chicago	1947

	J.D.	George Washington U.	1960
Harrison, Benjamin	B.A.	Miami (Ohio) U.	1852
Harrison, William	no deg.	Hampden-Sidney Coll.	1790
Hathaway, Stanley	A.B.	U. of Nebraska	1948
	LL.B.	U. of Nebraska	1950
Hatton, Frank	no deg.	no college	
Hay, John	B.A.	Brown U.	1858
Hayes, Rutherford	B.A.	Kenyon Coll.	1842
	LL.B.	Harvard U.	1845
Hays, William	grad.	Wabash Coll.	1900
	M.A.	Wabash Coll.	1904
Heckler, Margaret	B.A.	Albertus Magnus Coll.	1953
	LL.B.	Boston Coll.	1956
Hendricks, Thomas	grad.	Hanover Coll.	1841
Henshaw, David	no deg.	no college	
Herbert, Hilary	law deg.	U. of Alabama	1857
Herman, Alexis	B.A.	Xavier U., New Orleans	1969
	no deg.	U. of South Alabama	1972
Herrington, John	A.B.	Stanford U.	1961
	J.D.	U. of California, Berkeley	1964
Herter, Christian	B.A.	Harvard U.	1915
	no deg.	Columbia U. Sch. of Architecture	1916
Hickel, Walter	no deg.	high school	*ca.* 1935
Hills, Carla	A.B.	Stanford U.	1955
	LL.B.	Yale U.	1958
Hitchcock, Ethan	no deg.	no college	
Hitchcock, Frank	B.A.	Harvard U.	1891
	LL.B.	Columbian U. (now George Washington U.)	1894
	LL.M.	Columbian U. (now George Washington U.)	1895
Hoar, Ebenezer	grad.	Harvard U.	1835
Hobart, Garret	grad.	Rutgers U.	1863
Hobby, Oveta	no deg.	U. of Texas Law Sch.	1927
Hodel, Donald	B.A.	Harvard U.	1957
	J.D.	U. of Oregon	1960
Hodges, Luther	B.A.	U. of North Carolina	1919

Hodgson, James	A.B.	U. of Minnesota	1938
	no deg.	U. of Calif., Los Angeles	1948
Holt, Joseph	no deg.	St. Joseph's Coll.	*ca.* 1830
	no deg.	Centre Coll.	*ca.* 1831
Hoover, Herbert	B.A.	Stanford U.	1895
Hopkins, Harry	B.A.	Grinnell Coll.	1912
Houston, David	grad.	Coll. of South Carolina	1887
	M.A.	Harvard U.	1894
Howe, Timothy	no deg.	Maine Wesleyan Seminary	*ca.* 1839
Hubbard, Samuel	grad.	Yale U.	1819
Hufstedler, Shirley	B.A.	U. of New Mexico	1945
	LL.B.	Stanford U.	1949
Hughes, Charles	no deg.	Madison U. (now Colgate U.)	1878
	grad.	Brown U.	1881
	no deg.	New York Law Inst.	1882
	law deg.	Columbia U.	1884
Hull, Cordell	grad.	Cumberland U. Law Sch.	1891
Humphrey, George	grad.	U. of Michigan	1912
Humphrey, Hubert	no deg.	Denver Coll. of Pharmacy	1933
	B.A.	U. of Minnesota	1939
	M.A.	Louisiana St. U.	1940
Hunt, William	no deg.	Yale Coll.	*ca.* 1844
Huntington, Samuel	no deg.	read law	
Hurley, Patrick	B.A.	Indian U. (later Bacone Coll.)	1905
	LL.B.	National U.	1908
Hyde, Arthur	B.A.	U. of Michigan	1899
	LL.B.	U. of Iowa	1900
Ickes, Harold	B.A.	U. of Chicago	1897
	law deg.	U. of Chicago	1907
Ingham, Samuel	no deg.	no college	
Jackson, Andrew	no deg.	read law	
Jackson, Robert	grad.	Albany Law Sch.	*ca.* 1913
James, Thomas	no deg.	no college	
Jardine, William	B.S.	Agri. Coll. of Utah	1904
	no deg.	Grad. Sch. of Utah	1906
Jay, John	grad.	King's Coll. (now Columbia U.)	*ca.* 1764
Jefferson, Thomas	grad.	Coll. of William & Mary	1762

Jewell, Marshall	no deg.	no college	
Johnson, Andrew	no deg.	no college	
Johnson, Cave	no deg.	Cumberland U. (now U. of Nashville)	*ca.* 1814
Johnson, Louis	LL.B.	U. of Virginia	1912
Johnson, Lyndon	B.S.	Southwest Tex. St. Teacher's Coll.	1930
	no deg.	Georgetown U. Law Sch.	1935
Johnson, Reverdy	grad.	St. John's Coll.	1811
Johnson, Richard	no deg.	Transylvania U.	1800
Jones, Jesse	no deg.	no college	
Jones, William	no deg.	no college	
Kantor, Mickey	B.A.	Vanderbilt U.	1961
	J.D.	Georgetown U.	1968
Katzenbach, Nicholas	B.A.	Princeton U.	1945
	LL.B.	Yale U.	1947
	no deg.	Oxford U. (England)	1949
Kellogg, Frank	no deg.	read law	
Kemp, Jack	B.A.	Occidental Coll.	1957
	no deg.	Long Beach St. U.	*ca.* 1959
Kendall, Amos	grad.	Dartmouth Coll.	1811
Kennedy, David	B.A.	Weber Coll.	1928
	M.A.	George Washington U.	1935
	LL.B.	George Washington U.	1937
	grad.	Stonier School of Banking	1939
Kennedy, John F.	B.A.	Harvard U.	1940
Kennedy, John P.	grad.	Baltimore Coll.	1812
Kennedy, Robert	B.A.	Harvard U.	1948
	LL.B.	U. of Virginia	1951
Key, David	grad.	Hiwassee Coll.	1850
King, Horatio	no deg.	no college	
King, William	grad.	U. of North Carolina	1803
Kirkwood, Samuel	no deg.	read law	
Kissinger, Henry	A.B.	Harvard U.	1950
	M.A.	Harvard U.	1952
	Ph.D.	Harvard U.	1954
Kleindienst, Richard	A.B.	Harvard U.	1947
	LL.B.	Harvard U.	1950
Kleppe, Thomas	no deg.	Valley City (N.D.) Teacher's Coll.	1937
Klutznick, Philip	no deg.	U. of Kansas	1925

	no deg.	U. of Nebraska	1926
	LL.B.	Creighton U.	1929
Knebel, John	B.A.	U.S. Military Academy	1959
	M.A.	Creighton U.	1962
	J.D.	American U.	1965
Knox, Henry	no deg.	no college	
Knox, Philander	B.A.	Mount Union Coll.	1872
Knox, W. Franklin	B.A.	Alma Coll.	1898
Kreps, Juanita	A.B.	Berea Coll.	1942
	M.A.	Duke U.	1944
	Ph.D.	Duke U.	1948
Krug, Julius	B.A.	U. of Wisconsin	1929
	M.A.	U. of Wisconsin	1930
Laird, Melvin	B.A.	Carleton Coll.	1942
	no deg.	U. of Wisconsin Law Sch.	*ca.* 1948
Lamar, Lucius Q.C.	grad.	Emory Coll.	1845
Lamont, Daniel	no deg.	Cortland Normal Coll.	1871
Lamont, Robert	B.S.	U. of Michigan	1891
Landrieu, Moon	B.A.	Loyola U., New Orleans	1952
	LL.B.	Loyola U., New Orleans	1954
Lane, Franklin	no deg.	Hastings Law Sch.	1888
Lansing, Robert	grad.	Amherst Coll.	1886
Laurens, Henry	no deg.	no college	
Lee, Charles	A.B.	Coll. of New Jersey (now Princeton)	1775
Lee, Richard	no deg.	no college	
Legaré, Hugh	grad.	Coll. of Charleston (now U. of South Carolina)	1814
Levi, Edward	Ph.B.	U. of Chicago	1932
	J.D.	U. of Chicago	1935
	J.S.D.	Yale U.	1938
Lewis, Andrew	B.A.	Haverford Coll.	1953
	M.B.A.	Harvard U.	1955
Lincoln, Abraham	no deg.	read law	
Lincoln, Levi	grad.	Harvard Coll.	1772
Lincoln, Robert	grad.	Harvard Coll.	1864
Livingston, Edward	grad.	Coll. of New Jersey (now Princeton)	1781
Long, John	grad.	Harvard Coll.	1857

Lovett, Robert	grad.	Yale U.	1919
	no deg.	Harvard U. Law Sch.	1920
	no deg.	Harvard Business Sch.	1921
Lujan, Manuel	B.A.	Coll. of Santa Fe	1950
Lyng, Richard	Ph.B.	U. of Notre Dame	1940
Lynn, James	B.A.	Western Reserve U.	1948
	LL.B.	Harvard U.	1951
MacVeagh, Franklin	grad.	Yale U.	1862
	grad.	Columbia U. Law Sch.	1864
MacVeagh, Wayne	grad.	Yale U.	1853
Madigan, Edward	AA	Lincoln College	1955
Madison, James	B.A.	Coll. of New Jersey (now Princeton)	1771
Manning, Daniel	no deg.	no college	
Marcy, William	grad.	Brown U.	1808
Marshall, F. Ray	A.B.	Millsaps Coll.	1949
	M.A.	Louisiana St. U.	1950
	Ph.D.	U. of California, Berkeley	1954
Marshall, George	grad.	Virginia Military Inst.	1901
Marshall, James	grad.	Dickinson Coll.	1848
Marshall, John	no deg.	read law	
Marshall, Thomas	grad.	Wabash Coll.	1873
Martin, Lynn	B.A.	U. of Illinois	1960
Martinez, Mel	B.A.	Florida St. U.	1969
	J.D.	Florida St. U.	1973
Mason, John	grad.	U. of North Carolina	1816
	no deg.	Litchfield Law Sch.	*ca.* 1819
Mathews, F. David	A.B.	U. of Alabama	1958
	M.A.	U. of Alabama	1959
	Ph.D.	Columbia U.	1965
Maynard, Horace	grad.	Amherst Coll.	1838
McAdoo, William	no deg.	U. of Tennessee	*ca.* 1882
McClelland, Robert	grad.	Dickinson Coll.	1829
McCrary, George	no deg.	read law	
McCulloch, Hugh	no deg.	Bowdoin Coll.	*ca.* 1826
McElroy, Neil	B.A.	Harvard U.	1925
McGranery, James	grad.	Temple U.	1928
McGrath, James	Ph.B.	Providence Coll.	1926
	grad.	Boston U. Law Sch.	1928

McHenry, James	no deg.	Newark Acad.	*ca.* 1775
McKay, Douglas	grad.	Oregon St. Coll.	1917
McKean, Thomas	no deg.	read law	
McKenna, Joseph	grad.	Benicia Collegiate Inst.	1865
McKennan, Thomas	grad.	Washington Coll. (later Washington & Jefferson Coll.)	1810
McKinley, William	no deg.	Allegheny Coll.	*ca.* 1860
	no deg.	Albany Law Sch.	*ca.* 1867
McLane, Louis	no deg.	Newark Coll.	*ca.* 1801
McLaughlin, Ann	B.A.	Marymount Coll.	1963
	no deg.	Wharton Sch.	1987
McLean, John	no deg.	read law	
McNamara, Robert	A.B.	U. of California, Berkeley	1937
	M.B.A.	Harvard U.	1939
McReynolds, James	grad.	Vanderbilt U.	1882
	law deg.	U. of Virginia	1884
Meese, Edwin	B.A.	Yale U.	1953
	LL.B.	U. of California, Berkeley	1958
Meigs, Return	grad.	Yale Coll.	1785
Mellon, Andrew	no deg.	Western U. of Penn.	1872
Meredith, Edwin	no deg.	Highland Park Coll. (later Des Moines U.)	*ca.* 1894
Meredith, William	B.A.	U. of Pennsylvania	1812
Metcalf, Victor	grad.	Yale U.	1876
	law deg.	Hamilton Coll.	1877
Meyer, George	B.A.	Harvard U.	1879
Middleton, Henry	no deg.	no college	
Mifflin, Thomas	grad.	U. of Pennsylvania	1760
Miller, G. William	B.S.	U.S. Coast Guard Academy	1945
	J.D.	U. of California, Berkeley	1952
Miller, William H.	grad.	Hamilton Coll.	1861
Mills, Ogden	grad.	Harvard U.	1904
	grad.	Harvard U. Law Sch.	1907
Mineta, Norman	B.S.	U. of California, Berkeley	1953
Mitchell, James	no deg.	no college	
Mitchell, John	LL.B.	Fordham U.	1938
Mitchell, William	no deg.	Yale U.	*ca.* 1893
	grad.	U. of Minnesota	1895
	law deg.	U. of Minnesota	1896

Mondale, Walter	B.A.	U. of Minnesota	1951
	LL.B.	U. of Minnesota	1956
Monroe, James	no deg.	Coll. of William & Mary	1776
Moody, William	B.A.	Harvard Coll.	1876
Morgenthau, Henry	no deg.	Cornell U.	1913
Morrill, Lot	no deg.	Waterville Coll. (now Colby Coll.)	1831
Morton, Julius	no deg.	U. of Michigan	1853
	B.A.	Union Coll.	1856
Morton, Levi	no deg.	no college	
Morton, Paul	no deg.	no college	
Morton, Rogers	B.A.	Yale U.	1937
	no deg.	Columbia U. Coll. of Physicians	1938
Mosbacher, Robert	B.S.	Washington & Lee U.	1947
Mueller, Frederick	B.S.	Michigan St. U.	1914
Murphy, Frank	grad.	U. of Michigan	1912
	LL.B.	U. of Michigan	1914
Muskie, Edmund	B.A.	Bates Coll.	1936
	LL.B.	Cornell U.	1939
Nagel, Charles	grad.	Washington U.	1872
	no deg.	U. of Berlin (Germany)	1873
Nelson, John	grad.	Coll. of William & Mary	1811
New, Harry S.	no deg.	Butler U.	*ca.* 1880
Newberry, Truman	grad.	Yale U.	1885
Niles, John	no deg.	read law	
Nixon, Richard	B.A.	Whittier Coll.	1934
	J.D.	Duke U.	1937
Noble, John	grad.	Yale U.	1851
	grad.	Cincinnati Law Sch.	1852
Norton, Gale	B.A.	U. of Denver	1975
	J.D.	U. of Denver	1978
O'Brien, Lawrence	LL.B.	Northeastern U.	1942
O'Leary, Hazel	B.A.	Fisk U.	1959
	J.D.	Rutgers U.	1966
Olney, Richard	grad.	Brown U.	1856
	grad.	Harvard U. Law Sch.	1858
O'Neill, Paul	B.A.	Fresno St. Coll.	1960
	no deg.	Claremont Grad. Sch.	1961

	no deg.	George Washington U.	1965
	M.A.	Indiana U.	1966
Osgood, Samuel	grad.	Harvard Coll.	1770
Paige, Rod	B.S.	Jackson St. U.	1955
	M.S.	Indiana U.	1964
	Ph.D.	Indiana U.	1969
Palmer, Alexander	grad.	Swarthmore Coll.	1891
Patterson, Robert	grad.	Union Coll.	1912
	grad.	Harvard U. Law Sch.	1915
Paulding, James	no deg.	no college	
Payne, Henry	no deg.	no college	
Payne, John	no deg.	read law	
Peña, Federico	B.A.	U. of Texas	1968
	J.D.	U. of Texas	1972
Perkins, Frances	grad.	Mount Holyoke Coll.	1905
	no deg.	U. of Chicago	*ca.* 1906
	no deg.	U. of Pennsylvania	*ca.* 1908
	A.M.	Columbia U.	1910
Perry, William	B.S.	Stanford U.	1949
	M.A.	Stanford U.	1950
	Ph.D.	Pennsylvania St. U.	1957
Peterson, Peter	B.S.	Northwestern U.	1947
	M.B.A.	U. of Chicago	1951
Pickering, Timothy	grad.	Harvard Coll.	1763
Pierce, Franklin	B.A.	Bowdoin Coll.	1824
Pierce, Samuel	A.B.	Cornell U.	1947
	J.D.	Cornell U.	1949
	LL.M.	New York U.	1952
	no deg.	Yale U.	1958
Pierrepont, Edwards	grad.	Yale Coll.	1837
	no deg.	New Haven Law Sch.	*ca.* 1840
Pinkney, William	no deg.	read law	
Poinsett, Joel	no deg.	St. Paul's Sch. (Scotland)	*ca.* 1800
	no deg.	Woolwich Milit. Acad. (England)	*ca.* 1800
Polk, James	B.A.	U. of North Carolina	1818
Porter, James	no deg.	read law	
Porter, Peter	grad.	Yale Coll.	1791

Powell, Colin	B.S.	City Coll. of New York	1958
	M.B.A.	George Washington U.	1971
Preston, William	grad.	Coll. of William & Mary	1823
	no deg.	U. of Virginia Law Sch.	1825
Principi, Anthony	B.S.	U.S. Naval Academy	1967
	J.D.	Seton Hall U.	1975
Proctor, Redfield	grad.	Dartmouth Coll.	1851
	grad.	Albany Law Sch.	1859
Quayle, Dan	B.A.	DePauw U.	1969
	J.D.	U. of Indiana	1974
Ramsey, Alexander	no deg.	Lafayette Coll.	*ca.* 1839
Randall, Alexander	no deg.	read law	
Randolph, Edmund	grad.	Coll. of William & Mary	*ca.* 1775
Randolph, Peyton	no deg.	Coll. of William & Mary	*ca.* 1739
	no deg.	Inner Temple (England)	*ca.* 1740
Rawlins, John A.	no deg.	read law	
Reagan, Ronald W.	A.B.	Eureka Coll.	1932
Redfield, William C.	no deg.	no college	
Regan, Donald	B.A.	Harvard U.	1940
Reich, Robert	A.B.	Dartmouth Coll.	1968
	M.A.	Oxford U. (England)	1970
	J.D.	Yale U.	1973
Reno, Janet	B.A.	Cornell U.	1960
	LL.B.	Harvard U.	1963
Ribicoff, Abraham	no deg.	New York U.	1929
	LL.B.	U. of Chicago	1933
Richardson, Elliot	A.B.	Harvard U.	1941
	LL.B.	Harvard U.	1947
Richardson, William A.	grad.	Harvard U.	1843
	no deg.	Harvard U. Law Sch.	*ca.* 1846
Richardson, William B.	B.A.	Tufts U.	1970
	M.A.	Tufts U.	1971
Riley, Richard	B.A.	Furman U.	1954
	LL.B.	U. of South Carolina	1959
Robeson, George	grad.	Princeton U.	1847
Rockefeller, Nelson	A.B.	Dartmouth Coll.	1930
Rodney, Caesar	grad.	U. of Pennsylvania	1789
Rogers, William	A.B.	Colgate U.	1934
	LL.B.	Cornell U.	1937

Romney, George	no deg.	U. of Utah	1929
	no deg.	George Washington U.	1930
Roosevelt, Franklin	B.A.	Harvard U.	1903
	no deg.	Columbia U.	1907
Roosevelt, Theodore	B.A.	Harvard U.	1880
Root, Elihu	grad.	Hamilton Coll.	1864
	LL.B.	New York U. Law Sch.	1867
Roper, Daniel	no deg.	Wofford Coll.	*ca.* 1886
	grad.	Trinity Coll.	1888
Royall, Kenneth	B.A.	U. of North Carolina	1914
	J.D.	Harvard U.	1917
Rubin, Robert	A.B.	Harvard U.	1960
	no deg.	London Sch. of Economics	1961
	LL.B.	Yale U.	1964
Rumsfeld, Donald	A.B.	Princeton U.	1954
Rush, Richard	grad.	Coll. of New Jersey (now Princeton)	1797
Rusk, Dean	B.A.	Davidson Coll.	1931
	B.S.	Oxford U. (England)	1933
	M.A.	Oxford U. (England)	1934
Rusk, Jeremiah	no deg.	no college	
St. Clair, Arthur	no deg.	U. of Edinburgh (Scotland)	*ca.* 1755
Sargent, John	A.B.	Tufts Coll.	1887
Sawyer, Charles	grad.	Oberlin Coll.	1908
	grad.	U. of Cincinnati	1911
Saxbe, William	A.B.	Ohio St. U.	1940
	LL.B.	Ohio St. U.	1948
Schlesinger, James	A.B.	Harvard U.	1950
	A.M.	Harvard U.	1952
	Ph.D.	Harvard U.	1956
Schofield, John	grad.	U.S. Military Academy	1853
Schurz, Carl	no deg.	U. of Bonn (Germany)	1847
Schweiker, Richard	B.A.	Pennsylvania St. U.	1949
Schwellenbach, Lewis	law deg.	U. of Washington, Seattle	1917
Seaton, Frederick	grad.	Kansas St. Agri. Coll.	1931
Seward, William	grad.	Union Coll.	1820
Shalala, Donna	A.B.	Western Coll. for Women	1962
	M.S.	Syracuse U.	1968
	Ph.D.	Syracuse U.	1970

Shaw, Leslie	grad.	Cornell Coll.	1874
	no deg.	Iowa Coll. of Law	1876
Sherman, James	grad.	Hamilton Coll.	1878
	law deg.	Hamilton Coll.	1879
Sherman, John	no deg.	read law	
Sherman, William	grad.	U.S. Military Academy	1840
Shultz, George	B.A.	Princeton U.	1942
	Ph.D.	Mass. Inst. of Tech.	1949
Simon, William	B.A.	Lafayette Coll.	1952
Skinner, Samuel	B.S.	U. of Illinois	1960
	J.D.	DePaul U.	1966
Slater, Rodney	B.S.	Eastern Michigan U.	1977
	J.D.	U. of Arkansas	1980
Smith, Caleb	no deg.	Coll. of Cincinnati	1825
	no deg.	Miami (Ohio) U.	1826
Smith, Charles	grad.	Union Coll.	1861
Smith, Cyrus R.	no deg.	U. of Texas	1924
Smith, Hoke	no deg.	read law	
Smith, Robert	grad.	Coll. of New Jersey (now Princeton)	1781
Smith, William French	A.B.	U. of California, Berkeley	1939
	LL.B.	Harvard U.	1942
Snyder, John	no deg.	Vanderbilt U.	*ca.* 1916
Southard, Samuel	grad.	Coll. of New Jersey (now Princeton)	1804
Speed, James	no deg.	Transylvania U.	*ca.* 1833
Spencer, John	grad.	Union Coll.	1806
Stanbery, Henry	grad.	Washington Coll. (now Washington & Jefferson Coll.)	*ca.* 1819
Stans, Maurice	no deg.	Northwestern U.	1928
	no deg.	Columbia U.	1930
Stanton, Edwin	no deg.	Kenyon Coll.	*ca.* 1832
Stettinius, Edward	no deg.	U. of Virginia	1924
Stevenson, Adlai	no deg.	Centre Coll.	*ca.* 1857
Stimson, Henry	grad.	Yale U.	1888
	M.A.	Harvard Law School	1891
Stoddert, Benjamin	no deg.	no college	
Stone, Harlan	no deg.	Massachusetts Agri. Coll.	*ca.* 1890
	B.S.	Amherst Coll.	1894

	M.A.	Amherst Coll.	1897
	law deg.	Columbia U.	1898
Straus, Oscar	grad.	Columbia Coll.	1871
	grad.	Columbia U. Law Sch.	1873
Stuart, Alexander	no deg.	Coll. of William & Mary	*ca.* 1824
	grad.	U. of Virginia	1828
Sullivan, Louis	B.S.	Morehouse Coll.	1954
	M.D.	Boston U.	1958
Summerfield, Arthur	no deg.	no college	
Summers, Lawrence	S.B.	Mass. Inst. of Tech.	1975
	Ph.D.	Harvard U.	1982
Swanson, Claude	no deg.	Virginia A&M Coll.	*ca.* 1882
	grad.	Randolph-Macon Coll.	1885
	law deg.	U. of Virginia	1886
Taft, Alphonso	grad.	Yale Coll.	1833
Taft, William H.	B.A.	Yale U.	1878
	grad.	Cincinnati Law Sch.	1880
Taney, Roger	grad.	Dickinson Coll.	1795
Taylor, Zachary	no deg.	no college	
Teller, Henry	grad.	Alfred U.	1852
Thomas, Philip	grad.	Dickinson Coll.	1830
Thompson, Jacob	grad.	U. of North Carolina	1831
Thompson, Richard	no deg.	read law	
Thompson, Smith	grad.	Coll. of New Jersey (now Princeton)	1788
Thompson, Tommy	B.S.	U. of Wisconsin	1963
	J.D.	U. of Wisconsin	1966
Thornburgh, Richard	B.S.	Yale U.	1954
	LL.B.	U. of Pittsburgh	1957
Tobin, Maurice	no deg.	Boston Coll.	*ca.* 1919
Tompkins, Daniel	grad.	Columbia Coll.	1795
Toucey, Isaac	no deg.	read law	
Tracy, Benjamin	no deg.	read law	
Trowbridge, Alexander	A.B.	Princeton U.	1951
Truman, Harry	no deg.	Kansas City Law Sch.	1925
Tyler, John	grad.	Coll. of William & Mary	1807
Tyner, James	no deg.	read law	
Udall, Stewart	LL.B.	U. of Arizona	1948
Upshur, Abel	no deg.	Yale Coll.	*ca.* 1810

	no deg.	Princeton U.	*ca.* 1810
Usery, Willie	no deg.	Georgia Military Coll.	1941
	no deg.	Mercer U.	1949
Usher, John	no deg.	read law	
Van Buren, Martin	no deg.	read law	
Vance, Cyrus	B.A.	Yale U.	1939
	LL.B.	Yale U.	1942
Veneman, Ann	B.A.	U. of California, Davis	1970
	M.A.	U. of California, Berkeley	1971
	J.D.	Hastings Coll. of Law	1976
Verity, C. William	B.A.	Yale U.	1939
Vilas, William	grad.	U. of Wisconsin	1858
	grad.	U. of Albany Law Sch.	1860
Vinson, Frederick	law deg.	Centre Coll.	1911
Volpe, John	grad.	Wentworth Inst.	1930
Walker, Frank	no deg.	Gonzaga U.	1906
	grad.	U. of Notre Dame Law Sch.	1909
Walker, Robert	grad.	U. of Pennsylvania	1819
Wallace, Henry A.	grad.	Iowa St. Coll.	1910
Wallace, Henry C.	grad.	Iowa St. Agri. Coll.	1892
Wanamaker, John	no deg.	no college	
Washburne, Elihu	no deg.	Maine Wesleyan Seminary	*ca.* 1836
Washington, George	no deg.	studied surveying independently	*ca.* 1750
Watkins, James	B.S.	U.S. Naval Academy	1949
	M.S.	Naval Postgraduate Sch.	1958
Watson, W. Marvin	B.A.	Baylor U.	1949
	M.A.	Baylor U.	1950
Watt, James	B.S.	U. of Wyoming	1960
	J.D.	U. of Wyoming	1962
Weaver, Robert	B.A.	Harvard U.	1929
	M.A.	Harvard U.	1931
	Ph.D.	Harvard U.	1934
Webster, Daniel	grad.	Dartmouth Coll.	1801
Weeks, John	grad.	U.S. Naval Academy	1881
Weeks, Sinclair	B.A.	Harvard U.	1914
Weinberger, Caspar	A.B.	Harvard U.	1938
	LL.B.	Harvard U.	1941
Welles, Gideon	no deg.	American Acad.	1825

West, Roy	grad.	DePauw U.	1890
West, Togo	B.A.	Howard U.	1965
	J.D.	Howard U.	1968
Wheeler, William	no deg.	U. of Vermont	1840
Whiting, William	grad.	Amherst Coll.	1886
Whitney, William	grad.	Yale Coll.	1863
	no deg.	Harvard U. Law Sch.	1864
Wickard, Claude	grad.	Purdue U.	1915
Wickersham, George	no deg.	Lehigh U.	1875
	law deg.	U. of Pennsylvania	1880
Wickliffe, Charles	no deg.	read law	
Wilbur, Curtis	grad.	U.S. Naval Academy	1888
Wilbur, Ray	B.A.	Stanford U.	1896
	M.A.	Stanford U.	1897
	M.D.	Cooper Medical Coll.	1899
Wilkins, William	grad.	Dickinson Coll.	*ca.* 1801
Williams, George	no deg.	read law	
Wilson, Charles E.	grad.	Carnegie Inst. of Tech.	1909
Wilson, Henry	no deg.	no college	
Wilson, James	no deg.	Grinnell Coll.	*ca.* 1855
Wilson, William B.	no deg.	no college	
Wilson, William L.	grad.	Columbian Coll. (now George Washington U.)	1860
	no deg.	U. of Virginia Law Sch.	*ca.* 1860
Wilson, Woodrow	no deg.	Davidson Coll.	1874
	grad.	Coll. of New Jersey (now Princeton)	1879
	grad.	U. of Virginia Law Sch.	1881
	Ph.D.	Johns Hopkins U.	1886
Windom, William	no deg.	read law	
Wirt, William	no deg.	read law	
Wirtz, William	A.B.	Beloit Coll.	1933
	LL.B.	Harvard U.	1937
Wolcott, Oliver	grad.	Yale Coll.	1778
Wood, Robert	A.B.	Princeton U.	1946
	M.A.	Harvard U.	1947
	M.B.A.	Harvard U.	1948
	Ph.D.	Harvard U.	1950
Woodbury, Levi	grad.	Dartmouth Coll.	1809

Woodin, William	no deg.	Columbia U. Sch. of Mines	*ca.* 1890
Woodring, Henry	no deg.	Lebanon U.	*ca.* 1910
Work, Hubert	no deg.	U. of Michigan Med. Sch.	1884
	M.D.	U. of Pennsylvania Med. Sch.	1885
Wright, Luke	no deg.	U. of Mississippi	1868
Wynne, Robert	no deg.	no college	
Yeutter, Clayton	B.S.	U. of Nebraska	1952
	J.D.	U. of Nebraska	1963
	Ph.D.	U. of Nebraska	1966

Place of Birth

ALABAMA

Name	Birthdate	City or County
Blount, Winton M.	Feb. 1, 1921	Union Springs
Herman, Alexis	July 16, 1947	Mobile
Hitchcock, Ethan A.	Sept. 19, 1835	Mobile
Matthews, Forrest	Dec. 6, 1935	Grove Hill

ALASKA

Name	Birthdate	City or County
Udall, Stewart L.	Jan. 31, 1920	Saint Johns

ARIZONA

Name	Birthdate	City or County
Finch, Robert H.	Oct. 9, 1925	Tempe
Kleindienst, Richard G.	Aug. 1923	Winslow

ARKANSAS

Name	Birthdate	City or County
Clinton, William J.	Aug. 19, 1946	Hope
Snyder, John W.	June 21, 1895	Jonesboro

CALIFORNIA

Name	Birthdate	City or County
Babbitt, Bruce	June 27, 1938	Los Angeles
Brinegar, Claude S.	Dec. 16, 1926	Rockport
Dunlop, John T.	July 5, 1914	Placerville
Gardner, John W.	Oct. 8, 1912	Los Angeles
Herrington, John	May 31, 1939	Los Angeles
Hills, Carla A.	Jan. 3, 1934	Los Angeles
Kemp, Jack	July 13, 1935	Los Angeles
Lyng, Richard E.	June 29, 1918	San Francisco
McNamara, Robert S.	June 9, 1916	San Francisco
Meese, Edwin, III	Dec. 2, 1931	Oakland
Mineta, Norman	Nov. 12, 1931	San Jose
Nixon, Richard M.	Jan. 9, 1913	Yorba Linda
Richardson, William B.	Nov. 15, 1947	Pasadena
Veneman, Ann	June 29, 1949	Modesto
Watkins, James D.	Mar. 7, 1927	Alhambra
Weinberger, Caspar W.	Aug. 18, 1917	San Francisco

COLORADO

Name	Birthdate	City or County
Brannan, Charles F.	Aug. 23, 1903	Denver
Hufstedler, Shirley M.	Aug. 24, 1925	Denver

CONNECTICUT

Name	Birthdate	City or County
Acheson, Dean G.	Apr. 11, 1893	Middletown
Bush, George W.	July 6, 1946	New Haven
Forward, Walter	Jan. 24, 1786	East Granby
Gary, James A.	Oct. 22, 1833	Uncasville
Granger, Francis	Dec. 1, 1792	Suffield
Granger, Gideon	Sept. 19, 1767	Suffield
Hubbard, Samuel D.	Aug. 10, 1799	Middletown
Huntington, Samuel	July 3, 1731	Windham
Meigs, Return J., Jr.	Nov. 17, 1764	Middletown
Niles, John M.	Aug. 20, 1787	Poquonnock
Pierrepont, Edwards	Mar. 4, 1817	New Haven

Porter, Peter B.	Aug. 14, 1773	Salisbury
Ribicoff, Abraham A.	Apr. 9, 1910	New Britain
Smith, Charles E.	Feb. 18, 1842	Mansfield
Summers, Lawrence	Nov. 30, 1954	New Haven
Toucey, Isaac	Nov. 5, 1796	Newtown
Welles, Gideon	July 1, 1802	Glastonbury
Wolcott, Oliver, Jr.	Jan. 11, 1760	Litchfield

DELAWARE

Name	Birthdate	City or County
Bayard, Thomas F.	Oct. 29, 1828	Wilmington
Clayton, John M.	July 24, 1796	Dagsborough
McKennan, Thomas M. T.	Mar. 31, 1794	Dragon Neck
McLane, Louis	May 28, 1786	Smyrna
Rodney, Caesar A.	Jan. 4, 1772	Dover

DISTRICT OF COLUMBIA

Name	Birthdate	City or County
Brown, Ronald H.	Aug. 1, 1941	Washington
Dulles, John F.	Feb. 25, 1888	Washington
Gore, Albert, Jr.	Mar. 31, 1948	Washington
Seaton, Frederick A.	Dec. 11, 1909	Washington
Weaver, Robert C.	Dec. 29, 1907	Washington

FLORIDA

Name	Birthdate	City or County
Boyd, Alan S.	July 20, 1922	Jacksonville
Edwards, James	June 24, 1927	Hawthorne
Reno, Janet	July 21, 1938	Miami

GEORGIA

Name	Birthdate	City or County
Adams, Brock	Jan. 13, 1927	Atlanta
Bell, Griffin B.	Oct. 13, 1918	Americus
Carter, Jimmy, Jr.	Oct. 1, 1924	Plains

Cobb, Howell	Sept. 7, 1815	Cherry Hill
Crawford, George W.	Dec. 22, 1798	Augusta
Folsom, Marion B.	Nov. 23, 1893	McRae
Habersham, Joseph	July 28, 1751	Savannah
Lamar, Lucius Q. C.	Sept. 17, 1825	Putnam Co.
Rusk, D. Dean	Feb. 9, 1909	Cherokee Co.
Sullivan, Louis W.	Nov. 3, 1933	Atlanta
Usery, Willie J., Jr.	Dec. 21, 1923	Hardwick

HAWAII

ILLINOIS

Name	Birthdate	City or County
Ashcroft, John	May 9, 1942	Chicago
Block, John R.	Feb. 15, 1935	Galesburg
Bryan, William J.	Mar. 19, 1860	Salem
Cummings, Homer S.	Apr. 30, 1870	Chicago
Daley, William M.	Aug. 9, 1948	Chicago
Day, James E.	Oct. 11, 1914	Jacksonville
Derwinski, Edward J.	Sept. 15, 1926	Chicago
Donaldson, Jesse M.	Aug. 17, 1885	Shelbyville
Durkin, Martin P.	Mar. 18, 1894	Chicago
Goldberg, Arthur J.	Aug. 8, 1908	Chicago
Harlan, James	Aug. 26, 1820	Clark Co.
Harris, Patricia R.	May 31, 1924	Mattoon
Levi, Edward H.	June 26, 1911	Chicago
Lincoln, Robert T.	Aug. 1, 1843	Springfield
Madigan, Edward	Jan. 13, 1936	Lincoln
Martin, Lynn	Dec. 26, 1939	Evanston
Rawlins, John A.	Feb. 13, 1831	Galena
Reagan, Ronald W.	Feb. 6, 1911	Tampico
Rumsfeld, Donald	July 9, 1932	Chicago
Skinner, Samuel K.	June 10, 1938	Chicago
Stettinius, Edward R., Jr.	Oct. 22, 1900	Chicago
Wallace, Henry C.	May 11, 1866	Rock Island
West, Roy O.	Oct. 27, 1868	Georgetown
Wirtz, William W.	Mar. 14, 1912	DeKalb

INDIANA

Name	Birthdate	City or County
Barr, Joseph W.	Jan. 17, 1918	Vincennes
Butz, Earl L.	July 3, 1909	Albion
Denby, Edwin	Feb. 18, 1870	Evansville
Foster, John W.	Mar. 2, 1836	Pike Co.
Gresham, Walter Q.	Mar. 7, 1832	Lanesville
Hardin, Clifford M.	Oct. 9, 1915	Knightstown
Hay, John M.	Oct. 8, 1838	Salem
Hays, William H.	Nov. 5, 1879	Sullivan
Marshall, Thomas R.	Mar. 14, 1854	North Manchester
McCrary, George W.	Aug. 29, 1835	Evansville
New, Harry S.	Dec. 31, 1858	Indianapolis
Quayle, Dan	Feb. 4, 1947	Indianapolis
Tyner, James N.	Jan. 17, 1826	Brockville
Wickard, Claude R.	Feb. 28, 1893	Carroll Co.

IOWA

Name	Birthdate	City or County
Ballinger, Richard A.	July 9, 1858	Boonesboro
Good, James W.	Sept. 24, 1866	Cedar Rapids
Hoover, Herbert C.	Aug. 10, 1874	West Branch
Hopkins, Harry L.	Aug. 17, 1890	Sioux City
Meredith, Edwin T.	Dec. 23, 1876	Avoca
Wallace, Henry A.	Oct. 17, 1888	Orient
Wilbur, Curtis D.	May 10, 1867	Boonesboro
Wilbur, Ray L.	Apr. 13, 1875	Boonesboro

KANSAS

Name	Birthdate	City or County
Clifford, Clark McA.	Dec. 25, 1906	Scott
Curtis, Charles	Jan. 25, 1860	North Topeka
Glickman, Dan	Nov. 24, 1944	Wichita
Hickel, Walter J.	Aug. 18, 1919	Ellinwood
Norton, Gale	Mar. 11, 1954	Wichita
Woodring, Henry H.	May 31, 1890	Elk City

KENTUCKY

Name	Birthdate	City or County
Barkley, Alben W.	Nov. 24, 1877	Lowes
Blair, Montgomery	May 10, 1813	Franklin Co.
Breckinridge, John C.	Jan. 21, 1821	"Cabell's Dale"
Bristow, Benjamin H.	June 20, 1832	Elkton
Browning, Orville H.	Feb. 10, 1806	Cynthiana
Carlisle, John G.	Sept. 5, 1835	Campbell (now Kenton) Co.
Corwin, Thomas	July 29, 1794	Bourbon Co.
Crittenden, John J.	Sept. 9, 1787	Versailles
Davis, Jefferson	June 3, 1808	Christian (now Todd) Co.
Fall, Albert B.	Nov. 26, 1861	Frankfort
Francis, David R.	Oct. 1, 1850	Richmond
Guthrie, James	Dec. 5, 1792	Bardstown
Holt, Joseph	Jan. 6, 1807	Breckenridge Co.
Johnson, Richard M.	Oct. 17, 1781	Beargrass Creek (now Louisville)
Kreps, Juanita M.	Jan. 11, 1921	Lynch
Lincoln, Abraham	Feb. 12, 1809	Hodgen's Mill
McReynolds, James C.	Feb. 3, 1862	Elkton
Morton, Rogers C. B.	Sept. 14, 1914	Louisville
Speed, James	Mar. 11, 1812	Farmington
Stevenson, Adlai E.	Oct. 23, 1835	Christian Co.
Vinson, Frederick M.	Jan. 22, 1890	Louisa
Wickliffe, Charles A.	June 8, 1788	Springfield

LOUISIANA

Name	Birthdate	City or County
Landrieu, Moon E.	July 23, 1930	New Orleans
Marshall, F. Ray	Aug. 22, 1928	Oak Grove

MAINE

Name	Birthdate	City or County
Cohen, William	Aug. 28, 1940	Bangor
Hamlin, Hannibal	Aug. 27, 1809	Paris Hill
Howe, Timothy O.	Feb. 24, 1816	Livermore
King, Horatio	June 21, 1811	Paris
Long, John D.	Oct. 27, 1838	Buckfield
McCulloch, Hugh	Dec. 7, 1808	Kennebunk

Morrill, Lot M.	May 3, 1812	Belgrade
Muskie, Edmund S.	Mar. 28, 1914	Rumford
Rockefeller, Nelson A.	July 8, 1908	Bar Harbor
Washburne, Elihu B.	Sept. 23, 1816	Livermore

MARYLAND

Name	Birthdate	City or County
Agnew, Spiro T.	Nov. 9, 1918	Baltimore
Bonaparte, Charles J.	June 9, 1851	Baltimore
Creswell, John A. J.	Nov. 18, 1828	Port Deposit
Hanson, John	Apr. 3, 1715	Mulberry Grove, Charles Co.
Johnson, Reverdy	May 21, 1796	Annapolis
Kennedy, John P.	Oct. 25, 1795	Baltimore
Kirkwood, Samuel J.	Dec. 20, 1813	Harford Co.
Nelson, John	June 1, 1794	Fredericktown
Pinkney, William	Mar. 17, 1764	Annapolis
Stoddert, Benjamin	1751	Charles Co.
Taney, Roger B.	Mar. 17, 1777	Calvert Co.
Thomas, Philip F.	Sept. 12, 1810	Easton
Wirt, William	Nov. 8, 1772	Bladensburg

MASSACHUSETTS

Name	Birthdate	City or County
Adams, Charles F.	Aug. 2, 1866	Quincy
Adams, John	Oct. 30, 1735	Quincy
Adams, John Q.	July 11, 1767	Quincy
Bacon, Robert	July 5, 1860	Jamaica Plain
Bancroft, George	Oct. 3, 1800	Worcester
Bliss, Cornelius N.	Jan. 26, 1833	Fall River
Boutwell, George S.	Jan. 28, 1818	Brookline
Bush, George H.W.	June 12, 1924	Milton
Card, Andrew H., Jr.	May 10, 1947	Brockton
Crowninshield, Benjamin W.	Dec. 27, 1772	Boston
Cushing, Caleb	Jan. 17, 1800	Salisbury
Devens, Charles	Apr. 4, 1820	Charlestown
Dexter, Samuel	May 14, 1761	Boston
Endicott, William C.	Nov. 19, 1826	Salem
Eustis, William	June 10, 1753	Cambridge

Evarts, William M.	Feb. 6, 1818	Boston
Everett, Edward	Apr. 11, 1794	Dorchester
Folger, Charles J.	Apr. 16, 1818	Nantucket
Gerry, Elbridge	July 17, 1744	Marblehead
Gorham, Nathaniel	May 21, 1738	Charlestown
Hancock, John	Jan. 12, 1737	Quincy
Henshaw, David	Apr. 2, 1791	Leicester
Hoar, Ebenezer R.	Feb. 21, 1816	Concord
Kendall, Amos	Aug. 16, 1789	Dunstable
Kennedy, John F.	May 29, 1917	Brookline
Kennedy, Robert F.	Nov. 20, 1925	Brookline
Knox, Henry	July 25, 1750	Boston
Knox, W. Franklin	Jan. 1, 1874	Boston
Lincoln, Levi	May 15, 1749	Hingham
Marcy, William L.	Dec. 12, 1786	Southbridge
Maynard, Horace	Aug. 30, 1840	Westboro
Meyer, George von L.	June 24, 1858	Boston
Moody, William H.	Dec. 23, 1853	Newbury
O'Brien, Lawrence F.	July 7, 1917	Springfield
Olney, Richard	Sept. 15, 1835	Oxford
Osgood, Samuel	Feb. 3, 1748	Andover
Payne, Henry C.	Nov. 23, 1843	Ashfield
Perkins, Frances	Apr. 10, 1882	Boston
Pickering, Timothy	July 17, 1745	Salem
Regan, Donald T.	Dec. 21, 1918	Cambridge
Richardson, Elliot L.	July 20, 1920	Boston
Richardson, William A.	Nov 2., 1821	Tyngsborough
Smith, Caleb	Apr. 16, 1808	Boston
Tobin, Maurice J.	May 22, 1901	Boston
Volpe, John A.	Dec. 8, 1908	Wakefield
Weeks, Sinclair	June 15, 1893	West Newton
Whiting, William F.	July 20, 1864	Holyoke
Whitney, William C.	July 5, 1841	Conway

MICHIGAN

Name	Birthdate	City or County
Abraham, Spencer	June 12, 1952	Lansing
Brown, Jesse	Mar. 27, 1944	Detroit

Chapin, Roy D.	Feb. 23, 1880	Lansing
Humphrey, George M.	Mar. 8, 1890	Cheboygan
Lamont, Robert P.	Dec. 1, 1867	Detroit
Mitchell, John N.	Sept. 15, 1913	Detroit
Morton, Paul	May 22, 1857	Detroit
Mueller, Frederick H.	Nov. 22, 1893	Grand Rapids
Murphy, Frank	Apr. 13, 1890	Harbor Beach
Newberry, Truman H.	Nov. 5, 1864	Detroit
Summerfield, Arthur E.	Mar. 17, 1899	Pinconning

MINNESOTA

Name	Birthdate	City or County
Bergland, Robert S.	July 22, 1928	Roseau
Freeman, Orville L.	May 9, 1918	Minneapolis
Hodgson, James D.	Dec. 3, 1915	Dawson
Mitchell, William D.	Sept. 9, 1874	Winona
Mondale, Walter F.	Jan. 5, 1928	Ceylon
Stans, Maurice H.	Mar. 22, 1908	Shakopee

MISSISSIPPI

Name	Birthdate	City or County
Dickinson, Jacob McG.	Jan. 30, 1851	Columbus
Espy, Michael	Nov. 30, 1953	Yazoo City
Gregory, Thomas W.	Nov. 6, 1861	Crawfordsville
Paige, Rod	June 17, 1953	Monticello
Slater, Rodney	Feb. 23, 1955	Tutwyler

MISSOURI

Name	Birthdate	City or County
Colby, Bainbridge	Dec. 22, 1869	St. Louis
Davis, Dwight F.	July 5, 1879	St. Louis
Hannegan, Robert E.	June 30, 1903	St. Louis
Hyde, Arthur M.	July 12, 1877	Princeton
Klutznick, Philip M.	July 9, 1907	Kansas City
O'Neill, Paul	Dec. 4, 1935	St. Louis
Truman, Harry S	May 8, 1884	Lamar
Wood, Robert C.	Sept. 16, 1923	St. Louis

MONTANA

NEBRASKA

Name	Birthdate	City or County
Baldrige, Malcolm	Oct. 4, 1922	Omaha
Brownell, Herbert, Jr.	Feb. 20, 1904	Peru
Cheney, Richard B.	Jan. 30, 1941	Lincoln
Dern, George H.	Sept. 8, 1872	Hooper
Ford, Gerald R., Jr.	July 14, 1913	Omaha
Hathaway, Stanley K.	July 19, 1924	Osceola
Laird, Melvin R.	Sept. 1, 1922	Omaha
Peterson, Peter G.	June 5, 1926	Kearny
Yeutter, Clayton K.	Dec. 10, 1930	Eustis

NEVADA

NEW HAMPSHIRE

Name	Birthdate	City or County
Akerman, Amos T.	Feb. 23, 1821	Portsmouth
Cass, Lewis	Oct. 9, 1782	Exeter
Chandler, William E.	Dec. 28, 1835	Concord
Chandler, Zachariah	Dec. 10, 1813	Bedford
Chase, Salmon P.	Jan. 13, 1808	Cornish
Clifford, Nathan	Aug. 18, 1803	Rumney
Dearborn, Henry	Feb. 23, 1751	North Hampton
Dix, John A.	July 24, 1798	Boscawen
Fessenden, William P.	Oct. 16, 1806	Boscawen
Jewell, Marshall	Oct. 20, 1825	Winchester
Pierce, Franklin	Nov. 23, 1804	Hillsboro
Smith, William French	Aug. 26, 1917	Wilton
Stone, Harlan F.	Oct. 11, 1872	Chesterfield
Webster, Daniel	Jan. 18, 1782	Franklin
Weeks, John W.	Apr. 11, 1860	Lancaster
Wilson, Henry	Feb. 16, 1812	Farmington
Woodbury, Levi	Dec. 22, 1789	Francestown

NEW JERSEY

Name	Birthdate	City or County
Berrien, John M.	Aug. 23, 1781	Rocky Hill
Brewster, Benjamin H.	Oct. 13, 1816	Salem Co.
Burr, Aaron	Feb. 6, 1756	Newark
Cleveland, Grover	Mar. 18, 1837	Caldwell
Dent, Frederick B.	Aug. 17, 1922	Cape May
Dickerson, Mahlon	Apr. 17, 1770	Hanover Neck
Donovan, Raymond J.	Aug. 31, 1930	Bayonne
Edison, Charles	Aug. 3, 1890	Llewellyn Park
Frelinghuysen, Frederick T.	Aug. 4, 1817	Millstone
Garrison, Lindley M.	Nov. 28, 1864	Camden
Griggs, John W.	July 10, 1849	Newton
Hobart, Garret A.	June 3, 1844	Long Branch
Livingston, Edward	May 26, 1764	Clermont
McLaughlin, Ann D.	Nov. 16, 1941	Newark
McLean, John	Mar. 11, 1785	Morris Co.
Miller, William H. H.	Sept. 6, 1840	Augusta
Mitchell, James P.	Nov. 12, 1900	Elizabeth
Paulding, James K.	Aug. 22, 1778	Great Nine Partners
Randall, Alexander W.	Oct. 31, 1819	Ames
Robeson, George	Mar. 16, 1829	Oxford Furnace
Simon, William E.	Nov. 27, 1927	Paterson
Southard, Samuel L.	June 9, 1787	Basking Ridge
Trowbridge, Alexander B.	Dec. 12, 1929	Englewood

NEW MEXICO

Name	Birthdate	City or County
Lujan, Manuel, Jr.	May 12, 1928	San Ildefonso

NEW YORK

Name	Birthdate	City or County
Barr, William P.	May 23, 1950	New York City
Belknap, William W.	Sept. 22, 1829	Newburgh
Bennett, William J.	July 3, 1943	Brooklyn
Bissell, Wilson S.	Dec. 31, 1847	New London

Brady, Nicholas F.	Apr. 11, 1930	New York City
Brennan, Peter J.	May 24, 1918	New York City
Brown, Harold	Sept. 19, 1927	New York City
Butler, Benjamin F.	Dec. 17, 1795	Stuyvesant
Califano, Joseph	May 15, 1931	Brooklyn
Civiletti, Benjamin R.	July 17, 1935	Peekskill
Clinton, George	July 26, 1739	Little Britain
Colfax, Schuyler	Mar. 23, 1823	New York City
Collamer, Jacob	Jan. 8, 1791	Troy
Colman, Norman J.	May 16, 1827	Richfield Springs
Connor, John T.	Nov. 3, 1914	Syracuse
Cortelyou, George B.	July 26, 1862	New York City
Cuomo, Andrew	Dec. 6, 1957	Queens
Dickinson, Donald	Jan. 17, 1846	Port Ontario
Fairchild, Charles S.	Apr. 30, 1842	Cazenovia
Farley, James A.	May 30, 1888	Grassy Point
Fillmore, Millard	Jan. 7, 1800	Summerhill
Fish, Hamilton	Dec. 15, 1836	New York City
Flemming, Arthur S.	June 12, 1905	Kingston
Forrestal, James V.	Feb. 15, 1892	Matteawan
Gage, Lyman J.	June 28, 1836	De Ruyter
Hall, Nathan K.	Mar. 28, 1810	Skaneateles
Harriman, W. Averell	Nov. 15, 1891	New York City
Heckler, Margaret M.	June 21, 1931	Flushing
Hughes, Charles E.	Apr. 11, 1862	Glens Falls
James, Thomas L.	Mar. 29, 1831	Utica
Jay, John	Dec. 12, 1745	New York City
Kellogg, Frank B.	Dec. 22, 1856	Potsdam
Lamont, Daniel S.	Feb. 9, 1851	McGrawville
Lansing, Robert	Oct. 17, 1864	Watertown
Manning, Daniel	Aug. 16, 1831	Albany
Metcalf, Victor H.	Oct. 10, 1853	Utica
Morgenthau, Henry	May 11, 1891	New York City
Morton, Julius S.	Apr. 22, 1832	Adams
Mosbacher, Robert A.	Mar. 11, 1927	Mt. Vernon
Patterson, Robert P.	Feb. 12, 1891	Glens Falls
Pierce, Samuel	Sept. 8, 1922	Glen Cove
Powell, Colin	Apr. 5, 1937	New York City
Principi, Anthony	Apr. 16, 1944	New York City

Redfield, William C.	June 18, 1858	Albany
Rogers, William P.	June 23, 1913	Norfolk
Roosevelt, Franklin D.	Jan. 30, 1882	Hyde Park
Roosevelt, Theodore	Oct. 27, 1858	New York City
Root, Elihu	Feb. 15, 1845	Clinton
Rubin, Robert	Aug. 29, 1938	New York City
Schlesinger, James R.	Feb. 15, 1929	New York City
Schofield, John McA.	Sept. 29, 1831	Gerry
Seward, William H.	May 6, 1801	Florida
Sherman, James S.	Oct. 24, 1855	Utica
Shultz, George P.	Dec. 13, 1920	New York City
Spencer, John C.	Jan. 8, 1788	Hudson
Stanbery, Henry	Feb. 20, 1803	New York City
Stimson, Henry L.	Sept. 21, 1867	New York
Teller, Henry M.	May 23, 1830	Granger
Thompson, Smith	Jan. 17, 1768	Dutchess Co.
Tompkins, Daniel D.	June 21, 1774	Scarsdale
Tracy, Benjamin F.	Apr. 26, 1830	Oswego
Usher, John P.	Jan. 9, 1816	Brookfield
Van Buren, Martin	Dec. 5, 1782	Kinderhook
Wheeler, William A.	June 30, 1819	Malone
Williams, George H.	Mar. 23, 1823	New Lebanon
Wynne, Robert J.	Nov. 18, 1851	New York City

NORTH CAROLINA

Name	Birthdate	City or County
Badger, George E.	Apr. 17, 1795	New Bern
Branch, John	Nov. 4, 1782	Halifax
Burnley, James H., IV	July 30, 1948	High Point
Daniels, Josephus	May 18, 1862	Washington
Dobbin, James C.	Jan. 17, 1814	Fayetteville
Dole, Elizabeth H.	July 29, 1936	Salisbury
Eaton, John H.	June 18, 1790	Scotland Neck
Graham, William A.	Sept. 5, 1804	Vesuvius Furnace
Houston, David F.	Feb. 17, 1866	Monroe
Johnson, Andrew	Dec. 29, 1808	Raleigh
King, William R. deV.	Apr. 17, 1786	Sampson Co.
Polk, James K.	Nov. 4, 1795	Little Sugar Creek

Royall, Kenneth C.	July 24, 1894	Goldsboro
Smith, Hoke	Sept. 2, 1855	Newton
Thompson, Jacob	May 15, 1810	Leasburg
West, Togo	June 21, 1942	Winston-Salem

NORTH DAKOTA

Name	Birthdate	City or County
Christopher, Warren	Oct. 27, 1925	Scranton
Kleppe, Thomas S.	July 1, 1919	Kintyre

OHIO

Name	Birthdate	City or County
Alexander, Joshua W.	Jan. 22, 1852	Cincinnati
Alger, Russell	Feb. 27, 1836	Lafayette
Brown, Walter F.	May 31, 1869	Massillon
Daugherty, Henry M.	Jan. 26, 1860	Washington
Dawes, Charles G.	Aug. 27, 1865	Marietta
Day, William R.	Apr. 17, 1849	Ravenna
Dennison, William	Nov. 23, 1815	Cincinnati
Elkins, Stephen B.	Sept. 26, 1841	New Lexington
Fairbanks, Charles W.	May 11, 1852	Unionville Center
Foster, Charles	Apr. 12, 1828	Fostoria
Garfield, James A.	Nov. 19, 1831	Orange
Garfield, James R.	Oct. 17, 1865	Hiram
Grant, Ulysses S.	Apr. 27, 1822	Point Pleasant
Harding, Warren G.	Nov. 2, 1865	Blooming Grove
Harmon, Judson	Feb. 3, 1846	Newton
Harrison, Benjamin	Aug. 20, 1833	North Bend
Hatton, Frank	Apr. 28, 1846	Cambridge
Hayes, Rutherford B.	Oct. 4, 1822	Delaware
Hendricks, Thomas A.	Sept. 7, 1819	Zanesville
Hitchcock, Frank H.	Oct. 5, 1867	Amherst
Lynn, James T.	Feb. 27, 1927	Cleveland
McAdoo, William	Oct. 31, 1863	Marietta
McElroy, Neil H.	Oct. 30, 1904	Berea
McKinley, William	Jan. 29, 1843	Niles
Noble, John W.	Oct. 26, 1831	Lancaster

Rusk, Jeremiah	June 17, 1830	Malts
Sawyer, Charles	Feb. 10, 1887	Cincinnati
Saxbe, William	June 24, 1916	Mechanicsburg
Shalala, Donna	Feb. 14, 1941	Cleveland
Sherman, John	May 10, 1823	Lancaster
Sherman, William T.	Feb. 8, 1820	Lancaster
Stanton, Edwin McM.	Dec. 19, 1814	Steubenville
Taft, William H.	Sept. 15, 1857	Cincinnati
Verity, C. William	Jan. 26, 1917	Middletown
Wilson, Charles E.	July 18, 1890	Minerva
Windom, William	May 10, 1827	Belmont Co.

OKLAHOMA

Name	Birthdate	City or County
Hurley, Patrick J.	Jan. 8, 1883	Choctaw Indian Terr. (now Lehigh)
Knebel, John A.	Oct. 4, 1936	Tulsa
Miller, G. William	Mar. 9, 1925	Sapulpa

OREGON

Name	Birthdate	City or County
Andrus, Cecil D.	Aug. 25, 1931	Hood River
Goldschmidt, Neil E.	June 16, 1940	Eugene
Hodel, Donald P.	May 23, 1935	Portland
McKay, Douglas J.	June 24, 1893	Portland

PENNSYLVANIA

Name	Birthdate	City or County
Armstrong, John	Nov. 25, 1758	Carlisle
Black, Jeremiah	Jan. 1, 1810	Glades
Blaine, James G.	Jan. 31, 1830	West Brownsville
Boric, Adolph	Nov. 25, 1809	Philadelphia
Boudinot, Elias	May 2, 1740	Philadelphia
Bradford, William	Sept. 14, 1755	Philadelphia
Buchanan, James	Apr. 23, 1791	Cove Gap
Cameron, James	Mar. 14, 1833	Middletown
Cameron, Simon	Mar. 8, 1799	Maytown

Campbell, James	Sept. 1, 1812	Southwark
Carlucci, Frank	Oct. 18, 1930	Scranton
Coleman, William	July 7, 1920	Philadelphia
Dallas, George M.	July 10, 1792	Philadelphia
Franklin, Barbara H.	Mar. 19, 1940	Lancaster
Gates, Thomas	Apr. 10, 1906	Philadelphia
Haig, Alexander	Dec. 2, 1924	Bala-Cynwyd
Ickes, Harold L.	Mar. 15, 1874	Frankstown Twnshp.
Ingham, Samuel D.	Sept. 16, 1779	Great Spring
Jackson, Robert H.	Feb. 13, 1892	Spring Creek
Jones, William	ca. 1760	Philadelphia
Katzenbach, Nicholas	Jan. 17, 1922	Philadelphia
Knox, Philander C.	May 6, 1853	Brownsville
Lewis, Andrew	Nov. 3, 1931	Philadelphia
MacVeagh, Franklin	Nov. 22, 1837	Phoenixville
MacVeagh, Wayne	Apr. 19, 1833	Phoenixville
Marshall, George C.	Dec. 31, 1880	Uniontown
McClelland, Robert	Aug. 1, 1807	Greencastle
McGranery, James	July 8, 1895	Philadelphia
McKean, Thomas	Mar. 19, 1734	New London Twnshp.
McKenna, Joseph	Aug. 10, 1843	Philadelphia
Mellon, Andrew W.	Mar. 24, 1855	Pittsburgh
Meredith, William M.	June 8, 1799	Philadelphia
Mifflin, Thomas	Jan. 10, 1744	Philadelphia
Palmer, Alexander M.	May 4, 1872	Moosehead
Perry, William	Oct. 11, 1927	Vandergrift
Porter, James M.	Jan. 6, 1793	Selma
Ramsey, Alexander	Sept. 8, 1915	Harrisburg
Reich, Robery	June 24, 1946	Scranton
Rush, Richard	Aug. 29, 1780	Philadelphia
Schweiker, Richard	June 1, 1926	Norristown
Smith, Robert	Nov. 3, 1757	Lancaster
Thornburgh, Richard	July 16, 1932	Rosslyn Farms
Walker, Frank C.	May 30, 1886	Plymouth
Walker, Robert J.	July 19, 1801	Northumberland
Wanamaker, John	July 11, 1838	Philadelphia
Wickersham, George	Sept. 19, 1858	Pittsburgh
Wilkins, William	Dec. 20, 1779	Carlisle
Woodin, William H.	May 27, 1868	Berwick
Work, Hubert	July 3, 1860	Marion Center

RHODE ISLAND

Name	Birthdate	City or County
McGrath, Jame H.	Nov. 28, 1903	Woonsocket
Mills, Ogden L.	Aug. 23, 1884	Newport

SOUTH CAROLINA

Name	Birthdate	City or County
Byrnes, James F.	May 2, 1879	Charleston
Calhoun, John C.	Mar. 18, 1782	Abbeville
Hamilton, Paul	Oct. 16, 1762	St. Paul's Parish
Herbert, Hilary A.	Mar. 12, 1834	Lawrenceville
Hunt, William H.	June 12, 1823	Charleston
Jackson, Andrew	Mar. 15, 1767	Waxhaw
Laurens, Henry	Mar. 6, 1724	Charleston
Legaré, Hugh S.	Jan. 2, 1797	Charleston
Middleton, Henry	1717	Charleston
Poinsett, Joel R.	Mar. 2, 1779	Charleston
Riley, Richard	Jan. 2, 1933	Greenville Co.
Roper, Daniel C.	Apr. 1, 1867	Marlboro Co.

SOUTH DAKOTA

Name	Birthdate	City or County
Anderson, Clinton	Oct. 28, 1895	Centerville
Humphrey, Hubert	May 27, 1911	Wallace

TENNESSEE

Name	Birthdate	City or County
Alexander, Lamar	July 3, 1940	Maryville
Bell, John	Feb. 15, 1797	Nashville
Brock, William	Nov. 23, 1930	Chattanooga
Garland, Augustus	June 11, 1832	Covington
Hull, Cordell	Oct. 2, 1871	Olympus
Johnson, Cave	Jan. 11, 1793	Springfield
Jones, Jesse H.	Apr. 5, 1874	Robertson Co.
Kantor, Mickey	Aug. 7, 1939	Nashville
Key, David McK.	Jan. 27, 1824	Greenville
Wright, Luke E.	Aug. 29, 1846	Memphis

TEXAS

Name	Birthdate	City or County
Anderson, Robert	June 4, 1910	Burleson
Baker, James	Apr. 28, 1930	Houston
Bentsen, Lloyd	Feb. 11, 1921	Mission
Burleson, Albert	June 7, 1863	San Marcos
Cavazos, Lauro	Jan. 4, 1927	King Ranch
Cisneros, Henry	June 11, 1947	San Antonio
Clark, Tom C.	Sept. 23, 1899	Dallas
Clark, W. Ramsey	Dec. 18, 1927	Dallas
Connally, John B.	Feb. 27, 1917	Floresville
Duncan, Charles	Sept. 9, 1926	Houston
Eisenhower, Dwight	Oct. 14, 1890	Denison
Evans, Don	July 27, 1946	Houston
Garner, John N.	Nov. 22, 1868	Detroit
Hobby, Oveta C.	Jan. 19, 1905	Killeen
Johnson, Lyndon B.	Aug. 27, 1908	Stonewall
Lovett, Robert A.	Sept. 14, 1895	Huntsville
Nagel, Charles	Aug. 9, 1849	Colorado Co.
Peña, Federico	Mar. 15, 1947	Laredo
Smith, Cyrus R.	Sept. 9, 1899	Minerva
Watson, W. Marvin	June 6, 1924	Oakhurst

UTAH

Name	Birthdate	City or County
Kennedy, David M.	July 21, 1905	Randolph

VERMONT

Name	Birthdate	City or County
Delano, Columbus	June 5, 1809	Shoreham
Morton, Levi P.	May 16, 1824	Shoreham
Proctor, Redfield	July 1, 1831	Proctorsville
Sargent, John G.	Oct. 13, 1860	Ludlow
Shaw, Leslie M.	Nov. 2, 1848	Morristown
Taft, Alphonso	Nov. 5, 1810	Townshend
Vilas, William F.	July 9, 1840	Chelsea

VIRGINIA

Name	Birthdate	City or County
Barbour, James	June 10, 1775	Frascati
Barry, William T.	Feb. 5, 1785	Lunenburg
Bates, Edward	Sept. 4, 1793	Belmont
Bibb, George M.	Oct. 30, 1776	Prince Edward Co.
Breckinridge, John	Dec. 2, 1760	Staunton
Brown, Aaron V.	Aug. 15, 1795	Brunswick Co.
Chapman, Oscar L.	Oct. 22, 1896	Omega
Clay, Henry	Apr. 12, 1877	"The Slashes"
Conrad, Charles M.	Dec. 24, 1804	Winchester
Crawford, William H.	Feb. 24, 1772	Nelson Co.
Doak, William N.	Dec. 12, 1882	Rural Retreat
Ewing, Thomas	Dec. 28, 1789	West Liberty
Floyd, John B.	June 1, 1806	Smithfield
Forsyth, John	Oct. 22, 1780	Fredericksburg
Fowler, Henry H.	Sept. 5, 1908	Roanoke
Gilmer, Thomas W.	Apr. 6, 1802	Gilmerton
Glass, Carter	Jan. 4, 1858	Lynchburg
Goff, Nathan	Feb. 9, 1843	Clarksburg (now W.Va.)
Griffin, Cyrus	July 16, 1748	Richmond Co.
Grundy, Felix	Sept. 11, 1777	Berkeley Co.
Harrison, William H.	Feb. 9, 1773	Berkeley
Hodges, Luther H.	Mar. 9, 1898	Pittsylvania Co.
Jefferson, Thomas	Apr. 2, 1743	Shadwell
Johnson, Louis A.	Jan. 10, 1891	Roanoke
Lee, Charles	July 1758	Fauquier Co.
Lee, Richard H.	Jan. 20, 1732	Westmoreland Co.
Madison, James	Mar. 16, 1751	Port Conway
Marshall, James W.	Aug. 14, 1822	Clarke Co.
Marshall, John	Sept. 24, 1755	Germantown
Mason, John Y.	Apr. 18, 1799	Emporia
Monroe, James	Apr. 28, 1758	Westmoreland Co.
O'Leary, Hazel	May 17, 1937	Newport News
Payne, John B.	Jan. 26, 1855	Pruntytown (now W.Va.)
Preston, William B.	Nov. 29, 1805	Smithfield
Randolph, Edmund J.	Aug. 10, 1753	Williamsburg
Randolph, Peyton	Sept. 1721	Williamsburg

Stuart, Alexander H. H.	Apr. 2, 1807	Staunton
Swanson, Claude	Mar. 31, 1862	Swansonville
Taylor, Zachary	Nov. 24, 1784	Montebello
Thompson, Richard W.	June 9, 1809	Culpeper Co.
Tyler, John	Mar. 29, 1790	Greenway
Upshur, Abel P.	June 17, 1790	Northampton Co.
Washington, George	Feb. 22, 1732	Wakefield
Wilson, William L.	May 3, 1843	Middleway
Wilson, Woodrow	Dec. 28, 1856	Staunton

WASHINGTON

WEST VIRGINIA

Name	Birthdate	City or County
Baker, Newton D.	Dec. 3, 1871	Martinsburg
Fisher, Walter L.	July 4, 1862	Wheeling
Gore, Howard M.	Oct. 12, 1877	Harrison Co.
Strauss, Lewis L.	Jan. 31, 1896	Charleston
Vance, Cyrus R.	Mar. 27, 1917	Clarksburg

WISCONSIN

Name	Birthdate	City or County
Aspin, Les	July 21, 1938	Milwaukee
Cohen, Wilbur J.	June 10, 1913	Milwaukee
Eagleburger, Lawrence	Aug. 1, 1930	Milwaukee
Gronouski, John A.	Oct. 26, 1919	Dunbar
Krug, Julius A.	Nov. 23, 1907	Madison
Schwellenbach, Lewis	Sept. 20, 1894	Superior
Thompson, Tommy	Nov. 19, 1941	Elroy

WYOMING

Name	Birthdate	City or County
Watt, James G.	Jan. 31, 1938	Lusk

OTHER COUNTRIES

Name	Birthdate	City or Country
Albright, Madeleine K.	May 15, 1937	Prague, Czechoslovakia (now Czech Republic)
Biddle, Francis B.	May 9, 1886	Paris, France
Blumenthal, W. Michael	Jan. 3, 1926	Berlin, Germany
Campbell, George W.	Feb. 8, 1768	Tongue, Scotland
Celebrezze, Anthony J.	Sept. 4, 1910	Anzi, Italy
Chao, Elaine	Mar. 26, 1953	Taipei, Taiwan
Cox, Jacob D., Jr.	Oct. 27, 1828	Montreal, Canada
Dallas, Alexander	June 21, 1759	Jamaica, West Indies
Davis, James J.	Oct. 27, 1873	Thedegar, South Wales
Dillon, C. Douglas	Apr. 21, 1909	Geneva, Switzerland
Duane, William J.	May 9, 1780	Clonmel, Ireland
Gallatin, Albert	Jan. 29, 1761	Geneva, Switzerland
Gilpin, Henry D.	Apr. 14, 1801	Lancaster, England
Hamilton, Alexander	Jan. 11, 1757	Nevis, West Indies
Herter, Christian	Mar. 28, 1895	Paris, France
Kissinger, Henry A.	May 27, 1923	Furth, Germany
Lane, Franklin K.	July 15, 1864	Charlottetown, Canada
Martinez, Mel	Oct. 23, 1946	Sagua La Grande, Cuba
McHenry, James	Nov. 16, 1753	Ballymena, Ireland
Romney, George W.	July 8, 1907	Chihuahua, Mexico
St. Clair, Arthur	Mar. 23, 1734	Thurso, Caithness, Scotland
Schurz, Carl	Mar. 2, 1829	Liblar-am-Rhein, Germany
Straus, Oscar S.	Dec. 23, 1850	Otterberg, Germany
Wilson, James	Aug. 16, 1835	Ayshire, Scotland
Wilson, William B.	Apr. 2, 1862	Blantyre, Scotland

Marital Information

SINGLE

Name

Berrien, John M.

Brinegar, Claude S.

Buchanan, James

Crawford, George W.

Devens, Charles

Dickerson, Mahlon

Grundy, Felix

Henshaw, David

Hitchcock, Frank H.

Hubbard, Samuel D.

Johnson, Richard M.

Jones, William

King, William R. de V.

Legaré, Hugh S.

Marshall, Freddie R.

Marshall, James W.

McReynolds, James C.

Moody, William H.

Murphy, Frank

Nelson, John

Tyner, James N.

MARRIED

Name	Date	Spouse
Acheson, Dean G.	1917	Alice Stanley
Adams, Brockman	1952	Mary Elizabeth Scott
Adams, Charles F.	n.a.	Frances Lovering
Adams, John	1764	Abigail Smith
Adams, John Q.	1797	Louisa Catherine Johnson
Agnew, Spiro T.	1942	Elinor Isobel Judefind
Akerman, Amos T.	*ca.* 1850	Martha Rebecca Galloway

Alexander, Joshua W.	1876	Roe Ann Richardson
Alger, Russell A.	1861	Annette Henry
Anderson, Clinton P.	1921	Henrietta McCartney
Anderson, Robert B.	1935	Ollie Mae Rawlings
Andrus, Cecil D.	1949	Carol Mae May
Armstrong, John	1789	Alida Livingston
Arthur, Chester A.	1859	Ellen Lewis Herndon
Bacon, Robert	1883	Martha Waldron Cowdin
Badger, George E.	n.a.	Rebecca Turner
Badger, George E.	n.a.	Mary Polk
Badger, George E.	n.a.	Dilia (Haywood) Williams
Baker, James A., III	1953	Mary McHenry
Baker, James A., III	1973	Susan Winson
Baker, Newton D.	1902	Elizabeth Leopold
Baldridge, Malcolm	1951	Margaret Murray
Ballinger, Richard A.	1886	Julia A. Bradley
Bancroft, George	1827	Sarah H. Dwight
Bancroft, George	1838	Mrs. Elizabeth (Davis) Bliss
Barbour, James	1792	Lucy Johnson
Barkley, Alben W.	1903	Dorothy Boower
Barkley, Alben W.	1949	Mrs. Carlton S. Hadley
Barr, Joseph W.	1939	Beth Ann Williston
Barry, William T.	1824	Lucy Overton
Barry, William T.	n.a.	Catherine Mason
Bates, Edward	1823	Julia Davenport Coalter
Bayard, Thomas F.	1856	Louise Lee
Bayard, Thomas F.	1889	Mary W. Clymer
Belknap, William W.	n.a.	Cora LeRoy
Belknap, William W.	n.a.	Carrie Tomlinson
Belknap, William W.	n.a.	Mrs. John Bower
Bell, Griffin B.	1943	Mary Foy Powell
Bell, John	n.a.	Sally Dickinson
Bell, John	n.a.	Mrs. Jane (Ervin) Eatman
Bell, Terrel H.	1957	Alta Martin
Bennett, William J.	1982	Mary Elayne Glover
Benson, Ezra T.	1926	Flora Smith Amussen
Bergland, Bob S.	1950	Helen Elaine Gromm
Bibb, George M.	married twice; dates unavailable	names unavailable

Biddle, Francis V.	1918	Katherine Garrison Chapin
Bissell, Wilson S.	1889	Louisa Fowler
Black, Jeremiah	1836	Mary Forward
Blaine, James G.	1850	Harriet Stonwood
Blair, Montgomery	1838	Caroline Buckner
Blair, Montgomery	1847	Mary Elizabeth Woodbury
Bliss, Cornelius N.	1859	Elizabeth Mary Plummer
Block, John R.	1960	Susan Rathjo
Blount, Winton M.	1942	Mary Katherine Archibald
Blumenthal, W. Michael	1951	Margaret Eileen Polley
Bonaparte, Charles J.	1875	Ellen Channing Day
Boric, Adolph	1839	Elizabeth Dundas McKean
Boudinot, Elias	1762	Hannah Stockton
Boutwell, George S.	1841	Sarah Adelia Thayer
Boyd, Alan S.	1943	Flavil Juanita Townsend
Bradford, William	n.a.	Susan Vergereau Boudinot
Brady, Nicholas F.	1952	Katherine Douglas
Branch, John	n.a.	Elizabeth Foort
Branch, John	n.a.	Mrs. Eliza (Jordan) Bond
Brannan, Charles F.	1932	Eda V. Seltzer
Breckinridge, John	1785	Mary Hopkins Cabell
Breckinridge, John C.	1843	Mary Cyrene Burch
Brennan, Peter J.	n.a.	Josephine Brickley
Brewster, Benjamin H.	1857	Elizabeth von Meyerbach de Reinfeldts
Bristow, Benjamin H.	1854	Abbie S. Briscoe
Brock, William E., III	1957	Laura Handley
Brock, William E., III	1986	Saundra Mitchell
Brown, Aaron V.	n.a.	Sarah Burruss
Brown, Aaron V.	1845	Mrs. Cynthia (Pillow) Saunders
Brown, Harold	1953	Colene Dunning McDowell
Brown, Walter F.	1903	Katharin Hafer
Brownell, Herbert, Jr.	1934	Doris A. McCarter
Browning, Orville H.	1836	Eliza Caldwell
Bryan, William J.	1884	Mary Baird
Burleson, Albert S.	1889	Adele Steiner
Burnley, James H., IV	1969	Jane Nady
Burr, Aaron	1782	Mrs. Theodosia (Bartow) Prevost
Burr, Aaron	1833	Mrs. Eliza Jumel
Bush, George H.	1945	Barbara Pierce

Butler, Benjamin F.	1818	Harriet Allen
Butz, Earl L.	1937	Mary Emma Powell
Byrnes, James F.	1906	Maud (Burch) Perkins
Calhoun, John C.	1811	Floride Bouneau Calhoun
Califano, Joseph A., Jr.	1955	Gertrude Zawacki
Cameron, James D.	n.a.	Mary McCormick
Cameron, James D.	1878	Elizabeth Sherman
Cameron, Simon	n.a.	Margaret Brua
Campbell, George W.	1812	Harriet Stoddert
Campbell, James	1845	Emilie S. Chapron
Carlisle, John G.	1857	Mary Jane Goodson
Carlucci, Frank C., III	1976	Marcia Myers
Carter, James E., Jr.	1946	Rosalynn Smith
Cass, Lewis	1806	Elizabeth Spencer
Cavazos, Lauro F.	1954	Peggy Ann Murdock
Celebrezze, Anthony J.	1938	Anne Marco
Chandler, William E.	1859	Ann Caroline Gilmore
Chandler, Zachariah	1844	Letitia Grace Douglass
Chapin, Roy D.	1914	Inez Tiedeman
Chapman, Oscar L.	1920	Olga Pauline Edholm
Chapman, Oscar L.	1940	Ann Kendrick
Chase, Salmon P.	1834	Katherine Jane Garmiss
Chase, Salmon P.	1839	Eliza Ann Smith
Chase, Salmon P.	1846	Sarah Bella Dunlap Ludlow
Cheney, Richard B.	1964	Lynn Ann Vincent
Civiletti, Benjamin R.	1957	Gail Lundgren
Clark, Tom C.	1924	Mary Jane Ramsey
Clark, William R.	1949	Georgia Welch
Clay, Henry	1799	Lucretia Hart
Clayton, John M.	1822	Sarah Ann Fisher
Cleveland, Grover	1886	Frances Folsom
Clifford, Clark McA.	1931	Margery Pepperell Kimball
Clifford, Nathan	ca. 1827	Hannah Ayer
Clinton, George	1770	Cornelia Tappen
Cobb, Howell	1834	Mary Ann Lamar
Cohen, Wilbur J.	1938	Eloise Bittel
Colby, Bainbridge	1895	Nathalie Sedgwick
Colby, Bainbridge	1929	Anne (Ahlstrand) Ely
Coleman, William T., Jr.	1945	Lovida Hardin

Colfax, Schuyler	1844	Evelyn Clark
Colfax, Schuyler	1868	Ellen Wade
Collamer, Jacob	1817	Mary N. Stone
Colman, Norman Jay	1851	Clara Porter
Colman, Norman Jay	1866	Catherine Wright
Connally, John B.	1940	Ida Nell Brill
Connor, John T.	1940	Mary O'Boyle
Conrad, Charles M.	n.a.	M.W. Angela Lewis
Coolidge, Calvin	1905	Grace Anna Goodhue
Cortelyou, George B.	1888	Lily Morris Hinds
Corwin, Thomas	1822	Sarah Ross
Cox, Jacob D., Jr.	1849	Helen Finney
Crawford, William H.	1804	Susanna Girardin
Creswell, John A. J.	after 1850	Hannah J. Richardson
Crittenden, John J.	1811	Sally O. Lee
Crittenden, John J.	1826	Maria K. Todd
Crittenden, John J.	1853	Mrs. Elizabeth Ashley
Crowninshield, Benjamin W.	1804	Mary Boardman
Cummings, Homer S.	1929	Cecilia Waterbury
Curtis, Charles	1884	Anna E. Baird
Cushing, Caleb	1824	Caroline Wilde
Dallas, Alexander	1780	Arabella Maria Smith
Dallas, George M.	1816	Sophia Chew (or Nicklin)
Daniels, Josephus	1888	Addie Worth Bagley
Daugherty, Harry M.	1884	Lucy Matilda Walker
Davis, Dwight F.	1904	Helen Brooks
Davis, Dwight F.	1936	Pauline (Morton) Sabin
Davis, James J.	1914	Jean Rodenbaugh
Davis, Jefferson	1835	Sarah Knox Taylor
Davis, Jefferson	1845	Varina Howell
Dawes, Charles G.	1889	Caro D. Blymer
Day, James E.	1941	Mary Louise Burgess
Day, William R.	1875	Mary Elizabeth Schaefer
Dearborn, Henry	1771	Mary Bartlett
Dearborn, Henry	1780	Dorcas (Osgood) Marble
Delano, Columbus	1834	Elizabeth Leavenworth
Denby, Edwin	1911	Marion Thurber
Dennison, William	n.a.	(Miss) Neil
Dent, Frederick B.	1944	Mildred Carrington Harrison

Dern, George H.	1899	Lottie Brown
Derwinski, Edward J.	1946	Patricia Van Der Giessen
Dexter, Samuel	1786	Catherine Gordon
Dickinson, Donald McD.	1869	Frances Platt
Dickinson, Jacob McG.	1876	Martha Overton
Dillon, C. Douglas	1931	Phyllis Chess Ellsworth
Dix, John A.	1826	Catherine Morgan
Doak, William N.	1908	Emma Maria Cricher
Dobbin, James C.	n.a.	Louisa Holmes
Dole, Elizabeth Hanforth	1975	Robert Dole
Donaldson, Jesse M.	1911	Nell Graybill
Donovan, Raymond J.	1957	Catherine Sblendorio
Duane, William J.	n.a.	Deborah Bache
Dulles, John F.	1912	Janet Pomeroy Avery
Duncan, Charles W., Jr.	1957	Thetis Smith
Dunlop, John T.	1937	Dorothy Webb
Durkin, Martin P.	1921	Anna H. McNicholas
Eaton, John H.	before 1816	Myra Lewis
Eaton, John H.	1829	Margaret O'Neill
Edison, Charles	1918	Carolyn Hawkinson
Edwards, James	1951	Ann Norris Darlington
Eisenhower, Dwight D.	1916	Mary (Mamie) Geneva Doud
Elkins, Stephen B.	1866	Sarah Jacobs
Elkins, Stephen B.	1875	Hallie Davis
Endicott, William C.	1859	Ellen Peabody
Eustis, William	1810	Caroline Langdon
Evarts, William M.	1843	Helen Minerva Wardner
Everett, Edward	1822	Charlotte Gray Brooks
Ewing, Thomas	1820	Maria Willis Boyle
Fairbanks, Charles W.	1874	Cornelia Cole
Fairchild, Charles S.	1871	Helen Linklaen
Fall, Albert B.	1883	Emma Garland Morgan
Farley, James A.	1920	Elizabeth Finnegan
Fessenden, William P.	1832	Ellen Maria Deering
Fillmore, Millard	1826	Abigail Powers
Fillmore, Millard	1858	Mrs. Caroline (Carmichael) McIntosh
Finch, Robert H.	1946	Carol Crother
Fish, Hamilton	1836	Julia Kean
Fisher, Walter L.	1891	Mabel Taylor

Flemming, Arthur S.	1934	Bernice Virginia Moler
Floyd, John B.	1830	Shelly Buchanon Preston
Folger, Charles J.	1844	Susan Rebecca Worth
Folsom, Marion B.	1918	Mary Davenport
Ford, Gerald R., Jr.	1948	Elizabeth Bloomer
Forrestal, James V.	1926	Josephine Ogden
Forsyth, John	n.a.	Clara Meigs
Forward, Walter	1808	Henrietta Barclay
Foster, Charles	1853	Ann M. Olmstead
Foster, John W.	1859	Mary Parke McFerson
Fowler, Henry H.	1938	Trudye Pamela Hathcote
Francis, David R.	1876	Jane Perry
Freeman, Orville L.	1942	Jane Charlotte Shields
Frelinghuysen, Frederick T.	1842	Matilde E. Griswold
Gage, Lyman J.	1864	Sarah Etheridge
Gallatin, Albert	1789	Sophie Allegre
Gallatin, Albert	1793	Hannah Nicholson
Gardner, John W.	1934	Aida Marroquin
Garfield, James A.	1858	Lucretia Rudolph
Garfield, James R.	1890	Helen Newell
Garland, Augustus H.	1853	Virginia Sanders
Garner, John N.	1895	Ettie Rheiner
Garrison, Lindley M.	1900	Margaret Hildeburn
Gary, James A.	1856	Lavina W. Corrie
Gates, Thomas S., Jr.	1928	Millicent Ann Brengle
Gerry, Elbridge	1786	Ann Thompson
Gilmer, Thomas W.	1826	Anne Baker
Gilpin, Henry D.	1834	Eliza (Sibley) Johnston
Glass, Carter	1886	Aurelia McDearmon
Glass, Carter	1940	Mary (Scott) Meade
Goff, Nathan	1865	Laura Ellen Despard
Goldberg, Arthur J.	1931	Dorothy Kurgans
Good, James W.	1894	Lucy Deacon
Gore, Howard M.	1906	Royalene Corder
Gorham, Nathaniel	1763	Rebecca Call
Graham, William A.	1836	Susannah Sarah Washington
Granger, Francis	1816	Cornelia Rutson Van Rensselaer
Granger, Gideon	1790	Mindwell Pease
Grant, Ulysses S.	1848	Julia Boggs Dent

Gregory, Thomas W.	1893	Julia Nalle
Gresham, Walter Q.	1858	Matilda McGrain
Griffin, Cyrus	1770	Lady Christina Stuart
Griggs, John W.	1874	Carolyn Webster
Griggs, John W.	1893	Laura Elizabeth Price
Gronouski, John A.	1948	Mary Louise Metz
Guthrie, James	1821	Eliza C. Prather
Habersham, Joseph	1776	Isabella Rae
Haig, Alexander M., Jr.	1950	Patricia Fox
Hall, Nathan K.	1832	Emily Paine
Hamilton, Alexander	1780	Elizabeth Schuyler
Hamilton, Paul	1782	Mary Wilkinson
Hamlin, Hannibal	1833	Sarah Jane Emery
Hamlin, Hannibal	1856	Ellen Vesta Emery
Hancock, John	1775	Dorothy Quincy
Hannegan, Robert E.	1903	Irma Protzmann
Hanson, John	before 1749	Jane Contee
Hardin, Clifford M.	1939	Martha Love Wood
Harding, Warren G.	1891	Florence (Kling) De Wolfe
Harlan, James	1845	Ann Eliza Peck
Harmon, Judson	1846	Olivia Scobey
Harriman, William A.	1915	Kitty Lanier Lawrence
Harriman, William A.	1930	Mary (Norton) Whitney
Harris, Patricia R.	1955	William Beasley Harris
Harrison, Benjamin	1853	Caroline Lavinia Scott
Harrison, Benjamin	1896	Mary Scott Lord Dimmick
Harrison, William H.	1795	Anna Tuthill Symmes
Hathaway, Stanley K.	1948	Roberta Harley
Hatton, Frank	1867	Lizzie Snyder
Hay, John M.	1874	Clara L. Stone
Hayes, Rutherford B.	1852	Lucy Webb
Hays, William H.	1902	Helen Louise Thomas
Hays, William H.	1930	Jesse Herron Stutsman
Heckler, Margaret M.	1954	John Heckler
Hendricks, Thomas A.	1845	Eliza C. Morgan
Herbert, Hilary A.	1867	Ella B. Smith
Herrington, John	1961	Lois Haight
Herter, Christian A.	1917	Mary Carolina Pratt
Hickel, Walter J.	1941	Janice Cannon
Hickel, Walter J.	1945	Ermalee Strutz

Hills, Carla A.	1958	Roderick Maltman Hills
Hitchcock, Ethan A.	1869	Margaret D. Collier
Hoar, Ebenezer R.	1840	Caroline Downes Brooks
Hobart, Garret A.	1869	Jennie Tuttle
Hobby, Oveta C.	1931	William Pettus Hobby
Hodel, Donald P.	1956	Barbara Stockman
Hodges, Luther H.	1922	Martha Elizabeth Blakeney
Hodgson, James D.	1943	Maria Denand
Holt, Joseph	n.a.	Mary Harrison
Holt, Joseph	n.a.	Margaret Wickliffe
Hoover, Herbert C.	1899	Lou Henry
Hopkins, Harry L.	1913	Ethel Gross
Hopkins, Harry L.	1931	Barbara MacPherson Duncan
Hopkins, Harry L.	1942	Louise Hill (Macy) Brown
Houston, David F.	1895	Helen Beall
Howe, Timothy O.	1841	Linda Ann Haynes
Hufstedler, Shirley Mount	1949	Seth Hufstedler
Hughes, Charles E.	1888	Antoinette Carter
Hull, Cordell	1917	Rose Frances Whitney
Humphrey, George M.	1913	Pamela Stark
Humphrey, Hubert H., Jr.	1936	Muriel Fay Buck
Hunt, William H.	1848	Frances Ann Andrews
Hunt, William H.	1852	Elizabeth Augusta Ridgeby
Huntington, Samuel	1761	Martha Devotion
Hurley, Patrick J.	1919	Ruth Wilson
Hyde, Arthur M.	1904	Hortense Cullers
Ickes, Harold L.	1911	Anna Wilmarth Thompson
Ickes, Harold L.	1938	Jane Dahlman
Ingham, Samuel D.	1800	Rebecca Dodd
Ingham, Samuel D.	1822	Deborah Kay Hall
Jackson, Andrew	1791	Mrs. Rachel (Donelson) Robards
Jackson, Robert H.	1916	Irene Gerhardt
James, Thomas L.	1852	Emily 1. Freedbum
James, Thomas L.	n.a.	Mrs. E. R. Bordon
James, Thomas L.	n.a.	Edith Colborne
James, Thomas L.	1911	Mrs. Florence (MacDonnell) Gaffney
Jardine, William M.	1905	Effie Nebeker
Jay, John	1774	Sarah Livingston
Jefferson, Thomas	1772	Mrs. Martha (Wayles) Skelton
Jewell, Marshall	1852	Esther E. Dickinson

Johnson, Andrew	1827	Eliza McCardle
Johnson, Cave	1838	Elizabeth (Dortch) Brunson
Johnson, Louis A.	1920	Ruth Frances Maxwell
Johnson, Lyndon B.	1934	Claudia Alta (Lady Bird) Taylor
Johnson, Reverdy	1819	Mary Mackall Bowie
Jones, Jesse H.	1929	May Gibbs
Katzenbach, Nicholas de B.	1946	Lydia King Phelps Stokes
Kellogg, Frank B.	1886	Clara M. Cook
Kemp, Jack	1956	Joanne Main
Kendall, Amos	1818	Mary B. Woolfolk
Kendall, Amos	1826	Jane Kyle
Kennedy, David M.	1925	Lenora Bingham
Kennedy, John F.	1953	Jacqueline Lee Bouvier
Kennedy, John P.	1824	Mary Tennant
Kennedy, John P.	1829	Elizabeth Gray
Kennedy, Robert F.	1950	Ethel Skakel
Key, David McK.	1857	Elizabeth Lenoir
King, Horatio	1835	Ann Collins
King, Horatio	1875	Isabella G. Osborne
Kirkwood, Samuel J.	1843	Jane Clark
Kissinger, Henry A.	1949	Ann Fleischer
Kissinger, Henry A.	1974	Nancy Maginnes
Kleindienst, Richard G.	1948	Margaret Dunbar
Kleppe, Thomas S.	1958	Glendora Loew Gompf
Klutznick, Philip M.	1930	Ethel Ricks
Knebel, John A.	1959	Zenia Irene Marks
Knox, Henry	1774	Lucy Flucker
Knox, Philander C.	1880	Lillie Smith
Knox, W. Franklin	1898	Annie Reid
Kreps, Juanita M.	1944	Clifton H. Kreps, Jr.
Krug, Julius A.	1926	Margaret Catherine Dean
Laird, Melvin R.	1945	Barbara Masters
Lamar, Lucius Q.C.	1847	Virginia Longstreet
Lamar, Lucius Q.C.	1887	Henrietta (Dean) Holt
Lamont, Daniel S.	n.a.	Juliet Kinney
Lamont, Robert P.	1894	Helen Gertrude Trotter
Landrieu, Moon E.	1954	Vera Satterlee
Lane, Franklin K.	1893	Anne Claire Wintermute
Lansing, Robert	1890	Eleanor Foster

Laurens, Henry	1750	Eleanor Ball
Lee, Charles	1789	Anne Lee
Lee, Charles	n.a.	Margaret C. Scott Peyton
Lee, Richard H.	1757	Anne Aylett
Lee, Richard H.	1769	Anne (Gaskins) Pinckard
Levi, Edward H.	1946	Kate Sulzberger
Lewis, Andrew	1950	Marilyn Stoughton
Lincoln, Abraham	1842	Mary Todd
Lincoln, Levi	1781	Martha Waldo
Lincoln, Robert T.	1868	Mary Harlan
Livingston, Edward	1788	Mary McEvers
Livingston, Edward	1805	Louise Moreau de Lassy
Long, John D.	1870	Mary Woodward Glover
Long, John D.	1886	Agnes Pierce
Lovett, Robert A.	1919	Adele Quarterly Brown
Lujan, Manuel, Jr.	1951	Jean Couchman
Lyng, Richard E.	1944	Bethel Ball
Lynn, James T.	1954	Joan Miller
MacVeagh, Franklin	1868	Emily Eames
MacVeagh, Wayne	1856	Letty M. Lewis
MacVeagh, Wayne	1866	Virginia Rolette Cameron
Madison, James	1794	Dorothea (Dolley) (Payne) Todd
Manning, Daniel	1853	Mary Little
Manning, Daniel	1884	Mary Margaret Fryer
Marcy, William L.	1812	Dolly Newell
Marcy, William L.	1825	Cornelia Knower
Marshall, George C.	1902	Elizabeth Carter Coles
Marshall, George C.	1930	Katherine Boyce (Tupper) Brown
Marshall, John	1783	Mary Willis Ambler
Marshall, Thomas R.	1895	Lois Irene Kimsey
Mason, John Y.	1821	Mary Anne Port
Matthews, Forrest D.	1960	Mary Chapman
Maynard, Horace	1840	Laura Ann Washburn
McAdoo, William G.	1885	Sarah Houston Fleming
McAdoo, William G.	1914	Eleanor Randolph Wilson
McClelland, Robert	1837	Sarah E. Sabine
McCrary, George W.	1857	Helen Galett
McCulloch, Hugh	1838	Susan Mann
McElroy, Neil H.	1929	Mary Camilla Fry

McGranery, James P.	1939	Regina T. Clark
McGrath, James H.	1929	Estelle A. Cadorette
McHenry, James	1784	Margaret Allison Caldwell
McKay, Douglas J.	1917	Mabel Christine Hill
McKean, Thomas	1763	Mary Borden
McKean, Thomas	1774	Sarah Armitage
McKenna, Joseph	1869	Amanda F. Borneman
McKennan, Thomas M.T.	1815	Matilda Lourie Bowman
McKinley, William, Jr.	1871	Ida Saxton
McLane, Louis	1812	Catherine Mary Milligan
McLaughlin, Ann	1963	William Dore
McLaughlin, Ann Dore	1975	John McLaughlin
McLean, John	1843	Sarah Bella (Ludlow) Garrard
McNamara, Robert S.	1940	Margaret Craig
Meese, Edwin, III	1959	Ursula Herrick
Meigs, Return J., Jr.	1764	Sophia Wright
Mellon, Andrew W.	1900	Nora McMullen
Meredith, Edwin T.	1896	Edna C. Elliott
Meredith, William M.	1834	Catherine Keppele
Metcalf, Victor H.	1882	Emily Corinne Nicholsen
Meyer, George von L.	1885	Marion Alice Appleton
Middleton, Henry	1741	Mary Williams
Middleton, Henry	1762	Maria Henrietta Bull
Middleton, Henry	1776	Lady Mary Mackenzie
Mifflin, Thomas	1767	Sarah Morris
Miller, G. William	1946	Ariadna Rogojarsky
Miller, William H.H.	1863	Gertrude A. Bunce
Mills, Ogden L.	1911	Margaret Stuyvesant Rutherford
Mills, Ogden L.	1924	Mrs. Dorothy (Randolph) Fell
Mitchell, James P.	1923	Isabelle Nulton
Mitchell, John N.	n.a.	first wife unknown
Mitchell, John N.	n.a.	Martha (Beall) Jennings
Mitchell, William DeW.	1901	Gertrude Bancroft
Mondale, Walter F.	1955	Joan Adams
Monroe, James	1785	Elizabeth Kortright
Morgenthau, Henry	1916	Elinor Fatman
Morgenthau, Henry	1951	Marcelle Puthon
Morrill, Lot M.	1845	Charlotte Holland Vance
Morton, Julius S.	1854	Caroline Joy French

Morton, Levi P.	1856	Lucy Young Kimball
Morton, Paul	1880	Charlotte Goodridge
Morton, Rogers C. B.	1939	Anne Jones
Mosbacher, Robert A.	n.a.	first wife unknown
Mosbacher, Robert A.	1985	Georgette Paulson
Mueller, Frederick H.	1915	Mary Darrah
Muskie, Edmund S.	1948	Jane Gray
Nagel, Charles	1876	Fanny Brandeis
Nagel, Charles	1895	Anne Shepley
New, Harry S.	1888	Kathleen Virginia Mulligan
New, Harry S.	1891	Catherine McLaen
Newberry, Truman H.	1888	Harriet Josephine Bornes
Niles, John M.	1824	Sarah Robinson
Niles, John M.	1845	Jane Pratt
Nixon, Richard M.	1940	Thelma (Pat) Ryan
Noble, John W.	1864	Lisabeth Halstead
O'Brien, Lawrence F.	1944	Elva I. Brassard
Olney, Richard	1861	Agnes Thomas
Osgood, Samuel	1775	Martha Brandon
Osgood, Samuel	1786	Maria Bowne Franklin
Palmer, Alexander M.	1898	Roberta Bartlett Dixon
Palmer, Alexander M.	1923	Margaret Fallon Burrall
Paulding, James K.	1818	Gertrude Kemble
Payne, Henry C.	1869	Lydia Wood Van Dyke
Payne, John B.	1878	Kate Bunker
Payne, John B.	1913	Jennie Byrd Bryan
Patterson, Robert P.	1920	Margaret Tarleton Winchester
Perkins, Frances	1913	Paul Caldwell Wilson
Peterson, Peter G.	1953	Sally Hombagen
Pickering, Timothy	1776	Rebecca White
Pierce, Franklin	1834	Jane Means Appleton
Pierce, Samuel R., Jr.	1948	Barbara Wright
Pierrepont, Edwards	1846	Margaretta Willoughby
Pinkney, William	1789	Maria Rodgers
Poinsett, Joel R.	1833	Mrs. Mary (Izard) Pringle
Polk, James K.	1824	Sarah Childress
Porter, James M.	1821	Eliza Michler
Porter, Peter B.	1818	Letitia Breckinridge
Preston, William B.	1839	Lucinda Staples Redd

Proctor, Redfield	1858	Emily J. Dutton
Quayle, Danforth	1972	Marilyn Tucker
Ramsey, Alexander	1845	Anna Earl Jenks
Randall, Alexander W.	1842	Mary C. Van Vechten
Randall, Alexander W.	1863	Helen M. Thomas
Randolph, Edmund J.	1776	Elizabeth Nicholas
Randolph, Peyton	1745	Elizabeth Harrison
Rawlins, John A.	1856	Emily Smith
Rawlins, John A.	1863	Mary E. Hurlburt
Reagan, Ronald W.	1940	Jane Wyman
Reagan, Ronald W.	1952	Nancy Davis
Redfield, William C.	1885	Elise Mercein Fuller
Regan, Donald T.	1942	Ann Buchanan
Ribicoff, Abraham A.	1931	Ruth Siegel
Richardson, Elliot L.	1952	Ann Francis Hazard
Richardson, William A.	1849	Anna Maria Marston
Robeson, George	1872	Mary Isabelle (Ogston) Aulick
Rockefeller, Nelson A.	1930	Mary Todhunter Clark
Rockefeller, Nelson A.	1963	Margaretta Fitler Murphy
Rodney, Caesar A.	n.a.	Susan Hunn
Rogers, William P.	1936	Adele Langston
Romney, George W.	1931	Lenore La Fount
Roosevelt, Franklin D.	1905	Anna Eleanor Roosevelt
Roosevelt, Theodore	1880	Alice Hathaway Lee
Roosevelt, Theodore	1886	Edith Kermit Carow
Root, Elihu	1878	Clara Wales
Roper, Daniel C.	1889	Lou McKenzie
Royall, Kenneth C.	1917	Margaret Best
Rumsfeld, Donald	1954	Joyce Pierson
Rush, Richard	1809	Catherine E. Murray
Rusk, D. Dean	1937	Virginia Foisie
Rusk, Jeremiah McL.	1849	Mary Martin
Rusk, Jeremiah McL.	1856	Elizabeth M. Johnson
St. Clair, Arthur	1760	Phoebe Bayard
Sargent, John G.	1887	Mary Lorraine Gordon
Sawyer, Charles	1918	Margaret Sterrett
Sawyer, Charles	1942	Elizabeth De Veyrac
Saxbe, William	1940	Ardath Louise Kleinhans
Schlesinger, James R.	1954	Rachel Mellinger

Schofield, John McA.	1857	Harriet Bartlett
Schofield, John McA.	1891	Georgia Kilbourne
Schurz, Carl	1852	Margarethe Meyer
Schweiker, Richard	1955	Claire Coleman
Schwellenbach, Lewis B.	1935	Anne Duffy
Seaton, Frederick A.	1931	Gladys Hope Dowd
Seward, William H.	1824	Frances Miller
Shaw, Leslie M.	1877	Alice Crenshaw
Sherman, James S.	1881	Carrie Babcock
Sherman, John	1848	Margaret Sarah Cecilia Stewart
Sherman, William T.	1850	Elinor Byle Ewing
Shultz, George P.	1946	Helena Maria O'Brien
Simon, William E.	1950	Carol Girard
Skinner, Samuel K.	1960	Susan Thomas
Smith, Caleb	1831	Elizabeth B. Walton
Smith, Charles E.	1907	Nettie Nichols
Smith, Cyrus R.	1934	Elizabeth L. Manget
Smith, Hoke	1924	Mazie Crawford
Smith, Robert	1790	Margaret Smith
Smith, William French	1939	Margaret Dawson
Smith, William French	1964	Jean Vaugan
Snyder, John W.	1920	Evlyn Cook
Southard, Samuel L.	1811	Rebecca Harrow
Speed, James	1841	Jane Cochran
Spencer, John C.	1809	Elizabeth Scott Smith
Stanbery, Henry	1829	Frances E. Beecher
Stanbery, Henry	1840	Cecelia Bond
Stans, Maurice H.	1933	Kathleen Carmody
Stanton, Edwin McM.	1834	Mary Ann Lamson
Stanton, Edwin McM.	1856	Ellen M. Hutchinson
Stettinius, Edward R., Jr.	1926	Virginia Gordon Wallace
Stevenson, Adlai E.	1866	Letitia Green
Stimson, Henry L.	1893	Mabel Wellington White
Stoddert, Benjamin	1781	Rebecca Lowndes
Stone, Harlan F.	1899	Agnes Harvey
Straus, Oscar S.	1882	Sarah Lavanburg
Stuart, Alexander H.H.	1833	Frances Cordelia Baldwin
Summerfield, Arthur E.	1918	Miriam W. Graim
Swanson, Claude	1894	Lizzie Deane Lyons

Swanson, Claude	1923	Lulie (Lyons) Hall
Taft, Alphonso	1841	Fanny Phelps
Taft, Alphonso	1853	Louisa Torrey
Taft, William H.	1886	Helen Herron
Taney, Roger B.	1806	Anne P. C. Key
Taylor, Zachary	1810	Margaret Mackall Smith
Teller, Henry M.	1862	Harriet M. Bruce
Thomas, Philip F.	1835	Sarah Maria Kerr
Thomas, Philip F.	1876	Mrs. Clintonia (Wright) May
Thompson, Jacob	n.a.	Catherine Jones
Thompson, Richard W.	1836	Harriet Eliza Gardiner
Thompson, Smith	1794	Sarah Livingston
Thornburgh, Richard L.	1955	Virginia Hooton
Thornburgh, Richard L.	1963	Virginia Judson
Tobin, Maurice J.	1932	Helen M. Noonan
Tompkins, Daniel D.	1797	Hannah Minthorne
Toucey, Isaac	1827	Catharine Nichols
Tracy, Benjamin F.	1851	Delinda E. Catlin
Trowbridge, Alexander B.	1955	Nancy Horst
Truman, Harry S	1919	Elizabeth (Virginia Bess) Wallace
Tyler, John	1813	Letitia Christian
Tyler, John	1844	Julia Gardiner
Udall, Stewart L.	1947	Ermalee Webb
Upshur, Abel P.	1817	Elizabeth Dennis
Upshur, Abel P.	1824	Elizabeth Ann Brown
Usery, Willie J., Jr.	1942	Gussie Mae Smith
Usher, John P.	1844	Margaret Patterson
Van Buren, Martin	1807	Hannah Hoes
Vance, Cyrus R.	1947	Grace Elsie Sloane
Verity, C. William, Jr.	1941	Margaret Wymond
Vilas, William F.	1866	Anna M. Fox
Vinson, Frederick M.	1923	Roberta Dixon
Volpe, John A.	1934	Jennie Benedetto
Walker, Frank C.	1914	Hallie Victoria Boucher
Walker, Robert J.	1825	Mary Blechynder Bacle
Wallace, Henry A.	1914	Ilo Browne
Wallace, Henry C.	n.a.	Carrie May Broadhead
Wanamaker, John	1860	Mary Erringer
Washburne, Elihu B.	1845	Adele Gratiot

Washington, George	1759	Mrs. Martha (Dandridge) Custis
Watkins, James D.	1950	Sheila Jo McKinney
Watson, William M., Jr.	n.a.	Marion Baugh
Watt, James G.	1957	Leilani Bomgardner
Weaver, Robert C.	1935	Ella V. Hiath
Webster, Daniel	1808	Grace Fletcher
Weeks, John W.	1885	Martha A. Sinclair
Weeks, Sinclair	1915	Beatrice Dowse
Weinberger, Caspar W.	1942	Jane Calton
Welles, Gideon	1835	Mary Jane Hale
West, Roy O.	1898	Louisa Augustus
West, Roy O.	1904	Louise McWilliams
Wheeler, William A.	1845	Mary King
Whiting, William F.	1892	Anne Chapin
Whitney, William C.	1869	Flora Payne
Whitney, William C.	*ca.* 1895	Mrs. Edith Sibyl (May) Randolph
Wickard, Claude R.	1918	Louisa Eckert
Wickersham, George	1883	Mildred Wendell
Wickliffe, Charles A.	1813	Margaret Crepps
Wilbur, Curtis D.	1893	Ella T. Chilson
Wilbur, Curtis D.	1898	Olive Doolittle
Wilbur, Ray L.	1898	Marguerite May Blake
Wilkins, William	1815	Catherine Holmes
Wilkins, William	1818	Matilda Dallas
Williams, George H.	1850	Kate Van Antwerp
Williams, George H.	1867	Kate (Hughes) George
Wilson, Charles E.	1912	Jessie Ann Curtis
Wilson, Henry	1840	Harriet Malvina Howe
Wilson, James	1863	Esther Wilbur
Wilson, William B.	1883	Agnes Williamson
Wilson, William L.	1868	Nannine Huntington
Wilson, Woodrow	1885	Ellen Louise Axson
Wilson, Woodrow	1915	Edith (Boling) Galt
Windom, William	1856	Ellen P. Hatch
Wirt, William	1795	Mildred Gilmer
Wirt, William	1802	Elizabeth Washington
Wirtz, William W.	1936	Mary Jane Quisenberry
Wolcott, Oliver, Jr.	1785	Elizabeth Stoughton
Wood, Robert C.	1952	Margaret Byers

Woodbury, Levi	1819	Elizabeth Williams Clapp
Woodin, William H.	1899	Annie Jessup
Woodring, Henry H.	1933	Helen Coolidge
Work, Hubert	1887	Laura M. Arbuckle
Work, Hubert	1933	Ethel Reed Gano
Wright, Luke E.	1869	Kate Semmes
Wynne, Robert J.	1875	Mary McCabe
Yeutter, Clayton K.	1952	Jeanne Vierk

MARITAL INFORMATION MISSING

Abraham, Spencer

Albright, Madeleine

Alexander, Lamar

Aspin, Les

Babbitt, Bruce

Barr, William

Bentsen, Lloyd

Bowen, Otis

Brown, Jesse

Brown, Ronald

Bush, George W.

Card, Andrew

Chao, Elaine

Christopher, Warren

Cisneros, Henry

Clinton, William

Cohen, William

Cuomo, Andrew

Daley, William

Eagleburger, Lawrence

Esby, Michael

Evans, Donald

Franklin, Barbara

Glickman, Daniel

Goldschmidt, Neil

Gore, Albert

Herman, Alexis

Kantor, Michael

Madigan, Edward

Martin, Lynn

Martinez, Mel

Mineta, Norman

Norton, Gale

O'Leary, Hazel

O'Neill, Paul

Paige, Rod

Patterson, Robert

Peña, Federico

Perry, William

Powell, Colin

Principi, Anthony

Reich, Robert

Reno, Janet

Richardson, William B.

Riley, Richard

Rubin, Robert

Shalala, Donna

Slater, Rodney

Sullivan, Louis

Summers, Lawrence

Thompson, Tommy

Veneman, Ann

West, Togo

About the Editors

David B. Sicilia is Associate Professor of History at the University of Maryland, College Park. A specialist in modern U.S. history and business and economic history, he is coauthor of *The Entrepreneurs* (1986); *Labors of a Modern Hercules: The Evolution of a Chemical Company* (1990); *The Engine That Could: Seventy-five Years of Values Drives Change at Cummins Engine Company* (1997); and *The Greenspan Effect* (2000). Dr. Sicilia is Associate Editor of *Enterprise & Society: The International Journal of Business History.*

Robert Sobel (1931–1999) was Lawrence Stessin Distinguished Professor of Business History at New College of Hofstra University, where he taught for 43 years. Dr. Sobel authored many noteworthy books, including *The Great Bull Market* (1968); *The Age of Giant Corporations* (1972, 1984); *IBM: Colossus in Transition* (1981); *Coolidge: An American Enigma* (1998); and *The Pursuit of Wealth* (2000). He wrote popular columns for *Newsday* and *Barron's* and was editor of the Greenwood series Contributions in Economics and Economic History.